THE INTERPRETATION OF
THE FOURTH GOSPEL

THE
INTERPRETATION OF THE
FOURTH GOSPEL

BY

C. H. DODD
M.A., HON. D.D., F.B.A.
Professor Emeritus in the University of Cambridge

CAMBRIDGE
AT THE UNIVERSITY PRESS
1970

Published by the Syndics of the Cambridge University Press
Bentley House, 200 Euston Road, London N.W. 1
American Branch: 32 East 57th Street, New York, N.Y. 10022

International Standard Book Numbers
0 521 04848 6 clothbound
0 521 09517 4 paperback

First edition 1953
Reprinted 1954 1955 1958
1960 1963 1965 1968
First paperback edition 1968
Reprinted 1970

Printed in Great Britain
at the University Printing House, Cambridge
(Brooke Crutchley, University Printer)

PHYLLIDI

CONIVGI CARISSIMAE AMANTISSIMAE

HOC OPVS
QVOD IPSA SEMPER
SVADEBAT FOVEBAT EXSPECTABAT
QVINTO PERACTO LVSTRO
D.D.
AVCTOR
ANNO SALVTIS MCML

PREFACE

The scope of this book is restricted to the attempt to establish some general principles and lines of direction for the interpretation of the Fourth Gospel. Purely critical questions I have for the most part left aside. Nor have I in general pursued detailed exegesis of the text, apart from passages where such exegesis seemed indispensable for my main purpose. The book falls into three parts. In the first part I have surveyed some important sections of the field in which the thought of the Fourth Gospel has its background. In the second part, assuming this background, I have attempted to define, with such degree of precision as I could compass, some of the dominant concepts with which the evangelist operates. In the third part I have set out to trace the course of the argument through the whole gospel. I had at one time thought of adding a fourth part dealing with the relation of the Fourth Gospel to the historical tradition of early Christianity. This, however, does not seem to fall well within the main intention of the book, which in any case was tending to excessive length, and I have decided to reserve that topic. But since among the leading ideas of the gospel is the idea that certain historical events are a manifestation of the eternal and divine, I have added an appendix indicating briefly a line of thought which I should wish to follow upon the historical aspect of the Fourth Gospel. Some paragraphs in Part I, chs. 1 and 2, have been reproduced, by permission, from the *Bulletin of the John Rylands Library*, vol. 19, no. 2.

C.H.D.

CAMBRIDGE, 4 JANUARY 1950

The book has been read in proof, at every stage, by my friend and former pupil, the Rev. W. D. Davies, D.D., now Professor of the New Testament in Duke University, North Carolina. I am deeply indebted to him for many valuable corrections and suggestions, as also for verifying citations and references in the Bible and the Rabbinic Literature, and for compiling the Index to the latter. I am further indebted to my daughter, Mrs E. W. Heaton, for verifying and indexing citations and references in Greek (non-biblical) writers, and to my wife and Miss Audrey Bayley for assistance in preparing the indices. To all these I tender my most grateful acknowledgements.

C.H.D.

4 JUNE 1952

CONTENTS

PART I

THE BACKGROUND

PART II

LEADING IDEAS

ix

CONTENTS

Part III

ARGUMENT AND STRUCTURE

CONTENTS

APPENDIX

Wir sehnen uns nach Offenbarung,
Die nirgends würd'ger und schöner brennt
Als in dem Neuen Testament.
Mich drängt's, den Grundtext aufzuschlagen,
Mit redlichem Gefühl einmal
Das heilige Original
In mein geliebtes Deutsch zu übertragen.
Geschrieben steht: „Im Anfang war das Wort!"
Hier stock' ich schon! Wer hilft mir weiter fort?
Ich kann das Wort so hoch unmöglich schätzen,
Ich muß es anders übersetzen,
Wenn ich vom Geiste recht erleuchtet bin.
Geschrieben steht: Im Anfang war der Sinn.
Bedenke wohl die erste Zeile,
Daß deine Feder sich nicht übereile!
Ist es der Sinn, der alles wirkt und schafft?
Es sollte stehn: Im Anfang war die Kraft!
Doch, auch indem ich dieses niederschreibe,
Schon warnt mich was, daß ich dabei nicht bleibe.
Mir hilft der Geist! auf einmal seh' ich Rat
Und schreibe getrost: Im Anfang war die Tat!

GOETHE: *Faust*, Erster Teil, ll. 863–83

PART I
THE BACKGROUND

1. THE SETTING IN EARLY CHRISTIANITY

There is a scene in the early part of Goethe's *Faust*, where the hero, yearning for the light of revelation (which nowhere burns more brightly than in the New Testament), sets himself to translate the Gospel according to John. At the very first clause however he finds himself in a difficulty. How is it to be rendered? 'In the beginning was the Word.' But how can so high a value be set upon the mere word? Surely, 'In the beginning was the Thought'. But again, is it truly thought by which all things were made? Is it not rather Power? Or should he boldly render the sense of the passage, 'In the beginning was the Deed'?

The difficulty which baffled Faust at the beginning of his task is one which besets the student of the Fourth Gospel all through. He finds it impossible to satisfy himself regarding the meaning of the text without raising prior questions involving the whole universe of discourse within which the thought of the gospel moves. It is in general a sound maxim that any interpretation of the thought of a work as a whole should be based on a precise exegesis of the text. Through disregard of this maxim many elaborate interpretations of biblical and other documents have gone astray. It is true that exegesis always demands some kind of assumption regarding the general aim and the background of the work in hand; but in many cases this demand is fairly easily met, the required assumptions being such as are more or less obvious to the intelligent reader. But with such a work as the Fourth Gospel it is different. At every step the exegete is faced with the necessity of considering his text in the light of the ultimate meaning of the work. Thus Faust's difficulty was far from being one merely of translation or even of exegesis in the ordinary, restricted sense of the term. The question he raised is not a question of the meaning of the word λόγος, it is the question whether the proposition 'in the beginning was the Logos' belongs to a philosophy which gives primacy to abstract thought or to one which gives primacy to active power, or whether, indeed, the 'word' itself, as medium of communication, is after all an essential element in the author's meaning. That question cannot be decided either by the lexical meaning of the terms employed or by an elucidation of the propositions of which the Prologue is composed, in their proper interrelations. It receives an answer only when the student has made up his mind about the purport of the

3

gospel as a whole. Thus in the study of this gospel, exegesis of the text, and interpretation in the wider sense, are interdependent to an unusual degree.

In order to work towards a sound interpretation of the Fourth Gospel it is necessary to consider the work in its true context of thought, so far as that is possible for us at this date. If we approach it without regard to any such context, we are in danger of imposing upon it a subjective interpretation of our own, for we shall in fact be placing it in the context of our preconceived notions, which may be foreign to the intention of the evangelist. This has often been done.[1] How then shall we define the true context?

It has often been tacitly assumed that the context is sufficiently defined by the place which the Fourth Gospel occupies in the canon of Scripture. It is one of a group of four writings designated 'gospels', and it is as a member of this group that it has been most often studied. In the pre-critical period the aim of the student was to 'harmonize' it with the other three. When the critical movement arose, the emphasis shifted to the differences and contrasts which an unbiased comparison brought to light. We may not unfairly surmise that the effect of this stage of criticism upon many minds was to leave them with the impression that John was inferior to the Synoptics in every quality that a gospel should possess— in the historicity of its narrative, the accuracy of its reported discourses, and the truth of its picture of 'the Jesus of history'. Where they could interpret John from the standpoint of the Synoptics they found it wanting, and where it could not be understood from that standpoint they were at a loss. The fact is that the Fourth Gospel belongs only in part to the same class with the Synoptics. Its true context is only partially that which it shares with the other gospels.

At a later stage of criticism attention was drawn to those aspects of the Fourth Gospel in which it stands together with the theological literature of the New Testament, and particularly with the Pauline Epistles. It became customary to describe the Fourth Evangelist as 'the greatest of the followers of Paul', and his work as 'deutero-Pauline'.

---

[1] In a book entitled *The Call of the Carpenter* by the once famous American labour leader Bouck White, ὁ πατήρ μου ἕως ἄρτι ἐργάζεται, κἀγὼ ἐργάζομαι (John v. 17), is explained as meaning (I quote from memory) 'My father is a working-man to this day, and I am a working-man myself'. That the Greek words could bear that meaning is undeniable. If one insists on placing them in the context of a philosophy dominated by the idea of the class-war, then such an exegesis is natural. But we have no reason to suppose that John or his readers had ever heard of that philosophy.

That the evangelist has not escaped the powerful influence of the first great Christian theologian whose works are extant, is probable enough. But the actual range of Pauline influence upon Johannine thought has been exaggerated. Those who tie John down too closely to the Pauline tradition are inclined to undervalue his distinctive contribution to the religion and theology of early Christianity. Paul no doubt cleared up the Judaistic question, and asserted the ecclesiastical, spiritual, and intellectual independence of gentile Christianity once for all. He also set an example of using current modes of thought to illuminate the Christian Gospel. In this sense he may have prepared the way for Johannine Christianity. Further, his work at Ephesus must have directly influenced the circle within which the Fourth Gospel was written, if it did not influence the author.[1] It may be that Paul's 'cosmical Christology', as it is called, was a suggestive factor in stimulating the thought of the Fourth Evangelist. But it is not safe to assume that Paul was the only begetter of that Christology, and in any case the whole setting of it in Paul and in John is so different that it is precarious to postulate any direct connection— certainly any literary connection—between them. Paul's treatment of the doctrine of the Man from Heaven has little in common with the Johannine doctrine of the descending and ascending Son of Man, beyond their common foundation in the primitive Christian attribution of the title 'Son of Man' to Jesus, and possible non-Christian ideas which each approached in a different way. The distinctively Pauline presentation of Christianity, as we find it in the four *Hauptbriefe*, moves on lines strikingly different from Johannine thought. If in Colossians and Ephesians (assuming the latter to be Pauline) Paul approaches nearer to John, we may profitably observe that the development of thought, at least in Colossians, was called forth by contact with heretical or semi-Christian ideas of a 'Gnostic' cast in the province of Asia; and these ideas lead us directly into a world which, as we shall see, is more closely related to Johannine thought than anything which is specifically Pauline. Thus, it is only with caution that we can use Paul to interpret John. The resemblances which we note are largely in points where Paul himself was very likely not an originator. They belong to a Jewish-

[1] I assume here that the tradition which associates the Fourth Gospel with Ephesus is to be accepted. A case can be made out for Alexandria, and even for Antioch. But the Johannine epistles at any rate seem firmly rooted in the province of Asia. Whether or not they were the work of the evangelist, they are too closely connected with the gospel for an origin at geographically distant places to be considered probable.

Hellenistic strain which was probably in Christianity almost from the beginning.[1]

The fact is that the thought of this gospel is so original and creative that a search for its 'sources', or even for the 'influences' by which it may have been affected, may easily lead us astray. Whatever influences may have been present have been masterfully controlled by a powerful and independent mind. There is no book, either in the New Testament or outside it, which is really *like* the Fourth Gospel. Nevertheless, its thought implies a certain background of ideas with which the author could assume his readers to be familiar. How far are we able to reconstruct that background?

It is clear, to begin with, that the gospel has behind it the common Christianity of the early period, and that readers who shared the life and thought of the Church would find here much that was familiar, from which they could advance to its new and unfamiliar teaching. The evangelist presupposes the existence of the Church itself with its κοινωνία, under the leadership of 'the Twelve'. He presupposes the two primitive sacraments of Baptism and the Eucharist. He presupposes also the κήρυγμα in which the primitive Church made known its faith to the non-Christian public.

The *kerygma* is essentially a proclamation of the facts about Jesus in an eschatological setting which indicates the significance of the facts. It is prefaced, or accompanied, by the announcement that the prophecies are fulfilled in these facts, which must consequently be regarded as inaugurating a new age, and a new order of relations between God and man; and it is attested by an appeal to the experience of the Spirit in the Church. The literary form which came to be known as εὐαγγέλιον is based upon the *kerygma*, and the Fourth Gospel no less than the others.[2] The main topics recur, and in the same order, as they are found in Mark and in the primitive forms of *kerygma* in Acts: the preaching of John the Baptist, the inauguration of Jesus as Messiah, His ministry in Galilee, His removal from Galilee to Jerusalem,[3] His sufferings, death and resurrection, and the coming of the Holy Spirit.

[1] How long was it before the 'Hellenists' of Acts vi. 1 made themselves felt Not more, certainly, than three or four years after the Crucifixion.

[2] See my book *The Apostolic Preaching and its Developments*, especially pp. 164–75 (first edition), 65–73 (later editions).

[3] vii. 1–14, which, although visits to Jerusalem have been recorded previously, announces a formal migration, but see pp. 384–6 below.

It is in its treatment of the eschatological setting of the facts that the Fourth Gospel departs most notably from earlier renderings of the *kerygma*. The eschatology of the early Church has two sides. On the one hand we have the belief that with the coming of Christ the 'fulness of time' has arrived, the prophecies are fulfilled, and the Kingdom of God is inaugurated on earth. On the other hand we have the expectation of a consummation still pending in the future. There is some tension between the two in almost all New Testament writings. They differ among themselves with respect to the relation conceived to exist between the fulfilment which is already matter of history, and the fulfilment which belongs to the future. In the Fourth Gospel the language of 'futurist eschatology' is little used. The sense of realization has extended itself over almost the whole field, and expectation has shrunk correspondingly. It has not entirely gone, for the Lord is represented as forecasting for His Church a universality which the evangelist can hardly have supposed to be fully realized in his time, and as speaking of a day when the generations of the dead will be raised up. We need not regard such expectations as merely vestigial remains of the eschatology of the primitive Church. They are a part of the evangelist's own faith. But it is nevertheless true that they no longer have the full significance which belongs to the hope of the second advent in some other New Testament writings. The all-important fact for this evangelist is that the universality of the Christian religion is already given in the moment when Christ being 'lifted up' begins to draw all men to Himself; and that the eternal life to which the dead will be raised is already the possession of living men in union with Him. This is the fulfilment, the day which Abraham rejoiced to see, of which Moses wrote, to which the Scriptures testify. It is not therefore accurate to say that the Fourth Evangelist has abandoned the eschatological setting of the original *kerygma*. He has transformed it by altering the perspective. The formula often used, that John has turned eschatology into 'mysticism', is misleading, unless it is clearly understood that this 'mysticism' (if that is the right word)[1] is based upon a fulfilment of history, within history; and this is the essential burden of eschatology in its Christian form. The evangelist's own formula is ἔρχεται ὥρα καὶ νῦν ἐστιν.

Yet when all this is said, it remains that the terms in which the nature of the fulfilment through Christ is set forth are strange to normal early Christianity as known from other New Testament writings, and seem

[1] See pp. 197–200.

7

to carry the reader into other regions of thought. Similarly, while the instructed Christian reader would recognize the significance of allusions to Baptism and the Eucharist, there is no explicit reference to these as institutions of the Church—for example, no injunctions about baptism 'in the Name', as in Matthew, no account of the baptism of Jesus (which was treated as in some sort the prototype of Christian baptism), and no account of the institution of the Eucharist or command to repeat its celebration. What John says about rebirth ἐξ ὕδατος καὶ πνεύματος, and about the Bread of Life, while for the Christian reader it would be filled with meaning out of the sacramental life of the Church, carries a meaning of its own to readers with no Christian background, provided they are acquainted with certain forms of religious symbolism current beyond the frontiers of Christianity.

This in itself suggests that the evangelist has in view a non-Christian public to which he wishes to appeal. This suggestion finds some confirmation from a comparison of the opening of this gospel with that of Mark. In Mark, after a citation of prophecy, John the Baptist is introduced without any preparation, as a personage known to the reader, and then after a brief account of the preaching of John, it continues, 'About that time Jesus came from Nazareth of Galilee and was baptized by John in Jordan'. There is no attempt to explain who Jesus was. He comes abruptly on the scene, and we pass at once to a series of stories about Him. The Fourth Gospel begins with a Prologue which introduces on the one hand the eternal Logos, and on the other hand 'a man sent from God, whose name was John'. The Logos is incarnate in a human person, and the 'man sent from God' identifies Him. Then at last we learn that His name is Jesus Christ. It is clear that a reader who knew nothing at all about Christianity or its Founder could read that exordium intelligently, provided that the term 'logos', and the idea of a 'man sent from God', meant something to him. But these are ideas which are in no way distinctive of Christianity.

The impression produced by this opening becomes even stronger as we proceed. As I shall hope to show, the gospel could be read intelligently by a person who started with no knowledge of Christianity beyond the minimum that a reasonably well-informed member of the public interested in religion might be supposed to have by the close of the first century, and Christian ideas are instilled step by step until the whole mystery can be divulged. If he was then led to associate himself with the Church and to participate in its fellowship, its tradition and its sacraments, he would be able to re-read the book and find in it vastly more than had been obvious at a first reading.

The evangelist takes leave of his readers (according to what must have been originally intended for the conclusion of the book, xx. 31) with the words: 'This has been written in order that you may hold the faith that Jesus is the Christ the Son of God, and that, holding this faith, you may possess life by His name.' If we lay stress upon the tense of the verbs, we must say that while the aorists πιστεύσητε, σχῆτε, would necessarily have implied that the readers did not so far hold the Christian faith or possess eternal life, the continuous presents πιστεύητε, ἔχητε, do not exclude readers who were already Christians, and whose faith the writer may have wished to confirm by giving it a richer content. That he would welcome such readers is certain. Yet the continuous present could be justified, even as addressed to those who were not yet Christians, if the writer were thinking not so much of the moment of conversion, as of the continuing union with Christ, the condition of which is faith, and which means the perpetual possession of eternal life. If, without too narrowly observing grammatical forms, we try to enter into the author's intention, it must surely appear that he is thinking, in the first place, not so much of Christians who need a deeper theology, as of non-Christians who are concerned about eternal life and the way to it, and may be ready to follow the Christian way if this is presented to them in terms that are intelligibly related to their previous religious interests and experience.

It seems therefore that we are to think of the work as addressed to a wide public consisting primarily of devout and thoughtful persons (for the thoughtless and religiously indifferent would never trouble to open such a book as this) in the varied and cosmopolitan society of a great Hellenistic city such as Ephesus under the Roman Empire. In what follows I propose to take soundings here and there in the religious literature of that time and region, with a view to reconstructing in some measure the background of thought which the evangelist presupposed in his readers.

2. THE HIGHER RELIGION OF HELLENISM: THE HERMETIC LITERATURE

Augustine, in a well-known passage of the *Confessions* (VII. 9), writes:

Thou didst procure for me through a certain person...some books of the Platonists translated from Greek into Latin. There I read—not in so many words, but in substance, supported by many arguments of various kinds—that in the beginning was the Word, and the Word was with God, and the Word was God. The same was in the beginning with God. By him were all things made, and without him was not anything made. That which was made in him was life, and the life was the light of men. And the light shineth in darkness and the darkness comprehended it not. And that the soul of man, though it bear witness of the light, is not itself the light; but the Word of God, being God, is the true light that lighteth every man that cometh into the world. And that he was in the world and the world was made by him, and the world knew him not. But that he came unto his own and his own received him not, but as many as received him to them gave he power to become sons of God, even to them that believe on his name, I did not read there. Again I read there that God the Word was born not of the flesh nor of blood, nor of the will of man, nor of the will of the flesh, but of God. But that the Word was made flesh and dwelt among us I did not read there.

Augustine doubtless speaks for many readers of the Fourth Gospel at an even earlier period. They found that it fitted into the context of the Greek philosophy in which they had been trained. It is obvious that it has affinity with Platonic thought. When John speaks of ἄρτος ἀληθινός as distinguished from ordinary loaves, of ἡ ἄμπελος ἡ ἀληθινή and τὸ φῶς τὸ ἀληθινόν, a Platonist would readily understand him to be speaking of the eternal 'ideas' in contrast to their phenomenal representatives. It would not be necessary for him to be acquainted with Plato's writings. The theory of a world of eternal forms, of which phenomena are the shadows, reflections, or symbols, had found wide acceptance, and in one form or another it reappears in various types of religious philosophy in the Hellenistic world.

The Logos-doctrine, however, to which Augustine specially refers, is no part of the original system of Plato, though it appears in the neo-Platonism of Plotinus. That doctrine owed more to the Stoics. From the time of Posidonius, who gave the Stoic philosophy a strong infusion of Platonism, the two schools approached one another, and on the popular level philosophy often took the form of a platonizing Stoicism or stoicizing Platonism. This mixed philosophy was one of the fore-runners of neo-Platonism.

The fusion of Platonism and Stoicism provided an *organon* for thinkers of various tendencies who sought a philosophical justification for religion. A striking example is to be found in the so-called Hermetic literature. The extant Hermetic writings are the remnants of an extensive literature current in antiquity under the name of Hermes Trismegistus. The person so called was represented as a sage of ancient Egypt, deified after his death as the Egyptian Hermes, that is, the god Thoth. Much of this literature deals with astrology, magic or alchemy.[1] With this we are not here concerned. But the name of Hermes Trismegistus was also used by Greek writers on philosophical and religious subjects. A collection of such writings is extant in Greek MSS. of the fourteenth century and onwards, called by modern editors *Corpus Hermeticum*. Another im-portant tractate of the same kind is preserved in a Latin translation among the works of Apuleius, under the title *Asclepius*. The Greek original, known as Λόγος Τέλειος, is partly extant in fragments and citations. The Latin version was known to Augustine, who accepted it as the translation of an authentic work of *Mercurius Aegyptius, Mercurii majoris nepos*, and quoted or summarized substantial passages from it in *De Civitate Dei*.[2] Extensive fragments of other writings of similar character are preserved in the form of excerpts in Stobaeus, or are known from citations in ancient authors.

It seems by now to be generally accepted that these writings were produced, in Egypt, for the most part in the second and third centuries A.D. A date in the first century is perhaps not excluded for one or two tractates, and it is possible that some of the citations may be from *Hermetica* later than the third century. They are all original Greek works, and not, as was at one time held, translations from Egyptian.[3] Their teaching pre-

---

[1] We have now for the first time a full and authoritative account of the non-philosophical *Hermetica* in A. J. Festugière, *Hermès Trismégiste*, vol. I, as well as an admirable account in brief of the Hermetic literature by the same author under the title *L'Hermétisme* (Lund, 1948).   [2] VIII. 23 sqq.

[3] The monumental four-volume edition of the *Hermetica*, by W. Scott, completed by A. S. Ferguson (1924–1936), contains an immense amount of material for the study of this literature, but its text has proved to be unusable, since Scott emended the MS. text so irresponsibly that it amounts to a rewriting. We are fortunate now in having a thoroughly critical text (and on the whole a conservative text) in the Budé series,

supposes the fusion of Platonic and Stoic doctrine for which Posidonius (in the first century B.C.) is thought to have been mainly responsible. It does not presuppose the neo-Platonism of Plotinus and Proclus. The literature, however, represents a situation in which there had already been a considerable interpenetration of Greek and other cultures, and non-Greek influences have certainly affected various Hermetic writers in varying degrees. The *Hermetica*, in fact, are monuments of the cross-fertilization of Greek and oriental thought which was characteristic of the Near East in the Hellenistic and Roman periods. Compared with much of the other literature (if literature it may be called) which represents the syncretism of the period, the Hermetic writings of the *Corpus*, at least, show a dominant Greek strain in their sobriety and reasonableness, though they have a warmth of religious feeling which we (perhaps wrongly) regard as non-Greek.

The writers of the *Hermetica* do not form in any strict sense a school. The idea that there existed a Hermetic 'church', of which the *Corpus* was the sacred canon, is not supported by evidence. Their doctrines cannot be brought into any unified or consistent system of philosophy. But they share a common outlook and a common religious spirit, and they enable us to form a fairly coherent idea of the ways in which devout and intelligent people thought in the Hellenistic world under the Roman empire.[1] Most of these writings are probably later in date than the Fourth Gospel, though the earliest of them may not be very much later.[2] But the type of religious thought they represent can be traced to an earlier period. In particular, its essentials seem to be presupposed in Philo, for while the non-Hebraic strain in Philo's thought often recalls the

edited by A. D. Nock and A. J. Festugière (Paris, 1945). The two volumes so far published contain the *Corpus Hermeticum* and the Latin *Asclepius*. I have regularly cited these works in the Budé text (except where otherwise indicated). For the fragments and excerpts (promised in a forthcoming volume) I have had to turn to Scott, using his apparatus to restore the MS. text so far as practicable.

[1] In *The Bible and the Greeks* (1935), part II, I have discussed some of the *Hermetica* with the special intention of tracing the Jewish strain in the medley of thought which lies behind them. A. D. Nock has since expressed the view that Jewish influence may have effectively started the movement of thought represented by the *Hermetica* in general.

[2] In the forementioned book, pp. 201–9, I discussed the date of the first tractate in the *Corpus Hermeticum*. I should now be disposed to state with rather stronger conviction my provisional conclusion that this tractate is earlier than Valentinus, and consequently not later than about A.D. 125–30. [A *lapsus calami*, corrected in the second impression (1954), attributed Zosimus, who made extensive use of *C.H.* I, to 'the beginning of the third century'; for 'third', read 'fourth'.]

Hermetica quite strikingly, I can find no grounds for concluding that they were directly influenced by Philo.

Most of the writings of the *Corpus* are in the form of dialogues, in which the interlocutors are generally Hermes Trismegistus and one or other of his sons Tat and Asklepios. The teachings of the various *libelli*, though in general based upon the popular mixture of Stoicism and Platonism, are not uniform. In some points they contradict one another. This fact was observed by some of the later writers. Thus in *C.H.* xvi. 1 Asklepios writes to King Ammon, φανήσεται γάρ σοι καὶ τοῖς ἐμοῖς ἐνίοις λόγοις ἀντίφωνος.[1] What is common to all is a certain spirit or attitude. All the writers are primarily interested not in speculative philosophy but in religion. And it is a religion of a singularly pure and spiritual kind. They believe in God, the one God, Maker and Father of the universe. He is wise and good, and He alone. (οὗτος δὲ καὶ κρείττων καὶ εἷς καὶ μόνος ὄντως σοφὸς τὰ πάντα, xiv. 3.) The λεγόμενοι θεοί have as little claim to goodness in the absolute sense as have men.[2] In particular He is good because He gives all and claims nothing.[3] He demands from men no sacrifices except the λογικαὶ θυσίαι of praise and thanksgiving, and no service except the practice of virtue. 'The service of God is one thing alone, to refrain from evil' (θρησκεία δὲ τοῦ θεοῦ μία ἐστίν, μὴ εἶναι κακόν, *C.H.* xii. 23). The εὐσεβὴς ψυχή is never tired of praising (God) and blessing all men, and doing good in every way by word and deed, in imitation of its Father (ἡ δὲ τοιαύτη ψυχὴ κόρον οὐδέποτε ἔχει ὑμνοῦσα, εὐφημοῦσα δὲ πάντας ἀνθρώπους καὶ ἔργοις καὶ λόγοις πάντα εὖ ποιοῦσα μιμουμένη οὕτως τὸν πατέρα,[4] *C.H.* x. 21). It must however be observed that this recognition of social obligation as a part of religion is rare.

---

[1] Scott rejects this sentence, without sufficient reason, as far as I can see. He also says ἀντίφωνος means 'sounding in response' and not 'discordant'. But Liddell and Scott recognize the meaning 'discordant' here and in other passages. Nock and Festugière do not question the authenticity of the sentence, but think it may perhaps be no more than a commonplace, while admitting the possibility of the meaning given above, which still seems to me most probable.

[2] *C.H.* ii. 14 οὔτε γὰρ τῶν ἄλλων λεγομένων θεῶν οὔτε ἀνθρώπων οὔτε δαιμόνων τις δύναται κἂν κατὰ ποσονοῦν ἀγαθὸς εἶναι ἢ μόνος ὁ θεός.

[3] *C.H.* ii. 16 ὁ γὰρ ἀγαθὸς ἅπαντά ἐστι διδοὺς καὶ μηδὲν λαμβάνων. ὁ οὖν θεὸς πάντα δίδωσι καὶ οὐδὲν λαμβάνει. v. 10 πάντα δίδως καὶ οὐδὲν λαμβάνεις. Cf. xiv. 4 θεὸν μὲν διὰ τὴν δύναμιν, ποιητὴν δὲ διὰ τὴν ἐνέργειαν, πατέρα δὲ διὰ τὸ ἀγαθόν.

[4] So N.-F. Scott reads... τὸν θεὸν ὑμνοῦσα εὐφημοῦσά τε, καὶ πάντας κ.τ.λ., comparing M. Aurelius Antoninus v. 33, τί ἄρκεῖ; τί δὲ ἄλλο ἢ θεοὺς μὲν σέβειν καὶ εὐφημεῖν, ἀνθρώπους δὲ εὖ ποιεῖν, and this is perhaps to be preferred. Cf. *C.H.* x. 19 ἀγὼν δὲ εὐσεβείας τὸ γνῶναι τὸ θεῖον καὶ μηδένα ἀνθρώπων ἀδικῆσαι.

For the Hermetists as a whole the ethical demand of religion is for personal purification and detachment from material things. 'Since existent things are of two kinds, the corporeal and the incorporeal, which comprise respectively the mortal and the divine, the choice of one or the other lies before the man who would choose' (δύο γὰρ ὄντων τῶν ὄντων, σώματος καὶ ἀσωμάτου, ἐν οἷς τὸ θνητὸν καὶ τὸ θεῖον, ἡ αἵρεσις θατέρου καταλείπεται τῷ ἑλέσθαι βουλομένῳ, *C.H.* IV. 6). The Hermetists in general would have warmly agreed with James i. 27 that θρησκεία καθαρὰ καὶ ἀμίαντος παρὰ τῷ θεῷ καὶ πατρὶ αὕτη ἐστίν...ἄσπιλον ἑαυτὸν τηρεῖν ἀπὸ τοῦ κόσμου: it is in fact substantially their own language; but it would not have been natural to them to add, ἐπισκέπτεσθαι ὀρφανοὺς καὶ χήρας ἐν τῇ θλίψει αὐτῶν. It is upon God and the eternal world that their minds are set. The only way of salvation for man is knowledge of God (τοῦτο μόνον σωτήριον ἀνθρώπῳ ἐστίν, ἡ γνῶσις τοῦ θεοῦ, *C.H.* x. 15). The final evil is to be ignorant of the divine, but to be able to know it, to desire and hope for such knowledge, is the straight way (ἡ γὰρ τελεία κακία τὸ ἀγνοεῖν τὸ θεῖον, τὸ δὲ δύνασθαι γνῶναι καὶ θελῆσαι καὶ ἐλπίσαι ὁδός ἐστιν εὐθεῖα, *C.H.* XI. 21). The virtue of the soul is knowledge, for he who knows is both good and pious and already divine (ἀρετὴ ψυχῆς γνῶσις· ὁ γὰρ γνοὺς καὶ ἀγαθὸς καὶ εὐσεβὴς καὶ ἤδη θεῖος, *C.H.* x. 9). To possess such knowledge is to be a complete man, and not only so, but to be immortal and even a god (cf. *C.H.* IV. 4 οὗτοι μετέσχον τῆς γνώσεως καὶ τέλειοι ἐγένοντο ἄνθρωποι, *ibid.* 5 ὅσοι δὲ τῆς ἀπὸ τοῦ θεοῦ δωρεᾶς μετέσχον, οὗτοι, ὦ Τάτ, κατὰ σύγκρισιν τῶν ἔργων ἀθάνατοι ἀντὶ θνητῶν εἰσίν, *C.H.* x. 4 ἡ τοῦ ἀγαθοῦ θέα...πάσης ἀθανασίας ἀνάπλεως, *C.H.* I. 26 τοῦτό ἐστιν τὸ ἀγαθὸν τέλος τοῖς γνῶσιν ἐσχηκόσι, θεωθῆναι). Thus the Hermetists would have agreed with John: αὕτη ἐστὶν ἡ αἰώνιος ζωή, ἵνα γινώσκωσίν σε τὸν μόνον ἀληθινὸν θεόν (xvii. 3): and like the evangelist, they wrote ἵνα ζωὴν ἔχητε (xx.31). For it is because they believed that knowledge of God is the only way of salvation that they expounded their philosophy. Some of them proclaim it with what we can only call an evangelistic passion. 'Oh earth-born men,' cries the prophet of Poimandres, 'why have ye given yourselves over to death, when ye have the right to partake of immortality? Repent, ye who have made error your fellow-traveller and ignorance your consort. Depart from that light which is darkness! Leave corruption and partake of immortality!' (*C.H.* I. 28).

We must now ask, what is this 'knowledge' which the Hermetists proclaim as the only way of salvation? As most of the *libelli* are concerned with speculations about the nature of God and the eternal world, the origin and constitution of the visible world, the nature and destiny of man, and the like, we might reasonably conclude that this was what they meant by saving knowledge. It is at least clear that they thought such speculations very important. Not that they regarded them as speculations. For them they were divinely revealed truth. In the first *libellus* of the *Corpus*, the author relates how he saw a vision of creation, which was interpreted to him by the God Poimandres himself. And the fiction by which the teaching is generally put into the mouth of Hermes, the messenger and revealer of the gods,[1] is enough to show that the writers believed themselves to be transmitting revelation. To accept and believe the divinely revealed truth about God and the world is at the least a necessary preliminary to salvation, for we are thus secured against πλάνη, against erroneous ideas about life, its meaning and purpose. 'The evil of the soul', says Hermes to Tat, 'is ignorance. For the soul that knows nothing of existent things, nor of their nature, nor of the Good, is shaken blindly by bodily passions. This unhappy soul, being ignorant of itself, is slave to alien and oppressive bodies, carrying the body like a burden, not governing it but being governed by it. This is the evil of the soul' (*C.H.* x. 8). And again, 'Without philosophy it is impossible to be perfectly pious. But he who learns of what nature things are, and how they are ordered, and by whom, and to what end, will be thankful for all things to the Creator, as to a good father, a kindly fosterer, and a faithful guardian, and he who is thankful will be a pious man.... Let this, my child, be the end of piety, to which when you have attained, you will live nobly and die happily, because your soul knows where to fly aloft' (*Exc. ap.* Stob., Scott, II B, 2, 4).

It is thus clear that the Hermetists believed that their theological, cosmological and anthropological dogmas had in some sense saving power. At the same time there is sufficient evidence that γνῶσις is for them something more than metaphysics. One writer distinguishes between γνῶσις and ἐπιστήμη, which is scientific knowledge of the object. Γνῶσις, he says, ἐστιν ἐπιστήμης τὸ τέλος (*C.H.* x. 9). Although other writers do not make this distinction explicitly, yet many of them indicate that at its best γνῶσις is knowledge *of* God, and not merely knowledge about Him. After all, the most important thing we can know about God (they

---

[1] Hermes himself is sometimes taught by Νοῦς, or by Ἀγαθὸς Δαιμών, ὁ πρωτόγονος θεός. For the compiler of the *Corpus*, as probably for the author of *C.H.* XIII, the prophet of *C.H.* I is Hermes, though the tractate itself does not say so.

imply) is that it is His will, His nature and property to be known by men. God is the Good, and it is the property of the Good to be known (ἴδιον τοῦ ἀγαθοῦ τὸ γνωρίζεσθαι, *C.H.* x. 4). And again, 'God is not ignorant of man, but knows him altogether and desires to be known' (οὐ γὰρ ἀγνοεῖ τὸν ἄνθρωπον ὁ θεός, ἀλλὰ πάνυ γνωρίζει καὶ θέλει γνωρίζεσθαι, *C.H.* x 15). Man is τοῦ θεοῦ δεκτικὸς καὶ τῷ θεῷ συνουσιαστικός, capable of receiving God and of communing with Him. For he is the only animal with which God converses, τούτῳ γὰρ μόνῳ τῷ ζῴῳ ὁ θεὸς ὁμιλεῖ (*C.H.* XII. 19). 'Holy is God', runs the hymn in *Poimandres*, 'who wills to be known and is known to His own' (ἅγιος ὁ θεὸς ὃς γνωσθῆναι βούλεται καὶ γινώσκεται τοῖς ἰδίοις, *C.H.* I. 31).

But further, 'Like is known by like.'[1] Hence to know God is in some sort to partake of His nature. 'Unless you make yourself like God', says Nous to Hermes (ἐὰν μὴ σεαυτὸν ἐξισάσῃς τῷ θεῷ), 'you cannot rationally apprehend God, for like is apprehended by like (τὸ γὰρ ὅμοιον τῷ ὁμοίῳ νοητόν). Make yourself to grow into immeasurable greatness, leap beyond all body, rise above all time, and become an eternal being (αἰὼν γενοῦ), and you shall rationally apprehend God.... Become higher than all height, lower than all depth. Comprehend in yourself all sense-perceptions of created things, fire and water, dry and wet. [Imagine yourself] to be everywhere at once, in earth, in the sea, in heaven; yet unborn, in the womb, young, old, dead, and whatever there is after death. Apprehend all these things at once, times, places, qualities, quantities, and you shall be able to apprehend God' (*C.H.* XI. 20). We are reminded on one side of Plato's description of the philosopher as the 'spectator of all time and all existence'. But the Hermetist means something less rational, more mystical. Similarly in the *De Regeneratione* (Περὶ Παλιγγενεσίας) the reborn Tat exclaims, 'I am in heaven, on earth, in water, in air. I am in animals, in plants, in the womb, before the womb, after the womb, everywhere!' (*C.H.* XIII. 11). These writers seem to be attempting to describe what some mystics call the 'cosmic consciousness'—an experience of liberation from the limits of individuality and identification with the All. Accordingly in the *Key of Hermes* the knowledge of God is described in terms which are clearly those of mystic vision. 'Not yet are we able to open the eyes of the mind and behold the beauty, the imperishable, inconceivable beauty, of the Good. For you will see it, when you cannot say anything about it. For the

[1] Aristotle, *De Anima* I. 404b17 γινώσκεσθαι γὰρ τῷ ὁμοίῳ τὸ ὅμοιον, with references to Empedocles and to Plato's *Timaeus*. The idea is frequently enunciated.

knowledge of it is divine silence and annihilation of all senses.... Shining about all the mind, it shines also upon the whole soul and draws it up from the body, and changes it all into [divine] essence' (*C.H.* x. 5–6).

Such then is the goal of γνῶσις. The metaphysical speculations which bulk so largely in the *Hermetica* are propaedeutic to the vision of God. Thus after a long disquisition on astronomy Hermes says, 'He who is not ignorant of these things can apprehend God precisely. Indeed, if I may speak so boldly, he may behold Him with his own eyes (αὐτόπτης γενόμενος θεάσασθαι), and beholding become blessed' (*Exc. ap.* Stob., Scott, VI. 18). He adds, however, 'But it is impossible for one who is in the body to have such happiness. One must exercise the soul beforehand here, in order that when it goes there, where it is permitted to behold God, it may not miss the way. Those men who are lovers of the body will never behold the vision of the beautiful and the good.' Some of the other writers also take the view that the beatific vision is reserved for the next life, but some clearly conceive it to be possible in this life, as the hymn in the Latin *Asclepius* emphatically declares: 'gaudemus quod te nobis ostenderis totum; gaudemus quod nos in corporibus sitos aeternitati fueris consecrare dignatus. haec enim humana sola gratulatio, cognitio majestatis tuae'[1] (*Ascl.* 41).

It is in fact in their religious attitude to God that the unity of the Hermetic writings is to be sought. It is difficult to find in them anything like a consistent or uniform system of philosophy. Sometimes they use language which should strictly imply an immanence of God in the world amounting to a complete pantheism. At other times they strain language to emphasize His complete transcendence. Ordinarily they describe the deity in such terms as νοῦς, or τὸ ἓν καὶ τὸ πᾶν, or the like, avoiding any suspicion of anthropomorphism, and yet they speak at times of communion with God in terms which are applicable only to personal relations. But always they make it clear that to 'know' God is a profound religious experience satisfying the ultimate needs of the soul. This comes out most clearly in the hymns which are appended to some of the *libelli*—notably in those of the *Poimandres* and the Περὶ Παλιγγενεσίας.

In these hymns we meet with a recurrent devotional formula which reminds the reader of the religious language of the Fourth Gospel—the

[1] The Greek text of the Λόγος Τέλειος reads: χαίρομεν ὅτι σεαυτὸν ἡμῖν ἔδειξας, χαίρομεν ὅτι ἐν πλάσμασιν ἡμᾶς ὄντας ἀπεθέωσας τῇ σεαυτοῦ γνώσει. χάρις ἀνθρώπου πρός σε μία, τὸ γνωρίσαι (Nock-Festugière after Pap. Mimaut).

formula of Life and Light, used as a description either of God Himself or of the experience of communion with God. Thus in the *Poimandres*: 'I believe and testify: I enter into Life and Light. Blessed art Thou, O Father!' (πιστεύω καὶ μαρτυρῶ· εἰς ζωὴν καὶ φῶς χωρῶ. εὐλογητὸς εἶ πάτερ, *C.H.* I. 32). In the Περὶ Παλιγγενεσίας: 'O Holy Knowledge, enlightened by thee, through thee hymning the intellectual Light, I rejoice with the joy of mind!...Save, O Life; enlighten, O Light!' (γνῶσις ἁγία, φωτισθεὶς ἀπὸ σοῦ, διὰ σοῦ τὸ νοητὸν φῶς ὑμνῶν, χαίρω ἐν χαρᾷ νοῦ...σῷζε ζωή, φώτιζε φῶς, *C.H.* XIII. 18–19).

This conception of God as Life and Light clearly belongs to a religious tradition which is represented also in the Johannine writings. 'God is light, and in Him is no darkness at all'; 'In Him was life and the life was the light of men': such expressions would be entirely in place in a Hermetic writing. The precise significance of such expressions in the general thought of the *Hermetica* is less clear than their adequacy as devotional formulae. It is, however, in no way surprising that thinkers in the Platonic tradition should follow out the master's suggestion that where thought falters at the task of conceiving directly the absolute Good it should look to the sun, the light of this world, as the offspring and image of the Good. In one excerpt we actually have the statement, 'The sun is the image of the heavenly Creator-God' (ἥλιος εἰκών ἐστι τοῦ ἐπουρανίου δημιουργοῦ θεοῦ, *Exc. ap.* Stob., Scott, XXI. 2), and there are similar suggestions elsewhere, but these probably belong to the recrudescence of sun worship in the third century. The figure enabled the Hermetists to express the relation of God to the world by the metaphor of rays proceeding from a source of light (*C.H.* X. 22 τοῦ θεοῦ καθάπερ ἀκτῖνες αἱ ἐνέργειαι, cf. XII. 1; XVI. 16).

In some of the *Hermetica* the phenomenon of life in the universe is an absorbing interest. Thus in *C.H.* XII the world is defined as πλήρωμα τῆς ζωῆς (15), and we have the remarkable statement: 'As heaven, earth, water and air are parts of the world, so life and immortality...are parts of God' (ὥσπερ τοῦ κόσμου μέρη ἐστιν οὐρανὸς καὶ ὕδωρ καὶ γῆ καὶ ἀήρ, τὸν αὐτὸν τρόπον μέρη[1] ἐστι ⟨θεοῦ⟩ ζωὴ καὶ ἀθανασία..., 21). The suggestion surely is that as God is manifestly the cause of physical life in the world, so we can look to Him for life everlasting. Again in *C.H.* XI there is an argument from the unity of life in the universe to the unity of

[1] MSS. vary between μέρη and μέλη. The insertion of θεοῦ is an old conjecture of Turnebus. Scott accepts it in his text; N.-F. do not give it in the text, but supply it in translation. The whole context, I think, makes it necessary.

God: 'If all things are alive, and life is one, then God is one. And again, if all things are alive, both things in heaven and things on earth, and there is one life in them all brought into being by God, and this *is* God, then all things are brought into being by God' (εἰ δὲ πάντα ζῷα, μία δὲ καὶ ἡ ζωή, εἷς ἄρα καὶ ὁ θεός. καὶ πάλιν εἰ πάντα ζῷά ἐστι, καὶ τὰ ἐν οὐρανῷ καὶ τὰ ἐν τῇ γῇ, μία δὲ κατὰ πάντων ζωὴ ὑπὸ τοῦ θεοῦ γίνεται, καὶ αὕτη ἔστι θεός, ὑπὸ τοῦ θεοῦ ἄρα γίνεται πάντα, 14). 'For who beside Him is the maker of life and immortality?' (τίς γὰρ μετ' ἐκεῖνόν ἐστι ζωῆς καὶ ἀθανασίας ⟨καὶ⟩ μεταβολῆς ποιητής; 5). In a word, life is the same thing as the Beautiful and the Good, i.e. it is God (ἔστι δὲ τοῦτο, ὦ φίλτατε, ζωή, τοῦτο δέ ἐστι τὸ καλόν, τοῦτο δέ ἐστι τὸ ἀγαθόν, τοῦτό ἐστιν ὁ θεός, 13).

It is probable that in the general medley of religious beliefs characteristic of the Hellenistic world we must allow for the influence of Zoroastrianism and of Oriental sun-worship in the tendency to conceive God as light, and perhaps for the influence of Egypt, where *ankh*, life, was the attribute of various gods, in the tendency to conceive Him as life. But what is the origin of this liturgical formula which combines life and light? That question does not seem to have a clear answer. But it is possible that the use of both symbols in the Hebrew Scriptures contributed to the growth of the conception, for the influence of these Scriptures on certain of the *Hermetica* is undeniable. We recall that in one place at least in the Old Testament the two symbols are brought together:

...with Thee is the fountain of life:

In Thy light shall we see light (Ps. xxxvi. 9);

and we may observe that the collocation is already fixed for Philo.

In so far as the Hermetists follow the immanental or pantheistic theology of the Stoics, and identify God with the universe, the distinction between knowledge about the universe and knowledge of God tends to disappear, for in seeing the works of God we see God, and indeed are in some sort ourselves God. Thus the strongly Stoic author of *C.H.* v (Ὅτι ἀφανὴς θεὸς φανερώτατός ἐστιν) speaks in terms of pure pantheism: 'There is nothing in the whole world which is not He. He is existent things and non-existent things. For existent things are such as He has manifested, non-existent things such as He holds within Himself' (οὐδὲν γάρ ἐστιν ἐν παντὶ ἐκείνῳ [*sc.* κόσμῳ] ὃ οὔκ ἐστιν αὐτός. ἔστιν οὗτος καὶ τά ὄντα αὐτὸς καὶ τὰ μὴ ὄντα. τὰ μὲν γὰρ ὄντα ἐφανέρωσε, τὰ δὲ μὴ ὄντα ἔχει ἐν ἑαυτῷ, v. 9).[1] Accordingly the worshipper of God can say, 'Thou art whatsoever I am; Thou art whatsoever I do; Thou art whatsoever I say: for Thou art all' (σὺ εἶ ὃ ἂν ὦ, σὺ εἶ ὃ ἂν ποιῶ, σὺ εἶ ὃ ἂν λέγω· σὺ γὰρ πάντα εἶ, v. 11).[2] But there is little consistent pantheism in the *Hermetica*. Even the writer just quoted, the most definitely Stoic of them all except the author of the Λόγος Ἱερός (*C.H.* III), can speak of God as Father and Creator, and compare Him to a sculptor or a painter. Indeed it is difficult to take his pantheism with full seriousness in view of a long passage where he deduces the Creator from His created works in a tone which recalls Hebrew poetry: 'If you would see Him, consider the sun, consider the order of the stars. Who is He that guards their order?... Who is He that defined the manner and greatness of their course? This Great Bear that revolves about itself and carries the whole world round with it, who is He that possesses this instrument? Who is He that set bounds to the sea? Who is He that made the earth firm?'—and then, after a description of the wonders of the human frame—'Who is He that made all these things? Who is their mother, who their father? Who but the invisible God who created all things by His own will?' (*C.H.* v. 3, 4, 7).

On the other hand, the author of Νοῦς πρὸς Ἑρμῆν, though he is as markedly Platonic as the author of *C.H.* v is Stoic, and though his fundamental maxim is πηγὴ πάντων ὁ θεός, yet allows himself the pantheistically-sounding expression, αὐτουργὸς γὰρ ὢν ἀεί ἐστιν ἐν τῷ ἔργῳ, αὐτὸς ὢν ὃ ποιεῖ (*C.H.* XI. 14). It is clear that he is speaking of an immanence which by no means excludes a real transcendence. The thought of God's unceasing activity which is here expressed receives emphasis elsewhere in the same dialogue: 'God is not idle, else all things would be idle, for all things are full of God; but there is no idleness anywhere in the world or out of it. "Idleness" is an empty word whether applied to the Maker or to what is made', οὐ γὰρ ἀργὸς ὁ θεός, ἐπεὶ πάντα ἂν ἦν ἀργά· ἅπαντα γὰρ πλήρη τοῦ θεοῦ. ἀλλ' οὐδὲ ἐν τῷ κόσμῳ ἐστιν

[1] Cf. x. 2 τί γάρ ἐστιν θεός...ἢ τὸ τῶν πάντων εἶναι οὐκέτι ὄντων; XII. 22–3 τοῦτό ἐστιν ὁ θεός, τὸ πᾶν, ἐν δὲ τῷ παντὶ οὐδέν ἐστιν ὃ μὴ ἔστιν [*sc.* θεός]. All the same, if God is also the potentiality of things not yet existent, then the thought is not purely pantheistic. There is a curious suggestion of a philosophy not altogether unlike Samuel Alexander's.

[2] This is echoed in the language of a magical papyrus, Οἶδά σε, Ἑρμῆ, καὶ σὺ ἐμέ· ἐγώ εἰμι σὺ καὶ σὺ ἐγώ, which may well go back to a Hermetic liturgy, where its true purport would have been religious or mystical rather than philosophical. We may question whether in fact the apparent pantheism of *C.H.* v is not more properly religious and mystical than strictly metaphysical in spite of its philosophical colouring.

ἀργία οὐδαμοῦ οὐδὲ ἕν τινι ἄλλῳ· ἀργία γὰρ ὄνομα κενόν ἐστι, καὶ τοῦ ποιοῦντος καὶ τοῦ γενομένου (XI. 5). This thought, which recalls the Johannine ὁ πατήρ μου ἕως ἄρτι ἐργάζεται (v. 17), is elaborated in other passages of the *Corpus*. God is essentially the one Creator, transcending the universe, to which He imparts existence by communicating Himself to it.

Such is the prevailing view of the writers of the *Corpus*. Some of them are at greater pains to guard against a pantheistic identification of God with any other existence. 'What then is God?' asks Asklepios in the Λόγος Καθολικός, and Hermes replies, 'He who is no one of these things, but the cause of existence to them and to all and each of all existent things', ὁ μηδὲ ἓν τούτων ὑπάρχων, ὢν δὲ καὶ τοῦ εἶναι τούτοις αἴτιος καὶ πᾶσι καὶ ἑνὶ ἑκάστῳ τῶν ὄντων πάντων (*C.H.* II. 12). And again, 'God is not mind, but the cause of the existence of mind, nor πνεῦμα, but the cause of the existence of πνεῦμα, nor light, but the cause of the existence of light', ὁ οὖν θεὸς οὐ νοῦς ἐστιν, αἴτιος δὲ τοῦ νοῦν εἶναι, οὐδὲ πνεῦμα, αἴτιος δὲ τοῦ εἶναι πνεῦμα, οὐδὲ φῶς, αἴτιος δὲ τοῦ φῶς εἶναι (*ibid.* 14).

There is in some *libelli* a tendency to emphasize the 'otherness' of God by means of negations. The Good, according to the tractate called *The Bowl* (Κρατὴρ ἢ Μονάς), is like to itself but unlike all else (αὐτῷ μέν ἐστιν ὅμοιος, τοῖς δὲ ἄλλοις πᾶσιν ἀνόμοιον, IV. 9). Cf. XI. 5 μηδέποτε τῶν κάτω μήτε τῶν ἄνω ὅμοιόν τι ἡγήσῃ τῷ θεῷ. God in fact is 'das ganz Andere'. This does not mean merely that God is not to be identified with anything in the phenomenal order. The contrast between phenomena and noumena is always assumed when Platonism predominates. But sometimes doubts are expressed whether God can properly be said even to be νοητός, whether He can properly be said to have οὐσία at all, or is strictly ἀνουσίαστος (II. 4–5; cf. XII. 1). This is again Platonic. The Good is ἐπέκεινα τῆς οὐσίας (*Rep.* 504 b). One writer indeed pushes the transcendence of God to the point of an absolute dualism of God and the world. 'I thank God', he exclaims, 'that He has put it into my mind, as touching knowledge of the Good, that it is impossible for the Good to exist in the world. For the world is the totality of evil, and God the totality of good' (κἀγὼ δὲ χάριν ἔχω τῷ θεῷ, τῷ εἰς νοῦν μοι βαλόντι περὶ τῆς γνώσεως τοῦ ἀγαθοῦ, ὅτι ἀδύνατόν ἐστιν αὐτὸ ἐν τῷ κόσμῳ κἂν εἶναι. ὁ γὰρ κόσμος πλήρωμά ἐστι τῆς κακίας, ὁ δὲ θεὸς τοῦ ἀγαθοῦ, VI. 4). This pessimistic judgment recalls I John v. 19 ὁ κόσμος ὅλος ἐν τῷ πονηρῷ κεῖται. On this view, to know God one must turn from the world and seek the Good and the Beautiful, which are nowhere in the world: ἐὰν περὶ τοῦ θεοῦ 3ητῆς, καὶ περὶ τοῦ καλοῦ 3ητεῖς, VI. 5. But this absolute dualism is not characteristic of the *Hermetica*, which almost always represent the cosmos as in one way or another a revelation of God. They echo in various forms the closing sentence of the *Timaeus*, in which the cosmos is described as εἰκὼν τοῦ νοητοῦ θεὸς αἰσθητός. E.g. *C.H.* VIII. 2 πρῶτος γὰρ πάντων ὄντως καὶ ἀΐδιος καὶ ἀγέννητος ὁ δημιουργὸς τῶν ὅλων θεός. δεύτερος δὲ ὁ κατ᾽ εἰκόνα αὐτοῦ [*scil.* ὁ κόσμος], ὑπ᾽ αὐτοῦ γενόμενος καὶ ὑπ᾽ αὐτοῦ συνεχόμενος καὶ τρεφόμενος καὶ ἀθανατιζόμενος, ὡς ὑπὸ ἰδίου [1] πατρός, ἀεί3ωος[2] ὡς ἀθάνατος: Λόγος Τέλειος (= Latin *Asclepius*), 8 ὁ κύριος καὶ τῶν πάντων ποιητής, ὃν θεὸν καλεῖν νενομίκαμεν, ἔτι τὸν δεύτερον ἐποίησε θεὸν ὁρατὸν καὶ αἰσθητόν... ἐπεὶ οὖν τοῦτον ἐποίησε πρῶτον καὶ μόνον καὶ ἕνα, καλὸς δὲ αὐτῷ ἐφάνη καὶ πληρέστατος πάντων τῶν ἀγαθῶν, ἠγάσθη τε καὶ πάνυ ἐφίλησεν ὡς ἴδιον τόκον.[3] The κόσμος therefore is Son of God, bearing His likeness. Man similarly is the offspring of the κόσμος, and bears its likeness; cf. *C.H.* VIII. 5 τὸ δὲ τρίτον 3ῷον, ὁ ἄνθρωπος, κατ᾽ εἰκόνα τοῦ κόσμου γενόμενος, *et passim*. Thus we have the gradation of being: God, cosmos, man. Man accordingly knows God not immediately but through the mediation of the cosmos. 'Man became a spectator of the works of God, and he marvelled and recognized their Maker', θεατὴς γὰρ ἐγένετο τοῦ ἔργου τοῦ θεοῦ ὁ ἄνθρωπος καὶ ἐθαύμασε καὶ ἐγνώρισε τὸν ποιήσαντα (*C.H.* IV. 2). It is to be observed that the idea that man knows God through His Son the cosmos sometimes finds expression in terms which recall Christian language about the revelation of God in His Son Jesus Christ. Such statements as John i. 18, xiv. 9 *b*, would readily have been accepted by many Hermetists, though by the 'Son' they would have understood the cosmos.

This simple conception of mediation, however, is modified in two ways: (i) the emphasis on the transcendence of God leads to the introduction of further grades of being between God and the cosmos; and (ii) it is held that man is something more than a mere offspring of the cosmos, and is not wholly dependent on it for his knowledge of God.

[1] *Sic* MSS.: ἀϊδίου N.-F.

[2] MSS. ἀεί3ωον *vel* ἀεὶ 3ῶν.

[3] Verbally, there is some resemblance between this and John iii. 16 ἠγάπησεν ὁ θεὸς τὸν κόσμον, but there κόσμος is not the universe but mankind. In *C.H.* I. 12 the beloved ἴδιος τόκος is Man. However differently it works out, the thought of the evangelist is moving among concepts and images which are common to him and the Hermetists.

Some of the more distinctive features of the Hermetic philosophy are the product of these two tendencies.

In so far as the Hermetists are under Platonic influence, it is natural that they should make use of the conception of a noumenal world, transcendent and eternal, which is the archetype of the phenomenal world. Thus in *C.H.* xvi. 12 the κόσμος νοητός encompasses the κόσμος αἰσθητός and fills it ποικίλαις καὶ παντομόρφοις ἰδέαις. In the *Poimandres* it is revealed in a vision that the primal light, which is God, consists of innumerable δυνάμεις making up a world which is the ἀρχέτυπον εἶδος (*C.H.* 1. 8). In Philo the κόσμος νοητός is a mediating factor between God and the phenomenal world; but the Hermetists do not in general seem to make much use of the Platonic doctrine in this particular way. It reduces itself for the most part to a mere distinction between ὁρατά and νοητά, the former known by αἴσθησις, the latter by νόησις, and in this sense it is almost everywhere assumed. But that God made the phenomenal world through the νοητά, or that we must ascend to knowledge of God through knowledge of the νοητά, is scarcely made clear. It seems to have been more congenial to the Hermetists to conceive the divine element in the κόσμος as a cosmic soul than as the reflection of a transcendent world of ideas. This still leaves open the question how the transcendent God is related to the world which is His creation.

A very common mode of expression is to speak of the δυνάμεις or ἐνέργειαι of God as pervading the cosmos, and these are sometimes compared to rays (ἀκτῖνες) streaming from the eternal light. But in some tractates there is an attempt to define more explicitly an entity intermediate between God and the world. In the Λόγος Καθολικός God, or the Good, is wholly other than all existing things; but Space, τόπος, in which all things move and have their being, is divine, or may even be called in some sense God, and so is a sort of second God, mediating between the Absolute and phenomena (*C.H.* ii. 1–6). In *C.H.* xi the mediating entity is αἰών. Here the personified Νοῦς begins his exposition περὶ τοῦ παντὸς καὶ τοῦ θεοῦ with the formula ⟨ὁ⟩ θεός, ὁ αἰών, ὁ κόσμος, ὁ χρόνος, ἡ γένεσις. This hierarchy of being is expounded in a series of propositions defining the relations of God, Eternity, the World, Time and Generation in various ways. The thought is not very clear, but the intention seems to be to affirm that the world is not, as some would have it, the direct image of God, but the image of Eternity, which is His image (εἰκὼν τοῦ θεοῦ ὁ αἰών, τοῦ δὲ αἰῶνος ὁ κόσμος, xi. 15), and hence that knowledge of the cosmos *simpliciter* (cosmology) is not in itself the way to knowledge of God. We must rise through the world to Eternity which 'encompasses' the world, or, as we might put it, we must know the world *sub specie aeternitatis*, if we would know God. This is in fact implied pretty clearly in the maxim at the end of this dialogue,[1] which I have already quoted in another connection: 'leap out beyond all body, transcend all time, αἰὼν γενοῦ, καὶ νοήσεις τὸν θεόν'. This concept of αἰών recurs in the Latin *Asclepius*, 30: 'In ipsa enim aeternitatis vivacitate mundus agitatur, et in ipsa vitali aeternitate locus est mundi . . . ipse extrinsecus vivificatur ab aeternitate, vivificatque ea quae intra se sunt omnia.'

The concept goes back to the *Timaeus*, but its presentation in the Νοῦς πρὸς Ἑρμῆν and the Λόγος Τέλειος is not purely Platonic. It seems that we must allow for the probable influence of Iranian theology, which knows of a god Zirvan (Αἰών, Κρόνος = Χρόνος), and for the Egyptian practice of giving the title αἰών to the gods of polytheism, perhaps with the intention of suggesting an order of divinity lower than that of the supreme God. The familiar use of αἰών in the Gnostics is similar to this. If this equivocation in the term be allowed for, then the statement that the worshipper must himself become an 'aeon' is intelligible. The doctrine is then clear: Αἰών mediates between God and the world; by becoming an αἰών, by identifying himself with Αἰών, man knows God.

The concepts of Space and Eternity, however, as intermediate entities must be regarded as comparatively isolated experiments, which did not commend themselves to the Hermetists in general. More commonly an expression of the idea of mediation is sought by way of the concept Νοῦς. That God Himself is of the nature of νοῦς, mind or reason, is an idea common to almost all of these writers. Either God *is* νοῦς, or νοῦς is His οὐσία, so far as He may be said to possess οὐσία. Many of the writers are content to conceive His relation to the world in the simple form that in so far as the world is rational it bears the mark of its divine origin. But some of them are more subtle, and attempt in various ways to distinguish νοῦς in a measure from God in His absolute being and from the world. Thus in the dialogue just quoted νοῦς is an ἐνέργεια

---

[1] Scott divides this dialogue into two in the middle of 6, on the ground that the doctrine of 6b–22 is for the most part fairly normal Platonism, and does not make use of the concept of αἰών. The division does not seem to be called for. The recurrence of αἰών in 15 (which Scott excises) and 20 (which Scott emends away) seems to clamp the two parts together, and to supply the motive for the introduction of αἰών at the beginning—for as usual the motive of the dialogue is practical rather than theoretical. N.-F. accept the dialogue as a unity.

of the transcendent God, and in the Λόγος Καθολικός (*C.H.* ii) God is not νοῦς but the cause of the existence of νοῦς. *C.H.* xii bears the title Περὶ Νοῦ Κοινοῦ. It begins: 'Νοῦς, Ο Tat, is of the essence of God, if indeed there is an essence of God; and of what manner this may be, He alone knows exactly. Νοῦς, then, is not cut off from the essence of God, but as it were evolved out of it, like the light of the sun' ('Ο νοῦς, ὦ Τάτ, ἐξ αὐτῆς τῆς τοῦ θεοῦ οὐσίας ἐστίν, εἴ γέ τις ἔστιν οὐσία θεοῦ· καὶ ποία τις οὖσα τυγχάνει, οὗτος μόνος ἀκριβῶς [αὐτὸν][1] οἶδεν. ὁ νοῦς οὖν οὐκ ἔστιν ἀποτετμημένος τῆς οὐσιότητος τοῦ θεοῦ, ἀλλ' ὥσπερ ἡπλωμένος, καθάπερ τὸ τοῦ ἡλίου φῶς, *C.H.* xii. 1). Otherwise expressed, it is the soul of God (xii. 9). This νοῦς rules over all things, fate and law and everything else (πάντων ἐπικρατεῖ ὁ νοῦς, ἡ τοῦ θεοῦ ψυχή, καὶ εἱμαρμένης καὶ νόμου καὶ τῶν ἄλλων πάντων, *C.H.* xii. 9). The intention is clearly to preserve the unique and worshipful transcendence of God while doing justice to the evidence of His creation in the rationality of the universe and its laws.

Since, however, the aim of the tractate, as of the *Hermetica* in general, is practical rather than theoretical—to lead men to the knowledge of God which is salvation—the writer is even more interested in the anthropological than in the cosmological aspect of his doctrine of νοῦς. 'This mind', he proceeds, 'is God in men, and therefore some men are gods, and their humanity is near to deity.... But in irrational animals mind is nature. For where soul is, there mind is, as where life is, there soul is. But in irrational animals the soul is life void of mind. For mind is the benefactor of the souls of men.... All souls therefore over which mind presides, to them it shows its own light' (οὗτος δὲ ὁ νοῦς ἐν μὲν ἀνθρώποις θεός ἐστιν· διὸ καί τινες τῶν ἀνθρώπων θεοί εἰσι, καὶ ἡ αὐτῶν ἀνθρωπότης ἐγγύς ἐστι τῆς θεότητος.... ἐν δὲ τοῖς ἀλόγοις ζῴοις ἡ φύσις ἐστίν. ὅπου γὰρ ψυχὴ ἐκεῖ καὶ νοῦς ἐστίν·... ἐν δὲ τοῖς ἀλόγοις ζῴοις ἡ ψυχὴ ζωή ἐστι κενὴ τοῦ νοῦ. ὁ γὰρ νοῦς ψυχῶν ἐστὶν εὐεργέτης ἀνθρώπων.... ὅσαις ἂν οὖν ψυχαῖς ὁ νοῦς ἐπιστατήσῃ, ταύταις φαίνει ἑαυτοῦ τὸ φέγγος, *C.H.* xii. 1–3). Such men are delivered from the domination of fate (*ibid.* 9), since mind is supreme over fate.

Similarly in the *Key of Hermes* νοῦς is said to enter into the pious soul and lead it to the light of knowledge (εἰς δὲ τὴν εὐσεβῆ ψυχὴν ὁ νοῦς ἐμβὰς ὁδηγεῖ αὐτὴν ἐπὶ τὸ τῆς γνώσεως φῶς, *C.H.* x. 21; cf. John xvi. 13 ὅταν δὲ ἔλθῃ ἐκεῖνος, τὸ πνεῦμα τῆς ἀληθείας, ὁδηγήσει ὑμᾶς εἰς τὴν ἀλήθειαν πᾶσαν). If, on the other hand, a man does not possess νοῦς,

[1] αὐτόν *seclusi.*

he is not a man in the full sense, 'for man is (by definition) a divine animal, and does not fall into the same class with other earthly animals, but with the so-called gods in heaven above, or rather, if one may venture to speak the truth, the man who is man indeed is above them, or at the least they are equals in power' (ἡ δὲ τοιαύτη ψυχή, ὦ τέκνον, νοῦν οὐκ ἔχει· ὅθεν οὐδὲ ἄνθρωπον δεῖ λέγεσθαι τὸν τοιοῦτον. ὁ γὰρ ἄνθρωπος ζῷόν ἐστι θεῖον καὶ οὐδὲ τοῖς ἄλλοις ζῴοις συγκρινόμενον τῶν ἐπιγείων ἀλλὰ τοῖς ἐν οὐρανῷ ἄνω λεγομένοις θεοῖς· μᾶλλον δὲ εἰ χρὴ τολμήσαντα εἰπεῖν τὸ ἀληθές, καὶ ὑπὲρ ἐκείνους ἐστὶν ὁ ὄντως ἄνθρωπος, ἢ πάντως γε ἰσοδυναμοῦσιν ἀλλήλοις, *ibid.* 24). In *C.H.* IX all men possess νοῦς; in some it does not function but those in whom it does function are saved (οὐ πᾶς δὲ ἄνθρωπος...ἀπολαύει τῆς νοήσεως, ἀλλ' ὁ μὲν ὑλικὸς ὁ δὲ οὐσιώδης. ὁ μὲν γὰρ μετὰ κακίας ὑλικὸς...ἀπὸ τῶν δαιμόνων τὸ σπέρμα τῆς νοήσεως ἴσχει, οἱ δὲ μετὰ τοῦ ἀγαθοῦ οὐσιωδῶς ὑπὸ τοῦ θεοῦ σωζόμενοι, *C.H.* IX. 5). In *The Bowl* (Κρατὴρ ἢ Μονάς) only some men possess νοῦς, and this fact is accounted for by a myth which tells how God willed that this precious possession should be a prize to contend for, and therefore filled a great bowl with νοῦς and sent it down in charge of a herald, who proclaimed 'Immerse thyself in this bowl, O soul that art able, who believest that thou shalt ascend to Him who sent down the bowl, who knowest for what thou wert born' (βάπτισον σεαυτὴν ἡ δυναμένη εἰς τοῦτον τὸν κρατῆρα, ἡ πιστεύουσα ὅτι ἀνελεύσῃ πρὸς τὸν καταπέμψαντα τὸν κρατῆρα, ἡ γνωρίζουσα ἐπὶ τί γέγονας, *C.H.* IV. 4). 'As many therefore as understood the proclamation, and immersed themselves in νοῦς, these partook of knowledge and became perfect men by receiving νοῦς' (ὅσοι μὲν οὖν συνῆκαν τοῦ κηρύγματος καὶ ἐβαπτίσαντο τοῦ νοός, οὗτοι μετέσχον τῆς γνώσεως καὶ τέλειοι ἐγένοντο ἄνθρωποι τὸν νοῦν δεξάμενοι). Here the τέλειος ἄνθρωπος is the same as the οὐσιώδης ἄνθρωπος of *C.H.* X and the ὄντως ἄνθρωπος of *C.H.* IX, and he is immortal and divine (IV. 5, 7). According to the Latin *Asclepius* (Λόγος Τέλειος) man has a twofold nature. On the one side he is οὐσιώδης, bearing the image of God ('solum enim animal homo duplex est; et ejus una pars simplex, quae, ut Graeci aiunt, οὐσιώδης, quam vocamus divinae similitudinis formam', Lat. *Ascl.* 7); the other part is ὑλικόν. The origin of this twofold nature this writer describes as follows. Having made the world, God, being so great and good, willed that there should be another, who could look upon the world which He had made out of Himself, and thereupon He made man as the imitator of His reason and care. Man as so made was οὐσιώδης, but in order that he might make contact with the material world God provided him with a material body (*ibid.* 8). Here the οὐσιώδης ἄνθρωπος is one part of human nature; in the other passages cited he is a sub-species of the human race, so to speak. But in either case we have a humanity which is divine in a sense other than that in which the whole cosmos is divine. Similarly in *The Bowl*, God, having made the world, desired to adorn it, and therefore sent down man as an ornament of the divine body (ἠθέλησε καὶ τὴν γῆν κοσμῆσαι, κόσμον δὲ θείου σώματος κατέπεμψε τὸν ἄνθρωπον, *C.H.* IV. 1–2). There may be a hint that the honourable term κόσμος belongs to the universe only as completed by the presence of divine humanity.

Here then we have arrived at the conception of man as something more than an offspring of the cosmos, bearing the divine image at second hand. He shares in the divine principle of mind or reason not merely as the lower animals and the rest of the cosmos do, by being rationally ordered, but by being in some sort identified with divine Mind whereby he inwardly knows God from whose essence mind proceeds. It is note-worthy that several expressions used of the τέλειος or οὐσιώδης ἄνθρωπος recall what is said in the Fourth Gospel of the divine Man or Son of Man. The οὐσιώδης ἄνθρωπος is sent down by God to earth; He knows ἐπὶ τί γέγονε, and believes that he will ascend to Him who sent him. He has received νοῦς, and so is divine and immortal. Similarly in John the Son of Man has come from above, He speaks of God as ὁ πέμψας με (*passim*), He says ἐγὼ εἰς τοῦτο γεγέννημαι (xviii. 37), He knows that ἀπὸ θεοῦ ἐξῆλθεν καὶ πρὸς τὸν θεὸν ὑπάγει (xiii. 3), He says, ἀναβαίνω πρὸς τὸν πατέρα μου (xx. 17), He has been baptized with πνεῦμα (which is in some sort the Christian equivalent of νοῦς, i. 32–4), and possesses that unity with God which is the goal of the τέλειος ἄνθρωπος, 'I and my Father are one' (x. 30).

But further, this whole doctrine of νοῦς as the medium at once of creation and of knowledge has obvious points of contact with the Philonic and Johannine doctrine of the Logos, for the Logos also is that aspect of the divine through which the universe was made, and through which men know God and receive the right to become sons of God. Thus while on the one hand the Hermetic νοῦς has affinities with the Johannine πνεῦμα, on the other hand it is parallel with the Johannine Logos.

We may now profitably enquire whether there are traces of an actual Logos-doctrine in the *Hermetica*. Scott is inclined to confine the meaning of the term λόγος wherever possible to that of 'word'. Naturally, as in any Greek literature, there are numerous places where that is the inevitable translation. But the Hermetists do not always use λόγος as the simple equivalent of 'word'. There is an instructive passage in the Περὶ Νοῦ Κοινοῦ (*C.H.* XII. 12 sqq.). God has given to man, says Hermes, two things which distinguish him from the other animals, νοῦς and λόγος, and besides these, he adds, he possesses τὸν προφορικὸν λόγον.[1] This is the Stoic term invented to distinguish the sense of λόγος as 'word' from its sense as 'thought', λόγος ἐνδιάθετος. Thus Hermes distinguishes the gift of speech from the gift of λόγος which along with νοῦς is man's prerogative. This is borne out by what follows. Tat, understanding λόγος as speech, objects, 'Do not the other animals use λόγος?' No, Hermes replies, not λόγος but φωνή. Λόγος, he goes on, is common to all men. But surely, Tat objects, each nation has its own λόγος. Man, replies Hermes, is one, and his λόγος is one, but it is variously interpreted in spoken signs. Thus λόγος is the same in Egypt, Persia and Greece (*ibid.* 13). Clearly then λόγος is not a spoken word, for when Egyptians, Persians and Greeks speak, they utter different *words*. The articulate thought or meaning, however, lying behind the word is common to all men. It is λόγος in this sense that is here said to be the image of God, and in this sense it is also called the νοῦς of God (*ibid.* 14), or again λόγος is in νοῦς as νοῦς is in God (*Exc. ap.* Stob. XI. 2 (15)), or νοῦς is in ψυχή and λόγος in νοῦς, or conversely, νοῦς is in λόγος and λόγος in the soul (X. 13). As a psychological term therefore, λόγος stands for a faculty or activity of the soul which is intimately associated with νοῦς, and in some sort dependent on it. In some places it is definitely inferior to νοῦς, as in *The Bowl*, where all men possess λόγος, but only those who have received 'baptism' in the Bowl possess νοῦς (*C.H.* IV. 3), and apparently in *Exc. ap.* Stob. IVb1, where science and art (ἐπιστήμη καὶ τέχνη) are ἐνέργεια τοῦ λογικοῦ, i.e. λόγος is the intellectual faculty (διανοητικὸς λόγος, *Exc. ap.* Stob. XVIII. 5), as distinguished from the higher faculty of νοῦς, which is the organ of γνῶσις. But elsewhere λόγος is an aspect of νοῦς itself, or at least is the instrument by which it works. Thus in *Exc. ap.* Stob. XIX. 5 λόγος is τῆς οὐσίας τοῦ καλοῦ θεωρητικός, and with it is associated knowledge of superior things (συνυπάρχει τῷ λόγῳ ἡ τῶν τιμίων γνῶσις, *ibid.* 6). Hence ἐν λόγῳ γενέσθαι is equivalent to μετέχειν ζωῆς νοερᾶς, and while man

[1] Scott, followed by N.-F., excises these words as a gloss. But even if they are excised, the distinction between λόγος ἐνδιάθετος and λόγος προφορικός is implicitly made. But see N.-F. note *ad loc.*

is called ζῷον διὰ τὴν ζωήν, he is called λογικὸν διὰ τὸ νοερόν (*Exc. ap.* Stob. xx. 3–4). It is for this reason that the λογικὸν μέρος τῆς ψυχῆς is described as ἐπιτήδειον εἰς ὑποδοχὴν τοῦ θεοῦ (*C.H.* xvi. 15), *capax Dei.*

Thus while the Hermetists work by preference with the concept of νοῦς, they have also a fairly well established doctrine of λόγος in the psychological sense, and this must be borne in mind when we turn to the few passages which seem to speak of a cosmic λόγος. In *Exc. ap.* Stob. xii. 1 the Providence by which the world is governed is defined as 'the absolute λόγος of the heavenly God' (πρόνοια δέ ἐστιν αὐτοτελὴς λόγος τοῦ ἐπουρανίου θεοῦ). Λόγος here is surely something more than simply 'word'. The dialogue called *The Bowl* begins, 'The Creator made the whole world not with hands but by λόγος'—are we to render 'by His word', or 'by thought'? The dialogue goes on to say that after so creating the world, God adorned this divine body by sending down man, and while the cosmos is superior to the animals by its permanence, man is superior to the cosmos in possessing λόγος καὶ νοῦς, for he became spectator of the work of God and wondered and recognized his Maker (τὸν πάντα κόσμον ἐποίησεν ὁ δημιουργὸς οὐ χερσὶν ἀλλὰ λόγῳ....κόσμον δὲ θείου σώματος κατέπεμψε τὸν ἄνθρωπον....καὶ ὁ μὲν κόσμος τῶν ζῴων ἐπλεονέκτει τὸ ἀείζωον ⟨ὁ δὲ ἄνθρωπος⟩[1] καὶ τοῦ κόσμου τὸν λόγον καὶ τὸν νοῦν. θεατὴς γὰρ ἐγένετο τοῦ ἔργου τοῦ θεοῦ ὁ ἄνθρωπος, καὶ ἐθαύμασε καὶ ἐγνώρισε τὸν ποιήσαντα, *C.H.* iv. 1–2). It is probable that we may recognize here some influence from the creation-story in Genesis, where God spoke and the world came into being. But what is not present in the Genesis story is the suggestion that man, descending from God, possessed that same λόγος by which God made the world. The passage at least hints at a divine 'thought' which shaped the world, and which abides in man as a permanent endowment, so that he is capable of recognizing the divine workmanship. We are not far from the conception of the divine Wisdom by which the worlds were made, and which passing into holy souls maketh them to be friends of God and prophets (Wisd. vii. 27).

In the *Hermetica* (or perhaps a single *Hermeticum*) cited by Cyril of Alexandria we meet with indications of a fully developed doctrine of the cosmic logos recalling that of Philo. Here the creative λόγος of the Lord of all is the πρώτη δύναμις which proceeded from Him. It creates and gives life, and rules over all created things (*Fragmenta* (Scott), 27–9). The work from which these citations are made was probably later than the writings of the Hermetic *Corpus*, and neither in the *Corpus* nor in

[1] *Sic* N.-F. after Scott, rejecting his further emendations.

the excerpts in Stobaeus do we find any such clearly developed doctrine. There are, however, two *libelli* of the *Corpus* which approach such a doctrine, the *Poimandres* (*C.H.* I) and the Περὶ Παλιγγενεσίας (*C.H.* XIII). These two are in several ways so closely related to Johannine thought that it will be worth while to consider them in some detail.

In the first *libellus* of the Hermetic *Corpus*[1] the author relates how he was called and commissioned by the God Poimandres to be 'a guide of the human race, teaching them the words, how and in what manner they shall be saved' (I. 29). There is nothing in the text to indicate that the prophet is conceived as Hermes, and it might quite well be taken as the account given by some unknown prophet of his call. But in the Περὶ Παλιγγενεσίας Hermes is made to refer to teaching which he received from Poimandres (*C.H.* XIII.15), and we may take it that by the time the latter dialogue was composed the *Poimandres* was accepted as a Hermetic writing, as it certainly was by the compiler of the *Corpus*. In any case it contains teaching of the kind which we have seen to be characteristic of the Hermetic school, but this teaching is presented in a more imaginative way than is usual with writers of this school, with a freer use of myth; and along with the pedantry of the philosophical jargon with which we are familiar there is an almost poetical quality in it, fitly preparing the way for the noble hymn with which it concludes. Whether or not it was intended to be attributed to the mythical Hermes Trismegistus, there is no mistaking the note of genuine and first-hand religious experience which gives it warmth and elevation.

The seer relates how he was in a state of mystical contemplation when he heard his name called. 'Who art thou?' he asked. 'I am Poimandres, the mind of the Sovereignty' (ἐγὼ μέν εἰμι ὁ Ποιμάνδρης, ὁ τῆς αὐθεντίας νοῦς, I. 2). The strange name probably represents the Egyptian *Pe-eime-n-Re*, 'the Knowledge of Ra',[2] of which the Greek ὁ τῆς αὐθεντίας

---

[1] I have discussed the *Poimandres* somewhat fully in *The Bible and the Greeks*, pp. 99–209.

[2] Zosimus, alluding to this dialogue, gives the form Ποιμενάνδρης, which he no doubt understood as = ποιμὴν ἀνδρῶν. It is just possible, but no more, that the author of *C.H.* XIII was thinking of such an etymology when he wrote λόγον τὸν σὸν ποιμαίνει ὁ νοῦς, but there is no suggestion in the dialogue that the god is in any sense a shepherd. Reitzenstein, building on this dubious etymology, attempted to bring *C.H.* I into contact with the Ποιμήν of Hermas, and invented an Ur-poimandres as a source for Hermas: a notable example of cobweb-spinning. It seems much more probable that Poimandres is an intentionally mysterious name, and the Egyptian derivation, adopted by Scott from the Egyptologist F. Ll. Griffith, is reasonably probable.

νοῦς serves as translation. In response to the seer's prayer, 'I desire to learn about existent things, and to apprehend (νοῆσαι) their nature, and to know God', a revelation is vouchsafed to him. He sees a vision of boundless light, bright and gladsome; and after a little while, over against it, a turbulent, sounding ocean of darkness. Then a holy word out of the light (ἐκ φωτός τις¹ λόγος ἅγιος) falls upon the ocean of darkness, and forthwith pure fire, followed by air, rises out of the darkness and remains suspended above it, leaving a mixture of earth and water, agitated by the πνευματικὸς λόγος (1. 5). Poimandres now explains that the light is He Himself, Mind or God, and the φωτεινὸς λόγος is the Son of God. The seer turns again to the vision. He now sees that the light is not simple, but consists of innumerable δυνάμεις, constituting a boundless world. This, Poimandres explains, is the archetypal form (τὸ ἀρχέτυπον εἶδος, i.e. as other writers would put it, the νοητὸς κόσμος). How then, the seer asks, did the elements of fire, air, water and earth come into being? The reply is that the Counsel of God received the Word, beheld the beautiful world (the κόσμος νοητός) and imitated it (ἐκ βουλῆς θεοῦ, ἥτις λαβοῦσα τὸν λόγον καὶ ἰδοῦσα τὸν καλὸν κόσμον ἐμιμήσατο, 1. 8).

Next, Mind, or God, being Life and Light, gave birth to another mind, the Creator (ὁ δὲ νοῦς ὁ θεός...ζωὴ καὶ φῶς ὑπάρχων, ἀπεκύησε [λόγῳ]² ἕτερον νοῦν δημιουργόν, 1. 9). This Demiurge created the seven planets, whose administration is called Fate (εἱμαρμένη). This accomplished, the Word of God, which had previously descended upon matter, leapt upward and was united with the νοῦς δημιουργός. Together they imparted a rotary movement to the planets, and this rotation caused life to appear in the lower elements of earth and water. Since, however, the λόγος had deserted this lower sphere, the living things it produced were ἄλογα ζῷα.

Now comes a fresh stage. The Father of all, Mind, being Life and Light, gave birth to a Man, like to Himself (ἀπεκύησεν ἄνθρωπον αὐτῷ ἴσον), having his Father's image, and delivered all created things into his hand. Man beheld the created universe, and desired himself to create. Receiving permission from his Father, he descended into the sphere of the Demiurge. The planetary beings imparted to him their own qualities,³

¹ Τι codd. plerique: spatium fere vi litterarum A (see N.-F.).
² I bracket λόγῳ after Reitzenstein: see *The Bible and the Greeks*, p. 133.
³ It is a familiar astrological idea that the planets contribute the factors which make up the dispositions of men. Our own language retains traces of it when we speak of a man as 'jovial', 'mercurial', or 'saturnine'.

and thus equipped he reached the lower sphere, displaying to it the beautiful form of God (τὴν καλὴν τοῦ θεοῦ μορφήν). Lower nature fell in love with the human form divine. Man returned her love, and they came together. 'And hence', says the seer, 'of all living things on earth man is twofold, mortal because of the body, but immortal because of the essential man' (καὶ διὰ τοῦτο παρὰ πάντα τὰ ἐπὶ τῆς γῆς ζῷα διπλοῦς ἐστὶν ὁ ἄνθρωπος, θνητὸς μὲν διὰ τὸ σῶμα, ἀθάνατος δὲ διὰ τὸν οὐσιώδη ἄνθρωπον, I. 15); for from this union of divine Man with Nature sprang the ancestors of the human race. Thus 'from Life and Light man became soul and mind, soul from Life and mind from Light' (*C.H.* I. 17). Then God spoke with a holy word, 'Increase by increase and multiply by multiplying, all ye creatures, and let rational man recognize that he is immortal and that the cause of death is love of the body' (ὁ θεὸς εὐθὺς εἶπεν ἁγίῳ λόγῳ· Αὐξάνεσθε ἐν αὐξήσει καὶ πληθύνεσθε ἐν πλήθει, πάντα τὰ κτίσματα καὶ δημιουργήματα· καὶ ἀναγνωρισάτω ὁ ἔννους ἄνθρωπος[1] ἑαυτὸν ὄντα ἀθάνατον, καὶ τὸν αἴτιον τοῦ θανάτου ἔρωτα σώματος, 18). The myth has thus led up to the moral which the seer is concerned to enforce.

The myth (which I have simplified by omitting features not directly relevant to our purpose) has long been recognized as being a rendering of the myth of the creation and fall in Genesis. I have shown elsewhere in detail that it follows its biblical model even more closely than appears on the surface, with frequent echoes of the actual language of the LXX. The Hebrew myth is interpreted in terms of the Platonic-Stoic philosophy which is common to most of the Hermetic writers, much as writers of the last century set out to reconcile Moses with Darwin. But it is clear that Genesis, understood in the light of Jewish Hellenistic exegesis in Alexandria, is regarded as an inspired document revealing the truth about the beginnings of man and the universe. If you know this truth, then you are in possession of the secret of immortality.

The rest of the *libellus* is devoted to the elaboration of this theme. 'The man who knows himself has entered into the absolute Good, but he who has loved the body which is of the error of lust, he abides erring in darkness, suffering the things of death in his senses' (ὁ ἀναγνωρίσας ἑαυτὸν ἐλήλυθεν εἰς τὸ περιούσιον ἀγαθόν,[2] ὁ δὲ ἀγαπήσας τὸ ἐκ πλάνης ἔρωτος σῶμα, οὗτος μένει ἐν τῷ σκότει πλανώμενος, αἰσθητῶς πάσχων

---

[1] ἄνθρωπος B[1] ἔννους *cett.* ὁ ἔννους N.-F. ὁ ἔννους ἄνθρωπος Reitzenstein. Cf. 21. ὁ ἔννους ἄνθρωπος ἀναγνωρισάτω ἑαυτόν.

[2] This I take to mean the good which is ἐπέκεινα τῆς οὐσίας.

τὰ τοῦ θανάτου, I. 19). And what is it to 'know oneself'? 'God the Father is Light and Life, from whom man is sprung. If therefore you learn that you are yourself of life and light, you will enter into life again' (φῶς καὶ ζωή ἐστιν ὁ θεὸς καὶ πατήρ, ἐξ οὗ ἐγένετο ὁ ἄνθρωπος. ἐὰν οὖν μάθῃς σεαυτὸν ἐκ ζωῆς καὶ φωτὸς ὄντα...εἰς ζωὴν πάλιν χωρήσεις, I. 21). This passage into life is then described as an ascent (ἄνοδος) of Man corresponding to his primal fall. On his journey through the seven spheres he gives back the passions which he had received from the planets, and thus purified arrives where the powers praise God. Then in order they ascend to the Father (καὶ τότε τάξει ἀνέρχονται πρὸς τὸν πατέρα). Being changed into powers they are in God (δυνάμεις γενόμενοι ἐν θεῷ γίνονται). In short, this is the good end of those who have acquired knowledge—to be deified (τοῦτό ἐστι τὸ ἀγαθὸν τέλος τοῖς γνῶσιν ἐσχηκόσιν, θεωθῆναι, I. 26).

It is clear that we have here an individual rendering of the common teachings of the Hermetic school. The use of the Hebrew creation-myth as a vehicle for these teachings is almost peculiar to the *Poimandres*, though there is reason to suspect the influence of the Hebrew Scriptures on other *libelli*.[1] But there is nothing essential which could not be documented from other writings of the *Corpus*. I should agree with Reitzenstein and Scott in concluding that there is no sufficient reason for suspecting any Christian influence.[2] But parallels to Christian teaching are obvious. In particular there is an unmistakable 'Johannine' ring (if we may put it so) about much of the language. I give a list of the more striking parallels to the Fourth Gospel (see pp. 34–35).

A general review of the parallels shows that expressions in the Fourth Gospel referring to Christ correspond to expressions in the *Poimandres* referring sometimes to Poimandres, the divine Revealer, sometimes to the prophet himself, and sometimes to the heavenly Ἄνθρωπος. And since the Prologue to the Fourth Gospel points to Christ as the creative *Logos* incarnate, we may say that the Johannine conception of Christ has in some measure combined the roles assigned in the *Poimandres* to four distinct beings. While there is nothing to lead us to infer any

[1] The creation-myth of Genesis also underlies the Λόγος Ἱερός (*C.H.* III), but this tractate is Judaeo-Stoic, and stands apart from other *Hermetica*. See *The Bible and the Greeks*, pp. 210–34. For further examples of biblical influence see *ibid.* pp. 235–42.

[2] Scott however admits the possibility that the writer may have been influenced by his Christian neighbours 'not in his doctrine...but rather in his view of his own function as a teacher...as one on whom is laid the task of calling mankind to repentance'. But is this necessary?

THE BACKGROUND

Corpus Hermeticum I (*Poimandres*)

6 τὸ φῶς ἐκεῖνο ἐγώ...ὁ σὸς θεός.

12 ὁ δὲ πάντων πατήρ...ἀπεκύησεν ἄνθρωπον αὐτῷ ἴσον, οὗ ἠράσθη⎫
ὡς ἰδίου τόκου...παρέδωκε τὰ ἑαυτοῦ πάντα δημιουργήματα. ⎪

13 (ὁ ἄνθρωπος) ἔξων τὴν πᾶσαν ἐξουσίαν. ⎬

14 ὁ τοῦ τῶν θνητῶν κόσμου καὶ τῶν ἀλόγων ζῴων ἔχων πᾶσαν⎪
ἐξουσίαν. ⎭

19 οὗτος μένει ἐν τῷ σκότει πλανώμενος.

21 εἰς ζωὴν πάλιν χωρήσεις.
πῶς εἰς ζωὴν χωρήσω; cf. 24 ἔτι δέ μοι εἰπὲ περὶ τῆς ἀνόδου.

22 παραγίνομαι αὐτὸς ἐγώ...τοῖς ὁσίοις καὶ ἀγαθοῖς...καὶ ἡ παρουσία
μου γίνεται βοήθεια, καὶ εὐθὺς τὰ πάντα γνωρίζουσι καὶ τὸν
πατέρα ἱλάσκονται ἀγαπητικῶς.
πυλωρὸς ὢν ἀποκλείσω τὰς εἰσόδους τῶν κακῶν.

26 ἀνέρχονται πρὸς τὸν πατέρα.
ἐν θεῷ γίνονται.
καθοδηγὸς γίνῃ τοῖς ἀξίοις, ὅπως τὸ γένος τῆς ἀνθρωπότητος διὰ
σοῦ ὑπὸ θεοῦ σωθῇ.

29 καθοδηγὸς ἐγενόμην τοῦ γένους, τοὺς λόγους διδάσκων πῶς καὶ τίνι
τρόπῳ σωθήσονται.
ἐτράφησαν ἐκ τοῦ ἀμβροσίου ὕδατος.

30 θεόπνους γενόμενος ⟨μέχρι⟩[1] τῆς ἀληθείας ἦλθον.

31 ἅγιος ὁ θεὸς ὁ πατὴρ τῶν ὅλων.
ἅγιος ὁ θεός, ὃς γνωσθῆναι βούλεται καὶ γινώσκεται τοῖς ἰδίοις.
ἅγιος εἶ ὁ λόγῳ συστησάμενος τὰ ὄντα.

32 φωτίσω τοὺς ἐν ἀγνοίᾳ τοῦ γένους μου ἀδελφούς.
πιστεύω καὶ μαρτυρῶ.

εἰς ζωὴν καὶ φῶς χωρῶ.
ὁ σὸς ἄνθρωπος συναγιάζειν[2] σοι βούλεται, καθὼς παρέδωκας αὐτῷ
τὴν πᾶσαν ἐξουσίαν.

---

[1] I have restored the text after *C.H.* IX. 10, οὐ φθάνει μέχρι τῆς ἀληθείας.
Reitzenstein ⟨ἐπὶ τὸν κύκλον⟩ τῆς ἀληθείας. Scott leaves a lacuna, but suggests
in his note ⟨ἐπὶ τὸ πέδιον⟩ τῆς ἀληθείας. N.-F. take ἀληθείας with θεόπνους:
'Et me voici donc, rempli du souffle divin de la vérité.'

Gospel according to John

viii. 12   ἐγώ εἰμι τὸ φῶς τοῦ κόσμου (cf. I John i. 5 ὁ θεὸς φῶς ἐστιν).

⎧ v. 20   ὁ γὰρ πατὴρ φιλεῖ τὸν υἱόν,
⎪   καὶ πάντα δείκνυσιν αὐτῷ ἃ αὐτὸς ποιεῖ.
⎨ xiii. 3   πάντα ἔδωκεν αὐτῷ ὁ πατὴρ εἰς τὰς χεῖρας.
⎩ xvii. 2   καθὼς ἔδωκας αὐτῷ ἐξουσίαν πάσης σαρκός.

xii. 46   ἵνα πᾶς ὁ πιστεύων εἰς ἐμὲ ἐν τῇ σκοτίᾳ μὴ μείνῃ (contrast
          I John ii. 10 ἐν τῷ φωτὶ μένει).

v. 24   μεταβέβηκεν ἐκ τοῦ θανάτου εἰς τὴν ζωήν.

xiv. 5-6   πῶς οἴδαμεν τὴν ὁδόν; ...ἐγώ εἰμι ἡ ὁδὸς καί...ἡ ζωή.

xiv. 21   ὁ ἀγαπῶν με...κἀγὼ ἐμφανίσω αὐτῷ ἐμαυτόν. 23 ἐλευσόμεθα
          καὶ μονὴν παρ' αὐτῷ ποιησόμεθα.... 26 ἐκεῖνος διδάξει
          πάντα.

x. 3   τούτῳ ὁ θυρωρὸς ἀνοίγει.

xx. 17   ἀναβαίνω πρὸς τὸν πατέρα μου.

xiv. 20   ἐγὼ ἐν τῷ πατρί εἰμι, et simm. passim.

iii. 17   ἀπέστειλεν ὁ θεὸς τὸν υἱὸν εἰς τὸν κόσμον...ἵνα σωθῇ ὁ κόσμος
          δι' αὐτοῦ.

v. 34   ταῦτα λέγω ἵνα ὑμεῖς σωθῆτε. 24 ὁ τὸν λόγον μου ἀκούων...
        ἔχει ζωὴν αἰώνιον.

iv. 14   τὸ ὕδωρ ὃ ἐγὼ δώσω αὐτῷ γενήσεται ἐν αὐτῷ πηγὴ ὕδατος
         ἀλλομένου εἰς ζωὴν αἰώνιον.

xvi. 13   ὅταν ἔλθῃ ἐκεῖνος, τὸ πνεῦμα τῆς ἀληθείας, ὁδηγήσει ὑμᾶς εἰς
          τὴν ἀλήθειαν πᾶσαν.

xvii. 11   πάτερ ἅγιε.
i. 1-3   ὁ λόγος...ἦν ἐν ἀρχῇ πρὸς τὸν θεόν. πάντα δι' αὐτοῦ ἐγένετο.
⎧ xiii. 1   ἀγαπήσας τοὺς ἰδίους τοὺς ἐν τῷ κόσμῳ.
⎩ x. 14   γινώσκω τὰ ἐμὰ καὶ γινώσκουσί με τὰ ἐμά.

i. 9   τὸ φῶς τὸ ἀληθινὸν ὃ φωτίζει πάντα ἄνθρωπον.

⎧ i. 7   ἦλθεν εἰς μαρτυρίαν...ἵνα πάντες πιστεύσωσιν δι' αὐτοῦ.
⎨ i. 34   ἑώρακα καὶ μεμαρτύρηκα. Cf. I John v. 10 ὁ πιστεύων εἰς τὸν
⎩   υἱὸν τοῦ θεοῦ ἔχει τὴν μαρτυρίαν ἐν αὐτῷ.

viii. 12   ἕξει τὸ φῶς τῆς ζωῆς.

xvii. 19   ὑπὲρ αὐτῶν ἐγὼ ἁγιάζω ἐμαυτὸν ἵνα ὦσιν καὶ αὐτοὶ ἡγιασμένοι.

---

² N.-F. take transitively, 'ton homme veut te prêter aide dans l'œuvre de sancti-
fication', the ἐξουσία being presumably authority to consecrate. But verbs in -ζω
are not necessarily transitive: ἡσυχάζειν is to be, or become, quiet, as well as to
quieten, νηπιάζειν, to be childish, ἀκμάζειν, to be in one's prime, ἑλληνίζειν,
to behave as a Greek, etc. (see Moulton and Howard, *Grammar of New Testament
Greek*, II, pp. 409–10). So it is quite possible to understand, with Scott, 'thy man
wills to be holy, as thou art holy'.

direct literary relationship between the two writings, it will hardly be questioned that the similarities of expression suggest a common background of religious thought. It is therefore worth while to examine somewhat more closely certain points in the teaching of the *libellus*.

The conception of the divine as Life and Light we have seen to be found elsewhere in the *Hermetica*, but in this tractate it receives exceptional emphasis. The secret of immortality in fact is the knowledge that God is life and light and that we are His offspring. The purpose of the myth and its interpretation is to help the reader to realize these simple but momentous truths. The myth itself starts with a vision of infinite light, and this light is God. We must however remember that it is a myth, and we must not conclude that the writer thought of God as having a material substance visible as pure light. On the contrary, in so strongly Platonic a work we must suppose that God was conceived rather as the eternal reality of which visible light is the 'copy', in the language of other Hermetic writings as τὸ ἀρχέτυπον φῶς, or in Johannine language as τὸ φῶς τὸ ἀληθινόν. For in the development and interpretation of the myth the primal light is the κόσμος νοητός, and is never absorbed into the visible universe. The Hermetic writer has no more thought of God as material light than has the Johannine writer when he says ὁ θεὸς φῶς ἐστίν. But for both writers light, especially combined with life, is the most adequate symbol of the divine being.

Over against the primal light stands the chaotic ocean of darkness, not coeval with it, but μετ᾽ ὀλίγον ἐν μέρει γεγενημένον. Thus the light shines upon darkness, and by its power the universe takes shape out of chaos. Cf. John i. 5 τὸ φῶς ἐν τῇ σκοτίᾳ φαίνει καὶ ἡ σκοτία αὐτὸ οὐ κατέλαβεν ('did not overpower it', as in vi. 17 אD, xii. 35).[1] We have therefore a cosmological dualism. The universe originates in darkness which is antagonistic to the divine light, but is forced by it to submit to order and definition. The stuff of the world is non-divine, though its form is divinely imposed. In the Fourth Gospel the cosmological dualism of i. 5 is not ultimate, since *everything* came into being through the Logos, χωρὶς αὐτοῦ ἐγένετο οὐδὲ ἕν: the emphatic negative would seem to imply that the evangelist is ruling out a view that *something* existent did come into being without the Logos, e.g. the primeval ocean of darkness.

[1] In both writers we have a reduced survival (of which probably neither was conscious) of the primitive myth of the conflict of the Light-God with the monster of darkness.

No fewer than three intermediaries are involved in the creation of the world according to Poimandres—Λόγος, Βουλή and Νοῦς Δημιουργός. The part played by Βουλή is subordinate and somewhat obscure, but Λόγος and Νοῦς Δημιουργός have definite functions assigned to them. It is the part of Λόγος to cause the four elements to crystallize out of formless chaos, of Νοῦς Δημιουργός to create the astral bodies out of the higher elements of fire and πνεῦμα. Together they bring about the revolutions of the spheres which cause life to appear in the lower elements, earth, water, and air, and then their work is done. This curious division of labour may be due to the fact that the writer draws his cosmology from more than one source. In the Νοῦς Δημιουργός we may recognize the second νοῦς of some other *Hermetica*, though in them the term δημιουργός is usually kept for the supreme Creator.[1] Of greater interest for our present purpose is the Λόγος, which appears also in the two verses of the Fourth Gospel which alone are given to cosmology. The interpretation of these two verses is a notorious crux, and it may be that a study of the λόγος in *Poimandres* will throw some light upon it.

We turn back then to the vision of the First Things. First there was boundless light, then darkness below it. The seer proceeds (in language whose obscurity may be partly due to textual corruption):

ὡς εἰκάσαι με ἰδόντα[2] μεταβαλλόμενον τὸ σκότος εἰς ὑγράν τινα φύσιν ἀφάτως τεταραγμένην καὶ καπνὸν ἀποδιδοῦσαν ὡς ἀπὸ πυρὸς καί τινα ἦχον ἀποτελοῦσαν ἀνεκλάλητον γοώδη, εἶτα βοὴ ἐξ αὐτῆς ἀσυνάρθρως ἐξεπέμπετο, ὡς εἰκάσαι φωνὴν φωτός.[3]

This may be translated:

I seemed to see the darkness changing into a sort of moist nature, unspeakably agitated, giving out smoke as from a fire, and producing a sort of ineffable, glamorous noise; and then a cry was sent out from it inarticulately.

The words ὡς εἰκάσαι φωνὴν φωτός must be out of place, for the cry is explicitly said to proceed from chaos, and not from light. If Nock's emendation is accepted, the noise is the voice of the fire which is mingled in the chaotic mass until at a later stage it is separated out (the ὡς ἀπὸ πυρός of this sentence does not refer to the presence of fire in chaos: it is a mere comparison: the darkness was *like* smoke that rises from fire).

[1] E.g. *C.H.* VIII. 2, IX. 5.
[2] *Sic* Bᶜ, εἰδόντα *cett.*, εἶτα Reitzenstein, N.-F., who connect ὡς εἰκάσαι με with the foregoing sentence, which they emend, in my judgment, temerariously.
[3] *Sic* MSS., φωνὴ πυρός *vel* φύσεως Reitzenstein, φωνῇ πυρός N.-F. ('tel que je le comparerais à une voix de feu'), *transp.* Scott. *V. infr.*

We may perhaps understand that the fire, imprisoned in the chaotic mass, is 'groaning and travailing' to be released, and its release is recorded in the following sentence: ἐξεπήδησεν πῦρ ἄκρατον. But I am not fully convinced. The next stage is as follows: ἐκ τοῦ φωτός τις[1] λόγος ἅγιος ἐπέβη τῇ φύσει, 'a sort of holy word out of the light assailed the nature', i.e. the ὑγρὰ φύσις, the turbulent ocean of darkness. As a consequence fire, followed by πνεῦμα and air, flies aloft out of chaos, leaving behind earth and water mixed, κινούμενα...διὰ τὸν ἐπιφερόμενον πνευματικὸν λόγον. The last words recall Gen. i. 2 πνεῦμα θεοῦ ἐπεφέρετο ἐπάνω τοῦ ὕδατος. A comparison with the writer's biblical model shows that the assault of the λόγος upon chaos represents the statement of Genesis, εἶπεν ὁ θεός Γενηθήτω στερέωμα κτλ. (Gen. i. 6). Thus the ἅγιος λόγος is in the first place a word spoken by God. The words ὡς εἰκάσαι φωνὴν φωτός, which as we have seen are out of place, are plausibly conjectured by Scott to refer to the λόγος. Such an accidental transference in copying is not difficult to suppose.[2] The word is as it were (ὡς εἰκάσαι) the voice of the Light, answering the inarticulate cry of chaos. Similarly at a later stage the command to increase and multiply is introduced by the words ὁ θεὸς εἶπεν ἁγίῳ λόγῳ. At the same time the word once spoken remains rushing like a wind over the terraqueous mass, and keeping it in motion.[3] Again after its work is complete it leaves the lower world and is united with the νοῦς δημιουργός (10). Thus some sort of substantive existence is attributed to the λόγος. We must, however, remember that this whole vision of creation is in some sort symbolic, and needs interpretation. The light is not a real visible light, but a symbol of νοῦς or God. Similarly the λόγος may not be a real audible word. We turn therefore to the interpretation. 'That light', says Poimandres, 'is I, Mind, your God, who existed before the moist nature which appeared out of darkness; and the luminous word (λόγος φωτεινός) out of Mind is the Son of God.' The light therefore is not a real visible light, but a symbol for divine Mind; and the word is not a real audible word, but a symbol for the

[1] τι MSS., spatium fere vi litterarum A. ? τοῦ πρώτου(αου) conj. N.-F.

[2] Thus we have the equation, φῶς : φωνή :: νοῦς : λόγος, cf. 6. As φωνὴ φωτός, the λόγος is φωτεινός. Cf. the Gnostic Justin ap. Hippolytus, Refut. v. 26: when Elohim approached τὸ πέρας ἄνω τοῦ οὐρανοῦ, and begged for the gate to be opened, φωνὴ αὐτῷ ἀπὸ τοῦ φωτὸς ἐδόθη.

[3] The description of it as πνευματικός should mean, in a Hermetic writing, or in any writing influenced by Stoicism, that the λόγος is material, being of the nature of 'air in motion'. But the wind, like the light, may merely be part of the picture, symbolizing non-material existences. The λόγος cannot really be material, since it is ὁμοούσιος with νοῦς, which is essentially non-material (10).

Son of God. The seer is still at a loss—as indeed we, the readers, are. Τί οὖν; he asks. Unfortunately the reply is obscure, and the text uncertain. The MSS. (1. 6) read as follows:

οὕτως γνῶθι τὸ ἐν σοὶ βλέπων καὶ ἀκούων λόγος κυρίου ὁ δὲ νοῦς πατὴρ θεός. Pal.[1]

οὕτω γνῶθι τὸ ἐν σοὶ βλέπων καὶ ἀκοῦον λ. κ. ὁ δ. ν. π. θ. Q.

οὕτω(ς) γνῶθι τὸ ἐν σοὶ βλέπον καὶ ἀκοῦον λ. κ. ὁ δ. ν. π. θ. cett.

The text of the majority of MSS. would give the sense: 'learn thus—that in you which sees and hears is the λόγος of the Lord, and Mind is God the Father.' This is accepted by Nock-Festugière. That could only mean that the λόγος in man is the faculty of seeing and hearing, and it is the offspring of God. But λόγος as a psychological term in the *Hermetica* stands, as we have seen, for the intellectual faculty, for thought rather than perception, and even if the present writer could be supposed to use it in a different sense, it would be irrelevant at this point to say that the λόγος in man is the offspring of divine Mind. We are here concerned with cosmology. Anthropology follows in a later section. MSS. CQ seem to be right in reading βλέπων. The meaning then is 'learn in this way, by looking at that which is in yourself'. The seer is invited to understand the relation of νοῦς and λόγος in the universe on the analogy of the structure of human personality. Cf. *C.H.* XI. 19 οὕτω νόησον ἀπὸ σεαυτοῦ. Thus the meaning here probably is that the cosmical λόγος is the Son of God in the same sense as that in which λόγος as a psychological factor is the offspring of mind in man. Cf. Philo, *De Cher.* 7 ἠχεῖ μὲν γὰρ ὁ γεγωνὸς λόγος, πατὴρ δὲ τούτου ὁ νοῦς.[2] It seems therefore that we must in some way emend the MS. text to give the sense: 'Learn thus, by looking at that which is in yourself: the word is son and mind father; and these are not separate one from another, for the union of these is life.'[3] The statement is still obscure, but we may understand

[1] Scott cites this reading from C (Vaticanus), N.-F. from Pal. (Palatinus).

[2] For the purpose of this particular Scripture interpretation (Abraham = πατὴρ ἐκλεκτὸς ἠχοῦς) Philo takes the spoken word (γεγωνὸς λόγος) as the image or offspring of νοῦς. But λόγος is not *essentially* the spoken word but the thought expressed in the word (cf. *C.H.* XII. 12–13).

[3] The words καὶ ἀκούων (-ον) might have been interpolated because the copyist was influenced by the frequent association of βλέπειν καὶ ἀκούειν. In *The Bible and the Greeks*, p. 119, I suggested τὸ ἐν σοὶ βλέπων· εἰκὼν νοῦ λόγος, supporting it by comparing XII. 14 ὁ οὖν λόγος εἰκὼν ⟨τοῦ νοῦ⟩ καὶ νοῦς τοῦ θεοῦ. There however the words τοῦ νοῦ are a conjecture, though to my mind a probable one. Εἰκών is in any case correlative with 'son' or 'offspring'. I still suspect κυρίου of being a Christian interpolation, in spite of Festugière's defence of it.

39

it to mean that in man mind is prior to λόγος and yet inseparable from it in the living whole of experience; and so the λόγος through which the cosmos came out of chaos proceeds from the transcendent divine Mind, and yet is not separable from it. That is, λόγος here takes the place which in other dialogues is occupied by such mediating entities as αἰών, or the cosmic νοῦς, which 'is not cut off from the essence of God, but evolved out of it like the light of the sun' (C.H. XII. 1). It is therefore a double of the ἕτερος νοῦς δημιουργός of the present tractate, and the author in effect admits this when he says that after the separation of the elements was complete the λόγος was united with the demiurge, because it was of the same substance (ἐπήδησεν εὐθὺς ἐκ τῶν κατωφερῶν στοιχείων ὁ τοῦ θεοῦ λόγος εἰς τὸ καθαρὸν τῆς φύσεως δημιούργημα, καὶ ἡνώθη τῷ δημιουργῷ νῷ· ὁμοούσιος γὰρ ἦν, 10).

In a curious kind of interlude it is explained that in the differentiation of chaos into the discrete elements of matter the λόγος had the co-operation of the Counsel of God, βουλὴ θεοῦ, ἥτις λαβοῦσα τὸν λόγον καὶ ἰδοῦσα τὸν καλὸν κόσμον ἐμιμήσατο (8). In so far as the λόγος is a word, this would mean that the personified βουλή heard the command of God, looked up to the κόσμος νοητός from which it came, and in obedience to the command began the creation of a world which is a copy of the κόσμος νοητός. Interpreted, it might mean that there was already a divine plan implicit even in formless chaos, and that the thought of the transcendent Mind descending upon it brought it into operation. The term βουλή is not elsewhere used in the *Hermetica* except in the Περὶ Παλιγγενεσίας. It may be compared with the θέλησις or θέλημα of God in the *Key of Hermes* (C.H. X. 2), which, however, is not hypostatized, as well as with the Stoic πρόνοια (Scott). But it is closer to the βουλὴ θεοῦ of the LXX, which is brought into connection with σοφία and πνεῦμα (Wisd. ix. 13–17), and we must probably account for its appearance here as due to Jewish influence.[1] The author seems concerned to find a place for all intermediate entities given in his sources. The passage does not throw any significant light on his λόγος doctrine.

We conclude that the λόγος of the *Poimandres* is not simply a 'word'; it is the thought of God which imposed differentiation upon undifferentiated chaos, and it is virtually equated with the immanent reason of the universe (the νοῦς δημιουργός). Owing to the fortunate ambiguity of

[1] See *The Bible and the Greeks*, pp. 126–32. Reitzenstein's idea that a sexual union between λόγος and βουλή is intended is completely groundless, and most improbable in an author with a strong anti-sexual bias.

the Greek term λόγος it could be symbolized by an audible word proceeding from the primal light, and the same ambiguity facilitates the comparison between the λόγος issuing from the eternal mind and the words of a man expressing his mind.

Its appearance in the creation myth of the *Poimandres* is probably due to the Jewish doctrine of the creative Word of the Lord, since the Hermetist is here following the myth of Genesis as interpreted in Jewish-Hellenistic exegesis. He is probably not following Philo, but like Philo he had before him the LXX, and like him accepted the Stoic idea of the immanent λόγος. The author of the Fourth Gospel also had Genesis before him, and the cast of his thought clearly suggests that he was acquainted, if not with Philo, at least with Jewish thought proceeding on similar lines. His λόγος-doctrine must be placed in this context.

After the creation of the world, the *Poimandres* proceeds to an account of the origin of man. Here the cosmic intermediaries, λόγος, βουλή and νοῦς δημιουργός, play no part. Man is given a more direct relation to the supreme God. We have already seen that while many of the *Hermetica* are content to regard man as the offspring of the cosmos, and so standing at second remove from God, some of them attempt in various ways to attribute to him a higher dignity. The author of *Poimandres* has once again gone to his biblical source, as interpreted by Hellenistic-Jewish exegetes like Philo, who found in Gen. i. 26 an account of the creation of a heavenly or archetypal man. This man, according to *Poimandres*, was the offspring of God like the νοῦς δημιουργός (12). The same verb ἀπεκύησεν is used of both. He was equal to God, and very beautiful, as bearing the image of his Father. God loved him as His own child,[1] and gave all His creatures into his hand. But man, stirred by the ambition to create, like God, descended into the created sphere. The story of his descent is clearly a version of the story of the Fall of Adam in Genesis. It is definitely a fall of man from his high estate, for through it he became implicated with matter, which had come from the primeval darkness. It brought death into the world and all our woe. Because of it, man, 'being immortal and having authority over all things, suffers the mortal lot in subjection to fate. Being superior to the frame of things he has become a slave within the frame of things' (ἀθάνατος γὰρ ὢν καὶ πάντων τὴν ἐξουσίαν ἔχων, τὰ θνητὰ πάσχει ὑποκείμενος τῇ εἱμαρμένῃ. ὑπεράνω

[1] οὗ ἠράσθη ὡς ἰδίου τόκου, 1. 12: cf. Λόγος Τέλειος, 8 (cited p. 22 above), where the ἴδιος τόκος whom God loved is the κόσμος.

THE BACKGROUND

οὖν ὢν τῆς ἁρμονίας ἐναρμόνιος γέγονε δοῦλος, 15). Empirical humanity in short is θνητὸς διὰ τὸ σῶμα, ἀθάνατος δὲ διὰ τὸν οὐσιώδη ἄνθρωπον. The expression ὁ οὐσιώδης ἄνθρωπος we have already met in the *Hermetica*. It is equivalent to ὁ ὄντως ἄνθρωπος and ὁ τέλειος ἄνθρωπος. These terms, as we have seen, sometimes stand for a subspecies of the genus *homo*, sometimes for one element in the human soul; in either case for the divine in humanity. To these we must add a fourth term used in the *Poimandres*, ὁ ἔννους ἄνθρωπος (21). Apparently in the present tractate the last term is used, like τέλειος ἄνθρωπος in the *Bowl* (*C.H.* iv. 4) and ὁ ὄντως ἄνθρωπος in the *Key* (x. 24), for an individual man who has the capacity for recognizing his heavenly origin, and so regaining his immortality;[1] while the term ὁ οὐσιώδης ἄνθρωπος is used for the divine element in human nature. It seems to be implied that not every man is ἔννους, though this is hardly consistent with the doctrine that all men have in them something of the οὐσιώδης ἄνθρωπος, and it may not have been the author's real meaning. There is a similar uncertainty in other tractates. But so far there is no essential difference between the doctrine of the *Poimandres* and that of other *Hermetica*.

There are, however, two points peculiar to the *Poimandres*. In the first place, the present condition of man is due to a fall. In other tractates (Lat. *Ascl.* i. 7, *C.H.* iv. 2) the ὄντως ἄνθρωπος is sent down by God to earth to adorn it. In the *Poimandres* he sinfully lusts after the creature. This feature we must certainly attribute to Jewish influence. In the second place, the story of the fall of man is told in mythical form as if the primal man were an individual person. The question should be raised, how far the myth is to be taken literally. Did the author of *Poimandres* believe that there was a supernatural person who became the ancestor of the human race, or is he consciously using symbolism? It may be observed that a similar question is raised by a famous passage in the Book of Daniel (vii. 13, 27). Is the כבר־אנש thought of as a real supernatural being, the representative in heaven of the people of God on earth, or is he a purely visionary and symbolic figure, standing for 'the people of the saints of the Most High'? The author of the Similitudes of Enoch (I Enoch xlvi–li) apparently took him for a real supra-historical person,[2] but that does not settle the question for Daniel.

[1] Since the word of Poimandres, ὁ ἔννους ἄνθρωπος ἀναγνωρισάτω ἑαυτόν, calls forth the question οὐ πάντες ἄνθρωποι νοῦν ἔχουσι; to which the God replies, εὐφήμει, ὦ οὗτος. For the text, see p. 32, n. 1.
[2] But see pp. 241–242.

42

The figure of the heavenly Man in various forms appears over a wide range of religious literature. It is traced by Reitzenstein, Bousset and others to the primitive myth of the *Urmensch*, or primal Man, particularly in the form which this myth takes in Iranian religion. If this be its origin, then it certainly departed widely from its original significance, and few of the primitive traits of the *Urmensch* remain either in Daniel and Enoch, or in Philo and *Poimandres*. In any case, even if the figure of the divine Ἄνθρωπος is ultimately to be traced back to a personage of primitive mythology, it does not necessarily follow that the Hermetic writer thought of him as a real suprahistoric personage. Other features of the myth, as we have seen, are purely symbolic, and so may be the figure of Ἄνθρωπος. As the argument proceeds, the mythical figure is lost sight of. We are told how man, any man, may gain immortality and rise to unity with God. The stages of the ascent recapitulate the stages of the fall of Ἄνθρωπος, but it is no mythical being that is in view, but you or I.[1] The divine Man, child of God, has become, to put it so, the Man in men, of divine origin, and capable of redemption from the taint of matter and mortality into the life of God. He may never have been meant for anything else. On the other hand, in so far as the author took his Platonism seriously, he must have believed in the real existence of eternal archetypes (as indeed he speaks of τὸ ἀρχέτυπον εἶδος), and his Ἄνθρωπος is probably as real as they. He is in some sort the equivalent of the Platonic 'idea' of man, and the author means to say that this 'idea' of man is essentially divine, but has become implicated in the taint of matter, from which it needs to be released. The myth has dramatic detail which is merely picturesque, but it concerns a being fully real in the Platonic sense.

I have already shown how the language used in the *Poimandres* about Ἄνθρωπος recalls the language used in the Fourth Gospel about Christ. It is surely clear that whatever may have been the origin of the expression ὁ υἱὸς τοῦ ἀνθρώπου in Christian usage, in the Fourth Gospel it bears some sort of relation to the Ἄνθρωπος of *Poimandres*. The Son of Man is God's Son, beloved by His Father, and like Him; He is the light of the world and the life of men; He descends ἐκ τῶν ἄνω, and takes on a material body. He ascends again to His Father, and those who are united with Him have knowledge of God and enter into life and light.

---

[1] This becomes clear when the plural is substituted for the singular in 26. It may be that when in the hymn the prophet speaks of himself as ὁ σὸς ἄνθρωπος he implies that he himself is now fully identified with the οὐσιώδης ἄνθρωπος.

43

The differences are obvious and will be discussed later, but it is surely clear at least that the Son of Man in the Fourth Gospel has more affinity with the Ἄνθρωπος of *Poimandres* than with the Son of Man of Jewish Apocalyptic.

The thirteenth *libellus* of the Hermetic *Corpus*, entitled Περὶ Παλιγγενεσίας (*De Regeneratione*), is a dialogue between Hermes and his son Tat. In the course of it Hermes makes reference to the recorded teachings of ὁ Ποιμάνδρης ὁ τῆς αὐθεντίας νοῦς. Beyond what is written, says Hermes, Poimandres had not given him any further teaching, knowing that he was now capable of thinking out everything for himself (15). The implication is that the present *libellus* is dependent on the *Poimandres*, and is intended to supplement its teaching.

The *Poimandres*, as we have seen, was designed to lead men into the knowledge of God, that they might themselves become immortal and divine, and the hymn with which it closes indicates that the prophet himself has undergone this experience. But what is it that actually happens when a man becomes divine? The answer of the present dialogue is that he has been born again. Hermes himself, identified here with the prophet of *Poimandres*, has been born again. He has already taught Tat that no one can be saved before rebirth (μηδένα δύνασθαι σωθῆναι πρὸ τῆς παλιγγενεσίας, 1). Tat asks for an explanation. In the course of the conversation the metaphor of rebirth is developed: the father is the will of God, the womb wisdom, the seed the real Good (τὸ ἀληθινὸν ἀγαθόν), and the offspring a god, a child of God (θεοῦ θεὸς παῖς, 2; θεὸς καὶ τοῦ ἑνὸς παῖς, 14). In his new being the reborn is in fact the All in all, made up of all powers (τὸ πᾶν ἐν παντὶ ἐκ πασῶν δυνάμεων συνεστός,[1] 2). Not unnaturally, Tat cries Αἴνιγμά μοι λέγεις ὦ πάτερ! 'This kind of thing', Hermes replies, 'cannot be taught, but God brings it to our mind when He wills' (τοῦτο τὸ γένος ὦ τέκνον οὐ διδάσκεται, ἀλλ᾽ ὅταν θέλη ὑπὸ τοῦ θεοῦ ἀναμιμνήσκεται, 2). Tat pleads nevertheless for further enlightenment. 'What can I say, my child?' says Hermes. 'I have nothing to say but this: seeing in myself that an uncreated vision has come to pass by the mercy of God, I have both passed out of myself into an immortal body, and I am no longer what I formerly was, but I have been born in Mind' (τί εἴπω ὦ τέκνον; οὐκ ἔχω λέγειν πλὴν τοῦτο· ὁρῶν †τι† ἐν ἐμοὶ ἄπλαστον θέαν γεγενημένην ἐξ ἐλέου θεοῦ, καὶ ἐμαυτὸν ἐξελήλυθα εἰς ἀθάνατον σῶμα, καὶ εἰμι νῦν οὐχ ὁ πρίν, ἀλλ᾽ ἐγεννήθην ἐν

---

[1] *Sic* d: -τως MSS., N.-F.

νῷ,¹ 3). He goes on to explain that the body which has colour, touch and measure is not his real self: οὐκ ὀφθαλμοῖς τούτοις θεωροῦμαι νῦν, ὦ τέκνον (3). Tat must in the same way pass out of himself—like, he adds, people who dream in sleep, but without sleep (εἴθε ὦ τέκνον καὶ σὺ σεαυτὸν διεξελήλυθας, ὡς οἱ ἐν ὕπνῳ ὀνειροπολούμενοι, χωρὶς ὕπνου, 4). Tat feels the need of assistance. 'Tell me this also', he says, Τίς ὁ γενεσιουργὸς τῆς παλιγγενεσίας; The answer is Ὁ τοῦ θεοῦ παῖς ἄνθρωπος εἶς, θελήματι θεοῦ. Hermes then, himself a man who has become a child of God by rebirth, is to direct, under God, the process by which Tat is to pass through the same experience. After some further explanation he gives the command: 'Draw it into yourself, and it will come; will, and it happens; reduce to inactivity the senses of the body, and the birth of deity will be' (ἐπίσπασαι εἰς ἑαυτὸν καὶ ἐλεύσεται. θέλησον καὶ γίνεται. κατάργησον τοῦ σώματος τὰς αἰσθήσεις καὶ ἔσται ἡ γένεσις τῆς θεότητος). This is the attitude of mind which Tat must adopt. The first step in the process of rebirth is the cleansing of the soul from the taint of matter. 'Purify yourself from the irrational torments of matter' (κάθαραι σεαυτὸν ἀπὸ τῶν ἀλόγων τῆς ὕλης τιμωριῶν, 7). These 'torments' are ignorance, grief, incontinence, lust, injustice, πλεονεξία, falsehood, envy, guile, wrath, headstrongness (προπέτεια), and malice. They are inherent in the material body, the σκῆνος, which is derived from the zodiacal circle (12),² and through imprisonment in this body the 'immanent Man' is condemned to the life of the senses (διὰ τοῦ δεσμωτηρίου τοῦ σώματος αἰσθητικῶς πάσχειν ἀναγκάζουσι τὸν ἐνδιάθετον ἄνθρωπον,³ 7). The ἐνδιάθετος ἄνθρωπος is clearly the οὐσιώδης ἄνθρωπος of the *Poimandres*. Rebirth is the liberation of the immanent Man by the mercy of God from the 'torments' of the passions resident in the material body.

Enlightened now on the need for rebirth and on its nature, so far as this can be known without passing through the actual experience, Tat

¹ The text (which I give after N.-F.) is not in all respects satisfactory, but the meaning is sufficiently clear.
² Cf. the doctrine of the *Poimandres* that the passions are derived from the astral διοικηταί. The two lists have in common ἐπιθυμία, δόλος, ἀπάτη, προπέτεια.
³ Scott takes exception to the phrase ἐνδιάθετος ἄνθρωπος and excises it, on the ground that it is the actual, empirical man who is imprisoned in the body. But the meaning of the author (who depends on the *Poimandres*) must be that within the individual man is the οὐσιώδης ἄνθρωπος, but he is reduced to impotence by being enslaved to the body. It is thus the heavenly Man, immanent in the individual man, who is imprisoned, and for this being the expression ὁ ἐνδιάθετος ἄνθρωπος, coined on the model of the Stoic ἐνδιάθετος λόγος, is entirely appropriate. So N.-F. note *ad loc.*, who give parallels.

is ready to be reborn. 'Be silent now, my child, and speak not, and so mercy will not cease towards us from God' (8). We are now to imagine a period of solemn silence, while teacher and pupil wait upon God. Then Hermes speaks again. 'Rejoice now, my child; you are being purified by the powers of God for the construction of the λόγος in you' (χαῖρε λοιπόν, ὦ τέκνον, ἀνακαθαιρόμενος ταῖς τοῦ θεοῦ δυνάμεσιν εἰς συνάρθρωσιν τοῦ λόγου, 8). Then he calls the roll of the 'torments', as each in turn is expelled and replaced by the 'power' of God which is its contrary. 'Knowledge of God has come to us, and by its coming, my child, ignorance is driven away. Knowledge of joy has come to us, and at its coming, my child, grief will flee to those who have room for it. Next after joy I call continence—O sweetest power! Let us greet her, my child, most gladly! How she repels incontinence the moment she arrives!' Similarly καρτερία is invoked to expel lust, justice expels injustice, κοινωνία is invoked to expel πλεονεξία, and truth to expel falsehood. Here the list is broken off. 'See, my child, how the good is completed by the advent of truth, for envy has departed from us, and the good follows hard upon truth, together with life and light, and not one of the torments of darkness comes against us any more, but all have flown, with a rush of wings, vanquished away' (9). The dislocation of the order of τιμωρίαι is probably due to the combination of a scheme of twelve based on the Zodiac with a scheme of seven based on the seven planets, as in the *Poimandres*; but the abrupt close, where the advent of truth scatters the whole host of darkness and brings life and light, is perhaps more effective than a strictly symmetrical scheme would have been.

The crisis of rebirth is now over. 'We have been deified[1] by generation', says Hermes. 'Whosoever has attained by the mercy of God this divine generation, leaving behind the bodily senses, recognizes that he has been constituted out of divine elements, and is glad' (10).

Tat now utters the confession of the reborn: 'Father, being made steadfast by God, I now perceive not with the vision of the eyes, but with the intellectual energy which is through the powers. I am in heaven, in earth, in water, in air; I am in animals, in plants; in the womb, before the womb, after the womb, everywhere.' He has in fact become identical with τὸ πᾶν ἐν παντὶ ἐκ πασῶν δυνάμεων συνεστός, as Hermes had declared (2).

[1] MSS. ἐθεωρήθημεν: but Reitzenstein, Scott, N.-F. are surely right in reading ἐθεώθημεν.

He has, however, some further questions to ask; among them, 'Tell me, father, can this body made up of powers ever be dissolved?' 'Εὐφήμησον', cries Hermes; 'do you not know that you have become a god and child of the One?' (ἀγνοεῖς ὅτι θεὸς πέφυκας καὶ τοῦ ἑνὸς παῖς;). Tat expresses a desire to hear the Hymn of Rebirth (τὸν ὕμνον τῆς παλιγγενεσίας), which the powers sing to God in the Eighth Sphere (*Poim.* 26). Hermes commends him for his eagerness to put off the body (λῦσαι τὸ σκῆνος) and ascend to the place of the powers. But meanwhile, though Poimandres did not reveal any more than is written (in *C.H.* 1), yet Hermes himself, being reborn, knows the hymn of the powers. Tat desires to hear it. There follows a hymn similar to that in the *Poimandres*, recalling, like it, but even more strikingly, the poetry of the Hebrew Psalms.[1] Some verses from it must be quoted.

> All powers within me, praise the One and the All;
>> Sing with my will, all powers within me.
> Holy knowledge, enlightened by thee,
>> Through thee praising the noumenal Light,
>> I rejoice with the joy of Mind....
> O Life and Light, from you[2] to you the benediction proceeds.
>> I thank Thee, O Father, energy of the powers.
>> I thank Thee, O God, power of my energies.
>> Thy Logos praises Thee through me....
> The universe (τὸ πᾶν) which is within us,
>>> Save, O Life,
>>> Enlighten, O Light,
>>> Inspire, O God![3]
> Mind shepherds Thy Logos, O Spirit-bearer, Creator!
> Thou art God! Thy man cries this,
>> Through fire,
>> Through air,
>> Through earth,
>> Through water,
>> Through *pneuma*,
>> Through all Thy creatures.

[1] See *The Bible and the Greeks*, pp. 241–2.

[2] ὑμῶν Reitzenstein, Scott, N.-F., MSS. ἡμῶν. The emendation gives the finer sense, Life and Light (= God) being the source as well as the object of praise, as in Rom. viii. 27 the πνεῦμα (God within) inspires the prayer which is heard by God above.

[3] πνευμάτιϡε θεέ is Reitzenstein's emendation after Keil. MSS. have πνεῦμα θεέ. But the God of the Poimandres *libelli* is not πνεῦμα, though He is πνευματοφόρος. Scott re-writes the passage. See also pp. 218–219.

The hymn, we must remember, is sung by Hermes, who has been reborn into deity, or rather by the powers dwelling in him, and the hearing of it is the final stage in the initiation of Tat: 'By thy hymn and thy benediction my mind is further enlightened' (21). He is now permitted, under the instruction and guidance of Hermes, to utter a brief benediction ἐξ ἰδίας φρενός. 'Thou, my child, send up an acceptable sacrifice to God the Father; ἀλλὰ καὶ πρόσθες, ὦ τέκνον, "διὰ τοῦ Λόγου".' After a warning not to divulge this tradition of rebirth, the dialogue closes with the words 'Now you know with your mind both yourself and our Father', νοερῶς ἔγνως σεαυτὸν καὶ τὸν πατέρα τὸν ἡμέτερον.

There are obscurities in this tractate, and no wonder, when the author has undertaken the daring task of making us spectators while a man is actually reborn before our eyes! But it cannot be denied that he has created a 'numinous' atmosphere in which the reader feels that something of solemn import is taking place. And in spite of all obscurities it is possible to discover in a general way what he meant by being born again. Man's material body carries the ineradicable taint of sensual passions. He must be purified from the taint. Such purification can be effected only by the invasion of divine powers which expel the evil passions. These powers, which are conceived wholly in ethical terms, knowledge, joy, continence, etc., together constitute the divine λόγος, which by the mercy of God is formed in man, becoming a new body, divine and indissoluble. His real self is now a part of the divine νοῦς, and he is one with the whole universe. He is fit to worship God 'through the λόγος'. It is not he, his old individual self, that worships, but the λόγος, or, in other words, the divine powers that are within him. Rebirth in fact is the identification of a man with God through the indwelling of the λόγος. The doctrine is intimately connected with the general teaching of the *Hermetica*. As we have seen, most of these writings teach that a man may undergo an experience in which he is liberated from the life of the senses, attains knowledge of God, and becomes immortal and divine. The description of the reborn person in this dialogue is very near to the description of the *visio Dei* in Νοῦς πρὸς Ἑρμῆν (*C.H.* xi. 20, see p. 16). The idea of the liberation of the ἐνδιάθετος ἄνθρωπος from the 'prison of the body' is similar to that of the ascent of the οὐσιώδης ἄνθρωπος in the *Poimandres*. The idea of the new body constituted of divine powers recalls the teaching of *The Key* that the pious soul after separation from the body becomes all νοῦς, and is clothed with a body of pure fire (*C.H.* x. 18–19). The passage from the lower life to the higher, which is here called rebirth, is the baptism in νοῦς of *The Bowl*. The common stuff of Hermetic teaching is here; but there is a more definite attempt to present it in the form of an imaginative rendering of a personal experience.

Throughout this tractate, as in the *Poimandres*, there are expressions which recall the language of the Fourth Gospel and the First Epistle of John. I give a list of the more striking parallels (pp. 50–51).

Behind these verbal parallels lie real similarities of thought. In the Hermetic as in the Johannine writings, knowledge of God, conferring eternal life, is for those who have passed by rebirth from the realm of σῶμα or σάρξ into the realm of νοῦς or πνεῦμα. In both, purification is a stage in the attainment of eternal life, but not the final stage. In both, the status of 'child of God' is attained through the λόγος. As Hermes, a man, but the child of God, is the γενεσιουργὸς τῆς παλιγγενεσίας, so it is implied, if not stated, that through Christ, the incarnate Son of God, men are born again. As in the Hymn of Rebirth man worships God 'through the λόγος', so in the Farewell Discourses of the Fourth Gospel men pray to God in the name of Christ. It is noteworthy that in the Περὶ Παλιγγενεσίας, as in the Fourth Gospel, the cosmic functions of the Λόγος are in the background as compared with its functions in the salvation of men. The Logos-doctrine of this *libellus* is indeed peculiar. It appears to start from the psychological sense of λόγος which we have recognized in other *libelli*.[1] But here λόγος is not part of the common and original constitution of human nature, but implanted in it through rebirth. It is formed in man by the union of divine δυνάμεις (8 ἀνακαθαιρόμενος ταῖς τοῦ θεοῦ δυνάμεσιν εἰς συνάρθρωσιν τοῦ λόγου). The δυνάμεις in the *Hermetica* are always thought of as radiations (ἀκτῖνες) of the divine being. Thus the λόγος is the sum of emanations from the eternal Νοῦς, as, from another point of view, the human λόγος is the expression of νοῦς in man. In other *libelli* the δυνάμεις are cosmic forces, through which God creates the world, and it is unlikely that the author of the Περὶ Παλιγγενεσίας took a different view.[2] But as imparted to man, these δυνάμεις take the form of ethical qualities. Similarly, in the Fourth Gospel the cosmic aspect of the λόγος is affirmed briefly in the exordium,

---

[1] The sense of λόγος as 'word' is at most hinted at in the hymn ὁ σὸς λόγος ὑμνεῖ σε.

[2] When Tat is reborn, he feels himself to be present at once in every part of space and time, and in the Hymn the Reborn praises God in all the elements. These statements are intelligible if the δυνάμεις by which the cosmos is made and sustained are indwelling in the reborn man, but not otherwise.

THE BACKGROUND

C.H. xiii (Περὶ Παλιγγενεσίας)

1   αἰνιγματωδῶς καὶ οὐ τηλαυγῶς ἔφρασας περὶ θειότητος διαλεγόμενος.
    μηδένα δύνασθαι σωθῆναι πρὸ τῆς παλιγγενεσίας.

    πυθομένου (μου) τὸν τῆς παλιγγενεσίας λόγον μαθεῖν.
    ἐξ οἴας μήτρας ἄνθρωπος ἐγεννήθη.

2   ἡ σπορὰ τὸ ἀληθινὸν ἀγαθόν.
    τίνος σπείραντος; —τοῦ θελήματος τοῦ θεοῦ.

    τοῦτο τὸ γένος οὐ διδάσκεται, ἀλλ᾽ ὅταν θέλῃ ὑπὸ τοῦ θεοῦ ἀναμιμνή-
    σκεται.

3   ἐγεννήθην ἐν νῷ.

    οὐκ ὀφθαλμοῖς τούτοις θεωροῦμαι νῦν.

6   τὴν ἐν θεῷ γένεσιν.

7   κάθαραι σεαυτόν.

8   ἦλθεν ἡμῖν γνῶσις θεοῦ.
    ἦλθεν ἡμῖν γνῶσις χαρᾶς· παραγενομένης ταύτης ἡ λύπη φεύξεται.

9   τῇ δὲ ἀληθείᾳ καὶ τὸ ἀγαθὸν ἐπεγένετο ἅμα ζωῇ καὶ φωτί.
    οὐκέτι ἐπῆλθεν οὐδεμία τοῦ σκότους τιμωρία.

14 τοῦ ἑνὸς παῖς.

15 καλῶς σπεύδεις λῦσαι τὸ σκῆνος, κεκαθαρμένος γάρ.

18 χαίρω ἐν χαρᾷ νοῦ.

19 αἱ δυνάμεις αἱ ἐν ἐμοί...τὸ σὸν θέλημα τελοῦσιν.

    φώτιζε φῶς.

    ποιμαίνει ὁ νοῦς.

21 πέμψον δεκτὴν θυσίαν τῷ πάντων πατρὶ θεῷ...διὰ τοῦ λόγου.

Fourth Gospel and First Epistle of John

John xvi. 29   ἴδε νῦν ἐν παρρησίᾳ λαλεῖς καὶ παροιμίαν οὐδεμίαν λέγεις.

John iii. 3   ἐὰν μή τις γεννηθῇ ἄνωθεν οὐ δύναται ἰδεῖν τὴν βασιλείαν τοῦ θεοῦ.

John iii. 4   πῶς δύναται ἄνθρωπος γεννηθῆναι γέρων ὤν;

John iii. 4   μὴ δύναται εἰς τὴν κοιλίαν τῆς μητρὸς αὐτοῦ δεύτερον εἰσελθεῖν καὶ γεννηθῆναι;

I John iii. 9   σπέρμα αὐτοῦ ἐν αὐτῷ μένει.

John i. 13   οἳ οὐκ ἐξ αἱμάτων οὐδὲ ἐκ θελήματος σαρκὸς οὐδὲ ἐκ θελήματος ἀνδρὸς ἀλλ᾽ ἐκ θεοῦ ἐγεννήθησαν.

John xiv. 26   ἐκεῖνος ὑμᾶς διδάξει πάντα καὶ ὑπομνήσει ὑμᾶς πάντα.

John iii. 8   ὁ γεγεννημένος ἐκ τοῦ πνεύματος (πνεῦμα the Christian counterpart of νοῦς).

John xiv. 19   ὁ κόσμος με οὐκέτι θεωρεῖ, ὑμεῖς δὲ θεωρεῖτέ με.

John i. 13   ἐκ θεοῦ ἐγεννήθησαν.

John xv. 2   πᾶν τὸ καρπὸν φέρον καθαίρει αὐτό, cf. xiii. 10–11.

John xvii. 3   ἵνα γινώσκωσίν σε τὸν μόνον ἀληθινὸν θεόν.

John xvi. 20   ἡ λύπη ὑμῶν εἰς χαρὰν γενήσεται.

John xiv. 6   ἐγώ εἰμι ἡ ὁδὸς καὶ ἡ ἀλήθεια καὶ ἡ ζωή.

John xii. 35   ἵνα μὴ σκοτία ὑμᾶς καταλάβῃ.

John viii. 41   ἕνα πατέρα ἔχομεν τὸν θεόν.

John xv. 3   ἤδη ὑμεῖς καθαροί ἐστε διὰ τὸν λόγον ὃν λελάληκα ὑμῖν.

John xv. 11   ἵνα ἡ χαρὰ ἡ ἐμὴ ἐν ὑμῖν ᾖ.

John iv. 34   ἵνα ποιήσω τὸ θέλημα τοῦ πέμψαντός με.

John i. 9   τὸ φῶς τὸ ἀληθινὸν ὃ φωτίζει πάντα ἄνθρωπον.

John x. 11   ἐγώ εἰμι ὁ ποιμὴν ὁ καλός.

John xv. 16   ὅτι ἂν αἰτήσητε τὸν πατέρα ἐν τῷ ὀνόματί μου....

but in the rest of the work the incarnate Logos mediates to men a divine life essentially ethical in quality.

The question may be raised, whether Christian influence is to be traced in the Περὶ Παλιγγενεσίας where it differs from the common type of Hermetic teaching. It is certainly one of the later *Hermetica*—substantially later, it would appear, than the *Poimandres*—and it probably belongs to a period when Christianity was already widespread in Egypt. Biblical influence is almost as clear as in the *Poimandres*, and more so than in most of the *Hermetica*, but for the most part it could readily be accounted for here, as in the *Poimandres*, by an acquaintance with the LXX. But besides the Johannine echoes there are several expressions which recall New Testament language, such as σκῆνος for the body, the verb δικαιοῦσθαι, and the expression εὐλογία for a hymn of praise.[1] In such cases the question of priority is a delicate one. While Reitzenstein confidently denies any Christian influence, Scott allows some measure of such influence to be possible. But so far as the more essential elements are concerned, we may observe that the word for 'rebirth', παλιγγενεσία, at any rate is pre-Christian, being used by Chrysippus and the earlier Stoics, and by Philo, as well as in *C.H.* III. 3, and on the testimony of the *libellus* itself (1) the doctrine μηδένα δύνασθαι σωθῆναι πρὸ τῆς παλιγγενεσίας was found in the earlier *Hermetica*, the γενικοὶ λόγοι. Further, we have seen that apart from the term itself, and such metaphorical expressions as necessarily cohere with the figure of rebirth— 'womb' and 'seed'—the substance of the teaching in this dialogue can be documented from other *libelli*. We may fairly conclude that even if some Christian influence may have indirectly made itself felt, yet the doctrine is not likely to have been derived from Christian sources. Or if we went so far as to suppose that the impulse to use the figure of rebirth may have been partly due to Christian influence, it is in any case clear that the figure conveys to the Hermetist ideas entirely familiar to his

[1] We might add λογικὴ θυσία, but this comes from the *Poimandres*, and in both *libelli* such an expression is naturally related to the general character of the teaching they convey, whereas in Paul λογικὴ λατρεία has the appearance of a more or less technical expression taken over. Philo will throw light on the use of such expressions, by Paul and the Hermetist alike, but their origin probably lies outside Judaism and Christianity. Σκῆνος is common in non-Christian literature and goes back to Greek medical writers (see L. and S.), δικαιοῦσθαι is used in a sense which is etymologically correct, but quite different from biblical usage (see *The Bible and the Greeks*, p. 59, but I am not now prepared to allow any probability to the view that δικαιοῦσθαι here has been influenced by Christian usage), and εὐλογία is Jewish before it is Christian.

school, and not felt in any way as an alien intrusion. Thus we have probably to regard the idea of rebirth as belonging to the common background of thought, and the treatment of it by Hermetic and Christian writers respectively may usefully be compared for the sake of the light it may throw on either system of doctrine.[1]

What has here been said of one *libellus* may be said also of the whole body of Hermetic writings. It seems clear that as a whole they represent a type of religious thought akin to one side of Johannine thought, without any substantial borrowing on the one part or the other. It is when we have done justice to this kinship that we are likely to recognize the full significance of those elements in Johannine thought which are in striking contrast to the *Hermetica*, and in which we must seek the distinctively Christian teaching of the Fourth Gospel.

[1] If the author of the Περὶ Παλιγγενεσίας be supposed to have some acquaintance with the Fourth Gospel (which I think improbable), at any rate the tractate would supply evidence of the sense in which Johannine doctrine would be understood in religious circles of the type represented by the *Hermetica*, i.e. the kind of public which, as I take it, John had in view.

3. HELLENISTIC JUDAISM:
PHILO OF ALEXANDRIA

We have seen that the kind of religious philosophy propagated in the Hellenistic world by such writings as the *Hermetica* owed something to the influence of Judaism and of the Old Testament. In the easy give-and-take of civilized and intellectual life in the period, the influence was reciprocal. Hellenistic Judaism is a distinct phenomenon of the time. That the Fourth Evangelist expected to find readers among open-minded Jews who participated in the intellectual life of Hellenism we may take for granted. If we can discover what was in their minds, we may hope, here too, to find pointers to the meaning which the Fourth Gospel was intended to convey to its primary public.

The best known and most representative figure of Hellenistic Judaism is Philo of Alexandria, whose voluminous works enable us to form a fairly comprehensive estimate of the kind of religious philosophy which emerged within Judaism from the cross-fertilization of Hebrew and Greek thought in the cosmopolitan atmosphere of the great centre of Hellenistic culture in Egypt. If some recent critics are right in holding that much in the works of Philo is simply 'lifted' from earlier sources, they are not for that reason less valuable as evidence for our purpose.

Philo appears in his works as a loyal Jew—at least in intention—for whom the Scriptures of the Old Testament had absolute authority. But he is so steeped in Gentile thought—mainly in the popular Platonic-Stoic philosophy which meets us also in the *Hermetica*—that the Scriptures naturally interpret themselves to him in its terms. No doubt he wished to commend the Jewish religion to the Gentile public, by showing it to be, when rightly understood, a profoundly philosophical system, containing within it all the highest truths of philosophy, not as human speculations, but as divine revelation. But we should not think of his allegorical interpretation of Scripture as a mere accommodation for the sake of propaganda. It was for him the one true interpretation of the Old Testament, guaranteed as such, not only by its rationality, but also by his own religious experience, to which he repeatedly appeals.

It has always been recognized that Johannine thought has some sort of affinity with that of Philo. The fact that the Prologue to the Fourth Gospel equates Christ with the divine Logos called the attention of early

Christian theologians to the Logos-doctrine of Philo. It has often been assumed, in ancient and in modern times, that the Johannine Logos is identical with the Philonic. This is a matter that calls for investigation. Again, from an early date commentators have applied the method of allegorical exegesis, as practised by Philo, to the interpretation of the narratives of the Fourth Gospel, whether in the sense that the evangelist treated the traditional narratives as allegories, or in the sense that he constructed narratives which he intended to be understood allegorically. But here the parallel with Philo must be used with caution. Philo is applying to the sacred text of the Old Testament a method elaborated by Greek teachers in dealing with the sacred text of Homer. It is of the essence of the matter that the text is a *datum*. It must simply be accepted; it may not be altered or criticized. If the material it offers is intractable, allegorical exegesis is the way to make it available. To construct allegorical narratives deliberately would be an entirely different thing, with a different psychological basis; and even to mould traditional material into an allegorical form would be to do something different from what Philo has done. In the Fourth Gospel there are traces of allegorical interpretation of the Old Testament, but they are rare. The question whether the evangelist intended his own narratives to be allegorized by the reader must be carefully weighed, with the consciousness that if he did so he did something for which Philo affords no exact parallel.

There is, however, a real affinity between the two writers in their use of symbolism, which is not the same thing as allegory. There is an important range of symbolism common to both. Thus both of them use light as a symbol of the Deity in His relation to man and the world— a symbol which as we have seen is also characteristic of the *Hermetica*. 'God is light,' says Philo, 'for in the Psalms it is said "The Lord is my light and my saviour" (Ps. xxvi (xxvii). 1); and not only light, but the archetype of every other light, or rather more primitive and higher than every archetype' (ὁ θεὸς φῶς ἐστίν—'κύριος' γὰρ 'φωτισμός μου καὶ σωτήρ μου' ἐν ὕμνοις ᾄδεται—καὶ οὐ μόνον φῶς, ἀλλὰ καὶ παντὸς ἑτέρου φωτὸς ἀρχέτυπον, μᾶλλον δὲ παντὸς ἀρχετύπου πρεσβύτερον καὶ ἀνώτερον, *De Somn.* I. 75). Similarly Wisdom, which is also the divine Logos (*Leg. All.* I. 65), or alternatively proceeds from the Logos as its source (*De Fuga*, 97), is θεοῦ τὸ ἀρχέτυπον φέγγος (*De Migr. Abr.* 40). The Johannine equivalent of ἀρχέτυπον φῶς is φῶς ἀληθινόν (John i. 9). This light-symbolism is found everywhere in Philo's writings, in many different connections. One of the fundamental ideas associated with it is that of the self-revealing character of light. 'God saw before the beginning of things, using Himself as light' (ἑώρα ὁ θεὸς καὶ πρὸ γενέσεως, φωτὶ χρώμενος ἑαυτῷ, *Quod Deus*, 58). Again, 'Is not light seen by means of light? In the same way God, being His own ray, is beheld through Himself alone.... They pursue truth who form their idea of God by means of God Himself—light by means of light' (τὸ φῶς οὐ φωτὶ βλέπεται; τὸν αὐτὸν δὴ τρόπον καὶ ὁ θεὸς ἑαυτοῦ φέγγος ὢν δι' αὐτοῦ μόνου θεωρεῖται.... ἀλήθειαν δὲ μετίασιν οἱ τὸν θεὸν θεῷ φαντασιωθέντες, φωτὶ φῶς, *De Praem.* 45–6). A similar idea underlies the passage about the Light of the World in John viii. 12–14. Christ, being Himself the divine light, bears true witness of Himself, because He knows His own source and goal (ἐγώ εἰμι τὸ φῶς τοῦ κόσμου.... κἂν ἐγὼ μαρτυρῶ περὶ ἐμαυτοῦ, ἀληθής ἐστιν ἡ μαρτυρία μου, ὅτι οἶδα πόθεν ἦλθον καὶ ποῦ ὑπάγω).

Another cycle of symbolism is centred in the idea of God as the Fountain from which life-giving water streams. As John speaks of ὕδωρ ζῶν, and of πηγὴ ὕδατος ἁλλομένου εἰς ζωὴν αἰώνιον (iv. 10, 14), so Philo speaks of an ἀθανατίζον ποτόν or ποτὸν τῆς ἀθανασίας (*De Spec. Leg.* I. 303, *De Fuga*, 199), of which God, or His Logos (*De Somn.* II. 245), is the πηγή. The water is sometimes virtue, sometimes wisdom, but above all it is life itself. 'He says somewhere, "They have left me, the fountain of life" (Jer. ii. 13)... God therefore is the primaeval Fountain.... For God alone is the cause of the soul and of intelligent life. For matter is a dead thing, but God is something more than life; He is, as He Himself says, "the perennial Fountain of life"' (εἶπε γάρ που, Ἐγκατέλιπόν με πηγὴν ζωῆς...οὐκοῦν ὁ θεός ἐστιν ἡ πρεσβυτάτη πηγή....μόνος γὰρ ὁ θεὸς ψυχῆς καὶ ζωῆς καὶ διαφερόντως λογικῆς ψυχῆς καὶ τῆς μετὰ φρονήσεως ζωῆς αἴτιος. ἡ μὲν γὰρ ὕλη νεκρόν, ὁ δὲ θεὸς πλέον τι ἢ ζωή, πηγὴ τοῦ ζῆν, ὡς αὐτὸς εἶπεν, ἀέννάος, *De Fuga*, 197–8). Again, 'He exhorts the swift runner to hasten breathlessly to the most high divine Logos, which is the fountain of wisdom, in order that drawing from the stream he may find as a prize everlasting life instead of death' (προτρέπει δὴ τὸν μὲν ὠκυδρομεῖν ἱκανὸν συντείνειν ἀπνευστὶ πρὸς τὸν ἀνωτάτω λόγον θεῖον, ὃς σοφίας ἐστὶ πηγή, ἵνα ἀρυσάμενος τοῦ νάματος ἀντὶ θανάτου ζωὴν ἀίδιον ἆθλον εὕρηται, *De Fuga*, 97).

A third symbol common to Philo and John is that of the shepherd. Among many passages the following may be cited. 'To be a shepherd is so good a thing as to be justly attributed not only to kings and wise men and perfectly purified souls, but even to God the ruler of all....For he speaks thus: "The Lord is my shepherd, and I shall lack nothing"

(Ps. xxii (xxiii). 1). This psalm should be rehearsed by every lover of God, and in an especial sense by the universe. For like a flock, earth and water and air and fire and all plants and animals in them...are led according to right and law by God the Shepherd and King, who has set over them His true Logos and first-begotten Son, who takes over the care of this sacred flock like the vicegerent of a great king. For it is said somewhere, "Behold I am; I send my angel to thy face, to keep thee in the way" (Exod. xxiii. 20). So let the whole universe, the greatest and most perfect flock of the self-existent God, say "The Lord is my shepherd, and I shall lack nothing." And let each individual also say the same, not by voice that flows through tongue and mouth...but with the voice of the intelligence. For it is impossible for any lack of what is proper to exist while God is in command, Who is wont to bestow full and perfect goods upon all beings' (*De Agr.* 50–3, slightly abridged). And again, 'Moses says in his prayer, "Let the Lord God watch over this congregation, and this congregation of the Lord shall not be as sheep without a shepherd" (Num. xxvii. 16–17). For when the president of our composite nature, or overseer, or father, or what you please to call him, the true Logos, goes away and leaves the flock that is in us, the flock left neglected itself perishes, and there is great loss to the master. The cattle, widowed of the herdsman who would admonish and train them, have wandered far from rational and immortal life' (*De Post.* 67–8, slightly abridged). A superficial parallel with the passages about the shepherd and the flock in John x. 1–18, 25–9, is obvious. But the limits of the parallelism are no less obvious. Philo applies the figure in the first place to the universe, in which the Logos organizes the varied elements of nature into a cosmos, and secondarily to the individual soul, which needs the control and guidance of the Logos to bring its instincts, passions and desires into rational order.[1] John keeps close to the biblical idea of God as Shepherd of the community of Israel.

It is to be observed that all these symbols have warrant in the Old Testament, and this will be found to be true generally of the symbolism both of Philo and of the Fourth Gospel. Without any further examples being adduced, it will be clear that Philo's use of symbolism may

---

[1] The tendency to 'spiritualize' and individualize the teaching of the Old Testament is to be found also in the *Hermetica*; see *The Bible and the Greeks*, p. 187. It is characteristic of the Hellenistic mind. Together with an exaggerated interest in cosmology, it is largely responsible for Philo's distortions of the religion of the Old Testament. The Fourth Gospel is free from both tendencies.

reasonably be expected to throw some light on that of the Fourth Gospel. But a comparison of the two will be profitable only if we have some clear idea of the relation of the thought of Philo as a whole to Johannine thought.

For Philo, as for the Hermetists, and for the Fourth Evangelist, to know God is the chief end of man and his highest blessedness. It is God's will that men should know Him. 'He has called us to honour the God who truly is, not that He needs honour for Himself—for being most sufficient to Himself He needs no other—but because it is His will to lead the race of men, wandering in trackless wastes, into a way free from all error, in order that following nature they may attain the supreme end, which is knowledge of Him Who truly is, Who is the first and most perfect Good, from Whom as from a fountain all particular goods are poured upon the world and those in it' (ἐπὶ τὴν τοῦ πρὸς ἀλήθειαν ὄντος θεοῦ τιμὴν ἐκάλεσεν, ἑαυτοῦ τιμῆς οὐ προσδεόμενος—οὐ γὰρ ἑτέρου χρεῖος ἦν ὁ αὐταρκέστατος ἑαυτῷ—βουλόμενος δὲ τὸ γένος τῶν ἀνθρώπων ἀνοδίαις πλαζόμενον εἰς ἀπλανεστάτην ἄγειν ὁδόν, ἵν' ἑπόμενον τῇ φύσει τὸ ἄριστον εὕρηται τέλος, ἐπιστήμην τοῦ ὄντως ὄντος, ὅς ἐστι τὸ πρῶτον ἀγαθὸν καὶ τελεώτατον, ἀφ' οὗ τρόπον πηγῆς ἄρδεται τῷ κόσμῳ καὶ τοῖς ἐν αὐτῷ τὰ ἐπὶ μέρους ἀγαθά, De Decal. 81). This gift of knowledge, like all the gifts of God, is given fully and absolutely, but appropriated by men as they are able to receive it. The mass of men, as it is written in Gen. vi. 12, have corrupted His way—κατέφθειρε πᾶσα σάρξ τὴν ὁδὸν αὐτοῦ ἐπὶ τῆς γῆς: it is *His* way, not theirs, Philo observes, for the masculine αὐτοῦ cannot refer to σάρξ;[1] the meaning is, 'all flesh has corrupted the perfect way of the eternal and incorruptible which leads to God. This way is wisdom, for led by this straight and level way reason arrives at the goal; and the goal of the way is γνῶσις καὶ ἐπιστήμη θεοῦ' (*Quod Deus*, 142–3). This figure of the Way that leads to God is one that Philo frequently uses, and we may recall that in the Fourth Gospel the disciples anxiously confess that they do not know the Way (xiv. 5). There they receive their answer: Ἐγώ εἰμι ἡ ὁδός.... οὐδεὶς ἔρχεται πρὸς τὸν πατέρα εἰ μὴ δι' ἐμοῦ. For Philo, as we have seen, the Way is wisdom, or philosophy (cf. *De Cong.* 79 ἔστι γὰρ φιλοσοφία ἐπιτήδευσις σοφίας, σοφία δὲ ἐπιστήμη θείων καὶ ἀνθρωπίνων καὶ τῶν τούτων αἰτίων). The relation between Philo's Way and that of the Gospel we shall have to consider later. This wisdom which leads to God is the gift of God, and especially so in the revelation of Himself which He has

---

[1] The Hebrew בשׂר is masculine, but Philo follows the LXX unquestioningly— unlike John (see p. 245).

given in the Scriptures. This is fundamental with Philo. Man is not left to seek God by Himself. God reveals Himself to inspired men and prophets, and the greatest of them is Moses, whose authentic writings Philo finds in the Pentateuch. 'We pupils and acquaintances of Moses will never abandon the quest for the Self-existent, believing that the knowledge of Him is the consummation of happiness and age-long life, as the Law says that all those who adhere to God live—a necessary and philosophical doctrine, for the godless are indeed dead in their souls, but those who take their stand by God the self-existent live an immortal life' (ἡμεῖς γε οἱ φοιτηταὶ καὶ γνώριμοι τοῦ προφήτου Μωυσέως τὴν τοῦ ὄντος ζήτησιν οὐ μεθησόμεθα, τὴν ἐπιστήμην αὐτοῦ τέλος εὐδαιμονίας εἶναι νομίζοντες καὶ ζωὴν μακραίωνα, καθὰ καὶ ὁ νόμος φησὶ τοὺς προσκειμένους τῷ θεῷ ζῆν ἅπαντας (Deut. iv. 4), δόγμα τιθεὶς ἀναγκαῖον καὶ φιλόσοφον· ὄντως γὰρ οἱ μὲν ἄθεοι τὰς ψυχὰς τεθνᾶσιν, οἱ δὲ τὴν παρὰ τῷ ὄντι θεῷ τεταγμένοι τάξιν ἀθάνατον βίον ζῶσιν, De Spec. Leg. I. 345). Like the Jews in the Fourth Gospel, Philo searches the Scriptures because he believes that in them he has eternal life (John v. 39 ἐραυνᾶτε τὰς γραφὰς ὅτι ὑμεῖς δοκεῖτε ἐν αὐταῖς ζωὴν αἰώνιον ἔχειν: the verb ἐραυνᾶν is similarly used by Philo, De Somn. I. 41, Quod Det. 13, etc.). His 'philosophy', therefore, is not the speculation of the free and unaided human intellect. It starts from the appropriation of revealed truth. As we have seen, the Hermetists also believed that wisdom and knowledge came by revelation, and in their writings Hermes, the sage of remote antiquity, is the recipient and transmitter of divine revelation. Moses occupies much the same place for Philo. He is the hierophant, the mystagogue, by whom we are initiated into the mysteries of God. 'Even if we have closed the eye of the soul, and do not care or are not able to look up, do thou, O Hierophant, lift up thy voice and take command of us, and never cease to anoint our eyes until thou lead us as initiates to the hidden light of sacred words, and show us the beauties which are fenced off and invisible to the uninitiate' (κἂν ἡμεῖς καμμύσαντες τὸ τῆς ψυχῆς ὄμμα μὴ σπουδάζωμεν ἢ μὴ δυνώμεθα ἀναβλέπειν, αὐτός, ὦ ἱεροφάντα, ὑπήχει καὶ ἐπιστάτει καὶ ἐγχρίων μή ποτε ἀπείπῃς, ἕως ἐπὶ τὸ κεκρυμμένον ἱερῶν λόγων φέγγος ἡμᾶς μυσταγωγῶν ἐπιδείξῃς τὰ κατάκλειστα καὶ ἀτελέστοις ἀόρατα κάλλη, De Somn. I. 164). The use of such language, borrowed from the Mysteries, is as characteristic of Philo as of the Hermetists. He believes no more than they in any ritual or sacramental initiations,[1] but he and they believe

---

[1] In this point I cannot follow E. R. Goodenough, though his work By Light, Light is a valuable and illuminating discussion of many sides of Philo's teaching.

that there is a kind of spiritual initiation which by grace of God gives what the Mysteries offered, and what man by his unaided effort could never attain—vision of reality and eternal life. The initiate is enabled 'to touch the limits of the All, and press on to the all-beautiful and famous vision of the ingenerate' (τῶν τοῦ παντὸς ἅψασθαι περάτων καὶ πρὸς τὴν τοῦ ἀγενήτου παγκάλην καὶ ἀοίδιμον θέαν ἐπειχθῆναι, De Ebr. 152). And this is eternal life (ἀλλ' οὐ ζωὴ μέν ἐστιν αἰώνιος ἡ πρὸς τὸ ὂν καταφυγή; De Fuga, 78). The same idea in a transmuted form governs the thought of the Fourth Gospel: αὕτη δέ ἐστιν ἡ αἰώνιος ζωή, ἵνα γινώσκωσί σε τὸν μόνον ἀληθινὸν θεόν (John xvii. 3).

Again, for Philo as for the Hermetists, to know God is to be a son of God (οἱ δὲ ἐπιστήμῃ κεχρημένοι τοῦ ἑνὸς υἱοὶ θεοῦ προσαγορεύονται, De Conf. 145). The expression however does not carry quite the same implication. True to his Jewish upbringing, Philo keeps the distinction between God and man. He has no doctrine of rebirth by which the human becomes divine, nor does he ever say that by knowing God man is deified. On the contrary, 'God might sooner change to man than man to God' (θᾶττον γὰρ ἂν εἰς ἄνθρωπον θεὸν ἢ εἰς θεὸν ἄνθρωπον μεταβαλεῖν, Leg. ad Gaium, 118). Verbally at least this points to the possibility, which for the Fourth Evangelist is an actuality, of an incarnation of the divine. But the expression is rhetorical—Philo is denouncing the deification of the emperor—and hardly intended to be taken with full seriousness. For Philo God is eternally other than man. There is indeed in man a divine element by virtue of his creation in the image of God, and in this sense God may be called the Father of men, as indeed of all things; but in no way can man become God, or the son of God in an absolute sense. At his best he is the adopted son of God (μόνος γὰρ εὐγενὴς ἅτε θεὸν ἐπιγεγραμμένος πατέρα καὶ γεγονὼς εἰσποιητὸς αὐτῷ μόνος υἱός—of Abraham, De Sobr. 56). Philo is here in harmony with the whole biblical tradition, in both Testaments, though later Christian writers allowed themselves to speak of man as being deified through the incarnation of the Son of God.

Here we come at once upon the ambiguity or duality which runs through all Philo's thought. Up to a point he will use the language which is natural to the Hermetists, but it does not always mean exactly the same thing to him. On the one hand he shares the religious outlook of Greek thinkers deriving from Plato, whose God was the metaphysical Absolute, the One beyond the many. On the other hand he is deeply influenced by the piety of the Old Testament, which no amount of allegorical exegesis can wholly resolve into a mystical absorption into the One. Up to a point he is able to reconcile the two ways of religion, but in the end they remain unassimilated.

It was easy enough for Philo to find in the Old Testament itself support for his strenuous insistence, in Platonic vein, upon the unity and the transcendence of God, and his rejection of any approach to anthropomorphism. He is never tired of quoting the biblical maxim οὐχ ὡς ἄνθρωπος ὁ θεός, and if in certain parts of Scripture there are undoubted anthropomorphisms, he was only following the later writers of the Old Testament in explaining these away. Moreover, the LXX offered him a rendering of the divine Name which seemed to justify the conception of God as pure being. In Philo's Greek Bible, God replies to Moses's request to know His name in the words Ἐγώ εἰμι Ὁ ὬΝ· οὕτως ἐρεῖς τοῖς υἱοῖς Ἰσραήλ, Ὁ ὬΝ ἀπέσταλκέν με πρὸς ὑμᾶς (Exod. iii. 14). Thus Philo's favourite designation for God is Ὁ ὤν or Ὁ ὄντως ὤν. When however he turns this into the neuter, and speaks of Τὸ ὄν, Τὸ ὄντως ὄν, he is deserting the Old Testament, and assimilating the God of his fathers to the impersonal Absolute of the Platonists.

Again, while he has scriptural warrant for denying to God any trace of human weakness or limitation, and insisting on His complete transcendence of man and the world, he goes beyond his warrant in conceiving God as devoid of all passions and qualities, and defining Him only by negatives. It is in accordance with this conception of the divine that he speaks of that knowledge of God which is eternal life as καταφυγὴ πρὸς τὸ ὄν. It is a flight to pure Being, which is nothing else besides pure Being, for even the final knowledge of God is only knowledge that He is; *what* God is, is known only to Himself (ὁ δ᾽ ἄρα οὐδὲ τῷ νῷ καταληπτὸς ὅτι μὴ κατὰ τὸ εἶναι μόνον· ὕπαρξις γὰρ ἔσθ᾽ ἣν καταλαμβάνομεν αὐτοῦ, τῶν δέ γε χωρὶς ὑπάρξεως οὐδέν, *Quod Deus* 62; cf. ἐκεῖνο μὲν γάρ, ὃ καὶ ἀγαθοῦ κρεῖττον καὶ μονάδος πρεσβύτερον καὶ ἑνὸς εἰλικρινέστερον, ἀμήχανον ὑφ᾽ ἑτέρου θεωρεῖσθαί τινος, διότι μόνῳ θέμις αὐτῷ ὑφ᾽ ἑαυτοῦ καταλαμβάνεσθαι. τὸ δ᾽ ὅτι ἔστιν, ὑπάρξεως ὄνομα καταληπτὸν ὄν. . .οὐ πάντες. . .καταλαμβάνουσιν, κτλ., *De Praem.* 40; *et simm. pass.*). Of the stages preparatory to such knowledge Philo has much to say—the way of ascetic practice, by which the soul is freed from the bonds of matter, the way κάτωθεν ἄνω, of inference from the world to its Creator, the way of contemplation of the eternal ἰδέαι; of these we shall have to take some account afterwards. But for the present we are concerned with the consummation, the *Visio Dei.* 'If there are any who were able to apprehend Him from Himself, without employing any reasoning besides to help towards the vision, let them be enrolled among the pious and genuine worshippers and true friends of God. Of these is he who is called in Chaldaean "Israel", but in Greek "Seeing God"—not indeed seeing *what* God is—for that, as I have said, is impossible—but seeing *that* He is; not having learnt it from any other...but having received this new name from God Himself alone, who willed to reveal His own existence to His suppliant....Is not light seen by means of light? Even so God, being His own illumination, is beheld through Himself alone, no other co-operating or being capable of co-operating towards the pure apprehension of His existence' (εἰ δέ τινες ἐδυνήθησαν αὐτὸν ἐξ ἑαυτοῦ καταλαβεῖν ἑτέρῳ μηδενὶ χρησάμενοι λογισμῷ συνέργῳ πρὸς τὴν θέαν, ἐν ὁσίοις καὶ γνησίοις θεραπευταῖς καὶ θεοφιλέσιν ὡς ἀληθῶς ἀναγραφέσθωσαν. τούτων ἐστὶν ὁ Χαλδαϊστὶ μὲν προσαγορευόμενος Ἰσραήλ, Ἑλληνιστὶ δὲ ΟΡΩΝ ΘΕΟΝ, οὐχ οἷός ἐστιν ὁ θεός—τοῦτο γὰρ ἀμήχανον, ὡς ἔφην—ἀλλ' ὅτι ἔστιν, οὐ παρ' ἑτέρου τινὸς μαθών...ἀλλὰ παρ' αὐτοῦ μόνου μετακληθεὶς τὴν ἰδίαν ὕπαρξιν ἀναφῆναι θελήσαντος ἱκέτῃ....καὶ συνόλως τὸ φῶς οὐ φωτὶ βλέπεται; τὸν αὐτὸν δὴ τρόπον καὶ ὁ θεὸς ἑαυτοῦ φέγγος ὢν δι' αὐτοῦ μόνου θεωρεῖται, μηδενὸς ἄλλου συνεργοῦντος ἢ δυναμένου συνεργῆσαι πρὸς τὴν εἰλικρινῆ κατάληψιν τῆς ὑπάρξεως αὐτοῦ, *De Praem.* 43–5).

From this point of view, then, the knowledge of God is an intense mystical awareness of absolute being. But in other passages Philo uses language which sorts ill with this extremely abstract conception. In particular he frequently uses the language of worship, of faith and of love. We have already seen that he speaks of those who have the vision of God as ὅσιοι καὶ γνήσιοι θεραπευταί, and expressions of that kind are common enough to indicate clearly that worship is a moment in man's experience of God. But in the kind of mysticism which is unity or identity with God as pure being there is no place properly for worship, which implies an ultimate distance between the Creator and the creature. Philo here speaks as a Jew brought up on the Old Testament.

Again, he owes to the same source the concept of faith as an element in man's approach to God. Here the story of Abraham plays a decisive part in his thought. It was easy to allegorize the story as an account of the ascent of the soul to God. The Lord said to Abraham (Gen. xii. 1), ἄπελθε ἐκ τῆς γῆς σου—i.e. abandon the body, since the body of man is made of γῆ, as Moses said (Gen. iii. 19)—καὶ ἐκ τῆς συγγενείας σου—i.e. abandon sense, for αἴσθησις συγγενὲς καὶ ἀδελφόν ἐστι διανοίας—καὶ ἐκ τοῦ οἴκου τοῦ πατρός σου—i.e. turn from speech to silence, for νοῦς is the father and λόγος (ὁ κατὰ προφοράν) is its dwelling-place (*De Migr. Abr.* 1–6). Thus Abraham becomes the type of the soul that turns from things of sense to the invisible world, and so comes to the knowledge of Τὸ ὄν. This class of soul (τουτὶ τὸ γένος) 'constrained by an unspeakable longing to behold and ever hold converse with divine things, after it has explored and passed through the whole visible nature, forthwith goes after the incorporeal and intelligible, taking with it no one of the senses, but abandoning all of the soul that is irrational, and employing solely that part of it which is called reason and ratiocination' (ἱμέρῳ γὰρ τοῦ θεωρεῖν καὶ τοῖς θείοις ἀεὶ συνεῖναι κατεσχημένον ἀλέκτῳ, τὴν ὁρατὴν ὅταν ἅπασαν φύσιν διερευνήσῃ καὶ διεξέλθῃ, πρὸς τὴν ἀσώματον καὶ νοητὴν εὐθὺς μέτεισιν, οὐδεμίαν τῶν αἰσθήσεων ἐπαγόμενον, ἀλλ' ὅσον μὲν τῆς ψυχῆς ἄλογον μεθιέμενον, τῷ ὃ κέκληται νοῦς καὶ λογισμὸς μόνῳ προσχρώμενον, *De Praem.* 26). The allegorical method is nowhere employed with greater subtlety than in working out this theme from all the details of the story of Abraham. But after all, the Bible holds up Abraham as an example of faith, and Philo was too good a Jew not to give full value to the maxim that 'Abraham believed God and it was counted unto him for righteousness'. Accordingly place must be found for faith in the account of the way in which man knows God. Philo does indeed try to bring πίστις into the closest relation with the philosophical ideal of supersensible apprehension (ἡ πρὸς θεὸν πίστις καὶ ἀφανοῦς ὑπόληψις,[1] *De Somn.* I. 68), but there remains a hard core of meaning in the term which cannot be dissociated from personal piety. Πίστις after all implies a personal trust in God, and belief in that which He reveals. This aspect of personal piety is evident in a rhetorical passage where Philo sets forth the properties of faith: 'Faith in God is the only true and secure good, comfort of life, fulfilment of kindly hopes, barrenness of evils and fertility of goods, renunciation of misery, knowledge of piety, possession of happiness, the amelioration in everything of the soul that is stayed and founded upon the First Cause which can do all things and wills the best' (*De Abr.* 268). Such faith is an inseparable element in the

---

[1] The expression actually is τῆς πρὸς θεὸν πίστεως καὶ ἀφανοῦς ὑπολήψεως, leaving doubtful the construction of the genitive ἀφανοῦς. But 'conception of the invisible' seems a better meaning than 'invisible conception'. Philo frequently uses τὸ ἀφανές for invisible realities, e.g. *De Plant.* 20, *De Cher.* 96, *De Spec. Leg.* I. 6; without the article, *De Spec. Leg.* III. 194 ἐμφανὲς ἀφανοῦς μίμημα.

ultimate experience of the divine. The three patriarchs symbolize respectively faith, joy and the vision of God, and 'to have faith in God, to have lifelong joy, and always to see That which Is—what more profitable or more reverend thing could be conceived than this?' (τοῦ δὲ πιστεύειν θεῷ καὶ διὰ παντὸς τοῦ βίου χαίρειν, καὶ ὁρᾶν ἀεὶ τὸ ὄν, τί ἂν ὠφελιμώτερον ἢ σεμνότερον ἐπινοήσειέ τις; *De Praem.* 27).

Still more striking is the emphasis laid on love. Here again Philo found in the Old Testament an element in religion that could not be wholly interpreted in the terms of an ontological mysticism. Indeed no Jew could ever get away from the Shema: 'Hear, O Israel; the Lord our God is one Lord, and thou shalt love the Lord thy God.' And it is fundamental for Philo. 'To live according to God is defined by Moses as loving Him' (τὸ κατὰ θεὸν ʒῆν ἐν τῷ ἀγαπᾶν αὐτὸν ὁρίʒεται Μωυσῆς, *De Post.* 69). 'The thing that is demanded of thee, O mind, by God is neither burdensome and complicated nor difficult, but altogether simple and easy: that is, to love Him' (αἰτεῖται ὦ διάνοια παρά σου ὁ θεὸς οὐδὲν βαρὺ καὶ ποικίλον ἢ δύσεργον ἀλλὰ ἁπλοῦν πάνυ καὶ ῥάδιον· ταῦτα δέ ἐστιν ἀγαπᾶν αὐτόν, *De Spec. Leg.* I. 299–300). This attitude of love to God is contrasted with an inferior attitude of fear. The last-quoted passage continues, 'that is, to love Him as Benefactor, or if not, at least to fear Him as Ruler and Lord, to take all means of pleasing Him, to serve Him not carelessly but with the whole soul filled with a God-loving disposition, to embrace His commandments, and to honour righteousness' (ταῦτα δ' ἐστὶν ἀγαπᾶν αὐτὸν ὡς εὐεργέτην· εἰ δὲ μή, φοβεῖσθαι γοῦν ὡς ἄρχοντα καὶ κύριον, καὶ διὰ πασῶν ἰέναι τῶν εἰς ἀρέσκειαν ὁδῶν καὶ λατρεύειν αὐτῷ μὴ παρέργως ἀλλὰ ὅλῃ τῇ ψυχῇ πεπληρωμένῃ γνώμης φιλοθέου καὶ τῶν ἐντολῶν αὐτοῦ περιέχεσθαι καὶ τὰ δίκαια τιμᾶν). The terms κύριος and θεός denote God in His relation to the material and the spiritual sphere respectively. Those who live upon the lower plane are to fear Him as Lord, those who live upon the higher plane are to love Him as God. 'Of the sensible world He is called Master and Benefactor by the names Lord and God, but of the noumenal good Saviour and Benefactor and nothing else, not Master nor Lord. For the wise is the friend of God rather than His slave' (τοῦ μὲν γὰρ αἰσθητοῦ κόσμου δεσπότης καὶ εὐεργέτης ἀνείρηται διὰ τοῦ κύριος καὶ θεός· τοῦ δὲ νοητοῦ ἀγαθοῦ σωτὴρ καὶ εὐεργέτης αὐτὸ μόνον, οὐχὶ δεσπότης ἢ κύριος. φίλον γὰρ τὸ σοφὸν θεῷ μᾶλλον ἢ δοῦλον. παρὸ καὶ σαφῶς ἐπὶ Ἀβραὰμ φάσκει· Μὴ ἐπικαλύψω ἐγὼ ἀπὸ Ἀβραὰμ τοῦ φίλου μου, *De Sobr.* 55). Thus to fear God and keep His commandments is the lower way, appropriate to those who are still bound by the senses; the higher way is to love God, and this is the way of the wise; 'for to those who do not assign to the Self-existent any human part or passion, but in a godly manner honour It for Itself alone, love is most appropriate, and fear to the others' (τοῖς μὲν οὖν μήτε μέρος μήτε πάθος ἀνθρώπου περὶ τὸ ὂν νομίζουσιν, ἀλλὰ θεοπρεπῶς αὐτὸ δι' αὐτὸ μόνον τιμῶσι, τὸ ἀγαπᾶν οἰκειότατον, φοβεῖσθαι δὲ τοῖς ἑτέροις, Quod Deus, 69). 'These all are at once friends of God and befriended by Him; they love God and are loved by Him in return' (πάντας φιλοθέους ὁμοῦ καὶ θεοφιλεῖς, ἀγαπήσαντας τὸν ἀληθῆ θεὸν καὶ ἀνταγαπηθέντας πρὸς αὐτοῦ, De Abr. 50). The relation between the love of God and the knowledge of God is not explicitly stated, but as the knowledge of God makes men sons of God, so those who love Him are called His sons by adoption (De Sobr. 56), and as knowledge of God is eternal life, so to love God is life (ἡ ζωή σου τὸ ἀγαπᾶν τὸν ὄντα, De Post. 69), and whether we speak of knowledge or of love, it is the height of human happiness (knowledge τέλος εὐδαιμονίας, De Spec. Leg. I. 345; love of God πέραν ὅρων ἀνθρωπίνης εὐδαιμονίας, De Sobr. 56). It seems therefore that in Philo's conception of the knowledge of God there are included both the mystical awareness of pure being and a personal love for One Who also loves us.

If we put all this together, we see that Philo approximates to the idea of eternal life in the Fourth Gospel. For both of them eternal life is to know God—τὸν μόνον ἀληθινὸν θεόν, as they both say—and for both of them such knowledge is in part at least a matter of faith and love. And when Philo contrasts the slavish fear of God, as the attitude of those who do not really know Him, with the love of God, which is the attitude of those who know and are His friends, we are very near indeed to the language of the Fourth Gospel: οὐκέτι λέγω ὑμᾶς δούλους, ὅτι ὁ δοῦλος οὐκ οἶδεν τί ποιεῖ αὐτοῦ ὁ κύριος. ὑμᾶς δὲ εἴρηκα φίλους, ὅτι πάντα... ἐγνώρισα ὑμῖν (John xv. 15). This conception of the knowledge of God, however, is in Philo somewhat uneasily associated with a type of mysticism which finds its goal in pure awareness of absolute being.

Philo's philosophy, apart from its Hebraic sources, combines elements of Platonism and of Stoicism. According to the Platonic tradition the world of sensible experience—κόσμος αἰσθητός—is the copy of a higher world of eternal forms—κόσμος νοητός. The latter alone is fully real, and knowledge properly so called is knowledge of the κόσμος νοητός. The Stoics recognized no such supramundane existences. For them the rational principle is immanent in the universe, ὁ τοῦ κόσμου λόγος, ὁ τοῦ παντὸς λόγος. The world as we know it is there because the active principle, λόγος, acts upon the passive principle, ὕλη, and gives it form and meaning; and that is why we know it, because there is λόγος in us also. The Stoics are prepared to apply to λόγος the term 'God'. There is no other God than the immanent rational principle. The Platonists on the other hand seek God beyond the world. Either He is identified with the highest of the Ideas which make up the κόσμος νοητός, or He is the cause or ground of the κόσμος νοητός.

Now Philo was a theist, whose Jewish training led him to believe in a transcendent God not to be identified with the world or any part of it; a God who is the Creator of the world. He seeks in Platonic and in Stoic sources a philosophy which will give reasoned expression to the relation which such a God must bear to the world and to man. In the Old Testament God is said to have created the world by His word. The meaning was simply that God spoke and the world came into existence. But in his Greek Bible Philo read such expressions as τῷ λόγῳ τοῦ κυρίου οἱ οὐρανοὶ ἐστερεώθησαν (Ps. xxxii. 6). Elsewhere he read that the λόγος of God came to prophets and gave them knowledge of Him. In the fortunate ambiguity of the Greek word lay the possibility of understanding such statements in a sense approximating to that of the Stoics. The Stoics were right in finding in λόγος the principle both of reality and of knowledge; but wrong in identifying λόγος with God, for the λόγος proceeded from God. Again, Philo was familiar with the Wisdom theology, according to which God first created Wisdom and then through her created the world. Wisdom is thus the thought of God projected forth as the beginning of the work of creation. She is not identical with God, nor yet with the world. She proceeds from God, and gives form and reality to the world we know, and passing into holy souls makes them friends of God and prophets.[1] Logos, therefore, can be understood in terms of Wisdom. As in man there is a λόγος ἐνδιάθετος, which is the rational thought in the mind, and a λόγος προφορικός, which is the thought uttered as a word, so the divine Logos is in the first place a thought of God, His eternal Wisdom; and in the second place it is projected into formless and unreal matter, making of it a universe, real and rational.[2] In its former aspect it can be equated with the κόσμος νοητός: it is the τόπος of the Ideas (De Opif. 20).

The nature of the Logos and its relations with God, man and the universe is the subject of endless disquisitions in Philo's writings,

[1] Wisd. vii. 27.
[2] De Vit. Mos. II (III). 127.

incredibly complicated, and doubtfully consistent in detail. But the essentials of his Logos-doctrine are fairly simple and clear. We may consider some passages relevant to our purpose, following first the *De Opificio*, which gives a straightforward account of the Logos as cosmological principle. 'God, assuming, as God would assume, that a beautiful copy could never come into existence without a beautiful model...when He willed to create this visible world, first blocked out (προεξετύπου) the intelligible world, in order that using an incorporeal and godlike model he might make the corporeal world, a younger image of the elder (πρεσβυτέρου νεώτερον ἀπεικόνισμα) containing as many sensible *genera* as the other contained intelligible. The world consisting of ideas must not be spoken or thought of as being in space. Where it exists, we shall know by using a familiar illustration. When a city is being founded...sometimes there comes forward a man trained as an architect, and after surveying the favourable features of the site he first makes an outline in his mind (διαγράφει ἐν ἑαυτῷ) of almost all the parts of the city that is to be built—temples, gymnasia, council-chambers, markets, harbours, docks, alleys, the structure of the walls, the plan of the houses and public buildings. Then, receiving an impression of each of them in his soul, as if in wax, he models a city of the mind (πόλις νοητή)....Looking to this model he proceeds to construct the city of stone and wood, making the corporeal substances resemble each of the incorporeal ideas. In like manner we must think of God. When He designed to found the Great City, He first conceived its types, and from them composed a world of the mind (κόσμος νοητός), and then using it as a model completed the world of the senses' (*De Opif*. 16–19). Consequently, the κόσμος νοητός is simply the λόγος of God in the act of creating a world (οὐδὲν ἂν ἕτερον εἴποι τὸν νοητὸν κόσμον εἶναι ἢ θεοῦ λόγον ἤδη κοσμοποιοῦντος, *ibid*. 24). And the Logos is the image (εἰκών) of God, His seal (σφραγίς) stamped upon creation. Or, in personal metaphor, it is described as the firstborn Son of God (πρωτόγονος υἱός). The personification must not be taken seriously; Philo speaks of the visible world also as the μόνος καὶ ἀγαπητὸς αἰσθητὸς υἱός of God, born of the union of God with His own Wisdom or Knowledge (*De Ebr*. 30–1). So far as Philo means anything more than that both the κόσμος νοητός and the κόσμος αἰσθητός have their source in God, he probably has in mind the idea that the spoken word is the offspring of the mind (ἠχεῖ μὲν γὰρ ὁ γεγωνὸς λόγος, πατὴρ δὲ τούτου ὁ νοῦς, *De Cher*. 7).

The Logos, being the medium of the creation of the world, is also the medium of its divine government. For it is not only transcendent in the mind of God, but also immanent in the universe which was created through it. It is 'the captain and steersman of the universe' (ὁ δίοπος καὶ κυβερνήτης τοῦ παντός, *De Cher.* 36). It is the agent of God's gifts (ὑπηρέτης δωρεῶν) to the world (*Quod Deus*, 57). It is set by God over His flock, like the vicegerent of a king (*De Agr.* 51, *De Mut.* 114–16). On the other hand it is also the medium by which the world approaches God, the ἀρχιερεύς, the ἱκέτης, through whom this world aspires to the eternal; and 'it is necessary that he who is consecrated to the Father of the world should employ His son most perfect in virtue (the κόσμος νοητός = λόγος) as advocate (παράκλητος) for the forgiveness of sins and the supply of ungrudging benefits' (*De Vit. Mos.* II (III). 134).

In all respects the Logos is the medium of intercourse between God and this world. As some of the later Old Testament writers sought to avoid saying that the transcendent God had direct dealing with men, and spoke of His angel or His name, so Philo calls the Logos by such biblical terms as ἄγγελος (ἀρχάγγελος) and ὄνομα θεοῦ. And indeed his use of the term Logos itself has some affinity with the (probably later) use of the term מֵימְרָא as a periphrasis for the divine name.[1] But with Philo it is more than a periphrasis. It implies a definite *Weltanschauung*: by Logos Philo means the Platonic world of ideas, conceived not as self-existent, but as expressing the mind of the One God. It is this that mediates between God and our world.

From this point of view we must understand what he says about the Logos in relation to the knowledge of God. God Himself is unknowable save as to His ὕπαρξις, and even such knowledge of Him is only for the few who are perfect. But for those who are still seeking the goal, God is known in and through His Logos. Men should 'endeavour to see the Self-existent or, if they cannot, at least to see Its image, the most sacred Logos' (ἐφίεσθαι μὲν τοῦ τὸ ὂν ἰδεῖν, εἰ δὲ μὴ δύναιντο, τὴν γοῦν εἰκόνα αὐτοῦ τὸν ἱερώτατον λόγον, *De Conf.* 97). 'For the Logos is the God of us imperfect men, but the Primal God is the God of the wise and perfect' (οὗτος γὰρ ἡμῶν τῶν ἀτελῶν ἂν εἴη θεός, τῶν δὲ σοφῶν καὶ τελείων ὁ πρῶτος, *Leg. All.* III. 207). 'So long as a man is not yet perfect,

---

[1] Strack-Billerbeck's *Exkurs über den Memra Jahves* in *Kommentar zum neuen Testament aus Talmud und Midrash* (1924), II, pp. 302–33, shows conclusively that מימרא in the Targums is never the name of a personal mediating hypostasis. Moore, *Judaism* (1927), II, pp. 417 sqq. comes to the same conclusion.

he employs as the guide of his way the divine Logos; for there is an oracle, "I will send my angel before thy face"', etc. (Exod. xxiii. 20) (ἕως μὲν γὰρ οὐ τετελείωται, ἡγεμόνι τῆς ὁδοῦ χρῆται λόγῳ θείῳ· χρησμὸς γάρ ἐστιν, Ἰδοῦ ἀποστέλλω τὸν ἄγγελόν μου πρὸ προσώπου σου κτλ., *De Migr. Abr.* 174). But what does all this really mean? In spite of all personification, Philo is not really thinking of a personal guide and companion. The Logos is the world of Ideas. Knowledge of God comes by the discipline of contemplating the unseen archetypes.

But the relation of the Logos to men needs some further consideration. In reviewing the *Hermetica* I called attention to the concept of perfect, true or essential humanity (ὁ τέλειος, ὁ ὄντως, ὁ οὐσιώδης ἄνθρωπος). Sometimes these terms appeared to stand for a class of men, sometimes for the real or essential humanity in men (ὁ ἐνδιάθετος ἄνθρωπος). Further, we saw that in the *Poimandres* the οὐσιώδης ἄνθρωπος was identified with the pre-existent heavenly Man. Now in Philo we meet with a similar range of conceptions. He several times comments on Gen. iv. 26 καὶ τῷ Σὴθ ἐγένετο υἱός, ἐπωνόμασεν δὲ τὸ ὄνομα αὐτοῦ Ἐνώς· οὗτος ἤλπισεν ἐπικαλεῖσθαι τὸ ὄνομα κυρίου τοῦ θεοῦ. As Philo points out, the name Enosh means 'man': Χαλδαῖοι γὰρ τὸν ἄνθρωπον Ἐνώς (אֱנוֹשׁ) καλοῦσιν, ὡς μόνου πρὸς ἀλήθειαν ὄντος ἀνθρώπου τοῦ τὰ ἀγαθὰ προσδοκῶντος καὶ ἐλπίσιν χρησταῖς ἐφιδρυμένου (*De Abr.* 8), 'and that is why,' he goes on, 'desiring to praise the hopeful nobly, after saying that this person hoped in the Father and Maker of all, he adds, "this is the book of the beginning of men" (Gen. v. 1), although fathers and forefathers have already preceded. But those he considered to be the leaders of the mixed race, but this one of the most pure and well-filtered race, which is truly rational (ὄντως λογικόν).' Enosh in fact is ὁ κατ' ἐξοχὴν ἄνθρωπος, and his record is βίβλος γενέσεως τοῦ πρὸς ἀλήθειαν ἀνθρώπου (*ibid.* 9–11). What then is this πρὸς ἀλήθειαν ἄνθρωπος or κατ' ἐξοχὴν ἄνθρωπος? In the *Quod Det.* 22, Philo speaks of the πρὸς ἀλήθειαν ἄνθρωπος or ἀληθινὸς ἄνθρωπος as ἐν ἑκάστου τῇ ψυχῇ κατοικῶν. Similarly in the *De Somn.* I. 215 he speaks of the two temples of God, the one being the κόσμος in which the Logos is priest, the other the λογικὴ ψυχή, whose priest is ὁ πρὸς ἀλήθειαν ἄνθρωπος. This would naturally be explained by reference to the account of the creation of man. God made man of χοῦς and breathed into him the breath of life. Accordingly 'every man is in respect of his intelligence akin to the divine Logos, being an impress, or fragment, or effulgence of the blessed nature, but in respect of the structure of his body akin to the whole world' (πᾶς ἄνθρωπος κατὰ μὲν τὴν διάνοιαν ᾠκείωται λόγῳ θείῳ, τῆς μακαρίας φύσεως ἐκμαγεῖον ἢ ἀπόσπασμα ἢ ἀπαύγασμα γεγονώς, κατὰ δὲ τὴν τοῦ σώματος κατασκευὴν ἅπαντι τῷ κόσμῳ, *De Opif.* 146). Accordingly, in commenting on Gen. ii. 8 ἔθετο ἐκεῖ τὸν ἄνθρωπον ὃν ἔπλασεν, Philo observes, 'it is expressly said that God placed τὸν ἐν ἡμῖν πρὸς ἀλήθειαν ἄνθρωπον, τουτέστι τὸν νοῦν, among the most sacred growths and plants of virtue' (*De Plant.* 42). For Philo the story of Eden is the account of the origin of empirical humanity. There is however another Man, made in God's image, the pure archetype of Man, the Platonic Idea of Man, in fact. 'There are two kinds of man. The one is heavenly man, the other earthly. The heavenly, being made in the image of God, has no part in corruptible or earthly substance; the earthly was made of seminal matter, which he has called χοῦς. For this reason the heavenly man is said not to be created (πεπλάσθαι) but formed after the image of God (κατ' εἰκόνα τετυπῶσθαι θεοῦ), but the earthly to be the creature (πλάσμα) and not the offspring (γέννημα) of God. The man of earth is to be regarded as νοῦς in the process of being mingled with body, but not yet completely mingled' (*Leg. All.* 1. 31–2). In *De Fuga* 71 the term ὁ πρὸς ἀλήθειαν ἄνθρωπος is applied to this heavenly Man, who is νοῦς καθαρώτατος, as distinguished from the so-called νοῦς which is mingled with αἴσθησις. This heavenly Man again Philo finds in Zech. vi. 12 ἰδοὺ ἄνθρωπος ᾧ ὄνομα ἀνατολή. On this he comments, 'A strange appellation, if you think the reference is to man composed of soul and body; but if it refers to that incorporeal man, who is no other than the divine image, you will admit that the name Ἀνατολή has been given him most appropriately; for the Father of all caused him to spring forth (ἀνέτειλε) as His eldest (πρεσβύτατον) son, whom elsewhere he has called "first-born" (πρωτόγονον); and the Begotten, imitating His Father's ways, looked to His archetypal models and shaped the forms' (*De Conf.* 62–3). But elsewhere the eldest son is the Logos, and creation is the function of the Logos. This prepares us for passages in which Man is actually identified with the Logos. The Logos is called, according to *De Conf.* 146, ἀρχὴ καὶ ὄνομα θεοῦ καὶ ὁ κατ' εἰκόνα ἄνθρωπος καὶ ὁ ὁρῶν, Ἰσραήλ. Again, the phrase of Gen. xlii. 11 πάντες ἐσμὲν υἱοὶ ἑνὸς ἀνθρώπου is explained as meaning ἕνα καὶ τὸν αὐτὸν ἐπιγεγραμμένοι πατέρα οὐ θνητὸν ἀλλ' ἀθάνατον, ἄνθρωπον θεοῦ, ὃς τοῦ ἀϊδίου λόγος ὢν ἐξ ἀνάγκης καὶ αὐτός ἐστιν ἄφθαρτος (*De Conf.* 41). The Logos, as we have seen, is the κόσμος νοητός—or rather the κόσμος νοητός is λόγος θεοῦ ἤδη κοσμοποιοῦντος. If we may put it so, the heavenly Man is also λόγος θεοῦ ἤδη ἀνθρωποποιοῦντος.[1] In other words, whatever belongs to the world of Ideas is Logos: the heavenly Man, being the eternal archetype of mankind, is therefore Logos, and as such the first-born Son of God.[2] But as we have seen, there is a Logos immanent in the world, analogous to the λόγος προφορικός in man, as well as a transcendent Logos analogous to the λόγος ἐνδιάθετος. Similarly, there is not only a heavenly Man above us, but there is also a real man (ὁ πρὸς ἀλήθειαν ἄνθρωπος) indwelling in the soul of each. And this man is also νοῦς, and is also Logos. It is this fact that gives man kinship with the universal Logos, and enables him to rise by communion with it to knowledge of God. God is known through the Logos or κόσμος νοητός, but there is in man himself that which belongs to the κόσμος νοητός. In a word, 'Man is kith and kin to God in respect of participation in Logos, which although he seems to be mortal gives him immortality' (ἄνθρωπος...ἀγχίσπορος ὢν θεοῦ καὶ συγγενὴς κατὰ τὴν πρὸς λόγον κοινωνίαν, ὃς αὐτὸν καίτοι θνητὸν εἶναι δοκοῦντα ἀπαθανατίζει, De Spec. Leg. IV. 14).

It seems clear that behind all this lie speculations about Man to which the *Hermetica* also bear witness. And in dealing with the Johannine doctrine of the Son of Man Who is in heaven, Who is the Son of God, and identical with the Logos, in union with Whom men attain eternal life, we must take account of what Philo says of the ἀληθινὸς ἄνθρωπος. Indeed, in view of the evangelist's use of ἀληθινός would not the Philonic phrase ὁ ἀληθινὸς ἄνθρωπος have fitly expressed his meaning, if he had not been bound by tradition to the Aramaizing expression ὁ υἱὸς τοῦ ἀνθρώπου?

If we now assume this equation, λόγος = ἀληθινὸς ἄνθρωπος = ὁ κατ' εἰκόνα ἄνθρωπος = υἱὸς τοῦ ἀνθρώπου, the extent of parallelism between Philo and the Fourth Gospel becomes remarkable. To begin with the Prologue, the proposition, ἐν ἀρχῇ ἦν ὁ λόγος, may be directly documented out of the *De Opif.*, both going back to an interpretation of Gen. i. That the Logos was πρὸς τὸν θεόν is in effect affirmed in *Quod Deus* 31: this world, as being visible, is the younger son of God; the elder son, which is the κόσμος νοητός (=λόγος) God kept by Himself (ὁ μὲν γὰρ κόσμος οὗτος νεώτερος υἱὸς θεοῦ ἅτε αἰσθητὸς ὤν· τὸν γὰρ πρεσβύτερον—νοητὸς ἐκεῖνος—πρεσβείων ἀξιώσας παρ' ἑαυτῷ καταμένειν διενοήθη).

[1] Cf. *De Spec. Leg.* III. 37 ὁ ἀνθρώπινος νοῦς πρὸς ἀρχέτυπον ἰδέαν, τὸν ἀνωτάτω λόγον, τυπωθείς.
[2] Cf. *De Mut.* 181. 'Isaac' is not the name of a man, but of the ἐνδιάθετος υἱὸς θεοῦ.

With the twofold statement, ὁ λόγος ἦν πρὸς τὸν θεὸν καὶ θεὸς ἦν ὁ λόγος,[1] we may compare *De Somn.* I. 229–30, where ὁ θεός is said to be properly used of the Self-existent, and θεός without the article of the Logos. In the words πάντα δι' αὐτοῦ ἐγένετο we may recognize a precise formulation of the role of the Logos in creation based upon the principle enunciated in *De Cher.* 127: God is the αἴτιος ὑφ' οὗ γέγονεν ὁ κόσμος, and the Logos the ὄργανον δι' οὗ κατεσκευάσθη. In John i. 4 (whatever the precise exegesis of the clauses) the Logos is (as Philo might have said) the τόπος of life and light. Philo never says exactly this. He does say that the Logos is the τόπος of the divine δυνάμεις, and as God is the πηγὴ ζωῆς, and the source of the ἀρχέτυπον φῶς, and since the Logos is His εἰκών, His σκιά, His Son, the Johannine doctrine may fairly be said to be implicit in the Philonic. Similarly in John, Christ, who is Son of Man (ἀληθινὸς ἄνθρωπος=λόγος), is both ζωή and φῶς τοῦ κόσμου. As the Philonic Logos is the ἡγεμών of the way that man must tread to the knowledge of God (e.g. *De Migr. Abr.* 174 ἕως μὲν γὰρ οὐ τετελείωται, ἡγεμόνι τῆς ὁδοῦ χρῆται λόγῳ θείῳ), so Christ is the Way by which men come to the Father. Like the Philonic Logos, Christ is the Shepherd of God's flock, albeit in a different sense. As in Philo the Logos is ἀρχιερεύς and ἱκέτης for the world before God, so in John the prayers of men are directed to the Father through the Son. The Philonic term παράκλητος is applied to Christ by implication in John xiv. 16, and directly in I John ii. 1. As for Philo the Self-existent cannot be seen (except in so far as the vision of His ὕπαρξις and no more is granted to the perfect), but is known through the Logos, so according to the Fourth Gospel, θεὸν οὐδεὶς ἑώρακεν πώποτε, but ὁ ὢν εἰς τὸν κόλπον τοῦ πατρὸς ἐκεῖνος ἐξηγήσατο (John i. 18), and accordingly Christ can say ὁ ἑωρακὼς ἐμὲ ἑώρακεν τὸν πατέρα (xiv. 9). The Philonic identification of the Logos with the κόσμος νοητός may seem at first sight entirely strange to the thought of the Fourth Gospel; but we may recall that Christ is spoken of as ἀληθινὸν φῶς, ἄρτος ἀληθινός, ἄμπελος ἀληθινή. The ἀληθινόν in Philo is not the true as distinguished from the false, but the real as distinguished from the phenomenal. Thus the eternal reality (the Platonic ἰδέα) manifested in our experience of light, bread and vine is in each case the Logos. This is not so widely different from Philo's doctrine that the Logos as κόσμος νοητός comprehends in itself all the ἰδέαι (e.g. *De Sacr.* 83).

[1] θεός may no doubt be taken as a normal anarthrous predicate, but in any case John has avoided a statement of identity, ὁ θεὸς ἦν ὁ λόγος.

It seems clear, therefore, that whatever other elements of thought may enter into the background of the Fourth Gospel, it certainly presupposes a range of ideas having a remarkable resemblance to those of Hellenistic Judaism as represented by Philo. The treatment of those ideas is indeed strikingly different. In particular there is one decisive difference: the evangelist conceives of the Logos as incarnate, and of the ἀληθινὸς ἄνθρωπος as not merely dwelling as νοῦς in all men, but as actually living and dying on earth as a man. This means that the Logos, which in Philo is never personal, except in a fluctuating series of metaphors, is in the gospel fully personal, standing in personal relations both with God and with men, and having a place in history. As a result, those elements of personal piety, faith and love, which are present in Philo's religion but not fully integrated into his philosophy, come to their own in the gospel. The Logos of Philo is not the object of faith and love. The incarnate Logos of the Fourth Gospel is both lover and beloved; to love Him and to have faith in Him is of the essence of that knowledge of God which is eternal life. This however is to anticipate the results of further discussion.

4. RABBINIC JUDAISM

In the preceding chapters I have attempted a survey of some of the more important features in the Hellenistic background of the Fourth Gospel; for although Philo was himself a Jew, his place in the history of religious thought sets him more in the Greek than in the Hebrew succession. During the ascendancy of the *Religionsgeschichtliche Schule* in the latter years of the nineteenth century and the early years of the twentieth, it came to be generally held that the Fourth Gospel was to be understood almost entirely from a Hellenistic standpoint, and such Jewish, or Hebraic, elements as appear in it were consistently minimized. In recent years the balance has been redressed. This has been chiefly due to two factors.

First, the Semitic element in the language of the Fourth Gospel has been recognized and studied. Burney, *The Aramaic Origin of the Fourth Gospel* (1922), maintained that the Greek of the Gospel is only a thin disguise for Aramaic, that it is in fact translation Greek, the whole work having been originally written in Aramaic, which can often be recovered with reasonable certainty. Torrey, in his two books, *The Four Gospels* and *Our Translated Gospels* (1936), maintained a similar thesis for the whole four. The two writers naturally agree in many places in recognizing Aramaic idioms, but where they suggest retranslations they are often in disagreement about the original, and the cases of alleged mistranslation which both of them adduce rarely coincide. Matthew Black, *An Aramaic Approach to the Gospels and Acts* (1946), has criticized both. He does not regard the Fourth Gospel as entirely a translation from an Aramaic original, but he offers some examples (different from those of Burney and Torrey) where, in his opinion, a mistranslation from Aramaic has affected the sense of a passage. Meanwhile Adolf Schlatter, in his two books, *Die Sprache und Heimat des vierten Evangelisten* (1902) and *Der Evangelist Johannes* (1930), had discovered in the language of the gospel traces of Hebrew rather than of Aramaic idiom. He has richly illustrated Johannine expressions from the Hebrew of rabbinic writings. He holds that the writer was bilingual, like some of the authors of Talmud and Midrash, and that, writing in Greek, he betrayed his native idiom, as well as his acquaintance with the established phraseology of the rabbinical schools.

Semitists are thus far from agreement among themselves. The view that the gospel as it stands is a translation has found little favour either with Semitists or with Hellenists, and is entirely improbable. Opinions differ whether the undeniable Semitisms are due to the use, in some places, of Aramaic (or Hebrew) sources, written or oral, or simply to an author who thought in a Semitic idiom while he wrote in Greek. In any case, the evidence for an underlying Semitic idiom is irresistible. This in itself brings the gospel back into a Jewish environment, of which we must take account. Beyond this, I do not here discuss the question of language.

The second and more important factor is the fresh study of Judaism, and its application to problems of the New Testament. Until the early years of the present century Christian scholars found it almost impossible to make effective use of the documents of Rabbinic Judaism for want of a critical and chronological assessment of the material. This want is being remedied. The student of the New Testament is especially indebted to G. F. Moore, *Judaism* (1927), a comprehensive and authoritative account of the Jewish religion as it was in the early Christian period, based upon Rabbinic evidence accurately datable to that period; and to Strack-Billerbeck's *Kommentar zum neuen Testament aus Talmud und Midrash* (1922–8). To these add Israel Abrahams, *Studies in Pharisaism and the Gospels*, and the composite *Judaism and Christianity*, especially vol. II, *The Contact of Pharisaism with other Cultures*, ed. H. Loewe (1937).

In the present chapter, where I am mainly dependent on secondary sources, I draw largely upon the writers mentioned above.[1] My aim is not to attempt any comprehensive survey of the Jewish or Hebraic background of the gospels, but to indicate by means of some outstanding examples the way in which the thought and the methods of Rabbinic Judaism need to be taken into account for the interpretation of the Fourth Gospel. I shall select material under three heads, (1) The Torah, (2) The Messiah, and (3) The Name of God.

1. THE TORAH

The key-word of the Jewish religious vocabulary is תּוֹרָה. It is a word of wide meaning. Its original sense is 'direction', 'instruction', 'teaching'. It is used to cover (a) 'commandments, statutes and judgments', delivered by judges, kings or lawgivers—in fact, what we should call 'law'; (b) oracular responses delivered by priests at the local or national shrines; and (c) religious teaching given by prophets upon the nature and character of God, His dealings in history, His purposes for

[1] Unless otherwise stated, I usually owe quotations from Talmud and Midrash to Strack-Billerbeck (S.-B.).

His people, and His demands upon men. The Pentateuch, as a compilation of civil and religious institutions, and of the sacred history, was specifically called תּוֹרָה, but the word had also a wider connotation, including the prophetic teaching and later teaching regarded as a commentary upon the Torah proper. It stands in fact for the whole of religion regarded as divine revelation.

The LXX chose the Greek word νόμος to render תּוֹרָה, in all its senses. It is not a perfect equivalent. Νόμος in its Greek usage covers only the first of the three senses defined above, and on the other hand it has meanings which are alien from the idea of Torah, such as 'custom', 'rule', 'principle' in the abstract.[1]

If now we consider the use of the term νόμος by New Testament writers, we observe the following facts: (a) in the Synoptic Gospels and Acts, νόμος is the Pentateuch, but chiefly in its aspect as a code of civil and religious institutions—'law'; (b) in James, νόμος is not the Pentateuch as such, but the divine 'law', conceived partly in the Jewish way as specific enactments, and partly in the Stoic way as an immanent principle of action—the 'perfect law of liberty'; (c) in Paul νόμος is often the Pentateuch, or the code of civil and religious institutions comprised in it (ὁ νόμος τῶν ἐντολῶν ἐν δόγμασιν); but it has an extension of meaning in two directions: (i) it is used to cover the whole Old Testament, in the sense of a divine revelation (תּוֹרָה in its widest sense); (ii) it is also used in the Stoic manner for an immanent principle, and that in several different ways.[2]

Now in the Fourth Gospel νόμος is used, exactly as in the LXX, to cover both the narrower and the wider meanings of תּוֹרָה, but never in any sense which is not covered by תּוֹרָה. That is to say, it never strays away from the Jewish into the Greek field of meaning. To put the matter otherwise, whereas in Paul and James there are passages in which the substitution of תּוֹרָה for νόμος would obscure the sense, there is no such passage in the Fourth Gospel. This in itself is an important piece of evidence for the Jewish affinities of this work.

I propose now to examine all the uses of the term νόμος in this gospel. The references to νόμος in the narrative of the trial before Pilate (xviii. 31, xix. 7) are of no special significance. When Pilate says κατὰ τὸν νόμον ὑμῶν κρίνατε αὐτόν, he is thinking of the law governing the administration of justice in the Jewish community, like the νόμος of any

---

[1] I have discussed תורה = νόμος more fully in *The Bible and the Greeks*, pp. 25–41.
[2] See *The Bible and the Greeks*, l.c.

Greek city which enjoyed its own municipal institutions under the imperial system. But this was of course for the Jews a part of the Torah. Similarly when the Jews say, ἡμεῖς νόμον ἔχομεν, καὶ κατὰ τὸν νόμον ἐκεῖνον ὀφείλει ἀποθανεῖν, they are referring to that aspect of the Torah in which it served as a criminal code.

There are two other references to this aspect of the Torah. In vii. 51 Nicodemus, speaking in Sanhedrin, appeals to the provision that no man shall be condemned unheard: μὴ ὁ νόμος ἡμῶν κρίνει τὸν ἄνθρωπον, ἐὰν μὴ ἀκούσῃ πρῶτον παρ' αὐτοῦ, καὶ γνῷ τί ποιεῖ; The maxim referred to is stated in *Exod. R.* 21. 3 (*ap.* Schlatter): 'Flesh-and-blood, if it hear the words of a man, judges him; if it does not hear, it cannot establish his judgment.' Similarly in viii. 17, the law of evidence is cited: ἐν τῷ νόμῳ δὲ τῷ ὑμετέρῳ γέγραπται ὅτι δύο ἀνθρώπων ἡ μαρτυρία ἀληθής ἐστιν. The rule forbidding the admission of the evidence of a single witness in criminal causes is laid down in Num. xxxv. 30, Deut. xvii. 6, xix. 15. S.-B. cite from Siphre on Num. *l.c.* § 161 the maxim that wherever in Scripture a witness is mentioned, this shall be interpreted, on the basis of this fundamental passage, as implying at least two witnesses, unless the context makes it plain that *only* one is intended. Thus the evangelist is referring to well-known regulations of the Torah; and it is noteworthy that his formula of citation, here and elsewhere, corresponds closely to the Rabbinic formula, כָּתוּב בַּתּוֹרָה.

In all other places the reference is to Torah in its comprehensive sense, as the authoritative basis of the whole religious life and thought of the Jewish people. It is for the evangelist, as for the Rabbis, the Torah of Moses, νόμος Μωυσέως (vii. 23), i.e. it was given by Moses (vii. 19, οὐ Μωυσῆς ἔδωκεν ὑμῖν τὸν νόμον;) or, more properly, it was given by God through Moses (i. 17 ὁ νόμος διὰ Μωυσέως ἐδόθη). This is the language of Rabbinic Judaism; cf. Siphre on Deut. xxxi. 14, § 305 (*ap.* Schlatter) 'Blessed be God, who gave the Torah to Israel through Moses our teacher' (עַל יְדֵי משה רבינו).[1] Primarily it is found in the Pentateuch: thus νόμος is distinguished from προφῆται in i. 45: ὃν ἔγραψεν Μωυσῆς ἐν τῷ νόμῳ καὶ οἱ προφῆται: for the formula cf. Tanch. ויקרא 18. 10 (*ap.* Schlatter) משה כתב בתורה. Elsewhere however the whole Old Testament is νόμος = תּוֹרָה, as frequently in the Talmud. Thus in x. 34 and xv. 25 the Psalms are cited as νόμος, as in Sanh. 91 b Ps. lxxxiv.

[1] As Moses is the 'Rabbi' of Israel, so the Pharisees call themselves תלמידיו של משה (Joma 4a *ap.* S.-B.), cf. John ix. 28, where the Pharisees say ἡμεῖς τοῦ Μωυσέως ἐσμὲν μαθηταί.

5 is cited as Torah (this and other examples in S.-B.). Similarly in xii. 34 ἡμεῖς ἠκούσαμεν ἐκ τοῦ νόμου ὅτι ὁ χριστὸς μένει εἰς τὸν αἰῶνα must refer to prophetic passages such as Is. ix. 6–7, Ezek. xxxvii. 25, rather than to the Pentateuch.

The most general sense of νόμος is intended in vii. 49 ὁ ὄχλος οὗτος ὁ μὴ γινώσκων τὸν νόμον ἐπάρατοί εἰσιν. The phrase ὁ μὴ γινώσκων τὸν νόμον appears to describe the class known as עַמֵּי־הָאָרֶץ, i.e. those who did not study the Torah or follow its requirements scrupulously (see passages cited by S.-B. ad loc., Komm. II, pp. 494–5). The עַם־הָאָרֶץ is also called בּוּר 'empty', 'uncultivated', and הֶדְיוֹט, ἰδιώτης. During the first century the strict observers of the Torah were separating themselves from the mass of the population and forming חֲבוּרוֹת, intended to protect their members from defiling contacts in business or social life with עַמֵּי־הָאָרֶץ. With the process of separation mutual dislike and contempt grew between the two classes. The strongest expressions of contempt for the עַם־הָאָרֶץ are cited from the period beginning with Judah ha-Nasi (the compiler of the Mishna, c. A.D. 190–200); but already in the first century B.C. we find Hillel saying, 'A בּוּר fears not sin, and no עַם־הָאָרֶץ is pious.' R. Dosa ben Harkinas (c. A.D. 90) said, 'Morning sleep, and midday wine, and children's talk, and sitting in the meeting-houses of the עַמֵּי־הָאָרֶץ, drive a man out from the world' (Pirqe Aboth, in Charles, Pseudepigrapha, ii. 6, iii. 15). Nothing indeed comparable with the curse of John vii. 49 is attested for so early a period, but it cannot be said to be out of tune with the ethos of the time.[1]

In his references therefore to νόμος, the evangelist moves within the sphere of Rabbinic conceptions of Torah. Further, he shows familiarity with details of rabbinic exposition and practice.

Thus he is acquainted with the casuistry of the Sabbath Law. Take, for example, the passage vii. 22–4 διὰ τοῦτο Μωυσῆς δέδωκεν ὑμῖν τὴν περιτομήν,--οὐχ ὅτι ἐκ τοῦ Μωυσέως ἐστὶν ἀλλ' ἐκ τῶν πατέρων,--καὶ ἐν σαββάτῳ περιτέμνετε ἄνθρωπον. εἰ περιτομὴν λαμβάνει ἄνθρωπος ἐν σαββάτῳ ἵνα μὴ λυθῇ ὁ νόμος Μωυσέως, ἐμοὶ χολᾶτε ὅτι ὅλον ἄνθρωπον ὑγιῆ ἐποίησα ἐν σαββάτῳ; μὴ κρίνετε κατ' ὄψιν, ἀλλὰ τὴν δικαίαν κρίσιν κρίνατε.

---

[1] See S.-B.'s long note ad loc., Komm. II, pp. 494–519. Most of their evidence however is of later date. Various breaches of ordinances are charged against the עַם־הארץ, but essentially he is a person who does not study the Torah, and consequently does not obey it, on the principle כל־שאינו למד אינו עושה. Thus the Johannine ὁ μὴ γινώσκων τὸν νόμον is a proper equivalent.

Before coming to the main point of this passage, it is worth while to observe how continuously its language recalls that of the Old Testament and the Talmud. The expressions δοῦναι περιτομήν, λαμβάνειν περιτομήν, correspond to נָתַן, נָטַל אֶת־הַמִּילָה in the Talmud (examples in Schlatter). Πατέρες represents אָבוֹת, the regular designation of the patriarchs Abraham, Isaac and Jacob. The expression κρίνειν κατ' ὄψιν is a close equivalent to לְמַרְאֵה עֵינָיו שָׁפַט (Is. xi. 3, closer than the LXX κατὰ τὴν δόξαν κρίνειν), and τὴν δικαίαν κρίσιν κρίνειν follows Deut. xvi. 18 וְשָׁפְטוּ אֶת־הָעָם מִשְׁפַּט צֶדֶק (LXX καὶ κρινοῦσιν τὸν λαὸν κρίσιν δικαίαν).

To come now to the casuistry of the passage: it is admitted that the Torah permits circumcision on the Sabbath. This is good Rabbinic doctrine. Schlatter cites Pal. Ned. 38b 'circumcision repels the Sabbath commandment' (הַמִּילָה דוֹחָה אֶת־מִצְוַת הַשַּׁבָּת). S.-B. add numerous citations elaborating the principle in detail. From this Jesus is made to argue that it must be legitimate to heal a *whole* man on the Sabbath. Why ὅλον ἄνθρωπον? According to Tos. Shab. 15. 16 p. 134, R. Eliezer (c. A.D. 90) said: 'Circumcision repels the Sabbath. Why? Because on its account one makes oneself guilty of annihilating the Torah if it is not carried out at the appointed time. And is not an inference from the less to the greater[1] permissible? For the sake of one member he repels the Sabbath, and shall not the whole of him repel the Sabbath?' (עַל אֵבֶר אֶחָד מִמֶּנּוּ דוֹחֶה אֶת־הַשַּׁבָּת וְכוּלוֹ לֹא יִדְחֶה אֶת־הַשַּׁבָּת). Or, as the other Eliezer (ben Azariah, c. A.D. 100) puts it: 'If circumcision, which affects one of our 248 members, repels the Sabbath, how much more must the whole body repel the Sabbath?' (Joma 85 a–b, in S.-B.). Thus the evangelist puts into the mouth of Jesus an argument, on the principle קַל וָחֹמֶר, which was current among one school at least of Rabbis of his own time, to justify healing in critical cases on the Sabbath.

A further example of the evangelist's familiarity with Rabbinic thought and practice is afforded by the trial scene of ch. ix. A blind man whom Jesus has healed on the Sabbath is examined before a tribunal composed of 'Pharisees'. It is not the Sanhedrin, but it is some body which is competent to pronounce a sentence of expulsion from the Synagogue. The sentence is imposed on the ground that the man acknowledges as a prophet one who is a breaker of the Law. Apparently we have no

---

[1] קַל וָחֹמֶר, lit. 'light and heavy', is one of the thirteen rabbinic methods of interpretation, which may take the form either of an inference *a minori ad majus* or *a majori ad minus*. Here it is the former.

information regarding the process of expulsion, its grounds, or the authority competent to carry it out, which applies to the time of Jesus or to the period of the Gospel. S.-B. have shown (Excursus on *Synagogenbann, Komm.* IV, pp. 293 sqq.) that the doctrine of the three stages of excommunication, נדוי, שמתה and חרם, which older commentators cite, is a mediaeval misunderstanding of earlier statements, and that in any case these forms of excommunication are not tantamount to actual exclusion from the Jewish community, to which we know the Minim to have been subject at least from the second century, and which seems to be implied in the term ἀποσυνάγωγος. We have therefore no means of testing the accuracy of the evangelist's representation of the trial. But there are certain expressions in the narrative which do suggest knowledge of Jewish ideas and procedure.

At the outset of the trial the Pharisees are divided among themselves. The one party argues: Jesus is a breaker of the Law, a sinner, and therefore cannot be παρὰ θεοῦ, i.e. He cannot be a true prophet. The other party argues: Jesus has performed a miracle: therefore He is not a sinner (ix. 16). Schlatter observes that such a division would correspond to the known tendencies of the schools of Hillel and of Shammai respectively. The former tended to pay regard to the given facts of a situation, the latter to the logical application of a principle. The principle itself, that a sinner cannot perform a miracle, is stated in Berach. 58a (S.-B.) 'Does the All-merciful perform a miracle for liars?' Cf. also Berach. 20a: R. Papa (d. 376) said to Abaye (d. 338–9): 'What is the difference between the ancients, for whom miracles occurred, and ourselves, for whom no miracle happens?'...He answered, 'The ancients devoted themselves to the hallowing of the Name, and we have not devoted ourselves to the hallowing of the Name.' (The Name is hallowed by obedience to the Law, and in particular by specially meritorious actions.)

The man is now asked to state his opinion of Jesus. He replies, Προφήτης ἐστίν (ix. 17). It is assumed that if Jesus can be shown not to be a prophet, then the man's confession lays him open to a sentence of excommunication. His claim to be a prophet can be impugned (*a*) if the genuineness of the miracle can be disproved, (*b*) if He can be shown to be a sinner. The question at issue is, first of all, the reality of the alleged miracle. If it is real, then it would follow, not necessarily that Jesus is a prophet, but that He is, in the frequent phrase of the Talmud, 'worthy for whom a miracle should happen'. Evidence is therefore taken on this point, first from the parents of the man. Their evidence proving inconclusive, the man himself, being of age (ἡλικίαν ἔχει = יגדיל והגיע לפרק[1]), is called (ix. 18–21). He is solemnly warned in the formula Δὸς δόξαν τῷ θεῷ (ix. 24). This phrase is misunderstood by many commentators, who take it to mean, 'Give to God, not to Jesus, the credit for your cure.' But the Pharisees do not admit the reality of the cure and are therefore not likely to urge the man to praise God for it. The formula seems to be an exhortation to full and frank confession of the truth. Cf. Mishna San. 6. 2 (when a man is to be stoned):

When ten cubits from the stoning place they say to him, Confess: for it is the custom of all about to be put to death to make confession; and every one who confesses has a share in the world to come; for so we find it in the case of Achan. Joshua said to him: My son, ascribe glory to the Lord the God of Israel (שים כבוד לי׳), and make confession unto Him; and tell me now what thou hast done; hide it not from me. And Achan answered Joshua and said, Of a truth I have sinned against the Lord the God of Israel, and thus and thus have I done.[2]

Thus God is glorified by a full confession. The man in reply gives a plain account of his cure. The Pharisees, who had hoped for a confession that the cure was a bogus one, turn to abuse and threats—for the words Σὺ μαθητὴς εἶ ἐκείνου convey a threat, in view of the decision which is reported above, to expel adherents of Jesus from the Synagogue.[3] They add, Ἡμεῖς δὲ τοῦ Μωυσέως ἐσμεν μαθηταί—a description which as we have seen is applied specifically to Pharisees in the Talmud (ix. 28).

The man is now made to defend his adherence to Jesus on the ground that at least He cannot be a sinner, since God hears His prayers: οἴδαμεν ὅτι ὁ θεὸς ἁμαρτωλῶν οὐκ ἀκούει, ἀλλ' ἐάν τις θεοσεβὴς ᾖ καὶ τὸ θέλημα αὐτοῦ ποιῇ, τούτου ἀκούει. This is a good Rabbinic maxim: cf. Berach. 6b: R. Chelbo (c. 300) reported R. Huni (d. 297) as saying, 'Every man in whom is the fear of God (יִרְאַת אֱלֹהִים = יִרְאַת שָׁמַיִם = θεοσέβεια, Gen. xx. 11 LXX), his words are heard.' The Pharisees resent the man's posing as a Rabbi, and cut the proceedings short by expelling him from the synagogue (ix. 34).

There are therefore in the narrative several indications of the author's acquaintance with Jewish ideas and practices. It may well be that he

---

[1] Cf. Pal. Jebamoth 13b, of a girl עד שתגדיל ותגיע לפרק.

[2] Trans. Danby.

[3] There is some inconsistency here, for the resolution of the Pharisees is said to have been in the terms ἵνα ἐάν τις αὐτὸν ὁμολογήσῃ Χριστόν, ἀποσυνάγωγος γένηται, whereas no Messianic claim is mentioned in the course of the trial.

wrote with recollections in his mind of such proceedings against Minim in his time.

Without going any further, it seems difficult to deny that the evangelist (or his authority) had some considerable knowledge of Torah.[1] But it is to be observed that his attitude to it is external and detached. He cites it (viii. 17) in the words ἐν τῷ νόμῳ τῷ ὑμετέρῳ γέγραπται, that is, in the precise formula, כָּתוּב בְּתוֹרַתְכֶם, with which in dialogues in the Talmud and Midrashim (Mishna Aboda 3. 4, Lev. R. 4. 6, Qoh. R. 1. 8, 11. 1, ap. Schlatter) Gentile interlocutors refer to the Torah. Cf. x. 34 οὐκ ἔστι γεγραμμένον ἐν τῷ νόμῳ ὑμῶν; xv. 25 ὁ λόγος ὁ ἐν τῷ νόμῳ αὐτῶν γεγραμμένος, vii. 19 οὐ Μωυσῆς ἔδωκεν ὑμῖν τὸν νόμον; Though no one but a Jew would be likely to possess such knowledge of the Torah, the evangelist clearly feels himself to be outside the Jewish system.

The observation that the evangelist was one who knew the Torah but detached himself from it gives special point to those passages where he draws an explicit contrast between Christianity and the Torah, regarding the latter as superseded by the former. John i. 17 ὁ νόμος διὰ Μωυσέως ἐδόθη, ἡ χάρις καὶ ἡ ἀλήθεια διὰ Ἰησοῦ Χριστοῦ ἐγένετο. Here χάρις καὶ ἀλήθεια represents חֶסֶד וֶאֱמֶת. That these attributes of God were revealed in the Torah was the assumption of the Jewish religion. Cf. Midr. Ps. on Ps. xxv. 10, 'All Thy ways are חֶסֶד וֶאֱמֶת': 'Grace: that means God's acts of love; truth: that means the Torah.'[2] The evangelist holds that the real revelation of God's grace and truth is not in the Torah, but in Jesus Christ. A similar point is made in a striking way in v. 39 ἐραυνᾶτε τὰς γραφάς, ὅτι ὑμεῖς δοκεῖτε ἐν αὐταῖς ζωὴν αἰώνιον ἔχειν·...καὶ οὐ θέλετε ἐλθεῖν πρός με ἵνα ζωὴν ἔχητε.[3] Here ἐραυνᾶν represents (as it does in Philo) the Hebrew word דָרַשׁ, which is the technical expression for the intensive study of the Torah (whence 'Midrash'). The belief that such study was the way to eternal life is a commonplace of rabbinic teaching, e.g. Pirqe Aboth vii. 6, 'Torah...gives to them that practise it life in this age and in the age to come.' Mech. Exod. xiii. 3, 'Torah, in which is (life of) the age to come' attributed to R. Ishmael (c. A.D. 135). Pesiqta 102b, 'The words

[1] It may be observed that although this fact permits the inference that the evangelist (or his authority) was a Jew, it is not favourable to the view which identifies him with John son of Zebedee; for John the fisherman was ἀγράμματος καὶ ἰδιώτης (Acts iv. 13)=בּוֹר וְהֶדְיוֹט, two technical terms for those who were ignorant of Torah.

[2] See below, pp. 173-6.

[3] For the text and construction of this passage see pp. 329-30.

of Torah which are life of this age and life of the age to come' (numerous other examples in S.-B. *ad* Rom. iii. 2). The evangelist implicitly denies this. Not the Torah, but Christ, is the way to Life. Not 'words of Torah', but His words, are life (vi. 63).

This contrast of the Torah and the incarnate Word is one of the governing ideas of the gospel, appearing in various symbolic forms. Thus the water of the well of Jacob is contrasted with the living water, and the water of the Jews' purifying with the good wine which Jesus gives (iv. 12–14, ii. 6–10). In Talmud and Midrash the Torah is constantly compared to water, e.g. Siphre on Deut. 11. 22, § 48, 'As water is life for the world, so also the words of Torah are life for the world' (Prov. iv. 22 'My words are life to those that find them'); 'as water leads the impure up from his impurity, so the words of Torah lead a man from the evil way to the good way' (Ps. xix. 8 'The commandment of the Lord is pure, enlightening the eyes'); 'as water is to be had for the world without price, so are the words of Torah to be had for the world without price' (Is. lv. 1 'Ho, every one that thirsteth, come ye to the waters, and he that hath no money'). Similarly the Targum renders Is. xii. 3 ('Therefore with joy shall ye draw water out of the wells of salvation'): 'Ye shall receive with joy new teaching from the elect righteous.'[1]

Again, the manna given by Moses is contrasted with the true bread from heaven. It does not appear that the manna is used as a symbol of the Torah; but bread is so used. E.g. Pesiqta 80b: R. Berechiah comments on Prov. xxv. 21 'If thine enemy hunger, feed him with bread, i.e. with the bread of Torah; if he thirst, give him water to drink, i.e. the water of Torah.' Cf. Gen. R. 70. 5: A proselyte (גֵּר) asked the meaning of Deut. x. 18, '(The Lord) loveth the stranger (גֵּר), in giving him bread and raiment' (לֶחֶם וְשִׂמְלָה). R. Joshua interpreted it thus: 'bread means the Torah, as it is written (Prov. ix. 5): "Come, eat of my bread (*sc.* the bread of Wisdom)"; raiment means the scholar's robe; if a man gets Torah, he gets the scholar's robe.' Thus it was natural enough to think of Torah as the bread of Moses, and from this it is an easy step to the manna. This bread of Moses is superseded by the real bread from heaven: οὐ Μωυσῆς δέδωκεν ὑμῖν τὸν ἄρτον ἐκ τοῦ οὐρανοῦ, ἀλλ' ὁ πατήρ μου δίδωσιν ὑμῖν τὸν ἄρτον ἐκ τοῦ οὐρανοῦ τὸν ἀληθινόν (vi. 32).[2]

---

[1] These and other passages in S.-B.

[2] The argument is somewhat complicated by the fact that the gift of manna was expected to be restored by the Messiah (see S.-B. *ad loc.*), as לַחְמוֹ שֶׁל־עוֹלָם הַבָּא. According to Gen. R. 82 R. Joshua interpreted Prov. xxviii. 19, 'He that tilleth

Again, in Exod. R. 25. 7, Prov. ix. 5, 'Come eat ye of my bread and drink of the wine which I have mingled', is interpreted as follows:

God spoke: What caused you to eat of the manna and to drink of the well? It was because you accepted the statutes and ordinances; as it is written, There He made for them a statute and an ordinance (Exod. xv. 25). Thus by merit of my bread (i.e. the bread of Torah) you ate the bread of manna, and by merit of the wine that I mixed (i.e. the wine of Torah) you drank of the water of the well, as it is written, And drink of the wine that I have mingled.

Thus wine is a symbol of Torah. In the story of the miracle of Cana (John ii. 1–12) the wine supplied by Christ is contrasted both with the water of the καθαρισμός τῶν 'Ιουδαίων, and also with the inferior wine which was provided at the beginning of the feast (ii. 10). It is therefore possible that an allusion to the wine of Torah underlies the second contrast: as Christ gives ἀληθινὸς ἄρτος so also He gives οἶνος ἀληθινός, while the Torah offers only the shadow.

We have in fact an idea similar to that of the Epistle to the Hebrews. As there the religious institutions of Judaism are shadows of heavenly realities, so here the Torah is contrasted with ἀληθινά—the eternal realities of which the Torah offers only a counterfeit presentment.

With all this in view we can now see that the same contrast is implicit in the idea of φῶς ἀληθινόν (i. 9). For although the real light has in the gospel no expressed foil corresponding to the water of Jacob's well or the manna of Moses, yet the evangelist may now be assumed to have been aware of the well-established tradition which used light as a symbol of the Torah. Thus Siphre on Num. vi. 52, § 41 explains the clause of the priestly benediction, 'The Lord make His face to shine upon thee'—'i.e. the light of the Torah', referring to Prov. vi. 23, 'For the commandment is a lamp and the Torah is light.' Again, in Baba Bathra 4a Baba ben Buta addresses Herod the Great after he has put the Rabbis to death, 'Thou hast quenched the light of the world' (אוֹרוֹ שֶׁל עוֹלָם = τὸ φῶς τοῦ κόσμου, John viii. 12), citing the same passage from Proverbs. In Deut. R. 7.3 there is a comment on Cant. i. 3, 'Thy name is as ointment poured forth.' This is said to refer to the Torah: 'As oil is life for the world, so the words of Torah are life for the world. As oil is light for the world, so also are the words of Torah light for the world' (אורה לעולם).

his land shall have plenty of bread', 'He who serves God to the day of his death (עבד אדמתו read as מותו (יום) עד (אלהים) (עובד will be satisfied with the bread of the age to come.' See further below, pp. 335–6.

We can hardly doubt therefore that the evangelist is implicitly contrasting the real Light of the world with the Torah, which claims also to be a light for the world.

It is to be observed that most of the statements about the Torah find their scriptural justification in passages referring to Wisdom, especially the *locus classicus*, Prov. viii. 22 sqq. This identification of the Torah with Wisdom goes back to a period earlier than our rabbinic sources. It is found in the great Praise of Wisdom in Sirach xxiv,[1] a passage which contains many parallels to the Johannine and Rabbinic material we have been studying. With this passage in view, we are justified in concluding that the doctrine of Torah as the pre-existent thought of God revealed in time, which we find in Talmud and Midrash, is by no means a late creation, even though many of the *testimonia* may be relatively late. In its main outlines it formed a part of rabbinic teaching at the period of the Fourth Gospel, and we may safely infer that the author of that work was acquainted with it.

In view of all this it is instructive to observe that many of the propositions referring to the Logos in the Prologue are the counterparts of rabbinic statements referring to the Torah.

The Logos is said to have been pre-existent, with God from the beginning. Cf. Pesaḥim 54a Bar.: 'Seven things were created before the world was created: the Torah, Repentance, Paradise, Gehenna, the Throne of Glory, the Sanctuary, and the Name of the Messiah.' In substantiation of the pre-existence of the Torah Prov. viii. 22 is cited: 'The Lord created me as the beginning of His way, the first of His works of old.' Otherwise, Gen. R. 1 (4): 'Six things preceded the creation of the world: some of them were actually created, others entered into the mind of God, to be created afterwards. The Torah and the Throne of Glory were created; the Fathers, Israel, the Sanctuary and the Name of the Messiah entered into the mind of God to be created.' The idea recurs many times in various forms.

---

[1] Some critics regard Sir. xxiv. 23, which explicitly identifies Wisdom with the 'Book of the Covenant of the Most High', and with 'the Law which Moses enacted', as an interpolation into the Greek Sirach. In any case, however, it may be assumed to be pre-Christian. The identification may be a part of a deliberate effort on the part of the orthodox Rabbis to call a halt to dangerous Hellenizing tendencies. Wisdom was too easily represented as a kind of Jewish counterpart of Isis or the Syrian Astarte. She was recalled to safe and orthodox paths by being identified with Torah, but the identification opened the way to quasi-personifications of Torah. See W. L. Knox, *St Paul and the Church of the Gentiles*, ch. III.

The Logos was with God, εἰς τὸν κόλπον τοῦ πατρός. Cf. Aboth
d'R. Nathan 31 (8b): R. Eliezer ben Jose of Galilee (c. A.D. 150) said,
'Before the world was made the Torah was written and lay in the bosom
of God, and with the ministering angels uttered a song', citing Prov. viii.
30: 'Then I was by Him, as one brought up with Him; and I was daily
His delight, rejoicing always before Him.' Midr. Ps. on Ps. xc. 3 (after
the usual enumeration of the seven primeval things): 'On what was the
Torah written? With black fire on white fire, and it lay on God's knee
while God sat upon the throne of glory.' As the Logos is called the son
of God, so the Torah is in several places (cited by S.-B.) described (in
metaphor) as the daughter of God.

The Logos is the agent or instrument of creation. Cf. Pirqe Aboth iii. 19,
where the Torah is 'the precious instrument wherewith the world was
made'. In Gen. R. 11, R. Hoshaya the elder (c. 225) said: 'The Torah says,
"Through the רֵאשִׁית, the first principle, God made heaven and earth",
and the רֵאשִׁית is nothing other than the Torah, as it says (Prov. viii. 22)
"The Lord created me as the רֵאשִׁית of His ways."'

That the Torah, like the Logos, is life and light, we have already seen.
That the Torah, like the Logos, makes men sons of God, may be inferred
from the passage Pirqe Aboth, iii. 19 which may now be quoted in full:

> Beloved are Israel, that they are called sons of God. Greater love was it that
> it was known to them that they were called sons of God.... Beloved are Israel,
> in that to them was given the precious instrument wherewith the world was
> created. Greater love was it that it was known to them that there was given
> to them the precious instrument wherewith the world was created, as it is said,
> 'For a good doctrine I have given you; forsake not my Torah.'[1]

The evangelist therefore writes all through with the intention of
exhibiting the revelation in Christ as offering in reality that which Judaism
meant to offer, but failed to provide—a genuine knowledge of God conveying life to men. He is not interested, as Paul was, in the moral problem
presented by the failure to live up to the ethical demands of the Law.
The Law as such is not for him a way to the knowledge of God's will.
It stands over against the true revelation of God. It claims to be, but is
not, the divine Wisdom, the light of the world, the life of men. Divine
Wisdom is incarnate in Jesus Christ, in whom is the πλήρωμα of grace
and truth.

[1] After Herford in Charles's *Pseudepigrapha*.

2. The Messiah

The Fourth Gospel is the only New Testament document which uses the term Μεσσίας, a Greek transliteration of the Hebrew מָשִׁיחַ or the Aramaic מְשִׁיחָא, most probably the latter. It is introduced in i. 41, and there translated by the familiar χριστός, which takes its place everywhere else in the Gospel, except in iv. 25, where the Samaritan woman is made to say, οἶδα ὅτι Μεσσίας ἔρχεται, the explanation, ὁ λεγόμενος χριστός, being once more added.

It is notoriously difficult to produce satisfactory evidence of the absolute use of the term מָשִׁיחַ in pre-Christian Judaism. In the Old Testament מְשִׁיחַ יהוה is not infrequently used as an appellation of the legitimate reigning king, particularly of David and his dynasty; in other passages, perhaps, of the nation personified. There is no passage where it can with probability be held to apply (originally) to any figure expected to appear in the future. At the same time, since various prophecies do contemplate the appearance in the future of a prince of the house of David, in whose time the divine promises to Israel will be fulfilled, it would have been natural enough to apply to such a person the solemn title of the Davidic monarch, משיח יהוה. The first place where it is explicitly so applied is Ps. Sol. xvii. 36, at least if χρισ τός κύριος is, as it appears to be, a mistranslation of מָשִׁיחַ אֲדֹנָי. The person so designated is the Davidic monarch of the future age of bliss. But the absolute use of מְשִׁיחָא to designate such a personage does not seem to be found before it occurs in the Apocalypses of Baruch and Ezra round about A.D. 100 (though Dan. ix. 25–6 may afford a partial precedent for such a use).[1] Abrahams[2] points out that there was a tendency in Hebrew to omit the second member of a compound title (as נָגִיד for נָגִיד עַם אֵל, גָּאוֹן for גְּאוֹן יַעֲקֹב), and Dalman suggests that a special reason for the abbreviation may be found in the increasing reluctance to utter the name of God. At any rate the form מְשִׁיחָא is regularly found in the Targums. In the Babylonian Talmud the indeterminate משיח is found, as though a personal name, but as it is not attested for Palestine it is probably not ancient. Abrahams sums up, 'The name Messiah does not become common in Rabbinic usage till after the

---

[1] And also one recension of the so-called *Zadokite Fragment* (in Charles, *Pseudepigrapha*) ix. 10, if this work is pre-Christian; but we await further light from newly discovered material.

[2] 'The Personal Use of the Term "Messiah"', in *Studies in Pharisaism and the Gospels*, 1st series, pp. 136 sqq., which I am here following.

destruction of the Temple. Its application to Jesus occurs at the moment when the name began to be widely used, and the New Testament usage here, as in many other points, is parallel to Rabbinic development and forms a link in the chain.' It is therefore clear at least that the Fourth Evangelist did not take the title χριστός simply from Christian tradition, but was aware of its Aramaic original, which he correctly transliterates as μεσσίας.

We may enquire how far he shows acquaintance with Jewish messianic ideas.

(i) Like the Synoptic evangelists, the author of the Fourth Gospel is aware that the title Messiah is a royal title. He does not indeed use the form χριστὸς βασιλεύς, as Luke does, thereby providing the first known example of the term 'the anointed King', or 'King Messiah', מַלְכָּא מְשִׁיחָא, which becomes common later in the Talmud. But like Matthew and Mark he has the expression 'King of Israel' (i. 49). No parallel is cited from Rabbinic sources, but the phrase is a natural expression for the fundamental meaning of 'Messiah'. It is noteworthy that while 'King of Israel' is found in the other gospels only in Matt. xxvii. 42, Mark xv. 32, where it is used in mockery, John puts it in the mouth not only of the crowd at the Triumphal Entry, but of Nathanael when he confesses Christ (i. 49).[1] In the trial narrative, following the common tradition, he represents Pilate as using the title 'King of the Jews' (xviii. 33), a form which, we may safely say, is not likely to have been used by Jews, but which is natural enough in the mouth of a Roman. To the question, 'Are you the King of the Jews?' Jesus replies, 'Do you say this of your own accord, or have others said it to you about me?'—as much as to say, 'Am I to answer that question in the sense in which you, as a Roman, would naturally mean it; i.e. taking the word "king" in a political, worldly sense?' Pilate replies, in effect, that he is repeating a charge formulated by the Jews; they must take responsibility for the term he uses. Jesus then explains, 'My royalty is not a worldly royalty. I am not a king in the political sense.' Pilate seizes upon the admission which seems to be implied in the disclaimer. 'Well then, are you a king in some sense?' Jesus replies, '"King" is your word, not mine—σὺ λέγεις ὅτι βασιλεύς εἰμι. But my real function is that of witness to the truth' (xviii. 34-7). The evangelist's intention seems clear. The term 'king', i.e. Messiah, as applied to Jesus, is to be understood only in the sense of

[1] In the Old Testament מֶלֶךְ יִשְׂרָאֵל, βασιλεὺς τοῦ Ἰσραήλ, is a title of Jehovah, Is. xliv. 6, etc.

authority in the spiritual sphere, the authority which belongs to one who knows and communicates absolute truth. (A Greek reader would recall that according to the Stoics the wise man is the only true king.) The term Messiah, therefore, must in Christian usage, according to this evangelist, be stripped of a large part of its connotation in Jewish usage.

(ii) In vii. 25–44 the Jews are represented as discussing the Messianic claims of Jesus. Three tests of Messiahship are alleged:

(a) 'When the Messiah comes, no one knows whence He is' (vii. 27). This represents a doctrine well attested in Jewish sources—the doctrine that the Messiah has already come into the world, but is concealed in some unknown place until the day appointed by God for His appearance. The idea underlying this doctrine appears to be that the divine intervention may take place suddenly at any time, and the Messiah must be available for the role He is to play, and available as a grown man, ready to bear rule over Israel. Thus from His birth to the time of His appearance He is present in the world unknown. Various Rabbis attempted to guess the place of His concealment. Some said Rome, some 'the north', while others held that He had been caught up to Paradise for the time.[1] Most of the evidence for this theory of the hidden Messiah is late, but we have at least one authority for it which is very near in date to the Fourth Gospel: in IV Ezra xiii the Messiah is symbolized by the figure of a man arising out of the sea. This is interpreted in the words, 'Just as one can neither seek out nor know what is in the deep of the sea, even so can no one upon earth see My Son...but in the time of His day' (xiii. 52).

In view of this, we may fairly conclude that the Fourth Evangelist is giving expression to a belief held by Jews in his time. In the dramatic situation which he has composed, the Jews argue that Jesus cannot be the Messiah, because, so far from appearing from some unknown and mysterious quarter, he is a man of well-known and unpromising origin, a Galilaean. Jesus is made to admit that the Jews know His origin, but, with an irony characteristic of this gospel, a hint is given to the reader that His true origin is even more mysterious and august than that of the hidden Messiah of Jewish expectation; He comes, not from Rome or the north, or from any unknown place of concealment, but direct from God Himself: ἔστιν ἀληθινὸς ὁ πέμψας με, ὃν ὑμεῖς οὐκ οἴδατε (vii. 28).

(b) Certain of the Jews are inclined to accept Jesus as Messiah on the ground that He has performed many signs: even the Messiah could not be expected to perform more (vii. 31). In Jewish sources there is not

[1] See S.-B. II, p. 340.

very much about signs to be wrought by the Messiah (though there is much about signs heralding His coming); but it is always assumed in general terms that He will be equipped with miraculous powers; and as prophets were believed to have corroborated their message with miracles, and even Rabbis to have given miraculous proof of the rightness of their decisions on disputed points, we may assume that the Messiah would establish His claims in a similar, but even more striking way. S.-B. cite from Pes. R. a sign by which the Messiah will reveal His supernatural dignity, and from Sanh. an unhistorical story that Bar-cochba was challenged to perform a messianic sign, and failed. Thus we may take the evangelist to refer to current Jewish belief. The same belief is no doubt implied in the Synoptic prediction that false Messiahs will perform σημεῖα καὶ τέρατα (Mark xiii. 22 and parallels). On the other hand the Synoptic statement that the Jews demanded from Jesus a sign from heaven, which is probably historical, need have no reference to messianic claims, since the Talmud contains similar stories about Rabbis. This historical incident is represented in the Fourth Gospel by vi. 30. If we compare that passage with the one now under discussion, we may probably again recognize the evangelist's irony. The 'signs' which the people expect from the Messiah are mere miracles; yet when they see a miracle they fail to see the 'sign'; for to the evangelist a σημεῖον is not, in essence, a miraculous act, but a significant act, one which, for the seeing eye and the understanding mind, symbolizes eternal realities.

(c) The Messiah is to be born of the seed of David, and at David's village of Bethlehem (vii. 42). For the Davidic descent of the Messiah no special authorities need be cited; it is, apart from some temporary aberrations, a standard part of messianic belief from the prophetic period onwards. For the expectation of His birth at Bethlehem our evidence is less satisfactory. The prophecy of Micah v. 2 does not appear to be frequently cited. Where the belief was held that David himself would return as Messiah, naturally Bethlehem was the birthplace of the Messiah. But this belief, though it seems to be attributed to Aqiba, is not alluded to in the New Testament. In so far as the Messiah is thought of as a second David, it would be natural to assume that He would be like David in the place of His birth as in other respects. But no rabbinic passages to that effect are cited by the authorities before the fourth century. The doctrine of the Messiah's birth at Bethlehem is combined with the doctrine of His unknown whereabouts in the well-known story which is told in Midrash Echa and elsewhere, on the authority of R. Aibo (c. A.D. 320),

how the Messiah, Menahem ben Hezekiah by name, was born at Bethlehem
on the day of the destruction of the Temple, and forthwith snatched
away, no one knows where. Whether it was, as both John and Matthew
aver, established rabbinic doctrine in the first century that the Messiah
should be born at Bethlehem, does not seem certain. It seems possible
that so far from the Nativity stories in Matthew and Luke having been
composed for apologetic purposes, in order to meet a generally held
belief that the Messiah must be born at Bethlehem, it was the fact that
Jesus was actually born there that revived in Christian circles interest in
a prophecy which played little part in contemporary Jewish thought.
On the other hand we must allow for the possibility that interpretations
of the Old Testament which seemed to favour Christian claims may have
been deliberately abandoned in the rabbinic schools. However this may
be, it is significant that the Fourth Evangelist allows the objection
of the Jews to pass unanswered. This may be another case of his irony:
the reader is supposed to know that in saying 'the Scripture says that
the Messiah comes of the stock of David, and from Bethlehem, the village
where David was', the critics of Jesus are unconsciously corroborating
His claims; or it may be that he knew nothing of the story that Jesus
was born there. But in any case it is clear that he does not wish to rest
his argument for the Messiahship of Jesus upon either His Davidic
descent or His birth at Bethlehem. In this he is at one with Mark, and
differs from Matthew and Luke. In essentials, Jesus is for this evangelist
not the Messiah of Jewish expectation, but a more august figure.

(iii) In a similar controversial passage in ch. xii an allusion by Jesus
to His approaching death is represented as causing the Jews to argue
that one who is shortly to die cannot be the Messiah, since 'we have
heard out of the Torah that Messiah abides for ever' (xii. 34). In earlier
prophecy, from Is. ix. 7 onwards, the king who is to come (to whom the
title Messiah was most popularly given) is to bear rule 'for ever', the
scene of his rule being this world of history. In later apocalyptic the
scene of eternal dominion tends to shift from this familiar world to
another world which will appear when heaven and earth have passed
away. Dominion in this other world of course belongs to the Eternal
Himself, but whether it is exercised directly or through a vicegerent is
not entirely agreed. In the medley of apocalyptic documents known as
the Book of Enoch various views are represented. In the so-called
Similitudes of Enoch (chs. xxxvii–lxxi) it appears to be exercised through
a vicegerent called the Elect One, or the Son of Man, to whom occasionally

the title Messiah is given.[1] It would appear that the Elect One Himself 'abides for ever' in the strictest sense. When, about the close of the first century, learned discussion issued in the formulation of a more or less coherent doctrine, a distinction was drawn between 'the days of the Messiah', which close 'this age', and 'the age to come', which lies beyond the horizon of time. The Messiah is now no longer thought of as exercising eternal dominion. In the Apocalypses of Baruch and Ezra He reigns for a time and then dies (IV Ezra vii. 28–30), or returns to heaven (Apoc. of Baruch xxx. 1), and the Age to Come follows. The Fourth Gospel represents the Jews as taking the earlier view, which does not contemplate the death of the Messiah. Once again we observe the characteristic irony of the evangelist. For the Jews, the death of Jesus is a fatal disqualification for messiahship: the Messiah must abide for ever. The reader is intended to gather that the death of Jesus in fact sets the seal upon the eternity of His person and work: it is His entrance into glory.

The conclusion we draw is that the Fourth Evangelist, even more definitely than the Synoptics, is developing his doctrine of the person and work of Jesus with conscious reference to Jewish messianic belief. The Messiah of the Jews is to be a descendant of David, He is to appear no one knows whence, He is to work signs and to reign as king, and He is to abide for ever. Of Jesus the evangelist will not affirm that He is the Son of David; if He is a king, His kingship is of an entirely different order; His origin is mysterious indeed, since He comes from another world; He works signs, in a more profound sense than the Jews imagined; and the death which appears to be the end of Him is in fact the climax and seal of His manifestation as the eternal Saviour of the world. Thus while formally the evangelist claims for Jesus the Jewish title Μεσσίας, in fact the Jewish conception of Messiahship is set aside, and his doctrine of the Person of Christ is mainly worked out under other categories, which are not those of Rabbinic Judaism.[2]

The positive and significant elements in the Johannine Christology find little or no point of attachment to Jewish messianic ideas. The pre-existence of the Messiah is no part of current Jewish doctrine, unless it be in the apocalypses, to be more precise, in the Book of Enoch, or, to be still more precise, in the so-called Similitudes which form part of the Ethiopic Enoch but are not otherwise known. Dalman, S.-B., and G. F. Moore however agree in denying that even there a real pre-existence

[1] For uncertainties regarding the Similitudes of Enoch, see pp. 241–2.
[2] See below, pp. 228–62.

is intended.[1] What we have is only a presentation in visionary form of the orthodox rabbinic doctrine that the 'name of the Messiah' was present with God before the creation of the world; i.e. that His coming was a part of the aboriginal design of God for the universe which He purposed to create. Again, there is no hint in our Jewish authorities of any equation of the Messiah with Wisdom, or with the divine Word, or any other supposed mediating hypostasis. Not the Messiah, but the Torah, or Wisdom, is God's medium of self-revelation to men. And finally, there is no suggestion in our Jewish sources that the Messiah is divine, though He is associated with Jacob, Moses, and others, as one of those to whom God, according to rabbinic exegesis of certain scriptural passages, gave His own name of אֵל, as a king might confer his own title, *ad hoc*, upon his representative.

3. THE NAME OF GOD

The significance attached to the Name of God in the Old Testament needs no illustration. The name of a person is the symbol of his personal identity, his status, and his character; and so, for the Hebrew monotheist, the Name of God stands as a symbol for His sole deity, His glory, and His character as righteous and holy. As such it is used in various periphrases, rhetorical or reverential. To 'know the name' of God, or to 'know that His name is יהוה', is an expression which sums up the ideal attitude of Israel (or of the individual Israelite) to Jehovah. It is the vocation of the servant of God to 'declare His name' to other men (Ps. xxi (xxii). 23). In the good time coming the ideal relation of Israel to their God will be realized: 'My people shall know my name' (Is. lii. 6, cf. Jer. xvi. 21).

In Judaism after the Old Testament period the gradual withdrawal of the name יהוה from public use, and the ultimate suppression of its pronunciation, was accompanied (whether as cause or as consequence or as both) by a growing sense of the extreme power and sanctity of the actual name—the שֵׁם הַמְפוֹרָשׁ as it came to be called, meaning properly, it appears, the name as distinctly pronounced according to its letters and their sounds (see S.-B., *Komm.* I, p. 311), though other, sometimes fanciful, explanations of the term were offered. Pinchas ben Jair (*c*. A.D. 130–60) said: 'In this age the prayer of the Israelites is not heard, because they do not know the *shem hammephorash*; but in the age to come God will reveal it to them.' For this he cites various passages

[1] So also T. W. Manson, 'The Son of Man in Daniel, Enoch and the Gospels', in *Bulletin of the John Rylands Library*, vol. XXXII (1950), pp. 171–93.

of Scripture; in particular, Ps. xci. 14–15 'I will set him on high because he hath known my name; he shall call upon me and I will answer him'; Is. lii. 6

לָכֵן יֵדַע עַמִּי שְׁמִי לָכֵן בַּיּוֹם הַהוּא כִּי־אֲנִי־הוּא הַמְדַבֵּר הִנֵּנִי

Pinchas apparently understands this as follows: 'Therefore my people shall know my name, therefore, on that day, that *Ani-hu* is speaking: here am I.' That is to say, he treats אֲנִי הוּא as the Name of God, the *shem hammephorash*, which is to be revealed in the age to come. The expression אֲנִי הוּא is several times used in II Isaiah with especial weight and solemnity, in the sense 'I am', asserting the eternal self-existence of God, e.g. Is. xlviii. 12 אֲנִי הוּא אֲנִי רִאשׁוֹן אַף אֲנִי אַחֲרוֹן, 'I am; I am the first; also I am the last'; xliii. 10 'that you may know and believe me and understand כִּי אֲנִי הוּא'. The LXX render אני הוא, ἐγώ εἰμι, and appear to have taken it as the equivalent of a divine name. In Is. xliii. 25 they render אָנֹכִי אָנֹכִי הוּא מֹחֶה פְשָׁעֶיךָ by ἐγώ εἰμι ἐγώ εἰμι ὁ ἐξαλείφων τὰς ἀνομίας σου, 'I am "I AM", who erases your iniquities.' They appear also to have understood the name יהוה as having the same sense, for in Is. xlv. 18 (unless they had a different text) they render אֲנִי יהוה וְאֵין עוֹד by ἐγώ εἰμι καὶ οὐκ ἔστιν ἔτι, and in the following verse they seem to have rendered יהוה twice, once by ἐγώ εἰμι and once by κύριος: אֲנִי יהוה דֹּבֵר צֶדֶק becomes ἐγώ εἰμι ἐγώ εἰμι κύριος ὁ λαλῶν δικαιοσύνην, 'I am "I AM" the Lord, who speaks righteousness.'

There was however a tradition which gave for אֲנִי הוּא the slightly altered form אֲנִי וְהוּא, and this was said to be the *shem hammephorash*. According to R. Judah ben Ilai (*c.* A.D. 130–60), when at the Feast of Tabernacles the priests circled the altar chanting the Hosanna from Ps. cxviii. 25 אָנָּא יהוה הוֹשִׁיעָה נָּא, instead of אָנָּא יהוה they sang אֲנִי וְהוּא The intention was apparently to disguise the pronunciation of the sacred Name. But special significance was attached to the form אֲנִי וְהוּא, 'I and he'. It was taken to stand for the intimate association, or quasi-identification, of God with His people. Thus R. Abbahu (*c.* 300) commented on Ps. lxxx. 3 וּלְכָה לִישֻׁעָתָה לָּנוּ as follows: 'לְךָ is meant'; i.e. for לְכָה 'come', read לְךָ 'thyself'. The sentence is to be understood in the sense that in rescuing Israel God rescues Himself. Abbahu therefore took the disguised form of Ps. cxviii. 25 to be a prayer that God would help both His people and Himself, אֲנִי וְהוּא. Similarly R. Aqiba (d. A.D. 135) on II Kms. vii. 23, אֲשֶׁר פָּדִיתָ לְּךָ מִמִּצְרַיִם,

interpreted לְךָ as direct object of the verb, giving the sense 'thou hast redeemed thyself out of Egypt'. The same idea was found in Is. lxiii. 9 בְּכָל־צָרָתָם לֹא צָר, where by reading לֹו for לֹא we get the sense 'in all their affliction He had affliction' (so also the English A.V.); and in Ps. xci. 15 עִמּוֹ־אָנֹכִי בְצָרָה, 'I am with him in affliction.' While, on the one hand, the name אֲנִי וְהוּא thus signifies the solidarity of God with His people in their troubles, on the other hand it implies the duty of Israel to become like God. Thus Abba Shaul (c. A.D. 200) commented on Exod. xv. 2 זֶה אֵלִי וְאַנְוֵהוּ, 'Let us be like God; as He is merciful and gracious, so be thou merciful and gracious.' It appears that he read אנוהו as אֲנִי וְהוּא, 'I and he', implying a community of character between God and Israel, as elsewhere there is community of sufferings.

There is much else in a similar sense. It often appears little better than *Wortspielerei*, and most of the evidence is late. Yet the doctrine of the solidarity of God with His people is implicit in much of the Old Testament, and its explicit statement goes back at least to Aqiba. There seems no reason to reject R. Judah ben Ilai's statement that the form אֲנִי וְהוּא was actually employed by the priests in the temple (i.e. before A.D. 70). It is not impossible that the traditional interpretation of it may have had its beginnings during the period to which the Fourth Gospel belongs, and that the evangelist may have been aware of the profound idea that the Name of God can be known (that is, His true character can be apprehended) only where His intimate unity with His people is appreciated.

The form אֲנִי הוּא is represented in the LXX (as we have seen) by ἐγώ εἰμι. Is. xliii. 10 ἵνα γνῶτε καὶ πιστεύσητε καὶ συνῆτε ὅτι ἐγώ εἰμι seems to be echoed in John viii. 28 γνώσεσθε ὅτι ἐγώ εἰμι, and xiii. 19 ἵνα πιστεύητε...ὅτι ἐγώ εἰμι. It is difficult not to see here an allusion to the divine name אֲנִי הוּא. The implication would seem to be that God has given His own Name to Christ; and this is actually stated in xvii. 11. We may further recall that the Name is associated in the Old Testament with the glory of God. Thus, in one of the strongest statements of monotheism, Is. xlii. 8, we have אֲנִי יהוה הוּא שְׁמִי וּכְבוֹדִי לְאַחֵר לֹא־אֶתֵּן, which the LXX renders ἐγώ κύριος ὁ θεός, τοῦτό μου ἐστιν τὸ ὄνομα, τὴν δόξαν μου ἑτέρῳ οὐ δώσω. Now in John xii. 23 we have the statement, ἐλήλυθεν ἡ ὥρα ἵνα δοξασθῇ ὁ υἱὸς τοῦ ἀνθρώπου, and this is followed by the prayer, πάτερ δόξασόν σου τὸ ὄνομα (xii. 28). Later, in xvii. 5, Christ prays, δόξασόν με σύ, πάτερ, παρὰ σεαυτῷ τῇ δόξῃ ᾗ εἶχον πρὸ τοῦ τὸν κόσμον εἶναι παρὰ σοί. Thus the eternal glory of God is given to Christ, and in the same act the Name of God is glorified.

This would seem to be the presupposition of the use by Christ of the divine name ἐγώ εἰμι = אֲנִי הוּא.

But we have further to observe the sequel in each case where the name is so used. In viii. 28 we read, 'You will know that ἐγώ εἰμι, and I do nothing of my own initiative, but I speak just as my Father taught me; and He who sent me is with me—ὁ πέμψας με μετ' ἐμοῦ ἐστιν', cf. Ps. xc (xci). 5, μετ' αὐτοῦ εἰμι ἐν θλίψει. The ἐγώ εἰμι carries with it the solidarity of Christ with God. Again, in xiii. 20, after pronouncing the ἐγώ εἰμι, Christ goes on, ἀμήν, ἀμήν, λέγω ὑμῖν . . . ὁ ἐμὲ λαμβάνων λαμβάνει τὸν πέμψαντά με—a statement implying once again His solidarity with the Father. Cf. xvi. 32 οὐκ εἰμὶ μόνος, ὅτι ὁ πατὴρ μετ' ἐμοῦ ἐστίν, viii. 16 μόνος οὐκ εἰμί, ἀλλ' ἐγὼ καὶ ὁ πέμψας με. The phrase ἐγὼ καὶ ὁ πέμψας με is equivalent to אֲנִי וְהוּא as understood in the later tradition. It seems not impossible that John was already acquainted with it. The substitution of Christ for Israel in the expression of solidarity is in harmony with early Christian procedure in general, and in particular with that of the Fourth Gospel.[1]

With all this in mind, we may recall the rabbinic saying that while in this age the true name of God is unknown, in the age to come it will be revealed. According to John xvii. 6, 26, the mission of Christ in the world was to make known the Name of God, and this mission He fully discharged: ἐφανέρωσά σου τὸ ὄνομα τοῖς ἀνθρώποις, ἐγνώρισα αὐτοῖς τὸ ὄνομά σου.[2] It is difficult not to suppose that there is some reference here to the revelation of the *shem hammephorash*; and if so, then the Name takes the form, not merely of אֲנִי הוּא, ἐγώ εἰμι, but of אֲנִי וְהוּא, ἐγὼ καὶ ὁ πέμψας με. If the Name of God is the symbol of His true nature, then the revelation of the Name which Christ gives is that unity of Father and Son to which He bears witness.

Much of this will seem somewhat speculative, and the links in the chain of evidence are not all complete, but it is at least possible that one of the most distinctive ideas of the Fourth Gospel, and one which has been thought most remote from the Judaism within which Christianity arose, has its roots in reflections of Jewish Rabbis upon prophetic teaching about the relation between God and His people, in the light of the disasters which fell upon Israel during the period A.D. 70–135.[3]

[1] See pp. 244–7.

[2] It is to be noted that Ps. xxi (xxii). 23 (in a non-LXX translation), ἀπαγγελῶ τὸ ὄνομά σου τοῖς ἀδελφοῖς μου, is used as a *testimonium* to Christ in Heb. ii. 12. The entire Psalm was treated by early Christian interpreters as messianic.

[3] The suggestion that the Johannine doctrine of the unity of Father and Son might be connected with the *shem hammephorash*, אֲנִי וְהוּא, I owe to

5. GNOSTICISM

The terms 'Gnostic' and 'Gnosticism' are used by modern writers in a confusing variety of senses. If they refer, as by etymology they should refer, to the belief that salvation is by knowledge, then there is a sense in which orthodox Christian theologians like Clement of Alexandria and Origen, on the one hand, and Hellenistic Jews like Philo, and pagan writers like the Hermetists, on the other, should be called Gnostics; and in this wide sense the terms are used by many recent writers, especially in Germany. In this sense the Gospel according to John should be classed as Gnostic. Ancient writers use the term 'Gnostic' sometimes as the proper name of certain sects or schools of thought, while others appear to use it loosely with a note of sarcasm. I use it here in the way in which it has been generally used for many years by theologians in this country, as a label for a large and somewhat amorphous group of religious systems described by Irenaeus and Hippolytus in their works against Heresy (*Adversus Haereses* and *Refutatio Omnium Haeresium*), and similar systems known from other sources. This is a use of the term which has no warrant in these writers themselves, or in any ancient authorities, but it is convenient, and need not be misleading.[1]

Widely as these systems differ in detail, most of them have a certain family likeness, and the same *clichés* tend to recur in a way which encourages the attempt to find some common basis. The question of their relation to Christianity is much debated, and cannot be said to be settled. It is best not to ask, Were the Gnostics Christians? If we ask, Did the Gnostics consider themselves Christians? the answer would seem to be that some did and some did not. Two opposite views have been held. On the one hand the typical Gnostic systems are regarded as varying attempts, on the part of people who in intention at least accepted fundamental Christian beliefs, to expand, supplement and re-interpret those beliefs

G. Klein, *Der älteste christliche Katechismus* (1909), and I have drawn upon the material assembled in that work, pp. 44–9, supplementing it from S.-B., *Komm.* II, p. 797. S.-B. accept the statement that the form אני והוא was employed by the priests at the Feast of Tabernacles, but dismiss the interpretation of it as late.

[1] The most instructive discussion of the meaning of the terms, Gnostic and Gnosticism, known to me is R. P. Casey, 'The Study of Gnosticism', in *J.T.S.*, vol. XXXVI (1935), pp. 45–60.

in terms acceptable to the thinking religious public of the time. On the other hand, Gnosticism is regarded as a religious movement older than Christianity, and originally independent of it, which, being from the outset syncretistic in character, readily adopted Christian ideas into its systems as those beliefs became known to the wider public.

It will be well to set down a few more or less certain facts. First, there is no Gnostic document known to us which can with any show of probability be dated—at any rate in the form in which alone we have access to it—before the period of the New Testament. The attempts made by Reitzenstein and others to recover supposed earlier and pre-Christian sources are entirely speculative. Whatever plausibility they possess depends on the establishment of a prior probability that the non-Christian elements are anterior to the Christian elements in the documents as they stand.

Secondly, the typical Gnostic systems all combine in various ways and proportions ideas derived from Christianity with ideas which can be shown to be derived from, or at least to have affinities with, other religious or philosophical traditions. They draw from Greek religion and philosophy, from the Jewish scriptures, probably from Iranian and other oriental traditions. As compared with the *Hermetica*, and even with Philo, the Gnostic systems are generally speaking less Hellenic, more oriental, and certainly much more addicted to mythology.

Thirdly, the various Gnostic systems differ widely in the way in which they introduce and combine these disparate elements, and each system has to be considered separately, for what it is in itself. No general and all-embracing answer can be given to the question, What is the relation of Gnosticism to Christianity?

For example, the Naassene document cited at considerable length by Hippolytus (*Refut.* v. 1–11) appears to be in substance a commentary upon a hymn to Attis, the text of which is quoted (v. 9). In this hymn Attis, in the syncretistic fashion of the times, is identified with other divine figures, such as Pan, Osiris and Adonis. The writer takes the various names and titles given to the god in the hymn, and illustrates them by reference to other mythologies. His examples range over a wide field. Among other religions, he is acquainted with Judaism and Christianity, and as he quotes Homer, Empedocles and Anacreon, so he quotes the Old Testament, the canonical gospels, and apparently the apocryphal Gospel of Thomas. The work is in no sense an interpretation of Christianity. In so far as it has any particular religious aim, it would seem to be to show that all religions are manifestations of the one esoteric truth.

The Μεγάλη Ἀπόφασις attributed to Simon of Gitta, though generally thought to be a later product of his school, expounds a system which is obviously neither Christian nor Jewish in character, mainly by way of an allegorical exposition of passages from the Old Testament, very much in the manner which we associate with Philo, but which was no doubt widely practised in Hellenistic Judaism. The fragments known to us contain no more than three or four quotations from the New Testament, whereas in some parts of them references to the Old Testament are continuous. Similarly, the only recognition of Christianity attributed to Simon by Irenaeus is his statement that he himself had appeared in Judaea as the Son, and had seemed to suffer, and had now appeared in Samaria as the Father, while he visited other nations as the Holy Spirit. Simonianism, therefore, is not an interpretation of Christianity, unless to explain why Christianity is superseded is to interpret it.[1] The chief debt which Simonian Gnosticism owed to Christianity, perhaps, was the impulse which led it to recognize historical figures (Simon himself and Helen) as manifestations of celestial powers. This is a feature which is absent from other Gnostic systems, except where they make a place for Jesus Himself.[2]

Again, the *Book of Baruch* attributed to the Gnostic Justin is, so far as we know it from Hippolytus (*Refut.* v. 23–8), in the main a mythical adaptation of Old Testament material. Its system, such as it is, is almost entirely documented out of purely Jewish sources. But the writer freely illustrates his points by reference to pagan myths, such as those of Heracles, Leda, Ganymede and Danae. There is a short Christian episode in the scheme, which presents Jesus as the first initiate into true *gnosis*, and this could be removed without seriously affecting the system.

Basilides, to take one more example, is said to have taught among the Persians, and there is evident affinity between his scheme and Zoroastrianism. He documents it occasionally from the Old Testament, more frequently from the New Testament, both interpreted allegorically; but these biblical allusions are illustrative rather than constitutive. His celestial hierarchy, whatever its origin, contains names mostly taken from the vocabulary of Greek philosophy, νοῦς, λόγος, φρόνησις, σοφία, δύναμις,

[1] Some moderns however seem to take this view of 're-interpretation'.
[2] John the Baptist appears in the Mandaean system (if we are to reckon it with Gnosticism), but not as the manifestation of a celestial power. See pp. 119–120.

though three of these are also theological terms in the New Testament. The identification of νοῦς with Christ indicates a real attempt to interpret Christianity in more universal terms; and the historical figure of Jesus, as the first true Gnostic, the firstfruits, in fact, of redeemed humanity, plays a real part; for after He was enlightened (ἐφωτίσθη) the whole of the υἱότης which remained in the world 'followed Jesus', was cleansed, and ascended.[1] Basilides does give the impression of one to whom the central beliefs of Christianity are of real importance, and who seeks to interpret and commend them by relating them to a scheme of philosophy[2] in mythical form. The *gnosis* he seeks to convey is, for him, the Christian Gospel. But the whole framework of his system is of non-Christian origin, and could not possibly have been deduced from Christian doctrine.

The system of Valentinus, finally, is more definitely Christian in inspiration. While his celestial hierarchy is clearly akin to that of Basilides (in the form known to Irenaeus), its names have a biblical ring. Ἀλήθεια, λόγος, and ζωή, if not directly derived from Christian tradition, are yet important enough in the New Testament to give a certain Christian character to the Pleroma, while ἐκκλησία can owe its place there only to the Christian doctrine of the Church.[3] Moreover, the dramatic movement of the Valentinian myth is determined by biblical ideas—the creation of the world by Wisdom and its redemption by Christ. The tortuous elaborations of these ideas are designed to make the Christian doctrines more acceptable to the readers addressed, especially by relating them to such problems as those of the nature of the universe and of man, and the origin of evil, which profoundly interested thoughtful people of the period. Thus we may recognize Valentinus as a Christian thinker[4] concerned to provide Christianity with a more adequate theology, as it seemed to him, than the conservative teachers of the Church offered. At the same time, the general structure of his thought has so much in common with

[1] Hippolytus, *op. cit.* VII. 26. Irenaeus's account of Basilides, *Adv. Haer.* I. 19. 2, differs widely from that given in Hippolytus.
[2] Hippolytus attempts to derive the system of Basilides from the philosophy of Aristotle. The attempt is a *tour de force*; yet there is a philosophical basis beneath the mythology.
[3] On the other hand part of the masculine side of the Valentinian genealogy is identical with the group of mediating beings in the *Poimandres*: δημιουργός, λόγος, ἄνθρωπος; to these Valentinus has added the feminines ζωή, ἀλήθεια and ἐκκλησία, of which the last is purely Christian (with Jewish antecedents) and the other two are prominent in the Johannine presentation of Christianity.
[4] F. C. Burkitt's vindication of the essential Christianity of Valentinus in *Church and Gnosis* (1932) I find convincing.

Gnostic systems whose contact with Christianity is slight, that he may best be regarded as a mediator between Christianity and a Gnostic movement which in fact owed little to Christianity, though it might make use of Christian terms and ideas.

To sum up, it is impossible to answer our question in general terms, covering the whole body of Gnostic doctrine. If Valentinus is a Christian theologian of an adventurous type, Justin and the Naassene writer are nothing of the kind; still less 'Simon'. On the other hand, there is a certain general framework of thought which appears in all or almost all the Gnostic systems. There does seem to have been something which might be called a Gnostic movement, or at least tendency. It was essentially syncretistic, actuated by the belief that revealed truth was witnessed by various religions, or mythologies, and making use of Greek philosophical ideas at a remove. Contact with Christianity quickened this movement, already influenced by Judaism, and a rank growth of Christian, or semi-Christian and quasi-Christian, systems arose. The documents known to us represent this later development, parallel in time to the Christian theologians of the second and third centuries, and also to the main body of Hermetic writings.

In Gnosticism we meet again many of the ideas which are already familiar from Philo and the *Hermetica*, and the general background of thought may often seem to be very much the same. The object of the Gnostic teachers would seem to have been to put into the hands of the initiate the means of escape from the bondage of matter, and from fate and the rule of malign powers, and to give him the opportunity of attaining immortality. So far they have much in common with the Hermetists and with Philo. But it is difficult to trace in the extant Gnostic literature anything of that genuinely mystical piety which shines through Philo's extravagant allegories and the complicated metaphysics of the *Hermetica*. *Gnosis* is not in fact so much knowledge *of God*, in any profoundly religious sense, as knowledge *about* the structure of the higher world and the way to get there—γνῶσις τῶν ὑπερκοσμίων. It includes cosmology, but its special interest lies in that which is beyond the κόσμος and can be known only by revelation. This γνῶσις τῶν ὑπερκοσμίων is usually conveyed in the form of myths, in which various metaphysical concepts are more or less personified. How far the personification was meant to be taken seriously, how far the initiate was expected to rationalize the myth, it is difficult or impossible to say. But the predominance of myth is characteristic of Gnosticism, in contrast to the *Hermetica*, where it is used sparingly, and usually transparently, and to Philo, where scriptural passages understood as allegories take the place of myth, and are constantly rationalized. It may well be that the greater Gnostic teachers, like Valentinus and Bardaisan, meant the myth to be no more than the clothing for wisdom scarcely expressible by direct speech; but it seems certain that their less intelligent followers, like the author or authors of the *Pistis Sophia*, took the myths all too literally. In Mandaism we have the end-product of this degradation. It is perhaps because it is chiefly represented to us by its inferior exponents, or else by opponents who may have misunderstood it, that Gnosticism has so often the look of gross superstition. We shall do well not to pay too great attention to the mythical form. In any case, Gnosticism seriously claims to secure access to a realm of being altogether other than the world of sensible experience, through the communication of detailed knowledge of that world, rather than through any properly religious attitudes or activities.

The most cogent reason why in studying the background of the Fourth Gospel we should take account of Gnostic heresy is that readers of this gospel in the second century seem to have been aware of some affinity. On the one hand, those who down to a late date in the second century rejected it—Epiphanius's ἄλογοι—were, it is believed, ultra-conservative theologians who thought it smacked of heresy. On the other hand, it is certain that some Gnostics were profoundly interested in it. In reading through Irenaeus and Hippolytus on Heresies one is struck by the relative frequency and importance of quotations from the Fourth Gospel, or clear echoes of it. This is especially to be observed in the documents representing the teaching of Basilides and Valentinus. The first commentators on the Fourth Gospel (so far as we know) were the Valentinians Ptolemy, whose exposition of the Prologue is extant, and Heracleon, whose commentary is largely excerpted by Origen. Both are serious pieces of exegesis. Both, naturally, find the Valentinian system in the gospel, and perhaps do so without greater strain on the natural meaning than may sometimes be detected in more orthodox commentators. Yet when we have studied them as sympathetically as possible, it seems that we must conclude that the ideas which they are setting forth are not in fact derived from the text of the Fourth Gospel, however felicitously, sometimes, it may be used to illustrate them. If there is an affinity, it would seem to be due to some degree of common background behind the thought of orthodox and heretical teachers. It would of course be out of the question here to attempt any presentation of the Gnostic theologies, but it may be worth while to select some topics, and try to detect elements in Gnostic doctrine which may go back to an earlier stage, and belong to the general climate of religious thought in which the Fourth Evangelist and his readers lived. The attempt may also suggest some comparison of the different ways in which the evangelist and his Gnostic contemporaries treated such topics.

1. GNOSTIC DUALISM

All Gnostic systems rest upon a metaphysical dualism. Their authors are haunted by a sense of the misery and futility of human life in this world, and they connect this with our imprisonment in a material body, which is part of a material order of things. This material order is sharply contrasted with a higher order, entirely spiritual, having no contact with matter. Thus, 'Existent things are divided by Basilides into two adjacent and primary divisions. The one he calls κόσμος, the other ὑπερκόσμια.' These are separated by a στερέωμα or μεθόριον, which prevents contact between the two spheres (Hippolytus, *Refut.* VII. 23). Similarly, the Valentinians speak of a Totality (πλήρωμα) of aeons, a harmonious society or hierarchy of spiritual essences, bounded below by Ὅρος, by which the integrity of the Pleroma is safeguarded, and lower forms of existence shut out. The idea is that this material world, of which we are part, is separated off from a higher world above it, superior to it in all respects.

But this is not the whole story. For though man is part of this lower world, yet he has at least the desire to rise to the higher, and that would seem to indicate that there is some kind of aboriginal relation, at however far a remove, between this world and that. The various systems attempt in various ways to give an account of the way in which this relation is to be conceived. Thus according to Basilides:

In the beginning there were light and darkness.... When each of these came to recognition of the other, and the darkness contemplated the light, the darkness, as if seized with desire of the better thing, pursued after it, and desired to be mingled with it and to participate in it. But while the darkness did this, the light by no means received anything of the darkness into itself, nor desired anything of it, albeit it too suffered the desire to behold. So it beheld the darkness as if in a mirror. Thus a certain colour of light (*enfasis, id est color quidam lucis*) alone came to the darkness.... Hence there is no perfect good in this world, and what there is of good at all is very little.... Nevertheless by reason of this little bit of light, or rather of this sort of appearance of light, the creatures had power to generate a likeness tending towards that admixture which they had conceived from the light.[1]

In a more elaborate form of the Basilidian system the primal God, who must be called the Non-existent, since He is *ex hypothesi* the cause of all that exists, projected a seed having within it the universal germ (πανσπερμία) (Hippolytus, *Refut.* VII. 21). Out of this sprang first a threefold 'sonship' (υἱότης τριμερής). The first υἱότης was by nature so light that it sped immediately upwards to the non-existent God. The second flew up so far as it could (σπεύδει γὰρ πάντα κάτωθεν ἄνω ἀπὸ τῶν χειρόνων ἐπὶ τὰ κρείττονα, *ibid.* 22), but reaching a point at which it could not live in the rarer atmosphere (as a fish cannot live in air), it stayed at the μεθόριον. The third, being in need of purification, remained mingled with the bulk of the πανσπερμία. Out of this πανσπερμία, vivified by the presence of the third υἱότης, the great Archons were born, and they made the world we know. The upshot of this is that this world has in it an element which, though clogged by contact with grosser things, yet has affinity with the upper world, and tends to rise towards it. 'There was left in the πανσπερμία the third υἱότης...and it was necessary that this υἱότης should be revealed and restored to the upper place...as it is written, "the creation itself groaneth and travaileth together, awaiting the revelation of the sons of God". And these sons are we πνευματικοί' (Hippolytus, *Refut.* VII. 25). Thus there are in the world men who are by nature fit to be raised into the supramundane sphere.

In the system of Justin described by Hippolytus (*Refut.* v. 23–8) the myth is framed upon an allegorization of the Old Testament. There are three ἀρχαὶ ἀγέννητοι. First there is the supreme God, called Ἀγαθός, who dwells in light above. Then there is a pair: a male principle called Elohim (Ἐλωείμ), or the Father, and a female principle called Eden (Ἐδέμ). From them spring twelve angels associated with Elohim and twelve associated with Eden. The angels of Elohim make man out of the better part of Eden. Elohim puts into him πνεῦμα, Eden ψυχή. Elohim, in agreement with Eden (ἐκ κοινῆς εὐαρεστήσεως), creates heaven and earth and all that is in them. He then aspires upwards, for, like the Basilidian υἱότητες, he is ἀνωφερής. Arrived at the upper boundary of heaven, he beholds a light better than that which he had created, and seeks entrance. A voice out of the light[2] bids him enter, and he sits down

[1] Hegemonius, *Acta Archelai* LXVII. 7–11.
[2] Φωνὴ ἀπὸ τοῦ φωτός, *Refut.* v. 26; cf. *C.H.* I. 4–5.

at the right hand of Ἀγαθός. By thus leaving Eden, he was the cause of both good and evil. 'For by ascending to the Good he showed the way to those who wish to ascend, but by deserting Eden he became the cause of evils to the spirit of the Father which is in men' (ἀναβὰς γὰρ πρὸς τὸν Ἀγαθὸν ὁ πατὴρ ὁδὸν ἔδειξε τοῖς ἀναβαίνειν θέλουσιν, ἀποστὰς δὲ τῆς Ἐδὲμ ἀρχὴν κακῶν ἐποίησε τῷ πνεύματι τοῦ πατρὸς τῷ ἐν τοῖς ἀνθρώποις). For left to herself Eden took to bad ways, and her angels, led by Nahash, the Serpent (Ναάς), led men astray. Elohim however did not leave himself without witness, for his angels came to men and tried to persuade them to follow their Father in his upward ascent. But their persuasions were frustrated by Nahash until the angel Baruch, sent by Elohim, came to Jesus, the son of Joseph and Mary. He obeyed the call, resisted the seducements of Nahash, and ascended to the Good. Similarly, whoever is initiated into the mysteries of Elohim, and swears the oath, 'he enters to the Good, and sees that which eye hath not seen, nor ear heard, and which hath not entered into the heart of man, and drinks of the living water' (εἰσέρχεται πρὸς τὸν Ἀγαθόν, καὶ βλέπει ὅσα ὀφθαλμὸς οὐκ εἶδε καὶ οὖς οὐκ ἤκουσε καὶ ἐπὶ καρδίαν ἀνθρώπου οὐκ ἀνέβη, καὶ πίνει ἀπὸ τοῦ ζῶντος ὕδατος). This water, it is explained, is the water above the firmament of the evil creation, in which the πνευματικοί wash, as distinct from the waters below the firmament in which the χοϊκοὶ καὶ ψυχικοὶ ἄνθρωποι wash. Once again therefore we have a theory of the presence in this lower world of an element which tends to rise into the higher world, manifested in those members of the human race who are πνευματικοί.

The Valentinian system is more complicated than either of these.[1] Here the beginning of all things is the pair of 'Aeons', Deep (Βυθός), the First Father, and Silence (Σιγή), which is His thought (ἔννοια). From them proceed, by steps which are not quite the same in various forms of the system, Νοῦς and Ἀλήθεια, Λόγος and Ζωή, Ἄνθρωπος and Ἐκκλησία. These form the primary Ogdoad. From them proceed other aeons, all in pairs (συζυγίαι), making up a Pleroma of thirty. The youngest of the aeons is Σοφία. She is moved by desire to know the first Father, the Deep, and acting without her consort, the Willed or Designed (Θελητός), strives to move upwards towards Him, with disastrous results. She conceives a monstrous offspring, Ἐνθύμησις, Fancy, with which she travails desperately until she seems like to be completely undone. The

---

[1] Hippolytus, *Refut.* VI. 21–37, Irenaeus, *Adv. Haer.* I. 1–14 (Harvey), *Excerpta ex Theodoto*, printed among the works of Clement of Alexandria. I have attempted no more than a very broad and rough summary of the main features.

Ogdoad thereupon, to save her, produce a single aeon, Limit ("Ορος), also called Cross (Σταυρός). He delivers Sophia of her luckless offspring, and restores her to the harmony of the Pleroma. Her 'Ενθύμησις is driven out of the Pleroma, beyond the "Ορος, a monstrous birth, an abortion (ἔκτρωμα), called 'Αχαμώθ (a quasi-Hebrew form representing חָכְמָה, wisdom). She lay outside the Light and the Pleroma, in places of shadow and void, being shapeless and unformed. Then a new pair, Christ and Holy Spirit, proceeded from Νοῦς and 'Αλήθεια within the Ogdoad. Christ pitied Achamoth, and went down to her through the Cross, accompanied by Holy Spirit. He gave the formless form, and Achamoth became a kind of lower aeon, and is called Sophia after her parent, or alternatively Holy Spirit after the Spirit that accompanied Christ. Christ and Holy Spirit then returned to the Pleroma. Achamoth-Sophia was now aware of higher existences, and alternated between distress at her own condition, and joy in the thought of the Christ who had visited her. Out of her grief, fear and despair she produced matter; out of her aspiration towards Christ (her conversion, ἐπιστροφή) she produced τὸ ψυχικόν; and finally, having within her a sort of smell of incorruptibility (ὀδμήν τινα ἀφθαρσίας) left by Christ and Holy Spirit, she gave birth to τὸ πνευματικόν. She now set out to form a world in imitation of the eternal essences in the Pleroma. First, as an image of the first Father, she made out of τὸ ψυχικόν the Creator (Δημιουργός). He in turn created heaven and earth and all that therein is. But he worked blindly, not knowing what he was doing, imagining that he was himself the maker and lord of all, whereas in fact he was merely the tool of his mother Wisdom. When he came to the creation of mankind, first he made τὸν χοϊκὸν ἄνθρωπον, who is man κατ' εἰκόνα, being like his Creator, but not of the same substance (παραπλήσιον μὲν ἀλλ' οὐχ ὁμοούσιον). Then he breathed into him τὸν ψυχικόν, of his own substance; and this is man καθ' ὁμοίωσιν. Finally, without the knowledge of the Demiurge, ὁ πνευματικὸς ἄνθρωπος, of the substance not of the Creator but of Wisdom herself, was mingled with the other elements of humanity. The πνευματικὸς ἄνθρωπος is the antitype of the aeon 'Εκκλησία. Thus men are of three kinds, χοϊκοί or σαρκικοί, ψυχικοί, and πνευματικοί. The first are bound up with this perishable world, and cannot be saved. The third have an aboriginal affinity with the Pleroma, through their Mother, the second Wisdom (or Holy Spirit), and need no salvation, but are destined to ascend on high. The second class are capable of salvation, and it was for their sake that Jesus finally came from heaven.

This is the briefest possible outline of the common purport of the several Valentinian systems, all of which are far more complicated. Its interpretation is difficult enough.[1] But Valentinus would seem to have had before him the problem: if this world was created by the Wisdom of God (as the Old Testament affirmed), how comes it that it is such a poor sort of world? His answer is that the Wisdom which we see revealed in this world is a fallen Wisdom, having indeed in her some trace of her 'divine original', but disordered by undivine passion and ignorance. Only a 'premundane fall', not of man, but of the very principle by which the world came into being, can account for the evil which is deeply rooted in everything that we know—in everything but the finest part of the best men, the πνευματικοί. This minute seed of good (which Valentinus finds in the parables of the leaven and the mustard-seed) is in the world because the fallen Wisdom was in part redeemed before the world was. Not only was there a pre-mundane fall; there was also a pre-mundane redemption; and it is this fact that makes *our* redemption possible.

These three examples have been given in order to provide a basis of comparison with Johannine ideas. In John also we have the pervading idea of two orders of being, τὰ ἄνω and τὰ κάτω. To these terms correspond the verbs ἀναβαίνειν and καταβαίνειν (iii. 13, etc.), used by John with the same pregnant significance as in the Gnostics. The two orders are sharply distinguished in character: they are light and darkness (i. 5, viii. 12, xii. 46), spirit and flesh, and to belong to the one order excludes belonging to the other: 'that which is born of the flesh is flesh, and that which is born of the spirit is spirit' (iii. 6); those who are ἐκ τῶν κάτω cannot understand one who is ἐκ τῶν ἄνω (viii. 23). At the same time the lower order is not wholly out of relation to the higher. The light shines in darkness and the darkness does not overcome it (i. 5); just as in Basilides there is *color quidam lucis* in the darkness, which saves

---

[1] Burkitt, in *Church and Gnosis*, proposed to interpret the doctrine of the Pleroma psychologically. The aboriginal Deep is the unconscious mind, out of which a thought, ἔννοια, emerges, and this is the beginning of all concrete existence. Sophia is philosophy, which wrongly desires to search the ultimate deeps, and as a result produces only a disordered fancy (ἐνθύμησις). Only when philosophy submits to the Cross, which is at the same time the principle of limitation or definition, does its disordered fancy become a real world. This seems to throw a real light upon the way in which this strange system came to be formulated; but we surely have here something more than a mythological account of psychological processes. For the Σοφία of the Valentinians is not simply philosophy. She is clearly the creative Wisdom of the Old Testament.

the world from being wholly bad; and as in Valentinus the lower world has ὀδμήν τινα ἀφθαρσίας about it. In particular there are in the world men who having received the Logos (who is ἐκ τῶν ἄνω, who κατέβη) have the right to become children of God (John i. 12). In I John iii. 9 (see my note *ad loc.*) they are described as those in whom the σπέρμα τοῦ θεοῦ resides. This expression, used only here in the Johannine writings, is important in the vocabulary of Valentinianism. We hear of σπέρμα τῆς ἄνωθεν οὐσίας, ψυχαὶ δεκτικαὶ τοῦ σπέρματος, of σπέρματα τοῦ θεοῦ, τῆς 'Αχαμώθ, τῆς ἄνω ἐκκλησίας, all in reference to the πνευματικοί. It is the function of the Saviour to provide for the Seed a thoroughfare into the Pleroma (ἵνα τῷ σπέρματι δίοδον εἰς πλήρωμα παρασχῇ, *Exc. ex Theodoto*, 38; cf. 41 τὰ σπέρματα τὰ συνελθόντα αὐτῷ εἰς τὸ πλήρωμα, 42 διὸ καὶ τὰ σπέρματα ὁ 'Ιησοῦς διὰ τοῦ σημείου ἐπὶ τῶν ὤμων βαστάσας εἰσάγει εἰς τὸ πλήρωμα). Redemption will be complete ὅταν συλλεγῇ τὰ σπέρματα τοῦ θεοῦ (*Exc. ex Theodoto*, 49), just as, in John, Jesus dies ἵνα τὰ τέκνα τοῦ θεοῦ τὰ διεσκορπισμένα συναγάγῃ εἰς ἕν (John xi. 52). It might be argued that this is a case where the Gnostic writers are simply elaborating what they borrowed from the Fourth Gospel. But this appears less likely when we find in Basilides and Justin the same idea, substantially, in a much less Christian context. According to Basilides, as we have seen, there is a υἱότης immersed in the material world. No messenger from above came to redeem this 'sonship', as Basilides says with some emphasis. It was unnecessary, for just as naphtha can be ignited without actual contact with fire, so the hidden υἱότης takes fire, as it were, from the πνεῦμα which is at the μεθόριον. Thus the light of knowledge comes, and penetrates stage by stage, until the whole υἱότης which was left in the formlessness (ἀμορφία) has run upwards and arrived, being purified, above the μεθόριον (Hippolytus, *Refut.* v. 26–7) In Justin all men have remaining in them the πνεῦμα of their Father Elohim, and when they receive initiation into his mysteries they follow him upwards to the throne of the Good (*ibid.*). It is true that in both these systems Jesus appears as the first initiate to ascend; but He plays no more essential part than this, and the doctrine has not the aspect of being developed out of the comparatively small Christian element which appears in it. Moreover, the dependence of Basilides on Persian (Zoroastrian) ideas is manifest, and Justin has combined similar ideas with conceptions derived from the Old Testament. We cannot, moreover, ignore the resemblance to certain doctrines of the *Hermetica*. It is probable therefore that what we have in Valentinus, as in the others, is not a development from John, but rather a combination of certain Christian features with a scheme which in the main belongs to another tradition. It is in that case significant that there are in the Fourth Gospel traces of a similar scheme.

2. Gnostic Mediators

In the Johannine scheme the Logos plays the part of mediator between the upper sphere and the lower, both in the sense that He is the agent of the supreme God in creation, and in the sense that descending into this world He reveals the supreme God and makes a way for men to ascend. In the various Gnostic systems these functions are variously distributed among a number of beings. In all of them the immediate creator of the world is distinguished from the supreme Being, and in several of them the function of descending to reveal the true Gnosis is assigned to one or more supernatural beings. But the Logos seldom appears in any specially significant role. In the systems of Basilides and Valentinus Logos is one of a number of aeons, but is neither creator nor revealer, and the Valentinians explain that Jesus the Saviour is called Logos πατρωνυμικῶς because He is sprung from the aeons, among whom is Logos, and that in His incarnation He became an οὐράνιος λόγος through the descent of Holy Spirit. All this is best explained if we suppose that the general tradition to which the Gnostic systems point back did not work with the Logos idea, and that it is introduced into these systems because of the place it already had in Christian thought. The only important exception, perhaps, is a passage in the Naassene document to which I shall presently refer.

The other term which John uses for the Mediator is υἱὸς τοῦ ἀνθρώπου. This is of course a traditional Christian term; but we have already seen that as used by John it has some affinity with the idea of a heavenly Man found in Philo and the *Hermetica*. This idea plays a part in several of the Gnostic systems. It is to be observed that the Aramaic term lying behind υἱὸς τοῦ ἀνθρώπου, בַּר נָשָׁא, means 'man'. It is however unlikely that the Gnostic writers were acquainted with this fact; and indeed some of them distinguish Ἄνθρωπος from Υἱὸς τοῦ ἀνθρώπου,[1] making the latter the son of the former, according to the strict meaning of the Greek. When therefore we find the figure of the heavenly Ἄνθρωπος playing an important part, we may be fairly sure that we are not dealing with ideas originally derived from a reading of the gospels.

[1] E.g. Naassenes, Hippolytus, *Refut.* v. 6, Monoimos, *ibid.* VIII. 12, Sethians or Ophites, Irenaeus, *Adv. Haer.* I. 28.

In the Valentinian systems Ἄνθρωπος appears among the aeons of the primary Ogdoad, but plays no special part. His consort is Ἐκκλησία, the heavenly prototype of the πνευματικοί on earth. Thus Ἄνθρωπος is there solely to provide a heavenly prototype for the human race which is to be created when the lower world is formed on the model of the Pleroma.[1] We may suspect that as Logos is there because it already held an important place in Christian thought, so Ἄνθρωπος is there because the idea was important in one or other of the traditions upon which the Gnostics drew. The question is whether it came out of the Christian tradition or out of some other. Paul's doctrine of the heavenly Man suggests itself as a source. But although Paul's doctrine might give Christian sanction to the idea, there is nothing in the Valentinian use of the term which suggests a reference to Paul. There is no attempt to identify Anthropos with Christ, or with Holy Spirit. Moreover, as Reitzenstein pointed out, Paul's argument in I Cor. xv. 46–7 has a polemical tinge. He is arguing against a doctrine of the heavenly or spiritual Man which made Him prior to the χοϊκός. Such a doctrine is found in Philo and in some Hermetic and Gnostic writings. Thus we are encouraged to look in other directions for the source of the idea. In point of fact it is in the systems more remotely connected with Christianity than the Valentinian that Anthropos is important. In the Naassene document we read of an Ἀρχάνθρωπος called Adamas, who is to be identified with the Greek Hermes. Now Hermes is the Logos, the ἑρμηνεὺς καὶ δημιουργός of all things that were and are and shall be. Moreover, the earth produced an image of this Ἀρχάνθρωπος, a second Man whom the nations know under various names. The Chaldaeans call him Adam. He lay breathless, motionless, like a statue, until a soul was given him from above. This soul was brought down upon him from the Ἀρχάνθρωπος. The ἔσω ἄνθρωπος in all men is in fact Adamas, the Ἀρχάνθρωπος. When a man is reborn spiritually, this immanent humanity comes as it were into full being. The reborn is a τέλειος ἄνθρωπος, and in some sort identical with Adamas. It was to this that Jeremiah referred when he said (xvii. 9) ἄνθρωπός ἐστιν καὶ τίς γνώσεται αὐτόν; 'For the knowledge of man is the beginning of perfection, but the knowledge of God is achieved perfection' (Hippolytus, Refut. v. 8). It is difficult to reduce the teaching of the document to consistency, but the purport seems to be that there is a man in men, who is really the offspring and counterpart of the eternal,

[1] Cf. Valentinian frag. ap. Clem. Alex. Strom. (Stählin, 1906) II. viii. 36. 4 εἰς ὄνομα Ἀνθρώπου πλασθεὶς Ἀδὰμ φόβον παρέσχεν προόντος Ἀνθρώπου.

heavenly, divine Man, and when a man is initiated into Gnosis, he is delivered from his fleshly self, and becomes wholly identical with the true man within him. The affinities of all this are obviously with the Ἄνθρωπος doctrine of some of the *Hermetica*. It is given a Christian tinge, for Christ is said to be the true man in men: ὁ ἐν πᾶσι τοῖς γενητοῖς υἱὸς ἀνθρώπου (i.e. offspring of the Ἀρχάνθρωπος), κεχαρακτηρισμένος ἀπὸ τοῦ ἀχαρακτηρίστου λόγου (*ibid.* v. 7); and Jesus is the type of the 'perfect' man: ὁ ἀπὸ τοῦ ἀχαρακτηρίστου ἄνωθεν κεχαρακτηρισμένος τέλειος ἄνθρωπος (*ibid.* v. 8). It is clear that this identification of Christ with Ἄνθρωπος is secondary. The figure of Ἄνθρωπος is not derived from Christian sources.

In Irenaeus, *Adv. Haer.* I. 28 (Harvey) we seem to have a variant of the same doctrine, attributed here to the Sethians, also called Ophites, who say 'that there was a certain primal light in the power of Βυθός, blessed, incorruptible, and infinite; and this is the Father of all, and is called the First Man. And his Ἔννοια proceeding from Him they call ... the Son of Man, the Second Man.' The doctrine is Christianized by making Christ the offspring of the First Man and Holy Spirit, the female First Principle. Again, the Barbelo-Gnostics of Irenaeus, I. 27 have a somewhat obscure genealogy in which Ennoia and Logos give birth to Autogenes, and he produces *hominem perfectum et verum quem Adamantem vocant*, and as his consort *Agnitionem perfectam* (Γνῶσις τελεία). From them is born *lignum* (ξύλον), *quod et ipsum Gnosin vocant*. In this genealogy Christ is so to speak an elder collateral of Anthropos, being emanated at an earlier stage than Logos and Ennoia. Having in mind some other forms of the Ἄνθρωπος doctrine, we might interpret this as meaning that a man's true humanity emerges only when he embraces Gnosis, and so becomes an antitype of the heavenly pair who are the offspring of Logos and the thought of Logos.

It does in any case seem clear that Ἄνθρωπος was a figure in some non-Christian tradition to which these various systems go back,[1] and

[1] I do not here discuss the ultimate origin of the Ἄνθρωπος-myth. Reitzenstein finds it in Iranian religion. Bousset traces it back to Babylonian mythology. But the Babylonian and old Iranian myths seem to have very slender connection with the Philonic, Hermetic and Gnostic systems. These systems, as we have seen, on examination point to a fairly uniform common scheme lying behind them all. This common scheme is not attested, so far as I can see, in any earlier document. That is to say, the earliest documents for the Ἄνθρωπος-myth, in any form relevant to our purpose, are demonstrably exposed to Jewish influence, and Jewish speculations on Adam would seem to have been at least as influential as ideas borrowed from Iranian sources. See W. D. Davies, *Paul and Rabbinic Judaism*, ch. 3.

was brought into touch with Christian ideas in various ways. It seems difficult to resist the conclusion that John also is alluding to some such tradition. For him the Man is identical with the Logos (as in the Naassene document, and, as we have seen, in Philo), is the offspring of the supreme God, the Father, descends into the world to reveal knowledge of the Father, and, ascending again, draws after Him those who are born again and in whom He Himself abides. The language used in this sentence is in every respect both Johannine and Gnostic, but the difference between Johannine Christianity and Gnosticism emerges the more clearly because the terminology is so largely similar.

3. GNOSTIC REDEMPTION

What then is the Gnostic conception of redemption? It comes of course through Gnosis. Marcus the Valentinian taught 'that perfect redemption is simply knowledge of the unspeakable Greatness; for defect and suffering or passion (ὑστέρημα[1] καὶ πάθος) having come about through ignorance, the whole state of affairs produced by ignorance is dissolved by knowledge, so that knowledge is redemption of the inner man (ὥστε εἶναι τὴν γνῶσιν ἀπολύτρωσιν τοῦ ἔνδον ἀνθρώπου). It is not corporeal (for the body is corruptible), nor yet psychical, since the soul comes out of the Hysterema and is as it were the dwelling of the spirit.[2] Redemption therefore must be spiritual. For the spiritual man is redeemed through knowledge'[3] (Irenaeus, *Adv. Haer.* I. 14 (Harvey)).

What then is this knowledge? The Gospel, says Basilides, is knowledge of supramundane things, εὐαγγέλιόν ἐστιν ἡ τῶν ὑπερκοσμίων γνῶσις. It is in fact precisely the knowledge conveyed in the Gnostic myths— knowledge of the nature and origin of the heavenly aeons, of the nature and origin of this world and its rulers, of the nature and origin of man. Assuming that you are the kind of person capable of receiving this knowledge, and of ascending to the higher world, you will be enabled by receiving it to separate your true self from the material order to which it is essentially alien, and to find your way through the barriers which divide this world from the other. The knowledge that you possess will

---

[1] ὑστέρημα is the contrary of πλήρωμα: as the upper realm is completeness or totality, so the lower realm is essentially defect.

[2] Latin 'spiritus velut habitaculum', Greek *ap.* Epiphan. τοῦ πατρὸς ὥσπερ οἰκητήριον.

[3] 'Redimi enim per agnitionem interiorem hominem spiritalem', Greek διὰ Μωϋσέως for διὰ γνώσεως.

arm you against the powers that would hinder you on your way. Thus the initiate is instructed to say to the powers, when he meets them after death:

'I am a son from the Father—the Father pre-existent, the son in the present. I am come to see my own things and alien things; yet not wholly alien, but the things of Achamoth, who is female and made them for herself. I derive my race from the Pre-existent, and I am journeying to my home (εἰς τὰ ἴδια) from whence I came.' When he says this the powers flee, and he comes to those about the Demiurge. To them he says, 'I am a precious vessel, more precious than she who created you. If your Mother is ignorant of her own root, I know myself and I know whence I am, and I call upon immortal Wisdom, who is in the Father, and the Mother of your Mother, who has no Father and no Consort; but being female and born of a female she made you, not knowing her own Mother, but imagining herself alone. But I invoke her Mother.' When those about the Demiurge hear this they are greatly troubled, and condemn their root and the race of their Mother; and the departed goes on his way home, having cast off his chain, that is the soul.[1]

In a word, knowledge is power. He who knows what he is and whence he is can find the way home. He who knows the nature of the world and its governing powers can overcome these powers. Hence, he who brings knowledge to men is their Saviour. Thus in a Naassene hymn Jesus is made to say,

'Behold, O Father! this quest of evils upon earth is all astray from Thy spirit. But it seeks to escape bitter chaos, and knows not how it shall come through. Send me therefore, Father. Having the seals I will descend. I will traverse all aeons, and I will open all mysteries, and I will reveal the forms of gods. And having summoned Knowledge I will communicate the secrets of the holy way.'[2]

That is how Christ appears in the guise of a Gnostic redeemer. It is clear that whatever John meant by the knowledge which is eternal life through Christ, this was not what he meant. In the Fourth Gospel there is no more than a few verses of the Prologue dealing with the origins of the world and of man; and this is not set forth as the content of the revelation brought by Christ; it only indicates who He is and with what authority He speaks. What He reveals is God Himself, who so loved the world that He sent His Son. He reveals this by 'doing the works of God', and ultimately by giving Himself in order that the life

---

[1] Irenaeus, *Adv. Haer.* I. 14.   [2] Hippolytus, *Refut.* v. 10.

which is in Him may be set free for all men. The knowledge of God which He brings to men takes the form of love, trust and obedience directed to Him, whereby they are united to Him, and consequently to His Father, with Whom He is, whether on earth or in heaven, eternally one. The significance of the parallel and contrast is this. Both John and the Gnostics followed a deeply-grounded tendency, which sought redemption in γνῶσις. He and they believed that such γνῶσις was given in the Christian revelation. The different views they give of what the Christian γνῶσις is make Johannine Christianity, in spite of the common background, an entirely different thing from semi-Christian or near-Christian Gnosticism. But all this must await fuller treatment in later chapters.

6. MANDAISM

The Mandaean religion is practised at the present day by a small community resident in Iraq. Their cultus and beliefs were made known to Europeans by travellers in the East, but are now more accurately known through the publication of their sacred writings, which are written in a dialect of Aramaic. The chief of these are the Ginza ('Treasure') and the Book of John, both being collections of tractates originally more or less independent, along with liturgical texts.[1] None of the MSS. of the Ginza or the Book of John are older than the sixteenth century. The collection however is undoubtedly much older than this, dating probably from the early Islamic period, when the Mandaeans desired to be recognized by their conquerors, along with Jews and Christians, as 'people of the Book'. The compilation of the Mandaean Canon, therefore, cannot be dated much, if at all, before A.D. 700. That is not to say that certain of the writings contained in it may not be earlier, though considerable portions of the Ginza and of the Book of John were certainly written after the appearance of Islam, since they contain references to Mohammed and to the spread of his religion. The earliest allusion to the sect in literature is found in Theodore bar Khonai (A.D. 792). For any history of the Mandaeans and their beliefs before 700 we are dependent solely on inference and speculation. Some modern writers hold that it is possible to trace parts of the Mandaean literature, or at least the traditions which it represents, to the beginning of the Christian Era, or even farther back; and it is on the ground of such theories that the Mandaean question has played a part in discussions of Christian origins and in particular of the Fourth Gospel.

The Mandaean writings are an extraordinary farrago of theology, myth, fairy-tale, ethical instruction, ritual ordinances, and what purports to be history. There is no unity or consistency, and it is not possible to give a succinct summary of their teaching. It is neither consistently

---

[1] German translations by Mark Lidzbarski: *Das Johannesbuch der Mandäer* (1915); *Mandäische Liturgien*, in *Abhandlungen der kgl. Gesellschaft der Wissenschaften zu Göttingen* (1920); *Ginza, der Schatz, oder das grosse Buch der Mandäer* (1925). The present chapter is based mainly on a study of the Ginza in Lidzbarski's translation. For the history of Mandaism I have leaned heavily on Burkitt and Pallis (see references below).

monotheistic nor consistently dualistic. But in its main intention it is based upon a dualism not unlike that of the Manichees.

There is a realm of light, whose members are subjects of the 'high King of Light', otherwise called 'the Great Life'. Over against this there is a realm of darkness, ruled by Ruha d'Ḳudsha (the Holy Spirit) and her children the planets and the demons of the Zodiac. The universe is a kind of compromise between the two realms. The Mandaean Demiurge, Ptahil,[1] is the offspring of the beings of light, but there is something oblique about his birth. In one story his father Abathur looked into the waters of darkness, and saw his image there; and this image was his son Ptahil.[2] He is represented as foolish and rash.[3] By permission of the beings of light, and with their assistance, he makes out of the primeval chaos of darkness a world which has elements of light in it, but Ruha and her brood constantly interfere and spoil his work.[4] By craft they create the body of man,[5] which thus belongs to the realm of darkness. The soul of man however is sent down from the realm of light, and is by nature akin to the beings of light.[6]

Thus the soul in this world is a prisoner, tormented by the powers of evil. It can hope to escape only by the death of the body. Even then escape is not certain, for the soul on its way to the realm of light must pass a formidable series of guard-houses (*Maṭṭaratha*), in each of which a demon lurks to catch it.[7] Only the soul which has been prepared before-hand can win its way through. The preparation consists essentially in the due performance of the Mandaean ritual, combined with the com-

[1] He is obviously the Egyptian Ptah, the creator, the syllable -*il* being added on the analogy of Hebrew names of angels. An Aramaic etymology is offered in the Ginza, where the name is derived from √פתח, 'to open'.

[2] Ginza, Right-hand part (hereafter 'G.R.'), v. 1. p. 168. His dwelling is at the boundary between the world of light and the world of darkness—the proper place for the Demiurge in a Gnostic scheme. Cf. also xv. 3. p. 309. He will in the end be baptized and saved: Ginza, Left-hand part ('G.L.'), II. 14. pp. 55–6.

[3] G.R. v. 1. p. 169. His father Abathur acted presumptuously in sending him to a task of which he was incapable, cf. III. 93.

[4] G.R. III. pp. 94 sqq. It is curious that out of the multitude of mythical beings Ptahil emerges with something like an individual character. The picture of his helplessness before a job too big for him, and of his outwitting by the cunning demons, has something of humour and pathos. The reason no doubt is that the others are either good or evil: Ptahil, like ourselves, is a bit of each.

[5] So G.R. III. p. 100. Elsewhere Ptahil himself creates the corporeal Adam and Eve, after he was 'cut off from the light' (G.R. x. 241).

[6] G.R. x. p. 241, *et passim*.

[7] G.R. v. 3. pp. 180 sqq.

munication of a myth which declares that the powers of light have already overcome the powers of darkness.

The central part of the ritual is baptism in living (i.e. running) water, for such water contains the potency of the celestial water of life which flows in the realm of light. Baptism is frequently repeated, for by it alone the soul is kept pure from the taint of matter, and impregnated with the power of light. The person baptized wears a white robe which symbolizes the garments of light worn by celestial beings, and various other objects, particularly a crown and a staff, similarly symbolic, are employed in the rite. In the act of baptizing, the priest lays his hand upon the baptized, and names divine names over him, and when he emerges from the water he gives him his right hand, symbolizing his reception into the fellowship of the realm of light.[1]

The myth which is communicated to the faithful is intended to assure them that this ritual is grounded in ultimate realities, and has a divinely guaranteed efficacy. It is told in many varied forms, but the essential theme is the descent of a divine being—Manda d'Hayye[2] (Knowledge of Life), a son of the Great Life (or sometimes *his* son Hibil)—into the lower realm, his agonizing but victorious fight with the powers of darkness, and his triumphant ascent to the realm of light and reunion with the Great Life and all the celestial society.

The moral of the story is that as Manda d'Hayye (or sometimes Hibil-Ziwa: see below) entered the domain of the evil powers, endured their hostility, and won the victory; as he passed through the successive worlds that lie between this world and the realm of life and light, and overcame their demonic guardians; so the soul, now imprisoned in the world of darkness, can win through. More particularly, it is related that the divine champion before his descent received baptism, the robe, crown and staff, and the ceremonial hand-clasp (*kushṭa*) from the denizens of the world of light, and in the power of these descended without fear: 'he whom his Father arms, seals, baptizes and establishes need not fear the evil ones.'[3] Thus the ritual of Mandaean baptism is conceived as a re-enactment of the process whereby the divine

---

[1] See S. A. Pallis, *Mandaean Studies* (Eng. tr. 1919), pp. 160 sqq., where the Mandaean ritual is reconstructed from the Ginza, the Book of John, and liturgical texts.

[2] מַנְדָּע דְּחַיֵּא is not Mandaean, I understand, and it appears that the Mandaeans themselves do not know that it means 'knowledge of life', but take it to be simply the proper name of their deity. See Lidzbarski, *Joh. B.* xvii; Pallis, *op. cit.* p. 146, Casey, 'The Study of Gnosticism', in *J.T.S.* xxxvi, pp. 53–4.

[3] G.R. v. 1. p. 137.

champion was enabled to win the victory. It is to be observed that the
descent and ascent of Manda d'Hayye either precedes creation, or is
connected with the process of creation; in either case it took place before
man existed.

When man is created, the lower powers who produced his body are
not able to animate it. The Great Life thereupon sends down a soul,
which is either identical with, or the image of, the 'hidden Adam',
Adakas (אדם כאסיא = אדאכאס), a being of light, sometimes equated with
Manda d'Hayye, and Adam lives.[1] The planets, with Ruha their mother,
try all their arts to get him into their power, but the Great Life calls and
sends the three helpers, Hibil, Shitil and Enosh.[2] They provide Adam with
a wife, Hawwa, and enable him to found a family, and they teach him the
ritual (including the myth, which lies behind the ritual, of the victory over
the demons), by which he and his race may escape the dominion of the
planets and ascend to life on the death of the body.[3]

Thus the Mandaean religion is represented as founded upon a primitive
revelation. Into the mouth of the 'pure Messenger', who is Hibil or
Manda d'Hayye, are placed instructions upon theology and cosmology,
ethical and ritual commandments, and a forecast of the coming history
of the world, very much as in Jewish apocalypses similar matter is put
in the mouth of Enoch or of the Patriarchs.[4]

The history of the world is conceived as falling into successive epochs.[5]
The first three epochs, from Adam to Nu (Noah), are ended by catastrophes
which destroy all living except certain individuals. The souls of the dead
all ascend to the Light, and through the survivors the world is renewed.
After Noah the powers of evil increase their assaults upon mankind.
One of them, Adonai, brings the Jews out of Egypt, and gives the Law
through Misha bar Amra (Moses).[6] At last the seven planets lead all the
children of Adam astray. One of them, Nbu (Hermes, the planet
Mercury), is called also Christ. He revealed himself 'in another form',

---

[1] G.R. III. pp. 101–2.

[2] I.e. Abel, Seth and Enosh, G.R. III. 104–6.

[3] G.R. III. pp. 106–7.

[4] G.R. I. 79 sqq. pp. 12 sqq. (Hibil-Ziwa = Gabriel speaks), II. 1. 12 sqq. pp. 32 sqq.
(Hibil-Ziwa).

[5] G.R. I. 181 sqq. pp. 26 sqq., II. 1. 118 sqq. pp. 48 sqq.

[6] G.R. II. 1. 104 p. 45. The Jews are called יהוטאי, because they sinned (√חטא =
Hb. חטא). On the other hand, it is an offence in Jesus that he 'perverted the Torah',
G.R. II. 1. 147 p. 56; according to G.R. II. 1. 125 p. 50 there will be true believers
in the world from the time of Moses to the end of the age.

clothed with fire, calling Himself 'Jesus the Saviour'. Here I must quote the words of G.R. I. 200 sqq. pp. 28–9:

He says, 'I am God, the Son of God, whom my father has sent here.' He declares to you, 'I am the first Messenger, I am Hibil-Ziwa, who am come from on high.' But confess him not, for he is not Hibil-Ziwa. Hibil-Ziwa is not clothed with fire. Hibil-Ziwa does not reveal himself in that age. On the contrary, Enosh-Uthra comes and betakes himself to Jerusalem, clothed with a garment of water-clouds. He walks in bodily form, yet he is clothed with no bodily garment. There is no fiery wrath in him. He goes and comes in the years of Palṭus (Pilate), the king of the world. Enosh-Uthra comes into the world with the might of the high King of Light. He heals the sick, makes the blind to see, cleanses the lepers, lifts up the crippled who crawl upon the ground, so that they can walk, makes the deaf and dumb to speak, and raises the dead. He wins believers among the Jews, and shows them: There is life and there is death, there is darkness and there is light, there is error and there is truth. He converts the Jews to the name of the high King of Light.

Thereafter Enosh-Uthra ascends on high, the city of Jerusalem is laid waste, and the Jews dispersed. Finally comes Ahmaṭ, son of the sorcerer Bizbaṭ (Mohammed), and leads the souls of men astray.

A similar account, with many expansions, is given in G.R. II. I. 118 sqq., pp. 48 sqq. Here Enosh-Uthra exposes the deceptions of Jesus, and the Jews crucify Jesus as a deceiver, and imprison his followers, l.c. 156, p. 58.

The Mandaeans, then, record that shortly before the fall of Jerusalem two persons appeared in Judaea. Both were supernatural beings appearing in human form. One was Nbu, the evil planet Mercury, who appeared as Jesus. The other was Enosh, the third of the three Helpers of mankind, who appeared as—who? All the other personages who appear in the sketch of world history after Noah are historical characters—Abraham, Moses, Solomon, Jesus. Who was the historical character who embodied Enosh, as Jesus embodied Nbu?

In G.R. II. I. 151–2 p. 57 another figure is introduced.

Further, in that age a child will be born, whose name is called Johana, the son of the gray father Zakhria, who was granted to him in his old age at the end of 100 years. His mother Enishbai became pregnant with him, and bore him in her old age. When Johana grows up in that age of Jerusalem, faith will rest in his heart. He will take the Jordan and complete the baptism 24 years before Nbu takes a body and enters into the world. When Johana lives, in that age of Jerusalem, and completes the baptism, Jesus Christ comes, enters with humility, receives the baptism of Johana, and becomes wise through the wisdom of Johana. But then he perverts the speech of Johana, alters the baptism in Jordan, perverts the words of the truth, and preaches blasphemy and deceit in the world.

When Johana has finished his course, Hibil-Ziwa[1] or Manda d'Hayye[2] comes to him in the form of a child desiring baptism, but when he tries to enter the water the water retreats before him. Johana recognizes him, and is borne aloft to the world of light, baptized in the celestial Jordan, and clothed with garments of light.[3]

There is no doubt who is meant. It is the familiar figure of John the Baptist, son of Zachariah and Elizabeth, who baptized in Jordan, and to whom Jesus came for baptism.

Thus the false Messiah has two opponents, Johana and Enosh-Uthra. It is tempting to suggest that there were two accounts, in one of which Johana appeared, in the other Enosh-Uthra, and that these have been conflated in G.R. II. I. That is not impossible, but it cannot be proved. In any case, it is not legitimate to infer that Enosh-Uthra appeared in the form of John, as Nbu appeared in the form of Jesus. It is nowhere hinted that John was other than a man, miraculously born, indeed, but like all men possessing a body (as Enosh -Uthra does not), from which his soul is separated before he ascends. It is nowhere said that he was the divine Messenger. We are left with the question, Who is Enosh-Uthra? I will leave that question for the present, while I consider a theory which has been put forth, with weighty support, regarding the relations of Mandaism with John the Baptist and with the origins of Christianity.

The theory has two parts. First, it is argued that the kernel of Mandaism is a myth connected with the ancient Iranian mystery of redemption. Myth and mystery are pre-Christian, and underlie the formation of Christian doctrine, especially in its Johannine and Gnostic forms.[4] Secondly, it is argued that the Mandaean ritual and myth were actually formulated by John the Baptist, and that the Mandaeans of the eighth and following centuries are the successors of that Baptist sect to which allusions are found in Acts xviii. 24–xix. 7.[5] Christianity arose out of

---

[1] G.R. II, *l.c.*   [2] G.R. v. 4 p. 190.

[3] This story, greatly expanded, occupies the whole of G.R. v. 4.

[4] See Reitzenstein: *Das iranische Erlösungsmysterium* (1921).

[5] The amount that has been built upon that meagre and obscure section of Acts by writers of various schools is astonishing. The building is precarious indeed that rests upon so inadequate a foundation. It is by no means clear that the passage refers to a 'Baptist sect' at all. The twelve men of Ephesus are called μαθηταί, a word which, without further qualification, is constantly and invariably used of Christians.

this Baptist sect. Its members were called Nazoraeans, a name by which
the Mandaeans call themselves in their Scriptures. Jesus the Nazoraean,
a disciple of John, took the name over with him into the new sect which
he founded. The view of John presented in the New Testament answers
to the view of Jesus presented in the Mandaean literature. In each case
one of two kindred but now rival sects rebuts the claims made for the
leader of the other sect.

This theory has been maintained especially by M. Lidzbarski in his
Introductions to the Ginza and the Book of John, by R. Reitzenstein,[1]
and by R. Bultmann.[2]

Reitzenstein attempts to recover very early Mandaean sources from
certain portions of the literature, particularly from the long parallel
passages, G.R. I. 1–204 pp. 1–30, II. I. 1–165 pp. 30–61. These he regards
as variant recensions of an earlier *kleinere Sammlung* to which he gives the
title 'The Book of the Lord of Greatness', and which he supposes to have
had at one time an independent existence. Much of it is undeniably late,
but he believes it possible to recover from it, with help from some
passages of the Book of John, one or more original documents which
can be dated with some degree of accuracy. In particular one document (containing among other things the original nucleus of the passage
quoted above (p. 119) from G.R. I. 200–1) he believes to contain
authentic information about the early history of the 'Nazoraeans',
or proto-Mandaeans, and of their relations with nascent Christianity.
He confronts passages from this hypothetical document with parallel or
similar passages in the gospels, and decides that the Mandaean source
must be earlier.

The whole process of reconstruction is a masterpiece of characteristic
ingenuity, but it depends on too many arbitrary assumptions.[3] The
comparison with the gospels, for purposes of dating, is often acutely
drawn, but it needs always to be borne in mind that we are comparing
with them, not an existing document, but a reconstructed text from

---

[1] In 'Das mandäische Buch des Herrn der Grösse' (*Sitzungsb. d. Heidelberger
Akad. d. Wiss.* 1919).

[2] Most conveniently in an article in *Z.N.T.W.* XXIV (1925) pp. 100–46. Bultmann's
massive commentary on the Fourth Gospel did not come to my hand as a whole
until this book was complete.

[3] It is not too much to say that in Reitzenstein's later work much of ancient
literature became one vast jig-saw puzzle, to be dissected and reassembled by methods
which often had too little regard for the maxim that a chain is as strong as its weakest
link.

which evidences of later date have already been eliminated.[1] The recon-struction is too speculative to provide any trustworthy source of historical information.

Since we have embarked on this discussion because of its bearing on the study of the Fourth Gospel, we must take account of the special form of the theory put forth by Rudolf Bultmann in the article referred to above. According to Bultmann, the Fourth Gospel represents a Christian revision of the myth current in the Baptist (Nazoraean or Mandaean) sect, in which the leading ideas are those of the originally Iranian myth in its Mandaean form, and the claim is made for Jesus that He is in fact the divine Messenger who descends and ascends again for the salvation of men. The type of Christian thought which it represents, being very close to that of Mandaism, and of its founder John the Baptist, is actually more primitive than that represented by the Synoptic Gospels, which are the product of Jewish reaction.

In support of his thesis Bultmann adduces: (i) the polemic against the claims of John the Baptist, which have been regarded by many critics as directed against a Baptist sect; (ii) certain similarities of language and imagery between the Fourth Gospel and the Mandaean literature; and (iii) a whole series of statements about Jesus in the Fourth Gospel which can be paralleled with similar statements about the divine figures of Mandaism.

Bultmann sets out a formidable list of parallels, supported by similar parallels from such documents as the Odes of Solomon, the Acts of John, and the Acts of Thomas, including the Hymn of the Soul. The parallels are often striking. It cannot however be said that a simple comparison suggests that in all cases the Mandaean member of the parallel is prior to the Johannine. 'The Mandaean literature', says Bultmann, 'is especially instructive inasmuch as in it ideas, which in the Gospel according to John come to expression in brief turns of phrase and technical expressions, are formulated into more or less picturesque, or at least explicit scenes.' He implies that where this is the case, priority must be assigned to the Mandaean form. I cannot accept this as a sound critical principle. When, for example, he adduces the conversations between the Great Life and Manda d'Hayye (or Hibil), which precede the mission of the latter into

---

[1] As Lidzbarski observes, no document written in or near the first century could have called Pilate 'king of the world'. Reitzenstein naturally does not suppose the phrase to have occurred in the *Urschrift*, but there is no reason, other than its inacceptability in a first-century document, for excising it.

the lower world, and suggests that the simple allusions in the Fourth Gospel to the sending of the Son by the Father presuppose the elaborate mythical apparatus of the Mandaean passages, he is arguing against the natural presumption in such a case. Again, the ideas of the Good Shepherd and of the Vine are worked out in elaborate detail in the Book of John, whereas in the Fourth Gospel they are briefly touched upon. But I cannot believe that any unprejudiced reader of the several passages would suppose for a moment that the shorter form is dependent on the longer. The force of the parallels depends on the prior establishment of a presumption that the Mandaean corpus contains writings which are likely to have been both earlier than the Fourth Gospel and known to its author. If the Mandaeans were indeed founded by John the Baptist, then this presumption is at least not wildly improbable.

Now if John the Baptist stood in this intimate relation to the Mandaean religion, and if any part of its literature belongs to his time, we should expect some independent historical data about him to be preserved in it. But as a matter of fact, the Mandaean literature shows acquaintance only with the legends of his birth which are preserved in the Gospel according to Luke, with the fact that he practised baptism, and with the fact that Jesus was baptized by him. Apart from these elements in the story, all of which are attested by the New Testament, there is no single fact recorded in the Mandaean writings which can be supposed to make any contribution to our knowledge of the 'John of history'. Of the stories in the Book of John Lidzbarski says: 'That no new *historical* material was to be expected in them, one might have said beforehand, but even the assumption that ancient *legendary* formations might be found in them was doomed to disappointment' (*Johannesbuch*, p. 70). They are all fantasy and fairy-tale. This argument might not touch Bultmann deeply, since he thinks the gospels themselves contain very little trustworthy information about Jesus; but he would admit that the passion-narrative of the gospels has an historical core (even though there may be much legendary embellishment); whereas the Mandaeans do not even know how their supposed founder met his death, a point on which we are informed by Josephus as well as by the gospels.

Further, the beliefs about John against which the polemic of the Fourth Gospel seems to be directed are not those of the Mandaeans. 'He was not the Light, but was sent to bear witness about the Light.' There is nothing in the Mandaean literature to show that John was identified with 'the Light', or 'the High King of Light'. Nor does it represent John as

'Messiah'. The true rival of the false Messiah Jesus is not John but Enosh-Uthra.

Again, Mandaean baptism is a frequently repeated rite. The baptism of John, according to the New Testament, is a single eschatological sacrament, securing entrance into the redeemed community at the approaching judgment. If it be replied that this is a Christian perversion, then we must observe that the only evidence, outside Mandaism, which is alleged to prove the existence of a distinct sect of followers of John the Baptist, Acts xviii. 24–xix. 7, has no suggestion that Apollos or the twelve men of Ephesus gave up repeated baptisms in favour of the one baptism. Yet according to the theory we are discussing this was a main point of divergence between the two kindred sects. In the supposed situation even a Christian record could hardly avoid taking account of it.

In view of these considerations, the connection between John and the Mandaeans begins to wear thin. There is indeed no need to have recourse to any individual founder to explain the Mandaean baptismal rite. Frequent ritual lustrations were common in most ancient religions, including Judaism. The distinctive thing about Christian baptism, as to all appearance about its prototype, Johannine baptism, is its solitariness as a rite of initiation performed once for all.

It is a curious fact that the name of the Baptist in the Mandaean scriptures often has the Arabic form Jahja, under which John the Baptist appears in the Koran. Although Lidzbarski seeks to minimize the significance of this fact, the natural inference is that many of the allusions to John, particularly in the Book of John,[1] belong to the Islamic period. This lends colour to the view that the prominence of John the Baptist is a late development. The Moslem conquerors regarded as pagans all who could not produce a sacred book and a prophet. The Jews could appeal to Moses and the Old Testament, the Christians to Jesus and the Old and New Testaments. The Mandaeans compiled their canon, and set forth John the Baptist, who is mentioned with honour in the Koran, as their founder.[2] The information given about John, as we have seen,

[1] In this book the preaching of the Baptist is regularly introduced with the formula, 'Jahja preached at night, Johana in the evenings of the night.'

[2] Pallis, *Mandaean Studies*, p. 161, finds a similar ground for the Mandaean use of the name נצוריא. The form *an-Naṣara* is regularly used of Christians in the Koran. The Mandaeans, we know from G.R. 1. 199, were ready under pressure to profess themselves Christians, with mental reservations. To secure status under Moslem rule they adopted the name by which Christians were known to the conquerors. This explanation appears more probable than that offered by Reitzenstein and Bultmann.

apart from that which is mere fantasy or fairy-tale, might well have been derived from the New Testament. Even the account of the interview of John with Manda d'Hayye has traits which connect it with the Matthaean account of the conversation between Jesus and John before His baptism. Whether or not John figured at all in Mandaean tradition before the Islamic period, it seems clear that his *prominence* in the literature belongs to that period. It is chiefly in the Book of John that he takes his place as prophet and teacher of the Mandaeans, and it is in the Book of John that the Arabic form Jahja constantly occurs along with Johana. In the Ginza there are few allusions to him. The *locus classicus* is the passage already quoted, G.R. II. I. 151 sq. p. 57. In the parallel passage of G.R. I (200–201) John is not mentioned. He was therefore probably not mentioned in the older source which must underlie both passages. As we have noted, the material common to both recensions makes Enosh-Uthra, not John, the true counterpart and adversary of Jesus, the false Messiah.

This brings us back to the question we have not yet answered: Who is Enosh-Uthra? He appears in the narrative as a *Doppelgänger* of Jesus, only that Jesus comes in wrath, clothed in fire, whereas Enosh-Uthra appears clothed with clouds and is mild and beneficent. Suppose we ask first, Who is the Mandaean Jesus? The answer is given in a phrase of the Ginza which is no doubt an addition to the source, since it does not appear in both parallel forms of the document, but nevertheless correctly represents its intention: *m'shiha rumayya*, 'the Roman (i.e. Byzantine) Christ'.[1] The Jesus of the Ginza is the Christ of the Orthodox Church[2] which persecuted the Mandaeans. 'When he oppresses you say to him, "We belong to thee"; but confess him not in your hearts, neither fall away from your Lord the high King of Light.' This passage occurs in both versions of the document.[3] It belongs therefore to the source, which must accordingly belong to a period when the Christian Church had the upper hand, and tried to compel the Mandaeans to conform. They disavow the Christ represented by the persecuting Church, and set up against Him the true divine Messenger Enosh-Uthra.

---

[1] G.R. II. I. 140. Lidzbarski suggests a *Wortspiel*: רומיא = רַמְיָא ('the deceiver').

[2] This is not to say that the account given of Jesus comes from orthodox sources. That He is the son of Ruha d'Ḳudsha is an idea which is attested in the Gospel according to the Hebrews, and could have maintained itself only among unorthodox and Semitic-speaking Christians. The identification of Christ with Hermes, on the other hand, is attested by the Naassene document in Hippolytus, and must come from some syncretistic Gnostic Sect. But the fiery Jesus is intended for the Christ worshipped by the Orthodox Church.   [3] G.R. I. 199, II. I. 132.

Burkitt[1] seems right in deriving this figure from the Christ of Christian Gnosticism, or more particularly of the Marcionites. The Marcionite Christ is no man who dies, but a divine being clothed in the semblance of a man, and so is Enosh-Uthra. He is good and merciful, the opponent of the just but cruel God of the Old Testament and the Orthodox Church, and similarly Enosh-Uthra is merciful and the opponent of the wrathful Byzantine Christ. Now Theodore bar Khonai, the first writer to mention the Mandaeans, says that their founder, Ado, had learnt his doctrine from the Marcionites. Theodore would seem, after all, to be right at least so far, that behind the figure of Enosh-Uthra is the figure of Jesus as He was presented by the Marcionites in opposition to the Orthodox. Marcionism, however, cannot be the sole ancestor of Mandaism, since the latter differs radically from it (a) in the repudiation of celibacy, and (b) in the acceptance of elements from the Old Testament. It is true that for the Mandaeans the Adonai of the Old Testament is an evil power, but Abel, Seth and Enosh are among the powers of light. There are therefore other factors than Marcionism that went to the making of the Mandaean system—as indeed Theodore bar Khonai says there were.

If it be granted that Enosh-Uthra, in his appearance as the opponent of the wrathful Messiah, is a figure derived from heretical Christian sources, important consequences follow for the valuation of the Mandaean documents in relation to Christian origins. For Reitzenstein and Bultmann, the kernel of Mandaism is the doctrine of the divine Messenger, identical with the divine champion who overcame the demons, and with the primeval Man whose image or offspring is the human soul. This Messenger, as Enosh-Uthra, comes to men to redeem them from the evil world, and to enable the soul to win through to the world of light. This doctrine is supposed to lie behind the Johannine doctrine of the Son of Man, or even, as Reitzenstein would have it, to have been in the mind of Jesus Himself.

The myth of the primeval Man does not, in fact, appear to play any determinative part in the Mandaean system, though the Adakas or 'hidden Adam' of the creation-story, who is also in some passages Manda d'Hayye, goes back to that myth in some form. But it does not appear that Enosh is identified with him, even though the name Enosh means 'man'.[2] Since

---

[1] *J.T.S.* xxix (1928); cf. *Church and Gnosis*, ch. iv.

[2] The meaning of the name is exploited by Philo (*De Abr.* 7–12, etc.), but it would appear that the Mandaeans were as ignorant of its meaning, or as indifferent to it, as they were to the meaning of Manda d'Hayye (see p. 117). No doubt it is

Enosh comes 'clothed with water-clouds', it would be plausible to associate him with the figure who 'comes with the clouds of heaven' in Dan. vii. 13, if there were any evidence that the title 'Man' (בר־נשא) or its equivalent was current for a messianic figure before Christianity. But such evidence is lacking. In any case the Danielic figure is only 'like a man' (כבר־אנש). 'The Son of Man coming with the clouds' is an individual figure in the gospels, but in no document which is certainly earlier.[1] The close resemblance which the role of Enosh bears to that of Jesus in the gospels is most readily explained by derivation from Christian sources.

But if that is so, then the only appearance of an historical redeemer in the Mandaean literature is due to Christian influence. The divine messengers, Manda d'Hayye, Hibil, or elsewhere the three Uthras, Hibil, Shitil and Enosh, are concerned with the pre-mundane victory over demons, and they appear on earth to give the primitive revelation to Adam (or to Noah); but they do not appear again until the end of the world. There is no unequivocal appearance of the divine Messenger in history[2] apart from the appearance of Enosh-Uthra in the days of 'Palṭus the king of the world', which is a mere doublet of the Christian Gospel. Mandaism offers no real exception to the dictum of Edwyn Bevan that the idea of a personal redeemer of mankind is always the result of Christian influence.[3]

The theses therefore of Reitzenstein, that the common document lying behind the two parallel accounts of world history in G.R. I and II. I is a work of the first century, and that Mandaism represents the teaching of a pre-Christian Jewish sect founded by John the Baptist, from which Christianity emerged, fail to establish themselves in face of the inherent improbability that such a sect and its literature should have had a con-

---

possible that the choice of Enosh for this role goes back to a *milieu* in which a sense for the Hebrew meaning of the term was still alive; but for the Mandaeans the name is simply one of the trio Hibil, Shitil and Enosh.

[1] The Similitudes of Enoch are invoked; but for doubts regarding the authenticity, date and meaning of the so-called 'Son of Man' passages in Enoch, see pp. 241–2. In any case, the role of the Enochic 'Son of Man' has no close resemblance to that of Enosh in the Ginza. Still less likeness has the latter to the role of the *Urmensch* in any documents of relevant date. If Enosh-Uthra has any connection with pre-Christian ideas about a quasi-messianic figure called 'Man', it is likely to be *via* the Christian tradition.

[2] There are indeed passages where an Uthra is said to have delivered instructions to the Elect, but these are repetitions either of the primitive revelation or of the teaching of Enosh-Uthra.

[3] See *Hellenism and Christianity*, pp. 100–8.

tinuous existence from the first century to the eighth without attracting the attention of any extant writer during that long period.[1]

The other part of the theory however still remains open to investigation, viz. that the kernel of Mandaism is an ancient, pre-Christian mystery and myth of Iranian origin. Reitzenstein has sought to prove this in his book *Das iranische Erlösungsmysterium*. In this book he brings Mandaean material into comparison with a vast selection of Christian, Gnostic, Hellenistic and Zoroastrian texts, showing persuasively, if not always to complete conviction, how certain regulative ideas run through them all. The difficulty is to establish the date at which such ideas first appear in the particular combinations which are essential to a reconstruction of the myth and mystery. Too often the documents cited are of quite uncertain date, and we wander in a world almost as timeless as the world of the myth itself. When some more precise chronology is possible, it always, or almost always, turns out either that the document in question belongs to the fourth century or later, or that it belongs to an environment in which the influence of Christian or at least of Jewish thought is probable, so that it is hazardous to use the document to establish a pre-Christian, non-Jewish, mystery. While many of the ideas, and of the mythological conceptions employed, are of great antiquity, the combination of them into a myth of redemption such as Reitzenstein postulates does not seem to be proved for the period before the growth of the great Gnostic systems.

A good deal of Reitzenstein's line of argument seems to presuppose a maxim which he does not enunciate, but which would run as follows: Given two statements of an idea, the one in mythological terms, the other in philosophical, the former must be taken to be the earlier. Such a principle cannot be maintained. No doubt philosophers rationalized myths; but they also invented myths to teach their philosophy, as we know from Plato. Sometimes it may happen that an ancient myth is rationalized, and then in course of time the rationalization produces a fresh myth. For one type of mind truth must be expressed in rational, logical form; another type wants 'truth embodied in a tale': the one type will always rationalize poetry and mythology, the other type will always try to turn philosophy into a story. Only the highest type of mind, to which Plato

[1] What were Irenaeus and Hippolytus about, that they overlooked so important a rival of orthodox Christianity, when they cast their nets so widely? That they have mentioned a few doctrines and rites which bear some resemblance to Mandaism goes for little in a world pullulant with queer religions.

belongs, can hold together the rational and the imaginative in organic unity. At a lower level the pendulum swings.

Now let us look steadily at the Mandaean myth. Here is a god called Life, with his vicegerent, called Knowledge. Knowledge descends, breaks the bonds of fate, and makes a way for man to ascend into Life. The Mandaeans do not betray any consciousness that they are stating such a highly philosophical doctrine as that by knowledge and by knowledge alone man becomes a free agent and attains true life,[1] as is shown by the fact that they readily substitute for Life, the High King of Light, and for Knowledge, Glorious Abel (Hibil-Ziwa)! Reitzenstein scouts the idea that behind the mythology of Mandaism lies Greek philosophical thought. The crude myth must be the earlier. Thus the *Hermetica*, which do state a philosophical doctrine of the kind I have briefly summarized here, must be based on the Mandaean myth. But it is surely at least as likely that an enlightened doctrine of the Hermetic type has been debased, through centuries during which influences from the East have encroached upon Greek civilization, into this fantastic and often puerile story-telling.

Mandaism is best understood as fundamentally a Gnostic system, comparable though not identical with various Gnostic systems known to us, which combine elements drawn in varying degrees from Iranian, Babylonian, Egyptian, Jewish and Christian sources, with Greek philosophy somewhere in the background (in Mandaism very much in the background).[2] Much of it might be called Judaeo-Gnostic in the sense in which the systems of Simon and Justin might be so described (see pp. 99, 104–5). The influence of the Old Testament is pervasive. Such influence is rarely absent from Gnostic systems, but there seems here more of it than such systems usually show. Moreover the ethical portions of the literature often show close resemblance to Jewish *paraenesis* like that of the Testaments of the XII Patriarchs. The Christian element, as we have seen, appears to have come through heretical channels. But the sect remained exposed to Christian influence for a long time, as is shown

[1] As Pallis observes (*op. cit.* p. 160), the term מאדיתא, γνῶσις, is never used by the Mandaeans 'to express their sensations when the soul becomes united with the Realm of Light'. 'Knowledge' has become the mythical figure Manda d'Hayye, whose name is not good Mandaean, but survives as a fixed form whose source must be sought elsewhere.

[2] Such, broadly, is the conclusion of Pallis, in *Mandaean Studies*, where he attempts a careful analysis of the different strains. I differ from him in the estimate of Jewish influence, which he thinks was not direct, but mediated through Christianity, or even through Islam.

by references to persecution by Christian powers and to the danger of Christian proselytism, and by the fervid denunciations of Christian monachism.

It seems that we must conclude that the Mandaean literature has not that direct and outstanding importance for the study of the Fourth Gospel which has been attributed to it by Lidzbarski, Reitzenstein and Bultmann, since it is hazardous, in the presence of obvious and pervasive Christian influence, to use any part of it as direct evidence for a pre-Christian cult or mythology. It now becomes an addition to the fairly voluminous literature of Gnosticism; a valuable addition, since it is extant as a complete canon, while most of our Gnostic literature is more or less fragmentary; yet an addition, for our purposes, of limited value, because of the late date to which most of it must be attributed, coming down well into the Islamic period. Indeed it may well be that the chief value of this literature for the history of religion will prove to lie in the light it throws on religious conditions in the lands of the Euphrates at the time of the coming of Islam. For our purpose, however, it supplements the Greek and Coptic Gnostic literature with abundant material which may be used, with due caution, to illustrate the endless variations played upon the theme of the salvation of the soul through *gnosis*, and so indirectly to illustrate, by comparison and contrast, the ideas which lie behind the Fourth Gospel. But alleged parallels drawn from this medieval body of literature have no value for the study of the Fourth Gospel unless they can be supported by earlier evidence.[1]

[1] Loisy's *Le Mandéisme et les Origines Chrétiennes* (1934), which builds very largely on the liturgical texts, arrives at a similar conclusion.

PART II
LEADING IDEAS

1. SYMBOLISM

In Part I, we have surveyed the background of Johannine thought. The survey was of course far from exhaustive, but the results may be summarized as follows. While the evangelist stands within the general environment of primitive Christianity, and may have been in some measure influenced by Paul, he also shows affinities with certain tendencies in non-Christian thought. He is well aware of the teaching of Rabbinic Judaism, but only partly sympathetic to it. He is more sympathetically in touch with Hellenistic Judaism as represented by Philo. Like Philo himself, he is in contact with the higher pagan thought of the time, as represented to us by the Hermetic literature. 'Gnosticism' has in part the same roots as Johannine Christianity, and serves in some measure to illustrate Johannine conceptions, but more by contrast than by affinity. Mandaism turns out to be too late in date to be of any direct importance for our investigation, though in so far as it retains elements of earlier Gnosticism it may afford some illustrative parallels. Rabbinic Judaism, Philo and the *Hermetica* remain our most direct sources for the background of thought, and in each case the distinctive character of Johannine Christianity is brought out by observing the transformation it wrought in ideas which it holds in common with other forms of religion.

Part II will deal with the leading religious concepts employed in the Fourth Gospel, and will aim at defining their meaning in the context already indicated, which is assumed to be that of the readers to whom the work was originally addressed. But before beginning to deal with them it seems necessary to give some attention to the method adopted by the evangelist in presenting his teaching. The work lies before us in the form of a narrative with a brief philosophical or theological introduction. The latter part of the work, chs. xiii–xxi (or, if we isolate the appendix, xiii–xx), contains a full and detailed account of the trial, death and resurrection of Jesus Christ, preceded by a long and complex series of discourses set in the context of the Last Supper. All this corresponds to the Passion-narrative of the other gospels. In the former part of the work, chs. i–xii (or, if we set apart the proem, ii–xii), which corresponds to the account of the Ministry of Jesus in the other gospels, the narrative serves mainly as framework for a series of discourses (dialogues and monologues), all related to the dominant theme of eternal life. These discourses are made to hang upon a limited number of short narrative sections, presenting select episodes from the life of Jesus. In some cases at least, as in those of the Feeding of the Multitude, the Healing at Siloam, and the Raising of Lazarus, the contiguous discourses are so related to the narratives as to indicate that these are to be understood symbolically. It is reasonable to suppose that even where such direct indication is not given, the reader is intended to seek a similar symbolical interpretation. This makes it necessary to consider at the outset of our present task the nature of the symbolism of the Fourth Gospel.

The explicit use of symbolism is an obvious characteristic of this gospel—living water, bread of life, the true vine, the good shepherd, etc. It has long been recognized that the employment of such symbols is different from the use of parables in the Synoptic Gospels. The parable is a picture or a story of real life, presenting a situation which the hearers will recognize. Their judgment is invited upon the situation, either by implication or explicitly. The judgment so elicited is intended to be applied to a different situation which is present to the mind of the teller and the hearer of the parable. It is essential that the characters in the parable should be recognized as behaving as such characters might behave in real life, and the details of the parable are such as to create dramatic verisimilitude, and rarely have any independent significance. In general judgment is invited upon some single point, for the sake of which the parable is told. The further application of the judgment elicited is expected to be possible for the hearers, either from their knowledge of the context in the speaker's mind, or from their knowledge of the circumstances in which the question at issue arose, or from their general religious background. It is not always obvious to us, because we do not always possess the knowledge presupposed in the hearers, and the context and application which the evangelists have furnished are probably not always true to the original situation, since parables lend themselves to fresh applications in changed circumstances. But a study of the parables as a whole will justify the conclusion that no elaborate 'interpretation' of the details of a parable was necessary in order that it should serve its purpose with the original hearers.[1]

The difference between the Synoptic parables and the so-called allegories of the Fourth Gospel may be illustrated by a comparison of the parable of the Lost Sheep with the passage about the Good Shepherd in John x. 1–18. The parable draws a picture which exhibits the concern of a shepherd

[1] See my book *Parables of the Kingdom* (1935), ch. 1.

SYMBOLISM

over the loss of a single sheep out of a flock of one hundred. The details, which differ a little in Matthew (xviii. 12–14) and Luke (xv. 4–7), have clearly no independent significance. The judgment of the audience is invited: 'what do you think? if a man has a hundred sheep....' The answer is obvious: if a shepherd is fit to be a shepherd, that must be his attitude. The application to the situation in the ministry of Jesus is evident, in view of a whole body of narratives and sayings which indicate His concern about the 'lost sheep of the house of Israel' and the criticism it aroused. As a basis for any wider application, all we need to know is, 'The Lord is my shepherd.'

Now consider the Johannine 'allegory' of the Good Shepherd. It is at once obvious that there is not the same dramatic unity of time and place; and that the details of the picture have separate significance. The shepherd enters by the door (whereas robbers climb over the wall) and is admitted by the door-keeper; his sheep recognize his voice and follow where he leads (whereas they do not recognize the voice of a stranger or follow him); the good shepherd lays down his life for the sheep (whereas the hireling flees before the wolf). Long before the allegory is at an end, the figure of the shepherd is fused with that of Jesus Himself. It is not any earthly shepherd who came that the sheep might have life in abundance, nor is it any earthly shepherd who has other sheep, not of this fold, whom he must bring together. The shepherd in fact is all through a thin disguise for Jesus Himself, and the details are obviously selected, because they aptly symbolize aspects of His work. 'I am the good shepherd: I know my own and my own know me, as the Father knows Me and I know the Father; and I lay down my life for the sheep.' The pastoral imagery is only a fluctuating series of symbols for various aspects of the work of Christ. For this reason attention can be temporarily diverted from the shepherd who enters by the gate to the gate itself. No shepherd is also a gate (*pace* those ingenious commentators who suggest that the shepherd sleeps across the opening of the fold, making a gate of his body). But Jesus is both shepherd and gate, the giver of life and the way into life (cf. xiv. 6). Christ is the real subject of all the statements made, and shepherd and gate are cryptograms. For the interpretation of the symbolism we need to recall that in the Old Testament and the apocalyptic literature the people of God are represented as the flock of Jehovah, and Jehovah Himself or His representatives (Moses, David, etc.) as shepherds, and that evil rulers of Israel are denounced as unworthy shepherds (the hirelings of our passage); and it is even worth while

135

remembering that many of the first readers of the gospel would be aware that deities were not infrequently described in cult-language as shepherds, and that in Philo (and no doubt in other writings of Hellenistic Judaism) the Logos is the shepherd of the κόσμος and of the individual soul.

The same character of Johannine symbolism may be traced in the allegory of the vine, xv. 1 sqq. Certain operations belonging to viticulture are mentioned: the γεωργός tends the vine, cuts away barren branches, which are collected and burnt, and 'cleanses' other branches which, remaining as parts of the vine, bear fruit. But from the beginning and all through it is made clear that these are metaphors: Christ is the vine, His Father the γεωργός, His disciples the branches. This metaphorical application has determined the language used. Καθαίρειν is used of pruning in Philo, *De Somn.* II. 64, but it does not appear to have been common in the vocabulary of viticulture.[1] We may fairly suspect that the verb is used because it is applicable to that which Christ does for His disciples—ὑμεῖς καθαροί ἐστε διὰ τὸν λόγον ὃν λελάληκα ὑμῖν. Again, to speak of branches 'abiding in the vine' is surely no natural mode of expression: it is evidently chosen because it is the evangelist's characteristic way of describing the relation of the believer to Christ. The language indeed changes to and fro between the literal and the metaphorical in a way which would be bewildering, if the reader were not conscious all through that all the statements made really refer to Christ and His disciples, under the symbol of a vine and its branches, rather than to any earthly vine.

For the explication of the symbolism in this case we may turn first to the Old Testament, where the vine, or vineyard, is from Is. v. 1–7 a standing symbol of the people of God, planted, i.e. constituted as a nation, by Jehovah. In Ps. lxxix (lxxx). 9–15 the history of Israel from the Exodus is told in terms of the clearing of a vineyard, the import of a vine from abroad, its successful transplanting, and its prosperous growth; and then, with increasing neglect, the damage it suffers from trespassers and marauding animals. In Jer. ii. 21 Jehovah complains that although He planted a vine of fine quality, it has degenerated: ἐφύτευσά σε ἄμπελον καρποφόρον πᾶσαν ἀληθινήν, and this is echoed in the ἄμπελος ἀληθινή of John xv. 1.

[1] No example of καθαίρειν = to prune (apart from John xv. 2) is given in L.S. and M.M. I have gone through a number of vineyard leases and the like among the Oxyrhynchus papyri, which enter into elaborate detail about the various operations, without coming upon καθαίρειν. I do not think it was a word which a vinegrower would naturally have used.

A Hellenistic reader of the gospel would find the figure of God as γεωργός familiar enough. Numenius, the second-century philosopher who combined Platonism with elements of a revived Pythagoreanism, says, 'As is the relation of the γεωργός to the planter, so is the relation of the First God to the Demiurge. For the former sows the seed of ψυχή as a whole into the objects to which it is allotted, while the latter, as lawgiver, plants, distributes and transplants the seedlings that spring from it into us individually', ὥσπερ πάλιν λόγος ἐστι γεωργῷ πρὸς τὸν φυτεύοντα ἀναφερόμενος, τὸν αὐτὸν λόγον μάλιστα ἔχει ὁ πρῶτος θεὸς πρὸς τὸν δημιουργόν. ὁ μὲν γὰρ σπέρμα πάσης ψυχῆς σπείρει εἰς τὰ μεταλαγχάνοντα αὐτοῦ χρήματα σύμπαντα, ὁ νομοθέτης δὲ φυτεύει καὶ διανέμει καὶ μεταφυτεύει εἰς ἡμᾶς αὐτοὺς τὰ ἐκεῖθεν προκαταβεβλημένα (ap. Eusebius, Praep. Ev. XI. 18. 14). In the Hermetic tractate called Hermes to Asclepius the figure is simpler, inasmuch as no distinction is drawn between the γεωργός and the labourer who does the actual planting: 'Look at the γεωργός sowing into the ground, here wheat, there barley, and there some other seed; see him planting a vine and an apple-tree and other trees. Even so, God sows in heaven immortality, on earth mutability, but everywhere life and movement' (C.H. XIV. 10). In C.H. IX. 6 the κόσμος as ὄργανον τῆς θεοῦ βουλήσεως is ἀγαθὸς ζωῆς γεωργός. Philo uses the figure freely, attaching it to such Old Testament themes as the planting of the Garden of Eden and Noah's viticulture. All this must be taken into account; and of even greater significance is the primitive Christian use of vine-symbolism, of which something must be said presently. The immediate point is that here, even more than in the shepherd 'allegory', we are dealing with a kind of symbolism in which the images or figures employed, although they are taken from workaday experience, derive relatively little of their significance from the part they play in such experience. The symbol is almost absorbed into the thing signified. The meaning of the 'allegory' is only to a slight extent to be understood from a knowledge of what vines are as they grow in any vineyard; it is chiefly to be understood out of a rich background of associations which the vine-symbol had already acquired.

In like manner the images of bread and water retire behind the realities for which they stand, and derive their significance from a background of thought in which they had already served as symbols for religious conceptions. Thus bread, as we have seen, was held to be a symbol for the words of Torah, or for Wisdom. Manna, the bread from heaven, is not only in Jewish Apocalyptic one of the blessings of the messianic age, but in Philo it is a symbol of the Logos. Water, a very old and widespread religious symbol, has a more complicated background. It is a natural symbol for cleansing, and as such appears in the Siloam story (ix. 7) and in that of the Washing of the Feet (xiii. 5–10). In religious thought of the type of the *Hermetica* it has cosmological significance as the prototype of the lower creation: it is the residue of the ὑγρὰ φύσις after fire and πνεῦμα have been refined out of it to make the heavenly sphere. There may be a reference to this side of water-symbolism where water, standing for the lower life, is contrasted with wine, standing for the higher (ii. 1–12), and where baptism with water stands over against baptism with spirit (i. 26, 33). It is noteworthy that in the Gnostic Justin the water in which the ψυχικοί are cleansed is identified with the ὕδωρ τῆς πονηρᾶς κτίσεως, which is the 'waters beneath the firmament' of the Hebrew creation-story, and contrasted with the 'waters above the firmament', the ὕδωρ τοῦ ἀγαθοῦ 3ῆν, in which the πνευματικοί are cleansed. In Jewish thought the water which comes down from above is Torah, Wisdom, or Holy Spirit. Water as a symbol of life is very ancient and widespread, and occurs frequently in the Old Testament. Philo, as we have seen, makes great play with the passage in Jer. ii. 13 where God is described as πηγὴ ὕδατος 3ῶντος. Thus while water as a simple natural phenomenon, especially running water, which was called ὕδωρ 3ῶν, provides in itself a suggestive figure, it is the rich accumulation of symbolical meaning about the figure that gives its main significance to the water-symbol in the gospel.

In considering the background, however, we must give full weight to the use of water and of bread and wine in the primitive Christian sacraments. It was this which made these two symbols inevitable ones for the evangelist, whatever enrichment of content they may have received from diverse sources. He has not chosen to speak directly about the sacraments, but for the Christian reader the allusions are inescapable. Not only the symbolism of water and of bread of life has its roots here, but also the vine-symbolism. In the Synoptic accounts of the Last Supper the wine is called γένημα τῆς ἀμπέλου (Mk. xiv. 25 and parallels), and in the primitive, or very early, liturgy of the *Didache* this is linked up with Old Testament vine-symbolism in the thanksgiving for 'the holy Vine of David Thy servant, which Thou hast revealed to us through Jesus Thy Servant'.[1] The Johannine statements, 'I am the Vine', 'I am the Bread',

[1] See my article 'Eucharistic Symbolism in the Fourth Gospel', in *The Expositor*, 8th series, vol. II (1911), pp. 530–46.

are intended to give expression to the mysterious truth uttered in the words of Institution, 'Hoc est Corpus Meum: Hic est Sanguis Meus.'

We now pass to a further point. Both Vine and Bread have the epithet ἀληθινός, ἀληθινή. In Jer. ii. 21, where the expression ἄμπελος ἀληθινή occurs, the adjective renders the Hebrew אֱמֶת which expresses the idea of 'trustworthiness', and the meaning is, a plant which can be trusted to produce fruit after its kind. But this is one of a number of Hebrew terms which suffered a shift of meaning in passing into Greek.[1] Ἀληθινός properly means 'real', as opposed to that which is either fictitious or a mere copy, as when Aristotle speaks of τὰ ἀληθινά as opposed to τὰ γεγραμμένα, real objects as opposed to their pictured counterparts. Similarly Philo uses the term ἀληθινὸς ἄνθρωπος for the heavenly or archetypal Man, of whom empirical humanity is a copy.

In view of this we may say that when the evangelist speaks of ἄρτος ἀληθινός he means that spiritual or eternal reality which is symbolized by bread, and when he speaks of ἄμπελος ἀληθινή he means the reality which is symbolized by the vine. Similarly he uses the term φῶς ἀληθινόν. We may then recall that Plato, in a passage which had immense influence on religious thought, offered the sun as a symbol or image of the ultimate reality, the Idea of Good, and in his allegory of the Cave suggested that as artificial light is to the light of the sun (which relative to it is αὐτὸ τὸ φῶς), so is the sun itself to the ultimate reality (Rep. 506 D–517 A). It was probably largely through the influence of Plato (with a possible infusion of Zoroastrianism in a high state of dilution) that the conception of God Himself as the archetypal Light won currency in the religious world of Hellenism. Philo himself all but accepts this idea, but draws back, and says that God is πρεσβύτερον παντὸς ἀρχετύπου. The author of the First Epistle of John is willing to say ὁ θεὸς φῶς ἐστιν (i. 5). The evangelist does not use these words, but it is clear that in using the term φῶς he was barely conscious of using a symbol. When he has occasion to refer to empirical light (the light of the sun), he speaks of τὸ φῶς τοῦ κόσμου τούτου (xi. 9).

I do not suggest that the evangelist had direct acquaintance with the Platonic doctrine of Ideas; but there is ample evidence that in thoughtful religious circles at the time, and circles with which Johannine thought has demonstrable affinities, that doctrine had entered into the texture of thought. In any religious philosophy the conception of a κόσμος νοητός in some form or other was assumed—the conception of a world of invisible

[1] See below, pp. 170–8.

realities of which the visible world is a copy. It seems clear that the evangelist assumes a similar philosophy. His φῶς ἀληθινόν is the archetypal light, αὐτὸ τὸ φῶς, of which every visible light in this world is a μίμημα or symbol; his ἄρτος ἀληθινός is the reality which lies within and behind every visible and tangible loaf, in so far as it can properly be so called; and his ἄμπελος ἀληθινή is that which makes a vine a vine, at once its inner essence, and the transcendental real existence which abides while all concrete vines grow and decay.

From this we can understand his characteristic use of symbolism— I mean in particular the way in which the symbol is absorbed into the reality it signifies. Bread, vine, water, light, are not mere illustrations or analogies. A vine, in so far as it is a vine at all, bodies forth the eternal Idea of Vine; except in so far as it does so, it has no significance, indeed properly speaking no existence. Describe the eternal Vine, therefore, the ἄμπελος ἀληθινή, and you are describing every vine, in every respect which constitutes its vine-ness. What makes a shepherd a shepherd? The fact that he realizes in himself the eternal idea of shepherdhood, which is manifested in Christ. He enters by the door, knows his sheep, leads them to pasture, promotes their well-being, and risks his life to save them from danger.

In using the symbol of the shepherd, the evangelist has presented an avowedly fictitious and typical picture. In using the symbols of bread and water he has given, not fictitious pictures, but, ostensibly at least, accounts of historical incidents: the feeding of the multitude and the story of the blind man who was cured by washing in water. It is however evident that in each case the incident, though it is related as an historical occurrence, is no less symbolic, and that the relation of symbol to thing symbolized, where the symbol is an historical event, is not essentially different from the relation where the symbol is invented for the purpose. In a world in which everything derives its reality from the eternal Idea which it embodies or represents, there may be some things and events which more perfectly than others embody or represent the Idea. Such are the events of the life of Jesus. The healing of the blind by Christ *is* the cleansing of the soul from error, and its illumination with the light of life; for the water in which he washes is called Siloam, i.e. Ἀπεσταλμένος, and the One Sent is Christ. The feeding of the multitude with loaves *is* the nurturing of the soul with life eternal, for Christ who gives the bread *is* the Bread of Life. There is the same intrinsic unity of symbol and thing symbolized.

This points to the sense in which we must understand the word σημεῖον. In iv. 48, the evangelist refers in a depreciating way to σημεῖα καὶ τέρατα. The expression is common in the Old Testament, representing אותות וּמוֹפְתִים. מוֹפֵת, τέρας, means something wonderful or marvellous, a 'miracle', in the proper sense. But אות, σημεῖον, does not necessarily connote the miraculous. It is used by itself for a pledge or token, between man and man or between God and man; sometimes for a token of things to come, an omen. It is applied in particular to symbolic acts performed by the prophets. Thus in Ezek. iv. 1–3 the prophet is ordered to make a representation, with a tile and an iron plate, of a besieged city: σημεῖόν ἐστι τοῦτο τοῖς υἱοῖς 'Ισραήλ. The idea is that the act performed by the prophet is a significant act, which corresponds with something divinely ordained to happen in the real world. The prophets appear to have thought of such symbolic acts as more than mere illustrations. They were inspired by God, and in His unchanging purpose formed the necessary prelude to that which He had determined to perform. Ezekiel was caused to effect a sort of proleptic siege of Jerusalem; after that, nothing could prevent the siege from actually coming about. In the symbol was given also the thing symbolized.[1] It is an easy transition from this to the symbolic treatment of the acts of Jesus in the Fourth Gospel. Whether or not Jesus Himself did at times perform symbolic acts like those of the Old Testament prophets (as it is highly probable He did) it is certainly in the manner of the Fourth Evangelist to treat His acts as such. We may find here one source of the Johannine use of the term σημεῖον.

But we have to take account of another use of the term. Philo employs the verb σημαίνειν[2] with especial reference to the symbolical significance which he discovers in various passages of the Old Testament. Thus, commenting on Gen. xvi. 6, ἰδοὺ ἡ παιδίσκη ἐν ταῖς χερσί σου· χρῶ αὐτῇ ὡς ἄν σοι ἀρεστὸν ᾖ, he observes, 'The expression "in thy hands" means "at thy disposal", but it has the following further significance'; τὸ δὲ 'ἐν ταῖς χερσί σου' δηλοῖ μὲν τὸ 'ὑποχείριός ἐστί σοι'· σημαίνει δὲ καὶ τοιοῦτον ἕτερον (De Congressu 155). Δηλοῦν is used for the ordinary, literal meaning of the words, σημαίνειν for the underlying symbolical meaning which Philo finds in them. Accordingly, σημεῖον is used as a synonym for σύμβολον, e.g. Leg. Alleg. I. 58, commenting on Gen. ii. 9, where the trees of Paradise are described as 'fair to look upon and good

---

[1] See Wheeler Robinson, 'Prophetic Symbolism', in Old Testament Essays, ed. D. C. Simpson (1927).

[2] John uses the verb in an almost identical way, xii. 33, xviii. 32 [xxi. 19].

to eat'. 'It says', Philo observes, 'both "fair to look upon", which is the σύμβολον of the contemplative, and "good to eat", which is a σημεῖον of the useful and practical.' Again, in *Quis Rer.* 198, he cites Exod. xxx. 34 'Take unto thee sweet spices, stacte, and onycha, and galbanum; sweet spices with pure frankincense', and comments, 'The words, λάβε σεαυτῷ ἡδύσματα, στακτήν, ὄνυχα, in asyndeton, are σύμβολα of the weighty elements, water and earth. Then he makes a fresh start, with the conjunction, καὶ χαλβάνην ἡδυσμοῦ καὶ λίβανον διαφανῆ, and these again are in themselves σημεῖα of the light elements, air and fire.' The Philonic usage is not precisely that of the Fourth Gospel, which is in some ways nearer to the prophetic usage, but it clearly gives to σημεῖον the sense of 'symbol', and this is very near to the sense of a significant or symbolic act, which I take to be that of the Fourth Gospel.

In the prophets, the σημεῖον, or significant act, is usually a 'sign' of something about to happen in the working-out of God's purpose in history. In Philo, the σημεῖον, or σύμβολον, points to a hidden meaning, on the abstract, intellectual level. The Johannine σημεῖον is nearer to the prophetic; only it refers, in the first instance, to timeless realities signified by the act in time. Yet not wholly so. As we shall see, while in the first intention the feeding of the multitude signifies the timeless truth that Christ, the eternal Logos, gives life to men, and the healing of the blind that He is the Bearer of light, yet in the development of the argument we discover that Christ's work of giving life and light is accomplished, in reality and in actuality, by the historical act of His death and resurrection. In that sense, every σημεῖον in the narrative points forward to the great climax.

Those acts to which the term σημεῖον is explicitly applied in the gospel are in point of fact all such as are also regarded as miraculous; but as we have seen, the miraculous is no part of the original connotation of the word, nor is it in usage always applied to miracles. We can hardly doubt that the evangelist considered such acts as the cleansing of the Temple and the washing of the disciples' feet as σημεῖα. In both these cases he suggests a symbolical interpretation.

I conclude that the events narrated in the Fourth Gospel are intended to be understood as significant events, σημεῖα. In several cases a clue to their significance is supplied in the accompanying discourses. In other cases we are required to interpret them in accordance with the evangelist's known methods and conceptions. To a writer with the philosophical presuppositions of the evangelist there is no reason why a narrative

SYMBOLISM

should not be at the same time factually true and symbolic of a deeper truth, since things and events in this world derive what reality they possess from the eternal Ideas they embody.

Thus the very nature of the symbolism employed by the evangelist reflects his fundamental *Weltanschauung*. He writes in terms of a world in which phenomena—things and events—are a living and moving image of the eternal, and not a veil of illusion to hide it, a world in which the Word is made flesh. In the light of this, we proceed to the attempt to define as precisely as may be the leading ideas of the gospel, having before us the book as a whole, narrative and discourse, bound together by an intricate network of symbolism.

2. ETERNAL LIFE

We may find a natural starting point in the evangelist's own statement of the purpose of his book: he writes, ἵνα πιστεύοντες ζωὴν ἔχητε (xx. 31). This is indeed the purpose for which Christ came into the world: ἐγὼ ἦλθον ἵνα ζωὴν ἔχωσιν (x. 10). 'Life' therefore is a major theme of the book.[1] What then does the evangelist mean by 'life'?

In just short of half of the occurrences of the word ζωή[2] it has the epithet αἰώνιος, without any apparent difference of meaning. The terms ζωή and ζωὴ αἰώνιος belong to the common vocabulary of early Christianity, but except in the Fourth Gospel and I John the simple ζωή is preferred, the form ζωὴ αἰώνιος being absent from Hebrews, the epistles of James, Peter, and Jude, and Revelation. Both the simple and the compound term have Jewish precedent. 'Life' in the Old Testament, where there is generally no idea of immortality, means 'earthly life and well-being'.[3] The term ζωὴ αἰώνιος occurs only in the Greek versions of Dan. xii. 2 (=חַיֵּי עוֹלָם), i.e. in the one Old Testament book which teaches quite unequivocally the doctrine of a future life.

The word עוֹלָם, with αἰών as its equivalent, denotes properly a period of time of which the beginning or the end or both are out of sight, an indefinitely long rather than strictly an infinite period.[4] Ζωὴ αἰώνιος might therefore mean this earthly life indefinitely prolonged. In Enoch x. 10 it is even used for long life, where an ultimate termination is nevertheless contemplated. The wicked are said to hope vainly 3ῆσαι ζωὴν αἰώνιον, καὶ ὅτι 3ήσεται ἕκαστος αὐτῶν ἔτη πεντακόσια. Usually however the term is used for the life after death, conceived as indefinitely, or even infinitely, prolonged. It is so in Dan. l.c., and in Test. XII Patr. Asher. v. 2 (and vi. 6, some MSS.), Ps. Sol. iii. 16, and the corresponding Ethiopic phrase is used in that sense in Enoch xxxvii. 4, xl. 9.

The Targum of Onkelos uses חַיֵּי עָלְמָא in passages where the Old Testament speaks simply of 'life', but where later Judaism found references

---

[1] The term ζωή occurs thirty-six times in the gospel, and to these we must add sixteen occurrences of the verb 3ῆν, and three occurrences of 3ωοποιεῖν.

[2] Seventeen times.

[3] See Dalman, *Worte Jesu*, pp. 127 sqq.

[4] See Kittel, *Theologisches Wörterbuch zum N.T.*, s.v.

to the doctrine of a future life. In the Talmud חַיֵּי עוֹלָם[1] is used in antithesis to חַיֵּי שָׁעָה and here we may fairly find the meaning 'everlasting life'[2] as opposed to 'temporary life'. Under the influence of the developed doctrine the simple 'life' is also used to denote everlasting life beyond the grave. So in Ps. Sol. xiv. 6,[3] II Macc. vii. 9, 14,[4] and occasionally in the Talmud, but almost always with 'death' as an expressed counterpart.

Along with the usage of חַיֵּי עוֹלָם as the correlative of חַיֵּי שָׁעָה arose a different usage which distinguished two עוֹלָמִים, αἰῶνες: 'This Age' and 'The Age to Come'.[5] The doctrine of the two ages is found fully developed in IV Ezra, c. A.D. 100, but there appear to be references to it also in the Book of Enoch (xlviii. 7 'this world of unrighteousness', with lxxi. 15 'the world to come'), and it is implied in the language of Paul, the Synoptic Gospels, and the Epistle to the Hebrews. The doctrine evidently arose in apocalyptic circles, and was only slowly taken up in Rabbinic Judaism. References to it are scarce and not always certain in rabbinic sayings before the destruction of the Temple. But from the end of the first century it seems to have established itself.[6] Dalman thinks that in the Targum of Onkelos and the Targum of the Prophets, חַיֵּי עָלְמָא may be an abbreviation for חַיֵּי עָלְמָא דְּאָתֵי. If so, then ζωὴ αἰώνιος might be used in that sense. It is to be observed that where the doctrine of the two ages is in view, it is made more explicit that the difference between the life of This Age and the life of the Age to Come lies not merely in its infinite duration but also in its quality (IV Ezra vii. 12–13, viii. 52–4).

[1] The earliest example cited by Dalman is attributed to Eliezer ben Hyrcanos c. A.D. 100.

[2] The idea of infinite duration may have developed among the Jews under the influence of the Iranian conception of Zervan Akarana (ὁ ἄπειρος αἰών). See *Theol. Wört.*, l.c.

[3] διὰ τοῦτο ἡ κληρονομία αὐτῶν ᾄδης καὶ σκότος καὶ ἀπώλεια
καὶ οὐχ εὑρεθήσονται ἐν ἡμέρᾳ ἐλέους δικαίων,
οἱ δὲ ὅσιοι κυρίου κληρονομήσουσι ζωὴν ἐν εὐφροσύνη.

[4] II Macc. vii. 9 ὁ δὲ τοῦ κόσμου βασιλεὺς ἀποθανόντας ἡμᾶς ὑπὲρ τῶν αὐτοῦ νόμων εἰς αἰώνιον ἀναβίωσιν ζωῆς ἡμᾶς ἀναστήσει.... 14 σοῦ μὲν γὰρ ἀνάστασις εἰς ζωὴν οὐκ ἔσται.

[5] It is to be noted that in this case αἰών, עוֹלָם, is no longer an infinite period: הָעוֹלָם הַזֶּה lasts from that point in time at which the world was created to that point in time at which it will pass away, to give place to the new heaven and the new earth; then a new 'age' will begin. The Age to Come however is described in terms which place it outside the time series. Still it remains true that 'This Age' at any rate is a limited span of time.

[6] See Dalman, *Worte Jesu*, pp. 121 sqq., *Theol. Wört.*, s.v. αἰών, § 3.

In Jewish usage, then, we may distinguish three forms of expression which might lie behind the Christian use of the terms ζωή and ζωή αἰώνιος: (a) 'life' as contrasted with death; (b) 'life of the age', as contrasted with life of time; and (c) 'life of the Age to Come', as contrasted with the life of This Age. In all three cases there is reference to life beyond the grave.

In pagan religious and philosophical writers ζωή αἰώνιος is not found until long after our period. The simple ζωή is used in the *Hermetica* for the divine life into which man may enter, either here and now or after death. For life after death, however, the usual term is ἀθανασία. Philo agrees in general with pagan usage. He has ζωή αἰώνιος only once (*De Fuga*, 78), ἀλλ᾽ οὐ ζωή μέν ἐστιν αἰώνιος ἡ πρὸς τὸ ὂν καταφυγή, θάνατος δὲ ὁ ἀπὸ τούτου δρασμός;

In its preference for the form ζωή αἰώνιος the Fourth Gospel betrays the Jewish affiliation of its language. In v. 39 we have an explicit reference to Jewish doctrine: ἐραυνᾶτε τὰς γραφάς, ὅτι ἐν αὐταῖς δοκεῖτε ἔχειν ζωὴν αἰώνιον. Cf. Pirqe Aboth. vi. 7 'Great is Torah, for it gives to them that practise it life in this age and in the age to come'; and other passages cited pp. 82–3 above. Thus ζωή αἰώνιος is used in John with reference to the Jewish idea of the life of the Age to Come. Similarly in iv. 36, the harvester gathers a crop εἰς ζωὴν αἰώνιον. Cf. Tos. Peah. 4. 18 p. 24, where the proselyte King Monobazus of Adiabene (c. A.D. 50) is made to say, 'My fathers gathered treasures in This Age (בָּעוֹלָם הַזֶּה): I have gathered treasures לָעוֹלָם הַבָּא, for (or unto) the Age to Come'.[1] The equivalence of לָעוֹלָם הַבָּא and εἰς ζωὴν αἰώνιον is not exact, but the idea is similar. Take again xii. 25 ὁ μισῶν τὴν ψυχὴν αὐτοῦ ἐν τῷ κόσμῳ τούτῳ φυλάξει αὐτὴν εἰς ζωὴν αἰώνιον. This passage is the more significant because it is a Johannine rendering of a saying which is given in the Synoptics in various forms: Mark viii. 35, Matt. x. 39, xvi. 25, Luke ix. 24, xvii. 33. The Fourth Evangelist alone has given it a form which obviously alludes to the Jewish antithesis of the two ages: he who hates his soul בָּעוֹלָם הַזֶּה will keep it לָעוֹלָם הַבָּא, and consequently will possess חַיֵּי הָעוֹלָם הַבָּא. We may take it that in the other two passages where the phrase εἰς ζωὴν αἰώνιον occurs the *prima facie* reference at least is similar. These speak respectively of a fountain of living water ἀλλομένου εἰς ζωὴν αἰώνιον (iv. 14), and of βρῶσις μένουσα εἰς ζωὴν αἰώνιον (vi. 27).

The passages we have considered indicate at least that the evangelist is developing his doctrine of eternal life with reference to the Jewish

[1] Cited with its context in Moore, *Judaism*, II, pp. 91–2.

idea of the life of the Age to Come, qualitatively as well as quantitatively different from this life. There are further passages which use the simple term ζωή in a similar way. Thus v. 28–9 ἔρχεται ὥρα ἐν ᾗ πάντες οἱ ἐν τοῖς μνημείοις...ἐκπορεύσονται, οἱ τὰ ἀγαθὰ ποιήσαντες εἰς ἀνάστασιν ζωῆς, οἱ δὲ τὰ φαῦλα πράξαντες εἰς ἀνάστασιν κρίσεως. The antithesis ζωή–κρίσις corresponds to the language of Tos. Sanh. xiii. 2 p. 434, though the doctrine of that passage is different: 'The children of the wicked among the heathen shall not live (חיין), nor shall they be judged (נדונין).' The doctrine of the Johannine passage is similar to that of Dan. xii. 2 (LXX) πολλοὶ τῶν καθευδόντων ἐν τῷ πλάτει τῆς γῆς ἀναστήσονται, οἱ μὲν εἰς ζωὴν αἰώνιον, οἱ δὲ εἰς ὀνειδισμόν, οἱ δὲ εἰς διασπορὰν καὶ αἰσχύνην αἰώνιον. So closely indeed does it agree with the eschatology of popular Judaism and Christianity, and so different does it appear from the teaching of other passages in the Fourth Gospel which we must presently consider, that many commentators have attributed it to a redactor who did not fully understand the meaning of the evangelist. But as we have seen, there are several other passages in the gospel, not so easily detached or attributed to a redactor, which also imply the idea of ζωὴ αἰώνιος in the sense of a future life, like the Jewish 'Life of the Age to Come'. We must conclude that this is a part at least of what the evangelist meant by 'eternal life'.

There are however other passages which point to a different conception. In the dialogue preceding the Raising of Lazarus the evangelist appears to be explicitly contrasting the popular eschatology of Judaism and primitive Christianity with the doctrine which he wishes to propound. Jesus says to Martha, ἀναστήσεται ὁ ἀδελφός σου. Martha replies, 'I know he will rise again, ἐν τῇ ἀναστάσει ἐν τῇ ἐσχάτῃ ἡμέρᾳ' (xi. 23–4). This appears to be exactly the doctrine of v. 29. But the reply of Jesus does not express simple assent to this doctrine: 'I am the Resurrection and the Life. ὁ πιστεύων εἰς ἐμὲ κἂν ἀποθάνῃ ζήσεται, καὶ πᾶς ὁ ζῶν καὶ πιστεύων εἰς ἐμὲ οὐ μὴ ἀποθάνῃ εἰς τὸν αἰῶνα' (xi. 25–6). For the present we may give our attention to the latter part of this saying, leaving the ἐγώ εἰμι clause for later consideration. The doctrine of eternal life is stated in two forms. First: 'He who believes in me, even if he dies, will come to life' (giving to ζήσεται the ingressive sense which properly belongs to the form).[1] This may be taken as a confirmation of the popular eschatology as enunciated by Martha: faith in Christ gives the assurance that the believer will rise again after death. But the second statement is not the

[1] See Moulton, *Prolegomena*, p. 149.

147

simple equivalent of this: 'Everyone who is alive and has faith in me will never die.'[1] The implication is that the believer is already 'living' in a pregnant sense which excludes the possibility of ceasing to live. In other words, the 'resurrection' of which Jesus has spoken is something which may take place before bodily death, and has for its result the possession of eternal life here and now. It is significant that the narrative of the raising of Lazarus which follows is so constructed as to give a dramatic picture corresponding to the saying in v. 28–9. Lazarus, unlike the dead persons raised to life in the Synoptic Gospels, is already in the grave, and unlike them he comes to life at the bare word of Jesus. It certainly appears as though the evangelist had deliberately dramatized the saying, 'Those who are in the tombs will hear His voice and come forth.' The miracle of Lazarus's bodily resurrection, which anticipates the final resurrection, is a symbol of the real resurrection by which a man passes from a merely physical existence, which is death, into the life which is life indeed, and which is proof against the death of the body.

If this interpretation is on right lines, then v. 28–9 is no longer inconsistent with the verses which precede, 24–5 'He who hears my word and believes on Him who sent me possesses eternal life, and he does not come to judgment, but *has passed* from death into life. I solemnly assure you, the time is coming, *and now is*, when the dead will hear the voice of the Son of Man, and they who hear will come to life.' It is because the word of Christ has this power here and now that we can believe that it will have the same power hereafter. The same combination of ideas recurs in vi. 54 'He who eats my flesh and drinks my blood possesses eternal life, and I will raise him on the last day.' The evangelist agrees with popular Christianity that the believer will enter into eternal life at the general resurrection, but for him this is a truth of less importance than the fact that the believer already enjoys eternal life, and the former is a consequence of the latter.[2] It is in this sense that Christ, as the Bread of God, is described as ζωὴν διδοὺς τῷ κόσμῳ (vi. 33). In such passages we have, formally, a parallel to the pregnant use of 'life' in the sense of 'life of the Age to Come', which as we have seen occurs occasionally in the Talmud, with 'death' as its antithesis. But here the 'death' which is in view is rather the mode of existence of unenlightened, unredeemed

---

[1] οὐ...εἰς τὸν αἰῶνα is a strong expression for 'never'; cf. I Kms. xx. 15, II Kms. xii. 10, Ps. ix. 19, liv (lv). 23, cxxiv (cxxv). 1, etc. '...will not die eternally' is not a legitimate translation. But the expression is perhaps not uninfluenced by the fact that οὐ μὴ ἀποθάνῃ is felt as the equivalent of ζήσεται εἰς τὸν αἰῶνα.

[2] See further pp. 364–6.

humanity. We are reminded of the Greek idea which, beginning perhaps in Orphism, finds its succinct expression in Euripides' oft-quoted lines:[1]

$$\text{τίς οἶδεν εἰ τὸ ζῆν μέν ἐστι κατθανεῖν,}$$
$$\text{τὸ κατθανεῖν δὲ ζῆν;}$$

According to this conception the death of the body alone can release man from death into the life which is life indeed. But as we have seen, some of the Hermetic writings allow the possibility of beginning such a life here and now. For John this present enjoyment of eternal life has become the controlling and all-important conception.

When life is so conceived, the epithet αἰώνιος acquires a fresh shade of meaning. The believer possesses ζωὴ αἰώνιος here and now (iii. 36, v. 24, vi. 47, vi. 54). Inevitably the emphasis now falls on the qualitative rather than the quantitative aspect. As we have seen, Jewish usage has the expression חַיֵּי עוֹלָם, signifying 'everlasting' life, as contrasted with temporary life; and the expression חַיֵּי הָעוֹלָם הַבָּא, which implies a qualitative difference from the life of this age; but when the life of the Age to Come, with its specific quality, is transplanted into the field of present experience (which is never the case in Rabbinic Judaism), then the *chief* thing about it is its difference in quality from merely physical life. Its everlastingness is a function of its divine quality. We may then recall that Plato fixed the meaning of αἰώνιος as signifying 'eternal', in the strict sense of timelessness. This quality belongs to the divine or heavenly παράδειγμα, of which the visible universe is a copy.

The nature of the living being [*sc.* the κόσμος νοητός] was eternal (αἰώνιος). This quality it was impossible to attach to the created universe. So He [*sc.* ὁ γεννήσας πατήρ] thought to make a sort of moving image of eternity (εἰκὼ κινητόν τινα αἰῶνος). In constructing heaven, simultaneously He made an image of eternity which continues always as a unity, an image eternal by numerical process, namely that which we have called time. For days and nights, months and years did not exist before heaven came into existence; but at the moment when it came into existence He devised their origin. All these are parts of time: 'was' and 'will be' are aspects of time, and we are wrong in inadvertently applying them to everlasting essence (ἀΐδιον οὐσίαν). We say, 'it was', 'it is', 'it will be', but 'it is' is the only expression properly applicable to essence, while 'it was' and 'it will be' are properly said of the process which is in time. For these are motions, but that which is for ever immovably the same cannot become either older or younger with time; it cannot be said that it once came into existence, or that it has now come into existence, or that it will

[1] Frag. 639 (Dindorf).

be in future.... These are aspects of time, which imitates eternity and moves in a numerical cycle.[1]

This Platonic concept of eternity is taken over by Philo. The life of God, he says, is not time, but eternity, which is the archetype of time, and in eternity nothing is past or future, but only present (οὐ χρόνος ἀλλὰ τὸ ἀρχέτυπον τοῦ χρόνου καὶ παράδειγμα αἰὼν ὁ βίος ἐστιν αὐτοῦ· ἐν αἰῶνι δὲ οὔτε παρελήλυθεν οὐδὲν οὔτε μέλλει, ἀλλὰ μόνον ὑφέστηκεν, *Quod Deus*, 32). In this sense he comments on Deut. iv. 4 'Ye that did cleave unto the Lord your God are alive all of you this day.' 'To-day (σήμερον) is boundless and inexhaustible eternity (ὁ ἀπέρατος καὶ ἀδιεξίτητος αἰών). For periods of months and years and of time in general are notions of men, who reckon by number; but the true name of eternity is To-day' (*De Fuga*, 57). It is evident that when Philo uses the term ζωὴ αἰώνιος (*ibid.* 78), he means by it a life which, like that of God, is 'eternal' in the sense of 'timeless'. The thought of the Fourth Gospel has, as we have seen, some affinity with that of Philo. It appears that he too means by ζωὴ αἰώνιος 'eternal life' in the Platonic sense, at least so far, that it is a life not measured by months and years, a life which has properly speaking neither past nor future, but is lived in God's eternal To-day. To think of any end to such life would be a contradiction in terms. If therefore it is to be thought of in terms of time, that 'image of eternity' within which human experience lies, it must be thought of as everlasting. It is noteworthy that the evangelist, though he uses twice the expression ζῆν εἰς τὸν αἰῶνα (vi. 51, 58), which can hardly bear any sense other than that of 'live for ever', prefers negative equivalents like οὐ μὴ ἀποθάνῃ εἰς τὸν αἰῶνα (xi. 26), οὐ μὴ ἀπόλωνται εἰς τὸν αἰῶνα (x. 28; cf. also viii. 51–2). It is more philosophical to deny an ending to that which is in its nature eternal, than to affirm perpetuity in time of that which is strictly timeless.

In thus bringing the concept of ζωὴ αἰώνιος into the context of Greek philosophical thought, the evangelist has, however, avoided the abstract and static quality which adheres to Greek or Hellenistic 'mysticism', and this will become clearer as we proceed. Here the affiliation of his thought to Hebraic antecedents is of importance, for the Hebrew conception of life is always one of action, movement and enjoyment. Still more decisively is the idea filled with positive content through its association with a whole range of Christian ideas which we have still to study.[2]

---

[1] *Tim.* 37 D–38 A.

[2] I have developed this theme further in my Ingersoll Lecture (1950), *Eternal Life*; see *New Testament Studies* (Manchester Univ. Press, 1953), pp. 160–173.

3. KNOWLEDGE OF GOD

We seem now to have fixed, provisionally, pending the investigation of related concepts, the sense in which the Fourth Evangelist uses the term ζωή. He means by it life perfect and absolute, timeless in quality and therefore exempt from death. He conceives it as possible for men here and now, but to be realized in its fullness beyond the grave.

Such life for men consists in the knowledge of God: αὕτη ἐστιν ἡ αἰώνιος ζωή, ἵνα γινώσκωσίν σε τὸν μόνον ἀληθινὸν θεόν (xvii. 3). After our study of Philo, the *Hermetica*, and Gnosticism, we need only recall that the evangelist, in enunciating this maxim, is putting his teaching in line with a religious tendency dominant in his time over a wide area. His readers would recognize in him one more teacher who set out to do for his readers what the mysteries offered to do for their initiates, to lead them to such supernatural knowledge as should confer immortality. But this does not in itself decide the question, what this writer meant by γινώσκειν τὸν θεόν. Among the writers to whom I have referred there is no strict uniformity in this matter. For the Hermetists, saving knowledge is a discipline of cosmological, anthropological and theological speculation culminating in the mystical vision, which is at the same time deification. Gnosticism (in the narrower sense) has little mystical quality. For the typical Gnostic, γνῶσις is a quasi-scientific knowledge of that realm of being which transcends all human experience (γνῶσις τῶν ὑπερκοσμίων) communicated in terms of mythology—a knowledge which the soul can put to practical use when it leaves the body. For Philo, γνῶσις is attained through the understanding of the divine revelation given in Holy Scripture; it is on the one hand awareness of pure being, καταφυγὴ πρὸς τὸ ὄν, and on the other hand it has the quality of communion with God through faith and love.

We must therefore ask the question, what does the Fourth Evangelist understand by 'knowing God'?

In the article γινώσκειν in the *Theologisches Wörterbuch zum Neuen Testament*, Rudolf Bultmann has drawn out an elaborate comparison and contrast between the Greek and the Hebrew conceptions of knowledge. I will attempt to paraphrase briefly his conclusions, which seem to me, in their broad lines at least, to be convincing. The Greek conceives the process of knowing as analogous to seeing; that is, he externalizes the object of knowledge, *contemplates* (θεωρεῖ) it from a distance, and endeavours to ascertain its essential qualities, so as to *grasp* or *master* (καταλαβεῖν)[1] its reality (ἀλήθεια). It is the thing in itself, as static, that he seeks to grasp, eliminating so far as may be its movements and changes, as being derogatory to its real, permanent essence. Known and knower, therefore, stand over against one another, and direct communication between the two would be felt as introducing an element of κίνησις or γένεσις, and so as disturbing the pure apprehension of τὸ ὄν. This determines the Greek ideal of the βίος θεωρητικός.

The Hebrew on the other hand conceives knowledge as consisting in *experience* of the object in its relation to the subject. ידע implies an immediate awareness of something as affecting oneself, and as such can be used of experiencing such things as sickness (Is. liii. 3),[2] or the loss of children (Is. xlvii. 8), or divine punishment (Ezek. xxv. 14), or inward quietness (Job xx. 20), where either πάσχειν, or αἰσθάνεσθαι, rather than γινώσκειν, would be the true Greek equivalent. Thus it is the object in action and in its effects, rather than the thing in itself, that is known; and in knowing there is also an activity of the subject in relation to the object. To know anything is to concern oneself about it, to take account of it, the will as well as the intelligence being involved.

Accordingly, for the Greek, to know God means to contemplate the ultimate reality, τὸ ὄντως ὄν, in its changeless essence. For the Hebrew, to know God is to acknowledge Him in His works and to respond to His claims. While for the Greek knowledge of God is the most highly abstract form of pure contemplation, for the Hebrew it is essentially intercourse with God; it is to experience His dealings with men in time, and to hear and obey His commands.

It follows that γινώσκειν, though the nearest term in Greek corresponding to the Hebrew ידע, is not an exact equivalent. When now the Hebrew Scriptures appear in a Greek dress, a complex situation arises. In most places in the LXX ידע is represented by γινώσκειν.[3] This word

---

[1] This would seem to fit ἐπί-στασθαι (an alternative to γινώσκειν in translating ידע: used as a synonym in Acts xix. 15 τὸν μὲν Ἰησοῦν γινώσκω καὶ τὸν Παῦλον ἐπίσταμαι). The Greek knows a thing by '*over*-standing' it, where we '*under*-stand' (? by 'getting to the bottom' of it).

[2] Here, however, the passive participle יְדוּעַ is unexpected. The LXX help themselves out by translating, εἰδὼς φέρειν μαλακίαν.

[3] Where εἰδέναι is used, there seems to be no significant difference. Whatever difference of meaning the two words may originally have shown would seem to have practically disappeared by our period. There are places in the LXX where

cannot reproduce the precise connotation of the Hebrew original, with all its aura of association. To the Greek reader it inevitably suggests the ideas which he is accustomed to attach to it. At the same time, because it is embedded in a context of thought which after all is not Greek but Hebraic, it is likely to suffer some modification or extension of its normal meaning. Bultmann has perhaps not quite sufficiently allowed for these facts in maintaining the sharp distinction between Greek usage and Old Testament usage. So long as we are comparing purely Greek literature with the Hebrew Old Testament, the contrast holds good, but in Hellenistic Judaism, with its Greek Old Testament, the way is open for the development of fresh shades of meaning, neither Hebrew nor yet purely Greek. The term γινώσκειν is enlarging its territory, and the determination of its precise connotation in any particular place is a matter of delicate appreciation of the values of the context. As our exploration of the background of the Fourth Gospel has emphasized the vitality both of Jewish and of Gentile Hellenistic elements in it, this delicate discrimination of varieties of meaning over an expanding field of connotation is called for in Johannine interpretation.

From Greek and Hebrew usage alike Bultmann distinguishes the 'Gnostic'[1] usage of γινώσκειν and γνῶσις. The decisive new factors he finds in the influence of the mysteries with their ecstatic vision, and of magic with its secret formulae of power. The Gnostic form of knowledge is attached to the Greek in so far as it is a form of contemplation, θεωρία. It is ὀπτικὴ ἐπιστήμη, as Philo has it (De Spec. Leg. III. 100). But in its final form it lies beyond even the pure rational intuition of the eternal ideas which for Greek philosophy is the highest type of θεωρία. It is unlike all other knowledge; no longer an achievement of the human intellect, but a gift of God. It makes a man no longer that superior type of humanity, the philosopher, living the βίος θεωρητικός, but a being like God, or even a god himself. This is not properly Greek.

That the mystery-cults played a part in the development of this idea of γνῶσις is probable. But it is to be observed that such information about

γινώσκειν and εἰδέναι (for Hebrew ידע) are variant readings, with no difference of meaning, e.g. Is. lix. 8, Ps. lxxviii (lxxix). 6. So also in John xiv. 7; cf. viii. 19. Sometimes, as observed above, ἐπίστασθαι is used for ידע, with no difference of meaning.

[1] Including under the term 'Gnostic', as is customary with German writers, both the Christian and semi-Christian sects usually so called, and Hellenistic writers such as Philo and the Hermetists who share with them the doctrine of salvation by knowledge.

the mysteries as is available for our purpose belongs to a period when they had already become matter of theological interpretation. Just how the ancient mysteries, which seem to have begun as primitive vegetation or fertility cults, developed into vehicles for exalted religious ideas, we do not know. Was the idea of the knowledge of God in beatific vision, as it is described in the *Hermetica*, for example, a product of the cults, or was it read into them? In short, it is doubtful whether when we have uttered the blessed word 'mystery-religions' we have really come much nearer to accounting for the kind of religion which has its centre in γνῶσις, as mystical communion with God.

For communion it is. The Hermetists say that man is τῷ θεῷ συνουσιαστικός, capable of association (συνουσία) with God (*C.H.* XII. 19). And here the 'Gnostic' idea of γνῶσις departs perhaps more widely from normal Greek usage than the *Wörterbuch* article recognizes. God is now no longer an object of pure contemplation. He is actively in contact with men—τούτῳ γὰρ μόνῳ τῷ ζῴῳ ὁ θεὸς ὁμιλεῖ (*ibid.*). We have therefore moved away from the Greek conception of knowledge in the direction of the Hebrew, from pure contemplation to experience, an experience in which God and man are in active intercourse.

I have illustrated elsewhere[1] the extent to which the *Hermetica* and Hellenistic Judaism speak the same language, and I have shown that this cannot be wholly accounted for by the influence of Gentile thought upon Jewish writers, since the expressions in question can often be traced directly to the Old Testament—the Old Testament, it is true, in its Greek dress. Consider for example the following passages. I Kms. ii. 3 θεὸς γνώσεως κύριος: such an expression would fit properly into a Hermetic context, yet it is a literal translation of אֵל דֵּעוֹת יהוה. Jer. xi. 18 κύριε γνώρισόν μοι καὶ γνώσομαι. The Massoretic text reads, יהוה הוֹדִיעַנִי וָאֵדָעָה. The translators may have had a different text before them. In any case the Hebrew has suggested to them an expression that might well have been used by the Hermetic writer who praises God ὃς γνωσθῆναι βούλεται καὶ γινώσκεται τοῖς ἰδίοις (*C.H.* I. 31).

This thought, that our knowledge of God depends upon His will to communicate with men, is as characteristic of prophetic Judaism as it is of some *Hermetica*. Moreover, in both, our knowledge of God is the correlative of His knowledge of us. God 'knows' Moses, the prophets, Israel, those who fear Him (see below, pp. 160–3). Similarly, a Hermetist writes (*C.H.* x. 15) οὐ γὰρ ἀγνοεῖ τὸν ἄνθρωπον ὁ θεός, ἀλλὰ πάνυ

[1] In *The Bible and the Greeks*, part II.

γνωρίζει καὶ θέλει γνωρίζεσθαι. The formula οἶδά σε, Ἑρμῆ, καὶ σὺ ἐμέ, meets us in a magical papyrus,[1] but it is surely taken from the language of religion—very likely from the liturgy of a Hermetic cult. It has direct analogy with that idea of mutual 'knowledge' between God and man which is part of the Hebrew prophetic consciousness. In Hebrew the meaning was that God acknowledges, takes account of, concerns Himself with His servants; and that they acknowledge, take account of God, in hearing His word and yielding Him obedience. This characteristically Hebrew colouring is partly lost when ידע becomes γινώσκειν, but it is none the less true that γινώσκειν in such passages has a sense which is necessarily different from the purely Hellenic sense of the term, and which passes insensibly into the sense defined as 'Gnostic', which meets us in the *Hermetica*.

The extent to which, on occasion, the LXX hellenizes the thought of its Hebrew original may be illustrated by a very curious instance. In Hos. x. 12 and Jer. iv. 3 we have the expression נִירוּ לָכֶם נִיר, 'till for yourselves the untilled ground'. In Jeremiah it is rendered with reasonable correctness, νεώσατε ἑαυτοῖς νεώματα. The translator of Hosea however seems not to have known the rare root ניר. He has taken the substantive as the well-known word נִיר, a lamp, and has understood the prophet to be saying something about lighting a lamp. Accordingly he has rendered the phrase φωτίσατε ἑαυτοῖς φῶς γνώσεως. Now it is true that the idea of γνῶσις is simply intruded into the passage, and we have a clear example of Hellenistic influence upon a Jewish writer: φῶς γνώσεως is a thoroughly Hellenistic expression.[2] But it is clear that the translator, a Jew steeped in the Old Testament, felt that to 'light the light of knowledge' was a true part of Jewish piety. A consideration of this instance will give point to the conclusion that thinkers in Hellenistic Judaism and in circles represented by the *Hermetica* stood fairly close together in many respects, and in particular in respect of their conception of the knowledge of God. We can then understand the better how easily Philo fits into either of the two traditions. Much, I believe, that is non-Hellenic or Hellenic-with-a-difference in what we may call the higher paganism is actually due to this contact with a Judaism already partly

[1] Kenyon, *Greek Papyri in the British Museum*, I. cxxii. 49.
[2] Cf. *C.H.* x. 21 εἰς δὲ τὴν εὐσεβῆ ψυχὴν ὁ νοῦς ἐμβὰς ὁδηγεῖ αὐτὴν ἐπὶ τὸ τῆς γνώσεως φῶς, Latin *Asclepius*, 41 tua enim gratia tantum sumus cognitionis tuae lumen consecuti (but φῶς is absent from our text of the Greek original, the Λόγος Τέλειος).

hellenized. Consequently, the contrast between 'Old Testament' and 'Gnostic' conceptions of γνῶσις must not be too sharply drawn.

This is of importance for the consideration of the Johannine conception of γνῶσις. Its affinity with Hellenistic ideas as represented by Philo and the *Hermetica* I have already illustrated.[1] I would now call attention to the remarkable resemblance between certain Johannine expressions and the teaching of the Old Testament in its Greek dress.

It will be convenient to start with certain negative expressions. There are two places in the Fourth Gospel where it is said that the world does not 'know' God (or the Logos): xvii. 25 πατὴρ δίκαιε, καὶ ὁ κόσμος σε οὐκ ἔγνω, and i. 10 ἐν τῷ κόσμῳ ἦν καὶ ὁ κόσμος αὐτὸν οὐκ ἔγνω. We may take it that there is no reference here to the doctrine of the θεὸς ἄγνωστος, the God who is essentially unknown, and unknowable; for it is implied that God (through the Logos) is present in the world, to be known, as in *C.H.* v. 2 ἄφθονος γὰρ ὁ κύριος φαίνεται διὰ παντὸς τοῦ κόσμου· νόησιν ἰδεῖν καὶ λαβέσθαι αὐταῖς ταῖς χερσὶν δύνασαι, καὶ τὴν εἰκόνα τοῦ θεοῦ θεάσασθαι. We may compare the denunciation of pagan ἀγνωσία θεοῦ in Wisd. xiii. 1 sqq., where the gravamen of the charge is precisely that God is knowable through the world He has made, but that men are too stupid (μάταιοι φύσει) to perceive Him: ἐκ τῶν ὁρωμένων ἀγαθῶν οὐκ ἴσχυσαν εἰδέναι τὸν ὄντα. Here we are still well on Hellenistic ground. In some passages, however, of the Old Testament the pagan ignorance of God is spoken of in a different context of thought. Thus in Jer. x. 25 the prophet prays: ἔκχεον τὸν θυμόν σου ἐπὶ ἔθνη τὰ μὴ εἰδότα σε καὶ ἐπὶ γενεὰς αἳ τὸ ὄνομά σου οὐκ ἐπεκαλέσαντο. Ignorance of God is failure to acknowledge Him by invocation or worship. Moreover, the pagans' ignorance of God is shown by their persecution of God's people: κατέφαγον τὸν Ἰακὼβ καὶ ἐξανήλωσαν αὐτόν: that is to say, there is a criterion for knowledge of God in ethical behaviour.[2] We have the same parallelism, and the same ethical criterion, in Ps. lxxviii (lxxix). 6. With this in mind, we may observe that there is a parallelism of clauses also in John i. 10 ἐν τῷ κόσμῳ ἦν καὶ ὁ κόσμος αὐτὸν οὐκ ἔγνω· εἰς τὰ ἴδια ἦλθε καὶ οἱ ἴδιοι αὐτὸν οὐ παρέλαβον, where the second clause at least suggests that the will and not only the intelligence is at fault. To

---

[1] See pp. 14–17, 65 above.

[2] A limited ethical criterion, it may be said, since the sinners are denounced not because they did injustice *simpliciter*, but because they did injustice to the Jews. Yet Jeremiah less than most prophets is open to the charge of a narrow nationalism, and injustice and oppression are sinful even when we are ourselves their victims.

receive the Logos, or Word of God, implies (with the Old Testament background in view) something more than mere intellectual apprehension. In fact, the second clause echoes prophetic denunciations of God's own people (whether by οἱ ἴδιοι we understand historic Israel or a wider circle), for unwillingness to know Him; and the first clause may be taken to make a corresponding statement about humanity as a whole. God (through the Logos) is present, and revealed, in the world, but the world has not accepted the offer of 'knowledge' of God. As Paul put it, they did not *choose* to know God (οὐκ ἐδοκίμασαν τὸν θεὸν ἔχειν ἐν ἐπιγνώσει, Rom. i. 28); cf. Jer. ix. 6 οὐκ ἤθελον εἰδέναι με (corresponding to ἐμὲ οὐκ ἔγνωσαν in ix 3).[1] Thus in John i. 10, xvii. 25 there is an interweaving of Hellenistic and Hebraic conceptions. There is the Hebraic conception of a willing acknowledgement of God, and yet the term γινώσκειν unavoidably carries also a non-Hebraic nuance.

The prophetic denunciations of 'ignorance' of God on the part of His own people, to which I have just referred, are far more numerous than those which refer to the invincible ignorance of the pagan world, and more illuminating for our purpose. That God's people *ought* to 'know' Him is always assumed: it is unnatural that they should not know Him; but that they do not in fact know Him is the constant burden of prophecy. The *locus classicus* is Is. i. 3, which runs thus in the LXX: ἔγνω βοῦς τὸν κτησάμενον, καὶ ὄνος τὴν φάτνην τοῦ κυρίου αὐτοῦ· Ἰσραὴλ δέ με οὐκ ἔγνω, καὶ ὁ λαός με οὐ συνῆκεν. The sense of the verb is sufficiently defined by the illustration used. The village herd is driven at sundown into the compound. The intelligent ox and ass recognize their owner and his byre, and obediently take their places. Israel should similarly recognize its Owner, Jehovah, and range itself accordingly: ought to, but does not. The criterion in ethical behaviour emerges in the long and detailed castigation of social evils among the Jewish people which occupies most of the chapter. Similarly in Jer. ix, from which I have already cited ἐμὲ οὐκ ἔγνωσαν... οὐκ ἤθελον εἰδέναι με, 'ignorance' of God is shown in falsehood, treachery, adultery and the like. Again, where Isaiah announces αἰχμάλωτος ὁ λαός μου ἐγενήθη διὰ τὸ μὴ εἰδέναι αὐτοὺς τὸν Κύριον (v.13), he is clinching a denunciation of his fellow-countrymen for greed and rapacity (8–10), drunkenness and luxury (11–12a) and for taking no notice of the 'works of the Lord' (12b). Similarly where individual conduct is in question: in I Kms. ii. 12 the wicked sons of Eli are described as υἱοὶ λοιμοί, οὐκ εἰδότες τὸν κύριον.

[1] Similarly of the ἀσεβεῖς in Job xxxvi. 12: διὰ τὸ μὴ βούλεσθαι αὐτοὺς εἰδέναι τὸν κύριον, καὶ διότι νουθετούμενοι ἀνήκοοι ἦσαν.

These prophetic denunciations are echoed in places in the Fourth Gospel where the Jews are accused of not 'knowing' God. John viii. 54–55 might almost come out of an Old Testament prophetic book: ὑμεῖς λέγετε ὅτι Θεὸς ἡμῶν ἐστιν, καὶ οὐκ ἐγνώκατε αὐτόν. This comes near the end of a long discourse, or sequence of dialogues, comprising almost the whole of chs. vii and viii.[1] There is a good deal about 'knowing' in it, and it will be worth while noting some places, before coming back to viii. 54.

Jesus begins by proclaiming, 'My teaching is not mine; it is the teaching of Him who sent me. If anyone is willing to do His will, γνώσεται περὶ τῆς διδαχῆς' (vii. 16–17). Here we need not seek any special sense for γινώσκειν. It is a matter of understanding, and rightly valuing, that which Jesus teaches.

Next, the Jews raise the question whether Jesus is the Messiah. One difficulty they feel is that, according to what they have been taught, ὁ χριστὸς ὅταν ἔρχηται, οὐδεὶς γινώσκει πόθεν ἐστιν, whereas they know the origin of Jesus (vii. 27). With an irony characteristic of this Gospel, Jesus admits their claim, κἀμὲ οἴδατε καὶ οἴδατε πόθεν εἰμί (vii. 28). This is the language of everyday intercourse among men: Jesus is a visitor from Galilee, well known by sight and repute to the inhabitants of Jerusalem. But in a deeper sense their 'knowledge' is utter ignorance. You say you know πόθεν εἰμί, says Jesus, but in fact I come from One ὃν ὑμεῖς οὐκ οἴδατε. Knowledge of God comes into the question.

For a time the dialogue strays to other themes. Then Jesus offers Himself as the source of living water (vii. 38) and as the light of the world (viii. 12). We already know what these symbols imply. The eternal Logos, the mediator of the life and light which are of the very being of God, is offering Himself as life and light to men. The Jews cavil, and Jesus draws the inference: οὔτε ἐμὲ οἴδατε οὔτε τὸν πατέρα μου (viii. 19). So much for their claim, τοῦτον οἴδαμεν πόθεν ἐστιν. There follows a long and intricate passage introducing a variety of themes, but with the theme of 'knowledge' never far below the surface. Those who have been declared to have no knowledge of God are now said also to be no children of God. They are ἐκ τῶν κάτω, ἐκ τούτου τοῦ κόσμου (viii. 23); they are not ἐκ τοῦ θεοῦ (viii. 47). Their father is not God, but the devil (viii. 38b–44). Here again we have an interweaving of Hebraic and non-Hebraic ideas. It is the assumption of Judaism that God is the Father of His people Israel, and they His sons; they are supposed (at least) to know Him.

[1] Excluding, of course, vii. 53–viii. 11 in the T.R., which is no part of the original text of the Fourth Gospel. See pp. 345–54.

But at the same time it is a commonplace of 'Hellenistic mysticism' that through γνῶσις a man is deified, shares the divine nature, becomes θεὸς θεοῦ παῖς. That the evangelist was not conscious of a duality in his thought we may probably assume. His conception of γνῶσις θεοῦ finds room for both lines of thought in unity.

The Hellenistic line is prominent in a part of the discourse which I have just passed over, where the object of knowledge is ἀλήθεια: those who do not know God do not know ἀλήθεια, and consequently are not free men but slaves (viii. 31–6). The concept of ἀλήθεια we must presently examine.[1] We shall find that it is a term which in this gospel has almost entirely shed the Hebraic associations which lie behind it in the LXX. Knowledge of ἀλήθεια, that is, of things as they really are, or of reality itself, is a characteristically Greek conception, and that such knowledge brings freedom is congenial to Greek thought, both under Stoic influence, and in other circles where γνῶσις was held to be the way to escape the thraldom of εἱμαρμένη. As the discourse proceeds, however, we find that the evidence that the Jews do not know ἀλήθεια, do not know God, and are not His children, is found in their conduct. As the pagans in the time of Jeremiah (and of the author of Ps. lxxviii (lxxix)) showed that they did not 'know' God by persecuting His people, so the Jews of the first century show that they do not know God by persecuting Him whom God has sent: ζητεῖτέ με ἀποκτεῖναι, ἄνθρωπον ὃς τὴν ἀλήθειαν ὑμῖν λελάληκα, ἣν ἤκουσα παρὰ τοῦ θεοῦ . . . ὑμεῖς ποιεῖτε τὰ ἔργα τοῦ πατρὸς ὑμῶν (viii. 40). Their father is the devil, the primeval ἀνθρωποκτόνος (viii. 44). Thus it appears that failure to know God is a failure on the ethical plane. It is wilful rejection of God, and repudiation of His righteousness.

It is with all this complex development of thought behind us that we return to viii. 54–55 λέγετε ὅτι Θεὸς ἡμῶν ἐστιν, καὶ οὐκ ἐγνώκατε αὐτόν. It reiterates the language of the prophets, and, like them, contemplates a knowledge of God which is acknowledgement of His righteous will in action, and yet includes within it the idea of knowledge as pure apprehension of truth, or reality, as liberating power, and as a sharing of the divine nature; an idea which is not properly Hebraic, but belongs rather to the main tendency of Hellenistic religion.

On the basis, then, of negative expressions, characterizing ignorance, we have arrived at a provisional understanding of what 'knowledge' of

[1] See pp. 170–8.

God means. We may now test and expand our conclusions by considering passages which describe such knowledge positively. As I have
already observed, in the Old Testament, in 'Hellenistic mysticism'
and in the Fourth Gospel alike, man's knowledge of God is correlative with, and dependent on, God's 'knowledge' of man. I have
already referred to passages in the Hermetic writings which attest
this idea as current in Hellenistic circles. But it is far more prominent
in the Old Testament, where, in fact, God's knowledge of man is
the fundamental, permanent and certain thing, while man's knowledge
of God is problematical. The reason why it seemed best to start with
negative expressions is that there are so few passages in the Old Testament which categorically assert that man knows God. It is easy, as
we have seen, to produce passages which describe in terms of observed
fact what it means *not* to know God (e.g. Is. i, Jer. ix, cited above); it is
difficult to find passages which similarly describe in terms of observed
fact what it means to know God; for human knowledge of God is
tentative and uncertain.

In a comparison of the Fourth Gospel with the Old Testament, the
position is complicated by the fact that for John knowledge of God is
knowledge of Christ, as for Philo God is known in His Logos; and that
the Jesus of the gospel has a double role: He is, as Logos or Son, the
divine Object of man's knowledge, and at the same time the Subject of
God's knowledge of man; but He is also (as man) both the Object of
God's knowledge of man and the Subject of man's knowledge of God.
He is this (to anticipate the results of a subsequent discussion, see pp. 241–
62) both as human teacher and prophet, and as the representative 'Son
of Man' in whom all mankind is comprehended in its relation to God.
Bearing this in mind, we make a fresh start by considering passages
which bear upon God's 'knowledge' of man.

It is the constant assumption of prophetic teaching that Jehovah
'knows' Israel: e.g. Amos iii. 2 ὑμᾶς ἔγνων ἐκ πασῶν φυλῶν γῆς,
Hos. v. 3 ἐγὼ ἔγνων τὸν Ἐφράιμ καὶ Ἰσραὴλ οὐκ ἄπεστιν ἀπ' ἐμοῦ. The
meaning of the original in each case is fundamentally that which is proper
to the Hebrew ידע. Jehovah 'acknowledges' Israel, i.e. concerns
Himself personally with His people. Although the Greek γνῶναι would
not in itself suggest that meaning, yet the whole context in both prophets
makes it unavoidable. Jehovah 'knows' His people in the sense of calling
and electing them for His purpose, giving to them His revelation, and
judging them for their misdeeds.

Again, Jehovah 'knows' His prophets in a special way. Moses is the man ὃν ἔγνω κύριος αὐτὸν πρόσωπον κατὰ πρόσωπον (Deut. xxxiv. 10). Again, Jeremiah (xii. 3) gives expression to his prophetic consciousness in the words, σύ, κύριε, γινώσκεις με, adding, δεδοκίμακας τὴν καρδίαν μου ἐναντίον σου. Here the parallelism shows that even in Hebrew the idea of insight is included in the meaning of ידע. But in Jer. i. 5 it is clear that God's 'knowledge' of the prophet goes beyond insight, however penetrating: 'Before I formed you in the belly I knew you (יְדַעְתִּיךָ ἐπίσταμαί σε), and before you came out of the womb I sanctified you: I have appointed you a prophet to the nations.' It is God's will that is at work, choosing, sanctifying, appointing, determining the prophet's lot. Whether, however, we read such passages in Hebrew or in Greek, and whether the idea of insight and understanding, or that of choice and will, predominates, it is clear that they speak of God's relation to man as an 'I-Thou' relation (ὁ θεὸς ὁμιλεῖ τῷ ἀνθρώπῳ, as the Hermetist says; πρόσωπον κατὰ πρόσωπον, says the Deuteronomist).

In the post-prophetic period the individual pious Israelite appropriates the experience of the prophets to himself, and is conscious of being the object of God's 'knowledge'. Thus Ps. cxxxviii (cxxxix). 1–2:

> κύριε, ἐδοκίμασάς με καὶ ἔγνως με·
> σὺ ἔγνως τὴν καθέδραν μου καὶ τὴν ἔγερσίν μου.

The whole Psalm speaks of that perfect, interior insight into the heart of man which God alone possesses; and it ends with the prayer (23):

> δοκίμασόν με, ὁ θεός, καὶ γνῶθι τὴν καρδίαν μου·
> ἔτασόν με καὶ γνῶθι τὰς τρίβους μου.

But within this divine 'knowledge' of man is included much besides insight and understanding. God is his creator and controller (5). He gives guidance (10) and help (13). Again in Nahum i. 7 the faithful in Israel as a body are the objects of this divine 'knowledge', in a context which speaks of God's deliverance of His people from their enemies: χρηστὸς κύριος τοῖς ὑπομένουσιν αὐτὸν ἐν ἡμέρᾳ θλίψεως, καὶ γινώσκων τοὺς εὐλαβουμένους αὐτόν. Here the parallelism suggests that the 'kindness' of the Lord is much the same thing as His 'knowledge' of those who fear Him. God concerns Himself, in mercy, with His people. Yet when ידע becomes γινώσκων, the thought of God's insight into men cannot but enter in. The resultant idea is that of a personal relation of God with men, into which enter both a penetrating interior insight and a gracious concern for them.

There is one Old Testament passage which will serve particularly well for comparison with the Fourth Gospel, Num. xvi. 5 ἐπέσκεπται καὶ ἔγνω ὁ θεὸς τοὺς ὄντας αὐτοῦ καὶ τοὺς ἁγίους καὶ προσηγάγετο πρὸς ἑαυτόν, καὶ οὓς ἐξελέξατο ἑαυτῷ προσηγάγετο πρὸς ἑαυτόν. This is not an exact rendering of the Massoretic Text,[1] but the question of the true reading, or the original meaning, of the Hebrew is of less importance to us than the meaning given to the passage in Hellenistic Judaism, and the small verbal changes made by the translators are in themselves significant. The passage belongs to a story of a schism in Israel, and of how by supernatural means Jehovah declared Himself in favour of the one party against the other. But these Old Testament stories were regularly treated by Hellenistic Jewish interpreters as symbols of profound religious truths. This we know from Philo, and from other sources. It is in this spirit that the LXX translators have given us in their rendering of the verse before us what amounts to a summary of prophetic doctrine upon the subject of God's knowledge of His people. There are three points: (i) God 'knows' those who are His; (ii) He has chosen them; and (iii) He leads them to Himself. The close association of these three ideas secures the preservation of the Hebraic associations of the term 'know'; yet the words ἔγνω ὁ θεὸς τοὺς ὄντας αὐτοῦ could hardly fail to suggest to a Greek reader such sentiments as those of C.H. x. 15 (cited above), and C.H. i. 31 ὁ θεός...γινώσκεται τοῖς ἰδίοις, though this affirms the other side of this mutual 'knowledge'.

Now these three points clearly emerge in the teaching of the Fourth Gospel. (i) With ἔγνω κύριος τοὺς ὄντας αὐτοῦ cf. John x. 14 γινώσκω τὰ ἐμά. (ii) With οὓς ἐξελέξατο cf. John xiii. 18 ἐγὼ οἶδα τίνας ἐξελεξάμην, xv. 16 οὐχ ὑμεῖς ἐμὲ ἐξελέξασθε ἀλλ' ἐγὼ ὑμᾶς ἐξελεξάμην. (iii) With προσηγάγετο πρὸς ἑαυτόν cf. John vi. 44 οὐδεὶς δύναται ἐλθεῖν πρός με ἐὰν μὴ ὁ πατὴρ ἑλκύσῃ αὐτόν, xii. 32 πάντας ἑλκύσω πρὸς ἐμαυτόν. It is evident that the Johannine conception of God's knowledge of man is closely associated with those ideas of divine grace and election which belong to it in the prophetic writings.

In those passages the divine knower is Christ. Elsewhere He is the object of God's knowledge: x. 15 γινώσκει με ὁ πατήρ. We may compare the passages quoted from Jeremiah and the Psalms, and the reference to Moses ὃν κύριος ἔγνω; and recall that the relation of Jesus to the Father is in various ways expressed in terms corresponding to those of the

בֹּקֶר וְיֹדַע יְהוָה אֶת־אֲשֶׁר־לֹו וְאֶת־הַקָּדֹושׁ וְהִקְרִיב אֵלָיו וְאֵת אֲשֶׁר יִבְחַר־בֹּו יַקְרִיב אֵלָיו [1]
LXX represents a differently pointed text.

prophetic vocation: God sends Him, gives Him His word, instructs Him in His will.[1] In view of all this, it seems clear that when Jesus is said to be known by God, it is primarily in a sense analogous to that in which the prophets were said to be known by Him, though with that shift or extension of meaning which occurs when ידע becomes γινώσκειν.

We now turn to the other aspect of this two-sided relation: man's knowledge of God. In the Old Testament this may be expressed in either of two ways: the word 'God' may stand in the accusative as the direct object of the verb; or we may have a ὅτι-clause: γνῶναι ὅτι ἐγὼ κύριος, or the like. Both these forms of expression are found in the Fourth Gospel. I will take the former first.

(i) The fundamental proposition, αὕτη ἐστιν ἡ αἰώνιος ζωή, ἵνα γινώσκωσίν σε τὸν μόνον ἀληθινὸν θεόν (xvii. 3), has a true parallel in the LXX of Hos. vi. 2–3 ἐν τῇ ἡμέρᾳ τῇ τρίτῃ καὶ ἀναστησόμεθα καὶ ζησόμεθα ἐνώπιον αὐτοῦ, καὶ γνωσόμεθα· διώξομεν τοῦ γνῶναι τὸν κύριον. Whatever may have been the precise meaning of Hosea's original Hebrew,[2] there is no doubt that to a Greek reader this meant: 'we shall rise (from the dead) and live in His presence, and have knowledge; we shall press forward to know the Lord.' To know the Lord is to live before Him, that is, to have eternal life: which comes very near to the Hermetic maxim: τοῦτο μόνον σωτήριον ἀνθρώπῳ, ἡ γνῶσις τοῦ θεοῦ.

It is noteworthy that in this, and in nearly all Old Testament passages, man's knowledge of God is not present but future. Doubtless the prophets (whom God 'knew') were held to 'know' God. I Kms. iii. 7 speaks of Samuel πρὶν γνῶναι τὸν θεὸν καὶ ἀποκαλυφθῆναι αὐτῷ ῥῆμα κυρίου, implying that when the word of God came to him he did 'know' God. Yet I cannot discover a place where a prophet expressly says that he knows God. Again, while God's knowledge of Israel is confidently proclaimed by the prophets, they rarely affirm that Israel knows God. The claim of Israel in Hos. viii. 2 ἐμὲ κεκράξονται, Ὁ θεός, ἐγνώκαμέν σε is a false claim. Is. xxvi. 13 κτῆσαι ἡμᾶς, κύριε· ἐκτός σου ἄλλον οὐκ οἴδαμεν· τὸ ὄνομά σου ὀνομάζομεν implies that Israel 'knows' God (but only in the LXX). The pious in Israel are said to know God in

---

[1] See pp. 254–5.
[2] The M.T. reads ‏בַּיּוֹם הַשְּׁלִישִׁי יְקִמֵנוּ וְנִחְיֶה לְפָנָיו:‏
‏וְנֵדְעָה נִרְדְּפָה לָדַעַת אֶת־יהוה.‏

This is presumably the 'scripture' according to which Christ rose from the dead on the third day according to I Cor. xv. 4.

Ps. xxxv (xxxvi). 10 παράτεινον τὸ ἔλεός σου τοῖς γινώσκουσίν σε, and perhaps in Ps. lxxxvi (lxxxvii). 4. But such passages are exceptional. In Jer. ix. 24 (23) (a passage following close upon the condemnation of Israel for 'ignorance' of God, ἐμὲ οὐκ ἔγνωσαν . . . οὐκ ἤθελον εἰδέναι, ix. 3, 6) we have ἐν τούτῳ καυχάσθω ὁ καυχώμενος, συνίειν καὶ γινώσκειν ὅτι ἐγώ εἰμι κύριος ὁ ποιῶν ἔλεος καὶ κρίμα καὶ δικαιοσύνην ἐπὶ τῆς γῆς, ὅτι ἐν τούτοις τὸ θέλημά μου, λέγει κύριος. This aptly serves to illustrate the context of 'knowledge' of God, but it does not go so far as to say that anyone actually is entitled to boast such knowledge. In the large majority of cases knowledge of God is the object of exhortation, aspiration, or promise. In I Chron. xxviii. 9 David enjoins Solomon, γνῶθι τὸν θεὸν τῶν πατέρων σου καὶ δούλευε ἐν καρδίᾳ τελείᾳ καὶ ψυχῇ θελούσῃ. Jeremiah promises that, in the good time coming, under the new covenant this injunction will no longer be necessary: οὐ διδάξουσιν ἕκαστος τὸν πολίτην αὐτοῦ καὶ ἕκαστος τὸν ἀδελφὸν αὐτοῦ λέγων Γνῶθι τὸν κύριον· ὅτι πάντες εἰδήσουσίν με ἀπὸ μικροῦ αὐτῶν ἕως μεγάλου αὐτῶν (xxxviii. 34 = xxxi. 33).[1]

The Fourth Gospel contains similar promises for the future (viii. 28, 32, x. 38). But it is more significant that it also contains the affirmation that the disciples of Christ already possess knowledge of Him and of the Father. In x. 14–15 the mutual knowledge of Father and Son and the mutual knowledge of Christ and His flock are alike expressed by the verb γινώσκειν in the present tense; but the tense is perhaps rather 'gnomic' and timeless than strictly present in the temporal sense. In xiv. 7 we have variant readings:[2] according to the one text the disciples have

[1] For Judaism the study of Torah, no doubt, is a mode of 'knowing' God, upon one level, but knowledge of God in a more pregnant sense (or knowledge of the Name, for which see pp. 93–6) is a blessing yet to come.

[2] (a) ει εγνωκειτε με και τον πατερα μου αν ηδειτε BCL, etc.

(b) ει εγνωκειτε με και τον πατερα μου αν εγνωκειτε ΑΘ *text. rec.*

(c) ει εγνωκατε με και τον πατερα μου γνωσεσθε D.

(d) ܘܬܕܥܘܢ ܠܐܒܝ ܐܦ ܝܕܥܬܘܢ ܠܐ ܠܝ ܐܢ Syr. Sin.—evidently intended to be read as a question: 'If you have not known me, will you know also my Father?' Readings (a) and (b) give an 'unreal' conditional sentence, implying that the condition is not fulfilled. It is virtually identical with viii. 19 (addressed to unbelieving Jews) εἰ ἐμὲ ᾔδειτε καὶ τὸν πατέρα μου ἂν ᾔδειτε. The meaning here would be that the disciples have not 'known' Christ (in the full sense of θεάσασθαι τὴν δόξαν αὐτοῦ)—a fact which (in that case) Christ must be supposed to recognize in xiv. 9 with incredulous astonishment—else they would have had knowledge of God—which their present attitude puts in question; but from this moment, which is the moment when Christ is glorified (xiii. 31), having at last 'seen' Him, they do know God: ἀπ' ἄρτι γινώσκετε αὐτόν. Reading (c) gives a conditional

not so far 'known' Christ, and consequently do not yet know the Father; according to the other text they do know Christ, and consequently will know the Father; but there is no doubt about the conclusion of the verse: ἀπ' ἄρτι γινώσκετε αὐτὸν καὶ ἑωράκατε. Thus, whichever text we follow, the meaning is that from this moment ignorance of God is for Christ's disciples a thing of the past and, seeing and knowing Him, they know God.[1] We may add xiv. 17, which speaks of the Spirit of truth, which the world cannot receive because οὐ θεωρεῖ αὐτὸ οὐδὲ γινώσκει. On the other hand ὑμεῖς γινώσκετε αὐτό, ὅτι παρ' ὑμῖν μένει καὶ ἐν ὑμῖν ἔσται. Knowledge and vision of the Father, of the Son, and of the Paraclete are equipollent. In the dramatic situation, these statements are proleptic; but in intention chs. xiv–xvi are written as if out of the situation that arose after the death of Christ, in which the effects of His 'finished' work are realized (see pp. 396–8). It is clear that although chs. xiii–xvii, when compared with Hellenistic compositions, display much of the character of a scene of initiation (see pp. 420–3), the evangelist's meaning is different from that intended by any non-Christian Hellenistic writer. He means that through the incarnation of the Logos, consummated in His death, knowledge and vision of God were brought to men as never before. He is speaking of an historical fulfilment of the historical expectation of Israel expressed by the prophets; of the 'new covenant' under which all shall know God, from the least to the greatest. Here, in its

sentence 'implying nothing as to the fulfilment of the condition'. The perfect ἔγνωκα is in usage present. The meaning would be, 'If you know me, you will know the Father', an implicit assurance. This follows quite well on xiv. 6: no one comes to the Father except through Christ as 'way': conversely everyone whose 'way' is Christ arrives at the Father, or, in other words, everyone who knows Christ will come to know the Father. The argument then continues; from this moment the condition is fulfilled: the disciples do know God and have seen Him. Philip misunderstands: Christ replies with the rhetorical question, 'Can it be that you do not know me after the long time we have spent together?' The implied answer is 'Of course not'. Philip and the rest do know Christ: they have seen Him; *ergo*, they have seen the Father; and that justifies the statement of xiv. 7b, which Philip had misunderstood. Reading (*d*) has too little support to merit serious consideration; it might well be a corruption of (*c*), and in any case lends confirmation to γνώσεσθε. As between ἤδειτε (*a*) and ἐγνώκειτε (*b*) there is little to choose. As between the general text represented by (*a*) and (*b*) together on the one hand and (*c*) on the other, the weight of authority is scarcely decisive. The possibility of unconscious assimilation to viii. 19 should not be excluded, though on the other hand it is also possible that scribes may have altered reading (*a–b*) in order not to suggest that the disciples were in no better case than the unbelieving Jews; though this perhaps presupposes a better memory than scribes often show!

[1] See p. 397.

'realized eschatology', the Fourth Gospel stands apart from its Jewish and Hellenistic predecessors and analogues, and firmly within its Christian setting. All this must be considered more particularly hereafter; it does not throw very much light on our immediate question: what is γνῶσις θεοῦ?

It will assist our investigation to observe that knowledge of God in the Johannine sense either takes the form of a knowledge of Christ, or is dependent upon a knowledge of Christ. It is only between the Father and the Son that the relation of full mutual knowledge exists independently. The formula is (x. 14–15) γινώσκω τὰ ἐμὰ καὶ γινώσκουσί με τὰ ἐμά, καθὼς γινώσκει με ὁ πατήρ, κἀγὼ γινώσκω τὸν πατέρα. Similarly, in passages where the Jews are reproached with ignorance of God, Christ in contrast affirms His knowledge of Him: vii. 28–9 ἀλλ' ἐστὶν ἀληθινὸς ὁ πέμψας με, ὃν ὑμεῖς οὐκ οἴδατε· ἐγὼ οἶδα αὐτόν, ὅτι παρ' αὐτοῦ εἰμι κἀκεῖνός με ἀπέστειλεν, viii. 54–55 ὑμεῖς λέγετε ὅτι Θεὸς ἡμῶν ἐστιν, καὶ οὐκ ἐγνώκατε αὐτόν· ἐγὼ δὲ οἶδα αὐτόν. κἂν εἴπω ὅτι οὐκ οἶδα αὐτόν, ἔσομαι ὅμοιος ὑμῖν ψεύστης· ἀλλ' οἶδα αὐτόν, καὶ τὸν λόγον αὐτοῦ τηρῶ. The knowledge which Christ has of God is here associated on the one hand with His divine commission and on the other hand with His obedience to the divine word. It is the fulfilment of the prophetic ideal; for, as we have seen, the fact that the prophet is known by God implies as its correlative that the prophet shall know God too, while yet no prophet fully claims such knowledge. In Christ therefore we have, realized, the archetype of that true relation of man to God which is henceforth made possible in Him. We may observe that this is implied already in the Synoptic saying, Matt. xi. 27 (Luke x. 22) οὐδεὶς ἐπιγινώσκει τὸν υἱὸν εἰ μὴ ὁ πατήρ, οὐδὲ τὸν πατέρα τις ἐπιγινώσκει εἰ μὴ ὁ υἱός, καὶ ᾧ ἐὰν βούληται ὁ υἱὸς ἀποκαλύψαι. Where the Johannine statement advances beyond this is in representing Christ as occupying the place of God both as subject and as object in that divine-human relation of which His own relation with the Father is the archetype. If in His own relation to the Father, as knower and known, Christ realizes the prophetic ideal, it is only as more than a prophet, as the eternal mediating Logos, that He can reconstitute that relation for men by Himself standing in the place of God, as knower and known. Hence it is that the definition of ζωὴ αἰώνιος adds 'Jesus Christ' to 'the only real God' as object of knowledge (xvii. 3).

We have further to observe that in the group of passages before us knowledge of God is associated with vision of God: ἀπ' ἄρτι γινώσκετε αὐτὸν καὶ ἑωράκατε (xiv. 7). This identification of knowing with seeing is, as we have observed, characteristically Greek. Θεωρία has no such importance in Jewish piety, and the Old Testament lays little emphasis upon the vision of God as a form of religious experience.[1] Orthodox Judaism assumed that the vision of God is impossible to men in this life, and that it is a blessing reserved for the Age to Come.[2] The Fourth Evangelist can speak of men as knowing and seeing God, without actually contradicting the fundamental assumptions of Judaism, just because it is the presupposition of his whole view of religion that the Age to Come has come: eternal life is here. Nevertheless, the maxim holds good: θεὸν οὐδεὶς ἑώρακεν πώποτε (i. 18). Of one only can such direct vision of God be predicated: οὐχ ὅτι τὸν πατέρα ἑώρακέν τις εἰ μὴ ὁ ὢν παρὰ τοῦ θεοῦ, οὗτος ἑώρακεν τὸν πατέρα (vi. 46). The knowledge which Christ has of God, therefore, has that quality of direct vision which Hellenistic mystics claimed—falsely, in the evangelist's view—and which for Jewish thinkers was reserved for the supernatural life of the Age to Come. This knowledge which is vision He mediates to men in the sense, ὁ ἑωρακὼς ἐμὲ ἑώρακεν τὸν πατέρα (xiv. 9), ὁ θεωρῶν ἐμὲ θεωρεῖ τὸν πέμψαντά με (xii. 45).

Accordingly, the terms ὁρᾶν and θεωρεῖν are freely used with Christ as object. Sometimes they refer to the mere fact that Jesus was seen at Jerusalem and elsewhere, as any man is seen by his fellows. But sometimes they are used with a more pregnant meaning, the meaning once expressed in the words, θεάσασθαι τὴν δόξαν αὐτοῦ (i. 14).[3] The meaning is that those who, whether in actual physical presence, or in retrospect through the witness of the Church, contemplate the historic life of Jesus, and recognize the divine quality in it—His 'glory'—have attained a knowledge of Him which is the real 'vision of God'. It is clear that the evangelist is here working with a conception of 'knowledge of God', as vision, which

[1] The Old Testament speaks equivocally. It may well be that the pre-canonical tradition spoke oftener, and with less hesitation, of the Deity becoming visible to men's eyes, than the Massoretic editors wish us to perceive, and doubtless at one stage the prophetic 'vision' might include actual sight of God. But it is certain that a progressive disinclination to use such language can be observed. Contrast, e.g., Isaiah's blunt וָאֶרְאֶה אֶת־אֲדֹנָי (vi. 1) with Ezekiel's cumbrous paraphrases, הִנֵּה־שָׁם כְּבוֹד אֱלֹהֵי יִשְׂרָאֵל (viii. 4) and even דְּמוּת כְּבוֹד־יהוה (i. 28). The process went further in post-canonical exegesis, paraphrase and translation. For orthodox Judaism the idea of the invisibility of the Eternal was too valuable to be compromised.
[2] See the material adduced by S.-B. ad Matt. v. 8.
[3] The two meanings sometimes overlap, or suggest one another, and serve the Johannine irony: see vi. 36, ix. 37, xiv. 19, xvi. 16–17, vi. 40, 62, xii. 21, xx. 8, 20, 29.

on one side is close to that held by Hellenistic mystics; that he holds, as some of them do, that such vision is mediated; but that he finds the mediating principle (corresponding to the λόγος of Philo, the νοῦς of some *Hermetica*) not in abstractions, but embodied in a living person. This gives to the Johannine conception of knowledge (vision) of God a peculiar character of its own, to which no exact parallel can be found.

(ii) We now come to passages where the content of γνῶσις is expressed not in a direct object of the verb, but in a ὅτι-clause; and here again we may start with LXX parallels.[1]

In Is. xliii. 10–11 we read, γένεσθέ μοι μάρτυρες, καὶ ἐγὼ μάρτυς, λέγει κύριος ὁ θεός, καὶ ὁ παῖς ὃν ἐξελεξάμην, ἵνα γνῶτε καὶ πιστεύσητε καὶ συνῆτε ὅτι ἐγώ εἰμι· ἔμπροσθέν μου οὐκ ἐγένετο ἄλλος θεός, καὶ μετ᾽ ἐμὲ οὐκ ἔσται. ἐγὼ ὁ θεός, καὶ οὐκ ἔστιν παρὲξ ἐμοῦ σώζων. It will be obvious at once how much of this language is echoed in the Fourth Gospel. There is the idea of μαρτυρία—the 'witness' of God, and of His 'servant' (or 'son').[2] There is the idea of 'election', which, as we have just seen, is closely associated with God's 'knowledge' of man (see pp. 161–3).[3] We are evidently in touch with the main stock of Johannine thought. It is therefore significant that the expression ἵνα γνῶτε καὶ πιστεύσητε...ὅτι ἐγώ εἰμι has close parallels in the Fourth Gospel. Take first viii. 28 γνώσεσθε ὅτι ἐγώ εἰμι. In John and in Isaiah alike, the content of γνῶσις is the ἐγώ εἰμι (אֲנִי הוּא), which expresses the divine nature. In Isaiah it is the ἐγώ εἰμι of Jehovah: the knowledge of which he speaks is a recognition of the unique and eternal majesty of God as ruler of the universe and redeemer of His people. In John it is the ἐγώ εἰμι of Christ as Logos and Son of God: as the bearer and revealer, therefore, of that same majesty.

Again in John vi. 69 the disciples confess, ἡμεῖς πεπιστεύκαμεν καὶ ἐγνώκαμεν ὅτι σὺ εἶ ὁ ἅγιος τοῦ θεοῦ. The combination πιστεύειν καὶ γινώσκειν follows Isaiah closely; but for ὅτι ἐγώ εἰμι is substituted ὅτι σὺ εἶ ὁ ἅγιος τοῦ θεοῦ. The content of knowledge is the unique status of Christ Himself, which is an equivalent for knowledge of God. Cf. also xvii. 8 ἔγνωσαν ἀληθῶς ὅτι παρά σου ἐξῆλθον, καὶ ἐπίστευσαν ὅτι σύ με ἀπέστειλας.

---

[1] For some examples, see Ps. xlv. (xlvi). 11 (ὅτι ἐγώ εἰμι ὁ θεός), Is. xlix. 23 (ὅτι ἐγὼ κύριος), lx. 16 (ὅτι ἐγὼ κύριος ὁ σώζων σε), Ezek. *passim* (ὅτι ἐγώ εἰμι κύριος), Dan. (Θ.) iv. 29 (ὅτι κυριεύει ὁ ὕψιστος).

[2] E.g. iii. 11, 32, v. 31–2, 37–8, viii. 13–18, xv. 26–7.

[3] vi. 70, xiii. 18, xv. 16, 19.

Once again, in Jer. ix. 24 (23) the one thing upon which a man may legitimately pride himself is συνίειν καὶ γινώσκειν ὅτι ἐγὼ κύριος. Cf. John x. 38 ἵνα γνῶτε καὶ γινώσκητε ὅτι ἐν ἐμοὶ ὁ πατὴρ κἀγὼ ἐν τῷ πατρί. Knowledge is in the one case apprehension, or experience, of what it means to call God κύριος,[1] in the other case of the unity of Father and Son in the Godhead. For the evangelist surely the two amount to the same thing. To apprehend truly the nature of God is to apprehend Him in the unity of Father and Son.

Finally, the content of knowledge is enlarged to include the unity of men in and with Christ, in God: xiv. 20 ἐν ἐκείνῃ τῇ ἡμέρᾳ γνώσεσθε ὑμεῖς ὅτι ἐγὼ ἐν τῷ πατρί μου, καὶ ὑμεῖς ἐν ἐμοὶ κἀγὼ ἐν ὑμῖν. That is to say, γνῶσις is awareness of a relation of mutual indwelling of God and man. It is most illuminating to trace the development of this conception out of its Old Testament antecedents. For the prophets the height of religious knowledge is to apprehend in experience the unique majesty of God as Lord. For John this experience is made possible through the recognition of Christ as the revelation of God, of Christ as inseparably one with God; and it finds its completion in an experience of our own unity with Christ in God. At this point we are bound to recognize that the distinction between being in Christ and knowing that we are in Christ is hardly mcre than formal, that knowledge has in fact passed into union. In order therefore to complete our study of γνῶσις θεοῦ we shall have to consider the Johannine conception of mutual indwelling. But before coming to that it will be well to examine two other concepts closely related to γνῶσις, namely ἀλήθεια and πίστις.

[1] Including recognition of His moral character...ὅτι ἐγώ εἰμι κύριος ὁ ποιῶν ἔλεος καὶ κρίμα καὶ δικαιοσύνην ἐπὶ τῆς γῆς· ὅτι ἐν τούτοις τὸ θέλημά μου, λέγει κύριος.

4. TRUTH

Among the expressions used to denote the object of γνῶσις is ἀλήθεια: viii. 32 γνώσεσθε τὴν ἀλήθειαν καὶ ἡ ἀλήθεια ἐλευθερώσει ὑμᾶς. For a complete description therefore of the Johannine idea of the knowledge which is life eternal, we need to study the meaning of the term ἀλήθεια.

The adjective ἀληθής is in its earliest and most constant usage applied to statements which correspond to the facts. Its contrary is ψευδής. It means 'true', 'veridical'. This simple, normal, and fundamental use is common in the Fourth Gospel as in all Greek literature: e.g. x. 41 πάντα ὅσα εἶπεν Ἰωάνης περὶ τούτου ἀληθῆ ἦν: iv. 18 τοῦτο ἀληθὲς εἴρηκας. By an easy transference it is applied, in Greek literature after Homer, to persons who make such true statements, in the sense of 'veracious', and then in the extended sense of 'sincere'.

It is a further extension of meaning when the adjective is applied to objects of experience, whether persons or things, which are in fact what they appear or purport to be. The sense here is 'genuine', 'real'. This idea is in Hellenistic Greek more usually expressed by the adjective of secondary formation, ἀληθινός. Thus the astronomers apply this term to the real, as opposed to the apparent, risings and settings of the heavenly bodies, and Aristotle (*Pol.* III. 1281 b 12) speaks of τὰ ἀληθινά, real objects, as opposed to τὰ γεγραμμένα, their pictured copies. John uses ἀληθής in this sense in vi. 55 ἡ γὰρ σάρξ μου ἀληθής ἐστι βρῶσις, καὶ τὸ αἷμά μου ἀληθής ἐστι πόσις: and he occasionally uses ἀληθινός in the sense of 'veridical', e.g. iv. 37 ὁ λόγος ἐστιν ἀληθινὸς ὅτι ἄλλος ἐστὶν ὁ σπείρων καὶ ἄλλος ὁ θερίζων. But as a rule he reserves ἀληθινός, as we have seen,[1] for its more usual sense of 'real', e.g. φῶς ἀληθινόν, ἄρτος ἀληθινός, ἄμπελος ἀληθινή, ὁ ἀληθινὸς θεός, and so, surely, οἱ ἀληθινοὶ προσκυνηταί (iv. 23)—not 'sincere worshippers', but 'real worshippers', i.e. those whose religious exercises are in actual fact and reality an approach to God, and not a shadowy ritual which either counterfeits or at best merely symbolizes the approach to God.

In accordance with these varying uses of the adjectives, ἀλήθεια has a primary application to words or statements, with the meaning 'truth', as opposed to falsehood. As such, it may denote either the abstract quality of truthfulness, or the content of the statements, as agreeable

[1] See pp. 139–40.

to the facts. The two meanings easily pass into one another. Derivatively, ἀλήθεια may be applied to persons, in the abstract sense of 'veracity', 'sincerity'. The second main use of the term, in Greek literature after Homer, corresponds to the normal usage of ἀληθινός: it means 'reality' as opposed to mere appearance. Thus Thuc. II. 41 καὶ ὡς οὐ λόγων ἐν τῷ παρόντι κόμπος τάδε μᾶλλον ἢ ἔργων ἐστὶν ἀλήθεια, αὐτὴ ἡ δύναμις τῆς πόλεως, ἣν ἀπὸ τῶνδε τῶν τρόπων ἐκτησάμεθα, σημαίνει, 'that this is not mere verbal bombast for the occasion, but actual reality, is proved by the very power of our state, which we have acquired through this way of life'.

The Greek senses of the term are well summed up by Bultmann as follows:[1]

’Αλήθεια originally signifies a content of fact, or a state of affairs, in so far as it is seen, indicated, or expressed, and is completely manifested in such seeing, indication, or expression; with special reference to the fact that it might be concealed, falsified, or diminished. ’Αλήθεια is the *complete* or *real* state of affairs.... As in forensic language ἀλήθεια is the state of affairs to be proved, over against the various assertions of the parties, so in the historians it is the historical state of affairs over against myth, and in the philosophers that which really *is*, in the absolute sense.

In the philosophical use of the term the senses of 'truth' and 'reality' tend to run together. For Plato—and it is the Platonic tradition which is important for our purpose—there is a realm of ultimate reality, distinguished from the realm of phenomena which are only shadows, representations, or symbols of the real. ’Αλήθεια may accordingly be 'reality' itself, or the knowledge of reality, or the expression of such knowledge of reality in a philosophical doctrine, which is the 'truth'. Thus in *Rep.* 597 E, where the artist or poet, as an imitator, is described as τρίτος ἀπὸ τῆς ἀληθείας, the word ἀλήθεια clearly stands for 'reality'. In *Tim.* 29 C it is equally clearly the knowledge of reality: ὅτιπερ πρὸς γένεσιν οὐσία, τοῦτο πρὸς πίστιν ἀλήθεια.

The *locus classicus*, *Rep.* 508 D–509 A, illustrates the way in which the two senses flow together: Socrates is using the image of the sun and its light in illustration of the Idea of the Good.

Similarly then conceive the action of the soul: when it inclines to that upon which ἀλήθειά τε καὶ τὸ ὄν shines, it rationally apprehends and knows (ἐνόησέν τε καὶ ἔγνω), and appears to be rational: but when it inclines to that which is

[1] In *Theol. Wört.*, *s.v.*

mixed with darkness, that which comes into being and perishes, it forms opinions (δοξάζει) and peers shortsightedly up and down as it changes its opinions, and is as though it were not rational. Now this thing that affords ἀλήθεια to the objects of knowledge, and gives the power of knowing to the known, you must call the Idea of the Good. Since it is the cause of knowledge and of truth (ἐπιστήμης καὶ ἀληθείας) you must conceive it as an object of knowledge, and yet, though both knowledge and truth (γνῶσις καὶ ἀλήθεια) are such good things, you will do right to consider this even better than they. And as for ἐπιστήμη and ἀλήθεια, just as *there* it is right to consider light and vision to be sun-like but not the sun, so *here* it is right to consider both these like the Good, but it is not right to consider either of them the Good.

In the type of religious philosophy represented by the Hermetic writings, similarly, ἀλήθεια hovers between the senses of reality and the apprehension of reality. In *C.H.* XIII. 6 τὸ ἀληθές is defined thus: τὸ μὴ θολούμενον, τὸ μὴ διοριζόμενον, τὸ ἀχρώματον, τὸ ἀσχημάτιστον, τὸ ἄτρεπτον...τὸ ἀναλλοίωτον ἀγαθόν, τὸ ἀσώματον. *Exc. ap.* Stob. II A (Scott), a fragment Περὶ Ἀληθείας, lays down ἀλήθειαν εἶναι ἐν μόνοις τοῖς ἀϊδίοις (1) and continues, 'All things on earth, therefore, are not ἀλήθεια [*sic* MSS., Scott ἀληθῆ, unnecessarily] but ἀληθείας μιμήματα—not all, but a few of them.' (3) The contrary of ἀλήθεια is ψεῦδος, πλάνος, δόξαι, φαντασίαι. In answer to the question τί οὖν ἂν εἴποι[1] τις τὴν πρώτην ἀλήθειαν; Hermes replies, ἕνα καὶ μόνον, ὦ Τάτ, τὸν μὴ ἐξ ὕλης, τὸν μὴ ἐν σώματι, τὸν ἀχρώματον, τὸν ἀσχημάτιστον, τὸν ἄτρεπτον, τὸν μὴ ἀλλοιούμενον, τὸν ἀεὶ ὄντα.[2] In *C.H.* XIII. 9, on the other hand, ἀλήθεια is a δύναμις which, entering into the initiate, expels ἀπάτη (as γνῶσις expels ἄγνοια and ἐγκράτεια expels ἀκρασία).

In Philo ἀλήθεια is similarly associated with γνῶσις and ἐπιστήμη, and contrasted with δόξα (or δόκησις) and φαντασία (*Quod Det.* 162). The end of the investigation of νοητά is ἀλήθεια, whereas the end of the

---

[1] *Sic* Hense, MSS. εἶναι: εἶναι λέγεις Flussas, εἴποι τις ἀληθές Scott, unacceptably.

[2] The change from the neuter ἀληθές and the feminine ἀλήθεια to the masculine is significant. The Hermetist clearly means that the one and only God is Himself ἀλήθεια, and He alone. In the preceding paragraph the divine Sun, the Demiurge, is described as ἀληθές and as such to be worshipped μετὰ τὸν ἕνα καὶ πρῶτον. This appears to be a concession to a growing tendency to sun-worship. It may even be an interpolation, as Scott suggests, but is not necessarily so. In any case the eternal God and He alone is ἡ πρώτη ἀλήθεια. In spite of such passages, I doubt whether Bultmann is justified in giving *das Ewige, Göttliche*, as the meaning of ἀλήθεια in Hellenistic religious or philosophical writings (*Theol. Wört.* I, pp. 240, 251). Its *meaning* is 'reality', or 'the real' (or the apprehension of it); but according to these writings the real, and only the real, is eternal and divine.

investigation of ὁρατά is δόξα (*De Praem.* 28), and ἀλήθεια is δόξης πρεσβυτέρα καὶ παντὸς τιμιωτέρα τοῦ δοκεῖν (*De Abr.* 123). It is illuminated ἰδίῳ φέγγει νοητῷ καὶ ἀσωμάτῳ compared with which τὸ αἰσθητόν is like night compared with day (*De Vit. Mos.* II. 271). In countless passages this characteristically Hellenistic conception of ἀλήθεια recurs. Passages are, however, hard to find where the word clearly has the sense of 'reality', as distinguished from the apprehension of reality, though it is often on the verge of that meaning; as where the mind is said to gaze upon ἀλήθεια as upon a mirror, abandoning all φαντασίαι of the senses (*De Migr. Abr.* 190), or where the power of those who tell or write is contrasted with ἡ τῶν γινομένων ἀλήθεια (*ibid.* 110).

In the LXX ἀλήθεια is one of the terms used to translate אֱמֶת. This word is from the root אמן which expresses the idea, 'fix', 'confirm', 'establish'. Thus אֱמֶת is primarily the quality of firmness or stability; as a property of persons it means 'steadfastness', 'trustworthiness', and it is especially an attribute of God, as the One who is absolutely trust-worthy. In forensic language it stands for the 'validity' of legal enact-ments, judicial decisions, or evidence; and in particular the command-ments of God are אֱמֶת as being absolutely valid. It can be used of things which are genuine of their kind. זֶרַע אֱמֶת (Jer. ii. 21) is what a seedsman's catalogue would describe as 'guaranteed' or 'tested seed'. The LXX render here ἄμπελος ἀληθινή, an expression which to a Greek reader accustomed to the language of Hellenistic philosophy would suggest quite a different meaning: the 'real' vine, i.e. the Platonic idea of vine.[1]

It is evident that the meanings of the Hebrew and Greek words overlap, while their root-significance is quite different. Ἀλήθεια is fundamentally an intellectual category, אֱמֶת a moral category. Where אֱמֶת signifies the trustworthiness or validity of statements, its meaning approximates to that of ἀλήθεια as 'truth'. When it is used of persons who are steadfast, faithful or trustworthy, it suggests the sense of ἀληθής as 'sincere'. Where it is used of things which are 'genuine', it suggests the sense of ἀληθινός as 'real'. But the very far-reaching substitution of ἀλήθεια for אֱמֶת in the LXX has inevitably given a different colour to many passages. In any given passage it is a matter of very delicate appreciation to divine how far any shadow of the meaning of אֱמֶת clings to the Greek word. Certainly in the case of a Hellenistic-Jewish student of the Old Testament like Philo, the Hebrew associations of the term have receded far into the background. I can find no place in his works where the distinctively

[1] It is a meaning analogous to this which attaches to the phrase in John xv. 1.

Hebraic sense derived from אֱמֶת is to be discerned, and it is perhaps significant that Leisegang's Index to Philo cites no example of the biblical combination, ἔλεος καὶ ἀλήθεια.

In dealing with primitive Christian usage, the question how far the Greek of our documents carries with it a Semitic flavour is always a difficult one. It is noteworthy that in the Synoptic Gospels, where the Semitic background is in general most readily recognized, the words ἀληθής, ἀληθινός, ἀλήθεια are notably rare. Bultmann (*l.c.*) shows that there are passages in Paul, and in I Clement and Hermas, where ἀλήθεια preserves a more or less distinct reminiscence of אֱמֶת.

We have already found plentiful evidence that the Semitic element in the Fourth Gospel is by no means unimportant. We must therefore examine carefully its use of ἀλήθεια for possible traces of Hebrew influence.

There is, I think, only one passage in the gospel where a Greek reader would feel the expression to be definitely strange to the natural idiom of the language: iii. 21 ὁ ποιῶν τὴν ἀλήθειαν ἔρχεται πρὸς τὸ φῶς. The expression ποιεῖν ἀλήθειαν occurs in the Old Testament (Gen. xxxii. 10, xlvii. 29, II Esdr. xix (Neh. ix). 33; cf. Tob. iv. 6, xiii. 6). It represents the Hebrew עָשָׂה אֱמֶת, Aramaic עֲבַד קוּשְׁטָא. This expression, in accordance with the ordinary sense of אֱמֶת, means 'to practise fidelity', or, as we might say, 'to act honourably'. In this particular Johannine passage we should obtain excellent sense if we rendered, 'He who acts honourably comes into the light'; but it is doubtful whether Johannine usage in general would not require us to go beyond this simple sense.

There are other passages where Old Testament expressions seem to find an echo: xvi. 13 τὸ πνεῦμα τῆς ἀληθείας ὁδηγήσει ὑμᾶς εἰς τὴν ἀλήθειαν πᾶσαν (*v.l.* ἐν τῇ ἀληθείᾳ); cf. Ps. xxiv (xxv). 5 ὁδήγησόν με ἐπὶ τὴν ἀλήθειάν σου (*v.l.* ἐν τῇ ἀληθείᾳ). The Hebrew reads הַדְרִיכֵנִי בַאֲמִתֶּךָ, which means 'cause me to walk in Thy faithfulness'. Here אֱמֶת is that fundamental trustworthiness or rectitude which is an attribute of God, and to which by His help His servants may attain. This however is clearly not the sense of ἀλήθεια in John xvi. 13. The context speaks of things to be spoken, announced, and heard. The Paraclete hears the words of Christ, receives them, and announces them to the disciples. The content of these words is concisely summed up in the word ἀλήθεια, which is therefore not אֱמֶת, 'faithfulness', but 'truth'.

Again, iv. 23–4 οἱ ἀληθινοὶ προσκυνηταὶ προσκυνήσουσι τῷ πατρὶ ἐν πνεύματι καὶ ἀληθείᾳ· καὶ γὰρ ὁ πατὴρ τοιούτους ζητεῖ τοὺς προσκυνοῦντας αὐτόν. πνεῦμα ὁ θεὸς καὶ τοὺς προσκυνοῦντας ἐν πνεύματι καὶ ἀληθείᾳ δεῖ προσκυνεῖν; cf. Ps. cxliv (cxlv). 18 ἐγγὺς κύριος τοῖς ἐπικαλουμένοις αὐτόν, πᾶσι τοῖς ἐπικαλουμένοις αὐτὸν ἐν ἀληθείᾳ. The Hebrew is לְכֹל אֲשֶׁר יִקְרָאֻהוּ בֶאֱמֶת, i.e. those who appeal to Him with a sincere and steadfast reliance upon Him. This cannot be the meaning of the Johannine passage. There is no contrast between those whose approach to God is supported by a firm faith and those who lack such faith. The ἀληθινοὶ προσκυνηταί are those who are aware that God is πνεῦμα and accordingly worship Him ἐν πνεύματι: and they are contrasted with those who by confining His presence to Jerusalem or to Gerizim show that they do not realize His nature as πνεῦμα.[1] The contrast may be compared with that drawn in the Epistle to the Hebrews (viii. 1–7, etc.) between the σκιαί of the Levitical ritual and the ἀληθινὴ σκηνή in which the real sacrifice is offered. Ἐν ἀληθείᾳ therefore means 'on the plane of reality', i.e. of τὰ ὄντα as distinct from εἴδωλα or φαντασίαι. Again, take xvii. 17 ὁ λόγος ὁ σὸς ἀλήθειά ἐστιν; cf. Ps. cxviii (cxix). 160 ἀρχὴ τῶν λόγων σου ἀλήθεια. The Hebrew is רֹאשׁ־דְּבָרְךָ אֱמֶת. The parallel member of the verse indicates the sense: וּלְעוֹלָם כָּל־מִשְׁפַּט צִדְקֶךָ. The righteous judgment of God is eternal; and similarly His word may be summed up as absolute, immovable validity. This, rather than 'truth', is the primary suggestion of the Hebrew; but the transition from eternal 'validity' to 'truth' is an easy one, and the LXX rendering could hardly be understood by a Greek in any other sense than, 'The first principle of Thy words is truth.' The meaning intended by the evangelist is in all probability similar: 'Thy word is divine reality revealed.'

In i. 14, 17 we have the combination χάρις καὶ ἀλήθεια. This surely corresponds with the Old Testament expression חֶסֶד וֶאֱמֶת, which is variously translated, but most characteristically as ἔλεος καὶ ἀλήθεια.[2] There is, however, evidence that in the later stages of the LXX, and in Hellenistic Judaism after the Septuagintal period, χάρις came to be preferred to ἔλεος as a rendering of חֶסֶד,[3] and the combination of χάρις and ἀλήθεια is so unusual in Greek that we must suppose that the expression was derived from a Hebrew source. Moreover, χάρις and ἀλήθεια in Christ are contrasted with νόμος (i. 17). Now in the Old Testament we

[1] See pp. 223–5, 314.
[2] Ἔλεος καὶ ἀλήθεια, II Kms. ii. 6, Ps. xxiv (xxv). 10, lxxxiv (lxxxv). 11, lxxxviii (lxxxix). 15, Prov. xiv. 22; οὐκ ἔστιν ἀλήθεια οὐδὲ ἔλεος, Hos. iv. 1; ἐλεημοσύνη καὶ ἀλήθεια, Prov. xx. 22; ἐλεημοσύναι καὶ πίστεις, Prov. iii. 3, xv. 27 (xvi. 6), etc.
[3] Χάρις = חסד, Esther ii. 9 (חן וחסד, Esther ii. 17); Ecclus. vii. 33, xl. 17; also four times in Symmachus, once in Theodotion.

have such expressions as תּוֹרַת אֱמֶת, νόμος ἀληθείας (Mal. ii. 6), תּוֹרוֹת אֱמֶת, νόμους ἀληθείας (II Esd. xix. 13=Neh. ix. 13), תּוֹרָתְךָ אֱמֶת, ὁ λόγος σου ἀλήθεια (Ps. cxviii (cxix). 142). Thus according to Jewish belief the divine אֱמֶת is expressed in the Torah; according to the Fourth Gospel ἀλήθεια is expressed in Christ. The antithesis is in line with other antitheses that we have noted. But אֱמֶת as expressed in the Torah is not 'truth'. The sense is indicated by Exod. R. on xxix. 1 'As thou art אֱמֶת so is also Thy word אֱמֶת, for it is written "Thy word, O God, stands fast in heaven"' (Ps. cxix. 89).[1] Thus the quality indicated by אֱמֶת is permanent validity. This sense can hardly be supposed to come through to Greek readers of the words χάρις καὶ ἀλήθεια, though permanent validity and ontological eternity are analogous ideas in different frames of reference. Thus, while the mould of the expression is determined by Hebrew usage, the actual sense of the words must be determined by Greek usage. It is 'truth', i.e. knowledge of reality, that comes through Jesus Christ.

That such is the dominant sense of ἀλήθεια in this gospel becomes clear when we turn to expressions which have no Old Testament model. An important passage is xviii. 37 ἐγὼ εἰς τοῦτο γεγέννημαι καὶ εἰς τοῦτο ἐλήλυθα εἰς τὸν κόσμον, ἵνα μαρτυρήσω τῇ ἀληθείᾳ· πᾶς ὁ ὢν ἐκ τῆς ἀληθείας ἀκούει μου τῆς φωνῆς. We may take first the expression ὁ ὢν ἐκ τῆς ἀληθείας, for which it would be difficult indeed to cite any Old Testament or Hebrew parallel. It is parallel to such Johannine expressions as ἐκ τοῦ πνεύματος, ἐκ τοῦ θεοῦ, ἐκ τῶν ἄνω, all of which are applied to those who partake of the higher order of being, as opposed to those who are ἐκ τῆς σαρκός, ἐκ τῶν κάτω, ἐκ τοῦ κόσμου τούτου, ἐκ τοῦ διαβόλου. Ἀλήθεια therefore stands here for the realm of pure and eternal reality, as distinct from this world of transient phenomena.[2] Similarly, in the former part of the verse Jesus says that He has come to bear witness to 'the truth', i.e. to the divine reality as now revealed to men. There is the same movement of meaning between 'reality' and 'knowledge of reality' that we find in Greek philosophical language from Plato onwards.

And so, we return to the passage which I quoted first: viii. 32 γνώσεσθε τὴν ἀλήθειαν καὶ ἡ ἀλήθεια ἐλευθερώσει ὑμᾶς. It is now clear that what is here promised to the disciples of Christ is liberty through knowledge of

---

[1] Cited by Kittel, *Theol. Wört. s.v.* (Exod. R. 38. 1).

[2] With the very drastic revision of the idea of what *is* real which we shall have to observe in the development of Johannine thought.

divine reality. That the wise man is free,[1] that γνῶσις liberates from εἱμαρμένη, are commonplaces of Hellenistic popular philosophy. So we understand John to mean that the knowledge of that which is truly real sets men free, because it removes them from subjection to the σάρξ, the κόσμος, or τὰ κάτω, the sign of which is sin: πᾶς ὁ ποιῶν τὴν ἁμαρτίαν δοῦλός ἐστιν (viii. 34).[2] Such knowledge is given by the λόγος of Christ.

Such then is the characteristic sense of ἀλήθεια in the Fourth Gospel. It means eternal reality as revealed to men—either the reality itself or the revelation of it. It is probable that this pregnant meaning is to be read into the term even in expressions where we might seem to have only the current workaday sense of ἀλήθεια. Thus the phrase λαλεῖν or λέγειν τὴν ἀλήθειαν means in itself no more than to make a statement in accordance with the facts relevant to the situation, as opposed to telling a lie. These phrases occur repeatedly in viii. 40–6, with λαλεῖν τὸ ψεῦδος (44) as their natural antithesis. But the meaning throughout is controlled by the expression in 40 τὴν ἀλήθειαν λελάληκα ἣν ἤκουσα παρὰ τοῦ θεοῦ. It is *the* Truth, the revelation of eternal reality, that Christ declares. On the contrary the devil λαλεῖ τὸ ψεῦδος—not simply 'tells lies', but utters *the* Lie, the final denial of divine reality; and he does so because ἐν τῇ ἀληθείᾳ οὐχ ἕστηκεν: he has no standing-ground in the world of eternal reality, and so, οὐκ ἔστιν ἀλήθεια ἐν αὐτῷ, there is nothing in him which corresponds with the eternal reality.

Again, the expression ἐν τῇ ἀληθείᾳ is used in Greek in a merely adverbial sense (e.g. Plato, *Lach.* 183 D), 'really', 'in fact'. In John xvii. 19 the expression ἵνα ὦσιν καὶ αὐτοὶ ἡγιασμένοι ἐν ἀληθείᾳ might mean simply 'that they may be really sanctified'. But when we read the whole passage—ἁγίασον αὐτοὺς ἐν τῇ ἀληθείᾳ· ὁ λόγος ὁ σὸς ἀλήθειά ἐστιν... καὶ ὑπὲρ αὐτῶν ἐγὼ ἁγιάζω ἐμαυτόν, ἵνα ὦσιν καὶ αὐτοὶ ἡγιασμένοι ἐν ἀληθείᾳ—it is clear that we have a prayer that the disciples may be sanctified upon the plane of absolute reality. They will then be ἀληθινοὶ προσκυνηταί, whose worship is ἐν πνεύματι καὶ ἀληθείᾳ.

To conclude: the use of the term ἀλήθεια in this gospel rests upon common Hellenistic usage in which it hovers between the meanings of 'reality', or 'the ultimately real', and 'knowledge of the real'. On one side at least, the knowledge of God which is life eternal is an apprehension

---

[1] Cf. Philo's treatise, Περὶ τοῦ πάντα σπουδαῖον ἐλεύθερον εἶναι (*Quod omnis probus liber sit*).

[2] ῾Αμαρτίας is probably to be omitted, with D b Syr sin and Clem. Alex. It may well be due to a scribe too familiar with Pauline language. Cf. Rom. vi. 17, 20.

of ultimate reality—that reality which stands above the world of phenomena, and is eternal while they change and pass away. This eternal reality is manifested in Christ, who, as Logos, is Bearer not only of the divine χάρις but also of the divine ἀλήθεια, and through whom this ἀλήθεια is revealed to men. To put the matter even more strongly, He is not only the revealer of ἀλήθεια, He is Himself ἡ ἀλήθεια (xiv. 10).[1] The extent to which this identification of ultimate reality with a concrete Person known to history transforms the effective meaning of the term will appear hereafter. The form of expression at any rate indicates that the relation of men to Christ through which they 'know the truth' is more intimate than that of disciples to a teacher. To 'know the truth' they must not only hear His words: they must in some sort be united with Him who is the truth. Thus even when the concept of knowledge of God is most fully intellectualized, it remains true that it involves a personal union with Christ, which goes beyond mere intellectual apprehension. But this mediation of truth, knowledge, and life through Christ is a topic to which we must return later.

[1] Cf. the Hermetic fragment quoted above, p. 172, where after ἀλήθεια has been defined in purely abstract terms, we learn that in the end ἡ πρώτη ἀλήθεια is nothing other than God, ὁ ἀεὶ ὤν.

5. FAITH

Along with γινώσκειν the evangelist uses the term πιστεύειν, which is in fact considerably more frequent in the gospel. That there is some close association between the ideas is shown by the fact that in vi. 69 they are used together, πεπιστεύκαμεν καὶ ἐγνώκαμεν ὅτι σὺ εἶ ὁ ἅγιος τοῦ θεοῦ. An investigation therefore of the meaning of πιστεύειν is here in place.

In Greek literature the word is used both transitively and intransitively. Transitively used it means 'to entrust'. This use occurs once in the Fourth Gospel, ii. 24 οὐκ ἐπίστευεν αὐτὸν αὐτοῖς, but without any special significance. Intransitively used, the verb has two main meanings, 'to give credence to', 'to believe', and 'to have confidence in', 'to trust'. Normally, the verb in the latter sense is construed with a dative, in the former sense with a ὅτι-clause or the like. But the close connection of the two senses is well illustrated by Xenophon, *Mem.* I. i. 1–5. Socrates, it is there said, made statements and predictions on the ground of the warnings he received from his δαιμόνιον. He would not have done so εἰ μὴ ἐπίστευεν ἀληθεύσειν (if he had not been confident that he would be speaking truly). But, Xenophon proceeds, ταῦτα δὲ τίς ἂν ἄλλῳ πιστεύσειεν ἢ θεῷ; The belief that certain things are so is in the last analysis a trust in the veracity of God. Thus both a moral and an intellectual element enter into the sense of the word; but it would be true to say, by and large, that in Greek literature the intellectual element is the controlling one. Πίστις in the gods is primarily either belief that they exist, or belief in the veracity of their communications to men.[1]

In the Hermetic writings πιστεύειν comes to have a special connection with the idea of revelation. Thus in the tractate called Νοῦς πρὸς Ἑρμῆν, Hermes enquires of the God Νοῦς the truth about God and the universe, adding σοὶ γὰρ ἂν καὶ μόνῳ πιστεύσαιμι τὴν περὶ τούτου φανέρωσιν (*C.H.* xi. 1). There follows an exposition of the nature of the supreme God, of His unity, of His mediation to the world and to man, of His creative activity, leading to instructions for entering into the mystical experience of union with the whole creation, through which it is possible νοῆσαι τὸν θεόν (*ibid.* 20). Νοῦς concludes, 'These things have been revealed to you so far: in like manner think out (νόει) all the rest for

---

[1] I have discussed this more fully in *The Bible and the Greeks*, pp. 65–8, 198–200, where I have cited also some passages from Philo.

yourself, and you will not be deceived.' Thus it is by 'believing' or 'having faith in' the revealing deity that Hermes is put in the way of attaining for himself knowledge (δύνασθαι γνῶναι) or vision (σοι ὀφθήσεται) of God (*ibid.* 21). In the tractate called *The Bowl* (Κρατὴρ ἢ Μονάς) we learn that there is difficulty in attaining knowledge of God because τὰ ἀφανῆ δυσπιστεῖν ποιεῖ (*C.H.* iv. 9).[1] God, however, sent down a great Bowl filled with νοῦς, and His herald proclaimed βάπτισον σεαυτὴν ἡ δυναμένη (ψυχή) εἰς τοῦτον τὸν κρατῆρα, ἡ πιστεύουσα ὅτι ἀνελεύσῃ πρὸς τὸν καταπέμψαντα τὸν κρατῆρα, ἡ γνωρίζουσα ἐπὶ τί γέγονας (*ibid.* 4). Those who responded, μετέσχον τῆς γνώσεως, μετέσχον τῆς ἀπὸ τοῦ θεοῦ δωρεᾶς (*ibid.* 4–5). In the tractate called Περὶ Νοήσεως, Hermes gives Asklepios teaching about God, man and the world, and adds:

These things, Asklepios, would seem true to you, if you exercised intelligence (ἐννοοῦντι), but if you have no knowledge (ἀγνοοῦντι) they would be incredible (ἄπιστα). Τὸ γὰρ νοῆσαί ἐστι τὸ πιστεῦσαι, ἀπιστῆσαι δὲ τὸ μὴ νοῆσαι. For speech (ὁ λόγος) does not reach the truth, but mind (νοῦς) is great, and being guided up to a point by speech is capable of arriving at the truth. Thus, having embraced all things in thought (περινοήσας τὰ πάντα) and found them agreeable to what was interpreted by speech, it comes to have faith, and in that fair faith it comes to rest (ἐπίστευσε καὶ τῇ καλῇ πίστει ἐπανεπαύσατο) (*C.H.* ix. 10).[2]

In the LXX πιστεύειν is used to render הֶאֱמִין, the Hiphil of אמן, a root which conveys, as we have seen, the idea of firmness or stability. The Hiphil means 'to stand firm'. With the prepositions ל and ב it signifies to stand firm by virtue of one's relation to a person (or object), and so to rely firmly upon him (or it), i.e. to trust or credit a person. It thus approximates to the sense of πιστεύειν with the dative, and in fact this construction is almost invariably used in the LXX. The preposition ἐν occurs occasionally in one MS. or another, but never I think as a fully attested reading, and ἐπί occurs once only, Wisd. xii. 2 (where the attestation of the verb is not entirely satisfactory). Πιστεύειν with the dative fairly represents the Hebrew הֶאֱמִין ב. The only difference is that the intellectual element is more prominent in the Greek, while the moral element is more prominent, as it is fundamental, in the Hebrew.

---

[1] The affinity of this with Philo's definition of πίστις as ἀφανοῦς ὑπόληψις (*De Somn.* 1. 68) is manifest.

[2] See Festugière's note *ad loc.* The meaning seems to be that the speech of a teacher may bring you so far on the way to γνῶσις, but in the end you must trust your own insight or experience.

Further, הֶאֱמִין develops the sense of 'to be firmly convinced', and so can be used with a כִּי-clause. This is a fairly exact equivalent of πιστεύειν ὅτι, but it is rather rare in the Old Testament.

But the Hebrew verb is capable of a use for which, so far as I know, non-biblical Greek affords no parallel. It can be used absolutely, in its primary sense of 'to stand firm', either literally (as of the war-horse, Job xxxix. 24 [1]), or in the sense of having firmness, constancy, confidence, as a trait of character, or a moral attitude in certain circumstances. Thus in Is. vii. 9 we have the play upon words, אִם לֹא תַאֲמִינוּ כִּי לֹא תֵאָמֵנוּ 'If you do not stand firm, maintain your confidence, you shall not be made firm', i.e. given power to resist the enemy, a perfectly lucid and salutary maxim for a people under stress of war. It is evident that it is difficult to render this idea by the use of πιστεύειν, the verb which the LXX translators regarded as the proper equivalent of האמין. They have made an attempt, in which actually the sense is changed: ἐὰν μὴ πιστεύσητε, οὐδὲ μὴ συνῆτε. Again in Is. xxviii. 16, we have the saying: 'Behold, I lay in Zion for a foundation a stone, a tried stone, a precious stone of sure foundation: הַמַּאֲמִין לֹא יָחִישׁ.' The gnomic sentence, thus introduced abruptly in asyndeton, would seem to be conceived as if it were the inscription upon the corner-stone. The foundation which is laid *is* in fact the principle, הַמַּאֲמִין לֹא יָחִישׁ. Its significance is indicated by the context. Israel have made lies their refuge, but the hail will sweep away the refuge of lies. But amid the confusion and instability there is one sure foundation: 'He who has constancy will not hurry distractedly to and fro.' The LXX translators here rendered (with possibly a different reading for יָחִישׁ), ὁ πιστεύων οὐ μὴ καταισχυνθῇ. It is clear that this absolute use of πιστεύειν was felt difficult by Greek readers, and in אAQ the reading (clearly secondary) is ὁ πιστεύων ἐπ' αὐτῷ, and it is in this form that the passage is quoted in the New Testament (Rom. ix. 33, x. 11, I Pet. ii. 6). It is clear, however, that if the absolute use of πιστεύειν stands, its meaning is no longer 'to have constancy' amid a sea of distraction, but, in the religious sense, 'to have faith', and this is the sense appropriate to the other Isaianic passage in its Greek form: 'Unless you have faith you will never understand' ('credo ut intelligam!')—which is far from what Isaiah meant. If we press the question 'faith in what?' the answer is no doubt 'in God'. But the

---

[1] וְלֹא־יַאֲמִין כִּי־קוֹל שׁוֹפָר, which would appear to mean, 'he will not stand firm when the trumpet sounds'; but the text is thought to be corrupt, and is variously emended by editors; LXX, καὶ οὐ μὴ πιστεύσῃ ἕως ἂν σημάνῃ σάλπιγξ.

actual content of the verb is simply the quality of 'faith', as an ethical-psychological determination of the personality. Given the predominantly intellectual character of the Greek verb, Philo's ἀφανοῦς ὑπόληψις is a sufficiently apt definition (*De Somn.* i. 68).

It is this action of Hebrew religious conceptions upon the Greek philosophical idea, I believe, which prepares the way for the striking use of πιστεύειν in the hymn which closes the Hermetic tractate *Poimandres*, πιστεύω[1] καὶ μαρτυρῶ· εἰς ζωὴν καὶ φῶς χωρῶ (*C.H.* i. 32). The doctrine of the *Poimandres*, as of the *Hermetica* in general, is that knowledge is the way to life. It is evident, therefore, that 'to have faith' differs very little from 'to know';[2] and this close association of the two ideas in the *Hermetica* prepares us for their association in the Fourth Gospel.

I now turn to actual occurrences of πιστεύειν in this gospel.

(i) The characteristically Greek use which we have noted in Xenophon occurs in iv. 21 πίστευέ μοι, γύναι, ὅτι ἔρχεται ὥρα κτλ., xiv. 11 πιστεύετέ μοι ὅτι ἐγὼ ἐν τῷ πατρί. Here πίστευέ μοι no doubt means 'trust me'; but the trust is exhibited in the intellectual judgment that the words of Jesus are credible, exactly as Socrates 'trusted' his δαιμόνιον, which trust was exhibited in 'believing' its promptings. That is, it means 'believe me'; and the content of belief is given in the ὅτι-clause. We might translate 'Take my word for it: a time is coming....'.

(ii) The simple construction with the dative is frequent, as in ordinary Greek and in the LXX: but whereas in the latter the meaning is commonly 'trust', the context almost everywhere in the Fourth Gospel shows that the prevailing sense is 'believe'. Thus in ii. 22 we have ἐπίστευσαν τῇ γραφῇ καὶ τῷ λόγῳ ὃν εἶπεν ὁ Ἰησοῦς: v. 46 εἰ γὰρ ἐπιστεύσατε Μωϋσεῖ ἐπιστεύετε ἂν ἐμοί, and in the discussion in viii. 31–47 the repeated πιστεύειν μοι is correlated with τὴν ἀλήθειαν λέγειν, λαλεῖν, and alternates with expressions like ἀκούειν τὸν λόγον τὸν ἐμόν, τὰ ῥήματα τοῦ θεοῦ ἀκούειν.

(iii) Next, we have the equally idiomatic Greek usage of πιστεύειν with a ὅτι-clause, which happens also to coincide with the LXX usage representing the somewhat rare Hebrew כִּי הֶאֱמִין. The meaning here is 'to be convinced', 'to believe'. Apart from one instance noted above

---

[1] This is not quite the same as πιστεῦσαι in *C.H.* ix, *l.c.*, for there, although the verb is first used absolutely, it is explained in the words τοῖς ὑπὸ τοῦ λόγου ἑρμηνευθεῖσιν ἐπίστευσε, and so is not truly absolute as is the πιστεύω of *C.H.* i. 32. Scott's intrusion of ὅτι is uncalled for, and unhappy.

[2] Here the authors of *C.H.* i and ix have departed from Platonic principles, according to which πίστις is correlative to γένεσις, as ἀλήθεια to οὐσία (*Tim.* 29c).

FAITH

(*sub* i), the content of belief is in every instance the nature, mission, and status of Christ: ὅτι ἐγώ εἰμι (viii. 24, xiii. 19): ὅτι σὺ εἶ ὁ χριστός (xi. 27): ὅτι Ἰησοῦς ἐστιν ὁ χριστός (xx. 31): ὅτι ἐγὼ ἐν τῷ πατρὶ καὶ ὁ πατὴρ ἐν ἐμοί (xiv. 11): ὅτι σύ με ἀπέστειλας (xi. 42, xvii. 8): ὅτι παρὰ τοῦ πατρὸς ἐξῆλθον (xvi. 27): ὅτι ἀπὸ θεοῦ ἐξῆλθες (xvi. 30). That is to say, the content of πίστις is stated in much the same terms as the content of γνῶσις,[1] and it is not surprising that in the passage from which we started the two verbs are conjoined: πεπιστεύκαμεν καὶ ἐγνώκαμεν ὅτι σὺ εἶ ὁ ἅγιος τοῦ θεοῦ.

(iv) We now come to a form of expression for which there is no parallel, so far as I can discover, either in profane Greek or in the LXX: πιστεύειν followed by εἰς with the accusative. This would appear to be an alternative way of representing the Hebrew האמין ב. As an equivalent for the Hebrew preposition εἰς is quite natural. It would seem that πιστεύειν with the dative so inevitably connoted simple credence, in the sense of an intellectual judgment, that the moral element of personal trust or reliance inherent in the Hebrew and Aramaic phrase—an element integral to the primitive Christian conception of faith in Christ—needed to be otherwise expressed.[2] At any rate, the distinction between the two expressions seems to be preserved practically everywhere in the gospel,[3] and the construction with εἰς is so frequent that it must be considered the characteristic Johannine expression.[4] The sense of personal trust or confidence is clearly present in xiv. 1 μὴ ταρασσέσθω ὑμῶν ἡ καρδία· πιστεύετε εἰς τὸν θεόν, καὶ εἰς ἐμὲ πιστεύετε. The remedy for distraction and bewilderment is a firm reliance upon God and upon Christ. Yet this sense of personal trust is not always prominent in the expression. It often seems to imply a recognition of the claim of Jesus to be the revelation of God. This may perhaps best be illustrated by a negative instance: vii. 5 οὐδὲ γὰρ οἱ ἀδελφοὶ ἐπίστευον εἰς αὐτόν. The use of πιστεύειν in this form of expression implies the content of belief about Jesus expressed in the ὅτι-clauses which we have considered. While πιστεύειν with the dative means to

[1] See pp. 168–9 above.
[2] Another such fresh coinage is ἐπί (with accus. or dat.), which is found occasionally elsewhere in the New Testament, but not in the Fourth Gospel.
[3] The only exception is viii. 30–1, if the many who ἐπίστευσαν εἰς αὐτόν are to be identified with οἱ πεπιστευκότες αὐτῷ Ἰουδαῖοι, which is probable but not certain.
[4] Outside the Johannine writings it is found only in Matt. xviii. 6, Ac. x. 43, xiv. 23, xix. 4(?), Rom. x. 14, Gal. ii. 16, Phil. i. 29, I Pet. i. 8(?). Similarly, πιστός and πίστις are occasionally found with εἰς.

give credence to the words which Jesus speaks, πιστεύειν εἰς αὐτόν means to have a confidence in Him based upon an intellectual acceptance of the claims made for His person.

A phrase which needs special consideration is πιστεύειν εἰς τὸ ὄνομα αὐτοῦ (i. 12, ii. 23, iii. 18). It is apparent that the meaning does not substantially differ from that of πιστεύειν εἰς αὐτόν; but the use of ὄνομα is remarkable. It is peculiarly Johannine, and it goes along with his predilection for ὄνομα in other significant connections. No doubt the Semitic conception of the name as in some sort the symbol of the personality lies behind it. But it is perhaps worth while recalling that εἰς τὸ ὄνομα is specifically used in primitive Christianity of baptism. Various theories have been held about the meaning of baptism into the Name of Christ. The most probable is that which connects it with the use of ὄνομα with the implication of ownership on the one part, allegiance on the other.[1] To be baptized into the name of Christ is to take a step by which one passes into the absolute ownership of Christ and owes Him henceforth allegiance, as a δοῦλος to his κύριος. Is it not possible that, as baptism is always closely associated with faith, the evangelist has applied directly to faith a conception bound up with baptism? Thus πιστεύειν εἰς τὸ ὄνομα αὐτοῦ would be not simply to accept His claim, by intellectual assent, but to acknowledge that claim by yielding allegiance.

This emphatic sense might well be in place in i. 12: to receive the Logos in a sense which entitles one to become a child of God means to enter Christ's allegiance (not merely to believe His words or accept His claims).[2] Negatively, judgment falls on those who have not entered Christ's allegiance, but prefer darkness to light (iii. 18). But in ii. 23 it is less probable, since we are told of persons who ἐπίστευσαν εἰς τὸ ὄνομα αὐτοῦ, and yet Jesus οὐκ ἐπίστευεν αὐτὸν αὐτοῖς, because He knew them too well. It may be that πιστεύειν εἰς τὸ ὄνομα αὐτοῦ is no more than a variant, in these three places, of the commoner πιστεύειν εἰς αὐτόν.

Thus, as Bultmann (op. cit. s.v. γινώσκω, p. 713) observes, πιστεύειν takes over in Johannine language an element of the meaning of the Hebrew יָדַע which the Greek γινώσκειν was incapable of expressing: for יָדַע אֶת־הָאֱלֹהִים means to acknowledge God by way of submission to His will; and similarly πιστεύειν εἰς (Χριστόν), or πιστεύειν εἰς τὸ ὄνομα

---

[1] Examples in M.M. s.v. See also Deissmann, *Bible Studies* (1909), pp. 146–7, 197.
[2] Similarly I John v. 13 ταῦτα ἔγραψα ὑμῖν ἵνα εἰδῆτε ὅτι ζωὴν αἰώνιον ἔχετε, τοῖς πιστεύουσιν εἰς τὸ ὄνομα τοῦ υἱοῦ τοῦ θεοῦ.

FAITH

αὐτοῦ, means to acknowledge Christ and to accept Him as the revelation of God.

(v) We can now profitably turn to the absolute use of πιστεύειν. There are indeed a certain number of passages where the verb is used alone, but where the context clearly shows that some completing idea is to be supplied. Thus in iii. 18 we have ὁ μὴ πιστεύων ἤδη κέκριται, but the phrase clearly echoes ὁ πιστεύων εἰς αὐτόν of the preceding sentence, and in xii. 39 οὐκ ἠδύνατο πιστεύειν refers back to τίς ἐπίστευσεν τῇ ἀκοῇ; of xii. 38. With such cases we are not concerned, but only with such uses as are truly absolute. There are again places where πιστεύειν is used in the sense which, as we know from Acts, was generally current in the early Church, 'to be or become a Christian'. So in iv. 53 ἐπίστευσεν αὐτὸς καὶ ἡ οἰκία αὐτοῦ, which has a close parallel in Acts xvi. 34.

But there remain certain passages where πιστεύειν is used without any addition either expressed or clearly implied, and where the meaning is evidently something more than the *gemeinchristlich* sense of the phrase. Here we are reminded of that absolute use of πιστεύειν which we have found in the LXX and the *Hermetica*. Thus in i. 7 ἵνα μαρτυρήσῃ περὶ τοῦ φωτός, ἵνα πάντες πιστεύσωσιν δι' αὐτοῦ, the most natural meaning is 'that all might come to have faith'. In xi. 15 Jesus declares that He is glad of the opportunity offered by the death of Lazarus, ἵνα πιστεύητε— not, I think, in order that they may 'believe in' Him, specifically, though no doubt this is included; but that they may 'have faith'.

This absolute use of πιστεύειν is most common in passages which speak also of 'seeing'. Thus, vi. 36 καὶ ἑωράκατέ με καὶ οὐ πιστεύετε: xi. 40 ἐὰν πιστεύσῃς ὄψῃ τὴν δόξαν τοῦ θεοῦ, and again, vi. 46-7 οὐχ ὅτι τὸν πατέρα ἑώρακέν τις, εἰ μὴ ὁ ὢν παρὰ τοῦ θεοῦ, οὗτος ἑώρακεν τὸν πατέρα. ἀμήν, ἀμήν, λέγω ὑμῖν, ὁ πιστεύων ἔχει ζωὴν αἰώνιον. Most significant of all is xx. 25-9, the episode in which Thomas recognizes the risen Lord. The disciples say, ἑωράκαμεν τὸν κύριον. Thomas replies, ἐὰν μὴ ἴδω...οὐ μὴ πιστεύσω. Jesus appears to him and says, μὴ γίνου ἄπιστος ἀλλὰ πιστός—i.e. have faith. Thomas makes the confession, ὁ κύριός μου καὶ ὁ θεός μου, in which his faith is expressed. Then Jesus replies, ὅτι ἑώρακάς με, πεπίστευκας; μακάριοι οἱ μὴ ἰδόντες καὶ πιστεύσαντες. Even though at a pinch one might supply a ὅτι-clause with πεπίστευκας, the final πιστεύσαντες clearly refers to those who 'have faith'.

In these passages we discern a certain conception of a relation between faith and vision. In the first place, there is a form of vision, simple physical vision, which may exist without faith. Many of the contemporaries of Jesus saw Him in this sense, but without any saving effects. But when simple vision is accompanied by faith, it leads to vision in a deeper sense. No one, it is true, has direct vision of God; but he who has faith has eternal life: faith therefore is the equivalent of the life-giving vision, or knowledge, of God. Finally, in the Thomas-episode we have the transition: Thomas is of those who have seen Christ, physically, and, having faith, he has seen Him in the true sense: but more blessed are they who, without the physical sight of Him, have faith. 'If you have faith, you will see the glory of God', Jesus had said to Martha (xi. 40). In the prologue it is said ἐθεασάμεθα τὴν δόξαν αὐτοῦ: the evangelist speaks for those who have faith, and therefore vision. We may now recall Philo's equation of πίστις with ἀφανοῦς ὑπόληψις, and the Hermetic association of πίστις with knowledge, life and light.

Faith, then, is a form of vision. When Christ was on earth, to have faith was to 'see His glory'[1]—to apprehend and acknowledge the deity through the veil of humanity. Now that He is no longer visible to the bodily eye, faith remains the capacity for seeing His glory. This conception is vital to the evangelist's whole conception of the incarnation. Eternal life is the knowledge or vision of God. But no man has seen God at any time, as the mystics do vainly talk. He who has seen Christ has seen the Father. What, have the unbelieving Jews who saw Jesus seen the Father? No; to see the Father in Christ, to see His glory, was and always is the part of faith, ἀφανοῦς ὑπόληψις, and this is just as possible, and just as necessary, for us as for those who saw Him in the flesh. Thus πίστις is that form of knowledge, or vision, appropriate to those who find God in an historic Person of the past, a Person who nevertheless, through it, remains the object of saving knowledge, the truth and the life.

[1] On 'glory' see pp. 206–8, 373–4.

6. UNION WITH GOD

In examining the concept of knowledge of God, which is eternal life, we found that at a certain point this concept passed into a further idea of the relation between God and men, which may be defined as one of reciprocal or mutual immanence: 'You will know that I am in the Father, and you in me, and I in you' (xiv. 20, see p. 169). At this point we paused to examine the relations of γνῶσις with ἀλήθεια and with faith. Having cleared up these points we return to examine the idea of union with God by mutual indwelling.

It is to be observed that there is an obviously intentional parallelism between expressions used regarding the mutual indwelling, and the mutual knowledge, of God (Christ) and men. They may be tabulated as follows:

The Father knows the Son (x. 15)	The Son is in the Father (xiv. 10–11, 20, xvii. 21)
The Son knows the Father (x. 15)	The Father is in the Son (xiv. 10–11, xvii. 21, 23)
The Son knows men (x. 14)	Men are in the Son (xiv. 20, xvii. 21)
Men know the Son (x. 14)	The Son is in men (xiv. 20, xvii. 23, 26)
Men know (see) Father and Son (xiv. 7–8)	Men are in Father and Son (xvii. 21)

In both cases Christ mediates to men the relation in which He stands to the Father. We shall therefore assume that, as the general concept of γνῶσις θεοῦ lies behind the Johannine doctrine of γνῶσις, so behind the complex Johannine doctrine of mutual indwelling lies the more general concept ἐν θεῷ.

The expression ἐν θεῷ occurs with various shades of meaning in the religious language of Hellenism. There is an ancient and persistent usage in which the phrase is exactly parallel with similar prepositional phrases used with reference to men. Thus in Sophocles, *O.T.* 314, Oedipus appeals to Teiresias, as προστάτης and σωτήρ, to save Thebes from disaster: ἐν σοὶ γὰρ ἐσμέν, 'We are in your hands.' Similarly in *O.C.* 247, Antigone throws herself upon the compassion of the elders of Attica:

ἐν ὑμῖν ὡς θεῷ κείμεθα τλάμονες, 'We are dependent on you as on God'
Cf. Pindar, *Ol.* XIII. 104 νῦν ἔλπομαι μέν, ἐν θεῷ γε μὰν τέλος, 'I hope,
but the issue is in God's hands.'

Whatever may be the precise origin of this usage, its meaning is clear
enough. The preposition indicates complete dependence on a person,
whether human or divine. It may be that originally a man's fate was
thought of, with naïve realism, as an invisible something lying within
the hands of the person, God or man, who had power over him; but
in any case the local sense of the preposition has in effect been lost.

In the Hellenistic period, however, a usage appears in which the original,
local sense of ἐν is still felt. In the *Hermetica* the expression ἐν θεῷ is
frequently used of the relation of the universe to God as its Creator and
upholder. Thus, *C.H.* VIII. 5 'The world is caused by God and is in God;
and man is caused by the world and is in the world. God is the origin
of all things, encompasses them and holds them together', ὁ μὲν κόσμος
ὑπὸ τοῦ θεοῦ καὶ ἐν τῷ θεῷ, ὁ δὲ ἄνθρωπος ὑπὸ τοῦ κόσμου καὶ ἐν τῷ
κόσμῳ, ἀρχὴ δὲ καὶ περιοχὴ καὶ σύστασις πάντων ὁ θεός, *C.H.* IX. 9
'All things that exist...are in God and caused by God and depend on
Him', πάντα γὰρ ὅσα ἔστιν...ταῦτα ἐν τῷ θεῷ ἐστι καὶ ὑπὸ τοῦ θεοῦ
γινόμενα καὶ ἐκεῖθεν ἠρτημένα. Sometimes this relation is represented as
mediated. Thus *C.H.* XI. 2 'Αἰών is in God, and the world in αἰών, time
in the world, and γένεσις in time.' In a somewhat similar way the
immanence of man in God is expressed: *C.H.* XII. 13 'The soul is in the
body and νοῦς in the soul; λόγος in νοῦς, and νοῦς in God'; or, somewhat
differently, *C.H.* XI. 4 'God is in νοῦς, and νοῦς in the soul: ...and the
soul is full of νοῦς and of God.' It will be observed that the proposition
that man is in God (because he is in νοῦς) can be simply converted,
without change of meaning, into the proposition that God (as mediated
by νοῦς) is in man, so that the soul is full of God; just as the cosmological
doctrine that the world is in God can be otherwise expressed in the form
'The creator is in all things' (ὁ ποιῶν ἐν πᾶσίν ἐστιν, *C.H.* XI. 6). It is
a case of reciprocal immanence.

This mode of expression properly belongs to the Stoic pantheism.
Cf. Marcus Aurelius Antoninus, IV. 23 πᾶν μοι καρπὸς ὃ φέρουσιν αἱ σαὶ
ὧραι ὦ φύσις· ἐκ σοῦ πάντα, ἐν σοὶ πάντα, εἰς σὲ πάντα: Dio Chrysostom,
Orat. XII. 28, p. 384 'We are not situated afar from the divine, nor outside it by ourselves, but we are by nature in its very midst, or rather, we
are united with it, and attached to it in every possible way', ἅτε οὐ μακρὰν
οὐδ' ἔξω τοῦ θείου διῳκισμένοι καθ' αὑτούς, ἀλλ' ἐν αὐτῷ μέσῳ πεφυκότες,

μᾶλλον δὲ συμπεφυκότες[1] ἐκείνῳ, καὶ προσεχόμενοι πάντα τρόπον. Thus for Dio, ἐν θεῷ, or rather, ἐν τῷ θείῳ, is an expression for the most intimate union conceivable with the divine. It is this kind of language that is imitated in Acts xvii. 28 ἐν αὐτῷ γὰρ ζῶμεν καὶ κινούμεθα καὶ ἐσμέν. According to Norden, *Agnostos Theos*, p. 23, this use of the preposition goes back to the genuinely Attic usage we have noted, expressing 'unqualified dependence on a mightier'. The idea of dependence is certainly present in the *Hermetica* (cf. ἐκεῖθεν ἠρτημένα, *C.H.* ix. 9 above), but the dominant idea seems to be spacial. God is the περιοχή (*C.H.* viii. 5), or ὁ περιέχων (*C.H.* xi. 18), that which encompasses or embraces the universe, and so 'God holds all things, and nothing is external to Him and He external to nothing' (*C.H.* ix. 9). But the spacial metaphor is often transferred to the psychological plane. Thus in *C.H.* xi. 18 'All things are in God, not as lying in space'; on the contrary they are 'in God' as concepts are in the mind. 'Conceive the matter thus from your own experience. Command your soul to go to India, and it will be there more quickly than your command. Command it to go to the Ocean, and again it will speedily be there, not as having moved from place to place, but as being there (*ibid.* 19)....Behold what power, what speed you have! Are you capable of all these things, and is not God? Think of God, then, as containing all *concepts* in Himself' (τοῦτον οὖν τὸν τρόπον νόησον τὸν θεόν, ὥσπερ νοήματα πάντα ἐν ἑαυτῷ ἔχειν) (*ibid.* 20). It might be objected that this is an example of the immanence of the mind in the world, and so in form it is: the mind is in India, at the Ocean, and so forth. But the meaning is that the *idea* (νόημα) of India is present to the mind. It is in fact this psychological approach which justifies the equivalence of the ideas, 'the world in God', and 'God in the world'. Thus the relation intended by the expression ἐν θεῷ is analogous to the relation of a thought to the mind that thinks. That this makes not only the universe, but also human personality, adjectival to the divine substance, is an objection that would not occur to our authors, nor if it did occur would it have been felt as an objection. For in the thought of the *Hermetica* and of 'Hellenistic mysticism' in general the separate personality of the individual is an insecure and vanishing concept.

Nevertheless, their interest is not so barely metaphysical as this quasi-pantheistic language might seem to imply. I have already pointed out that in *C.H.* v, which is in expression perhaps more unreservedly pan-

---

[1] Cf. Rom. vi. 5 σύμφυτοι γεγόναμεν τῷ ὁμοιώματι τοῦ θανάτου αὐτοῦ.

theistic than any other Hermetic tractate, the tone is that of rapt and exalted worship.

When shall I praise thee?...For what shall I praise thee?...Wherefore shall I praise thee? As being mine? As having any property of thine own? As being another? Nay, thou art whatever I am, thou art whatever I do, thou art whatever I say. For thou art all, and there is nothing else. Even that which is not, thou art. Thou art all that has come into being: thou art that which has not come into being—Mind that thinks, Father that creates, God that works, good and making all things (*C.H.* v. 11).

The language of metaphysical pantheism is used to express a sense of most intimate unity with God which is profoundly religious. This genuinely religious experience of union with God with a background of pantheistic thought seems properly to be called mystical.

This deeply religious or mystical significance of the expression ἐν θεῷ is most strikingly brought out in *C.H.* XIII (*De Regeneratione*). Here Tat is 'born again' through waiting on 'the mercy of God', by which the divine δυνάμεις, ethically conceived, are implanted in him εἰς συνάρθρωσιν τοῦ λόγου. Thus the divine Logos is constituted in him. Since the Logos is the cosmic principle, this means that he is identified with the universe, and bears to God the relation which the universe bears to Him. Thus the reborn can speak of 'the universe that is in me', τὸ πᾶν τὸ ἐν ἐμοί, or conversely he can say, ἐν οὐρανῷ εἰμι, ἐν γῇ, ἐν ὕδατι, ἐν ἀέρι· ἐν ζῴοις εἰμι, ἐν φυτοῖς, ἐν γαστρί, πρὸ γαστρός, μετὰ γαστέρα, πανταχοῦ. But the universe is 'in God'. Hence the whole process can be described as ἡ ἐν θεῷ γένεσις. The author has deliberately sought to give a religious and ethical content to the metaphysical pantheism of his school.

Beside this philosophical use of the expression ἐν θεῷ we must also consider the more widely current adjective ἔνθεος or ἔνθους, whence the verb ἐνθουσιάζειν, and the noun ἐνθουσιασμός. It is not quite clear whether the form ἔνθεος is the grammatical equivalent of ἐν θεῷ, on the analogy of most adjectives of this formation, e.g. ἔντοπος, ἔνδημος, ἐνάλιος, ἐνόριος, ἔγκαιρος, etc., or whether it means 'containing God', on the analogy of ἔμψυχος, ἔμπνους, ἐναίματος, ἔνοινος, ἔνσπορος, ἔγκαρπος,[1] and a few others. But as we have seen it matters little from which end the relation is regarded. In any case the meaning of ἔνθεος is well established. The adjective denotes possession by a god, exhibiting itself in ecstasy

[1] Observe that our own language falls into a similar ambiguity, for we speak of a man being '*in* his right mind', '*in* his senses', of a tree being '*in* flower', '*in* fruit', even of a cow being '*in* calf'.

or sacred frenzy, like that of the worshippers of Dionysus, or, on a higher religious level, in the inspiration of the prophet.

It is in this sense that the word and its derivatives are freely employed by Philo, especially with reference to Moses and the prophets. He frequently speaks of ἔνθεος κατοχή (or κατοκωχή), ἔνθεος μανία, and the like. It is particularly interesting that Philo claims to have experience of such inspiration.

I am not ashamed [he says] to relate my own experience, which I have had thousands of times. Sometimes when I wish to turn to my customary writing of philosophical doctrines, and know quite well what I am to write, I have found my mind sterile and barren, and have gone away with nothing done.... At other times I have come with my mind empty, and suddenly I have become full of thoughts invisibly sown or dropped like snow from above, so that I have been frenzied with divine possession (ὑπὸ κατοχῆς ἐνθέου κορυβαντιᾶν), and unconscious of the place, the company, myself, and spoken and written words (*De Migr. Abr.* 34–5).

What Philo supposed to happen in such cases he sets forth in various passages.

So long as our own mind, pouring as it were noonday light into the whole soul, shines about us and encompasses us, we are in ourselves [ἐν ἑαυτοῖς as opposed to ἐν θεῷ], and are not possessed. But when this light reaches its setting, then, as might be expected, ecstasy and divine possession and madness fall upon us. For when the divine light shines, the human sets, and when it sets, then the other rises and shines. And this is wont to happen to the prophetic kind. The mind that is in us is banished at the coming of the divine spirit, and at its departure returns home.... For the prophet, even when he appears to speak, is in truth silent, and Another uses his organs of speech, his mouth and tongue, to declare whatsoever He wills (*Quis Rer.* 264–6).

One might expect to find that Philo would connect this condition of ecstasy with the knowledge or vision of God which is eternal life, but he does not appear directly to do so. In one passage at least he appears to say that it may bring one to the verge of vision, but no further. The mind, he says, is able to penetrate all parts of the visible universe, and beyond it to the κόσμος νοητός of eternal Forms. Then,

possessed by a sober intoxication, it is in ecstasy (ἐνθουσιᾷ), like the Corybants, filled with longing and desire for something other and better, and led by this desire to the utmost circumference of the noumenal world (πρὸς τὴν ἄκραν ἀψῖδα τῶν νοητῶν), it thinks to approach the great King himself; but just when it is striving to see, the pure and unmixed rays of the total light stream upon it like a torrent, so that the eye of the understanding is darkened by the dazzling radiance (*De Opif.* 71).

The term ἔνθεος, therefore, Philo seems to use only in the limited sense of prophetic ecstasy, which is close to its current use in Greek paganism. The expression ἐν θεῷ he uses occasionally, but without any suggestion of the ecstatic condition. Thus he says of Abel, 'Most paradoxically, he is killed and yet lives: he is killed out of the mind of folly, and he lives the blessed life in God (τὴν ἐν θεῷ ζωὴν εὐδαίμονα) (*Quod Det.* 48). The meaning does not seem to be clearly different from that of ἡ πρὸς θεὸν ζωή, τὸ κατὰ θεὸν ζῆν, expressions which occur elsewhere, indicating the life of virtue or wisdom, divinely given and directed, lived in dependence on God, in conformity with His will. Cf. also ἡ ἐν θεῷ χαρά (*De Ebriet.* 62), ἡ ἐν θεῷ ἀνάπαυσις (*De Fug.* 174). Even the last expression does not seem to have any specifically 'mystical' implications. The meaning of the phrase in Philo might quite well be derived from the well-established Greek use of it to denote dependence on God, or it might follow the usage of the LXX where such expressions as 'rejoice in the Lord', 'in the Lord is everlasting strength', leave the particular connotation of the preposition quite vague.

So far, then, our search for possible antecedents of Johannine usage has revealed a fairly wide range of imprecise meaning—dependence on God, conformity with His will, and the like—and two specific meanings: ecstatic possession by the divine, and, in a quasi-pantheistic sense, a 'mystical' inclusion in, or absorption into, the divine being.

We have still to enquire whether any help is to be found in Christian usage prior to the Fourth Gospel. Here Paul comes into question. He uses the expression ἐν θεῷ five times. In two cases, Rom. ii. 17, v. 11, the expression is καυχᾶσθαι ἐν θεῷ, a quite ordinary use of ἐν which does not help us at all; cf. Isocrates, *Panegyricus*, 121 οὐκ ἐν ἐκείνῳ ἔχομεν τὰς ἐλπίδας τῆς σωτηρίας. In Eph. iii. 9 it is a matter of a mystery 'hidden in God', which we may fairly take as a psychological use: the secret was 'in' God's mind, as it might be in a human mind. In I Thess. ii. 2 ἐπαρρησιασάμεθα ἐν τῷ θεῷ ἡμῶν, the meaning may be 'in dependence on God' or the like, after the vague manner of similar expressions in Philo. Only in Col. iii. 3 do we find a use which in any way recalls that of the Fourth Gospel: 'Your life is hidden with Christ in God.' Here we may probably recognize a half-unconscious spacial metaphor, helped out by the verb κέκρυπται. But there is no exactitude of meaning.

It is however the Pauline expression ἐν Χριστῷ which, especially since Deissmann's famous monograph on the subject,[1] has been commonly assumed to be the basis of the Johannine usage. According to Deissmann this is a spacial metaphor. Christ is regarded in the aspect of πνεῦμα, as a kind of spiritual space, if the expression may be allowed, within which the believer lives, as in an atmosphere. If so, then the Pauline usage might be compared with the 'mystical' sense of ἐν θεῷ, and we might recall that as Dio Chrysostom speaks of our being συμπεφυκότες τῷ θείῳ, so Paul speaks of our being σύμφυτοι with the likeness of Christ's death (or with Christ in the likeness of His death). This is what is usually meant by speaking of Paul's 'Christ-mysticism', as distinct from the 'God-mysticism' of Hellenistic writers. (Acts xvii. 28 does not represent normal Pauline usage.[2]) An examination however of the wide range of the expression ἐν Χριστῷ in the epistles seems rather to justify Schweitzer's view[3] that it is closely related to the idea of the solidarity of all believers in the Body of Christ, which is the Church. The metaphor is still spacial; but it is not a case of the individual living 'in Christ' as in a surrounding atmosphere, but of his forming part of an organic society in which Christ is active. Hence we can understand that Paul never speaks of Christ as being 'in God' as we are in Him. Col. iii. 3 might indeed be regarded as implying this; but it is significant that in this case the formula is σὺν τῷ Χριστῷ ἐν τῷ θεῷ. In II Cor. v. 19 we have θεὸς ἦν ἐν Χριστῷ,[4] but there is no correlative, Χριστὸς ἐν θεῷ. This differentiates the Pauline usage from the Johannine, for it is essential to the latter that the relation ἐγὼ ἐν τῷ πατρὶ καὶ ὁ πατὴρ ἐν ἐμοί is the direct archetype of the relation ὑμεῖς ἐν ἐμοὶ κἀγὼ ἐν ὑμῖν, and there is no suggestion of this in Paul. While therefore it would be rash to exclude Pauline influence, we cannot safely assume that the Johannine usage depends directly upon the Pauline, or may be directly explained from it.

We now turn to examine the Johannine expressions in their contexts in the gospel itself.

[1] *Die neutestamentliche Formel 'In Christo Jesu'*, von Adolf Deissmann, Marburg, 1892.

[2] It does not necessarily follow that the author of Acts has radically misrepresented Paul, who was capable of adopting in *ad hominem* argument language which he would not wish to be pressed too far.

[3] In *Die Mystik des Apostels Paulus*, 1930.

[4] Unless the sentence should be construed with ἦν καταλλάσσων, as an analytic present of continuous action: 'God was engaged in reconciling the world to Himself by the agency of Christ.' But the other construction seems more natural, 'God was in Christ, reconciling the world to Himself.'

We may begin with a passage dealing directly with the relation of Christ to the Father. In x. 30 Christ makes the great declaration 'I and the Father are one.' The Jews are scandalized; Jesus defends Himself, first by appeal to Scripture, and then with the clinching argument, 'If I am not doing the works of my Father, do not believe me; but if I am, then even if you do not believe me, believe the works, that you may know and recognize that the Father is in me, and I in the Father' (x. 37–8). Again in xiv. 8–11 there is a conversation with the disciples of similar purport: 'He who has seen me has seen the Father. How then can you say, Show us the Father? Do you not believe that I am in the Father and the Father in me? the words which I am speaking to you I do not speak of myself, and the Father who dwells in me is doing His works. Believe me, I am in the Father and the Father in me; or at least believe because of the works themselves.'

From these passages we learn (a) that the expression, 'I in the Father and the Father in me', is intended to describe a unity between Father and Son so close that to see the Son is tantamount to the *visio Dei*; and (b) that the relation so described is either constituted by, or at least manifested in, an activity which, though its proximate agent is the Son, is in reality that of the Father. We may now recall other passages which speak of the 'works' of God. 'My Father is working until now, and I am working' (v. 17). 'The Son can do nothing of Himself, but what he sees the Father doing; for what He does, the Son does likewise' (v. 19). 'I do nothing of myself, but as the Father taught me, I speak these things, and He who sent me is with me; He has not left me alone, because I do always what is pleasing to Him' (viii. 28–9). 'We must work the works of Him who sent me while it is day' (ix. 4). In the light of such passages as these it is clear that the relation described in the words, 'I in the Father and the Father in me', is conceived as a dynamic and not a static relation; it consists in an activity originating with the Father and manifested in the Son. It may be described as obedience to the word of the Father, or imitation of His works, but at bottom it is nothing so external as mere obedience or imitation. It is the sharing of one life, which is of course life eternal or absolute. 'The living Father has sent me, and I live διὰ τὸν πατέρα' (vi. 57). 'As the Father has life in Himself, so He has granted to the Son to have life in Himself' (v. 26). We cannot miss here the reference to the 'living God' of the Old Testament. Finally this sharing of life and activity is rooted in the love of God. 'The Father loves the Son, and shows Him what He Himself does' (v. 20); 'the

Father loves the Son, and has placed everything in His hands' (iii. 35).
And conversely, 'I love the Father and as the Father commanded me,
so I do' (xiv. 31).

The idea, therefore, that the Son is in the Father and the Father in the
Son is at least closely related to the idea that the love of the Father for
the Son, returned by Him, establishes a community of life between Father
and Son, which exhibits itself in that the Son speaks the Father's word
and does His works. Thus the glory of the Father is revealed in the Son:
'Now is the Son of Man glorified and God is glorified in Him; if God is
glorified in Him, then also God will glorify Him in Himself' (xiii. 32).[1]

This connection of ideas recurs where the relation of Father and Son
is expressly treated as archetype of the relation of Christ and His disciples.
The two decisive passages are in ch. xiv and ch. xv, respectively.

We have already considered xiv. 8–11 (p. 194 above), which deals
with the relation of Father and Son. We now read on:

I assure you, he who has faith in me will do the works I am doing; and
because I am going to the Father, he will do greater works still; in fact, anything
he asks in my name I will do,[2] in order that the Father may be glorified in the
Son. If you love me, you will observe my commands.... After a short while
the world will see no more of me, but you will see me; because I live, you will
live too. Then you will know that I am in the Father, and you in me and I in
you.... Anyone who loves me will observe my commands, and my Father will
love him, and we will come to him and make our dwelling with him. He who
does not love me does not observe what I say—not that it is my word but the
word of the Father who sent me (xiv. 12–15, 19–20, 23–4).

Along with this we may read vi. 56–7: 'He who eats my flesh and
drinks my blood dwells in me and I in him   As the living Father sent me,
and I live because of the Father, so he who feeds upon me will live
because of me.'

If we put these passages together, the thought is clear. At every point
the unity of Father and Son is reproduced in the unity of Christ and
believers. As the love of the Father for the Son, returned by Him in
obedience, establishes a community of life between Father and Son,
which exhibits itself in that He speaks the Father's word and does His
works, so the disciples are loved by Christ and return His love in

---

[1] For the Johannine use of the terms δόξα, δοξάζειν, see pp. 206–8, 373–4.

[2] The 'greater works' which the disciples are to do are after all done by Christ
in response to their prayer to the Father in His name. Consequently, the 'glory'
of them is Christ's, that is to say, God's. Such seems to be the sequence of thought.

obedience; in doing so, they share His life, which manifests itself in doing His works; it is really He who does them (just as the works of Christ are done by the Father), and by the doing of them the Father is glorified in the Son. This is what is meant by the expression, 'I in you and you in me'.

The other passage, xv. 1–12, is based upon the symbol of the vine, which in itself suggests a unity like that of a living plant, in which a common life, flowing from the central stem, nourishes all the branches and issues in fruit.[1] It is made clear that what is meant is the unity of the disciples in the love which is perfectly mutual between Father and Son, manifesting itself, once again, in obedience to the word or command of Christ (which is the word of the Father given to Him), which issues in action. The expressions,

> Abide in me and I in you (xv. 4);
> Abide in me and let my words abide in you (xv. 7);
> Abide in my love (xv. 9);

are all equivalent, and each has its correspondence with the archetypal relation of Father and Son. Finally, the command of Christ is, 'Love one another as I have loved you' (xv. 12). The triangle of relations is complete: the Father, the Son, and the disciples dwell in one another by virtue of a love which is the very life and the activity of God. In the Father, it is the love that gave the Son for the world; in the Son it is the love that brings forth perfect obedience to the Father's will, and lays down life for the disciples; in the disciples it is the love that leads them to obey His command and to love one another; and by their obedience the Father is glorified in the Son.

Finally, the idea of unity by mutual indwelling receives classical expression in the prayer of Christ in ch. xvii. With the passages in mind which we have already examined, we may now read the relevant clauses of the prayer with some measure of precise understanding of its closely packed meaning. For the disciples Christ prays, simply, 'that they may

---

[1] Here the Johannine idea of mutual indwelling comes closest to the Pauline ἐν Χριστῷ, which is exemplified not only in the σῶμα Χριστοῦ, but also in the olive-tree which is the true people of God, from which the unfruitful branches have been severed, in order that through faith new branches might be grafted into it (Rom. xi. 16–24). For John, as for Paul, the individual's inherence in Christ is inseparable from the unity of individual believers with one another in the Church. (See my note on κοινωνία, *Commentary on Johannine Epistles*, pp. 6–8.) Yet the way in which the idea is grounded and worked out is so different that it is unlikely that John owes it to Paul.

be one, as we are' (xvii. 11; cf. x. 30). Then, as the thought broadens, He prays for all who in time to come will become Christians: 'that they may all be one, as thou, Father, art in me and I in thee, that they may be in us... that they may be one as we are one; I in them and thou in me, that they may be made perfectly one' (xvii. 20–23). It is clear that for the evangelist, as for Hellenistic writers whom I have cited, the idea, ἐν θεῷ, with its correlative, 'God in us', stands for the most intimate union conceivable between God and men. But it clearly does not mean for him, as it does for some of them, an impersonal inclusion, or absorption, into the divine, conceived pantheistically; nor does it mean, as for some others, an ecstatic possession by a divine afflatus. It is so far like the former that it involves a real community of being, a sharing of life; and it is so far like the latter that it is a dynamic relation and not a static, producing the effects of an incursion of divine energy through which men may speak the words and do the works of God. But it is unlike both in being a personal relation with a living God, mediated through a concrete, historical personality, in whom that relation is original and perfect. It is not a question of inhering as it were adjectivally in the absolute Substance. God is 'the living Father'. His life is the outpouring of love. Nor is the divine love conceived abstractly, as when a Hermetic writer speaks of God loving the universe as His own offspring (Λόγος Τέλειος = *Asclepius* 8). It is a radically personal form of life, manifested in the concrete activity of Christ in laying down His life for His friends (xv. 13, in the context of some of the strongest expressions of the idea of mutual indwelling); by which we know that God so loved the world that He gave His Son (iii. 16). It is by becoming first the objects of this love, and then in turn the subjects of the same love, directed towards Christ and towards one another, that we become one by mutual indwelling both with Father and Son and with one another in Him; but all this, at every stage, in terms of living action—doing the works of God, bearing fruit to His glory.

This is perhaps the place to say something upon the question, which has been much discussed in recent years, whether the type of religion represented by the Fourth Gospel can or cannot properly be described as 'mysticism'. In this country at least it has been customary to describe John in some such terms as 'the greatest of Christian mystics', and to regard the Fourth Gospel as naturalizing the mystical form of religion within Christianity. Some however would vigorously deny that the term 'mystical' is properly applicable. To some extent the dispute seems to be about words. There are few terms in the English language so loosely used as the terms 'mystic', 'mystical', 'mysticism'.[1] In this book I have used the term 'Hellenistic mysticism' for a type of religion which should by this time be fairly clearly recognizable. Using the term in this sense, Walter Bauer has written, in his commentary on this gospel:

Much is said today about the mysticism of the Gospel according to John, and this is doubtless right, if one has regard to the language used. But the question may be asked—it is no more than a question—how far the author really experienced and felt what he speaks of.... Did he experience anything more than conversion to Christianity? Did he, as a Christian believer, have the 'vision' (*hat er als Gläubiger 'geschaut'*)? Did he experience hours in which he felt himself one with Christ and God, or has he only adopted ideas and expressions of a mystically coloured piety already petrified in literature, and made them serve his own purposes? In any case [Bauer replies to his own question] he never trod or recommended the way of ecstasy. The vision of God is known to John only in the sense that the Father is seen in the Son. The Father Himself is and remains withdrawn from the eyes of men. Relations to God and Christ are established through the keeping of the commandments. It is there that knowledge of God and love to Him and to Christ find their appropriate expression.... This conception of what makes a Christian, as the keeping of commandments, makes it unlikely that the Christian life should reach its highest points at moments when the other world mysteriously interpenetrates this world.[2]

If the mystic is one whose religious life is expressed in ecstasy, or one who experiences an impersonal absorption in the divine, then Bauer is certainly right in refusing the name to the Fourth Evangelist. But to suggest that he was merely using stereotyped terms in vogue, without attaching any particular meaning to them, is precarious; and to reduce his conception of the Christian life to a kind of legalism ('keeping the commandments') is certainly to misunderstand him. His thought has two inseparable strains. On the one hand we have the language of γνῶσις θεοῦ, of vision, of the indwelling of man in God and of God in man. On the other hand we have the insistence on the deed, the fruit.

---

[1] We have not even the distinction which is drawn in German between '*Mystik*' and '*Mysticismus*'. Consider the variety of literature commonly to be found in a second-hand bookseller's catalogue under the heading 'Mysticism'! Among those who affect the Marxist jargon it appears (so far as it is more than a convenient term of opprobrium) to apply to any way of thinking which admits the reality of a non-material factor in human experience. Such terms are well avoided in discussion by those who aim at precision of thought, unless they are carefully defined and restricted.

[2] *Das Johannesevangelium* (1925), p. 240 (my translation).

Both these strains must be taken seriously. They do not lie side by side unassimilated. They are so fused that both acquire definition and fullness of meaning through their combination. It is not by denying, or emptying of real meaning, either the one set of concepts or the other that we are likely to understand the teaching of the Fourth Evangelist. It is his special characteristic that he combines these two aspects of the religious life in so remarkable a way. The idea in which they meet is that of the divine ἀγάπη. That such ἀγάπη will express itself in acts of brotherly love, to the laying down of life, is for him in the nature of the case. But while it expresses itself in obedience to the law of charity, the love of God is not to be identified with, or restricted to, law-abiding obedience.

The term ἀγάπη differs in meaning from ἔρως.[1] Plato in the *Symposium* 210–12 has given an account of a type of 'mystical' experience based on ἔρως, which is the upward striving of man towards union with a higher order of being. 'Αγάπη is characteristically the love which gives itself. It has its origin in God, the highest of beings, who, loving His creatures, raises them to Himself. Man cannot have ἀγάπη except in so far as the love of God acts upon him and in him: ἡμεῖς ἀγαπῶμεν, ὅτι αὐτὸς πρῶτος ἠγάπησεν ἡμᾶς (I John iv. 19). There is in the last resort no ἀγάπη but the love of God. The glory of God is manifested wherever His love becomes effective: supremely in the self-offering of Christ; and also in those who through Christ live by the love of God.

If now we are thinking in terms of union with God, is not love, as a matter of fact, the only kind of union *between persons* of which we can have any possible experience? 'Cosmic emotion' is not very uncommon, and it is possible for the philosopher to interpret it as unity with 'God' in a pantheistic sense, and so to give a religious colour to what is really a theory of the universe. It is also possible to interpret certain abnormal psychical states as 'possession' by the divine Spirit. But in neither case have we evidence that union with a personal God is attained. For the only kind of personal union, I repeat, with which we are acquainted is love. John says that this is in truth the kind of union with God given in the Christian religion. He makes use of the strongest expressions for union with God that contemporary religious language provided, in order to assure his readers that he does seriously mean what he says: that through faith in Christ we may enter into a personal community of life

---

[1] See *Theologisches Wörterbuch zum N.T.*, *s.v.* ἀγάπη: also A. Nygren: *Agape and Eros* (Eng. trans. Hebert and Watson, 1932–9). I may refer to what I have written in my *Commentary on the Johannine Epistles*, pp. 107–13.

with the eternal God, which has the character of ἀγάπη, which is essentially supernatural and not of this world, and yet plants its feet firmly in this world, not only because real ἀγάπη cannot but express itself in practical conduct, but also because the crucial act of ἀγάπη was actually performed in history, on an April day about A.D. 30, at a supper-table in Jerusalem, in a garden across the Kidron valley, in the headquarters of Pontius Pilate, and on a Roman cross at Golgotha. So concrete, so actual, is the nature of the divine ἀγάπη; yet none the less for that, by entering into the relation of ἀγάπη thus opened up for men, we may dwell in God and He in us. Whether this should be called 'mysticism' I do not know.[1]

[1] In these paragraphs I have in part anticipated the results of further discussions, but this seemed the best place to attempt some clarification of this particular issue.

7. LIGHT, GLORY, JUDGMENT

In an earlier chapter I drew attention to the use of formulae coupling 'life' and 'light' in Hellenistic religious language, and observed that in the Fourth Gospel the same conjunction is to be found. Our present investigation of the leading concepts of Johannine thought started with the concept of life. We found that John conceives ζωὴ αἰώνιος, the life of God, to be accessible to men here and now, though it implies for its fulfilment an order of existence beyond space and time. It consists in 'knowledge' of God, which is also communion with God, or 'dwelling in' God. So far, he speaks the common language of Hellenistic mysticism. But for him the knowledge of God which is union with God is not metaphysics, nor direct super-sensuous vision of the absolute, nor yet mystical ecstasy or 'enthusiasm'. It is conditioned by a relation to the historical manifestation of the Logos. It is here that ἀλήθεια, absolute reality as revealed, is to be found. Hence knowledge takes the form of faith, which is both an acceptance of the fact that Jesus Christ is the revelation of the eternal God, and a personal attachment to Him. It is not a stage preliminary to knowledge, but is itself the knowledge of God which is communion with Him and constitutes eternal life. It is a way of 'seeing' God.

So far we have followed a line of thought which started from the concept of life. We have now to take account of the twin-concept of light, and this will mean in some measure retracing our steps. The wide use of the term φῶς as a symbolic expression for the absolute or eternally real, often in sharp contrast with the σκότος of error or unreality, is supposed to owe something to the influence of Zoroastrianism, with its antithesis of light and darkness, the realms of Ahura-mazda and Angro-mainyu. Yet light seems to be a natural symbol for deity. Sun-worship was certainly one of the living faiths of the ancient world, and it had a revival under the Roman Empire. To the naïve observer, the light of the sun is both the cause of life on earth and at the same time the medium by which we become aware of phenomena. Plato gave philosophical status to this conception when he used the sun as a symbol of the Idea of Good, which is at once the *ratio essendi* and the *ratio cognoscendi* of the universe, and which he identified—or at any rate was understood to identify—with the supreme God. It was mainly due to Plato, so far as

I can see, that in the Hellenistic world religious thinkers of a philosophical cast generally adopted this particular kind of symbolism; and it was in terms of a philosophy which at least intended to be Platonic that they rationalized the mythology they adopted, whatever its sources.

By using the symbol of light it was possible to give an account of the relation of the absolute to phenomena, of God to the universe. Light communicates itself by radiations, which are emanations (so it was supposed) of its own substance. Similarly, the ἐνέργειαι of the universe are ἀκτῖνες τοῦ θεοῦ, or τοῦ νοῦ (*C.H.* x. 22; cf. II. 12, XVI. 16). Thus God is the light by whose diffused radiations we apprehend the phenomenal world. As we rise in the scale, we are illuminated by those superior radiations which are the 'ideas' constituting the κόσμος νοητός, until at last the mystic beholds the Light itself (which is God) not by any borrowed light but by itself.[1] This line of thought I have illustrated from Philo and the *Hermetica*.

In these and similar writings, as we have noted, light is commonly associated with life as a description of the real, or the divine. Philosophy is here taking a fresh draught from its original fount in naïve religious feeling, and at the same time responding to the growingly intense longing for an assurance of immortality, for, as we have seen, in such writings ζωή means both physical vitality and something more. If the source of light, by which we know, is also the source of life, then as we advance in knowledge to vision of the Light, we also partake of the Life. Among the sources from which this doctrine of life and light in unity[2] was drawn, it seems that we must include the Hebrew Scriptures. In the Old Testament both terms are freely used to express that ultimate blessedness or salvation which is God's gift to men. In this sense, and in this sense alone, God may be said to *be* His people's light. The two terms are associated in Ps. xxxv (xxxvi). 10 παρὰ σοῦ πηγὴ ζωῆς, ἐν τῷ φωτί σου ὀψόμεθα φῶς.[3] The Hebrew writer was of course innocent of metaphysics; but if his teaching is to be provided with philosophical justification, a philosophy like that of Plato or of the *Hermetica* suggests

---

[1] Cf. Philo, *De Praem.* 45 τὸ φῶς ἆρ' οὐ φωτὶ βλέπεται; τὸν αὐτὸν δὴ τρόπον καὶ ὁ θεὸς ἑαυτοῦ φέγγος ὢν δι' αὐτοῦ μόνου θεωρεῖται.... 46 ἀλήθειαν δὲ μετίασιν οἱ τὸν θεὸν θεῷ φαντασιωθέντες, φωτὶ φῶς. (Note also the association of φῶς and ἀλήθεια.)

[2] Cf. *C.H.* XIII. 12 ζωὴ δὲ καὶ φῶς ἡνωμέναι εἰσίν.

[3] For life and light in conjunction cf. (beside Ps. xxxv. 11) Ps. lv (lvi). 14 ἐν φωτὶ ζώντων, Job xxxiii. 28 ἡ ζωή μου φῶς ὄψεται. See *The Bible and the Greeks*, pp. 133–6.

itself. It is thus that Philo treats the passage from Ps. xxvi (xxvii). 1, which is one of his fundamental texts (see pp. 55–6 above). It will be well to have the relevant passage from Philo before us: πρῶτον μὲν ὁ θεὸς φῶς ἐστι—'κύριος' γὰρ 'φωτισμος μου καὶ σωτήρ μου' ἐν ὕμνοις ᾄδεται— καὶ οὐ μόνον φῶς, ἀλλὰ καὶ παντὸς ἑτέρου φωτὸς ἀρχέτυπον, μᾶλλον δὲ παντὸς ἀρχετύπου πρεσβύτερον καὶ ἀνώτερον (De Somn. I. 75). Philo, we observe, draws back from the statement that God is light:[1] He is the archetype of light, or rather, as Creator, prior to this, as to all archetypes. Here his inherited Hebraic belief in the personal transcendence of God (rather than Platonism) modifies his acquired Hellenism. Similarly, although in I John i. 5[2] we have the blunt statement ὁ θεὸς φῶς ἐστιν, the evangelist seems, like Philo, to have preferred to avoid it. His equivalent for Philo's φωτὸς ἀρχέτυπον is φῶς ἀληθινόν (i. 9); both are speaking of the eternal 'idea' of light, of which all empirical lights are transient copies.[3] This archetypal light, John says, was 'in' the Logos,[4] and it is in some sort interchangeable with life (i. 3–4). The Logos is the τόπος of the archetypal life and light; they are (as we might say) aspects of the Logos; while, for John as for Philo, the eternal fons deitatis, the Father to whom the Logos is Son, is prior to all archetypes. If now we read the propositions contained in the Prologue, i. 5–10, with reference to the φῶς ἀληθινόν, which is their immediate subject, we learn that the archetypal light shone in the darkness (of not-being, ignorance and error), and resisted the assaults of the darkness.[5] It is in the world (since the ἐνέργειαι of the visible universe are ἀκτῖνες of archetypal light). It en-

[1] But so also does the author of C.H. II. 14.

[2] The epistle I believe not to be the composition of the evangelist: see my Commentary on the Johannine Epistles, pp. xlvii–lvi.

[3] The ἀρχέτυπον φῶς of C.H. II. 13, if we accept the text of Stobaeus: it is an ἀκτίς of νοῦς=θεός, who is Himself αἴτιος τοῦ φῶς εἶναι, but not Himself φῶς. Cf. also C.H. I. 7–8, where the ἀρχέτυπον εἶδος is visible (to the mind's eye) as light.

[4] I shall not here discuss the question whether we should punctuate, with Origen, Comm. in Joann. (Brooke) II. 16 (10)–21 (15), pp. 69–74, at ἕν, or, with Chrysostom, In Johann. Hom. (Migne) v. 1, at γέγονεν. The question may have some theological importance, but for our present purpose it need not be decided. In any case the intimate connection of ζωή and φῶς 'in' the Logos is affirmed, as in viii. 12 the light is defined as φῶς τῆς ζωῆς (cf. perhaps ὁ λόγος τῆς ζωῆς in I John i. 1, but see my note ad loc.). In Philo and the Hermetica too the relations among these highest abstractions are stated in varying terms, without any ultimate variation in meaning.

[5] Cf. C.H. I. 5, where the λόγος, proceeding from φῶς, assails the chaos of darkness.

lightens every man[1] (since in every man there dwells that essential humanity (οὐσιώδης ἄνθρωπος, ἐνδιάθετος ἄνθρωπος) which is (as *Poimandres* has it) the offspring of 'the Father of all who is life and light'). The majority of mankind however are not aware of the presence of the light (they do not rise from contemplation of phenomena to recognition of their archetypes), but those who 'receive' the light, the 'enlightened' minority, have that knowledge of God which makes them sons of God and sharers in His life.[2]

I do not suggest that this is an adequate or final interpretation of the relevant clauses of the Prologue;[3] but taken at their face value they fall in so aptly with the current teaching of 'Hellenistic mysticism' that we cannot but conclude that the evangelist intended to indicate a metaphysic of this kind as the presupposition of his theology. Beyond this point he betrays no interest in metaphysics. The doctrine of the archetypal light becoming immanent in the world and in man is not the substance of his Gospel. The determining fact of the Gospel, to speak in these terms, is that the archetypal light was manifested in the person of Jesus Christ. He is the Light in which we see light; that is, He is ἀλήθεια, reality revealed, as He is also ζωή. He mediates to man that knowledge of God which is eternal life. Thus when John speaks of the light coming into the world (iii. 19, xii. 46) he is always thinking of the appearance of Jesus Christ in history.

It is as incarnate that, having 'come into the world', He becomes τὸ φῶς τοῦ κόσμου (viii. 12, ix. 5). The expression is modelled on a Hebraic pattern. In Rabbinic tradition[4] Israel, or Jerusalem, is אוֹרָה לְעוֹלָם, אוֹר שֶׁל־עוֹלָם; the Torah and the Temple are both called אוֹרוֹ שֶׁל־עוֹלָם;

---

[1] It is not necessary for our present purpose to decide whether the words ἐρχόμενον εἰς τὸν κόσμον should be connected with ἄνθρωπον or with φῶς, but in my own judgment there is scarcely any doubt that πάντα ἄνθρωπον ἐρχόμενον εἰς τὸν κόσμον represents the very common Hebrew expression כָּל־בָּאֵי הָעוֹלָם, meaning 'every mortal man' (see examples *apud* Schlatter *ad loc*. Note especially Lev. R. 31. 6: אתה מאיר...לכל באי עולם which exactly = σὺ φωτίζεις πάντας ἐρχομένους εἰς τὸν κόσμον). The attempt, on the other hand, to connect ἐρχόμενον with ἦν produces a type of sentence alien from this writer's style.

[2] For the distinction between the two classes of men cf. *C.H.* I. 22, where the prophet asks, οὐ πάντες γὰρ ἄνθρωποι νοῦν ἔχουσιν; to which the God replies, Εὐφήμει, ὁ οὗτος, λαλῶν· παραγίνομαι αὐτὸς ἐγὼ ὁ νοῦς τοῖς ὁσίοις καὶ ἀγαθοῖς καὶ καθαροῖς καὶ ἐλεήμοσι, τοῖς εὐσεβοῦσι, καὶ ἡ παρουσία μου γίνεται βοήθεια καὶ εὐθὺς τὰ πάντα γνωρίζουσι.

[3] See pp. 268–285.

[4] See S.-B. *ad* Matt. v. 14, from which the evidence here summarized is taken.

even an individual teacher of Torah like Jochanan ben Zakkai (a contemporary of the evangelist) is in one place called נֵר עוֹלָם, though in a parallel passage we have נֵר יִשְׂרָאֵל, which is possibly more original. (נֵר, however, recalls the description of John the Baptist as λύχνος ὁ καιόμενος καὶ φαίνων in John v. 35.) In several places where language of this kind is used, it is made clear that all such 'lights of the world' are only derivative: the ultimate אוֹרוֹ שֶׁל-עוֹלָם or נֵרוֹ שֶׁל עוֹלָם is God Himself. It appears that in the present passage the Jews are not supposed to understand the statement 'I am the light of the world' as a claim to divine attributes, for they do not object, as they do in other places, that Jesus is 'making himself a god', or 'making himself equal with God' (cf. x. 33, v. 18). It is sufficient for the situation as dramatized by the evangelist, that they understand Him to be claiming to mediate the Word of God to men in an authoritative way. But this is Johannine irony. The reader knows well enough that He who says ἐγώ εἰμι τὸ φῶς τοῦ κόσμου is Himself the φῶς ἀληθινόν.

That he is intended to have in mind ideas associated with φῶς in Hellenistic thought seems to follow from the way the argument develops in viii. 12 sqq. The Jews object that the claim to be 'the light of the world' is unsupported by any evidence beyond the speaker's own statement, and this proves nothing, since according to the Torah, 'No man is accredited by his own words...no man may give evidence in his own cause.'[1] The reply of Jesus is that His evidence on His own behalf is to be accepted because He knows whence He comes and where He is going, whereas His adversaries do not know this (viii. 14). This is in itself somewhat obscure as an argument; yet we may say that if a person had perfect knowledge of himself, a knowledge necessarily shared by no one else, then his own testimony would be in fact the only testimony available. But if we leave out of sight the dramatic situation, and consider the evangelist's own view, as indicated in the Prologue, then we recall that in the kind of philosophy to which his thought is akin the specific attribute of light is that while all other things are seen and known by means of light, light is known by itself alone: φῶς φωτὶ βλέπεται. Thus the real meaning of Jesus's reply is that His claim is self-evidencing. Indeed, a claim to be 'the light' could not possibly be substantiated by anything except the shining of the light. It is the purport of the whole gospel that the work of Christ is self-evidencing; His ἔργα are luminous (v. 36, xiv. 11).

[1] See passages cited by S.-B. *ad loc.*

LEADING IDEAS

This is expressed in the Prologue in the proposition that in the incarnate Christ men saw the 'glory' of the eternal Logos. To this statement we must now turn. The climax of the series of statements about the eternal light in the Prologue is the statement that the Logos, the τόπος of both life and light, σὰρξ ἐγένετο, and the effect of this, the evangelist adds, was that ἐθεασάμεθα τὴν δόξαν αὐτοῦ (i. 14). The association of δόξα with φῶς goes back to the Old Testament.

The term δόξα[1] in Greek means either 'opinion' (which, Plato said, stands somewhere between knowledge and ignorance), or else 'reputation', and in particular a good reputation, and so 'honour', 'distinction'. It is still somewhat obscure how the word acquired a new meaning which made it capable of translating the Hebrew כָּבוֹד, Aramaic יְקָרָא. It seems that it does not bear this meaning anywhere except where Jewish influence is probable.[2] כָּבוֹד means the manifestation of God's being, nature and presence, in a manner accessible to human experience; and the manifestation was conceived in the form of radiance, splendour, or dazzling light (originally, perhaps, the lightning flash accompanying the thunder which for the naïve religious mind is the voice of God: cf. John xii. 29, a striking example of Johannine irony, amounting here almost to sarcasm). In Judaism of the Christian era, the שְׁכִינָה ('dwelling', or presence of God) was conceived as light.

It is therefore not surprising that δόξα and φῶς are found in parallelism referring to the manifestation of the power of God for the salvation of His people. Thus, in Is. lx. 1–3 φωτίζου, φωτίζου,[3] Ἰερουσαλήμ, ἥκει γάρ σου τὸ φῶς, καὶ ἡ δόξα κυρίου ἐπί σε ἀνατέταλκεν.... ἐπὶ δὲ σὲ φανήσεται κύριος, καὶ ἡ δόξα αὐτοῦ ἐπὶ σὲ ὀφθήσεται· καὶ πορεύσονται βασιλεῖς ἐν τῷ φωτί σου καὶ ἔθνη τῇ λαμπρότητί σου; and again (ibid. 19) ἔσται σοι κύριος φῶς αἰώνιον καὶ ὁ θεὸς δόξα σου. Similarly, Is. lviii. 8 ῥαγήσεται πρόιμον τὸ φῶς σου.... καὶ ἡ δόξα τοῦ θεοῦ περιστελεῖ σε.

In the Fourth Gospel the ordinary Greek use of δόξα is common (e.g. v. 41, 44, vii. 18, xii. 43); but in the four places which speak of 'seeing' the glory of God or of Christ (i. 14, xi. 40, xii. 41, xvii. 24)

---

[1] See the article δόξα in Kittel's *Theologisches Wörterbuch*; also A. M. Ramsey, *The Glory of God and the Transfiguration of Christ*, chs. I and II.

[2] Yet even Philo (according to Kittel, *l.c.*) has only one example, and Josephus none. Kittel distinguishes however an intermediate meaning, which Philo and Josephus have, in which δόξα refers to the outward 'splendour' or 'magnificence' of monarchs and the like, which symbolizes the 'honour' which they claim.

[3] 'Be enlightened': somewhat different from the Hebrew קוּמִי אוֹרִי, but natural enough in the process of Hellenizing the Old Testament.

and in the one place which speaks of 'manifesting' the glory (ii. 12), we must recognize the biblical meaning of the term. In xii. 41 we have a reference to the vision of Isaiah described in ch. vi of his book. Isaiah says bluntly, 'I saw the Lord.' John, in accordance with the general tendency of contemporary Judaism, says εἶδεν τὴν δόξαν αὐτοῦ.[1] Clearly, therefore, δόξα here means the manifestation of God's presence and power, כבוד or יקרא. So when in xvii. 24 Christ prays for His disciples, ἵνα θεωρῶσιν τὴν δόξαν τὴν ἐμὴν ἣν δέδωκάς μοι ὅτι ἠγάπησάς με πρὸ καταβολῆς κόσμου, he is using language of Hebraic ancestry to denote the *visio Dei*. Such vision of God is promised to faith in xi. 40; there, however, as something attainable in this life, and explicable in terms of i. 14, where in consequence of the incarnation of the Logos, i.e. of the eternal Light, ἐθεασάμεθα τὴν δόξαν αὐτοῦ, δόξαν ὡς μονογενοῦς παρὰ πατρός. There is here no longer any thought of visible light or radiance accompanying Christ in His earthly life; but not less really, the evangelist holds, the divine presence and power were apprehensible by those who had the faculty of faith. It is in this sense that in and through the σημεῖα He manifested His glory, ἐφανέρωσεν τὴν δόξαν αὐτοῦ (ii. 11). It is with these passages in view that we must understand the Johannine use of δοξασθῆναι with especial reference to the death of Christ (vii. 39, xii. 16, 23, xiii. 31).[2] If the actions of Christ are to be taken as equivalents for the radiance in which the power and presence of God are brought within human experience, or in other words, in which the eternal light is apprehended by means of itself, φωτὶ φῶς, then the action in which He most fully expressed Himself, namely His

---

[1] That the glory which Isaiah saw was the manifestation of the Logos (the archetypal light) would fit aptly into Philo's theory (see pp. 68–9, 72 above). In Johannine terms it explains itself through xvii. 24 and i. 14. Christ as Logos, as Son of the Father, is invested with the nature, character and power of the Eternal, from eternity (πρὸ καταβολῆς κόσμου); the manifestation of this nature, character and power, in time, takes place in the words and works of the incarnate Logos, in which, accordingly, the כבוד, δόξα, is 'manifested', and 'seen' by those who have faith. Such 'seeing' is the *visio Dei* under the conditions of life in time (ὁ ἑωρακὼς ἐμὲ ἑώρακε τὸν πατέρα), and the pledge of the ultimate *visio Dei* beyond this life.

[2] In passages of the Old Testament δοξασθῆναι is used in the sense of being 'transfigured' by a supernatural radiance: see Exod. xxxiv. 29 sqq. In the Fourth Gospel there is no 'transfiguration' of Christ in that sense: all the actions of His incarnate life are full of δόξα, apparent to the faculty of πίστις (=ἀφανοῦς ὑπόληψις). If there is any one moment of 'transfiguration', it is that in which He dedicates Himself to death, variously represented by xii. 23–8, xiii. 31, xvii. 5. See pp. 373–4, 396, 403.

self-devotion to death in love for mankind, is the conclusive manifestation of the divine glory. In developing this thought, the evangelist plays subtly upon the varying meanings of the word δόξα,[1] suggesting that by such a death Christ both 'honours' God (by complete obedience), and gains 'honour' Himself; but the 'honour' which He gains is no other than the 'glory' with which the Father has invested Him; in other words the revelation of the eternal majesty of God in His love for mankind. Thus if in the incarnate life of Christ the eternal, archetypal light is manifested, its final manifestation is in His death.

All this is by way of explication of what the evangelist means by τὸ φῶς τοῦ κόσμου. We must now return to the passages which contain this expression, for further examination. In viii. 12–16, the thought passes swiftly from 'light' to 'judgment'. 'I judge no one,' says Christ, 'and if I judge, my judgment is absolute' (ἀληθινή). This cryptic saying is not here developed. In ix. 6 sqq. the statement, 'I am the light of the world', is illustrated dramatically, after the evangelist's manner, by a scene in which Jesus gives sight to the blind. The story, however, immediately passes on to the judgment which the unenlightened pass upon the enlightened: the 'Pharisees', assembled as a court of judgment, condemn the man to whom Christ had given light, and, by implication, Christ Himself. In the sequel, by a dramatic *paraprosdokia*, Christ turns upon His self-constituted judges and pronounces their condemnation (ix. 41).[2] The whole passage may be taken as a comment on viii. 12–16. The claim of Jesus to be the light of the world, and the Jews' rejection of His claim, are dramatized in a scene where the cure of blindness is a manifest fact which the Jews refuse to acknowledge (though it is a fact that shines by its own light, cf. ix. 26), and thereby pronounce judgment on themselves.

The theme of κρίσις needs further investigation. The Greek word κρίνειν has the fundamental meaning 'to separate, discriminate': the act of the judge or court of justice is conceived as the discrimination of truth from falsehood, or of the innocent from the guilty. The Hebrew שָׁפַט, which it is used to translate, has no such associations: it denotes an act of sovereignty, expressed either in legislation or in the administra-

---

[1] Cf. xii. 23, 28, xiii. 31–2, xiv. 13. See pp. 373–4 below. This playing upon different senses of a word—or rather, this ranging up and down the scale of its possible meanings and making one meaning fill out another—is a part of this writer's technique.

[2] For a fuller examination of this episode, see pp. 357–8.

tion of justice, in rewarding the good and punishing the wicked. In Philo the original sense of κρίνειν is still quite alive. Thus in *De Mut.* 106–10 he says that the term κρίσις has two significations: (i) ἔκκρισις καὶ ἀπό-κρισις, an example of which is to be found in the case of public games, in which a large number of the competitors who appear are disqualified, πρὸς τῶν ἀθλοθετῶν ἐξεκρίθησαν, and (ii) τὸ κριτικὸν καὶ δικαστικὸν εἶδος, the process of judgment, narrowly so called, i.e. the administration of justice. In *Leg. All.* III. 118 sqq. he comments on the passage in Exod. xxviii. 26 which speaks of the High Priest's breastplate: τὸ λόγιον τῶν κρίσεων, τὴν δήλωσιν καὶ τὴν ἀλήθειαν. The λόγιον, he says, signifies λόγος ὁ κατὰ διάκρισον, the discriminating word (the spoken word, γεγωνὸς λόγος), which should possess σαφήνεια and ἀληθότης. Thus κρίσις signifies διάκρισις, separation or discrimination. It is essentially τῶν ἀγαθῶν καὶ κακῶν κρίσις, discrimination between good and evil (*De Vit. Mos.* I. 146). In allegorizing the story of Abraham's vision (Gen. xv. 9–20) in *Quis Rer.* 311, he interprets the flaming torches which passed between the divided bodies of the sacrificial victims as signifying the judgment of God which divides the contraries of which the entire world is composed: αἱ δὲ λαμπάδες τοῦ πυρὸς αἱ δᾳδουχούμεναι τοῦ δᾳδούχου θεοῦ κρίσις εἰσίν, αἱ λαμπραὶ καὶ διαυγεῖς, αἷς ἔθος μέσον τῶν διχοτομημάτων, λέγω δὲ τῶν ἐναντιοτήτων, ἐξ ὧν ἅπας ὁ κόσμος συνέστηκε, διάγειν.

All this should help to clarify the close connection which the Fourth Gospel makes between light and judgment. The evangelist starts from the common Christian belief that Christ, as Son of Man, is 'judge of quick and dead' (v. 27). He came for judgment, and since His judgment is the judgment of God Himself, it is just (v. 30) and absolute (or authentic, ἀληθινή, not simply 'true', viii. 16), unlike the judgments of men which are κατ' ὄψιν. So far the evangelist stands upon common ground with the general beliefs of primitive Christianity, which themselves were adapted from Jewish eschatology. But over against these statements, we have another series of statements which are formally in contradiction to them and state that Christ has *not* come to judge (iii. 17, viii. 15, xii. 47). We shall probably not be wrong in finding in such passages a protest against what the evangelist regarded as a crude misinterpretation of the idea of Christ as Judge. If we consider the teaching of the Apocalypse—a writing ironically enough attributed to the author of this gospel—we shall be able to form some conception of this crude misinterpretation. That the real purpose of Christ in coming into the world was this negative and destructive action the evangelist will not allow. In that sense Christ says, 'I did not come to judge the world but to save the world' (xii. 47), 'The Father did not send the Son into the world to judge the world, but in order that the world might be saved through Him' (iii. 17), 'I judge no one' (viii. 15). And yet tradition was right in affirming that He comes to judge the quick and the dead.

The reconciliation of the apparent contradiction is to be found by recalling that κρίσις has a meaning not included in the meaning of מִשְׁפָּט. It means 'to discriminate'; and the medium of discrimination is light. Christ came into the world as life and light, to save the world and not to condemn it. But what happens when light shines into dark places? We might find an answer in Ephesians v. 8–14, a reference which will serve to show that the evangelist was not introducing a wholly new idea. The point of departure here is the hymn which is quoted (v. 14)—a hymn which, from its citation in the epistle, we may suppose to have been current in that region to which the Fourth Gospel belongs. The hymn proclaims Christ as the Enlightener—virtually as φῶς τοῦ κόσμου—and also as Giver of life to the dead. Without suggesting any kind of direct literary dependence, we may recognize that we have both in Ephesians and in the Fourth Gospel an adaptation to Christian uses of the 'light mysticism' current in Hellenistic circles. In applying the quotation the author of Ephesians calls attention to the fact that the coming of the Life-giver who is also the Enlightener has the effect of making evil manifest and convicting the sinner, whose evil deeds might otherwise remain concealed: τὰ δὲ πάντα ἐλεγχόμενα ὑπὸ τοῦ φωτὸς φανεροῦται (v. 13). In a similar sense our evangelist says, 'This is what is meant by κρίσις: the light has entered the world, and men preferred darkness to light, because their deeds were evil. Everyone who does evil hates the light. He will not come to the light, in order that his deeds may not be shown up; whereas he whose deeds conform to reality comes to the light, so that his deeds may be manifested as wrought in God'[1] (iii. 19–21). The purpose and intention of the coming of Christ are in no sense negative or destructive, but wholly positive and creative; but by an inevitable reaction the manifestation of the light brings into view the ultimate distinction between truth and falsehood, between good and evil. Hence it is κρίσις, discrimination. Men by their response to the manifestation of the light declare themselves, and so pronounce their own 'judgment'.

[1] That which is ἐν θεῷ εἰργασμένον belongs to the realm of reality: hence its author may be said ποιεῖν τὴν ἀλήθειαν: see pp. 174, 176–8.

It is this fact that is exhibited dramatically in the denouement of the trial-scene in ix. 41.

Similarly in xii. 46–50 Christ came into the world as light, with the intention that men should not longer walk in darkness (but should have, as in viii. 12, the φῶς τῆς ζωῆς). His words (which are, according to vi. 63, πνεῦμα καὶ ζωή) convey life and light to the world. Inevitably, those who do not respond to His words, but prefer darkness to light, condemn themselves. Hence the word of judgment on the 'Last Day' is no other than the revelation of life and light which Christ gave in His incarnation. For the 'word' which He spoke is the 'commandment' of the Father, and that commandment is ζωὴ αἰώνιος.

Beside the words He spoke, there are the deeds of Christ, which are σημεῖα 'manifesting His glory', and their impact similarly discriminates between the opposed reactions of men to the light. From this point of view the story of the ministry is a story of κρίσις, for it tells of the sifting of men, until (to use Philo's illustration) all unworthy competitors in the great contest have been disqualified, and only the chosen few remain, who have come through the test. The final effulgence of eternal light, however, is to be seen in the passion and death of Christ, in which He is 'glorified'. That is why, immediately before His passion, Christ exclaims, νῦν κρίσις ἐστι τοῦ κόσμου τούτου (xii. 31). While His whole ministry is κρίσις, its culmination in His death is the very moment of κρίσις, because now the last recesses of the unapproachable light wherein God dwells have been laid open. In the presence of this revelation the powers of evil finally declare themselves by their rejection of the light; and in so declaring themselves condemn themselves to extirpation: νῦν ὁ ἄρχων τοῦ κόσμου τούτου ἐκβληθήσεται ἔξω (xii. 31).

The idea of the death of Christ as judgment is not absent from Christian thought outside the Johannine writings. For Paul the Cross is both the revelation of God's righteousness and the condemnation of sin;[1] and also, in it God triumphs over principalities and powers;[2] and this latter idea, at least, is found in other parts of the New Testament.[3] But nowhere are such ideas given so profound, consistent and even logical an expression as they are in the Fourth Gospel, where the interpretation of the coming of Christ through the categories of life and light supplies the needed structure of thought to carry such a paradoxical conception. We are in the presence of a great creative achievement of religious thought.

[1] Rom. iii. 25–6, viii. 3, etc.   [2] Rom. viii. 37–9, Php. ii. 8–11, Col. ii. 14–15.
[3] I Pet. iii. 18–22, Rev. i. 18 sqq.

In the whole field of 'Hellenistic mysticism' there is, so far as I know, no real parallel to this profound conception of judgment as the inevitable accompaniment of the revelation of light and life. A remote parallel in the Hermetic tractate called *The Bowl* (Κρατὴρ ἢ Μονάς) will serve to bring out the contrast rather than the likeness between the two. Here the Creator of the universe sends down to men a great bowl filled with νοῦς, proclaiming, 'The soul that will, let it baptize itself in the bowl.' Those who do so receive νοῦς (and νοῦς is often figured as light), and so are united with the eternal νοῦς which is God. Those who refuse are abandoned to irrationality and mortality (*C.H.* IV. 4–5). We can trace something like this general *schema* behind the Fourth Gospel. The Logos enters the world as light; to those who receive Him He gives the right to become children of God; the others walk in darkness. But here, for a vague and abstract νοῦς is substituted a concrete revelation of that which is truly divine in an historic life; for a hypothetical act of choice which in the end belongs to the realm of mythology, we have the actual facts of men's response to an historical revelation; and finally, the moral passion and realism of the Johannine idea of judgment are almost entirely missing from the Hermetic discourse. The current conceptions of the higher religion of Hellenism have been taken up but entirely transformed.

8. SPIRIT

The term πνεῦμα is conventionally defined as ἀὴρ κινούμενος (cf. Philo, *Quod Det.* 83). It is thus applied primarily to the wind (cf. Plato, *Definitiones*, πνεῦμα κίνησις ἀέρος περὶ τὴν γῆν), and to the breath of living beings, both of which are examples of air in motion. From these two fundamental meanings two main lines of usage derive, the one metaphysical, the other psychological (or physio-psychological).

To take the latter first, from an early period πνεῦμα stands along with ψυχή for the 'breath-soul', that invisible factor in the human being which seems to be inseparable from the function of breathing, and in default of which the man ceases to live. The distinction, and the relation, between πνεῦμα and ψυχή are differently stated by different schools of thought. The influential Stoic school defined the ψυχή as πνεῦμα ἔνθερμον.[1] Others distinguished the two in various ways, which do not especially concern us.

Of more immediate importance is the metaphysical development. The impression of movement and force which the mind derives from contemplating the effects of wind seems early to have suggested that life and movement in the world of nature are due to the presence of some element analogous to the breath-soul in man. The Pythagoreans spoke of an ἄπειρον πνεῦμα encompassing the universe, which the world breathes in (ἀναπνεῖ),[2] or of 'one πνεῦμα pervading the whole universe like a ψυχή, which also unites us with other living things'.[3] The expression πνεῦμα διῆκον δι' ὅλου τοῦ κόσμου was adopted by the Stoics. They conceived it as a very tenuous form of air, partly akin to fire, having its proper residence in the sphere remotest from the earth, but also diffused through the whole, and appearing in living beings as the soul. Its precise status among the elements, and its distinction from and relation to air and fire, and to the peculiar kind of air known as αἰθήρ, are points in which writers differ, and which remain somewhat ambiguous. In any case this diffused, tenuous kind of air has the property of thought (as indeed has the ψυχή in us, which is the same thing). To this 'living and thinking gas' (Scott's phrase) the Stoics gave the name of God. 'The

---

[1] See Ritter and Preller[8], § 508.
[2] Evidence in R.-P. § 75.
[3] Sextus Mathematicus *ap.* R.-P. § 73.

Stoics affirm an intelligent (νοερόν)[1] God: an artificer-fire (πῦρ τεχνικόν) proceeding to the originating of a universe, embracing all the seminal λόγοι, by virtue of which things come into being severally according to destiny (εἱμαρμένη), and a πνεῦμα pervading the whole universe, but receiving various appellations by reason of the mutations of matter through which it has passed.'[2] Clearly this divine πνεῦμα is not easily distinguishable from the λόγος in which all particular λόγοι are summed up.[3]

In the LXX πνεῦμα almost invariably translates the Hebrew רוּחַ, which has the same two primary meanings, 'wind' and 'breath'. The line however along which the usage of the term developed seems to have been different. It appears that the fundamental idea of רוּחַ is that of 'active power or energy, power superhuman, mysterious, elusive, of which the wind of the desert was not so much the symbol as the most familiar example'.[4] This 'elemental force, incalculable and irresistible and invisible', might descend upon men and possess them, enabling them, or impelling them, to perform impossible feats of strength or cunning.[5] In particular, it caused the 'prophetic' frenzy.[6] Thus נָבִיא, προφήτης, and אִישׁ הָרוּחַ, ἄνθρωπος πνευματοφόρος, stand in parallelism, Hos.ix. 7.[7] As the idea of prophecy was elevated and refined, רוּחַ, πνεῦμα, was held

---

[1] Cf. *C.H.* III. 1 πνεῦμα λεπτὸν νοερόν: the tractate is not properly Hermetic at all, but Judaeo-Stoic (see my discussion in *The Bible and the Greeks*, pp. 210–34): the πνεῦμα comes from Gen. i. 2, the epithet νοερόν from Stoicism. Similarly there is a πνεῦμα νοερόν in Wisdom (Wisd. vii. 22), but the author of the Book of Wisdom probably did not use the term in quite the same sense.

[2] From the *Placita Philosophorum ap.* R.-P. § 494. It appears from Diogenes Laertius VII. 148 cited *ibid.* § 513 that the προσηγορίαι are those of the gods of popular paganism, Zeus from 3ῆν, Hera from ἀήρ, and so forth.

[3] One sometimes has the feeling that the Stoics, like some modern materialists, are dodging the necessity of postulating some existence other than matter by applying a term (πνεῦμα), properly applicable to a material substance, to a postulated substance to which they assign essentially non-material attributes.

[4] H. Wheeler Robinson, *The Christian Experience of the Holy Spirit*, p. 8. This, however, does not necessarily mean that רוח, either as 'wind' or as 'spirit', is non-material. For the materiality of the spirit in rabbinic Judaism see passages cited by W. D. Davies, *Paul and Rabbinic Judaism*, 1948, pp. 183–5.

[5] Jud. xiv. 6, רוח יהוה, πνεῦμα κυρίου, leapt upon Samson and he tore a lion in pieces, *ibid.* vi. 34 πνεῦμα κυρίου ἐνεδυνάμωσεν τὸν Γεδεών, καὶ ἐσάλπισεν ἐν κερατίνῃ καὶ ἐφοβήθη Ἀβιέζερ ὀπίσω αὐτοῦ.

[6] I Kms. xix. 20–4.

[7] Cf. I Cor. xiv. 37 προφήτης ἢ πνευματικός. I raise the question whether in Hos. ix. 7 and Zeph. iii. 4 we should not read πνευματόφορος, 'borne by πνεῦμα' (cf. II Pet. i. 21 ὑπὸ πνεύματος ἁγίου φερόμενοι) rather than πνευματοφόρος, 'bearing πνεῦμα', as in Swete's text: πνευματοφόρος is an epithet of God in *C.H.* XIII. 19, and should properly be confined to Him.

responsible for higher intellectual achievements, wisdom and insight, yet without ever losing the sense that these were due to an influx of supernatural power. As a psychological term, רוּחַ seems at first to have denoted the passionate, strongly emotional side of human nature, expressing itself in outbursts of anger or uncontrollable impulses.[1] Later, and less characteristically, it is used in parallelism with נֶפֶשׁ, ψυχή, and with little apparent difference of meaning. It is the principle of life, which God imparts to man at his beginning, and recalls at death.[2]

The two concepts, therefore, expressed by רוּחַ and by πνεῦμα respectively, lie close together, in spite of certain differences, and it is natural that when in Hellenistic Judaism רוּחַ became πνεῦμα the Hebrew and the Greek ideas associated with the term should act and react upon one another. Such reaction we must certainly recognize on both sides of the dividing line, while there are other uses of πνεῦμα for which, it seems, other influences in the Hellenistic medley must be held mainly responsible. In popular usage πνεῦμα denoted an individual disembodied being, a 'spirit', whether a superhuman being (in Greek properly δαίμων), or the 'ghost' of a dead man.[3] This does not seem

[1] The connection between the invasion of the divine רוח and human passion is well illustrated by I Kms. xi. 6 καὶ ἐφήλατο πνεῦμα κυρίου ἐπὶ Σαούλ, ὡς ἤκουσεν τὰ ῥήματα ταῦτα, καὶ ἐθυμώθη ἐπ' αὐτοὺς ἡ ὀργὴ αὐτοῦ σφόδρα.

[2] See Ps. ciii (civ). 29–30 ἀντανελεῖς τὸ πνεῦμα αὐτῶν καὶ ἐκλείψουσιν... ἐξαποστελεῖς τὸ πνεῦμά σου καὶ κτισθήσονται: their πνεῦμα is His πνεῦμα: cf. Is. lvii. 16 πνεῦμα γὰρ παρ' ἐμοῦ ἐξελεύσεται καὶ πνοὴν πᾶσαν ἐγὼ ἐποίησα. In this limited sense spirit may be said to act creatively in the cosmos, but the extent to which the idea of the Creator Spiritus is present in the Old Testament and in rabbinic literature has often been greatly exaggerated. See W. D. Davies, op. cit. pp. 188–90.

[3] So in Isis to Horus (Κόρη Κόσμου), a work which, though it has affinities with the Hermetic literature, stands much nearer to popular mythology; see Excerpt XXIII in Scott's Hermetica, passim. In the Old Testament (possible marginal cases apart) there is perhaps only one such πνεῦμα which clearly acts like an individual person, III Kms. xxii. 21. They abound in the Enochic literature. A common source, neither Hebrew nor Greek, is indicated. It is said to be Iranian. In the New Testament πνεύματα ἀκάθαρτα are common in the Synoptic Gospels, and the Epistle to the Hebrews knows both angelic πνεύματα (i. 7, based on Ps. ciii (civ). 4, LXX, an inexact rendering of the Hebrew), and πνεύματα of just men made perfect in the world beyond (xii. 23). The Apocalypse knows of seven πνεύματα, which are represented as torches burning before the throne of God (iv. 5), or as the seven eyes of the Lamb, sent forth into all the earth (v. 6), and which constitute, with the Eternal and the Lamb, an eccentric and not-too-orthodox Trinity (i. 4–5). They appear to be next of kin to the seven Amesha Spentas of Zoroastrianism. That this muddled fantasy-thinking proceeded from the same mind that produced the notably sober and rational doctrine of πνεῦμα which we find in the Fourth Gospel— credat Judaeus Apella, non ego!

to be either Hebrew or Greek in origin. We need not here enquire further into it, since the usage has not affected the Fourth Gospel, as it is also rare in the kind of Hellenistic writings with which John has closest affinity.

In the *Hermetica* πνεῦμα is, in accordance with their Stoic tendency, one of the higher material elements, along with fire and air.[1] It is especially the source, or medium, of life. Thus in *C.H.* IX. 9, 'all things that exist are in God, have their being from God, and depend on Him: some of them are active through bodies, others cause movement through soul-essence (διὰ οὐσίας ψυχικῆς), and others cause life through spirit (διὰ πνεύματος ζωοποιοῦντα)'. In a *Discourse of Hermes to Asclepius*, cited by Cyril of Alexandria, we read: 'This πνεῦμα, of which I have often spoken before, all things need; for carrying all things, according to their deserts, it quickens and nurtures them; it is dependent on the holy fountain; it is a helper for spirits, and the cause of life to all, the only generative thing there is' (τούτου τοῦ πνεύματος, οὗ πολλάκις προεῖπον, πάντα χρῄζει· τὰ πάντα γὰρ βαστάζον κατ' ἀξίαν τὰ πάντα ζωοποιεῖ καὶ τρέφει, καὶ ἀπὸ τῆς ἁγίας πηγῆς ἐξήρτηται, ἐπίκουρον πνεύμασιν, καὶ ζωῆς ἅπασιν ⟨αἴτιον⟩[2] ἀεὶ ὑπάρχον, γόνιμον ἓν ὄν, Frag. 24 (Scott)). In the highly mythological *Isis to Horus* (Κόρη Κόσμου), Excerpt XXIII. 20 (Scott), the Creator appoints 'powers all-creating and spirit all-fashioning, generative for ever of all things that are to be, universally' (παν⟨τ⟩ούργους[3] δυνάμεις καὶ πάντεχνον πνεῦμα γεννητικὸν τῶν εἰς ἀεὶ μελλόντων ἔσεσθαι καθολικῶς πάντων).

The πνεῦμα in man is derived from the 'aether' (*C.H.* I. 17) and so is called αἰθέριον πνεῦμα (Scott, Excerpt XXIX), and at death it returns to the aether as the breath we draw in from the air is exhaled into the air again (*Isis to Horus*, Excerpt XXVI. 12). In life it is related to the ψυχή in ways which are variously described and need not detain us.

---

[1] *C.H.* I. 5; see my discussion in *The Bible and the Greeks*, pp. 121–5, 138.

[2] I insert αἴτιον after Scott. His numerous other emendations seem to be unnecessary. Is αει of MSS. the wreckage of αιτιον?

[3] Scott reads παντούργους for MSS. πανούργους. Παντοῦργος is certainly more correct in this sense (see L. and S.); but with such a writer as this no very high standard of correct Greek, perhaps, is to be expected. Apart from this, the MS. text of the words quoted seems sound, though there is perhaps some uncertainty in the rest of the sentence. See Scott. (If the MSS. are right in reading ἐχαρισάμην, § 20 is to be taken as a continuation of the speech of ὁ θεός in § 19, but in that case διέταξε above would have to be corrected into the first person. Scott conjectures χαρισάμενος, but he has rewritten the entire section and transferred it arbitrarily to a different part of the text.)

If the Hermetic writers had been orthodox Stoics, all this would have fallen well enough within the conception of πνεῦμα as a kind of gas diffused through the universe, with its maximum concentration in the region farthest from the earth, and having certain peculiar and exalted properties manifest in nature and in man. But their Stoicism is crossed by a Platonic strain for which the divine is essentially immaterial, non-sensible and transcendent. There is consequently a recurrent ambiguity in their thought about πνεῦμα in relation to the divine, and to man and the world. If πνεῦμα has the exalted and quasi-divine attributes and functions attributed to it, and if at the same time the divine is transcendent and entirely non-material, then does πνεῦμα belong properly to the sphere of αἰσθητά, or rather to that of νοητά? In the *Poimandres*, the Logos which is the cause of movement in the material universe is called πνευ-ματικὸς λόγος (*C.H.* I. 5). This should mean that it is itself material, though composed of the finest, and, so to speak, least material kind of matter conceivable. But the Logos is ὁμοούσιος with the νοῦς δημιουργός (*ibid.* 10) and the νοῦς δημιουργός is certainly not material, being the direct offspring of the primal νοῦς. The Logos therefore is not material, although it is πνευματικός. Further, in the Λόγος Καθολικός there is a discussion of motion, in which the writer maintains that matter is incapable of initiating motion, which must always originate ὑπὸ τῶν ἐντός...τῶν νοητῶν, ἤτοι ψυχῆς ἢ πνεύματος ἢ ἄλλου τινὸς ἀσωμάτου· σῶμα γὰρ σῶμα...οὐ κινεῖ (*C.H.* II. 8). This seems clear enough; πνεῦμα belongs to the sphere of νοητά and ἀσώματα. Yet a little later we learn that spaces which seem to us to be empty are in fact μεστὰ ἀέρος καὶ πνεύματος, where πνεῦμα again takes its usual place among the higher and finer material elements. Later in the same tractate there is a list of 'radiations' (ἀκτῖνες) of νοῦς (which is emphatically said to be ἐλεύθερος σώματος παντός). According to the MSS. of the *Corpus Hermeticum* this list includes, along with τὸ ἀγαθόν and ἀλήθεια, τὸ ἀρχέτυπον τοῦ πνεύματος. If this reading is right, we must suppose that the writer has attempted to resolve the contradiction—motion can be initiated only by νοητά: πνεῦμα causes motion: πνεῦμα is one of the material elements—by assigning, not πνεῦμα itself, but the archetype of πνεῦμα to the sphere of νοητά.[1] But in Stobaeus, where the same passage is excerpted, the MSS. read τὸ ἀρχέτυπον φῶς. Upon one point, however, this writer is clear and emphatic: God is not identical with πνεῦμα, but its Creator. He is αἴτιος τοῦ εἶναι πνεῦμα, as He is also αἴτιος τοῦ νοῦν εἶναι and αἴτιος

[1] But he has gained nothing by this: all archetypes are νοητά.

τοῦ φῶς εἶναι. Only two appellations are properly given to Him: τὸ ἀγαθόν[1] and πατήρ. For this writer, therefore, the identification of God with νοῦς or with φῶς, which is to be found in some *Hermetica*, is as illegitimate as the (Stoic) deification of the πνεῦμα διῆκον διὰ παντὸς τοῦ κόσμου. The author of Κρατὴρ ἢ Μονάς puts it less confusedly: God is οὔτε πῦρ οὔτε ὕδωρ οὔτε ἀὴρ οὔτε πνεῦμα, ἀλλὰ πάντα ἀπ' αὐτοῦ (*C.H.* IV. 1).

In the *De Regeneratione* (*C.H.* XIII) there are two references to πνεῦμα in passages where the context is obscure and the text not too certain; but in both cases it is clear that πνεῦμα is brought into close contact, if not equated, with life and light (i.e. with the very being of God). In *C.H.* XIII. 12 there is a crabbed argument about the twelve powers of the Zodiac and their role in the composition of our lower nature, and the ten divine δυνάμεις which expel those powers in the process of regeneration; and there is much play with numerical symbols. The ten δυνάμεις (through which, as we have learnt *ibid.* 8, the divine Logos is constituted in the regenerate) are symbolized by the decad (the number 10); but (here a step in the argument is unexpressed) the new nature wrought in us by the decad is life and light, and (the writer proceeds) these are one, ζωὴ δὲ καὶ φῶς ἡνωμέναι εἰσιν. Hence their proper symbol is unity (the number 1); 'hence is generated the number 1 [which is the number] of spirit', ἔνθα ὁ τῆς ἑνάδος ἀριθμὸς πέφυκε τοῦ πνεύματος. So Festugière (note *ad loc.*) understands the sentence: divine δυνάμεις = 10 = 1 = πνεῦμα = life and light.

In the concluding prayer or hymn of the regenerate (*ibid.* 19–20), God is addressed (according to the MSS.) in these terms: σῶζε ζωή, φώτιζε φῶς, πνεῦμα, θεέ...πνευματοφόρε, δημιουργέ, σὺ εἶ ὁ θεός. In the very next sentence we have the familiar list of elements, πῦρ, ἀήρ, γῆ, ὕδωρ—and πνεῦμα. It is quite intelligible that God should be called πνευματοφόρος in the sense that, being Himself transcendent, He controls and orders the immanent 'thinking gas' which is the medium of motion and life in the universe: but it is certain that this writer did not think God was Himself πνεῦμα in the sense of a 'thinking gas'. Most editors, therefore, have emended πνεῦμα θεέ in one way or another and N.-F. obelize it. The easiest emendation is Keil's πνευμάτιζε, though the word is not known to

---

[1] Yet the author has said that τὸ ἀγαθόν, like the archetype of πνεῦμα (or of φῶς), is an ἀκτίς of νοῦς. Unless his copyists have done him grievous wrong, the author of the Λόγος Καθολικός is muddled. Some editors however understand the two προσηγορίαι differently, but (I think) with less probability. See N.-F. *ad loc.*

L. and S. The prayer would then run, 'O Life, save us [i.e. make us alive]; O Light, enlighten us; O God, inspire us [i.e. endue us with πνεῦμα as vehicle of the higher mode of existence]', a perfectly appropriate petition to the πνευματοφόρος.[1] Yet it is not certain that we are not demanding more consistency of expression than we can reasonably expect from a writer of this type. If (as I think) Festugière is substantially right in his exegesis of § 12, then the same symbol (the number 1) stands both for life and light in union, and for πνεῦμα. If therefore God is invoked as life and light, it would not be improper to add πνεῦμα as a third divine title; but we should have no confidence in deducing from this a considered metaphysical doctrine of God as πνεῦμα.[2]

We conclude that the Hermetic writers tended to think of πνεῦμα as the vehicle or medium of life and movement in the universe, of life, movement and thought in man; that its name carried for them a kind of aura of divinity; but that they were confused and uncertain about its precise ontological status, accepting on the whole the Stoic idea of a material or quasi-material πνεῦμα diffused in the universe and immanent in man, but always haunted by a sense that it was in some peculiarly close association with the non-material sphere, and with the transcendent God whom most of them acknowledged, after their Platonic teachers.

In Philo there is no greater consistency in the use of πνεῦμα. He gives it its usual place among the material elements (e.g. *De Ebriet.* 106 οὐρανός, γῆ, ὕδωρ, πνεῦμα, and elsewhere with variations). It is frequently used for wind. The νοῦς in man can be described as ἔνθερμον καὶ πεπυρωμένον πνεῦμα (*De Fuga*, 134), and πνεῦμα can be defined as ἡ ψυχῆς οὐσία (*Quod Det.* 80). In this sense however πνεῦμα is *not* 'air in motion': it is 'a kind of type or stamp of divine power, which Moses calls the image, showing that God is the archetype of rational nature, and man is the copy or reproduction of it' (...οὐκ ἀέρα κινούμενον, ἀλλὰ τύπον τινὰ καὶ χαρακτῆρα θείας δυνάμεως, ἣν ὀνόματι κυρίῳ Μωυσῆς εἰκόνα

---

[1] Reitzenstein has adduced a mass of evidence to show that in certain circles it was held that by appropriate rituals a man might be transsubstantiated from σῶμα to πνεῦμα (ἀποβαλλόμενος τὴν τοῦ σώματος παχύτητα...πνεῦμα τελειοῦμαι... γίνονται πνεύματα φυγόντες τὸ σῶμα, etc.): possibly πνευματίζειν might express this, though I do not find an example. See *Die Hellenistischen Mysterienreligionen* (1920), pp. 159–73. Here again we find a parallel in the Enochic and other apocalyptic literature of popular Judaism, in the idea of a transsubstantiation of the righteous dead into forms of light or glory.

[2] Reitzenstein's 'πνεῦμα *als Gottesbezeichnung*' seems to belong to the host of πνεύματα which we know from *Isis to Horus* and similar documents, rather than to the high God; it is chiefly characteristic of magical formulae.

καλεῖ, δηλῶν ὅτι ἀρχέτυπον μὲν φύσεως λογικῆς ὁ θεός ἐστιν, μίμημα δὲ καὶ ἀπεικόνισμα ἄνθρωπος, *ibid.* 83). Philo is of course influenced by the account of the creation of man in Genesis. He frequently quotes Gen. ii. 7, sometimes as it stands in MSS. of the LXX, sometimes with πνεῦμα for πνοήν. In *De Opif.* 135 he says, 'That which He breathed into man is nothing other than πνεῦμα θεῖον, which settled a colony here (ἀποικίαν τὴν ἐνθάδε στειλάμενον) from that blessed and happy nature, for the benefit of our race.' Hence man may be described, in respect of his νοῦς or διάνοια, as τῆς μακαρίας φύσεως ἐκμαγεῖον ἢ ἀπόσπασμα ἢ ἀπαύγασμα (*De Opif.* 146). Yet as θεῖον ἀπόσπασμα, the νοῦς is (apparently) *not* πνεῦμα since πνεῦμα is a kind of σῶμα (*De Somn.* 1, 30, 34). The ambiguity is never wholly removed.[1]

Even more influential, perhaps, with Philo is the biblical idea of the prophetic πνεῦμα. In *De Gig.* 19 sqq., commenting on Gen. vi. 3 οὐ καταμενεῖ [οὐ μὴ καταμείνῃ LXX] τὸ πνεῦμά μου ἐν τοῖς ἀνθρώποις [add τούτοις LXX] εἰς τὸν αἰῶνα διὰ τὸ εἶναι αὐτοὺς σάρκας, he says:

The term θεοῦ πνεῦμα means in one sense air flowing from earth (ἀὴρ ῥέων ἀπὸ γῆς), the third element, which rides upon water (as he says in the Creation-story, πνεῦμα θεοῦ ἐπεφέρετο ἐπάνω τοῦ ὕδατος)...but in another sense it is unadulterated knowledge (ἀκήρατος ἐπιστήμη), of which every wise man of course partakes....Of this kind is the πνεῦμα of Moses....The πνεῦμα which rests upon him is the wise πνεῦμα, divine, indivisible, inseparable, comely (ἀστεῖον), which everywhere exists in fullness throughout the universe; the πνεῦμα which confers benefits without suffering loss, and when it is imparted or added to others is not diminished in understanding, knowledge or wisdom. And so the πνεῦμα θεοῦ may rest (μένειν) in the soul, but it cannot dwell there permanently (διαμένειν); and what wonder?...The chief cause of ignorance is the σάρξ, and affinity with the σάρξ. And he himself confesses this when he says that the divine πνεῦμα could not abide διὰ τὸ εἶναι αὐτοὺς σάρκας.

In the *Life of Moses* he represents Moses as the 'inspired' prophet: 'he becomes divinely possessed, inspired by the πνεῦμα which was accustomed to come upon him, and utters prophetic oracles' (ἔνθους γίνεται καταπνευσθεὶς ὑπὸ τοῦ εἰωθότος ἐπιφοιτᾶν αὐτῷ πνεύματος καὶ θεσπίζει προφητεύων, *De Vit. Mos.* 1. 175). Philo claims himself to have experience of such inspiration. He sometimes describes it in terms of

---

[1] It appears that recent physical theory finds itself confronted with an irresoluble contradiction between the wave theory and the molecular theory of radiation. Somewhat similarly, ancient thinkers failed to reconcile the concepts of πνεῦμα as material and as immaterial.

divine possession (ἐνθουσιασμός), sometimes in terms of πνεῦμα:[1] e.g. *De Somn.* II. 252 ὑπηχεῖ δέ μοι πάλιν τὸ εἰωθὸς ἀφανῶς ἐνομιλεῖν πνεῦμα ἀόρατον, καὶ φησίν, κτλ.[2] There was Hellenistic precedent for this association of πνεῦμα with the attainment of higher knowledge. Granted that the ψυχή in us is part of the divine πνεῦμα which is the vehicle of life and movement in the universe, then a reinforcement of the πνεῦμα in us from its cosmic source might naturally enlarge our mental powers. Thus the pseudo-Platonic *Axiochus*, 370 C, reviews the marvellous achievements of science (especially in physics and astronomy), and asks, how could the human mind attain such heights, εἰ μή τι θεῖον ὄντως ἐνῆν πνεῦμα τῇ ψυχῇ, δι' οὗ τὴν τῶν τηλικῶνδε περίνοιαν καὶ γνῶσιν ἔσχεν?[3] This passage (or some similar one) seems to be imitated in Philo, *De Vit. Mos.* II. 265. Philo has been holding up for admiration the profundity of the teaching of Moses: αἱ τοιαῦται εἰκασίαι συγγενεῖς προφητείας εἰσίν· ὁ γὰρ νοῦς οὐκ ἂν οὕτως εὐσκόπως εὐθυβόλησεν, εἰ μὴ καὶ θεῖον ἦν πνεῦμα τὸ ποδηγετοῦν πρὸς αὐτὴν τὴν ἀλήθειαν. In *C.H.* XII. 19 there is a list of ways in which God converses (ὁμιλεῖ) with men: by dreams, by omens (διὰ συμβόλων), by birds (augury), by entrails (*haruspicium*), διὰ πνεύματος, by the oak. That is why, the author adds, man professes to know things past, present and future (ἐπίστασθαι τὰ προγεγενημένα καὶ ἐνεστῶτα καὶ μέλλοντα). Πνεῦμα may here stand for prophetic 'inspiration'; but since it is coupled with διὰ δρυός, which, it seems, must refer to the oracle of the oak at Dodona, it is possible that it refers to the oracle of Delphi, where the Pythia was believed to enter the prophetic ecstasy through the effects of a vapour or gas rising from the cleft over which the sacred tripod was placed: such a vapour might well be described as πνεῦμα (so Scott *ad loc.*). Apart from this one passage, πνεῦμα as vehicle of revelation does not seem to occur in the *Hermetica*, and it is

---

[1] The Stoic physics and cosmology, it must be remembered, stood for the 'modern science' of the period. If you spoke of being 'in God', you risked being thought δεισιδαιμονέστερος. But if you suggested that the warm gas in us which the vulgar call the soul was reinforced by an influx of the same gas from the cosmic reservoir, and that it came to the same thing, then you were being 'scientific'. The same device, *mutatis mutandis*, is not unknown to some writers of the present day. It was a boon to Philo that his Bible encouraged him to use the 'scientific' term πνεῦμα.

[2] Cf. the detailed description of the prophetic 'ecstasy', *Quis Rer.* 257–66, where the θεῖον πνεῦμα plays a part. See pp. 191–2.

[3] But of course the author of the *Axiochus* is not thinking of anything like prophetic 'inspiration'. He means that the astonishing powers of the human intellect prove that it is itself in some sort divine.

certainly not characteristic of 'Hellenistic mysticism' in general. When the Hermetist says that in the beatific vision the incorruptible Good shines about the human νοῦς and changes it all into οὐσία (*C.H.* x. 6, cited pp. 16–17), he means something very like what Philo means when he says that in ecstasy the νοῦς in us is unseated at the arrival of divine πνεῦμα, since it is not right (θέμις) for mortal to dwell with immortal (*Quis Rer.* 265); but Philo uses the term πνεῦμα because he understands the experience in terms of prophecy as described in the Old Testament. The attempt to bring into a single concept the 'cosmic' πνεῦμα of Stoicism and the prophetic πνεῦμα of the Jewish scriptures goes far to account for Philo's usage, with its inevitable inconsistencies.[1]

It is apparently the idea of prophetic inspiration that lies behind the doctrine of Jewish eschatology that the Messiah, or the People of God in the age to come, or both, will be invested with the divine πνεῦμα; and this doctrine provided the mould for primitive Christian ideas. The tradition of the early Church, largely embodied in the apostolic κήρυγμα, and attested in the Synoptic Gospels and the Acts, declared that John the Baptist had predicted a baptism ἐν πνεύματι ἁγίῳ, that Jesus was 'anointed' πνεύματι ἁγίῳ, that during His ministry He promised πνεῦμα ἅγιον to His disciples, and that after His resurrection this promise was fulfilled.

The author of the Fourth Gospel has faithfully reproduced these main articles of the tradition (i. 32–3, iii. 34, vii. 39, xiv. 16–17, xx. 22). It is to be noted that only where he is in immediate contact with them does he use the current early Christian term πνεῦμα ἅγιον: in the Baptist's witness to the divine proclamation, οὗτός ἐστιν ὁ βαπτίζων ἐν πνεύματι ἁγίῳ (i. 33), and in his account of the actual gift of the Spirit to the disciples after the resurrection (xx. 22). It does not however follow that the meaning he attached to the term πνεῦμα coincided exactly with its meaning in other New Testament writings.

[1] The evidence adduced by Reitzenstein (*Die Hellenistischen Mysterienreligionen* (1920), pp. 159 sqq.) shows that the idea of a transfiguration into divine essence, as either the consequence or the pre-condition of γνῶσις, or indeed as identical with its attainment, was sometimes described as a change into πνεῦμα. But this evidence is largely drawn from magical papyri—a class of document which ransacked the vocabulary of almost all known religions of the near East, including Judaism and Christianity—with some support from semi-Christian Gnosticism. His citations from Philo and the New Testament seem in the main to show a use of πνεῦμα more or less directly derived from Old Testament ideas of the prophetic πνεῦμα. It seems probable that the use of the term πνεῦμα in relation to the attainment of γνῶσις is mainly due to the Hellenization of ideas derived from the Old Testament, though this biblical influence has often seeped through several strata of popular superstition, before we meet it in writings of the Hellenistic underworld.

(i) He shows himself aware of the original sense of πνεῦμα as 'wind':
iii. 8 τὸ πνεῦμα ὅπου θέλει πνεῖ, καὶ τὴν φωνὴν αὐτοῦ ἀκούεις,[1] ἀλλ' οὐκ
οἶδας πόθεν ἔρχεται καὶ ποῦ ὑπάγει. The fact that he can immediately
pass to the use of πνεῦμα for the medium of regeneration shows that in
his mind there was no final or absolute distinction between these two
uses, whether he thought in Greek terms of ἀὴρ κινούμενος, or in terms
of Hebrew thought for which 'the wind of the desert was not so much
the symbol as the most familiar example' of superhuman power (see p. 214).

(ii) In xi. 33 (ἐνεβριμήσατο τῷ πνεύματι) and xiii. 21 (ἐταράχθη τῷ
πνεύματι) we have a psychological use of the term. Since both passages
refer to violent emotion, we should perhaps see a closer connection with
Hebraic than with Greek psychology, though the distinction is a fine one
(see p. 215). It is probable that πνεῦμα in xix. 30 is the 'breath-soul'
which leaves the man at death, though it is just possible that the evangelist
intended to suggest a secondary meaning (see p. 428).

(iii) In xiv. 17, xv. 26 the Spirit which is to be given to the disciples
is defined as τὸ πνεῦμα τῆς ἀληθείας. In xvi. 13 we read, ὅταν ἔλθῃ
ἐκεῖνος, τὸ πνεῦμα τῆς ἀληθείας, ὁδηγήσει ὑμᾶς εἰς τὴν ἀλήθειαν πᾶσαν:
with which we may compare Philo's θεῖον πνεῦμα τὸ ποδηγετοῦν πρὸς
αὐτὴν τὴν ἀλήθειαν (De Vit. Mos. II. 265 cited above, p. 221). In
C.H. x. 21, the guide is νοῦς: εἰς δὲ τὴν εὐσεβῆ ψυχὴν ὁ νοῦς ἐμβὰς ὁδηγεῖ
αὐτὴν ἐπὶ τὸ τῆς γνώσεως φῶς. In C.H. XII. 12 νοῦς and λόγος together
are our guides (ὁδηγηθήσεται ὑπὸ ἀμφοτέρων). In C.H. IV. 11, Hermes
says to Tat: 'Believe me, my child; you will find the upward road;
or rather, the (divine) image itself will lead you', πίστευσόν μοι, τέκνον,
εὑρήσεις τὴν πρὸς τὰ ἄνω ὁδόν· μᾶλλον δὲ αὐτή σε ἡ εἰκὼν ὁδηγήσει.
To be led to τὰ ἄνω, or to the φῶς γνώσεως or to ἀλήθεια, is no more
than a variety of expression, and if in John πνεῦμα plays the part of guide,
it is clearly analogous to νοῦς and to the image of God. Again in iv. 23
we have the virtual hendiadys ἐν πνεύματι καὶ ἀληθείᾳ. As we have seen
(pp. 174–8 above) ἀλήθεια has in the Fourth Gospel in general its Hellenistic
sense of reality, reality as apprehended, or knowledge of reality. Thus
πνεῦμα has some very close relation to reality, unseen and eternal. It is
(as for Philo) the vehicle by which knowledge of such reality is given to

---

[1] For comparison and contrast we may note *Isis to Horus*, Excerpt XXIII. 36,
where the sound of roaring winds is the sound of the disembodied spirits passing
by—only that where we have to say 'wind' and 'spirit', the Hellenistic writer,
like John, has one word for both: ὡς δὲ καὶ τῶν συγγενῶν φυσ[σ]ώντων ἐν ἀέρι
πνευμάτων ἀκοῦσαι, τλημόνως οἴσομεν ὅτι μὴ συμπνέομεν αὐτοῖς.

men. But also, it is so conjoined with ἀλήθεια that it appears as if for John πνεῦμα could itself stand for the world of ultimate reality, as can νοῦς (or κόσμος νοητός) in Hellenistic writers.

(iv) The specific association of πνεῦμα with life, which we have noted elsewhere (cf. p. 216), occurs also here: vi. 63 τὸ πνεῦμά ἐστιν τὸ ζωοποιοῦν—a maxim which would be entirely at home in (for example) any Hermetic tractate. There, it might well mean that the principle or vehicle of life in the universe and in man is the immanent 'thinking gas'. Here, it clearly has no such meaning. In the next sentence we are told that the ῥήματα of Christ are πνεῦμα καὶ ζωή—another virtual hendiadys. It is not πνεῦμα in the Hellenistic sense, but νοῦς, which finds expression in words. Once again, we seem to have a use of πνεῦμα in which it is analogous in some respects to νοῦς, and yet preserves the sense of life-giving power.

(v) Being the vehicle of life, πνεῦμα is the medium of rebirth (iii. 5). As such it is contrasted with σάρξ, the medium of natural birth (cf. i. 13). In the verses which follow, the contrast of πνεῦμα and σάρξ corresponds with that of τὰ ἄνω and τὰ κάτω, and rebirth is (by implication) equated with ascent from the lower to the higher sphere. Thus the antithesis πνεῦμα-σάρξ corresponds with the antithesis νοητά-αἰσθητά, or νοῦς-ὕλη, in Hellenistic writings. But although in such writings πνεῦμα sometimes approximates to the status of νοητά, its correlative in this sense is never (apart from biblical or Jewish influence) σάρξ. On the other hand, in the Old Testament πνεῦμα and σάρξ, representing רוּחַ and בָּשָׂר, form a standing pair of contraries. The contrast between them is precisely that between God and mortal man, as we have it expressed with especial clarity and force in the parallelism of Is. xxxi. 3 מִצְרַיִם אָדָם וְלֹא־אֵל וְסוּסֵיהֶם בָּשָׂר וְלֹא־רוּחַ. The LXX has obscured the force of this passage in translation; but cf. II Chron. xxxii. 8 μετ' αὐτοῦ βραχίονες σάρκινοι, μεθ' ἡμῶν δὲ κύριος ὁ θεὸς ἡμῶν, Ps. lv (lvi). 5 ἐν τῷ θεῷ ἤλπισα, οὐ φοβηθήσομαι τί ποιήσει μοι σάρξ, Dan. ii. 11 (Theodotion), θεοὶ ὧν οὐκ ἔστιν ἡ κατοικία μετὰ πάσης σαρκός, Gen. vi. 3 οὐ μὴ καταμείνῃ τὸ πνεῦμά μου ἐν τοῖς ἀνθρώποις τούτοις εἰς τὸν αἰῶνα διὰ τὸ εἶναι αὐτοὺς σάρκας (see Philo's comment, p. 220). For Hebraic thinkers the contrast is not so much one of 'substance' (οὐσία), but rather of power and its opposite. God is known as רוּחַ because He exhibits His irresistible and mysterious power, as the 'living God', while human flesh is feeble, powerless, the victim of natural processes (πᾶσα σὰρξ χόρτος...ἐξηράνθη ὁ χόρτος, Is. xl. 6–7). In view of this, we shall be disposed to understand the comparison with the wind (iii. 8) with reference to its 'mysterious, elusive' power, rather than to its merely physical character as ἀήρ κινούμενος. It is this mysterious power, רוח יהוה rather than αἰθέριον πνεῦμα, that is the secret of rebirth.

We have here, therefore, a singularly close interweaving of Hebraic and Hellenistic conceptions. There is the underlying antithesis of τὰ ἄνω and τὰ κάτω, of which the former is the sphere of πνεῦμα καὶ ἀλήθεια. It is, as we have seen, just possible for a genuinely Hellenistic writer to use πνεῦμα in this sense, but not to use σάρξ as its opposite. The proper terms of the antithesis, for him, would be νοητά and αἰσθητά, or the like. The evangelist however has chosen the properly Hebraic antithesis of πνεῦμα-σάρξ, and this implies that the higher or divine order of things, while it is certainly the sphere of absolute reality, or pure being, is rather to be thought of in terms of life and power.

(vi) This decides the meaning of the definition, πνεῦμα ὁ θεός (iv. 24).[1] Verbally, it might seem to echo the Stoic definition of God as πνεῦμα διῆκον δι' ὅλου τοῦ κόσμου. As we have seen, the materialism of that definition was seldom completely transcended by Hellenistic writers who used the term πνεῦμα, however they might wish to maintain a non-material, Platonic, conception of deity. That, no doubt, is why Origen felt some uneasiness about the Johannine definition. His comment is worth quoting:

Many writers have made various affirmations about God and His οὐσία. Some have said that He is of a corporeal nature, fine and aether-like; some that He is of incorporeal nature; others that He is beyond οὐσία[2] in dignity and power. It is therefore worth our while to see whether we have in the Scriptures starting-points (ἀφορμάς) for making any statement about the οὐσία of God. Here [John iv. 24] it is said that πνεῦμα is, as it were, His οὐσία.[3] For he says, πνεῦμα ὁ θεός. In the Law He is said to be fire, for it is written, ὁ θεὸς ἡμῶν πῦρ καταναλίσκον (Deut. iv. 24, Heb. xii. 29), and in John to be light, for he says,

---

[1] It should be observed that to translate 'God is a spirit' is the most gross perversion of the meaning. 'A spirit' implies one of a class of πνεύματα, and, as we have seen, there is no trace in the Fourth Gospel of the vulgar conception of a multitude of πνεύματα.

[2] ὑπερέκεινα (sic leg. pro ὑπὲρ ἐκεῖνα) οὐσίας πρεσβείᾳ καὶ δυνάμει; cf. Plato, Rep. 509 B οὐκ οὐσίας ὄντος τοῦ ἀγαθοῦ, ἀλλ' ἔτι ἐπέκεινα τῆς οὐσίας πρεσβείᾳ καὶ δυνάμει ὑπερέχοντος, a passage clearly echoed here.

[3] οἱονεὶ οὐσία εἶναι αὐτοῦ τὸ πνεῦμα: for the expression cf. C.H. XI. 1 τοῦ δὲ θεοῦ ὥσπερ οὐσία ἐστίν...ἡ σοφία, VI. 4 ἡ οὐσία τοῦ θεοῦ, εἴ γε οὐσίαν ἔχει, τὸ καλόν ἐστι, XII. 1 ὁ νοῦς ἐξ αὐτῆς τῆς τοῦ θεοῦ οὐσίας ἐστίν, εἴ γέ τις ἔστιν οὐσία θεοῦ, etc.: everywhere the same hesitation to speak of the οὐσία of God—and always, perhaps, because Plato had said that the Good is ἐπέκεινα τῆς οὐσίας.

ὁ θεὸς φῶς ἐστι, καὶ σκοτία ἐν αὐτῷ οὐκ ἔστιν οὐδεμία (I John i. 5). If we are to take these statements at their face value, without concerning ourselves with anything beyond the verbal expression, it is time for us to say that God is σῶμα; but what absurdities would follow if we said so, few realize.

Then follows a long discussion in terms of Hellenistic (Platonic-Stoic) metaphysics, after which he comes to his conclusion:

God is called light by a transference from corporeal light to invisible and incorporeal, being so called because of His power in enlightening the eyes of the mind (νοητοὺς ὀφθαλμούς); and He is called a consuming fire, by analogy with (νοούμενος ἀπό) the corporeal fire which is destructive of matter. I take a similar view of the expression, πνεῦμα ὁ θεός. We are made alive (ζωοποιούμεθα) by πνεῦμα in respect of the intermediate and commonly so-called life, when the πνεῦμα surrounding us [sc. the Stoic pervasive gas] breathes the breath of life, corporeally so called. Hence (I suppose) God is called πνεῦμα, as leading us to *real* life (ἀληθινὴν ζωήν). For πνεῦμα is said, according to the Scripture, to make alive (ζωοποιεῖν)—clearly not in the sense of the intermediate life but of the more divine (ζωοποίησιν οὐ τὴν μέσην ἀλλὰ τὴν θειοτέραν); for the γράμμα also kills and causes death, not in the sense of the separation of soul from body, but in the sense of the separation of the soul from God.[1]

We may now draw together what we have learnt in this study. John defines deity as πνεῦμα. If we are to use the trinitarian formula, he speaks, not of Father, Son and Spirit, but of Father, Son and Paraclete, the term πνεῦμα being appropriated to Deity as such. Πνεῦμα connotes reality, or absolute being (νοῦς or νοητά), and as such is bracketed with ἀλήθεια. But it is reality as living, powerful and life-giving (after Hebraic ante-cedents) in contrast to the powerless σάρξ, which in turn belongs to the sphere of ὕλη. The only way for man to rise from the lower life to the higher is by being born ἐκ πνεύματος, which is also to be born ἐκ τοῦ θεοῦ. This rebirth is made possible through the descent of the 'Son of Man' from τὰ ἄνω to τὰ κάτω. This descent is otherwise expressed in the terms, ὁ λόγος σὰρξ ἐγένετο. The Logos, being θεός, has the nature of πνεῦμα, and consequently is said to be both ἀλήθεια and ζωή. Being πνεῦμα (not, of course, being 'the Holy Spirit'), He became σάρξ, partook fully in the experience of this lower world, and gave Himself to death (the characteristic mark of σάρξ), in love for mankind. It is this, and this alone, that makes possible for man the ἀνάβασις which is also rebirth ἐκ πνεύματος. Until Jesus was thus 'glorified', οὔπω ἦν πνεῦμα—there was for man no actual participation in ἀλήθεια or in ζωὴ ἀληθινή. It is only in connection

---

[1] *Comment. in Jo.* XIII. 21–3, Brooke, vol. I, pp. 267–70.

with the incarnation that the idea of birth ἐκ πνεύματος makes sense. Accordingly, the gift of the Spirit to the Church is represented, not as if it were a separate outpouring of divine power under the forms of wind and fire (as in the Acts), but as the ultimate climax of the personal relations between Jesus and His disciples: ἐνεφύσησεν[1] καὶ λέγει αὐτοῖς, Λάβετε πνεῦμα ἅγιον (John xx. 22). The ἐνεφύσησεν clearly echoes Gen. ii. 7, where John may conceivably have read, as Philo seems sometimes to have read, ἐνεφύσησεν εἰς τὸ πρόσωπον αὐτοῦ πνεῦμα ζωῆς, καὶ ἐγένετο ὁ ἄνθρωπος εἰς ψυχὴν ζῶσαν. But the subject of ἐνεφύσησεν in John is Jesus Christ, who, in the σάρξ, suffered, died and rose again. This is what is meant by rebirth ἐκ πνεύματος into ζωὴ αἰώνιος. But already I have anticipated the results of subsequent discussions.

[1] Note how the primitive conception of πνεῦμα as breath is still alive, as is that of πνεῦμα as wind.

9. MESSIAH

The first chapter of the gospel, after the end of the Prologue, is occupied by a series of 'testimonies' to Jesus, leading up to a solemn declaration on His part. The evangelist has so composed this introduction as to bring in the principal titles given to Jesus in the primitive Church: 'Messiah', or 'Christ' (i. 417, both Aramaic and Greek forms being given, and the title being further defined as 'He of whom Moses wrote in the Law, and the prophets' (i. 45); 'King of Israel' (i. 49); 'Son of God' (i. 34, 49); 'Son of Man' (i. 51). All these recur in other parts of the gospel, and with them the titles 'The Holy One of God' (vi. 69), and 'The Coming One' (ὁ ἐρχόμενος, xii. 13), which also occur in the other gospels (Mark i. 24, Luke iv. 34, Matt. xi. 3, xxi. 9, Mark xi. 9, Luke vii. 19, xiii. 35; cf. Heb. x. 37). In none of the Synoptic Gospels, and indeed in no other New Testament writer, do these Messianic titles receive such prominence as here. This prominence is particularly marked in the introductory chapter. It is as though the evangelist had intended to emphasize the fact that his own distinctive teaching rested directly on the messianic beliefs of the primitive Church, and with this aim had begun his work by calling the roll of the traditional messianic titles of the Lord. For in primitive Christian usage they are all messianic, though for the most part they cannot be shown to have been current in this sense in pre-Christian Judaism.

As for the title 'Messiah' itself, I have already observed that no other New Testament writer shows himself so fully aware of the Jewish ideas associated with it as does the Fourth Evangelist. He develops his teaching, in part, by way of opposition to such ideas. This is no doubt due to the effect of controversy with the Jews in the period during which the gospel was written. That the Messiah is Son of David, he appears to set aside (like Mark) as at best irrelevant to the true Christian doctrine of the Messiah. That He should appear from some unknown place of concealment, as Jewish tradition averred, is not true in the sense intended, though the actual mystery of His origin is even deeper than the Jews supposed. That the Messiah should 'abide for ever' is indeed profoundly true, but not in the sense that the Messiah is exempt from death.[1] In such ways the evangelist takes up the points made by Jewish controversialists against

[1] See above, pp. 91–2.

Christian belief. Nowhere else in the New Testament do we find Christian belief in the Christ so clearly at issue with the Jewish beliefs out of which in the last resort it arose.

One element indeed in the Jewish messianic idea receives unexpected prominence in this gospel, and it is that element which is probably most ancient, and certainly most persistent—the Messiah as king. Whereas in Matthew and Mark the title 'King of Israel' is used only in mockery, it is accepted by John as a legitimate title of Christ, being given to Him both by Nathanael in the chapter of testimonies, and by the multitude at the Triumphal Entry. In this case we have again an implicit polemic against current Jewish interpretations; for the Galileans who after the Feeding of the Multitude try to seize Jesus and make Him king are as grossly mistaken as Pilate, who imagines that His kingdom is of this world. Yet a king He is. The dialogue between Pilate and Jesus in the narrative of the Trial is significant. Jesus neither accepts explicitly nor rejects the appellation 'king', but in saying, 'My kingdom is not of this world', He admits by implication that He is a king in a non-worldly sense; and this sense is explained in the words 'For this I was born, and for this I came into the world, to bear witness to the Truth. Everyone who belongs to the Truth hears my voice' (xviii. 37). That is to say, the kingship of the Messiah is the sovereignty of the Truth which He reveals and embodies. In virtue of this He demands obedience from men.

We may usefully compare (and contrast) the way in which Philo sublimates, or etherializes, the concept of kingship. For example, in *De Agric.* 41 sqq. he elaborates the Stoic commonplace that the wise alone are kings, and as such are rightly called by the poetical epithet 'shepherds of the people'. Various such 'shepherds' are mentioned in scripture, in particular Jacob, who fed the flock of Laban (with an allegorical meaning), and Moses ὁ πάνσοφος who was shepherd of the flock of Jethro; which flock signifies the mind which welcomes delusion rather than reality and prefers seeming to being (διανοίας τῦφον πρὸ ἀληθείας ἀσπαζομένης καὶ πρὸ τοῦ εἶναι τὸ δοκεῖν ἀποδεχομένης). This is not far from the Johannine conception of the kingly office of Christ as μαρτυρεῖν τῇ ἀληθείᾳ. In *Quod Det.* 22 sqq. the πρὸς ἀλήθειαν ἄνθρωπος who dwells in each man's soul is at once ruler, king, judge and arbiter, and at times taking the office of witness or accuser invisibly convicts us within (ἔστι δ' ὅτε μάρτυρος ἢ κατηγόρου λαβὼν τάξιν ἀφανῶς ἡμᾶς ἔνδοθεν ἐλέγχει as in John xviii. 37 the messianic King is He who 'bears witness to the truth').[1] In *De Somn.* 1. 191 the offices of the Logos are enumerated. To some He is like a king and gives imperative orders (τοῖς μὲν ὡς βασιλεὺς ἃ χρὴ πράττειν ἐξ ἐπιτάγματος παραγγέλλει); to others He is διδάσκαλος, σύμβουλος, or φίλος (two of these offices also of Christ). These passages will suffice to show that the evangelist's re-interpretation of kingship is in no way alien from the intellectual *milieu* in which he wrote, though it is not directly derivative. As thus interpreted, the messianic kingship relates itself closely to ideas which play an important part in the distinctive thought of the gospel: 'I am ἡ ἀλήθεια'; 'The Father loves the Son and has given everything into His hand'; 'If you love me, keep my commandments.'

It is however the titles 'Son of God' and 'Son of Man' that the evangelist has selected to bear the weight of his interpretation of the Person of Christ. In this he is again in harmony with the Synoptic tradition. We shall presently go on to consider these titles and the ideas associated with them, but meanwhile we must take account of one of the series of titles in the 'chapter of testimonies' which I have so far passed over, namely, 'Lamb of God', ὁ ἀμνὸς τοῦ θεοῦ, or, more fully, ὁ ἀμνὸς τοῦ θεοῦ ὁ αἴρων τὴν ἁμαρτίαν τοῦ κόσμου (i. 29, 36).

Among the familiar titles which compose the rest of the series, the title 'Lamb of God' stands out as peculiar to the Fourth Gospel. Its origin and meaning present a difficult problem. The sentimental explanation which makes it refer to the innocence and gentleness of the character of Jesus cannot be taken seriously. Such characterization is entirely strange to the manner of the evangelist. We must try to approach the meaning from a study of the background and from the context in the gospel itself.

There are two other places in the New Testament where the term ἀμνός is used with reference to Christ. (i) Acts viii. 32 cites Is. liii. 7 ὡς ἀμνὸς ἐναντίον τοῦ κείροντος αὐτὸν ἄφωνος, and explains the passage as fulfilled in Christ. (ii) I Pet. i. 18–19 'You were emancipated from the futile way of life handed down from your fathers, not with perishable things such as silver or gold, but with precious blood, as of an unblemished and spotless lamb, namely the blood of Christ' (τιμίῳ αἵματι ὡς ἀμνοῦ ἀμώμου καὶ ἀσπίλου Χριστοῦ). It is to be observed that Christ is not here *called* 'lamb', but His blood is compared to that of a sacrificial lamb; for the epithet ἄμωμος is a constant epithet of sacrificial animals in the

[1] But in John it is the Paraclete, taking over the functions of Christ, who ἐλέγξει τὸν κόσμον (xvi. 8).

Old Testament, and the ἀμνὸς ἄμωμος appears in various rites. We may presume that the author of I Peter has in mind a general reference to sacrifice, without closely defining what kind of sacrifice. It has been thought that he has in mind the Paschal Lamb, since the Passover was in part a feast of the 'redemption' of Israel. But in the LXX ἀμνὸς ἄμωμος is never applied to the paschal victim, nor indeed is the term ἀμνός so applied at all, except in a variant.[1] The paschal victim is defined as a שֶׂה, i.e. a head of small cattle, which, it is laid down, may be either a sheep or a goat: LXX, πρόβατον τέλειον ἄρσεν ἐνιαύσιον...ἀπὸ τῶν ἀρνῶν καὶ τῶν ἐρίφων (Exod. xii. 5). The Paschal reference therefore does not leap to the eye. On the other hand it is possible that the writer had in mind Is. liii. 7 ὡς ἀμνὸς ἐναντίον τοῦ κείροντος ἄφωνος, since the allusion to redemption with silver and gold seems to be a reminiscence of Is. lii. 3 οὐ μετὰ ἀργυρίου λυτρωθήσεσθε, and Is. liii. 6–12 underlies I Pet. ii. 21–5. It may be therefore that the idea of the ἀμνός was suggested to the author of the epistle by Is. liii. 7, and since the same chapter speaks of the Servant as a sin-offering (אָשָׁם, περὶ ἁμαρτίας, 10), the thought of the sacrificial ἀμνὸς ἄμωμος has been combined in his mind with that of Isaiah's ἀμνός led to the slaughter. In any case, I Peter does not appear to give any precise clue to the meaning of ἀμνός in the Fourth Gospel.

A different word for 'lamb', ἀρνίον, is used throughout the Apocalypse of John as a title for Christ, or, as we might perhaps better put it, as a synonym for 'Messiah'. The Lamb shares the throne of God (xxii. 1, 3), receives with Him the praises of the inhabitants of heaven, and is the bridegroom at the marriage feast which represents the final consummation of the divine purpose for humanity. Two distinct elements seem to enter into the conception. On the one hand, the Lamb is sacrificed (v. 6, 12, vii. 14, etc.) for the redemption of man (v. 9). On the other hand, the Lamb is the leader or shepherd (vii. 17) of the people of God. He stands on Mount Sion, surrounded by myriads of saints (xiv. 1–5); he makes war against the enemies of God and overcomes them (xvii. 14); and the kings and great ones of the earth hide themselves from his wrath (vi. 16). The association of these ideas of violence and power with the figure of a lamb is at first sight paradoxical. But an explanation is found in the Jewish apocalyptic tradition. Thus in Enoch lxxxix sqq.[2] the people of

---

[1] Exod. xii. 5. A reads ἀπὸ τῶν ἀμνῶν καὶ τῶν ἐρίφων, but B has ἀρνῶν. Elsewhere the species is not defined.

[2] This belongs to the portion of the Book of Enoch which is extant (though defective) in Greek, and therefore may be used with confidence.

God is represented symbolically as a flock, and its successive leaders as sheep or rams, bell-wethers, we might say, which from time to time lead the flock. Thus David is represented as a lamb (ἀρήν), which becomes a ram, a ruler and leader of the sheep (εἰς κριὸν καὶ εἰς ἄρχοντα καὶ εἰς ἡγούμενον τῶν προβάτων, lxxxix. 46). Ultimately a great conflict and deliverance is described in these terms:

> But behold lambs were borne by those white sheep, and they began to open their eyes and to see and to cry to the sheep...and I saw in the vision how the ravens flew upon those lambs and took one of those lambs, and dashed the sheep in pieces and devoured them. And I saw till horns grew upon those lambs, and the ravens cast down their horns; and I saw till there sprouted a great horn of one of those sheep...and it cried to the sheep, and the rams saw it and all ran to it...and those ravens fought and battled with it and sought to lay low its horn, but they had no power over it....And I saw till a great sword was given to the sheep, and the sheep proceeded against all the beasts of the field to slay them, and all the beasts and the birds of the heaven fled before their face (xc. 6–19, Charles's translation).

According to Charles this passage represents the Maccabaean revolt, the great horned sheep being Judas Maccabaeus. Other authorities have found in the great horned sheep the Messiah Himself. In any case it is clear that we have here a prototype of the militant seven-horned 'Lamb' of the Apocalypse of John. There is a similar passage in the *Testaments of the Twelve Patriarchs, Joseph* xix. 8. The symbolism of the context is highly zoological: there are sheep and deer, cows and a heifer; and then, 'there came forth a lamb (ἀμνός), and on its left all the beasts and all the reptiles attacked, and the lamb overcame them and destroyed them'.[1] The figure thus symbolized is the coming deliverer commonly styled 'Messiah'. There can be little doubt that in this tradition of apocalyptic symbolism we must find the origin of the 'Lamb' of the Apocalypse of John. The 'Lamb' is the Messiah, and primarily the militant and conquering Messiah; but in the Christian writing, which has in view the historical crucified Messiah, the bell-wether of God's flock is fused with the lamb of sacrifice.[2]

---

[1] Following the Armenian version. The Greek and Slavonic texts have Christian interpolations, including the phrase ὁ ἀμνὸς τοῦ θεοῦ ὁ αἴρων τὴν ἁμαρτίαν τοῦ κόσμου in one MS. Charles has defended the substantial integrity of the Armenian text (*The Greek Versions of the Testaments of the Twelve Patriarchs* (1908), pp. 210–11).

[2] Enoch has ἀρήν, *Apoc. Joh.* ἀρνίον, *Test. Jos.* ἀμνός. In the LXX all three are used to translate כֶּבֶשׂ, ἀρήν and ἀμνός also for טָלֶה. If there is any such connection as I here postulate, it must have been established in the pre-Greek stage of these writings or of the tradition behind them.

MESSIAH

We now turn to the 'Lamb of God' in John. In view of the background, four interpretations seem to be possible: (i) the lamb of the sin-offering; (ii) the paschal lamb; (iii) the ἀμνός of Is. liii, i.e. the suffering Servant; (iv) the young ram which is ἄρχων καὶ ἡγούμενος τῶν προβάτων, i.e. the Messiah as 'King of Israel'.

(i) The interpretation of the Lamb as a sacrifice for sin finds support in the additional clause, ὁ αἴρων τὴν ἁμαρτίαν τοῦ κόσμου, though we should beware of giving to αἴρειν ἁμαρτίαν the sense of 'to bear sin'. The meaning is 'to remove sin', as in I Kms. xv. 25 καὶ νῦν ἆρον δὴ τὸ ἁμάρτημά μου καὶ ἀνάστρεψον μετ᾽ ἐμοῦ, καὶ προσκυνήσω κυρίῳ τῷ θεῷ σου. It should however be noted that the lamb is not in the Old Testament the characteristic sin-offering. As the author to the Hebrews knew, it was 'the blood of bulls and goats' that was believed to take away sin, and it was the 'scapegoat' that carried away the sin of Israel into the wilderness. But waiving this point, it seems unlikely that the evangelist should have introduced in this allusive way a reference to an idea which otherwise does not appear in his gospel, that of the death of Christ as an expiatory sacrifice. It is true that in I John ii. 2 Christ is an ἱλασμός, but this is one of the points in which the Fourth Gospel differs markedly from the epistle. There might be some suggestion of an expiatory sacrifice in the words of Caiaphas, 'It is expedient that one man should die for the people' (xi. 50), but if so, the evangelist has pointedly given a different turn to the idea (xi. 52).

(ii) The most widely favoured interpretation is that which finds an allusion to the paschal lamb. We have to ask whether this gospel shows other allusions to the Passover as a type of the death of Christ. Commentators usually find such an allusion in xix. 36 'No bone of his shall be broken.' This is supposed to be a citation of the regulation for the paschal victim in Exod. xii. 46 ὀστοῦν οὐ συντρίψετε ἀπ᾽ αὐτοῦ, and Num. ix. 12 ὀστοῦν οὐ συντρίψουσιν ἀπ᾽ αὐτοῦ. The Johannine form, ὀστοῦν οὐ συντριβήσεται αὐτοῦ, is indeed near enough to be a free citation of one of these passages. But it might equally be a free citation of Ps. xxxiii (xxxiv). 21:

> Κύριος φυλάσσει πάντα τὰ ὀστᾶ αὐτῶν,
> ἓν ἐξ αὐτῶν οὐ συντριβήσεται.

Now of the other Scriptures said to have been fulfilled in the events of the Crucifixion, two are from Psalms ('They parted my garments among them', Ps. xxi (xxii). 19, and 'I thirst', Ps. lxviii (lxix). 22), and the remaining one from Zech. xii. 10. The original reference in the last of these is somewhat obscure; but if we take 'No bone of his shall be broken' to be a reference to Ps. xxxiii (xxxiv). 21, then we have a consistent series of three citations from Psalms which speak of the afflictions of the righteous and their deliverance.[1] A reference, on the other hand, to the paschal ritual would stand isolated.

It is however often held that the Fourth Evangelist has deliberately altered the date of the Crucifixion in order to synchronize the death of Christ with the killing of the paschal victims on Nisan 14. If so, it is somewhat strange that he has not said anything to call attention to this synchronism. The statements of the gospels on the date of the Crucifixion are notoriously obscure, but on the whole it seems that the date given in the Fourth Gospel represents an alternative tradition of great antiquity, which may even be historically correct, so that there is no reason to seek for symbolic reasons for it.

The only other passage which is adduced in support of this paschal symbolism is vi. 4, where the Feeding of the Multitude is dated at a time when 'the Passover, the feast of the Jews, was near'. It is not quite certain that the words τὸ πάσχα formed part of the original text, but it is highly probable. It is likely enough that the evangelist intended to suggest a connection between Passover and the Eucharist, which is alluded to in the discourse of ch. vi. But in the discourse itself the prototype of the Bread of Life is not Passover but the manna, and there is nothing in it which even remotely suggests the paschal symbolism.

Thus paschal allusions in the gospel are by no means clear or certain. We come back to the phrase ὁ ἀμνὸς τοῦ θεοῦ, without any sure conviction that paschal symbolism was so definitely in the writer's mind that he could suggest it by such a phrase. That the title is paschal in character becomes less likely when we observe that ἀμνός is not, as I have already pointed out, the term for the paschal victim in the Old Testament, and that in any case it is not the function of the paschal victim to 'take away sin'; for although there may have been an expiatory element in the primitive rite underlying the Passover, no such idea was connected with it in historical times. It is therefore unlikely that readers could be expected

---

[1] The Psalms of the Righteous Sufferer, closely allied to the poems of the Suffering Servant in II Isaiah, are among the principal sources of *testimonia* for all New Testament writers. See my book, *According to the Scriptures* (Nisbet, 1952), ch. II.

to catch an allusion to the Passover here, in the absence of any clear indication in the context, or indeed in the gospel at large.

(iii) The interpretation which finds in the expression ὁ ἀμνὸς τοῦ θεοῦ an allusion to the Servant of the Lord in Is. liii has much to commend it. Not only is that chapter cited in xii. 38, but it seems clear, as we shall see presently, that the idea of the Servant was one that had a special significance for the evangelist. Moreover, in the present passage, the phrase ὁ αἴρων τὴν ἁμαρτίαν τοῦ κόσμου would aptly fit the suffering Servant of Is. liii, for his life is made a sin-offering, and he bears the iniquity of many. The question is, whether the term ἀμνός (רָחֵל), which in Is. liii. 7 is no more than an incidental comparison among other comparisons, could without further elucidation have been used as a title of the Servant. It is to be observed that the precise point of comparison with the ἀμνός in Isaiah, the silence of Christ before His judges (ἀμνὸς ἄφωνος), is a trait of the Passion narrative which is obscured in John, who, though at xix. 9 he has preserved from tradition the statement, ὁ δὲ Ἰησοῦς ἀπόκρισιν οὐκ ἔδωκεν αὐτῷ, has elsewhere represented Jesus as making a spirited defence both before Pilate (xviii. 34–7, xix. 11) and before Annas (xviii. 20–3). The Servant dies as a sin-offering, but this is not the point of comparison with רָחֵל, ἀμνός.

The view has recently found some acceptance, that the reference to the Servant of the Lord was originally more direct than appears in our text of the gospel. It was suggested by C. J. Ball that ἀμνός here is a mistranslation of the Aramaic טַלְיָא, taken in the sense of the Hebrew טָלֶה. טָלֶה means 'lamb'; but טַלְיָא in Aramaic corresponds to the Greek παῖς, both in the sense of 'boy' and in that of 'servant'. Adopting this suggestion, C. F. Burney argued that the expression ὁ ἀμνὸς τοῦ θεοῦ represents an Aramaic original טליא דאלהא, intended as the equivalent of the Isaianic phrase עבד יהוה, 'the Servant of the Lord'.[1] This theory has been adopted by Joachim Jeremias in the *Theologisches Wörterbuch, s.v.* It should be observed that in taking this view it is not necessary to adopt Burney's theory that the Fourth Gospel as a whole was translated from Aramaic, since it is conceivable that a saying attributed to the Baptist may have been handed down in an Aramaic form. Nevertheless there are difficulties about the theory. As I have elsewhere observed, 'ἀμνός in the LXX never translates טָלֶה. No examples are adduced of טַלְיָא as a rendering for עֶבֶד. Even the Syriac versions go back from παῖς to עַבְדָּא, except where they take it to mean "son". Thus we lack evidence

[1] *The Aramaic Origin of the Fourth Gospel* (1922), pp. 104–8.

in support of the view either that the Aramaic-speaking Church (or John the Baptist) could have spoken of the עבד יהוה as טליא דאלהא, or that a bilingual translator who took טַלְיָא in the sense of "lamb" would have chosen ἀμνός as its equivalent' (*J.T.S.* xxxiv, p. 285).

This theory of an Aramaic original, therefore, attractive as it is, has not sufficient ground to stand on. We are left with the Greek term ἀμνός. While a reference to the Servant would be quite consonant, as such, with the evangelist's outlook, I should doubt whether the expression ὁ ἀμνὸς τοῦ θεοῦ would carry that reference to his readers. We must, moreover, take into account the fact that, although he shows himself profoundly interested in the idea of the Servant, he does not elsewhere make use of the Isaianic doctrine of the Servant's expiatory death. Indeed, he seems deliberately to avoid the idea of expiation in connection with the death of Christ. Would he have introduced it here in such an allusive way? Thus while it would be rash to deny that the evangelist, whose mind is extremely subtle, and capable of packing much diversity of meaning into a phrase, may have had in the back of his mind some reminiscence of the ἀμνός of Is. liii. 7, it seems unlikely that such a reminiscence provided the primary and constitutive meaning of the expression, ὁ ἀμνὸς τοῦ θεοῦ.

(iv) We are left with the idea of the lamb as a symbol of the Messiah as leader of the flock of God, i.e. as 'King of Israel'. That this idea, grounded in apocalyptic symbolism, was known in the region with which the Fourth Gospel is connected, namely the Province of Asia, is proved by the Apocalypse of John, which notoriously shares with the Fourth Gospel a number of locutions which may fairly be regarded as characteristic of Ephesian Christianity. And although the evangelist has no sympathy with apocalyptic eschatology, he is certainly not unaware of it. The chief difficulty is that the term used in the Apocalypse of John is not ἀμνός but ἀρνίον. Nevertheless in the Jewish apocalypses which lie behind it ἀμνός, as well as ἀρήν, κριός and πρόβατον, is used of the bell-wether of the flock. While the author of the Apocalypse of John chose the term ἀρνίον, other Greek-speaking Christians who thought of the Messiah in apocalyptic terms may well have selected ἀμνός, which is in fact better suited than ἀρνίον to describe a young horned ram, since ἀρνίον, to Greeks for whom the diminutive form still had force, might suggest an infant sheep, while ἀμνός is the regular equivalent of כֶּבֶשׂ, which denotes the young adult animal.

That the evangelist understood 'The Lamb of God' to be a synonym for 'The Messiah' appears from the context. The Baptist says, 'Behold the Lamb of God.' Andrew hears him, and says to his brother Simon Peter, 'We have found the Messiah' (εὑρήκαμεν τὸν Μεσσίαν, i. 41). Moreover the idea of the Messiah as 'King of Israel', which is suggested by the horned lamb or young wether as leader of the flock, is, as we have seen, one that John accepts, and interprets in his own way.[1]

It remains to explain the addition, ὁ αἴρων τὴν ἁμαρτίαν τοῦ κόσμου. I have pointed out that it is illegitimate to understand αἴρειν ἁμαρτίαν as 'to bear sin', implying an interpretation of the death of Christ as a piacular sacrifice. It means 'to remove sin', as in I John iii. 5 ἐφανερώθη ἵνα τὰς ἁμαρτίας ἄρῃ, i.e. to abolish or do away with sin. To make an end of sin is a function of the Jewish Messiah, quite apart from any thought of a redemptive death. E.g.: Testament of Levi, xviii. 9 (of the priestly Messiah from Levi):

> ἐπὶ τῆς ἱεροσύνης αὐτοῦ ἐκλείψει ἡ ἁμαρτία
> καὶ οἱ ἄνομοι καταπαύσουσιν εἰς κακά.

Ps. Sol. xvii. 29 (of the Messiah Son of David):

> οὐκ ἀφήσει ἀδικίαν ἐν μέσῳ αὐτῶν αὐλισθῆναι ἔτι
> καὶ οὐ κατοικήσει πᾶς ἄνθρωπος μετ' αὐτῶν εἰδὼς κακίαν.

Apocalypse of Baruch, lxxiii. 1–4 (of 'My Messiah'):

> And it shall come to pass when He has brought low everything that is in the world,
> And has sat down in peace for the age on the throne of His Kingdom...
> Judgements and revilings and contentions and revenges
> And blood and passions and envy and hatred
> And whatsoever things are like these,
> Shall go into condemnation when they are *removed*.

Primitive Christian Messianism, which repudiated or radically transformed many elements of Jewish belief, retained and emphasized this function of the Messiah, in a sublimated or 'etherialized' form:

> God exalted Him at His right hand as Prince and Saviour, to give to Israel repentance and forgiveness of sins (Acts, v. 31).

> God raised up His Servant and sent Him to bless you by turning each one from his wickednesses (Acts, iii. 26).

> You shall call His name JESUS, for He Himself will save His people from their sins (Matt. i. 21).

---

[1] I am indebted for the first suggestion of this interpretation to F. Spitta, *Streitfragen der Geschichte Jesu* (1907), pp. 172–224, though I do not consider all his evidence admissible.

Thus the expression, 'God's Lamb who removes the sin of the world', in the sense 'God's Messiah who makes an end of sin', is entirely intelligible on the basis of primitive Christian messianic belief with its Jewish background.

I conclude that the expression ὁ ἀμνὸς τοῦ θεοῦ, in its first intention, is probably a messianic title, virtually equivalent to ὁ βασιλεὺς τοῦ 'Ισραήλ, taken over by the evangelist from a tradition which also underlies the Apocalypse of John. It is possible enough that other ideas may be in some measure combined in it, for our author's thought is subtle and complex. Since he certainly used *testimonia* from the prophecy of the suffering Servant in Is. lii. 13–liii. 12, reminiscences of the ἀμνός of Is. liii. 7 may have had some influence (though John probably knew well enough that ἀμνός is a mistranslation for רָחֵל). It is even possible that in speaking of the removal of sin he recalled that the Servant was a sin-offering, and thought of the lamb of sacrifice—but if so, in a highly sublimated sense (cf. vi. 51, x. 15, xvii. 19). Yet none of these possible lines of meaning are followed up in the gospel. All the more probable does it seem that for the evangelist 'Lamb' was a traditional messianic title, like 'Messiah' itself and 'King of Israel', and that it is introduced in ch. i as such. If that is so, it would seem to be by no means impossible that it may have been used, in its apocalyptic sense, by John the Baptist, and so have passed into early Christian usage in certain circles.

In this introductory chapter, then, it would seem that the evangelist has deliberately set his feet firmly upon the ground of the common Christian tradition, in order to advance from this to his distinctive teaching.

For the sake of completeness we may here notice two more titles, which do not seem in the same way to belong to the common tradition, and yet have no special relation to distinctively Johannine ideas.

(i) Ὁ σωτὴρ τοῦ κόσμου, iv. 42. The title σωτήρ, which in the Old Testament (representing always some derivative from the root ישׁע) is sometimes given to human deliverers of Israel from its enemies, but mostly to God Himself, is in the New Testament most common in works of relatively late date: it occurs ten times in the Pastoral Epistles (mostly with θεός), five times in II Peter, and once in Jude, as well as in I John iv. 14, where we have, as here, σωτὴρ τοῦ κόσμου. In the Synoptic Gospels it is confined to Luke. 'God my Saviour' in Luke i. 47 echoes a very frequent expression in the Old Testament. In Luke ii. 11 alone Christ is called σωτήρ. Among the various renderings of the apostolic *kerygma* in the Acts, σωτήρ is confined to the brief summary in v. 30–2, in a passage which is under some suspicion of being a secondary variant of ch. iv,[1] and to the speech attributed to Paul in ch. xiii, which may be coloured by Pauline usage, since the apostle uses the term in Phil. iii. 20; and it occurs also, in a rather different connection, in Eph. v. 23. There is thus little ground for supposing that the primitive tradition gave the title σωτήρ to Christ. This is somewhat surprising, since it would seem to suggest itself naturally from the etymology of the name Jesus; but so it is. On the other hand, in the Hellenistic world it was a very common attribute of pagan gods (and of emperors), and it seems likely that it was in Hellenistic Christian circles that it gained currency. The evangelist may even have been conscious of a certain dramatic propriety in putting it in the mouth of Samaritans, who in this gospel represent in some sort the Gentile world over against the Jews. No explanation of the term is offered. The reader is left to gather from the tenor of the work as a whole in what sense Christ is Saviour.

(ii) Ὁ προφήτης, vii. 40, with the addition of ὁ ἐρχόμενος εἰς τὸν κόσμον, vi. 14. This is not treated by the evangelist as a messianic title, for in vii. 40 it is suggested by some of the crowd as an *alternative* to the title ὁ χριστός favoured by others. In vi. 14 the recognition of Jesus as 'the coming Prophet' leads the crowd to attempt to make Him king. Here therefore it is quasi-messianic; yet the evangelist clearly regards it as in any case an inadequate, or even misleading, description of the real status of Jesus. In i. 21 John the Baptist, having repudiated the title ὁ χριστός, is offered the alternatives, Elijah or ὁ προφήτης, both of which he rejects. Again, therefore, ὁ προφήτης is not strictly a messianic title, though it has some analogy with messianic titles. The meaning of the term as used by this evangelist (and by him alone) is enigmatic. Other places where Jesus is acknowledged by various persons as a prophet are not relevant. A suggestion which has in late years been widely accepted[2] is that we have here the influence of the idea of the one prophet who is incarnated in different historical individuals at various periods. This idea plays a part in Manichaean and Mandaean doctrine, and it is important in Islam. The only early Christian documents which are cited in support are the pseudo-Clementine *Homilies* and *Recognitions*, but these are assigned to a date far too late to provide evidence relevant to the Fourth

[1] See my discussion in *The Apostolic Preaching* (1936), pp. 29–36.
[2] See Bauer *ad* i. 21.

Gospel.[1] In the Elkesaite document summarized by Hippolytus, *Refut.* x. 29, it is χριστός who is thus reincarnated repeatedly; the term προφήτης is not used. The suggested theory therefore lacks probability. It is possible that the evangelist had in mind the prophetic figure called תָּאֵבָה, who in Samaritan eschatology is understood to have corresponded to the Messiah;[2] or he may have that thought of the 'prophet like unto Moses' of Deut. xviii. 15. In Acts iii. 22–3 this prophecy is regarded as fulfilled in Christ. It may well be however that the Fourth Evangelist did not accept the identification. It is in any case clear that for him the title ὁ προφήτης is not an appropriate one, though it may represent a stage towards a true estimate of the status of Jesus. It has no further significance for the development of his distinctive teaching.

[1] Carl Schmidt, *Studien zu den Pseudoclementinen*, in *Texte und Untersuchungen*, 1929, dates the *Grundschrift* underlying both *Homilies* and *Recognitions* about A.D. 220–30. If earlier sources were incorporated in the work, their identification and dating are speculative.
[2] If this goes back to so early a period. Our Samaritan evidence is late.

10. SON OF MAN

The phrase ὁ υἱὸς τοῦ ἀνθρώπου is freely used in the Fourth Gospel as a designation for Jesus, as in the Synoptic Gospels, where it occurs alike in Mark, in the material common to Matthew and Luke, and in passages peculiar to Matthew and to Luke respectively. It thus belongs to the common tradition behind the gospels, and John has undoubtedly taken it from that tradition. For him as for the other evangelists it is characteristically a self-designation of Jesus (xii. 34 is no real exception), and it is just about as frequent in the Fourth Gospel as in Mark (Mark fourteen times, John thirteen, if we follow אB and Sinaitic Syriac in reading τὸν υἱὸν τοῦ ἀνθρώπου in ix. 35, against the T.R. τὸν υἱὸν τοῦ θεοῦ). The precise meaning of the term in the Synoptics is a problem in itself, to which we must not here be diverted. In the Old Testament υἱὸς ἀνθρώπου frequently renders the Hebrew בֶּן־אָדָם, in the sense of 'human being', e.g. Ps. viii. 5 (in parallelism with ἄνθρωπος, אֱנוֹשׁ), and once the Aramaic בַּר־אֱנָשׁ, Dan. vii. 13 (both LXX and Theodotion). Both these passages are cited in the New Testament as *testimonia* to Christ; Dan. vii. 13 in Mark xiv. 62 and parallels, and Ps. viii. 5 in Heb. ii. 6–9. The use of the latter passage, however, as a *testimonium* did not originate with the *Auctor ad Hebraeos*, since Ps. viii. 7 is cited in I Cor. xv. 27, along with Ps. cix (cx). 1 (which in Mark xiv. 62 is associated with Dan. vii. 13) in a passage which later goes on to refer to Christ as ἄνθρωπος (i.e. בַּר־אֱנָשׁ, בַּר־נָשָׁא). To put it broadly, Ps. viii. 5 is applied to Christ as the representative Head of humanity (of ideal, or redeemed humanity), and Dan. vii. 13 is applied to Him as the 'Coming One' to whom everlasting dominion is given, 'at the right hand of God'. As such, He is also called 'Messiah', but Mark indicates (viii. 30–1, xiv. 61–2) that 'Son of Man' is the preferred title.

There is little evidence to show that in pre-Christian Judaism the term 'Son of Man' was used as a messianic title. In Dan. vii. 13, the figure who is 'like a human being' (ὡς υἱὸς ἀνθρώπου, כְּבַר־אֱנָשׁ) is expressly identified with 'the people of the saints of the Most High', i.e. with the true and final People of God to whom ultimate dominion is promised. In the Ethiopic Book of Enoch, xlvi. 1–3, the apocalyptic description of Dan. vii is imitated, and a 'being whose countenance had the appearance of a man' is thereinafter referred to in an Ethiopic expression which apparently represents ὁ υἱὸς τοῦ ἀνθρώπου, perhaps=הַו בַּר־נָשׁ. This figure appears to be identified with the 'Elect One', who is also called Messiah. It is, however, not entirely clear that an individual figure of any kind is intended. It has been plausibly argued that here, as in Dan. vii, the Son of Man is symbolic of the 'congregation of the elect'.[1] According to Enoch lxx–lxxi Enoch himself is apparently identified with the Son of Man.[2] The whole question is still open. But the evidence of the Similitudes of Enoch is not entirely satisfactory, for the following reasons: (i) these portions of the Ethiopic book have no parallel in any of the extensive Greek fragments (which do not contain any passage referring to the Son of Man); a comparison of these fragments with the parallel parts of the Ethiopic does not encourage complete confidence in the fidelity or integrity of the Ethiopic version; (ii) the Ethiopic has three different terms which Charles renders by 'Son of Man', adding that the translator 'can only have had one and the same phrase before him' (why?); the three terms in question he renders 'filius hominis', 'filius viri', and 'filius prolis matris viventium'. 'The mother of all living' (from Gen. iii. 20) is a phrase used by 'Gnostics' of the Christian era (e.g. Hippolytus, Refut. v. 7, 16), as well as in the Manichaean system. It is difficult to feel quite sure that we have before us a faithful version of a homogeneous pre-Christian text. It was announced that an Aramaic MS. of Enoch was among the scrolls discovered in a cave near the Dead Sea. We must await its publication. It may settle the whole matter; or again it may not.[3] Meanwhile, it ought not to be affirmed as proven upon the evidence of the Ethiopic Book of

---

[1] T. W. Manson, 'The Son of Man in Daniel, Enoch and the Gospels', in *Bulletin of the John Rylands Library*, vol. xxxii (1950), pp. 171–93, now speaks of a characteristic 'oscillation' between the individual and the corporate sense.

[2] This identification is crucial for Otto's interpretation, in *Reich Gottes und Menschensohn* (1934). Charles excised lxxi as an interpolation, and his translation of lxx. 1 eliminates the identification. Dr Matthew Black allows me to refer to an article shortly to be published, in which he maintains that lxx–lxxi is indeed to be separated from the rest of the Similitudes, but as belonging 'to an older, not to a younger stratum of the Enoch tradition', and as representing a pre-Christian Jewish apocalyptic belief in 'the Head of the Elect, who, at the beginning of history and at its end, is . . . the immortalized patriarch, the Elect One, the Son of Man'. The Similitudes, he thinks, may have grown out of it by a re-writing of the Enoch legend in support of a doctrine of a supernatural Messiah, foreign to the original conception of I Enoch.

[3] But according to W. F. Albright, in *The Old Testament and Modern Study*, 1951, p. 23, the text is that of 'part of the long lost Book of Lamech, showing very close affinities to the first part of the Book of Enoch as well as to the so-called Book of Noah, embedded in our extant Enoch'.

Enoch that 'Son of Man' was a messianic title recognized as such in pre-Christian Judaism.[1]

In the Apocalypse of Ezra, xiii, the seer beholds 'as it were the form of a man arising out of the sea', and 'flying with the clouds of heaven'. The expression obviously recalls Daniel's כְּבַר־אֱנָשׁ. He is subsequently referred to as 'the man' or 'this man' (presumably הַו בַּר־נָשׁ) and in the interpretation of the vision he performs messianic functions, and is apparently to be identified with 'my Son' (xiii. 52) who is the Messiah (xii. 32). Here then, in a document pretty closely contemporary with the Fourth Gospel, the 'Son of Man' of Daniel seems to be identified, or fused, with the 'Messiah'. Yet Moore comments, 'The whole drama moves on a fantastic stage...and the Messiah is a symbol, not a person' (*Judaism*, II, p. 338).

Moore produces some evidence that Jewish interpreters may have sought the Messiah in Dan. vii at an earlier period; but it is not conclusive, and in any case the actual phrase 'Son of Man' does not appear to be used in a messianic sense. The Danielic figure is called עֲנָנִי ('Cloud-man'); or בַר־נִפְלִי ('Son of νεφέλη, Cloud') (*op. cit.* pp. 334–7).

As we have noted, the Hebrew and Aramaic expressions translated by υἱὸς ἀνθρώπου mean no more than 'man', or 'human being'. In I Cor. xv Paul uses the simple ἄνθρωπος of Christ in connection with *testimonia* which elsewhere are associated with the expression 'Son of Man'. We may take it that he, and probably also the author of the Fourth Gospel, were aware that the proper equivalent of the primitive Christian term for Christ, which was presumably בַּר־נָשָׁא, was ὁ ἄνθρωπος. At any rate, the statements about the Son of Man which are actually made in the Fourth Gospel recall the figure of the heavenly Ἄνθρωπος as we have met it in Hellenistic documents. Whatever may have been the remoter origins of this conception,[2] it meets us in a common and characteristic form in the Hermetic literature,[3] in Hellenistic Judaism as represented by Philo,[4] and in early semi-Christian, or near-Christian, 'Gnosticism'[5]—that is to say, in an area of religious thought which, though exposed to various influences, shows most markedly the influence of Platonism and of the

---

[1] See also J. Y. Campbell in *J.T.S.* xlviii (1947), pp. 146–8. I am disposed to agree with him that in the present state of the matter 'the evidence of the Book of Enoch' (I should say, rather, of the Similitudes) 'is quite inadequate to prove anything at all about Jewish messianic expectations, or messianic titles, in the time of Jesus'.

[2] For speculations upon this subject see e.g. Bousset, *Hauptprobleme der Gnosis* (1907), pp. 160–223; Reitzenstein, *Poimandres*, pp. 81 sqq.

[3] See pp. 31–2, 41–3.   [4] See pp. 69–71.   [5] See pp. 109–12.

more speculative Judaism. The idea is that of a Being who is the archetype of the human race, and at the same time the true or essential humanity (ἀληθινός, οὐσιώδης ἄνθρωπος) resident or immanent (ἐνδιάθετος) in individuals of the human species; who is the offspring of the Supreme God and destined to be reunited with Him. If we now recall what is said about the Man in some of the sources I have referred to, we shall find that they are often echoed, though with a difference, in the Fourth Gospel.

The Johannine Son of Man is the Son of God; He descended from heaven and ascends to heaven again (iii. 13, vi. 62, etc.). He is in intimate union with God, 'dwelling in Him'. He is archetypal at least in the sense that His relation to the Father is the archetype of the true and ultimate relation of men to God (see above, pp. 166–7, 194–5). Moreover, He is represented symbolically by light, bread, the vine; in relation to the empirical light, bread and vine He is ἀληθινός, the ultimate reality lying behind phenomenal existences, or that which ultimately they mean. The φῶς ἀληθινόν, for example, is what Philo calls ἀρχέτυπον φωτός. It is, in other words, the Platonic Idea of light. It is no long step from that to say that for John the Son of Man is the ἀληθινὸς ἄνθρωπος, the real or archetypal Man, or the Platonic Idea of Man.

Again, the Hellenistic heavenly Man, dwelling either in all men, or in those who are τέλειοι ἄνθρωποι, represents, or sums up in Himself, humanity as such. Similarly for John the true life for men is attained only by those in whom Christ dwells, and who dwell in Him. He is the Vine, they the branches. That is to say, as Son of Man He is in some sort the inclusive representative of ideal or redeemed humanity. He descends into the world and dies in order that He may draw all men to Him (xii. 32). He ascends to God in order that where He is they may be also (xiv. 3). For this conception of the solidarity of believers with Christ there was precedent in the Christian tradition. Not only is it impressively worked out in Paul's doctrine of the Body of Christ, but it is implied in such Synoptic sayings as Matt. xxv. 40 'Inasmuch as you did it to one of the least of these my brethren, you did it to me'; Matt. x. 49 'He who receives you receives me'; Luke x. 16 'He who hears you hears me, and he who rejects you rejects me.' This is one of the few Synoptic sayings which have a close parallel in the Fourth Gospel: xiii. 20 'He who receives whomever I send receives me.' Such solidarity is a part of what the Fourth Evangelist means by describing Christ as Son of Man.

This corporate significance of the term is not alien from the Jewish and Old Testament tradition lying behind the gospels. In Dan. vii, as we have noted, the כְּבַר־אֱנָשׁ is a symbolic figure standing for 'the people of the saints of the Most High', i.e. for the ideal Israel of the future. In Ps. lxxix (lxxx). 18 υἱὸς ἀνθρώπου (in parallelism with ἀνὴρ δεξιᾶς σου) is apparently a personification of Israel as God's people, first oppressed, then delivered by the power of God.[1] That the evangelist was not unaware of this identification of the Son of Man with ideal Israel appears from the way in which he first introduces the title in i. 51: 'You will see the heaven opened and the angels of God ascending and descending upon the Son of Man.'

The reference to Gen. xxviii. 12 cannot be avoided: '[Jacob] dreamed, and behold a ladder set up on the earth, and the top of it reached to heaven; and behold the angels of God עֹלִים וְיֹרְדִים בּוֹ.' I leave the last words untranslated for the moment, because the Hebrew word בּוֹ is ambiguous. It might mean 'on him', or, since סֻלָּם is masculine, it might mean 'on the ladder'. The LXX has come down on the side of the latter meaning, rendering ἐπ' αὐτῆς, in agreement with the feminine κλῖμαξ. Jewish exegetes were divided. Burney and Odeberg cite from Bereshith Rabba 70. 12:

[Interpretations of] R. Ḥiya and R. Yannai [first half of third century]. The one scholar says, 'Ascending and descending upon the ladder', and the other says, 'Ascending and descending upon Jacob'. The explanation 'Ascending and descending upon the ladder' is to be preferred. The explanation 'Ascending and descending upon Jacob' implies that they were taking up and bringing down upon him. They were leaping and skipping over him and rallying him, as it is said, 'Israel in whom I glory' (Is. xlix. 3), 'Thou art he whose εἰκών (אִיקוֹן) is engraved on high.' They were ascending on high and looking at his εἰκών (אִיקוֹנִין = εἰκόνιον), and then descending below and finding him sleeping. (Burney's translation; the Hebrew text in Odeberg.)

It seems clear that John knew and accepted the interpretation which understood Gen. xxviii. 12 to say that the angels of God ascended and descended upon Jacob, or Israel, and that for 'Israel' he substituted

---

[1] And note that in the earlier part of the same Psalm (9–15) Israel is God's Vine. The LXX, handling the original somewhat drastically, has brought 'Vine' and 'Son of Man' into direct parallelism:

κατάρτισαι αὐτὴν ἣν ἐφύτευσεν ἡ δεξιά σου
καὶ ἐπὶ υἱὸν ἀνθρώπου ὃν ἐκραταίωσας σεαυτῷ   (16).

If we single out any one passage in the Old Testament which might be regarded as the scriptural basis for the Johannine idea of the Son of Man, Ps. lxxix (lxxx) would take precedence of Dan. vii.

'Son of Man'. As Burney well puts it, 'Jacob, as the ancestor of the nation of Israel, summarizes in his person the ideal Israel *in posse*, just as our Lord, at the other end of the line, summarizes it *in esse* as the Son of Man' (*Aramaic Origin*, p. 115). For John, of course, 'Israel' is not the Jewish nation, but the new humanity, reborn in Christ, the community of those who are 'of the truth',[1] and of whom Christ is king. In a deeper sense He is not only their king, He is their inclusive representative: they are in Him and He in them.

The same Midrash on Gen. xxviii. 12 suggests, as Odeberg shows in his note on John i. 51, a further aspect of John's treatment of the Son of Man idea. It connects the descent of the angels upon Jacob, or Israel, with the prophecy of Is. xlix. 3 δοῦλός μου εἶ σύ, Ἰσραήλ, καὶ ἐν σοὶ ἐνδοξασθήσομαι. In the next verse but one of the same prophecy Israel responds, δοξασθήσομαι ἐναντίον Κυρίου. Similarly in the Fourth Gospel the Son of Man is glorified, and God is glorified in Him: xiii. 31 νῦν ἐδοξάσθη ὁ υἱὸς τοῦ ἀνθρώπου καὶ ὁ θεὸς ἐδοξάσθη ἐν αὐτῷ, xii. 23 ἐλήλυθεν ἡ ὥρα ἵνα δοξασθῇ ὁ υἱὸς τοῦ ἀνθρώπου.

That this is no accidental parallel appears from a closer study of the Isaianic context. The mission of the Servant in this passage is, first, to gather Israel together to the Lord, συναγαγεῖν τὸν Ἰακὼβ πρὸς αὐτόν (xlix. 5). With this we may compare John xi. 52, which defines the purpose of the death of Christ as 'to gather together into one the scattered children of God', ἵνα καὶ τὰ τέκνα τοῦ θεοῦ τὰ διεσκορπισμένα συναγάγῃ εἰς ἕν. Secondly, the Servant is called to be a 'light of the Gentiles' (xlix. 6), to say to those who are in darkness, 'Be revealed' (xlix. 9). So in the Fourth Gospel Christ is the Light of the World, and he who believes in Him and follows Him will not walk in darkness (xii. 46, viii. 12). Finally, as a result of the mission of the Servant, 'They shall feed in the ways, and on the bare heights shall be their pasture. They shall not hunger nor thirst...for He that has mercy on them shall lead them, even by springs of water shall He guide them' (xlix. 9–10). The echoes of this language in the Fourth Gospel are manifest (x. 3, 9, iv. 14, vi. 35).

It is to be observed that in Is. xlix the Servant is in part identified with Israel, and in part appears as a messenger of God to Israel. That is to say, the individual and the corporate aspects of the idea are confused, or combined. The term 'Son of Man' is similarly capable of an individual and a corporate sense. It would appear that the evangelist found in the

---

[1] Much as in Philo Ἰσραήλ = ὁρῶν θεόν stands for that select γένος of men who have the vision of God.

Servant of the Lord an embodiment of the people of God, and applied what is said of him to the Son of Man, conceived as embodying collectively in Himself redeemed humanity.

It is possible that we should also find in the Servant passages of the Second Isaiah a clue to the mysterious idea of the 'exaltation' of the Son of Man. In Is. lii. 13 the LXX has Ἰδοὺ συνήσει ὁ παῖς μου, καὶ ὑψωθήσεται καὶ δοξασθήσεται σφόδρα (הִנֵּה יַשְׂכִּיל עַבְדִּי יָרוּם וְנִשָּׂא וְגָבַהּ מְאֹד). The parallel would encourage us to understand that when John says, δεῖ ὑψωθῆναι τὸν υἱὸν τοῦ ἀνθρώπου (iii. 14, xii. 34), he means much the same as when he speaks of the Son of Man being glorified. The word ὑψωθῆναι was used in primitive Christianity for the 'exaltation' of Christ to the right hand of God (Acts ii. 33, v. 31). That Christ is exalted, as He is glorified, in His death, is a turn of thought essential to the whole Johannine position. What underlies it, I have already suggested in dealing with the concept of δόξα. In his Old Testament exemplar, the evangelist would readily understand Is. lii. 13 in the light of liii. 7–8. The Servant is 'exalted and glorified exceedingly' in His death.

If this connection of thought be considered valid, we can see how easily the evangelist could connect the work of the suffering Servant, who is also the Son of Man, in gathering together the scattered children of God, with the death of Christ. We then have a suggestive background for the saying in xii. 32 κἀγὼ ἐὰν ὑψωθῶ ἐκ τῆς γῆς, πάντας ἑλκύσω πρὸς ἐμαυτόν. This, the evangelist comments, He said σημαίνων ποίῳ θανάτῳ ἤμελλεν ἀποθνήσκειν. In His death the Son of Man draws all men into union with Himself, and so affirms His character as inclusive representative of the redeemed race.

In the light of this we may turn to iii. 13–14 οὐδεὶς ἀναβέβηκεν εἰς τὸν οὐρανὸν εἰ μὴ ὁ ἐκ τοῦ οὐρανοῦ καταβάς, ὁ υἱὸς τοῦ ἀνθρώπου. καὶ καθὼς Μωυσῆς ὕψωσεν τὸν ὄφιν ἐν τῇ ἐρήμῳ, οὕτως ὑψωθῆναι δεῖ τὸν υἱὸν τοῦ ἀνθρώπου. The ascent of the Son of Man is here equated with His exaltation. John conceives the 'uplifting' of the Son of Man as making possible for men that union with Him by which they too ascend to the Father.[1] Cf. vi. 62 ἐὰν θεωρῆτε τὸν υἱὸν τοῦ ἀνθρώπου ἀναβαίνοντα. As the 'looking' at the serpent caused Israel to 'live', so the 'contemplation' of the Son of Man in His exaltation brings life eternal. It is in His death above all that He is exalted, and, in 'drawing' men to Him, uniting them with Him, affirms the character which specifically belongs to the Son of Man, the character of the inclusive representative of true humanity.

[1] See further below, pp. 306–7, 375–9.

It is probably in a similar sense that we are to understand viii. 28 ὅταν ὑψώσητε τὸν υἱὸν τοῦ ἀνθρώπου, τότε γνώσεσθε ὅτι ἐγώ εἰμι. The solemn affirmation, ἐγώ εἰμι, here as elsewhere, is an echo of the ἐγώ εἰμι, אני הוא, by which in the Second Isaiah Jehovah declares Himself as the Self-existent, and is to be taken as declaring that in Christ the Self-existent is fully revealed. The knowledge of Him, then, as the revelation of the Self-existent will come only ὅταν ὑψώσητε τὸν υἱὸν τοῦ ἀνθρώπου.[1]

Within the same context of thought we may place what is said of the Son of Man in the discourse on the Bread of Life in ch. vi. Here we are first told that the Son of Man gives τὴν βρῶσιν τὴν μένουσαν εἰς ζωὴν αἰώνιον, which, unlike the manna of Moses, is ἄρτος ἀληθινός. It is, in fact, ὁ καταβαίνων ἐκ τοῦ οὐρανοῦ. We already know from iii. 13 that ὁ ἐκ τοῦ οὐρανοῦ καταβάς is no other than the Son of Man. It is as Son of Man that Jesus says, ἐγώ εἰμι ὁ ἄρτος τῆς ζωῆς. When the Jews crudely misunderstand Him, He explains His meaning in the words, 'Unless you eat the flesh of the *Son of Man*, and drink His blood, you have no life in you.... He who eats my flesh and drinks my blood, dwells in me and I in him.' That is, to eat and drink the flesh and blood of Christ is to become incorporate in the Son of Man, and to share His life. When the hearers are still 'scandalized' by this σκληρὸς λόγος, they are reminded once more that it is only in the contemplation of the Son of Man ascending where He was before, that is, of His exaltation in death, that its meaning can be understood. Incorporate with Him, they ascend in Him out of τὰ κάτω into τὰ ἄνω, out of darkness into light, out of death into life eternal.

Thus the term 'Son of Man' throughout this gospel retains the sense of one who incorporates in Himself the people of God, or humanity in its ideal aspect. But while the concept employed is substantially identical with that of the heavenly Man as known over a wide range of Hellenistic thought, the reality to which the concept is applied is different. The Hellenistic Ἄνθρωπος is a metaphysical abstraction. No doubt for those who accepted the Platonic 'realism' the Idea of Man was a 'real' existence, more real than empirical individuals of the human race. Nevertheless its reality is of the kind arrived at by abstracting from the concrete actuality of experience. To ask whether the Man is a person is a question which hardly has a meaning. The mode of expression alternates bewilderingly between the philosophical and the mythical. Philosophically, the Man is no other than νοῦς, reason or mind in general. Mythically, He acts as

[1] See further below, pp. 375–9.

a person, but in relations with other mythical figures which clearly amount to no more than the personification of abstractions. It was in fact one of the weaknesses of all ancient thought that it had no clear conception of personality. In the Fourth Gospel, on the other hand, there is never any doubt that the evangelist is speaking of a real person, that is, of a concrete, historical individual of the human race, 'Jesus of Nazareth, the Son of Joseph' (i. 45). He labours, grows weary, thirsts, feels joy and sorrow, weeps, suffers, and dies. His relations with other men are such as can be expressed in terms of love, trust and obedience, and that not in any symbolic or sublimated sense, but as men love, trust and obey one who is their master and teacher (xiii. 13). His 'glory' is the transfiguration of a human life by a supreme act of self-sacrifice; He lays down His life for His friends, as many a man has done (xv. 13). And yet, says the evangelist, in all this He was much more than one individual among the many. He was the true self of the human race, standing in that perfect union with God to which others can attain only as they are incorporate in Him; the mind, whose thought is truth absolute (xiv. 6), which other men think after Him; the true life of man, which other men live by sharing it with Him (xiv. 6, 20, vi. 57).

It is clear that this conception raises a new problem. It challenges the mind to discover a doctrine of personality, which will make conceivable this combination of the universal and the particular in a single person. A naïve individualism regarding man, or a naïve anthropomorphism regarding God, makes nonsense of the Johannine Christology. Ancient thought, when it left the ground of such naïve conceptions, lost hold upon the concrete actuality of the person. It denied personality in man by making the human individual no more than an unreal 'imitation' of the abstract universal Man, and it denied personality in God by making Him no more than the abstract unity of being. A Christian philosophy starting from the Johannine doctrine of Jesus as Son of Man should be able to escape the *impasse* into which all ancient thought fell, and to give an account of personality in God and in ourselves.

11. SON OF GOD

The idea of a being affiliated to a deity, in one sense or another, was extremely widespread in the ancient world. In Greek mythology there were family relationships among the gods, and as the tendency towards monotheism increased, these mythical relationships afforded the opportunity for expressing the subordination of lesser deities to the one supreme God. Thus Hermes and Apollo were sons of Zeus, and philosophical apologists for religion could interpret this as meaning that such deities of popular worship were manifestations or emanations of the one God. Again, there were demigods and heroes sprung from the unions of gods with mortals, and royal clans like the Heraclidae traced their descent from such beings.

In Egypt, and among various oriental peoples, the reigning king was divine, and was described as the son of the god worshipped as the special patron of the royal house, whether this was understood to mean that his descent could be traced to the god, or that his actual birth was miraculous, or that he was in some sense an 'epiphany' of the god himself. In the Hellenistic period the Greek settlers and conquerors readily accepted such ideas, bringing them into connection with their inherited mythology of demigods and heroes, as well as with the practice, which had never been entirely obsolete, of raising men of exceptional distinction (like, e.g., Brasidas the Lacedaemonian and Demetrius Poliorcetes) to the rank of heroes. Alexander was hailed by Ammon as his son, and was later provided with a miraculous birth.[1] After him the Hellenistic sovereigns of Egypt and Syria inherited the divine status of their native predecessors. Antiochus IV was θεὸς ἐπιφανής. Θεὸς ἐκ θεῶν was a title of the Ptolemies. The Roman emperors stepped into their shoes. Augustus was *divi filius*, υἱὸς θεοῦ. He and his successors were officially raised to divine rank after death, but in the East they were worshipped in their lifetime as gods.

Thus the idea of divine or deified men was familiar. At the same time the rationalization of mythology associated with the name of Euhemerus, which itself was doubtless influenced by this familiar idea, taught men to think of the gods themselves as no more than great men and benefactors

[1] On this see Tarn, *Alexander the Great*, vol. I, pp. 42-4, 77-81, vol. II, pp. 347-73.

of the race deified after death. The distinction between gods and men wore thin. 'Man on earth is a mortal god; God in heaven is an immortal man' (*C.H.* x. 25) was a maxim widely current in various forms.

It is in this atmosphere of thought that we have to understand the ascription of divinity to prophets and wonderworkers of the Hellenistic world. The θεῖος ἀνήρ is a figure of the period. His divinity is often expressed in the phrase 'son of God', or the like.[1] Apollonius of Tyana was hailed as son of Zeus. The title seems sometimes to have been justified by a birth-legend. According to Lucian, Alexander of Abonoteichos (δῖος Ἀλέξανδρος) claimed that he was descended from Perseus, and that although his ostensible parents were obscure persons, his real father was the Homeric hero Podaleirios (Lucian, *Alexander* 11).

How far such stories were taken seriously we cannot say. But in more spiritual circles the view was held that a man might become divine, or realize his inherent divinity, by an initiation into the knowledge of God. In the Hermetic tractate *De Regeneratione* it is assumed that Hermes, one of the traditional gods of Greece, identified with the Egyptian Thoth, was once a man (though indeed a man of divine descent), but had been 'born again', and so became θεὸς θεοῦ παῖς. The teaching of the tractate is that any man who undergoes a similar rebirth may also become 'a god, a child of God'. Similarly, some of the mysteries, at least in their reformed character in the Hellenistic and Roman periods, appear to have offered deification to their devotees, and the form of initiation into the mysteries of Isis, as described for example by Apuleius, seems to have been based upon the rites by which the Egyptian Pharaohs entered upon their divinity.

In popular Hellenistic usage therefore the expression υἱὸς θεοῦ reflects a certain confusion of divinity and humanity. On the one hand it represents a reduction of the idea of God, and on the other hand an extravagant estimate of the great man—intelligible, perhaps, to our generation from the surprising language which has been used about certain contemporary leaders. In more philosophical, and perhaps more deeply religious circles, this very assimilation of God and man seemed to demand a greater emphasis upon the absolute transcendence of the ultimate *fons deitatis*, the Unknown God, whose relation to the world and to man

---

[1] But the strolling prophets of Syria known to Celsus (Origen, *c. Cels.* VII. 9), who have played far too large a role in these discussions, may have been Christian ecstatics, for the formula ὁ θεὸς ἢ θεοῦ παῖς ἢ πνεῦμα θεῖον smacks of primitive Christian trinitarianism.

can be conceived only through a series of mediating essences. For some writers this whole cosmos is the only true son of God, and man can know God only through the cosmos. For others, the cosmos itself is not the creation of the supreme God, but of a subordinate creator or creators, who again may be described as God's children. Or again, it may be that not the visible cosmos, but its intelligible archetype, the κόσμος νοητός, is the son of God. For Philo, the κόσμος νοητός, or the Logos of which it is an aspect, or with which it is identified, is the firstborn Son (πρωτόγονος or πρεσβύτατος υἱός) of God, while the visible cosmos is His younger Son. In a somewhat similar sense, apparently, the Hermetic tractate *Poimandres* describes the creative word, Logos, as υἱὸς θεοῦ.[1] In all such ways of speech, the term 'Son of God' is clearly metaphorical. While popular religion spoke of subordinate divinities as sons of the high gods, philosophical religion took over the term to describe the mediating essences through which the supreme God creates the world and reveals Himself to man, and meant by it some kind of emanation, best conceived on the analogy of the relation of speech to the mind that frames it, or of a thought to the mind that thinks.

Among the Jews the situation was different. Philo the Jew, indeed, whom I have cited among Hellenistic writers, approximates to Hellenistic ideas, though he carefully guards himself against their cruder forms, and repudiates, for instance, the idea that a man can in any circumstances become God (see p. 60). But the Hebrew-thinking Jew was never tempted to assimilate divinity and humanity in any way, nor did he confuse creation with procreation.

The term 'son of God' is indeed not infrequently found in Jewish writings, but its significance is always metaphorical. Israel is the son of Jehovah, not in the sense that the Israelites were descended from Him, as the Heraclidae were descended from Heracles. It signifies that Jehovah, by a free act of grace, has chosen to place Israel in a relation of peculiar intimacy with Him, as the objects of His care and discipline, and demands from them a loyalty and obedience like that which a good son pays to the head of the family. The king of Israel is God's son, not in the sense in which the Egyptian monarchs or the Roman emperors were so called, but as the representative of the people of Jehovah before their God. 'Thou art my son, this day have I begotten thee' (Ps. ii. 7), appears to be a Hebrew adaptation of the Babylonian formula of *adoption*. If Israel, or the king of Israel, is the son of God, he is so by adoption, not by

[1] See above, pp. 39–40.

procreation. And when in Hellenistic Judaism the term υἱὸς θεοῦ is applied to a private individual (e.g. Wisd. ii. 18), the meaning is not either that he was miraculously born, or that he has been deified by initiation, but that he lives within the divine care and discipline, in loyal obedience to the law of God. It has rather the aspect of an expression borrowed from the environment, and given a reduced significance in accordance with the traditional idea of Israel as son of God by grace and adoption.

The question whether in pre-Christian Judaism the title 'son of God' was used of the Messiah is not entirely settled. The evidence is not satisfactory. The application however of the title both to the nation as a whole (Exod. iv. 22, Hos. xi. 1) and to its anointed king (II Sam. vii. 14, Ps. ii. 7) might easily have led to its application to an ideal figure who was conceived as the perfect representative of the Davidic monarchy, and as embodying in Himself the ideal relation of Israel to God and to the world. But the first clear and explicit allusion to 'My son the Messiah' in Jewish literature appears to occur in IV Ezra, which is about contemporary with the Fourth Gospel.

In the Synoptic Gospels the title is primarily messianic, as is clear from (a) the question of the High Priest, 'Art thou the Messiah, the Son of the Blessed?' (Mark xiv. 61), and (b) the Matthaean form of Peter's confession, 'Thou art the Messiah, the Son of the living God' (Matt. xvi. 16). And as we have seen, it is as a messianic title that it is introduced by the Fourth Evangelist in the chapter of testimonies. The messianic idea itself, however, is a fluid one, and Christian messianic belief departs so widely from its Jewish antecedents, that it is not profitable to attempt to determine the meaning of the expression 'son of God' from that of 'Messiah'.

This brief survey of the background will have shown that the expression 'son of God' might suggest to various classes of readers in the public to which the Fourth Gospel might appeal a wide variety of ideas. It might suggest a man of god-like character or power, a prophet or initiate, the Messiah of the Jews, or a supernatural being mediating the knowledge of the supreme God. All this is too vague to serve as more than a general starting-point for our investigation of the usage in the gospel itself. We must examine closely what the evangelist actually says about the Son of God. Certainly there is no other writing known to me in which the idea of divine sonship is treated with anything like such fullness and precision.

First, we may observe that all through the gospel the Son of God is presented as one 'sent' by the Father. The verbs πέμπειν and ἀποστέλλειν, used apparently without any difference of meaning, occur in this connection over forty times in all parts of the gospel. God is referred to as ὁ πατήρ μου, or, ὁ πατὴρ ὁ πέμψας με, or simply, ὁ πέμψας με. We may therefore take it to be a regulative idea that the Son of God is He who is commissioned or delegated by God to mankind. In other words, He comes 'in the name' of the Father (v. 43). It is as God's representative that men receive or reject Him; ὁ ἐμὲ λαμβάνων λαμβάνει τὸν πέμψαντά με (xiii. 20), ὁ ἐμὲ μισῶν καὶ τὸν πατέρα μου μισεῖ (xv. 23).

As the Father's delegate, the Son speaks the words of God, and does the works of God, both however in strict subordination to the Father. 'I do nothing of myself, but as the Father taught me, I am speaking thus.... I do always what pleases Him' (viii. 28 sq.). Entire obedience to the Father is the inseparable condition of the mission of the Son: 'My food is to do the will of Him who sent me' (iv. 34).

This description of the status and function of the Son of God recalls the language of the Old Testament prophets. The prophet is one sent by Jehovah. Isaiah heard the divine voice proclaim, 'Whom shall I send, and who will go for us?' and replied, 'Here am I; send me' (Is. vi. 8). And if we observe that in John the Son is 'sanctified and sent *into the world*' (John x. 36), this finds a parallel in Jeremiah's conviction that he was consecrated before birth to the prophetic office: 'Before thou camest forth out of the womb I sanctified thee: I have appointed thee a prophet unto the nations' (Jer. i. 5). Again, if the Son is said to know the Father and to be known by Him, this again is not without parallel in the prophets. That the Lord knows His servants the prophets is repeatedly stated, and in some measure at least the prophet knows Him: 'Surely the Lord will do nothing, but he revealeth his secret unto His servants the prophets' (Amos iii. 7), 'Let him that glorieth glory in this, that he understandeth and knoweth me, saith the Lord' (Jer. ix. 24). It is at least the ideal of the prophet that he should know God as he is known by God.[1] In his work he is dependent on God and obedient to His will. 'What the Lord saith unto me, that will I speak', says Micaiah ben Imlah (III Kms. xxii. 14); and the strange symbolic actions (σημεῖα) performed by the prophets are done by direct inspiration of God, and are in some sort the acts of God Himself.[2]

[1] See above, pp. 163–4.
[2] See H. Wheeler Robinson, *Prophetic Symbolism*, in *Old Testament Essays*, ed. D. C. Simpson (1927), pp. 1–17.

The prophet is thus the delegate of God, and His representative to men. To accept the prophet's word is to accept the word of the Lord; to reject him is to reject the Lord. 'They have not rejected thee, but they have rejected me', says Jehovah to Samuel (I Sam. viii. 7). Cf. John xii. 48–9.

Finally, as the representative of God, the prophet has a delegated authority over mankind. 'The Lord said unto me, See, I have this day set thee over the nations and over the kingdoms, to pluck up and to break down, and to destroy and to overthrow; to build up and to plant' (Jer. i. 10). Similarly, 'the Father loves the Son and has given everything into His hand' (John iii. 35). In particular, 'He has given Him authority to execute judgment' (v. 27).

It appears then that John has deliberately moulded the idea of the Son of God in the first instance upon the prophetic model. It is as prophet that Jesus appears to those who have not fully penetrated His secret (iv. 19, ix. 17). The human mould, so to speak, into which the divine sonship is poured is a personality of the prophetic type. Upon this plane, the difference between prophet and Son is that the latter possesses in an absolute sense that which the prophets possess ideally but not in full actuality, and possesses permanently what they perhaps possess intermittently and *ad hoc* (cf. viii. 35 ὁ υἱὸς μένει [ἐν τῇ οἰκίᾳ] εἰς τὸν αἰῶνα). It is not that the Son possesses inherently or independently that which the prophets possess derivatively, for strong emphasis is laid upon the Son's absolute dependence on the Father, especially in the important discourse, v. 17 sqq., to which we must return in a moment. Such dependence is of the essence of sonship. 'The living Father sent me and I live διὰ τὸν πατέρα' (vi. 57). 'I am the Vine and my Father the γεωργός' (xv. 1).

The absolute dependence of the Son on the Father being presupposed, it is impossible to overstate the extent to which divine powers and prerogatives are exercised by the Son. To return to the discourse of v. 17 sqq., the two supreme prerogatives of God as Creator and Ruler of the universe are vested in the Son, namely ζωοποίησις and κρίσις. 'As the Father awakens the dead and gives them life, so the Son gives life to whom He will.... For as the Father has life in Himself, so He has granted to the Son to have life in Himself.' We may observe how this idea is illustrated in the story of the raising of Lazarus. This story is intended to set forth Christ as 'the resurrection and the life', that is to say as Him who 'awakens the dead and gives them life'. In the story He comes to the tomb, and orders the stone to be removed, saying 'If you have faith you will see the glory of God' (xi. 40). Then, when the stone is removed, 'Jesus lifted up his eyes to heaven and said, "Father, I thank thee that thou hast heard me; I knew that thou always hearest me"' (xi. 41), and then, 'Lazarus, come forth' (43). The evangelist has represented Jesus as working the miracle in the consciousness of an uninterrupted dependence on the Father. His prayer is always heard; the supply of divine power is continuous; the only appeal of Son to Father is in the form of a thankful acknowledgement of delegated power and authority. It is as the Son, aware that the Father has granted Him to have life in Himself, that Christ awakens the dead. The deed is in fact not His, but the Father's, though He is the immediate agent. 'The words which I say to you I am not speaking of myself, and the Father who dwells in me does His works' (xiv. 10).

Similarly, to return to v. 17 sqq., 'the Father judges no one, but has given all judgment to the Son....He has given Him authority to execute judgment, because He is the Son of Man....I can do nothing of myself: as I hear I judge, and my judgment is just because I seek not my own will but the will of Him who sent me' (v. 22, 27, 30). The judgment is passed, as we have seen, in a sense automatically, through the reaction of men to the revelation of the light in Christ. The process is clearly described in xv. 22–4, 'If I had not come and spoken to them, they would have had no sin; but as it is, they have no excuse for their sin. He who hates me hates my Father also. If I had not done among them works which no one else ever did, they would have had no sin; but as it is, they have both seen and hated both me and my Father.' Thus κρίσις and ζωοποίησις are obverse and reverse of the same process. Positively, the work of Christ is to bring life and light; negatively, it results in judgment upon those who refuse the life and turn away from the light. The 'signs', again, are so recorded as to bring out this double significance. Christ gives life to the impotent man at Bethesda. The Jews seek to kill Him. He pronounces their judgment: 'You will not come to me that you may have life....I have come in the name of my Father and you do not receive me....Do not suppose that I will accuse you to the Father. Your accuser is Moses.... If you do not believe his writings, how can you believe my word?' (v. 39–47) Again, Christ breaks the Bread of Life for the multitude. As a result, many were 'scandalized', and went away and walked no more with Him—self-condemned (vi. 60–1, 66). He gives sight to the blind. The Jews cavil, and again He pronounces judgment: 'I have come into the world for judgment, that those who do not see may see, and those who see may become blind....If you were blind, you would have no sin; but as it is, you say, "We can see", and your sin remains' (ix. 39–41). The would-be judges are judged. With a similar irony, after the raising of Lazarus, the chief priests and Pharisees sit in judgment on Jesus, not perceiving that they are thereby judging themselves (xi. 45–53). Finally, in His passion and death, in which above all Christ gives life to the world, the sin of the world is most effectively judged. 'Now is the judgment of this world' (xii. 31).

My intention in recalling these passages is to show how the evangelist is concerned all through to exhibit the work of the Son as having the two inseparable aspects of ζωοποίησις and κρίσις, and to represent these as the distinctively divine activities;[1] for to give life is the work of the Creator, and to judge is the work of the Ruler of the universe. To be Son of God is to exercise these functions in continuous and absolute dependence on the Father. It is thus the nature of the work which He accomplishes which finally distinguishes the Son from the prophet.

In such work, the unity of Father and Son is complete. 'I do nothing of my own initiative: as the Father taught me, I am speaking thus. He has not left me alone, because I always do what pleases Him' (viii. 28–9). 'I am not alone, because the Father is with me' (xvi. 32). 'If I judge, my judgment is absolute (ἀληθινή), because I am not alone, but I and He who sent me' (viii. 16). The form of statement in the last of these passages is especially noteworthy. In the act of judgment it is not only Christ who is at work, but Father and Son in unity—ἐγὼ καὶ ὁ πέμψας με. In the whole work of Christ there is a twofold agency. It is the work of the Son; it is equally, and indistinguishably, the work of the Father. At every point in it He can say, μόνος οὐκ εἰμί, ἀλλ᾽ ἐγὼ καὶ ὁ πέμψας με. Father and Son are subjects of the same activity. This is otherwise expressed in the form ἐγὼ καὶ ὁ πατὴρ ἕν ἐσμέν (x. 30). This statement is made with express reference to the work of ζωοποίησις ('I give them eternal life and they shall never perish', x. 28), and it is corroborated by the argument, 'If I do not do my Father's works, do not believe me; but if I do, then believe the works, that you may know and recognize that the Father is in me, and I in the Father' (x. 38). It is in this unity with the Father in exercising the divine prerogatives of vivifying and judging that the unique sonship of Christ is manifested.

[1] See further, pp. 320–8.

All this is stated by the evangelist in terms of the historic mission of Jesus. It is as the man, 'Jesus of Nazareth the son of Joseph', that He heals the sick, gives sight to the blind, feeds the hungry, and raises the dead, and finally gives Himself for the life of the world. All these are σημεῖα of the work of God, which is ζωοποίησις and κρίσις. It is as the 'teacher sent from God' that He speaks the words which are spirit and life. But the occurrence of such 'signs' in the history of a living man calls for explanation. It raises the question, which is put repeatedly: Πόθεν ἐστιν; (vii. 27–8, viii. 14, ix. 29–30, xix. 9).

The evangelist's answer to this question is unequivocal. Though the Son of God lives a human life on earth, He is a stranger to this world. John works, like most religious thinkers of his time, with a *Weltanschauung* which is, *prima facie* at least, dualistic. There are two planes of being, denominated, as in the *Hermetica* and other similar literature, τὰ ἄνω and τὰ κάτω, or, in accordance rather with Jewish precedent, πνεῦμα and σάρξ, where πνεῦμα corresponds pretty closely with the Hellenistic νοῦς.[1] Thus the sphere of τὰ ἄνω corresponds with the κόσμος νοητός. It is the seat of ἀληθινά, absolute realities. The life of man lies in the sphere of τὰ κάτω, of σάρξ. God on the other hand is πνεῦμα, and can properly be worshipped only ἐν πνεύματι καὶ ἀληθείᾳ, 'in spirit, that is, in reality' (John iv. 23). 'That which is born of the σάρξ is σάρξ, and that which is born of the πνεῦμα is πνεῦμα' (iii. 6). There is a fixed separation between the two planes. It is possible for man to pass from the lower sphere to the higher only by being born again (γεννηθῆναι ἄνωθεν, ἐκ πνεύματος, iii. 3, 5, cf. γεννηθῆναι ἐν νῷ, *C.H.* xiii. 3).

Jesus, however, is not Son of God by virtue of rebirth (as was Hermes, *C.H.* xiii. 3, 14). He belongs aboriginally and inseparably to the sphere of τὰ ἄνω; so John viii. 23 ὑμεῖς ἐκ τῶν κάτω ἐστέ, ἐγὼ ἐκ τῶν ἄνω εἰμί· ὑμεῖς ἐκ τούτου τοῦ κόσμου ἐστέ, ἐγὼ οὐκ εἰμὶ ἐκ τοῦ κόσμου τούτου. His appearance in the world is a κατάβασις, and it culminates in an ἀνάβασις, which is possible only for one whose native sphere is τὰ ἄνω (iii. 13)— and for those who, being united with Christ and born again, are 'drawn' by Him into the sphere of life. He Himself did not become Son of God by ascending from the earthly sphere to the heavenly, but those who share His ascent become children of God. Moreover, He is continuously aware of His origin and destiny, while these are unknown to men; viii. 14 οἶδα πόθεν ἦλθον καὶ ποῦ ὑπάγω. This awareness is a function of His permanent sense of being 'in the Father'. On earth He is still ὁ ὢν εἰς

[1] See above, pp. 19, 103–9, 224–5.

τὸν κόλπον τοῦ πατρός (i. 18; for His ἐξήγησις of the Father takes place in His earthly ministry).[1]

More specifically, 'He knew that He came out from God and was going to God' (xiii. 3). Similar expressions occur frequently. The phrases used are παρὰ τοῦ θεοῦ, ἀπὸ τοῦ θεοῦ, ἐκ τοῦ θεοῦ.

In so far as the prepositions retain anything of their original shades of meaning, these three forms of expression would indicate slightly different aspects of the matter.

Παρά has properly the sense 'beside', 'alongside'. In that sense it is used with the dative. With the accusative, it denotes motion towards a position beside some person or object. With the genitive, it denotes motion away from such a position. Thus, ὁ ὢν παρὰ τοῦ θεοῦ might properly mean, 'He who, having been beside God (cf. xvii. 5 παρὰ σοί), has moved from such a position into the earthly sphere'; and that may be what the phrase is intended to suggest. This meaning however cannot be pressed, since John the Baptist is described as ἀπεσταλμένος παρὰ θεοῦ. The phrase παρὰ τοῦ θεοῦ, therefore, must be given a more general meaning, such as would include prophets and messengers of God.

Ἀπό denotes properly separation, and is also frequently used where the effective cause of an action, whether personal or impersonal, is in question. It is sometimes, like ὑπό, the preposition of the agent. Thus, so far as the phrase ἀπὸ θεοῦ denotes anything more than departure or separation, it would be congruous with the idea of the mission of the Son: ἀπὸ θεοῦ ἦλθεν would imply 'he came, sent by God'. The distinction, however, between ἀπό and παρά is not very clearly observed in the gospel.

Ἐκ properly denotes extraction or origin; ἐξῆλθον ἐκ τοῦ πατρὸς καὶ ἐλήλυθα εἰς τὸν κόσμον (xvi. 28) can hardly mean anything else than 'I issued out of the Father and came into the world'; cf. viii. 42 ἐγὼ γὰρ ἐκ τοῦ θεοῦ ἐξῆλθον καὶ ἥκω, οὐδὲ γὰρ ἀπ' ἐμαυτοῦ ἐλήλυθα, ἀλλ' ἐκεῖνός με ἀπέστειλεν, where the distinction between ἐκ and ἀπό is in view; Christ's coming was not initiated by Himself—He came, not ἀπ' ἐμαυτοῦ but ἀπὸ τοῦ θεοῦ, since the Father sent Him; but not only so—He had His origin in the being of the Father. It is in this precise sense, and not in any vaguer sense which the words might also bear, that He is ἐκ τοῦ

---

[1] Hence the reading, ὁ ὢν ἐν τῷ οὐρανῷ (iii. 13), gives at any rate a perfectly good sense. The authority of ℵB is against it, but the support of Θ and *fam*. 1, the Curetonian Syriac, Old Latin, and Bohairic versions, with a formidable array of patristic quotations, is not to be despised.

θεοῦ. In this sense, applicable to no prophet or messenger, Jesus is Son of God.

The evangelist does not mean that the man Jesus of Nazareth had a divine parentage, such as current legends attributed to demigods and heroes, or to θεῖοι ἄνθρωποι like the later Apollonius of Tyana or Alexander of Abonoteichos. About His extraction, on the earthly plane, there is no mystery: κἀμὲ οἴδατε καὶ οἴδατε πόθεν εἰμί. Nor does John betray any knowledge of, or interest in, the doctrine of the virgin birth of Christ, as it meets us in the First and Third Gospels and in Ignatius.[1] In any case, it is evident that it is not by reason of a miraculous conception that He is designated Son of God; for that would mean that He began to be Son of God at birth; but this is emphatically not the evangelist's view. Christ existed on the heavenly plane before He appeared on earth, and was already the 'beloved Son' of God. In xvii. 5 He speaks of 'the glory which I possessed at thy side (παρὰ σοί) before the world existed', and in xvii. 24 of 'my glory which thou gavest me because thou lovedst me before the foundation of the world'.

This pre-temporal (or more properly, non-temporal) existence of the Son is affirmed with emphasis, and assumed all through the gospel. We are to understand that in the case of Jesus, to come παρὰ τοῦ θεοῦ does indeed mean to come from a place by God's side in heaven, and to come ἀπὸ τοῦ θεοῦ means to be sent not (as it might be) from Galilee to Jerusalem, but from τὰ ἄνω to τὰ κάτω. To His pre-existence, the evangelist believes, the Old Testament bears witness. The vision of 'the

[1] The reading ὅς...ἐγεννήθη in i. 13 is poorly attested, and its insertion is all too easily explicable. That ἡμεῖς ἐκ πορνείας οὐκ ἐγεννήθημεν (viii. 41) presupposes slanders upon the birth of Jesus, and that these in turn imply His virgin birth, is possible but no more. The emphatic ἡμεῖς could easily mean 'We Jews as distinct from Gentile nations' (cf. stories about the origins of Ishmaelites, Moabites, Ammonites, and Midianites in Gen. xvi. 4–16, xix. 30–8, xxv. 1–6). It is also possible that the evangelist was acquainted with the tradition of the miraculous birth, but regarded it as an esoteric mystery which he would not divulge, as he has also refused to divulge the baptism of Jesus and the institution of the Eucharist. On the other hand, the words Ἰησοῦν υἱὸν τοῦ Ἰωσὴφ τὸν ἀπὸ Ναζαρέτ (i. 45) occur in a formal confession of Christ by Philip, one of the first disciples, and can hardly have been intended to be entirely erroneous. The intention appears to be to identify Jesus as the son of Joseph from Nazareth, and then to designate Him as the Messiah of whom Moses and the prophets wrote, as Son of God, and as King of Israel; these titles being understood, not as contradicting Philip's description of His human identity, but as affirming that He who is, on the human plane, 'Jesus son of Joseph' is *also* that which these titles imply. It is this 'and also' that raises the Christological problem, as John conceives it, and his doctrine of incarnation is the answer.

Lord' which came to Isaiah was a vision of the glory of Christ: 'Isaiah saw His glory and spoke of Him' (xii. 41).[1] But the most explicit and illuminating statement is in viii. 56-8. The whole context calls for examination.

Jesus has said, 'Anyone who listens to what I say will never see death' (viii. 51). His opponents retort that since not only the prophets, but even Abraham, the father of the chosen race, is unquestionably dead, the implication is that the followers of Jesus, and *a fortiori* Jesus Himself, are in a position superior to that of the father of the chosen race; which is absurd. 'Are you greater than our father Abraham?' To this Jesus replies: 'Your father Abraham was delighted to see my day; he saw it, and he rejoiced.' The statement could be justified from rabbinic inter-pretations of Gen. xxiv. 1, which says that Abraham בָּא בַּיָּמִים, trans-lated, rightly, 'was advanced in years'. The literal meaning, however, is 'entered into the days'. A rabbinic tradition which appears in various places explained it to mean that Abraham was allowed a vision of all the 'days', or periods of time, to come, including the great events in the history of his descendants, and including the age to come (see S.-B. *ad loc.*). This tradition, as such, seems to be traceable to the middle of the third century but no farther back. Yet we learn that Rabbi Nathan (*c.* A.D. 160) observed that Abraham 'saw' the parting of the Red Sea and the giving of the Law, so that the tradition may well be older than appears. If so, then it would justify the statement that Abraham 'saw the day' of the Messiah. The Jews in the Fourth Gospel, however, misunderstand what Jesus says: 'You are not yet fifty years old', they say, 'and have you seen Abraham?'—i.e. were you a contemporary of Abraham? To this Jesus replies, πρὶν Ἀβραὰμ γενέσθαι, ἐγὼ εἰμί. The point of this, in the first place, lies in the contrast of the verbs, γενέσθαι, to come into being, in the aorist, and εἶναι, to be, in the continuous present. The implication is that Jesus does not stand within the temporal series of great men, beginning with Abraham and continuing through the suc-cession of the prophets, so as to be compared with them. His claim is not that He is the greatest of the prophets, or even greater than Abraham himself. He belongs to a different order of being. The verb γενέσθαι is not applicable to the Son of God at all. He stands outside the range of temporal relations. He can say ἐγὼ εἰμί. This is the אֲנִי הוּא of the Old

---

[1] This is justified by the maxim, θεὸν οὐδεὶς ἑώρακεν πώποτε (i. 18, vi. 46). Similarly, Philo denied the direct vision of God, but affirmed vision of His Logos (see pp. 68–9).

Testament, the declaration of the unique and eternal self-existence of God. It is possible, as was suggested above (pp. 93–6), that John had in mind the rendering of this divine name in the form אֲנִי וְהוּא, 'I and He', implying that the true name of God is that which declares His solidarity with His people (and so with the Messiah as the inclusive representative of the people of God). However that may be, it is clear that in the mouth of Jesus it is justified by the maxim μόνος οὐκ εἰμί, ἀλλ᾽ ἐγὼ καὶ ὁ πέμψας με (viii. 16). That which is from all eternity is the unity of Father and Son, in a mutual 'knowledge', an 'indwelling', of which the real character is ἀγάπη. This is the ultimate mystery of Godhead which Jesus revealed to the world—ἐγνώρισα αὐτοῖς τὸ ὄνομά σου καὶ γνωρίσω, ἵνα ἡ ἀγάπη ἣν ἠγάπησάς με ἐν αὐτοῖς ᾖ (xvii. 26).

The conclusion might be stated thus: The relation of Father and Son is an eternal relation, not attained in time, nor ceasing with this life, or with the history of this world. The human career of Jesus is, as it were, a projection of this eternal relation (which is the divine ἀγάπη) upon the field of time. It is such, not as a mere reflection, or representation, of the reality, but in the sense that the love which the Father bore the Son 'before the foundation of the world', and which He perpetually returns, is actively at work in the whole historical life of Jesus. That life displays the unity of Father and Son, in ways which may be described as 'knowledge' or 'indwelling', but are such, not in the sense of withdrawn contemplation like that recommended by 'Hellenistic mysticism', but in the sense that the love of God in Christ creates and conditions an active ministry of word and deed, in which the words are πνεῦμα καὶ ζωή, and the deeds are σημεῖα of the eternal life and light; a ministry which is also an aggressive conflict with the powers hostile to life, and ends in a victory of life over death through death. The love of God, thus released in history, brings men into the same unity of which the relation of Father and Son is the eternal archetype.

12. LOGOS

The word λόγος has an extremely extensive range of meanings.[1] Those which most concern us here are the two which the Stoics distinguished as λόγος ἐνδιάθετος and λόγος προφορικός—the λόγος in the mind and the uttered λόγος—i.e. 'thought' and 'word'. For us these concepts are distinct as they were not for Greek-speaking persons. Λόγος as 'word' is never the mere word as an assemblage of sounds (φωνή) but the word as determined by a meaning and conveying a meaning (φωνὴ σημαντική, Aristotle, De Interp. 4). Λόγος as 'thought' is neither the faculty nor the process of thinking as such, but an articulate unit of thought, capable of intelligible utterance, whether as a single word (=ῥῆμα), a phrase or sentence, or a prolonged discourse, or even a book. Whether or not it is actually uttered (or written) is a secondary matter, almost an accident; in any case it is λόγος. Behind it lies the idea of that which is rationally ordered, such as 'proportion' in mathematics or what we call 'law' in nature. These are examples of the same thing that we experience as articulate thought or meaningful speech.

In the LXX λόγος almost always renders דָּבָר (or its Aramaic equivalent מִלָּה), a term whose range of meaning overlaps that of λόγος but is not co-extensive with it. It is derived from the root דבר which means to speak, and דָּבָר is essentially the spoken word as means of communication. In the Old Testament דְּבַר יהוה is frequently used of God's communication with men, His self-revelation, especially through the prophets, to whom 'the word of the Lord came'. The totality of God's self-revelation is denominated תּוֹרָה, a term which is often parallel or virtually synonymous with דְּבַר יהוה.

The whole idea of revelation in the Old Testament is determined by the analogy of the word spoken and heard, as distinct from the idea of revelation as vision. It preserves the ontological distance between God and man, while affirming that God, of His personal choice, approaches men and deals with them in a way they can understand, and expects their response; as one man communicates with another by means of spoken words, inviting a response, without invading the prerogatives of individual personality. The idea that God similarly addresses a 'word' to what we call inanimate things, and that by means of such a 'word' He

[1] See *Theologisches Wörterbuch*, s.v.

called the ordered universe out of primeval chaos, is a refinement upon the idea of the 'word' that came to men through the prophets, to bring order and justice into human affairs under the rule of Torah.

We have to observe that for the Hebrew the word once spoken has a kind of substantive existence of its own.[1] A blessing, for example, once pronounced continues to bless, and a curse once uttered works itself out. This is true even of your words or mine, still more of the Word of God. Consider such expressions as the following:

As the rain cometh down and the snow from heaven,
And returneth not thither, but watereth the earth...
So shall my word [דְּבָרִי, τὸ ῥῆμά μου] be that goeth forth out of my mouth:
It shall not return unto me void,
But it shall accomplish that which I please,
And it shall prosper in the thing whereto I send it.   (Is. lv. 10–11.)

Ὁ παντοδύναμός σου λόγος ἀπ' οὐρανῶν ἐκ θρόνων βασιλείων
ἀπότομος πολεμιστὴς εἰς μέσον τῆς ὀλεθρίας ἥλατο γῆς,
ξίφος ὀξὺ τὴν ἀνυπόκριτον ἐπιταγήν σου φέρων,
καὶ στὰς ἐπλήρωσεν τὰ πάντα θανάτου,
καὶ οὐρανοῦ μὲν ἥπτετο βεβήκει δ' ἐπὶ γῆς.   (Wisd. xviii. 15–16.)

If it be said that these are mere poetical embroidery of language, it must nevertheless be admitted that the readiness to use such language points to an habitual tendency of thought to attribute to the spoken word an existence and activity of its own; and in fact such a tendency is deeply impressed upon the Hebrew language.[2]

For the use of the term λόγος in the religious thought of Hellenism, the account already given of the teaching of Philo, of the Hermetic literature, and of some of the semi-Christian, or near-Christian, 'Gnostic' sects, may suffice for our present purpose. It does not seem necessary to trace a Logos-doctrine backward through the history of Greek philosophy to its alleged source in Heraclitus (who, it appears, may not have meant what his Stoic and early Christian commentators supposed him to mean); still less to explore its alleged antecedents in Egyptian

---

[1] For an illuminating example of the persistence of this idea among Semitic-speaking people in Palestine, see Adalbert Merx, *Die vier kanonischen Evangelien*, 1902, on Matt. v. 47.

[2] It is not however exclusively Hebraic. It would appear to be common in primitive thought, and has left traces in various languages. Homer's 'winged words', which 'escape the barrier of the teeth', and 'fly', are an example. But in Hebrew the conception appears to be more continuously alive: the word is sent, comes, goes, endures, and so forth.

or Iranian religion. Any ideas derived from such sources must have already become naturalized in the more or less popular thought of the Hellenistic world, before they can be supposed to have had any influence upon the evangelist or his readers. The relevant evidence seems to show that in circles with which the evangelist and his readers may be supposed to have been in touch the conception of a mediating divine hypostasis or hypostases was extremely widespread, and that in some such circles the term λόγος was used to denote such an hypostasis. It does not prove, as is sometimes loosely suggested, that the term λόγος was very widely current in this sense. The range, in fact, in which really significant parallels to Johannine usage may be hopefully sought is relatively narrow.

Our next step should be to examine the use of the term λόγος throughout the Fourth Gospel. We may distinguish the following ways in which it is used.

(i) The term λόγοι in the plural is used in the plain and simple sense of 'words' spoken by Jesus or by others. It is interchangeable with ῥήματα.

(ii) The singular λόγος is used for a 'saying', 'statement', or 'discourse' Thus, in ii. 19–22, Jesus says, 'Destroy this temple and in three days I will raise it up.' He is misunderstood by both the crowd and the disciples; but the latter, after His resurrection, are said to have understood and believed it: ἐπίστευσαν τῇ γραφῇ καὶ τῷ λόγῳ ὃν εἶπεν ὁ Ἰησοῦς. In iv. 39 'Many of the Samaritans believed διὰ τὸν λόγον τῆς γυναικὸς μαρτυρούσης ὅτι Εἶπέν μοι πάντα ἃ ἐποίησα.' In iv. 37 ὁ λόγος ἐστὶν ἀληθινός, the λόγος is a proverbial saying. In xii. 38, xv. 25 it is a passage cited from the Old Testament. A λόγος in this sense is composed of λόγοι in the sense of ῥήματα. The expression ὅτε ἤκουσεν ὁ Πειλᾶτος τοῦτον τὸν λόγον (xix. 8) does not differ in sense from ὁ Πειλᾶτος ἀκούσας τῶν λόγων τούτων (xix. 13).

(iii) Λόγος is used collectively for the whole of what Jesus said to His disciples and to the world, His 'message', conceived as revelation and as a 'command' to be obeyed. Thus Jesus says, v. 24, ὁ τὸν λόγον μου ἀκούων ἔχει ζωὴν αἰώνιον, and to His disciples, xv. 3, ὑμεῖς καθαροί ἐστε διὰ τὸν λόγον ὃν λελάληκα ὑμῖν. In xiv and xv the expressions, τὸν λόγον μου τηρεῖν, τοὺς λόγους μου τηρεῖν, τὰς ἐντολάς μου τηρεῖν, alternate without any difference of meaning.

While however in all such cases λόγος is that which is spoken and heard, it is, in accordance with the fundamental connotation of the Greek term, to be understood as the uttered word *with* its meaning, or rational content. As such it is distinguished from λαλιά. 'Why do you not understand my λαλιά?' asks Jesus of the Jews (viii. 43), and replies, 'Because you cannot hear my λόγος.' Thus λόγον ἀκούειν is not simply to receive with the sense of hearing a connected series of sounds, but to apprehend the meaning which those sounds convey—much as a Hermetic writer says that all men of every nation have one λόγος, whether they be Greeks, Egyptians or Persians, though their φωνή differs (*C.H.* XII. 12–13). Thus the λόγος of Christ is the sum total of His spoken words (λόγοι or ῥήματα), regarded as containing His thought or meaning, but His uttered words, nevertheless, as is shown by the fact that what is said of His λόγος can also be said of His ῥήματα. Compare, for example, viii. 31 ἐὰν ὑμεῖς μείνητε ἐν τῷ λόγῳ τῷ ἐμῷ...γνώσεσθε τὴν ἀλήθειαν, with xv. 7 ἐὰν μείνητε ἐν ἐμοὶ καὶ τὰ ῥήματά μου ἐν ὑμῖν μείνῃ, ὃ ἐὰν θέλητε αἰτήσασθε καὶ γενήσεται ὑμῖν, and again v. 24 ὁ τὸν λόγον μου ἀκούων ἔχει ζωὴν αἰώνιον, with vi. 68 ῥήματα ζωῆς αἰωνίου ἔχεις, and vi. 63 τὰ ῥήματα ἃ ἐγὼ λελάληκα ὑμῖν πνεῦμά ἐστιν καὶ ζωή ἐστιν.

It is clear that for the evangelist the uttered words of Christ, constituting His λόγος, His total message to the world, are in a specific sense a life-giving power, and the medium through which He gives Himself to men. We may probably trace here something of the Hebraic conception of the word as having in some sort a substantive existence and a power of its own.

(iv) Λόγος is used of the 'Word of God', His self-revelation to men. In accordance with Jewish tradition, adopted by the Christian Church in general, this is conceived as embodied in the Old Testament. Thus in x. 34–5, Jesus cites from Ps. lxxxi (lxxxii). 6 'I said, You are gods', and comments, 'He called them gods πρὸς οὓς ὁ λόγος τοῦ θεοῦ ἐγένετο.' A similar idea is implied in v. 37–8 'The Father who sent me, He has borne witness concerning me. You never heard His voice (φωνή), you never saw His form, and you have not His word (λόγος) abiding in you.... You search the Scriptures...but you will not come to me that you may have life.' We might paraphrase thus:

God bears witness to me. True, God has not a voice to be heard, any more than He has a form to be seen; nevertheless there is such a thing as the Word of God. You believe that you have that word in the Scriptures, and you study them in the hope that they will give you that knowledge of God which is eternal life. But you fail to understand their true purport, which would point you to me as the real mediator of eternal life. That shows that though the *words* of Scripture are in your minds, the λόγος of God which they embody is not a power in you.

The established distinction is suggested between φωνή and λόγος. God has, unlike men, no φωνή, or at any rate none which can be heard by men.[1] But He has a λόγος, which can be recognized in the Scriptures by those who have it abiding in them.

But in a more profound and ultimate sense the Word of God is to be found in the λόγος of Christ: ὁ λόγος ὃν ἀκούετε οὐκ ἔστιν ἐμὸς ἀλλὰ τοῦ πέμψαντός με. So in xvii. 14 Jesus says, ἐγὼ δέδωκα αὐτοῖς τὸν λόγον σου. He adds, xvii. 17, ὁ λόγος ὁ σὸς ἀλήθειά ἐστιν.[2] Thus the λόγος of Christ is the λόγος of God, and that is ἀλήθεια, the ultimate reality revealed. Λόγος is clearly the content of Christ's teaching, the thought or meaning it conveys, and not merely the utterance. At the same time it is not to be dissociated from the uttered words, for in the same context, xvii. 8, Jesus says, τὰ ῥήματα ἃ δέδωκάς μοι δέδωκα αὐτοῖς, without appreciable difference of meaning.

We conclude that, along with other quite ordinary uses of the term, the Fourth Evangelist uses the term λόγος in a special sense, to denote the eternal truth (ἀλήθεια) revealed to men by God—this truth as expressed in words (ῥήματα), whether they be the words of Scripture or, more especially, the words of Christ. Λόγος in this sense is distinguished from λαλιά and φωνή. The divine λόγος is not simply the uttered words. It *is* ἀλήθεια. That is to say, it is a rational content of thought corresponding to the ultimate reality of the universe. But reality is conceived to be revealed, not, as in some contemporary teaching, in contemplation or ecstatic vision, but as spoken and heard. This form of expression preserves the distance between God and man, which is characteristic of biblical religion in general, and is blurred in much Hellenistic thought. The idea of revelation in John is governed by the category of 'hearing the word of the Lord', however that category may be extended. Hence, while the λόγος of God is rational content of thought, it is always in some sense uttered, and because it is uttered becomes a life-giving power for men.

It is never expressly said in the body of the gospel, apart from the Prologue, that Christ *is* this divine λόγος. He utters the λόγος which the

---

[1] The φωνὴ ἐκ τοῦ οὐρανοῦ of xii. 28 (which is taken by the hearers to be either a thunder-clap or the voice of an angel) is to be understood in the light of the rabbinic belief in the בַּת קֹל. This is described as an echo of the heavenly speech; that is to say, it is not the voice of God, but represents the word of God. See S.-B. on Matt. iii. 17; Moore, *Judaism*, I, pp. 421 sq.

[2] Cf. Ps. cxviii (cxix). 142 'Thy law is truth' (אמת has become ἀλήθεια), 160 'The sum of thy word is truth' (see pp. 82, 173–6).

Father has 'given' Him, and so 'gives' it to men to be a power unto life. But in view of the equation of the divine λόγος with ἀλήθεια, it is significant that Christ says, ἐγώ εἰμι ἡ ἀλήθεια (xiv. 6). He not only 'gives' the word which is truth, He *is* it; just as He not only gives life, but *is* life. This is admirably illustrated in the discourse of ch. vi. Here Christ gives the bread of life, but He *is* the bread; and His comment on this is, 'The words (ῥήματα) that I speak to you are life' (vi. 63). All that Christ is, is in His words, and He is the truth and the life. It is only a step from that to say, He is the Logos. This step is taken in the Prologue.

We turn, then, to the Prologue, which for this purpose may be taken as extending to i. 18. I shall not here discuss various critical questions which have from time to time been raised; as, for example, whether the Prologue was from the first designed by the evangelist as an exordium to the whole work, or was added, by him or by a redactor, at a later stage; or again, whether it first existed independently, or was composed by the evangelist or the redactor. At all events, when the Fourth Gospel was published and received by the Church, the Prologue stood as an integral part of it. It is for us to interpret it as such, whatever its previous history may have been.

The Prologue differs from the rest of the gospel in that it treats, though very briefly, of cosmology and anthropology, that it uses the term λόγος in a cosmological connection, and that it affirms that in Christ, as the unique Son of God, the λόγος was incarnate. In interpreting the Prologue it is necessary to observe the exegetical point that the term λόγος is the direct subject of propositions only in verses 1–3 and 14. In verse 4 a transition is made to φῶς, and φῶς, not λόγος, is formally the subject of the propositions made in verses 9–12. While, however, φῶς is formally the subject, the corresponding pronoun, referring to the subject of the sentence, is in the masculine, αὐτόν, not agreeing with φῶς, which is neuter. There seem to be two possibilities: either (*a*) the propositions in question really refer to the masculine λόγος, here considered in its aspect as light; or (*b*) the thought of incarnation is already in the evangelist's mind, and the propositions of verses 9–12 refer to Christ as incarnate. These are not strictly exclusive alternatives. In what follows here I shall assume (*a*); the possible implications of (*b*) I shall consider later.

The main question which we have to discuss might be formulated thus: is the term λόγος to be translated 'word', and is the whole Logos-doctrine to be understood from the Hebraic conception of the דְּבַר יהוה,

or has λόγος a sense approximating rather to the Stoic 'rational principle', on the analogy of its predominant use in Philo?

Let us start with the hypothesis that the λόγος of the Prologue is the Hebraic דְּבַר יהוה. In considering the question, it is well to bear in mind that this term is largely interchangeable with תּוֹרָה; cf. Is. ii. 3 (= Mic. iv. 2), where the two terms, in the LXX νόμος and λόγος κυρίου, are in parallelism. Thus the 'word' of God can always be conceived as having a permanent, concrete embodiment in the Torah.

As we have seen, the author of *Poimandres*, in adapting to his purpose the creation narrative of Genesis, uses λόγος primarily in the sense of 'word'. The ἅγιος λόγος ἐκ τοῦ φωτός is the divine answer to the inarticulate cry of chaos (and is perhaps described as φωνὴ φωτός). And yet he speaks of the word as ὁ ἐπιφερόμενος πνευματικὸς λόγος; it rushes over the dark waters like a stormy wind (the רוּחַ אֱלֹהִים of Genesis), and subsequently leaps up to heaven to join the Demiurge (*C.H.* i. 5, 10).

We may therefore assume that for the author of the Prologue too the statement of Genesis that God spoke carried with it more meaning than a similar statement would naturally convey to us. It meant that by His utterance God brought into being a word which existed substantively, and mediated creative power. The word, then, *was*, i.e. existed substantially—ὁ λόγος ἦν—not merely, was spoken. It so existed before the world was, ἐν ἀρχῇ (verse 1). In the act of creation the word was to go forth from God, but before creation was begun it was 'with God', ἦν πρὸς τὸν θεόν. It existed as a hypostasis distinguishable from God, and yet it remained with Him (verse 2); cf. Ps. cxviii (cxix). 89 εἰς τὸν αἰῶνα, κύριε, ὁ λόγος σου διαμένει ἐν τῷ οὐρανῷ.

For creation by the word we have ample scriptural authority, e.g. Ps. xxxii (xxxiii). 6 τῷ λόγῳ κυρίου οἱ οὐρανοὶ ἐστερεώθησαν. This is here stated in the words, πάντα δι' αὐτοῦ ἐγένετο (verse 3), to which the evangelist, guarding against doctrines which attributed the origin of certain existences to inferior creators, or regarded matter as self-existent, adds, καὶ χωρὶς αὐτοῦ ἐγένετο οὐδὲ ἕν.

The next stage is the manifestation of the power of God's word in life and light (verse 4). This may best be illustrated from rabbinic sayings which (interpreting the Scriptures) declare the Torah (which is the word of God) to be life and light to men (see pp. 82–5). Since the evangelist is particularly concerned here with revelation, the aspect of the word as light takes the foremost place (verse 9). For this there is direct scriptural warrant in Ps. cxviii (cxix). 105. I shall here assume that the propositions in verses 9–12, of which φῶς is the direct subject, actually refer to the λόγος.

That the word of the Lord, as light or revelation, was (before the incarnation) in all the world, ἐν τῷ κόσμῳ ἦν (verse 10), is a proposition which, though it cannot be supported by direct quotations from the Old Testament, is in harmony with the general thought of Judaism. Ps. xviii (xix) brings together the praise of the Torah and the praise of God's glory in creation, and this glory is expressed in terms of the spoken word: ῥῆμα, λαλιαί, λόγοι, φωναί, φθόγγος, which go out εἰς τὰ πέρατα τῆς οἰκουμένης (verses 4–5). When the Torah was given on Sinai, according to a widespread rabbinic tradition, the voice of God sounded all over the world; some added, in all the languages of the nations (numerous passages to that effect in S.-B. *Komm.* II. 604–5). And although much Jewish teaching tended to narrow the range of revelation to the chosen people, there was always a strain which affirmed that some knowledge of God was vouchsafed to all mankind. Paul could have cited good rabbinic authority for his view that τὸ γνωστὸν τοῦ θεοῦ was manifest to the Gentiles through His created works (Rom. i. 19–20; see citations in S.-B. *ad loc.*). That is to say, the creative word of God ἐν τῷ κόσμῳ ἦν. Mankind, however, as a whole declined to acknowledge His word; ὁ κόσμος αὐτὸν οὐκ ἔγνω (verse 10). (On this, see above, pp. 156–9.)

Now comes a fresh stage. The light which is the word of God εἰς τὰ ἴδια ἦλθεν, καὶ οἱ ἴδιοι αὐτὸν οὐ παρέλαβον (verse 11). That is to say, the word of the Lord through Moses and the prophets came to His own people Israel, and Israel rejected it. This might serve as a brief but not inadequate summary of the whole prophetic movement—indeed of most of the history of Israel as it is presented in the Old Testament. Nevertheless there was always a faithful 'remnant'. 'Those who received the word, to them it gave the right to become children of God' (verse 12). It is ἐξουσία, 'right' or 'authority', that is given, not 'power',[1] and ἐξουσία is given by a competent legislative or judicial pronouncement; in this case, by the authoritative 'word' of the Ruler of the universe. That God did in fact authorize men to claim the status of sonship can be proved from scripture. The word of the Lord came to Moses, saying,

[1] The rendering of ἐξουσία by 'power', here and elsewhere, making it indistinguishable from δύναμις, is one of the most misleading mistranslations in our Authorized Version, as may be observed in the writings of some moderns who discuss the 'Christian doctrine of power' without turning up the Greek text of the New Testament.

'Israel is my son, my firstborn' (Exod. iv. 22); 'You are sons of the Lord your God' (Deut. xiv. 1). Κληθήσονται καὶ αὐτοὶ υἱοὶ θεοῦ ζῶντος says Hosea (i. 10).[1] Conversely, if they prove בָּנִים לֹא אֵמֻן בָּם, then the sentence is given; ἡμάρτοσαν, οὐκ αὐτῷ τέκνα (Deut. xxxii. 20, 5).[2] For rabbinic pronouncements, see S.-B. *Komm.* I. 219–20. The evangelist finds this doctrine of the sonship of God's people in Ps. lxxxi (lxxxii). 6 ἐγὼ εἶπα, Θεοί ἐστε καὶ υἱοὶ ὑψίστου πάντες.[3] His comment on it is illuminating: 'He called them gods, to whom the word of God came' (x. 35). Ἐκεῖνοι πρὸς οὓς ὁ λόγος τοῦ θεοῦ ἐγένετο are those who, according to i. 12, received the word, and were given the right to be children of God (in so far, *bien entendu*, as they heeded it).

The verse which follows, i. 13, is merely a comment on the idea 'children of God', but even so it might be illustrated from Ps. ii. 7 υἱός μου εἶ σύ· ἐγὼ σήμερον γεγέννηκά σε. If readers of the gospel were aware of the current Jewish interpretation of that text with reference to the true Israel (see S.-B. *Komm.* III. 674–5), they might find here documentation for the statement that those who received the word of God ἐκ θεοῦ ἐγεννήθησαν.

The following verse, i. 14, in which we reach the climax of the Prologue with the words ὁ λόγος σὰρξ ἐγένετο, takes us beyond the range of Jewish ideas, and we shall not expect anything in the way of Old Testament documentation. Yet as the writer proceeds, καὶ ἐσκήνωσεν ἐν ἡμῖν, καὶ ἐθεασάμεθα τὴν δόξαν αὐτοῦ...πλήρης χάριτος καὶ ἀληθείας, we find we are still moving among Jewish conceptions. The glory of the Lord is especially associated with the giving of the Torah (the word of God); the word ἐσκήνωσεν may echo the Hebrew שׁכן, from which was formed the word שְׁכִינָה, properly the 'dwelling', or 'presence' of God,

---

[1] That men are sons of God only because God speaks the word and 'calls' them sons, is a conception deeply rooted in Scripture. Hence in the Beatitudes, υἱοὶ θεοῦ κληθήσονται (Matt. v. 9). What God 'calls' men, that in fact they are, for His word possesses and confers ἐξουσία. The author of I John does not seem to have understood this, since he feels it necessary to explain that Christians not only are called, but are, children of God (iii. 1)—a distinction which would not, I think, have occurred to a writer whose thought ran in a Hebraic and biblical mould, like the evangelist.

[2] The Hebrew text here is obscure, and thought to be corrupt, but the LXX no doubt represents the current understanding of the passage.

[3] Although the author does not carry the quotation to the end of the sentence, it is clear that the words υἱοὶ ὑψίστου are essential to his argument; a neat instance of a principle which I believe to be of wide application, that the citation of a few words is often intended as a pointer to a larger context. See my book, *According to the Scriptures* (Nisbet, 1952), ch. II.

frequently used as a periphrasis for God Himself (cf. Burney, *Aramaic Origin*, pp. 35–7); and χάρις καὶ ἀλήθεια represents (though with a characteristic shift of meaning) חֶסֶד וֶאֱמֶת which in the Old Testament is the content of the Torah or word of the Lord (see pp. 82, 175–6). In verse 17, the χάρις and ἀλήθεια through Christ are explicitly contrasted with the Torah.

Whatever weight we may be prepared to allow to such parallels, it is at least clear that on this interpretation of λόγος the Prologue presents an orderly process of thought moving to a climax, in which most of the propositions in i. 1–14 find a suitable place. By the word of the Lord all things were made. It was manifested in the world as life and as the light of revelation, which is open to every man born. But mankind as a whole failed to recognize the word of God. He then sent His word to Israel through the prophets, but again Israel rejected the word, apart from a faithful remnant, to whom the word of God gave the right of sonship. Finally, the light which is the word of God was focused in an individual who was not one of a community of children of God, but His unique Son, μονογενὴς παρὰ πατρός.

The Logos-doctrine of the Prologue, therefore, can in great part at least be interpreted without much difficulty upon Old Testament presuppositions, the term λόγος having the meaning of 'word'. Such an interpretation has the advantage, in particular, of giving a good point to the contrast drawn in i. 17. Further, as we have seen, in the rest of the gospel λόγος appears never to be used without reference, explicit or implicit, to the spoken word, and it often alternates with ῥῆμα.

Moreover, the idea of Christ as Word—the spoken word of God though conceived in some sort hypostatically—is to be found in writings emanating from a circle whose thought certainly resembles that of the Fourth Gospel in some respects. I mean the Epistles of Ignatius and the Odes of Solomon. For example, Ignatius, *ad Magn.* VIII. 2 εἷς θεός ἐστιν, ὁ φανερώσας ἑαυτὸν διὰ Ἰησοῦ Χριστοῦ, τοῦ υἱοῦ αὐτοῦ, ὅς ἐστιν αὐτοῦ λόγος ἀπὸ σιγῆς προελθών. A word which 'proceeds from silence' is clearly, in some sense, a spoken word. Again, Od. Sol. xii. 11–12 'For the mouth of the Most High spoke to them, and the interpretation of Himself had its course by Him; for the dwelling-place of the Word is man, and His truth is love.' Here there is parallelism between the statement that the mouth of the Most High spoke, and the statement that the dwelling-place of the Word is man. This is the Word which was incarnate in Christ, as in Od. Sol. xli. 13–14, etc. We may observe that in a cosmological passage

where the Odist wishes to give expression to both sides of the meaning
of the Greek term λόγος, he writes,

ܘܥܠܡܐ ܒܪܐ ܒܡܠܬܗ܂ ܘܒܡܚܫܒܬܐ ܕܠܒܗ

'The worlds were made by His word, and by the thought of His heart'
(Od. xvi. 20). ܡܠܬܐ is the spoken word, ܡܚܫܒܬܐ the thought lying
behind it. Λόγος in Greek may be both; but if we follow the guidance
of the Odes we should conclude that in these circles it was taken, when
applied to Christ, to mean ܡܠܬܐ, 'word'. There is therefore a very strong
case to be made out, stronger than has sometimes been recognized, for
the view that the Logos of the Prologue is the Word of the Lord.

Yet there are grounds for thinking that although the evangelist had in
mind the thought of the creative and prophetic word of the Old Testament,
it does not account for the whole of the doctrine of the Prologue. In particular, there are two of the propositions in i. 1–14 which present great
difficulty, if λόγος be taken as precisely equivalent to 'word', or 'Torah':
θεὸς ἦν ὁ λόγος, and ὁ λόγος σὰρξ ἐγένετο. The latter is difficult on any
construction of the term λόγος, because it is an entirely fresh expression
for a fact *ex hypothesi* unprecedented and unique; yet to think of a 'word',
in anything like the Old Testament sense of the term, being incarnated,
is so extremely difficult that we are justified in raising the question
whether some other meaning of λόγος would not ease the matter. The
statement that the Word was God, if 'word' be taken in its Old Testament
sense, is equally difficult; and even if for 'word' we understand 'Torah'
(which would be legitimate) the difficulty is not greatly relieved. In a
Jewish *milieu* determined by reference to the Old Testament, the statement
that the Torah is God could scarcely find a home.[1]

I have pointed out above (pp. 269–72) that while in the Old Testament
the term תּוֹרָה is often parallel and almost synonymous with דְּבַר יהוה,
and the equation of the λόγος of the Prologue with the Torah of Rabbinic
Judaism facilitates the understanding of its successive propositions on
an Old Testament basis, much of what the rabbinic literature says about
the Torah, especially where it is in some sort personified, has been

---

[1] F. C. Burkitt, in *Church and Gnosis*, pp. 94–9, made a characteristically
brilliant attempt, the most thoroughgoing attempt known to me, to retain the
meaning 'word' quite strictly all through. I do not attempt here to examine it,
but I think it is fair to say that while over a great part of the Prologue his interpretation is at least highly plausible, it breaks down on these two clauses, where the
explanations offered are forced and unconvincing.

transferred from Wisdom, as part of a process by which orthodox Rabbinism resisted the danger of excessive approximation to Hellenism in Wisdom-speculation. The concept of חָכְמָה, σοφία, in the Wisdom literature represents the hypostatized thought of God, immanent in the world. As such, it replaces the Word of the Lord as medium of creation and revelation. There are obvious and striking similarities between certain of the propositions of the Prologue and passages in the Wisdom literature.[1] Some of them may be tabulated as follows:

Fourth Gospel	Wisdom literature
ἐν ἀρχῇ ἦν ὁ λόγος.	κύριος ἔκτισέν με ἀρχὴν ὁδῶν αὐτοῦ (Prov. viii. 22).
ὁ λόγος ἦν πρὸς τὸν θεόν.	ἤμην παρ' αὐτῷ (Prov. viii. 30).
	τὴν τῶν σῶν θρόνων πάρεδρον σοφίαν (Wisd. ix. 4).
πάντα δι' αὐτοῦ ἐγένετο.	ὁ ποιήσας τὰ πάντα ἐν λόγῳ σου, καὶ τῇ σοφίᾳ σου κατεσκεύασας ἄνθρωπον (Wisd. ix. 2).
	ἤμην παρ' αὐτῷ ἁρμόζουσα (Prov. viii. 30).
	ὁ θεὸς τῇ σοφίᾳ ἐθεμελίωσεν τὴν γῆν (Prov. iii. 19).
	ἡ πάντων τεχνῖτις σοφία (Wisd. vii. 22).
ἐν αὐτῷ ζωὴ ἦν.	αἱ γὰρ ἔξοδοί μου ἔξοδοι ζωῆς (Prov. viii. 35).
ἡ ζωὴ ἦν τὸ φῶς τῶν ἀνθρώπων.	(σοφία) ἀπαύγασμά ἐστιν φωτὸς ἀιδίου (Wisd. vii. 26).
τὸ φῶς ἐν τῇ σκοτίᾳ φαίνει, καὶ ἡ σκοτία αὐτὸ οὐ κατέλαβεν.	(σοφία) φωτὶ συνκρινομένη εὑρίσκεται προτέρα, τοῦτο μὲν γὰρ διαδέχεται νύξ, σοφίας δὲ οὐκ ἀντισχύει κακία (Wisd. vii. 29–30).
ἐν τῷ κόσμῳ ἦν.	διατείνει ἀπὸ πέρατος εἰς πέρας εὐρώστως, καὶ διοικεῖ τὰ πάντα χρηστῶς (Wisd. viii. 1).
	ἐν πάσῃ τῇ γῇ, καὶ ἐν παντὶ λαῷ καὶ ἔθνει ἐκτησάμην (Sir. xxiv. 6).
ὁ κόσμος αὐτὸν οὐκ ἔγνω.	ἐμίσησαν γὰρ σοφίαν (Prov. i. 29).

[1] See J. Rendel Harris, *The Origin of the Prologue to St John's Gospel*, 1917.

Fourth Gospel	Wisdom literature
εἰς τὰ ἴδια ἦλθεν καὶ οἱ ἴδιοι αὐτὸν οὐ παρέλαβον.	Wisdom went forth to make her dwelling among the children of men, and found no dwelling-place (Enoch xlii. 2).
ὅσοι δὲ ἔλαβον αὐτὸν ἔδωκεν αὐτοῖς ἐξουσίαν τέκνα θεοῦ γενέσθαι.	εἰς ψυχὰς ὁσίας μεταβαίνουσα φίλους θεοῦ καὶ προφήτας κατασκευάζει (Wisd. vii. 27).
ἐσκήνωσεν ἐν ἡμῖν.	ὁ κτίσας με κατέπαυσεν τὴν σκηνήν μου, καὶ εἶπεν, Ἐν Ἰακὼβ κατασκήνωσον (Sir. xxiv. 8).
δόξαν ὡς μονογενοῦς παρὰ πατρός.	ἔστιν γὰρ ἐν αὐτῇ πνεῦμα...μονογενές...ἀτμὶς γάρ ἐστιν τῆς τοῦ θεοῦ δυνάμεως καὶ ἀπόρροια τῆς τοῦ παντοκράτορος δόξης (Wisd. vii. 22, 25).

This list of parallels, which is not exhaustive, is sufficient to show that in composing the Prologue the author's mind was moving along lines similar to those followed by Jewish writers of the 'Wisdom' school. It is difficult to resist the conclusion that, while the Logos of the Prologue has many of the traits of the Word of God in the Old Testament, it is on the other side a concept closely similar to that of Wisdom, that is to say, the hypostatized thought of God projected in creation, and remaining as an immanent power within the world and in man.

In such a setting it is somewhat less difficult to find an approach to the enigmatic statement, ὁ λόγος σὰρξ ἐγένετο, for, although it would be idle to look for any real anticipation of the Johannine doctrine of incarnation, the idea of the immanence of Wisdom in men, making them friends of God, provides a kind of matrix in which the idea of incarnation might be shaped. But we are still far from anything which could justify the statement θεὸς ἦν ὁ λόγος, even though the functions assigned to Wisdom are often clearly those which are elsewhere assigned to God Himself.[1]

---

[1] Cf. Wisd. x sqq. The passage begins by attributing the acts of God recorded in Genesis to Σοφία, as distinct from God (cf. x. 9–10 σοφία...ἔδειξεν αὐτῷ βασιλείαν θεοῦ). From xi. 8 onward, however, such acts are attributed directly to God (addressed in the second person). The transition from the one to the other is almost imperceptible: see xi. 1–4. At the same time, though Wisdom is the εἰκών of God, the ἀπαύγασμα of eternal light, and so forth, such a statement as θεὸς ἦν ἡ σοφία is unthinkable.

With Wisdom we are already half-way to Philo's Logos, which is in many places almost a doublet of Wisdom, as it certainly has the Wisdom-concept for one of its ancestors. I have already pointed out some parallels between passages referring to the Logos in Philo and the propositions of the Prologue (pp. 71–2). Consider the following examples, where the Philonic passages are only a few pointers to a whole range of affinity:

Fourth Gospel	*Philo*
ἐν ἀρχῇ ἦν ὁ λόγος.	Before creation, God conceived in His mind the κόσμος νοητός, which is His λόγος (*De Opif.* 17. 24).
ὁ λόγος ἦν πρὸς τὸν θεόν.	God sent forth His younger son, the κόσμος αἰσθητός, but kept the elder, the κόσμος νοητός=λόγος, παρ' ἑαυτῷ (*Quod Deus*, 31).
θεὸς ἦν ὁ λόγος.	The anarthrous θεός may be used of the λόγος, while ὁ θεός is reserved for the Self-existent (*De Somn.* 1. 229–30).
πάντα δι' αὐτοῦ ἐγένετο.	God is the αἴτιος ὑφ' οὗ γέγονεν, the λόγος is ὄργανον δι' οὗ (*De Cher.* 127).
ἐν αὐτῷ ζωὴ ἦν.	No direct statement, but cf. *De Fuga* 97, *De Post.* 68–9.
The λόγος is φῶς ἀληθινόν.	τὸ μὲν παράδειγμα ὁ πληρέστατος αὐτοῦ λόγος, φῶς—'εἶπε' γάρ φησιν 'ὁ θεός· γενέσθω φῶς' (*De Somn.* 1. 75). The νοητὸν φῶς is θείου λόγου εἰκών (*De Opif.* 33). The φῶς ἀσώματον is the πρεσβύτατος or πρωτόγονος υἱός (=λόγος) (*De Conf.* 60–3).
ὅσοι ἔλαβον αὐτὸν αὐτοῖς ἐξουσίαν ἔδωκεν τέκνα θεοῦ γενέσθαι.	Μωυσῆς ὁμολογεῖ φάσκων, Υἱοί ἐστε κυρίου τοῦ θεοῦ [Deut. xiv. 1]... κἂν μηδέπω μέντοι τυγχάνῃ τις ἀξιόχρεως ὢν υἱὸς θεοῦ προσαγορεύεσθαι, σπουδαζέτω κοσμεῖσθαι κατὰ τὸν πρωτόγονον αὐτοῦ λόγον

LOGOS

Fourth Gospel

Philo

...εἰ μήπω ἱκανοὶ θεοῦ παῖδες
νομίζεσθαι γεγόναμεν, ἀλλά τοι...
λόγου τοῦ ἱερωτάτου· θεοῦ γὰρ
εἰκὼν λόγος ὁ πρεσβύτατος (*De
Conf.* 145–7).

θεὸν οὐδεὶς ἑώρακεν πώποτε· ὁ ὢν
εἰς τὸν κόλπον τοῦ πατρός,
ἐκεῖνος ἐξηγήσατο.

εὐπρεπές...ἐφίεσθαι μὲν τοῦ τὸ ὂν
ἰδεῖν, εἰ δὲ μὴ δύναιντο, τὴν γοῦν
εἰκόνα αὐτοῦ, τὸν ἱερώτατον λόγον
(*De Conf.* 97).

While therefore the statements of the Prologue *might* be understood
all through on the assumption that λόγος is the Word of the Lord in the
Old Testament sense, yet it seems certain that any reader influenced by
the thought of Hellenistic Judaism, directly or at a remove, would inevitably
find suggested here a conception of the creative and revealing λόγος in
many respects similar to that of Philo; and it is difficult not to think that
the author intended this. His λόγος is not simply the uttered word or
command of God; it is the meaning, plan or purpose of the universe,
conceived as transcendent as well as immanent, as the thought of God,
formed within the eternal Mind and projected into objectivity. From the
human point of view it is a rational content of thought, expressed in the
order of the universe, but it is this not, as with the Stoics, in the sense
that the order of the universe is self-originated, self-contained, and self-
explanatory, but in the sense that its order and meaning express the mind
of a transcendent creator. Thus from another point of view the λόγος
is God Himself as revealed; it is, in a Pauline phrase, τὸ γνωστὸν τοῦ
θεοῦ, that of God which is knowable; for as Philo puts it, all that man can
know of ultimate Deity is His ὕπαρξις, the fact that He is; beyond that,
we know Him only in His λόγος, His thought which is the principle of
reality in the universe. This thought however is not merely a meaning
or plan visible in the universe; it is also the creative power by which the
universe came into being and is sustained. It is, again in Pauline phrase,
θεοῦ δύναμις as well as θεοῦ σοφία, or as Philo has it, it is the sum of all
δυνάμεις. It is God's power in action as well as His thought. This is the
Hebraic element in Philo's thought, and it is stronger in John's. It is
perhaps only the sense of 'word' inherent in λόγος, with the suggestion
of power that always attaches to the word in Hebraic thought, that makes
it possible for λόγος as a metaphysical term to bear this dynamic

meaning. But it is only in Greek that a term is available which means both 'thought' and 'word'. It is noteworthy that in Origen's commentary on the Fourth Gospel, interpretations which depend upon taking λόγος in the sense of 'word' alternate with others which imply the sense of 'rational principle', without any apparent consciousness in the author that he is passing from one meaning to another. In other languages than Greek we are bound to come down on one side or the other.

The ambiguity which (from our point of view) enters into the Johannine conception of the Logos could be understood if we assumed that the author started from the Jewish idea of the Torah as being at once the Word of God and the divine Wisdom manifested in creation, and found, under the guidance of Hellenistic Jewish thought similar to that of Philo, an appropriate Greek expression which fittingly combined both ideas.

The most serious objection that is raised against interpreting λόγος in the Prologue in a sense similar to that which it bears in Philo is that the term is not elsewhere in the gospel used in any such sense. This objection is not fatal, for the following reasons:

(a) It is only in the Prologue that the evangelist deals with cosmology. It is only here, therefore, that he could have any occasion to use λόγος in a cosmological sense.

(b) In the rest of the gospel λόγος is not *merely* an uttered word, but the word with its rational content, as distinct from φωνή and λαλιά. When it is the word of God that is in question, this λόγος is identified with ἀλήθεια, which does not mean simply 'what is true', or 'veracity', but reality itself as rationally apprehended (see pp. 171–2, 176–8). This however is very close to the meaning of λόγος in Philo.

(c) The use of symbolism in the gospel implies a metaphysic not unlike that of Philo, and this metaphysic is indicated by the evangelist's use of the term ἀληθινός. Christ is φῶς ἀληθινόν, ἄρτος ἀληθινός, ἄμπελος ἀληθινή; all ἀληθινά are summed up in Him. If we speak of them in Platonic terms as ἰδέαι, then in Christ we find the ἰδέα τῶν ἰδεῶν. If we use Stoic language, then the λόγοι of light, bread, and vine are comprehended in the inclusive λόγος. This is precisely what Philo means by λόγος. It is the highest ἰδέα, or the τόπος of the ideas. Although, therefore, the evangelist does not, outside the Prologue, use λόγος in a cosmological sense, yet his implied philosophy would lead naturally to such a use of the term.

(*d*) Throughout the gospel Christ is spoken of as 'Son of Man', which, as I have shown, is best understood as the virtual equivalent of ἄνθρωπος ἀληθινός, the real or essential man, or the Idea of Man. In Philo the ἄνθρωπος ἀληθινός is identified with the λόγος, or, to speak more accurately, that aspect of the cosmical Logos which is specially related to mankind is the ἀληθινὸς ἄνθρωπος. Since, therefore, the evangelist is concerned with cosmology only in the Prologue, and elsewhere only with the mediation of God to *man*, it is not surprising if the term 'Son of Man' suffices him everywhere except in the one passage where he deals, however briefly, with the mediation of God to the universe. It can hardly be an accident, in any case, that even where the term λόγος is not used, functions which in Philo belong to the Logos are assigned to Christ. It is the conception of Christ as Logos in the sense of the sum of all ἀληθινά that provides the ground and justification for our author's distinctive doctrine of Christ's mediation: He mediates to men knowledge of God and union with God in the sense that His own relation to the Father is archetypal (see pp. 160, 166–7, 187).

I conclude that the substance of a Logos-doctrine similar to that of Philo is present all through the gospel, and that the use of the actual term λόγος in the Prologue, in a sense corresponding to that doctrine, though it is unparalleled in the rest of the gospel, falls readily into place.

If now we read the Prologue again, assuming that what we may for convenience call the Philonic conception of the Logos is present with and in the Hebraic conception of the Word of the Lord, the cosmological doctrine is more clear and straightforward, and the crucial proposition about the incarnation becomes more intelligible. As we have seen, it is possible to understand the cosmology of the Prologue on the assumption that the Logos is simply the Word of God, but certain of the expressions used are, on that assumption, somewhat harsh and forced.

Thus the expression ὁ λόγος ἦν πρὸς τὸν θεόν is a peculiar one if the meaning is 'the Word was with God'. If λόγος is a 'word', then πρὸς τὸν θεόν ought to mean, 'addressed to God';[1] but the paraphrase in I John i. 2, ἡ ζωὴ ἦν πρὸς τὸν πατέρα, makes it certain that the expression was understood to mean *apud deum*. And although with a Hebraic

---

[1] As Burkitt rightly urges in *Church and Gnosis*. Origen, in his discussion of the meaning of ὁ λόγος ἦν πρὸς τὸν θεόν, takes as starting point such Old Testament expressions as λόγος κυρίου ὃς ἐγένετο πρὸς Ὠσηέ, πρὸς Ἡσαΐαν, πρὸς Ἰερεμίαν, etc., and presses the difference between γενέσθαι and εἶναι: *Comm. in Joann.* (Brook), II. 1 sqq.

conception of the substantiality of the spoken word it is not impossible to speak of the word which a person has spoken remaining 'with' the speaker, it would be difficult to find an exact parallel, and the expression remains odd. It is true that the Torah is said to be with God, in His presence, lying upon His knees, but it is the Torah *as Wisdom*, as the relevant passages from the Talmud, cited by Strack-Billerbeck, clearly show. Now Philo says that God, while He sent forth His younger son, the κόσμος αἰσθητός, kept His elder son, the κόσμος νοητός, which is the λόγος, by Him, παρ' ἑαυτῷ. Surely John's meaning is the same.

Again, as we have seen, θεὸς ἦν ὁ λόγος is a strange expression. On Hebrew premisses, it is difficult to accept the statement that the 'word', as such, was God; nor is it much easier if we substitute 'Torah', or even 'Wisdom', for 'word'. If the meaning is that the word was divine, as being God's word, we should have expected θεοῦ ἦν ὁ λόγος, or θεῖος ἦν ὁ λόγος. On the other hand the term θεός is properly applied to the Philonic λόγος, while the term ὁ θεός is reserved for the *Fons deitatis* (πηγὴ τοῦ λόγου).

It is perhaps worth observing that the propositions ἐν ἀρχῇ ἦν ὁ λόγος—θεὸς ἦν ὁ λόγος—πάντα δι' αὐτοῦ ἐγένετο, are such as would have been directly intelligible and acceptable to any Stoic. They would have seemed to him a paraphrase of his own doctrine: τὸ μὲν οὖν πάσχον εἶναι τὴν ἄποιον οὐσίαν, τὴν ὕλην, τὸ δὲ ποιοῦν τὸν ἐν αὐτῇ λόγον, τὸν θεόν· τοῦτον γὰρ ἀίδιον ὄντα διὰ πάσης αὐτῆς δημιουργεῖν ἕκαστα (Diog. Laert. VII. 134). It is surely not to be supposed that the coincidence is accidental. Where the Stoic could not have followed John is in the proposition ὁ λόγος ἦν πρὸς τὸν θεόν. The assumption of a God beyond the world would have seemed to him uncalled for. But it is just here, of course, that Philo, under the influence of Platonism as well as of the Old Testament, differs from the Stoics with whom he has so much in common.

The opening sentences, then, of the Prologue are clearly intelligible only when we admit that λόγος, though it carries with it the associations of the Old Testament Word of the Lord, has also a meaning similar to that which it bears in Stoicism as modified by Philo, and parallel to the idea of Wisdom in other Jewish writers. It is the rational principle in the universe, its meaning, plan or purpose, conceived as a divine hypostasis in which the eternal God is revealed and active.

Let us then apply this conception to the proposition ὁ λόγος σὰρξ ἐγένετο. We have already seen that there is great difficulty in explaining this statement if λόγος be taken to mean simply 'word'. The idea of an incarnation of the λόγος as creative reason, though it still remains mysterious, is prepared for in the thought of the Logos immanent in man, as the equivalent of the divine, essential humanity, ἀληθινὸς ἄνθρωπος, as well as in the doctrine of that divine Wisdom which passing into holy souls makes them to be friends of God and prophets, the Wisdom which, like the Logos here, 'tabernacles' with men. That there should be any more precise antecedents for the Johannine expression is not to be expected, since the evangelist is, *ex hypothesi*, describing a unique and unprecedented fact. But it seems that the idea of a divine hypostasis, which is the very thought of God, embodying itself, as it were, in this visible world, and so in a sense 'becoming' the life which is the reality of the universe and the light of men, is a fitting subject for the proposition ὁ λόγος σὰρξ ἐγένετο, which states that this same divine hypostasis now embodied itself in a human individual, and so 'became flesh'.

The transition from the cosmical Logos to the Logos incarnate is assisted if we take the propositions in i. 9–13 to refer, as by their position they should naturally refer, to the pre-incarnate Logos. Read with the ideas of Wisdom and the Philonic Logos in mind, they state that the divine Wisdom pervading the world which was created by Wisdom was un-recognized, since mankind, though made in the image of God and par-taking of His Logos,[1] did not receive His word. Only by such an alternation of terms in English can the twofold meaning of λόγος have justice done to it. The sense of the passage may be aptly illustrated from Rom. i. 19–21, and all the more so because there is no possibility of literary dependence between the two passages, Paul having a different line of approach and a different terminology.

That of God which can be known is manifest among them, because God Himself manifested it to them. For His invisible attributes from the foundation of the world—that is to say, His everlasting power and deity—are contemplated when they are intellectually grasped through His works; so that the pagans are inexcusable, because although they knew God they did not glorify Him as God or give thanks, but were stultified in their reasonings, and their senseless mind was darkened.

But, John proceeds, this was not universally true. There were some who received the word of God, into whose souls Wisdom entered, making them not only friends of God and prophets, but children of God, generated

[1] Cf. *De Opif.* 146 πᾶς ἄνθρωπος κατὰ μὲν τὴν διάνοιαν ᾠκείωται λόγῳ θείῳ, *De Spec. Leg.* IV. 14 ἄνθρωπος...ἀγχίσπορος ὢν θεοῦ καὶ συγγενὴς κατὰ τὴν πρὸς λόγον κοινωνίαν. Thus mankind is ἴδιον to the Logos.

by no physical process and by no merely human act of will, but by the creative will of God. Thus the Logos, or Wisdom, which was the original principle of creation, acts creatively once again in giving men a new birth as sons of God. It does not seem necessary to confine this divine generation to pre-Christian Israel. That there are children of God scattered abroad through the world is stated in xi. 52, and it is unlikely that the evangelist was thinking only of Jews of the Dispersion. They are the 'other sheep not of this fold', whom it is Christ's mission to gather into one.[1] Thus it is quite consistent with his thought to interpret the τέκνα θεοῦ of i. 12 in the sense that already before the coming of Christ there were in the world those in whom the divine Logos was present, and who therefore had the 'right' to be children of God.

If this be the intention of verses 9–11, then the incarnation of the Logos appears as the final concentration of the whole creative and revealing thought of God, which is also the meaning of the universe, in an individual who is what humanity was designed to be in the divine purpose, and therefore is rightly called the 'Son of Man', that is to say, ὁ ἀληθινὸς ἄνθρωπος.

This gives an intelligible and consistent scheme, which is congruous with the use of terms, and with the general run of ideas, in the gospel itself, and in those circles of religious thought most akin to it. All this, however, assumes that the whole passage down to i. 13 refers to the pre-incarnate Logos. But it remains true that the language of verses 11–13, at least, would be equally in place as a description of the historical ministry of Jesus Christ: 'He came to His own place [which for this evangelist is Jerusalem, the holy city of the people of God], and His own people [the Jews] did not receive Him. But to those who received Him [His disciples], He gave the right to be children of God [by giving them the new birth, ἐξ ὕδατος καὶ πνεύματος], that is to say, those who believe in His name' [= ? who give Him their allegiance].

The last phrase would seem most naturally to be used of adhesion to Jesus Christ, or to the Christian Church, in view of the common Christian use of πιστεύειν, of the use of πιστεύειν εἰς τὸ ὄνομα in the gospel itself (see p. 184) and of its possible relation to εἰς τὸ ὄνομα in the baptismal formula (Matt. xxviii. 19, Acts viii. 16, I Cor. i. 13–15). Moreover, as we have noted, the use of the masculine pronoun with reference to the subject of the proposition, in spite of the fact that the expressed subject is the neuter φῶς, might readily be explained if the evangelist had in mind the incarnate Christ as the real subject of all these propositions.

[1] The Samaritans of ch. iv and the Greeks of ch. xii are among them.

But again, it may be that references to the incarnate Logos do not begin with verse 11, but with verse 9, if ἦν...ἐρχόμενον be taken as an analytic form of the continuous present: 'The real light, which enlightens every man, was (at that moment) coming into the world'—at the moment, that is, when John gave his testimony—so that in effect the transition from the pre-incarnate to the incarnate Logos would come at verse 6. From that time on 'He was in the world, though the world did not recognize Him.' John the Baptist himself, indeed, confesses that he did not recognize Him (οὐκ ᾔδειν αὐτόν, i. 30) until the moment of manifestation when the πνεῦμα descended upon Him. In i. 14 the καί might be taken as resumptive—'and so', or 'in short, the Logos became flesh'.

Again, however, on this line of interpretation, there seems no reason why we should not push the transition even farther back; for it is certainly the evangelist's view that life was in Jesus Christ when He exercised His historical ministry (cf. v. 26), and that this life was the light of men (cf. viii. 12, ix. 5, xii. 46). Thus it is only the first three verses of the gospel that necessarily refer to the pre-incarnate Logos. The rest *could* be understood as referring to the historical appearance of Jesus Christ.

The chief difficulty about such a view (apart from the linguistic arguments in favour of the alternative construction of verse 9, which I believe to be formidable, see p. 204 n. 1) is that the kind of reader whom John wished to reach (as it appears) would have no clue whatever to show that he was speaking of an historical character, or describing events in an historical life, until the expression, ὁ λόγος σὰρξ ἐγένετο, pulled him up short, and prepared for the explanation which follows in verses 15–18. Upon the view of the gospel as a whole to which our study so far has led, it seems that we must allow that the reader in the Hellenistic world for whom this Prologue is the first introduction to the Christian faith should be able to read it with a straightforward understanding of its meaning at least on one level, based upon his previous acquaintance with the terms used. I believe the meaning set forth in pp. 279–82, or something like it, is that which he would naturally attach to the whole passage. That, however, is not to say that this is the only level of meaning intended by the evangelist. For we shall find that it is one of the most marked features of this gospel that the argument constantly moves on two levels, and the *prima facie* meaning carries with it a further meaning, which comes to light only when the passage is re-read in view of the gospel as a whole.

In the case of the Prologue, I suggest that the true solution of the problem may be found if we take with the fullest seriousness the implications of the proposition, ὁ λόγος σὰρξ ἐγένετο, in the light of the whole story that follows. The Logos did not merely descend upon Jesus, enter into Him, or abide in Him. The Logos *became* the σάρξ or human nature which He bore. The life of Jesus therefore *is* the history of the Logos, as incarnate, and this must be, upon the stage of limited time, the same thing as the history of the Logos in perpetual relations with man and the world. Thus not only verses 11–13, but the whole passage from verse 4, is *at once* an account of the relations of the Logos with the world, *and* an account of the ministry of Jesus Christ, which in every essential particular reproduces those relations. 'The light shines in darkness'— that is a description of the created universe, in which pure reality is set over against the darkness of not-being: it is also a description of the appearance of Jesus on earth, as this evangelist sees it, and as he describes it in detail in the whole of his gospel. 'The darkness did not overcome it'—the world, in spite of the presence of non-divine elements in it, does not relapse into not-being, because light is stronger than darkness, reality and the good than unreality and evil. Similarly, the opposition to Jesus, even when it seemed to triumph in the crucifixion, failed to conquer Him. 'The real light that enlightens every man who enters the world' is to be seen in the universal mission of Christ, to draw all men to Himself, to gather together the scattered children of God. For that purpose He was in the world, but unrecognized by the world. As the Logos comes to men, who, as λογικοί (unlike irrational creatures, ἄλογα), are its proper home, but is not truly 'received' by them, so Jesus came to the Jewish people, His own people, and found no response. As those who admit the divine Logos, or Wisdom, to their souls, become sons of God, so Jesus gave to His disciples 'words of eternal life', and they were born again.

This double significance is thoroughly characteristic of the method of this evangelist. We have already seen, in examining his use of symbolism, that the particular events which he describes are for him important both as events in time and as 'signs' of eternal realities. The events of the life of Jesus are σημεῖα, in the last resort, just because in them the Logos became flesh. The gospel is a record of a life which expresses the eternal thought of God, the meaning of the universe. It is through a knowledge of this life that the eternal Logos is apprehended, and not otherwise. Though the evangelist recognizes a 'reception' of the Logos apart from the incarnation, yet this is a given possibility for mankind only because the Logos is He who became flesh, and, Christ having come, it is in 'believing in

His name' that the Logos is received. We do not start with cosmology, ascending to knowledge of God through His works in creation and the eternal forms behind them. We start with faith in Jesus, which involves the recognition that the meaning which we find in Him is the meaning of the whole universe—that, in fact, that which is incarnate in Him is the Logos. That is the direction of thought, and that is where John differs decisively from Philo and other thinkers of a similar tendency. Cosmology is not for him a path to knowledge of God and eternal life. Only he who knows God in Jesus Christ, knows what the Logos is, by which the world was made. In the light of its conclusion, the beginning of the Prologue may be read in this fashion: 'The ground of all real existence is that divine meaning or principle which is manifested in Jesus Christ. It was this principle, separable in thought from God, but not in reality separate from Him, that existed before the world was, and is the pattern by which, and the power through which, it was created. The life that is in the world, the light that is in the mind of man, are what we have found in Christ.' The evangelist does not, like some 'Gnostics', set out to communicate an account of the origin of the universe, as a way to that knowledge of God which is eternal life, and then fit Christ into the scheme. He says, in effect, 'let us assume that the cosmos exhibits a divine meaning which constitutes its reality. I will tell you what that meaning is: it was embodied in the life of Jesus, which I will now describe.'

We might put it thus, that the Prologue is an account of the life of Jesus under the form of a description of the eternal Logos in its relations with the world and with man, and the rest of the gospel an account of the Logos under the form of a record of the life of Jesus; and the proposition ὁ λόγος σὰρξ ἐγένετο binds the two together, being at the same time the final expression of the relation of the Logos to man and his world, and a summary of the significance of the life of Jesus. We may regard the Prologue as giving, in the barest skeleton outline, a philosophy of life, or *Weltanschauung*, which is to be filled in with concrete detail out of the gospel as a whole. In the third part of this book I shall try to show how the whole shape of the gospel is determined by the idea expressed in the words, ὁ λόγος σὰρξ ἐγένετο, with the content of the term λόγος supplied by the Prologue as a whole.

PART III
ARGUMENT AND STRUCTURE

INTRODUCTORY

Having now defined the principal concepts with which the Fourth Evangelist works, I propose to follow the argument of the gospel chapter by chapter.

The book naturally divides itself at the end of ch. xii. The division corresponds to that which is made in all the gospels before the beginning of the Passion-narrative. But here it is made more formal. The gospel is divided at this point virtually into two books. What follows in chs. xiii–xx—or xxi, if we include the appendix—may properly be called The Book of the Passion. The earlier chapters correspond to the account of the Ministry in the other gospels. The way in which John regards it may be gathered from the opening words of the epilogue which he has supplied in xii. 37–50 τοσαῦτα δὲ αὐτοῦ σημεῖα πεποιηκότος....
We may fitly call it The Book of Signs. This book begins with ch. ii. Ch. i forms a proem. I shall therefore examine the gospel under these three heads: A. The Proem; B. The Book of Signs; C. The Book of the Passion.

The purpose of this present discussion is to trace the argument which runs through the whole gospel, and to see how it is reflected in the structure of the book. At this point it is necessary to note that according to many recent critics any such enterprise is precarious at best, and probably futile, since (as they contend) the text of the work as it has come down to us does not represent its order as designed by the author. The original order is supposed to have suffered some primitive disarrangement, whether fortuitous or deliberate, which has resulted in inconcinnities and disjunctures sufficient to impair, if not to destroy, any continuity which the argument may once have possessed.

Many attempts have been made to improve the work by rearrangement of its material. Some of these have been (as it were) canonized by being adopted in large and important editions of the Fourth Gospel, and in modern translations. I have examined several of these rearrangements, and cannot sufficiently admire the patience and endless ingenuity which have gone to their making. It is of course impossible to deny that the work may have suffered dislocation, and plausible grounds may be alleged for lifting certain passages out of their setting, where there seems to be some *prima facie* breach of continuity. Unfortunately, when once the gospel has been taken to pieces, its reassemblage is liable to be affected by individual preferences, preconceptions and even prejudices. Meanwhile the work lies before us in an order which (apart from insignificant details) does not vary in the textual tradition, traceable to an early period. I conceive it to be the duty of an interpreter at least to see what can be done with the document as it has come down to us before attempting to improve upon it. This is what I shall try to do. I shall assume as a provisional working hypothesis that the present order is not fortuitous, but deliberately devised by somebody—even if he were only a scribe doing his best—and that the person in question (whether the author or another) had some design in mind, and was not necessarily irresponsible or unintelligent. If the attempt to discover any intelligible thread of argument should fail, then we may be compelled to confess that we do not know how the work was originally intended to run. If on the other hand it should appear that the structure of the gospel as we have it has been shaped in most of its details by the ideas which seem to dominate the author's thought, then it would appear not improbable that we have his work before us substantially in the form which he designed.

After dealing briefly with the Proem, I shall proceed to the Book of Signs, chs. ii–xii. This seems naturally to divide itself into seven episodes, each consisting of one or more narratives of significant acts of Jesus, accompanied by one or more discourses designed to bring out the significance of the narratives.

The second main division, which I have proposed to call the Book of the Passion, extends from the beginning of ch. xiii to the end of the work. It seems pretty clear that it was originally planned to end at xx. 30–1, where it is provided with a formal conclusion. Ch. xxi, whether the work of the evangelist or of another, has the character of a postscript, and falls outside the design of the book as a whole.

The Book of the Passion is constructed on a pattern broadly similar to that of each individual episode of the Book of Signs. There is a single continuous narrative, that of the arrest, trial, crucifixion and resurrection of Jesus Christ, in chs. xviii–xx; and a long series of discourses, partly dialogue and partly monologue, in chs. xiii–xvii, commonly called the Farewell Discourses. If in this case the narrative follows the discourses, instead of the discourses following the narrative, as is the general rule in the Book of Signs, that difference is necessitated by the difference in situation.[1] The narrative includes a certain amount of dialogue, chiefly in the account of the trial of Jesus, as well as in the post-resurrection narratives. The discourses similarly include a narrative element, in the account of incidents at the Last Supper. But the character of chs. xiii–xvii as discourse, and of chs. xviii–xx as narrative, is unmistakable.

Having in view the parallelism in structure with the episodes of the Book of Signs, we should be disposed to expect that the discourses would serve to elucidate the significance of the narrative. Such appears to be the intention of the evangelist. That however is to anticipate to some extent the results of this enquiry.

[1] As we shall see, the Farewell Discourses presuppose the Passion to such an extent that they may be said to be logically subsequent to the Passion-narrative; but to have placed them after this narrative would have wrecked the dramatic pattern of the gospel.

A. THE PROEM: PROLOGUE
AND TESTIMONY

Chapter i forms a proem to the whole gospel. It falls into two parts: 1–18, commonly designated the Prologue, and 19–51, which we may, from the nature of its contents, conveniently call the Testimony.

In order to define the function of this chapter in relation to the argument which follows, we may begin with the second part of the chapter, and compare it with the opening of the Gospel according to Mark. Mark i. 1–15 constitutes similarly an introduction or proem to the gospel. It brings John the Baptist on the scene, to act as herald for the coming Messiah; then records the divine testimony to Jesus at His baptism; and then, after the temptation in the wilderness, brings Jesus to Galilee with the momentous proclamation, πεπλήρωται ὁ καιρὸς καὶ ἤγγικεν ἡ βασιλεία τοῦ θεοῦ.

The section in John which I have proposed to call the Testimony covers much the same ground. It begins with the testimony of John the Baptist. And it is to be observed that while in Matthew and Luke the Baptist has much of the character of the preacher of righteousness which attaches to him in Josephus, in John as in Mark he is simply a witness to the coming of the Messiah. In the Fourth Gospel however his testimony is more detailed and definite than in Mark. In fact the testimony of the Baptist here absorbs what Mark has given as from his own pen. In the first place, the Baptist is made to cite precisely the scripture which Mark cites in his own person in the exordium: 'The voice of one crying in the wilderness, "Make straight the way of the Lord"' (i. 23). Thus the Baptist himself declares his own ministry to be the immediate prelude to the great divine Event. Next, he not only foretells, as in Mark, the coming of the Messiah: he designates Jesus as the Messiah (i. 29–34). He does this on the basis of a divine revelation. The supernatural designation of Jesus as Messiah is not directly recorded, as it is in Mark: it is reported by the Baptist, who saw the Spirit descending like a dove, and therefore, under divine guidance, recognized Jesus as Son of God, and as Him who should baptize with Holy Spirit. We have a remarkable interweaving of Mark's account of the witness of the Baptist, 'He will baptize with Holy Spirit', and of the Messianic designation of Jesus, 'Thou art my Son the Beloved.' The only peculiarly Johannine element is the title 'Lamb of God', which the Baptist applies to Jesus along with the more usual title 'Son of God'. This title is, as I tried to show (pp. 230–8), at least in its prior associations, an eschatological one. The horned lamb or ram is an apocalyptic figure for the divinely appointed leader of the people of God.

So far then we are clearly upon the same ground as in Mark i. 1–11, and in the apostolic *kerygma* as attested by Acts x and xiii. Jesus is designated as the Messiah, the inaugurator of the new order of the Spirit, and attested as such by the final representative of the prophetic succession. Mark has summoned confirmatory testimony at various points of the gospel, as for example the confessions of the demoniacs, of Peter, of Bartimaeus, and of the centurion at the Cross. John also introduces the confessions of Peter and of others in the course of his gospel. But in addition he has enlarged his introductory chapter with a further series of testimonies. The stories of Andrew and Peter, Philip and Nathanael are often described as the 'call' of these disciples, and they have affinity with 'vocation-stories' in the Synoptics: but it is not clear that the evangelist thought of the incidents he describes exactly as Mark thought of the calling of the fishermen and the publican. What is clear is that they are narrated at this point for the sake of the confirmatory testimony they afford to the Messiahship of Jesus. The evangelist has summoned as witnesses, to corroborate the testimony of the Baptist, a number of well-known or typical personages. The first confesses Jesus as 'Messiah', using the Aramaic term; the second as 'him of whom Moses wrote in the Law, and the prophets'; the third as 'the Son of God, the King of Israel'. It all constitutes a striking appeal to the standing tradition of the coming Messiah, who is the fulfilment of all prophecy, and a declaration that Jesus Christ is that fulfilment.

Mark, after recording the designation of Jesus as Messiah, brings Him upon the scene in Galilee, and represents Him as making in His own person the announcement: 'The time is fulfilled and the Kingdom of God is upon you.' Similarly John brings the chapter of testimony to a climax with an utterance of Jesus Himself: 'I solemnly assure you: you will see heaven opened and the angels of God ascending and descending upon the Son of Man.' I have already discussed the use of the term 'Son of Man' in this passage (pp. 245–6). Here we need only observe that in the primitive Christian tradition it is reserved as the typical self-designation of Jesus. Twice in Mark, where Jesus has been addressed by others as 'Messiah', He replies substituting the term 'Son of Man' (viii. 29–31, xiv. 61–2). Similarly here, after the witnesses have heaped together traditional messianic titles, Jesus replies with this mysterious formula. John clearly intends to affirm the primitive tradition that it was the title 'Son of Man' that Jesus had used to denote His dignity, mission and destiny, and he makes Him utter it with all solemnity here at the close of the chapter of testimony. As in Mark the whole narrative from this point falls under the rubric 'The time is fulfilled and the Kingdom of God is upon you', so in John the rest of the gospel is controlled by this revelation of the Son of Man. Both 'Kingdom of God' and 'Son of Man' stand for eschatological realities now declared to be present within history. The mysterious language about the open heaven and the ascending and descending angels is to be understood, as I showed, on the basis of Jewish exegesis of Jacob's vision, in which it is brought into connection with the Isaianic Servant of the Lord. The Son of Man, like the Servant, is the inclusive representative of the true Israel of God, upon whom the glory rests. The angels of the glory go to and fro, keeping the heavenly and the earthly in perpetual unity. The language is highly mythological and symbolic. Its meaning could otherwise be expressed in two phrases of the Prologue: 'the μονογενής in the bosom of the Father'; 'the Logos made flesh'.

It would therefore be improper to understand the declaration made to Nathanael as a promise of a revelation to be made after the incarnate life of Christ, that is to say, as a reference to a second Advent. Nor would it be possible to find the promised vision of the Son of Man in any particular recorded incident in the life. The whole series of 'signs' which follows, culminating in the supreme sign of the cross and resurrection, *is* the vision of the heaven opened and the angels of God ascending and descending upon the Son of Man. And these 'signs' are history. 'The Logos was made *flesh*—and we beheld His glory.' Whatever else, therefore, the Gospel story is to be, it is to be a realized apocalypse.

How then does the Prologue, i. 1–18, fit in with this conception of the intention of i. 19–51? Formally, since 19–51 corresponds to Mark i. 4–15, it should in some sense correspond to the opening verses of Mark, which enunciate the theme of the fulfilment of prophecy. And so it does. I have tried to show that whatever else the Logos of the Fourth Gospel is, on one side it is the Word of the Lord, by which the heavens were framed, which came through the prophets to Israel, was rejected by the people at large, but found acceptance with the faithful remnant, to whom it gave the status of God's children. This prophetic word, says the evangelist, was not merely fulfilled in the sense that what it declared came true. It was fulfilled in a deeper sense. The Word itself, the word which proceeds from the mouth of God and cannot return to Him void, found actual embodiment, and worked creatively as at the beginning. How could the writer more impressively have stated the fundamental conviction of the apostolic *kerygma*, that the whole meaning of prophecy is exhaustively realized in the Gospel story? The same idea of the fulfilment of the Word of God appears again in i. 17 in the contrast of the Law of Moses with Christ. The Torah was conceived as the Word of the Lord: its content and character were described as חֶסֶד וֶאֱמֶת, 'grace and truth'. The evangelist affirms that the Torah did not, in the full sense, bring grace and truth, but Christ does. The Torah therefore is but a shadow of the true Word of God, which came in its full reality in Jesus Christ.

But, as we have seen, it is impossible to confine the term Logos to the meaning 'word'. It is also the divine Wisdom, the Hebrew analogue at once of the Platonic world of Ideas and of the Stoic Logos: it is that thought of God which is the transcendent design of the universe, and its immanent meaning. Here we are in a world of conceptions to which eschatology is strange. Eschatology is cast in a temporal mould. It speaks of this age and that which is to come. The primitive eschatological Gospel of Christianity declared that that which was to come has come: 'Old things have passed away: behold new things have come into being.' The Prologue on the other hand is based upon the philosophical conception of two orders of being, distinguished not by succession in time, but by the greater or less measure of reality which they possess. There is the order of pure reality, transcendent and eternal, which is the very thought of God, and there is the empirical order, which is real only as it expresses the eternal order. The world at various levels—the lower creation, the human race, spiritually enlightened humanity—displays an increasing penetration of the lower order by the higher, an increasing dominance of light over darkness, of being over not-being, of truth over error. In terms of such a philosophy, the absoluteness of the Christian revelation is affirmed in a proposition which declares that in one single area of the universe of space and time phenomena have completely absorbed the reality of the eternal archetype, and that this area is co-extensive with the life, death and resurrection of Jesus Christ. The evangelist's term for the phenomenal order of being, so far as it is manifested in humanity, is σάρξ (iii. 6). Accordingly, the fundamental proposition takes the form, ὁ λόγος σάρξ ἐγένετο.

The Prologue thus represents a thoroughgoing reinterpretation of the idea which in the later part of the chapter is expressed in terms of the 'realized eschatology' of the primitive Church. The Logos-doctrine is placed first, because, addressing a public nurtured in the higher religion of Hellenism, the writer wishes to offer the Logos-idea as the appropriate approach, for them, to the central purport of the Gospel, through which he may lead them to the historical actuality of its story, rooted as it is in Jewish tradition, ἡ γὰρ σωτηρία ἐκ τῶν Ἰουδαίων ἐστιν (iv. 22). There is a far-reaching equivalence of the two propositions: 'The Logos became flesh and dwelt among us, and we beheld His glory'; and 'You will see heaven opened and the angels of God ascending and descending on the Son of Man.' Both of them contain in brief the substance of what the evangelist is now about to relate.

B. THE BOOK OF SIGNS

First Episode. The New Beginning (ii. 1–iv. 42)

Chapters ii. 1–iv. 42 contain two distinct narratives, and two passages of discourse, all of which prove to have, in a broad sense, a common theme: a theme which may perhaps best be characterized by Paul's aphorism, τὰ ἀρχαῖα παρῆλθεν· ἰδοὺ γέγονεν καινά (II Cor. v. 17).[1] In ii. 1–10 water is replaced by wine; in ii. 14–19 a new temple is foretold; the dialogue with Nicodemus in ch. iii is about new birth; the dialogue with the Samaritan woman in ch. iv contrasts both the φρέαρ of Jacob with 'living water', and the ancient cults of Jerusalem and Gerizim with the worship ἐν πνεύματι καὶ ἀληθείᾳ for which the time is ripe. We may therefore best treat these two chapters as forming a single complex act or episode, consisting of two σημεῖα, or significant actions, and two discourses developing their significance.

(i) The narrative of the Miracle of Cana, ii. 1–11, presents, at the very beginning of the Book of Signs, a particularly striking example of a feature of this gospel which will frequently recur. We may call it the Johannine irony. On the face of it we have here a naïve tale about a marvel at a village wedding. There is realism in the story, an eye for character and for seemingly trivial detail (the stone waterpots hold from seventeen to twenty-five gallons apiece); there is even a touch of homely humour in the remark of the ἀρχιτρίκλινος, 'Everyone puts the best wine on the table first, and brings on the poor stuff when the company is drunk; but you have kept your good wine to the last.' And yet we are told, 'Jesus did this as the beginning of His signs, and so manifested His glory.' Those last words recall (and are clearly intended to recall) the words of the Prologue: 'The Word became flesh and made His abode among us, and we beheld His glory.' The story, then, is *not* to be taken at its face value. Its true meaning lies deeper. We are given no direct clue to this deeper meaning, as we are for some other σημεῖα. It must be sought from a consideration of the general background of thought presupposed in the first readers.

The messianic banquet is an established Jewish and primitive Christian symbol. A γάμος provides imagery in several of the Synoptic parables.

[1] So Walter Bauer *ad loc.* quoting the Monarchian prologue to this gospel: 'ut veteribus inmutatis nova omnia quae a Christo instituuntur appareant.'

In the Johannine Apocalypse it appears as the 'marriage-supper of the Lamb' (Rev. xix. 7–9). The imagery passed into the Eucharistic symbolism of the Church. In early Christian art the scene of the Miracle of Cana often forms a counterpart to that of the Multiplication of the Loaves, in allusion to the Bread and Wine of the Eucharist; and it may well be that even for the earliest Christian readers of John ii. 1–11 the eucharistic complex of ideas was in mind, and was intended to be in mind. Yet no explicit allusion is made, and the non-Christian reader would have no inkling of it. In the tradition of the teaching of Jesus which is preserved in the Synoptic Gospels 'new wine' occurs in a context which refers to the shattering effect of His impact upon existing institutions;[1] yet it cannot be said to be a stated symbol of His teaching or ministry, any more than is the accompanying image of a new patch on an old garment. In all this we may find valid indications of the context of thought and imagination within which the present passage may have shaped itself in the writer's mind; but it does not supply a plain clue which the contemporary reader might be expected to seize.

Perhaps the best clue for him is provided by Philo, in a passage where he is speaking about Melchizedek, who 'brought forth bread and wine' for Abraham (Gen. xiv. 18). He recalls that the Ammonites and Moabites churlishly refused bread and water to Israel in the wilderness; 'but Melchizedek', he goes on, 'shall bring forth *wine instead of water* and give our souls a pure draught, that they may become possessed by that divine intoxication which is more sober than sobriety itself; for he is the priest-logos, and has for his portion the Self-existent'[2] (*Leg. Alleg.* iii. 79 sqq.). Ἀντὶ ὕδατος οἶνον, that is what our story is about. Without expecting to get from Philo a rigorous definition of the wine of God, which might be applied directly to the Fourth Gospel, we may profitably review some of the ideas he associates with it.

In *De Somn.* ii. 249, the Logos, as οἰνοχόος τοῦ θεοῦ καὶ συμποσίαρχος, pours sacred goblets of true joy (τῆς πρὸς ἀλήθειαν εὐφροσύνης). In *Quod Deus Immutabilis*, 158, commenting on Num. xx. 17–20 as an allegory of the quest of σοφία, he says, 'He would not drink from a cistern (λάκκος), to whom God gives pure draughts of wine (μέθυσμα), sometimes through the ministry of some messenger (or angel) whom

---

[1] Mark ii. 22 and parallels.

[2] The passage might also be rendered, 'The term "priest" here means the Logos, having for his portion the Self-existent', but the construction adopted above is more probable.

He has appointed cupbearer (οἰνοχοεῖν), and sometimes from His own hand, without any intermediary between Giver and recipient.' In *Leg. Alleg.* I. 84 μεθύει τὴν νήφουσαν μέθην is said of the man who praises God as He should be praised, 'when the mind goes out of itself and offers itself to God'.[1] In *De Somn.* II. 183 the οἰνοχόος receives cups of perennial grace (ἀεννάων χαρίτων λαβὼν προπόσεις). *Ibid.* 190 there is a vine which pertains to εὐφροσύνη; the μέθυσμα from it is undiluted sagacity (ἡ ἄκρατος εὐβουλία); the cupbearer draws from the divine bowl which God Himself has filled with virtues to the brim (ἐπὶ χείλη, cf. ἕως ἄνω, John ii. 7). Again, in *De Fuga* 166, the αὐτομαθὴς καὶ αὐτοδίδακτος σοφός 'has not gained improvement by studies and exercises and labours, but at once at his birth has found finished wisdom dropped like rain from heaven above, and drawing in its pure draught has feasted and continued drunk with that sober intoxication which goes with rightness of reason (μετ' ὀρθότητος λόγου)'. Thus the wine which the Priest-logos brings forth ἀντὶ ὕδατος stands for God's gifts of grace, joy, virtue, wisdom, and the like; in fact for all those things which for Philo characterize the higher or spiritual life. We may therefore recognize in it an apt symbol for all that the Fourth Evangelist conceives Christ to have brought into the world—without for the present defining it further. Later we shall learn more about the ἀληθινὴ ἄμπελος and its fruit.

What then is the water which is replaced by this wine of God? The evangelist has given us a hint when he says that the waterpots were there κατὰ τὸν καθαρισμὸν τῶν 'Ιουδαίων. They stand for the entire system of Jewish ceremonial observance—and by implication for religion upon that level, wherever it is found, as distinguished from religion upon the level of ἀλήθεια (cf. iv. 23–4). Thus the first of signs already symbolizes the doctrine that ὁ νόμος διὰ Μωϋσέως ἐδόθη· ἡ χάρις καὶ ἡ ἀλήθεια διὰ 'Ιησοῦ Χριστοῦ ἐγένετο (i. 17).[2]

It is thus that the glory of Christ is manifested—by a sign which sets forth the truth that with His coming the old order in religion is superseded by a new order. It is surely not without significance that this manifestation

---

[1] We are reminded of the worship ἐν πνεύματι of John iv. 23–4.

[2] Similarly Origen: 'At His former visit [to Cana] He brings us joy (εὐφραίνει ἡμᾶς)...and gives us to drink of the wine that proceeds from His power, which was water when it was drawn, but became wine when Jesus transformed it. And truly before Jesus the Scripture was water, but from the time of Jesus it has become wine to us.' Origen sees rightly that the water 'of the Jews' purifying' is the γράμμα of the Old Testament, but confines the transformation too narrowly to giving it a 'spiritual' interpretation. See Origen, *Comm. in Joann.* XIII. 62, pp. 277–8.

takes place τῇ ἡμέρᾳ τῇ τρίτῃ. The difficulty of basing a convincing chronology of events upon this datum is notorious. But the 'third day' was in Christian tradition from earliest times the day when Christ manifested His glory in resurrection from the dead. It is in accordance with the view taken by this evangelist that the whole of the incarnate ministry of the Word should have the character of the 'third day' of His glory.

(ii) From Galilee we are taken to Jerusalem, and here there is to hand an inevitable symbol of the old order in religion: the Temple with its sacrificial system. The evangelist has used for his purpose the narrative of the Cleansing of the Temple which appears also in the Synoptic Gospels. It is given here with little substantial difference from the Marcan version, though with no great measure of verbal agreement.

It is in the comments appended to the act of 'cleansing' that the distinctively Johannine element appears. The two citations of the Old Testament which Mark places in the mouth of Jesus, from Is. lvi. 7 and Jer. vii. 11, do not appear in John; but they are apparently replaced by two different *testimonia*. In driving out the traders, Jesus says, 'Do not make my Father's house a trading-place (οἶκον ἐμπορίου).' It seems possible that there is an allusion to Zech. xiv. 21 'In that day there shall be no more a כְּנַעֲנִי in the house of the Lord', if כְּנַעֲנִי is to be taken in the sense of 'trafficker' rather than 'Canaanite'. After all, the prophet has just invited 'all the families of the earth' to come up to Jerusalem for the Feast of Tabernacles, and there seems no reason for a last-minute exclusion of Canaanites. There is a pretty clear allusion to that chapter of Zechariah in John vii (see below, pp. 349–50), and it is probable that here also the evangelist intends us to have in mind the prophecy of the 'Day of the Lord', and to see it fulfilled in the expulsion of 'traffickers' from the Temple.[1]

In what follows, the significance of the whole scene is made more precise. The Jews demand a sign in justification of Jesus's action—as in Mark they ask for His authority. He replies, 'Destroy this temple and in three days I will raise it up.' The meaning is not at once clear. Is the destruction and subsequent rebuilding of the temple the 'sign' desired? But for John a 'sign' is something that actually happens, but carries a meaning deeper than the actual happening. The destruction of the temple, however, with its subsequent rebuilding, is not (certainly is not in the evangelist's view) anything that actually happens: the expression

[1] For the second *testimonium* see below, p. 301.

is metaphorical, and stands for something quite different from the destruction and restoration of a building. In vi. 30, after the Feeding of the Multitude, the Jews similarly demand a sign, suggesting that it might take the form of a renewal of the divine gift of manna. But in response, Jesus does not promise any significant event yet to happen; He offers an interpretation of what has already happened. That is to say, He invites His questioners to see in the actual occurrence of the Feeding of the Multitude the σημεῖον which they desire. As yet, though they have eaten of the loaves, they have not seen the σημεῖον.[1] It seems best to understand the present passage in a similar sense. In the words 'Destroy this temple and in three days I will raise it up', Jesus is not promising a significant event yet to come, but inviting His questioners to see in the actual occurrence of the Cleansing of the Temple the σημεῖον they desire.[2] The purging of the temple—that is, the expulsion of the sacrificial animals from its courts—signifies the destruction and replacement of the system of religious observance of which the temple was the centre: a new 'temple' for an old one. The auditors (according to John's regular technique) understand the statement with strict literalism, in order to prepare the way for a deeper interpretation. This deeper interpretation, the evangelist adds, could be fully understood only in the light of the resurrection of Christ (ii. 21–22).

The thought now becomes highly complex. The main idea, that of the replacement of the old temple (or order of religion) by a new one, is plain enough, and that is where the reader is intended to start. But this idea is placed within the context of the death and resurrection of Jesus Christ. The second *testimonium*, 'The zeal of thy house will eat me up', is cited from Ps. lxviii (lxix). 10. This Psalm belongs to a group of Psalms of the Righteous Sufferer, which provided from early times many *testimonia* to the Passion of Christ.[3] The implication is that, just as the Righteous Sufferer of the Psalm paid the price of his loyalty to the temple, so the action of Jesus in cleansing the temple will bring him to grief. In the Synoptic tradition the Cleansing leads directly to the Passion.[4]

---

[1] See below, pp. 334–5.

[2] So Origen, *Comm. in Joann.* x. 24, p. 184 (in cleansing the temple) 'I believe He wrought a deeper sign (σημεῖον βαθύτερον), so that we understand that these things are a symbol (σύμβολον) that the service of that temple is no longer to be carried on by way of material sacrifices (κατὰ τὰς αἰσθητὰς θυσίας)', etc.

[3] Ps. lxviii. 5 cited in John xv. 25; 10, in Rom. xv. 3; 22, in Matt. xxvii. 48, John xix. 28–9; 26, in Acts i. 20.

[4] For what here follows, see *Parables of the Kingdom*, pp. 98–101.

The story is embedded in a context which speaks of the rejection of Israel: the Blasted Fig-tree, the Mountain cast into the Sea, the Wicked Husbandmen. The authorities are incensed by these sayings, and seek to put Jesus under arrest. After a series of controversies on various points, there follows the forecast of the ruin of the temple (Mk. xiii. 2), which is brought up against Jesus at His trial (xiv. 58), in a form which resembles John ii. 19 'I will destroy this temple (made with hands) and in three days will build another (not made with hands).'[1] We may conclude that the saying in question was from the first associated both with the idea of the supersession of the old order of Jewish religion, and with the death of Jesus: with His death and, surely, with His resurrection; for the 'three days' are too intimately linked with the resurrection to be used without implicit reference to it. Thus John is true to a standing tradition he when says that the saying could not be understood fully until after the resurrection, which also threw light upon the Scripture (upon Ps. lxviii in the first place, but also upon the whole corpus of *testimonia*). It is with all this in mind that we are to read John ii. 21 'He was speaking of the temple of His body.' The association, or identification, of the temple which is to be destroyed and raised up with the body of Christ is in no way forced upon the passage: it is implicit in the tradition; since the process by which the transition is made from the old to the new is identical with the process of Christ's death and resurrection. John has only made it explicit. His Christian readers at Ephesus, however, might be expected to carry their understanding of the passage a little further. In documents which are certainly connected with Ephesus the Church is both σῶμα Χριστοῦ and ναὸς Θεοῦ.[2] The instructed reader, therefore, would conclude that the new order in religion which Christ inaugurates is that of the Church which is His Body.[3] That the evangelist intended this is highly

[1] If we are to compare the Marcan and Johannine forms of the saying, we must observe that the sophisticated Greek χειροποίητος (Hdt., Plato, etc., but adopted in LXX for אֱלִיל) and ἀχειροποίητος are almost certainly secondary, and that διὰ τριῶν ἡμερῶν is more elegant Greek than ἐν τρισὶν ἡμέραις, whereas in John the use of the imperative in the protasis of a conditional sentence (representing a well-known Hebrew idiom) and the unliterary ἐν τρισὶν ἡμέραις suggest that we are nearer to primitive Semitic forms of the saying: we should translate 'If this temple is destroyed, I will raise it up in three days.' The conditional form is dramatically appropriate.

[2] I Cor. xii. 27, iii. 16—written at Ephesus—and Eph. iv. 12, ii. 21—probably addressed, if not to Ephesus itself, at least to readers in the province of Asia.

[3] Cf. Origen, *Comm. in Joann.* x. 35 (20), p. 197 τό τε ἱερὸν καὶ τὸ σῶμα τοῦ Ἰησοῦ κατὰ μίαν τῶν ἐκδοχῶν τύπος μοι φαίνεται εἶναι τῆς ἐκκλησίας, κ.τ.λ.

probable; but it is not essential to the following of his argument, and would not suggest itself to his Hellenistic readers.

To sum up: it seems clear that both the Miracle of Cana and the Cleansing of the Temple are σημεῖα which signify the same fundamental truth: that Christ has come to inaugurate a new order in religion. The fresh element which the second σημεῖον introduces is the cryptic allusion to the death and resurrection of Christ,[1] which at this stage the uninstructed reader is to note with the expectation of clarification as the work proceeds. Meanwhile, the general theme is to be further illustrated in two discourses which follow.

(iii) The first of the two discourses takes the form of a dramatic dialogue, iii. 1–10, passing into monologue from that point on. Various attempts have been made to determine at what point the conversation with Nicodemus is supposed to end, and a fresh exposition to begin. But in fact, although the discourse wanders from the immediate point of rebirth, there is continuity down to iii. 21. The transition from dialogue to monologue is characteristic of this writer's manner.

Jesus is confronted with a representative of the old order which is being superseded; a peculiarly favourable and friendly representative— 'the teacher of Israel'. All the greater emphasis, therefore, falls upon His inexorable pronouncement, ἐὰν μή τις γεννηθῇ ἄνωθεν,[2] οὐ δύναται ἰδεῖν τὴν βασιλείαν τοῦ θεοῦ.[3] Nicodemus, playing the part expected from the interlocutors in Johannine debates, professes to take the statement with strict literalness, and so prepares the way for a clarification of the meaning. It is however dramatically appropriate that an orthodox Jewish Rabbi should find the idea of rebirth strange, for in fact, in spite of the oft-quoted maxim, 'The proselyte is like a new-born child', and

---

[1] This association with the Passion would encourage the instructed reader to see also in the wine of Cana a eucharistic symbol of the Passion, though no hint of it appears on the surface.

[2] It is not necessary here to discuss whether ἄνωθεν here means 'from above', or 'over again'. It is probable that the evangelist was well aware of the ambiguity, and intended to suggest both meanings. In iii. 31 ἄνωθεν certainly means 'from above'.

[3] Βασιλεία τοῦ θεοῦ does not occur in this gospel outside the present discourse, though the evangelist is interested in the βασιλεία of Christ (xviii. 36) and indeed makes more of the kingly aspect of Messiahship than any other New Testament writer; see pp. 229–30. The use however of the term 'Kingdom of God', as one of the terms for the new order in religion, lies well within the tradition of primitive Christianity as represented by the Synoptic Gospels. See *Parables of the Kingdom*, pp. 43–51.

some similar *façons de parler*, the native Rabbinic Judaism seems to have had in this period no real doctrine of regeneration.[1] It is sometimes suggested[2] that the direct antecedent of the Johannine doctrine of regeneration is to be found in such ideas as that expressed in the Synoptic saying, 'Unless you become like little children, you will never enter into the Kingdom of heaven' (Matt. xviii. 3). But the present saying moves in a different sphere of thought. The real approach in Judaism and primitive Christianity to the Johannine doctrine of rebirth is by way of the eschatological conception of the transfiguration of the blessed into forms of heavenly glory in the Age to Come.[3] This is called ἡ παλιγγενεσία in Matt. xix. 28. It is in accordance with the Johannine transmutation of eschatology that this 'rebirth', instead of lying in a scarcely imaginable future, becomes the condition of entering the 'Kingdom of God' (or 'eternal life') here and now, and, in doing so, ceases to be conceived as crude miracle on the quasi-physical plane, and acquires a genuinely religious significance.

In answer to Nicodemus's ἀπορία, the idea of rebirth is elucidated. Rebirth is necessary because there are two levels of existence, the one the sphere of σάρξ, the other of πνεῦμα. On each level like produces like. If for πνεῦμα we substituted νοῦς,[4] it would at once become clear how close we are to the widespread Hellenistic conception of the two orders of existence, the upper world (τὰ ἄνω) which is the sphere of νοῦς, in which alone dwell light and immortality, and the lower world (τὰ κάτω) which is the sphere of ὕλη or of darkness. Various forms of 'Hellenistic mysticism' envisage the problem of man's deliverance from ὕλη and his ascent to the realm of νοῦς, and offer to solve it by various kinds of initiation. For example, in *C.H.* IV, called *The Bowl* (Κρατὴρ ἢ Μονάς), a man may attain γνῶσις and become perfect through 'baptism' in the great Bowl which God has filled with νοῦς (IV. 4; cf. 6). In *C.H.* XIII (Περὶ Παλιγγενεσίας) the initiate says, ἐγεννήθην ἐν νῷ, and this is παλιγγενεσία (XIII. 1, 3). In similar terms our evangelist speaks of ὁ γεγεννημένος ἐκ τοῦ πνεύματος. The main theme of the discourse, then, is the passage of man out of the lower order of existence, the realm of σάρξ, into the higher order of existence, the realm of πνεῦμα in which alone ζωὴ αἰώνιος

---

[1] See material collected by Strack-Billerbeck *ad loc.* vol. II, pp. 420–3.

[2] Cf. Origen, *Comm. in Joann.* (Brooke) Frag. 35 ἐπὶ ταύτην τὴν γέννησιν παρορμῶν ὁ Ἰησοῦς τοῖς γνωρίμοις ἔλεγεν· Ἐὰν μὴ στραφῆτε καὶ γένησθε ὡς τὰ παιδία, κ.τ.λ.

[3] E.g. Enoch xxv. 6, l. 1, II Baruch li. 1–10. Cf. also I Cor. xv. 51–2.

[4] See pp. 223–5.

is his portion. It is this passage into the higher order of existence which has been symbolized by the changing of water into wine and by the cleansing (= transformation, or destruction and renewal) of the temple.

The dialogue on rebirth leaves Nicodemus still perplexed: 'How can these things be?' are his last words before lapsing into silence. The reader will not expect at this early stage to have in hand full materials for answering Nicodemus's question; but he has read the Prologue, and he will observe that the expression of iii. 5, 6, 8, ἐκ πνεύματος γεννᾶσθαι, echoes the expression ἐκ θεοῦ γεννᾶσθαι, which is found in i. 13. There it was explained that to be a 'child of God' is not the result of any process comparable with that of physical birth, 'from blood, from fleshly desire, from the will of the male'. It is by 'receiving the Logos' that man gains the right (ἐξουσία) to be God's child. This effectively dissociates the idea of rebirth, in the Johannine sense of the term, from all mythological notions of divine generation such as were current in wide circles of Hellenistic society, and it must be taken to overrule the whole discussion of the theme in the present passage.

The monologue into which the discourse develops after Nicodemus's retirement at iii. 11 works with the ideas of the Prologue. It speaks of the Μονογενής, the Son of the Father, who is the bearer of life and light. As in the Prologue the Logos, the μονογενὴς παρὰ πατρός,[1] the bearer of life and light, became flesh and revealed (or explained, ἐξηγήσατο) the Father, so in iii. 11–21 the μονογενὴς υἱὸς τοῦ πατρός descended from heaven bringing life and light to the world. This, we are to understand, is the background of the idea of rebirth, as it is intended here. The incarnation of the Logos is, in other terms, the descent of the Son of Man, or heavenly Man, into the lower sphere, the realm of σάρξ. It is the heavenly Man alone (as a Hellenistic reader would at once concede) who, having descended, ascends to heaven again. His descent and ascent open to men the possibility of receiving eternal life, that is, of ascending to the sphere of πνεῦμα; in other words, the possibility of rebirth. The possibility becomes an actuality for those who have faith in the Son— which is tantamount (in terms of the Prologue) to 'receiving the Logos', with the consequent ἐξουσία to be children of God.

[1] The term υἱός is not found in the Prologue, unless we accept the reading ὁ μονογενὴς υἱός in i. 18; but one who is μονογενής relatively to a πατήρ can be no other than the only son, although μονογενής (from μόνος and γένος) does not mean (at this period at any rate) 'only-begotten' (μονογέννητος), but 'alone of his kind', 'unique'.

So far the thought of this discourse, understood with reference to the Prologue, provides a perspicuous guide to the meaning of rebirth. The evangelist, however, after a manner to which he is addicted, slips in a further statement which for the moment remains in part cryptic, but will become perspicuous in the further development of the scheme of the gospel. 'As Moses lifted up the serpent in the wilderness, so the Son of Man must be lifted up, in order that everyone who has faith in him may possess eternal life.' The relevance of this to the discussion, up to a point, is fairly clear. The verb ὑψοῦσθαι is a synonym for ἀναβαίνειν. In the language of the primitive Church it is one of the ways of speaking of the Ascension of Christ. It appears, then, that the ἀνάβασις, or ὕψωσις, of which the evangelist is speaking is in some respect *like* the ὕψωσις of the brazen serpent which Moses set up before the dying Israelites in the wilderness. What is the point of comparison? There is nothing in the context to give guidance. Readers of the LXX however would remember that the serpent was, in the words of the Book of Wisdom, σύμβολον σωτηρίας (Wisd. xvi. 6): it signified the means through which men passed from death to life. The Book of Numbers recorded that there was great mortality among the people, but when the brazen serpent was set up, the dying man ἀπέβλεψεν ἐπὶ τὸν ὄφιν καὶ ἔζη (Num. xxi. 9). Upon this the author of Wisdom comments, that they were not saved διὰ τὸ θεωρούμενον, but by God the Saviour of all. Pursuing a similar line of interpretation, a rabbinic commentary says the meaning of Num. xxi. 13–14 is not that the serpent killed or made alive, but that 'every time that Israel direct their gaze on high and make their heart subservient to their Father in heaven, they are healed'.[1] For Philo also, the 'looking' at the serpent gives the clue to the meaning of the passage. The serpent, for him, is the counterpart of the serpent that tempted Eve. The latter stands for ἡδονή, the former for σωφροσύνη; and so, 'if the mind, stung by Pleasure, the serpent of Eve, is able to look with the faculties of the soul (ψυχικῶς) at the beauty of Temperance, the serpent of Moses, and *through it at God Himself*, he will live: only let him look and contemplate' (*Leg. All.* II. 81). Indirectly, therefore, the whole transaction symbolizes the attainment of life through the vision (or knowledge) of God; which, allowing for the usual shift of emphasis when we pass from Palestinian to Hellenistic Judaism, is not fundamentally

---

[1] Rosh ha-Shana iii. 8, *apud* S.-B. *ad loc.*, cited in full by Odeberg, *ad loc.* p. 107 (his translation is quoted above). His long note, pp. 98–113, assembles many comments from various sources.

dissimilar to the rabbinic interpretation. But it fits in with non-Jewish Hellenistic ways of thinking. Thus in the Hermetic tractate known as *The Bowl* (Κρατὴρ ἢ Μονάς), the author speaks of 'the image of God (τοῦ θεοῦ εἰκών), which if you behold exactly and contemplate with the eyes of the heart...you will find the way to the higher sphere (τὴν πρὸς τὰ ἄνω ὁδόν); or rather, the image itself will guide you; for this vision has a property of its own: it puts constraint on those who behold, and draws them up (ἀνέλκει), as they say the magnet draws iron'.[1] It appears then that for Hellenistic thinkers the elevation of the brazen serpent might readily signify the means by which, through His 'image', the mind might be drawn upward to the vision of God which confers eternal life. So far, a Hellenistic reader having some acquaintance with the teachings of Hellenistic Jews like Philo might be expected to follow the writer's thought. But it remains that ὑψοῦσθαι is a somewhat unexpected word in the context, and there is something cryptic, or oracular, about the saying which awaits further explication. As the work proceeds, the term ὑψοῦσθαι will acquire new and outstanding significance.[2]

The verses 13–15, therefore, are directly relevant to the theme of rebirth into eternal life. The possibility of such rebirth is conditioned by the descent of the Son of Man and His ascent, or 'elevation'. This descent-ascent is now traced to its originating cause, which is the love of God for the world. The statement in iii. 16 is quite fundamental to our author's position, and the reader is intended to bear it in mind during the following discussions, though little further is said about the love of God until with ch. xiii it becomes a dominant theme.

With verse 17 the argument moves from the idea of life to that of light—a constant transition in this gospel, for the Logos is the union of life and light. Thus in order to have a balanced statement, it is necessary to add that while Christ's coming into the world is in its prime intention the opening of the way of rebirth into eternal life, it is also the coming of light, and light judges, inevitably. It judges, in the sense that men pass judgment on themselves by their response to Christ. There are some who prefer darkness to light. They are self-condemned. This is the judgment

[1] *C.H.* iv. 11. In iv. 5 those who are initiated into γνῶσις through the process there called 'baptism' in νοῦς are described as ἑαυτοὺς ὑψώσαντες. Our evangelist would repudiate the suggestion that a man can 'lift himself' into the sphere of life, but he would readily agree that the Son of Man, being lifted up, draws men up like a magnet: in fact he says as much: κἀγὼ ἐὰν ὑψωθῶ ἐκ τῆς γῆς, πάντας ἑλκύσω πρὸς ἐμαυτόν (xii. 32).

[2] See pp. 375–9.

of the world, effected by the coming of Christ—who nevertheless came not to judge but to give life.

Thus the discourse, starting from the idea of rebirth, as initiation into eternal life, has become a kind of programme of the whole work of Christ, setting forth briefly certain ideas which will come up for fuller discussion as the work proceeds: notably those of the 'elevation' of the Son of Man, of the love of God for the world, and of light and judgment.

The passage next following, iii. 22–36, has the appearance of making a fresh departure. There is a change of scene, a brief narrative providing the setting for a dialogue in which the chief speaker is John the Baptist, and a succeeding monologue. Down to verse 30 the words of the Baptist seem directly appropriate to the dramatic situation; but from 31 onwards the discourse becomes more general, and has often been regarded as representing the evangelist's reflections in his own person, as distinct from the Baptist's reply. It is doubtful how far it is possible, here or elsewhere in this gospel, to draw a clear line between reported dialogue or discourse and the evangelist's reflections. What we constantly observe is that dramatic dialogue, often marked by vivid characterization of the interlocutors, melts imperceptibly into monologue, with a certain variation of style, it is true, but without any change so marked that we can say with confidence, 'Here Jesus, or the Baptist, is speaking, and here the evangelist.' In the present case, however, it has been noted that verses 31–6, unlike 22–30, contain many echoes of the ideas and language of the dialogue with Nicodemus and the discourse following. Thus we have the ideas of the higher and lower spheres of existence, and of Christ's descent from the one to the other, with the words ἄνωθεν, ἐκ τῆς γῆς, ἐκ τοῦ οὐρανοῦ; we have the description of Christ as 'the Son', and the reference to His 'sending' (ἀπέστειλεν, 17, 34); we have references to the love of God, to eternal life, to faith and to the Spirit; and we have the emphasis on μαρτυρία, on μαρτυρία based upon 'seeing', and in both passages we have the complaint that the μαρτυρία is rejected. Such echoes are lacking in 22–30.

Upon such grounds it has been proposed to regard verses 31–6 as the direct continuation of the discourse in iii. 11–21, and to remove verses 22–9 as an accidentally displaced section. The suggestion is a tempting one, though it is not so easy, when these verses have been removed from their present context, to find an entirely satisfactory place for them elsewhere, and upon this point those critics who propose a rearrangement are not agreed.

THE NEW BEGINNING

If, by way of experiment, we disregard verses 22–30, we find that verses 31–6 are indeed germane to the preceding discourse, but they cannot be said to be an appropriate continuation of it. It is pretty certain that if our MSS. had given verse 31 immediately after verse 21, critics would have pointed out a disjuncture; for there is no immediate connection between the thought of judgment by the light in verses 17–21 and the supremacy of Christ as the One who descends from heaven and bears witness to what He has seen, which is the theme of 31–2. These verses hark back to 11–14. The whole section, 31–6, is not so much a continuation of the preceding discourse as a recapitulation of its leading ideas, with some additional points. Such a recapitulation is quite in accord with our author's technique, but there is no ground for insisting that such a recapitulation must follow immediately upon the passage which it recapitulates: it may so follow, or it may not.

We may therefore enquire whether our author, wishing to bring in this recapitulatory passage, may not have selected the little dialogue-*pericope*, iii. 25–30, as an effective introduction for it. It seems possible to suggest a motive for the selection. In the dialogue on rebirth there is one expression which we have not yet considered. We have seen that the evangelist speaks of birth ἐκ πνεύματος, an expression which would convey meaning to any Hellenistic reader who was prepared for the substitution of πνεῦμα for νοῦς. But the expression he actually uses is ἐξ ὕδ·xτος καὶ πνεύματος. The instructed Christian reader would immediately recognize a reference to Baptism, as the sacrament through which the Spirit was given to believers, and by which they were initiated into that new order of life described as the Kingdom of God, which was historically embodied in the Church. For him, the unfamiliar element in the maxim of iii. 5 would be the description of Christian initiation as rebirth: the role of water and Spirit in initiation would be well known. But the intelligent outsider, lacking this clue, might well be puzzled about the association of water with Spirit as the source of eternal life.[1] It is true that water is a widespread symbol of life—and a very natural one in view of the importance of moisture to all organic existence—and that water-rites of various kinds, designed for the promotion of vitality or its restoration after suspension, were not uncommon in the ancient world. But this does not go very far towards explaining the meaning of the expression γεννηθῆναι ἐξ ὕδατος καὶ πνεύματος. The evangelist appears to have

[1] But cf. *C.H.* iv. 4 βάπτισον σεαυτὴν ἡ δυναμένη εἰς τοῦτον τὸν κρατῆρα... ὅσοι μὲν οὖν...ἐβαπτίσαντο τοῦ νοός, οὗτοι μετέσχον τῆς γνώσεως. The expressions are analogous, with the substitution of πνεῦμα for νοῦς.

309

deliberately exercised reserve about the Christian sacraments in writing for a public which included pagans whom he wished to influence towards the Christian faith. So he would not say plainly that initiation into the higher order of life is by way of baptism accompanied by the gift of the Spirit. Indeed, he may well have felt that to put it in that way would risk misleading such readers as he had in view. But he could bring in the idea of Baptism allusively. He has already had much to say about John the Baptist. In particular, he has recorded that John was sent to baptize ἐν ὕδατι (i. 26, 31, 33—the threefold repetition of ἐν ὕδατι is impressive), and that he declared Jesus to be ὁ βαπτίζων ἐν πνεύματι ἁγίῳ, on the ground that he had himself seen the Spirit descending and remaining on Him (i. 33). Thus the association of ideas, ὕδωρ-πνεῦμα, is established, although so far it is an association of contrast. Now in iii. 22, after the discourse which contains the saying about birth from water and Spirit, we are told that Jesus was baptizing, and that the fact was reported to John the Baptist, who was simultaneously engaged in baptizing at another place (iii. 26). The implication is that the two are regarded as competing practitioners of the same ritual, viz. baptism in water. But the reader is not to forget that Jesus is ὁ βαπτίζων ἐν πνεύματι ἁγίῳ. The implication is that the water-baptism administered by Jesus (and therefore also the water-baptism of the Church, though this is not brought to the surface) is also baptism ἐν πνεύματι. This is quite intelligible in the context of Johannine thought. The opening of the eyes of the blind by Jesus (partly through an act of 'washing', i.e. baptism) is also spiritual enlightenment (ix. 5–7), and we are to learn that the 'living water' which proceeds from Christ is the Spirit (vii. 38–39). The contrast drawn between Jesus as the baptizer ἐν πνεύματι and John the Baptist is the same contrast, essentially, as that which is in view in the following verses. Jesus is the Messiah, John only His forerunner; Jesus is the bridegroom, John the bridegroom's friend; He must increase, John must decrease; for, finally, Jesus is ὁ ἄνωθεν ἐρχόμενος, ὁ ἐκ τοῦ οὐρανοῦ.[1] And so we come back to the conjunct ideas of the Spirit and of life (rebirth) (34–6). In the sentence οὐ γὰρ ἐκ μέτρου δίδωσιν τὸ πνεῦμα (iii. 34), it is difficult—perhaps impossible—

---

[1] I leave undecided the question whether ὁ ὢν ἐκ τῆς γῆς applies to John the Baptist, in contrast to Christ, who is ἐκ τοῦ οὐρανοῦ. Origen says the heretics took that view, which he rejects (if frag. 49 *ap.* Brooke is rightly attributed to him). But Chrysostom accepted it, *In Joh. Hom.* (Migne), xxx. 1. He may well be right, and in that case the series of contrasts is continued.

to decide whether the subject of the verb is God or Christ.[1] If we take the latter view, then the statement is a repetition of i. 33 οὗτός ἐστιν ὁ βαπτίζων ἐν πνεύματι ἁγίῳ. If we take the former view, the reference is to i. 32 τὸ πνεῦμα καταβαῖνον καὶ μένον ἐπ' αὐτόν,[2] which explains how it is that Christ is equipped to baptize ἐν πνεύματι. In either case, we are led to the thought of Christ both as possessing the Spirit and as baptizing in Spirit, and in consequence mediating eternal life to the believer (iii. 36). We therefore conclude that the evangelist's intention is to link the ideas of ὕδωρ and πνεῦμα through the idea of baptism, and in particular baptism by Jesus (the Church's baptism), in contrast to John's baptism. If that is so, then we see why he has prefaced the recapitulatory passage, iii. 31–6, with the passage which (alone in the gospels) states that Jesus Himself baptized.[3]

It seems best therefore to regard iii. 22–6 as an explanatory appendix to the dialogue with Nicodemus and the discourse which grows out of it, the whole of ch. iii being concerned with the idea of initiation into eternal life (or rebirth), in conjunction with a rich complex of ideas which are required for its proper understanding.

(iv) The second discourse takes the form of a highly wrought dramatic dialogue, with an appropriate narrative setting. The principal interlocutor is a Samaritan woman whom Jesus meets at Jacob's well, but the disciples also take part, and at the end a body of Samaritans appears as chorus and makes a final comment.

The main dialogue runs from iv. 7 to 27. It falls into two parts, dividing at verse 15. The theme of 7–15 is ὕδωρ ζῶν, an expression which, with characteristic Johannine irony, at its first introduction appears to bear no more than its common meaning of 'running water', but turns out in verse 14 to mean the water of eternal life. Water has already served as a symbol. In the story of Cana it stands for the lower order of life which

---

[1] The *Textus Receptus*, inserting ὁ θεός, represents the dominant exegetical tradition; but Christ is taken as subject in a note from the *Catenae* printed as a fragment of Origen (no. 48) in Brooke's edition (vol. II, p. 264), and in a note attributed to Ammonius in Cramer's *Catena Patrum* (vol. II, p. 213).

[2] This would harmonize with the citation from the Gospel according to the Hebrews *ap.* Jerome, *In Jes.* XI. 2: cum ascendisset Dominus de aqua, descendit fons omnis spiritus sancti et requievit super eum.

[3] The statement is repeated in iv. 1, but immediately corrected in iv. 2, in a parenthesis which ruins the sentence, and perhaps has a better claim to be regarded as an 'editorial note' by a 'redactor' than anything else in the gospel except the colophon, xxi. 24–5.

Christ changes into the wine of life eternal. In iii. 5 it is associated with πνεῦμα as the source of the higher life. I have suggested that there is an implicit contrast between the mere water of John's baptism and the water of Christ's baptism which is also πνεῦμα. In the present passage there is an explicit contrast between two kinds of water: there is on the one hand the water of Jacob's well of which the patriarch and his sons (i.e. the Israelite nation) drank,[1] the water which in any case satisfies only temporarily; and on the other hand the 'water which keeps springing up to life eternal'. The former kind of water is clearly identical with the water of the Jews' καθαρισμός which was in the water-pots of Cana, and about which there was an inconclusive controversy between a Jew and disciples of the Baptist (iii. 25). In rabbinic tradition water was a frequent symbol of the Torah, as cleansing, as satisfying thirst, and as promoting life. It appears that the evangelist has taken up this symbol and turned it to depreciation of the ordinances of Judaism as commonly accepted in his time. The Torah is indeed water, but it is water belonging to the lower order of existence: it is not water of eternal life.

While in the Old Testament water has almost invariably honourable associations, in Hellenistic thought, being one of the denser elements, it tends to be associated with τὰ κάτω, at any rate in writers with any philosophical bias, however tenuous. Philo is in this point generally Hellenistic. But there are places where his dependence on the Old Testament leads him to find in water a symbol of higher realities. Thus in *De Post.* 127 sqq. he comments on Gen. ii. 6 πηγὴ δὲ ἀνέβαινεν ἐκ τῆς γῆς καὶ ἐπότιζε πᾶν τὸ πρόσωπον τῆς γῆς. 'Thus', he says, 'the Logos[2] of God waters the virtues, for it is the beginning and fountain of noble deeds.' Again, in *Leg. All.* II. 86, commenting on Deut. viii. 15, 16 he observes that the ἀκρότομος πέτρα of that passage is 'the Wisdom of God, from which He waters God-loving souls'.

With this complex background in view, it is not difficult to see how the evangelist could find in water-symbolism an effective illustration of

---

[1] Not only Jacob and his sons, but, the evangelist adds, their dumb cattle too. This water belongs to the material order of creation and to the animal life of man. Odeberg, *ad loc.* pp. 163–8, cites a number of passages from Gnostic and Mandaean literature drawing a contrast between the two kinds of water, sometimes identified with the waters above and below the firmament in Gen. i. 7; but these passages are probably all post-Johannine, and indeed, as he points out, some of them at least evidently depend in the last instance on our present passage.

[2] Λόγος here may be said to lean towards its Hebraic sense of 'word', but in Philo its Hellenistic connotation is never absent.

the idea which he expressed succinctly in the Prologue: 'The Torah was given through Moses; grace and truth came through Jesus Christ.' By the symbol of water this discourse is linked with the foregoing. It makes an advance upon it in that while iii. 5–8 speaks of the initiation of the new life, the present passage speaks of its continuance, through the same supply of 'living water' from which men are reborn into the realm of Spirit—the water which Christ gives.

The interlocutor, however, as usual, fails to understand; for the woman's rejoinder, 'Sir, give me this water, to save me the trouble of coming so far to draw', is evidently intended to indicate a crass inability to penetrate below the surface meaning. The dialogue accordingly takes a fresh turn. It reverts to the symbol through which the theme of the new life was presented in the second of the significant narratives with which the First Episode was introduced—the symbol of the temple cleansed (i.e. renewed, or destroyed and rebuilt). For although the word 'temple' is not used, there is a clear allusion to the Jewish and Samaritan temples, in Jerusalem and on Gerizim (iv. 20–1).

The transition is made in the dialogue of verses 16–18. On the level of dramatic narrative, the Samaritan woman is led to disclose the loose life she is living. Without expecting to discover exact allegorical equivalents for her five husbands and her paramour, we can hardly be wrong in recognizing (with most commentators) an allusion to the popular syncretistic cults of Samaria, combining the worship of the God of Israel with pagan elements in a way which the prophets had stigmatized as 'adulterous'. The readers, however, whom the evangelist had in mind would not be specially interested in such local cults, and we must probably suppose him to have something of wider interest in mind. It was not in Samaria alone that a mixture of Jewish tradition with extraneous elements produced strange religious systems which competed for converts in the Hellenistic world.[1] The so-called 'Gnostic' heresies described by Irenaeus and Hippolytus provide evidence of their existence, and also show how such syncretistic systems might be used as a basis for aberrant forms of Christian propaganda. Even before Marcion forced the whole Christian world to face the question in principle, it must have been a matter of controversy whether Christian missionaries were obliged to take their stand upon the Old Testament and the 'pure' Jewish tradition, or whether they might not properly make use of syncretistic modes of religious thought in their approach to the Hellenistic public. It may well be that

[1] Though Samaria was regarded as fertile in such cults.

such early controversies lie behind our author's insistence that as between 'pure' or traditional Judaism and any such form of syncretism as might be typified by Samaritan cults, the preacher of Christianity need be in no doubt, 'for salvation is derived from the Jews'—the approach to Christianity is through Judaism. If it is the forerunners of second-century 'Gnostic' heresies whom he has in mind, his comment is apt: ὑμεῖς προσκυνεῖτε ὃ οὐκ οἴδατε.[1]

But this is not the main point. Whether it is the temple at Jerusalem or the temple on Gerizim, whether pure traditional Judaism or the 'adulterated' version offered by the Samaritan cults, all such ways of religion belong to τὰ κάτω; they are in the sphere of σάρξ. In contrast, Christ inaugurates worship ἐν πνεύματι, or, in terms more familiar to Hellenistic readers, worship ἐν ἀληθείᾳ, that is, on the plane of full reality. Religion on the level of the temple-cults of Jerusalem and Gerizim (and all analogous cults) operates with the sensible and the material, τὰ αἰσθητά. It is this kind of religion that has been symbolized by the water 'of the Jews' purifying', and by the water of Jacob's well, as well as by the temple that needs to be cleansed (i.e. renewed, or destroyed and rebuilt). In Christ a new kind of religion is inaugurated, symbolized by the wine of Cana, the 'living water' which He gives, and the new temple which He will raise up. It is now defined in explicit terms: it is the worship of God ἐν πνεύματι (as a Hellenistic writer might have said ἐν νῷ), and it is ἐν ἀληθείᾳ, that is, it operates with that which is ultimately real.[2] Such worship is clearly the correlate of birth ἐκ πνεύματος, whereby a man rises from the sphere of σάρξ to that of πνεῦμα. In his regenerate condition, he receives, on the one hand, perennial supplies of spiritual life ('living water') from God, and, on the other hand, renders to God the worship of a spiritual being, due to Him who is πνεῦμα.[3] The main dialogue then ends with an express avowal by Christ that He is the 'Messiah'—with the implication that 'Messiah' means not only the messenger who will 'announce' certain religious truths (iv. 25), but the inaugurator of a new

[1] The supreme deity of the Valentinians is the unknowable Βυθός, of the Basilidians, the Non-existent. The purport of this verse is not unlike that of Acts xvii. 23.

[2] The grammatical form, in which a single preposition governs both substantives, indicates that πνεῦμα καὶ ἀλήθεια forms a single concept.

[3] At this point, the Hellenistic reader would understand that Christianity is a λογικὴ or νοητὴ θρησκεία, opposed to the material rites of popular paganism; and he might be quite open to such a message. How different, in the end, Johannine Christianity is from any mere 'spiritualizing' of religion he must wait to see. Conceivably, he might have taken the hint that the new temple for spiritual worship is nevertheless a σῶμα (ii. 21).

era in religion, of which it may be said, not only ἔρχεται ὥρα (iv. 21), but ἔρχεται ὥρα καὶ νῦν ἐστίν (iv. 23). This introduces what is to be the central theme of the dialogue which forms the conclusion of the whole scene (iv. 27–42).

This concluding dialogue exhibits in a rudimentary form a dramatic technique which the evangelist has used more elaborately elsewhere.[1] The action takes place on two stages, a front stage and a back stage, as we might put it. The return of the disciples and the departure of the woman (27–8a) divide the *dramatis personae* into two groups. On the front stage Jesus converses with His disciples (31–8). Meanwhile (ἐν τῷ μεταξύ) on the back stage the woman converses with her fellow-townsmen and induces them to accompany her to the place where she left Jesus (28b–30, 39). The two groups then converge, and move together to the town, where Jesus makes a short stay (40). The scene is thus at an end, but a final sentence uttered by the Samaritans (41–2), like the concluding chorus of a Greek play, sums up the meaning of the whole.

The conversation between the woman and the Samaritans (iv. 28–30, 39) moves within the limits of popular messianic concepts. She goes to the town with the idea that Jesus may indeed be the Messiah, as He has claimed to be. The Messiah she takes to be the One who will announce the whole truth in matters of religion—for such is the implication, in the context, of the words, ἀναγγελεῖ ἡμῖν ἅπαντα. Of Jesus she can attest that He has shown complete knowledge of her own past: a knowledge which is at least the mark of a prophet (iv. 19), and may be more. Upon such grounds many of the Samaritans accept the claims of Jesus. But meanwhile (and here we have an example of the Johannine irony) the conversation of Jesus with His disciples has indicated how much more than that the Messiahship of Jesus means.

The transition from the conversation of Jesus with the woman to His conversation with the disciples is effected (with complete dramatic verisimilitude) through the idea of food and the satisfaction of hunger (iv. 31)—the counterpart of water and the satisfaction of thirst. Jesus, the giver of living water, has no need that anyone should give Him food. Yet He is Himself dependent—on God who sent Him. It is by doing the will of God that He lives. This theme, of the dependence of Christ on the Father, introduced here so delicately, is elaborated in the discourse which follows in ch. v, and briefly summarized in vi. 57 ἀπέστειλέν με ὁ ζῶν πατήρ, κἀγὼ ζῶ διὰ τὸν πατέρα. But the conclusion of the sentence

[1] See pp. 347–8.

in iv. 35 is of special significance. It is a part of the will of God, by which Christ lives, that He shall bring His work to *completion*—ἵνα. . .τελειώσω αὐτοῦ τὸ ἔργον. That the word τελειοῦν is intended to carry full weight is shown by its recurrence in xvii. 4, where Jesus, on the eve of His departure, solemnly pronounces, ἐγώ σε ἐδόξασα ἐπὶ τῆς γῆς, τὸ ἔργον τελειώσας ὃ δέδωκάς μοι ἵνα ποιήσω. His mission is, not only to teach or to 'announce', but to complete the work of man's salvation; that is, in terms of the various parts of this episode, to effect the transformation of water into wine, to raise the new temple, to bring (through His descent and ascent) the possibility of birth ἐκ πνεύματος, to give living water which springs up to life eternal—in a word, to open to mankind a truly spiritual or divine life. That God in His own good time would bring about this great transformation of human life was the prophetic hope of Judaism. But—'You say, Four months from sowing to harvest: the time is not yet.' To which Jesus replies, 'The fields are already white for reaping. Already the reaper is taking his pay. He is gathering the crop— for life eternal' (iv. 35).

The passage is the counterpart of that place in the Synoptic Gospels (Matt. ix. 35–x. 1, Luke x. 1–2) where Jesus, sending out His disciples, assures them, ὁ θερισμὸς πολύς. It states the ultimacy, the finality, of the appearance and work of Christ as unequivocally as does that other Synoptic saying: ἔφθασεν ἐφ' ὑμᾶς ἡ βασιλεία τοῦ θεοῦ (Matt. xii. 28, Luke xi. 20).

The whole passage, therefore, from ii. 1 to iv. 42 (if we may pause a moment for retrospect) constitutes a compact episode in the presentation of the ministry of Jesus Christ. The dominant idea—that of the inaugura- tion of a new order of life for mankind through the incarnation of the Logos—is held up in various lights, turned round to exhibit different aspects, and linked with other ideas belonging to the Johannine theology in such a way that the entire episode may be said to contain the whole Gospel, for those who have sufficient command of the material. At the same time, for the less instructed outside public to which in part—perhaps primarily—the work is addressed, the argument proceeds step by step, from the known to the unknown, to build up one stage in the complex structure of Johannine Christianity. It presupposes no indispensable ideas beyond those which a serious and intelligent Hellenistic reader might fairly be expected to entertain, with the Prologue as his guide to the resetting of these ideas. There are allusions which must for the present remain cryptic for such a reader, and they warn him that he must persevere with his reading; but a full understanding of them is not essential to an understanding of the present stage of argument, which emerges perspicuous and definite.

The composition is carefully balanced and articulated. The details (even some which at first sight may seem casual) are seen by a careful reader to be subservient to the total impression. The two narratives are realistic and dramatic; rooted in normal human life, in Galilee and Jerusalem, with its incidents of marriage and merry-making, public worship and trade; and they fit naturally into the picture of the historical ministry of Jesus as it was handed down in tradition and presupposed in every presentation of the Gospel. This gives content to the term σάρξ in the fundamental proposition, ὁ λόγος σὰρξ ἐγένετο. At the same time the appended discourses point to the element of λόγος, the eternal reality embodied in the temporal events. These discourses again have dramatic propriety. In the first, the interlocutor is a Jew and a Rabbi, standing at the centre of the older dispensation of divine truth; in the second, a Samaritan woman, standing on the periphery, and apt to represent the wider gentile world; for with John, as with Paul, the Gospel is 'to the Jew first and also to the Greek'. In chs. iii and iv alike, the main discourse, or dialogue, has a supplement or appendix, bringing out a point implied in the main discourse, but otherwise left obscure. The discourses are linked throughout by unobtrusive cross-references, especially through the symbolism employed. The last discourse is linked in its first part with the first narrative (through the idea of 'water' which needs to be replaced either by 'wine' or by 'living water'), and in its second part with the second narrative (through its reference to the worship of God in the temple). The final utterance, 'This is indeed the Saviour of the world', fittingly gathers up, not only the teaching of the second discourse, but that of the entire episode; for the precise content of the somewhat vague (and widely used) title σωτήρ is to be understood from all that has been laid before the reader in these chapters.

Second Episode. The Life-giving Word (iv. 46–v. 47)

The Second Episode, iv. 46–v. 47, consists of two narratives and one discourse. The narratives are both stories of healing, such as bulk largely in the Synoptic Gospels, but are sparingly introduced in the Fourth Gospel. In fact, there is in this gospel only one healing-story outside the present episode (not to reckon the Raising of Lazarus), namely, that of the healing of the Blind Man at Siloam in ch. ix. As we shall see,[1] that narrative owes its place in the Book of Signs to its particular character— it is the healing of *blindness* (i.e. the giving of light for darkness). We may therefore ask, what particular character attaches to the narratives of the Nobleman's Son and the Impotent Man at Bethesda, and accounts for their position?

The first is an account of the recovery of a patient who was actually at the point of death (iv. 47, 49); and the recovery is effected by the mere word of Jesus, even at a distance. The word itself is significant: it is thrice repeated: ὁ υἱός σου ζῇ (iv. 50, 51, 53—the second time παῖς replaces υἱός with no difference of meaning).

The second narrative is about a man who had spent more than half a lifetime in such a devitalized condition that he could not even make use of means of healing which lay within his reach. He too is restored by the word of Jesus; more precisely, perhaps, by the word and by obedience to the word, since it is only in obeying the command, ἔγειρε, ἆρον τὸν κράβαττόν σου, καὶ περιπάτει, that the healing becomes effective.

We may say, therefore, that both narratives tell how the word of Christ gave life to those who were as good as dead, either in the sense of being at the point of death or in the sense of living chronically in a state of suspended vitality. In each case the life-giving Word is the pivot of the story.

If we now turn to the discourse (v. 19 sqq.) we find that its dominant theme is enunciated in the words, ὁ υἱὸς οὓς θέλει ζωοποιεῖ (v. 21). As the discourse proceeds we learn that this work of ζωοποίησις becomes effective through the hearing of the word (v. 24). It is the same idea that is illustrated in the two narratives, which we may therefore properly describe as σημεῖα of the life-giving Word. Primarily, it is the word which Christ speaks; but the evangelist does not intend his readers to forget that Christ is Himself the Word, in whom is life (i. 4). 'Christ was the Word and spake it' is a maxim true to the intention of this evangelist.

[1] See p. 357.

The entire passage, therefore, iv. 46–v. 47, forms a single complete episode. We may now examine it somewhat more closely.

(i) The first narrative in the Second Episode, that of the healing of the Nobleman's Son, is linked with the First Episode by the reference to Cana of Galilee, which is emphatically identified as the place ὅπου ἐποίησεν τὸ ὕδωρ οἶνον. The evangelist clearly holds it significant that the distressed father meets Jesus on the very ground where He had 'manifested His glory' in transforming power, lifting human life to a new level. It is the same power which is once again manifested in restoring the dying boy to life. We may note a progression in thought from the one incident to the other. In ch. ii, the work of Christ is represented as the simple enhancement of life (water becomes wine). In ch. iv it is the rescue of life from the immediate threat of death and destruction.[1] The progression reaches its culmination, as we shall see, in ch. xi, where life is actually victorious over death, in the raising of Lazarus.

(ii) The second narrative is linked with the preceding episode by the recurrence of the symbol of water. We have previously had the water of Jewish purifications, and the water of Jacob's well, as symbols of the ineffective ordinances of religion on the level of mere σάρξ, as opposed to religion ἐν πνεύματι καὶ ἀληθείᾳ. In the Bethesda narrative we have, once again, water which offers healing (or newness of life), but has not been effective to heal a cripple of thirty-eight years' standing. In the light of what has gone before, we should think of the 'law given through Moses' (or any religious system on that level). Over against it is set the life-giving word of Christ. It may not be illegitimate to press the symbolism a little further. There lies the healing water, but the cripple remains unhealed: so the Torah promised life to men, but the Gospel tradition knew of 'publicans and sinners' for whom it did nothing: the sick who needed a physician (Mark ii. 16–17). Of them the cripple of Bethesda may serve as representative. But how, it may be said, could the Torah, beneficent as it was, benefit those who refused to make use of its means of grace? The man might have been healed long ago, perhaps, if he had stepped down into the pool. Precisely; and that is why the

---

[1] This is substantially the view of Origen, *Comm. in Joann.* XIII. 57 (56) p. 271, where the δύο ἐπιδημίαι ἐν Κανᾷ are discussed, the first visit bringing εὐφροσύνη, the second πᾶσαν τὴν καταλειπομένην ἀσθένειαν καὶ τὸ πρὸς θάνατον κινδυνῶδες περιαιροῦσα.

first word of Jesus is, '*Have you the will* to become a healthy man?' The reply is a feeble excuse. The man has not the will. The law might show the way of life; it was powerless to create the will to live. The will to live, together with the power to live, is given in the word of Christ. We have one more exemplification of the maxim, ὁ νόμος διὰ Μωϋσέως, ἡ χάρις καὶ ἡ ἀλήθεια διὰ 'Ιησοῦ Χριστοῦ.

(iii) The transition from the narrative of the healing at Bethesda to the discourse which follows is made by way of a dialogue which arises with dramatic propriety out of the situation. At the close of the narrative we learn (v. 9b) that the healing took place on a Sabbath, and this provoked criticism from 'the Jews'. The motive is one which is prominent in the Synoptic Gospels, and was certainly deeply rooted in the tradition. John however has given it a new turn. Jesus claims that in healing (i.e. giving life) on the Sabbath He is doing what God is always doing (ὁ πατήρ μου ἕως ἄρτι ἐργάζεται, κἀγὼ ἐργάζομαι, v. 17). This puts the controversy at once on the highest theological level. The *apologia* of Jesus falls into two parts, intimately related. We may put the division at v. 30.

(*a*) The first, and main, part of the discourse, v. 19–30, elaborates the theme of God's perpetual activity. In order to appreciate the significance of what is said, it will be well to bear in mind that the statement of Gen. ii. 3, that 'God rested from His works on the seventh day', had given rise to debate and speculation in Jewish circles. It is reported that four eminent Rabbis, Gamaliel II, Joshua ben Chananiah, Eliezer ben Azariah, and Aqiba, on a visit to Rome, were challenged on the point whether God observes His own law, with the Sabbath law as instance. The particular solution they offered does not concern us, but it is to be noted that they assumed that God does in fact continue to work, and sought to justify the apparent breach of the command.[1] Any date at which these four Rabbis would be likely to be together would not be far from the date of composition of the Fourth Gospel.[2] But this was certainly not the first time the question had been raised. Philo concerns himself with it, in terms of Hellenistic Judaism. The Greek demand that the Absolute shall be changeless and immobile might well seem to be met

---

[1] S.-B. *ad loc.* citing Exod. Rabb. 30.9. The four Rabbis proved that God carried no burden beyond His own dwelling (=heaven and earth), or to a distance greater than His own stature; His 'work' therefore falls within permissible limits.

[2] All four Rabbis are of the so-called second generation (100–130). S.-B. date the journey to Rome *c.* 95, I do not know on what grounds.

by the statement of the Old Testament that God rested. Thus in *De Cher.*
86–90 he explains the expression σάββατον θεοῦ [1] in the sense that 'God,
being immutable and unchangeable, is by nature unwearying; and that
which has no part in weakness, even though it do all things, will never
cease resting through eternity; and so it is the property of God alone
to rest'. In fact, 'that which in existent things is at rest is one, God'
(τὸ γὰρ ἐν τοῖς οὖσιν ἀναπαυόμενον, εἰ δεῖ τἀληθὲς εἰπεῖν, ἕν ἐστιν, ὁ θεός).
We observe, however, the qualification, κἄν πάντα ποιῇ, which is
necessary in order to allow for another element in the conception of God,
namely that of unwearying *activity*. This was certainly congruent with
the Hebrew conception of the 'living God', and it was also strongly
emphasized in certain strains of Hellenistic teaching.[2] Thus Philo (*op. cit.*)
explains that the divine 'rest' (ἀνάπαυλα) does not mean abstention from
good deeds (ἀπραξία καλῶν), since the Cause of all things is by nature
active (δραστήριον) and never stops doing the most excellent things.
It means 'completely unlaborious activity, without suffering and with
perfect ease' (τὴν ἄνευ κακοπαθείας μετὰ πολλῆς εὐμαρείας ἀπονωτάτην
ἐνέργειαν—which echoes Aristotle's ἐνέργεια ἀκινησίας, *Eth. Nic.* VII. 14.
1154b27). Thus Philo, like the later Rabbis just cited, feels obliged to
qualify the statement of Gen. ii. 3. In *Leg. All.* I. 5–6 he goes so far as
to explain away the statement that God rested on the seventh day. It is
impossible, he says, that this should really be the meaning, 'for God never
ceases creating, but as it is the property of fire to burn and of snow to be
cold, so it is the property of God to create'. In fact (he points out) the
scripture does not say that God rested. The verb is the transitive and active
κατέπαυσεν, not the middle ἐπαύσατο. The meaning is that God caused
inferior creative agencies (or apparently creative agencies, τὰ δοκοῦντα
ποιεῖν) to cease, while He continued to create. A little later, however, he
modifies this position. God, he says, rests (παύεται) from creating mortal
things, when He begins to create divine things (the number 6 symbolizing
finite perfection, the number 7 absolute perfection, *op. cit.* 16). Here
therefore the solution of the problem is sought by distinguishing between
diverse works of God; from some He rests, from others He never rests,
even on the Sabbath. The same general line is followed by a much later
rabbinic ruling. Rabbi Pinchas (*c.* A.D. 360) said in the name of Rabbi
Hoshaya (*c.* 225) 'God rested (on the seventh day) from work on His

[1] An expression which, he says, occurs πολλαχοῦ τῆς νομοθεσίας. In our LXX
texts it does not seem to occur, but it may be said to be implied in τὰ σάββατα
κυρίου (Lev. xxiii. 38) and τὰ σάββατά μου *passim*. The LXX usually has the dative
κυρίῳ, representing the Hebrew שבת ליהוה.   [2] Cf. *C.H.* v. 9, xi. 5, 14, etc.

world, but He did not rest from His work on the wicked and His work on the righteous. He works with both: He shows to these something of their reward, and to those something of their punishment.'[1] In other words, God rested from the work of creation, but not from the moral government of the universe.

It seems clear that our evangelist is following a generally similar line of thought when he isolates for special consideration two aspects of divine activity which are indubitably perpetual, ζωοποιεῖν and κρίνειν, and claims that Christ performs both these 'works'. It might be held that 'judgment' here corresponds with 'His work upon the wicked and His work upon the righteous'. In that case we should have to assume that the argument runs: it is admitted that God perpetually judges His world; but it has been shown (iii. 17–21) that judgment is not a substantive work of God, but an inevitable accompaniment or consequence of His work for the salvation of men. Hence we must conclude that the work of salvation (ζωοποιεῖν), as well as the work of judgment, is part of God's perpetual activity.[2]

Perhaps however we may more readily find an analogy in Philo's doctrine of the two supreme divine 'powers', the δύναμις ποιητική and the δύναμις βασιλική, which represent the primary differentiation of the Logos. This doctrine appears in many parts of the Philonic corpus. The most straightforward statement of it, perhaps, is in the fragments of the *Quaestiones in Exodum*, ad Exod. xxv. 22 'The First of all is He who is elder than the One, the Monad, and the Beginning (ἀρχή). Next is the Logos of the Self-existent, the seminal essence of all beings. And from the divine Logos, as from a fountain, the two powers are separated. The creative power (ἡ ποιητική), by virtue of which the Creator established and ordered all things, is named θεός, and the kingly power (ἡ βασιλική), by virtue of which the Creator rules that which has come into being, is named κύριος.'[3] Of these two powers the cherubim which overshadowed the Ark are symbols (*De Fuga* 100). In *De Cher.* 27 the two appear in slightly different guise as 'goodness'[4] and 'authority': κατὰ τὸν ἕνα

---

[1] S.-B. *ad loc.* citing Gen. Rabb. [11. 10]. The Rabbi goes on to prove from Scripture that the rewarding of the righteous and the punishing of the wicked are properly called 'works' of God.

[2] For ζωοποίησις as divine prerogative in Jewish sources see A. Schlatter, *Der Evangelist Johannes*, p. 148, ad John v. 21.

[3] Harris, *Fragments of Philo Judaeus*, pp. 66–7. Cf. also *De Vit. Mos.* II. 99.

[4] Cf. *De Migr. Abr.* 182, where Philo speaks of the δύναμις καθ' ἣν ἔθηκε καὶ διετάξατο καὶ διεκόσμησε τὰ ὅλα, and adds, αὕτη δὲ κυρίως ἐστὶν ἀγαθότης.

ὄντως ὄντα θεὸν δύο τὰς ἀνωτάτω εἶναι καὶ πρώτας δυνάμεις ἀγαθότητα καὶ ἐξουσίαν. 'By goodness He generated the universe, and by authority He rules (ἄρχειν) that which was generated. The third between them, joining both, is the Logos, for by the Logos God both rules and is good. So the cherubim (at the gate of Paradise) are symbols of rule (ἀρχῆς) and goodness, the two powers, and the fiery sword is the symbol of the Logos.'[1]

Philo, then, operates with the conception of two fundamental 'powers' or attributes of God, which, having regard to the two alternative schemes of nomenclature, we may describe as creative goodness and kingly authority. The former attribute, Philo expressly says, must find continuous exercise, even on the seventh day of rest. He does not, I think, anywhere say explicitly that the attribute of kingly authority must similarly find perpetual exercise, but we may safely assume that he would not have differed from the later rabbinic ruling that God cannot rest for a moment from the moral government of the universe. John similarly speaks of two divine activities, ζωοποιεῖν and κρίνειν. The former is clearly a function of the creative power of God,[2] the latter of the kingly power.[3] The maxim, ὁ πατήρ μου ἕως ἄρτι ἐργάζεται, is specifically true in respect of these two activities: even on the Sabbath, as always, God gives life and judges. The words which follow, κἀγὼ ἐργάζομαι, imply that the life-giving work which Jesus has performed on the Sabbath is an instance of the divine activity of ζωοποίησις, and as such is exempt from the sabbath restrictions.

[1] In *De Fug.* 101, while the two powers are represented by the cherubim, the Logos is represented by no visible shape, being itself the image of God; but its presence is indicated by the words λαλήσω σοι ἄνωθεν τοῦ ἱλαστηρίου ἀνὰ μέσον τῶν δυεῖν χερουβίμ (Exod. xxv. 22). Thus the Logos is like a charioteer (ἡνίοχος), driving his team of 'powers', while ὁ λαλῶν (i.e. the supreme God Himself) is the rider (ἔποχος) who gives orders to the charioteer. Similarly, frag. *ad* Exod. *l.c.* ὑπὲρ δὲ τούτων κατὰ τὸ μέσον φωνὴ καὶ λόγος καὶ ὑπεράνω ὁ λέγων. Observe that λόγος here, as so frequently in Philo, retains its sense of 'word', even where it has full ontological significance. Similarly, in the passage from *De Cher.* above λόγῳ might be rendered, 'by a word'; yet such a rendering would fall short of Philo's total meaning.
[2] If we are to follow Philo's distinction, in *Leg. All.* I. 16, between the creation of θνητά, from which God rests on the seventh day, and of τὰ θεῖα καὶ ἑβδομάδος φύσει οἰκεῖα, from which He never rests, John's ζωοποίησις would clearly fall in the latter category, since he is concerned all through with ζωὴ αἰώνιος, or life on the plane of πνεῦμα and ἀλήθεια.
[3] Cf. *Vit. Mos.* II. 99 ἡ βασιλικὴ (δύναμις) ᾗ τῶν γενομένων ἄρχει καὶ σὺν δίκῃ βεβαίως ἐπικρατεῖ. Δίκη and κρίσις are conjoined, *De Mut.* 106, 110.

In the development of the discourse, however, the sabbath-question is forgotten, and attention is concentrated on the claim that Christ, as Son of God, has both authority and power to exercise the two divine functions of ζωοποίησις and κρίσις. 'As the Father wakens the dead and vitalizes them, so the Son vitalizes whom He will' (v. 21). The work of ζωοποίησις necessarily entails the work of judgment (cf. iii. 17–21), and the Son is vested with authority to judge (v. 27). No one should be surprised that the Son should judge the world, since He is vested with the power of life (v. 28): the ποιητική and the βασιλική δυνάμεις are correlative. Hence, we are to understand the 'sign' of Bethesda (as well as that of the Nobleman's Son) in the sense: 'Whoever hears my word... possesses eternal life and does not come up for judgment, but has passed from death to life' (v. 24).

The present discourse, therefore, advances, at least in explicit statement, beyond anything in the preceding episode. It makes the express claim that Jesus does what God alone can do. Any such claim necessarily raised a problem for monotheism. The Jewish insistence upon a severe monotheism met with a challenge wherever open-minded Jews were in contact with movements in paganism which in many ways were sympathetic, yet remained prone to polytheistic ways of thought. Such paganism could so easily come to terms with Jewish belief in ὁ ὕψιστος, or ὁ ὤν, and yet always keep other deities in reserve, to whom in practice, whatever philosophical explanations or justifications might be alleged, the worship was offered which Jews believed should be offered only to the One God.[1] Hellenistic-Jewish propagandists were inclined to go as far as they could in the way of compromise, sometimes to danger point. Even the conceptions of Wisdom and the Philonic Logos needed to be carefully guarded. It seems likely that in certain quarters the tendency to syncretism had gone further than our surviving sources admit. In reaction, orthodox Rabbinic Judaism became nervously anxious to guard against any suspicion of acknowledging 'two principles', שתי רשויות.[2] The claim here

---

[1] Did any philosophic pagan ever suffer martyrdom for refusing to sacrifice to the gods or the divine emperor?

[2] See Moore, *Judaism*, I, pp. 364–7. The dualism in view seems usually to be either (a) the distinction between the supreme Deity and the Demiurge, or (b) the recognition of an evil power of divine status, after the manner of Zoroastrian dualism. Later, Catholic Christianity was attacked as containing the heresy of 'two powers'. Moore observes that the arguments employed in anti-Christian controversy of the third century 'are in large part the same as are found earlier in discussions of the "two powers" in which both parties were Jews'. Among the earliest mentions of two powers, he observes, are *Siphre* on Deut. xxxii. 29 § 329, and *Mechilta* on Exod. xx. 2.

advanced for Jesus inevitably raises the question, whether it involves a departure from monotheism. If He can exercise the divine functions of ζωοποίησις and κρίσις, does that mean He is a δεύτερος θεός? The title 'Son of God' was in a Hellenistic context dangerously ambiguous.

The Jews are represented as understanding Jesus to claim that God is his ἴδιος πατήρ, i.e. his father in a sense other than that in which any Israelite might speak of Him as 'our Father in heaven'. Not only so, the words, ὁ πατήρ μου ἕως ἄρτι ἐργάζεται κἀγὼ ἐργάζομαι, they allege, imply that Jesus was 'making himself equal to God', ἴσον ἑαυτὸν ποιῶν τῷ θεῷ. The precise meaning and implications of the charge we must now investigate.

In Greek thought the idea of 'equality with God' is a fluctuating one.[1] The epithet ἰσόθεος can be used as a tribute to virtue, but also as little more than a fulsome compliment. It can also carry more serious implications. In the Hellenistic age, when, partly under oriental and Egyptian influences, the latent belief in the 'divinization' of men of eminent power or wisdom revived, it suggested that the person so described was in some sort more than merely human. The θεῖος ἄνθρωπος came to be an established and recognized type. One of the most notorious of them, Apollonius of Tyana, in a letter attributed to him, observes, 'What wonder is it if, while other men consider me equal to God (ἰσόθεον), and some even consider me a god (θεόν), my native place, so far, ignores me?'[2] In some quarters it was held that initiation into the mysteries conferred some kind of divinity, and in the more refined doctrine of the *Hermetica* divinization, or deification, takes place in the mystical vision or 'knowledge' of God. In *C.H.* XI. 20 (cited p. 16) we are told 'unless you make yourself equal to God (ἐὰν μὴ σεαυτὸν ἐξισάσῃς τῷ θεῷ) you cannot apprehend God, for like is known by like'.[3] In the *Poimandres* (see pp. 30–44) initiation into γνῶσις is represented as a process in which the initiate becomes identified with

According to Moore, *Mechilta* is based on the work of R. Ishmael (*c.* 120–130), with much additional material largely from Aqiba and his school, and *Siphre* on Deut. xxxii is basically from the school of Aqiba. It seems therefore that the polemic against the 'two powers' may with great probability be traced to a period not far removed from that of the Fourth Gospel. It may well be earlier.

[1] It is well illustrated by the citations in Wetstein's note *ad loc.*

[2] *Epistles of Apollonius*, xliv, in Philostratus, *Life of Apollonius of Tyana*, ed. Conybeare, 1912, vol. II, p. 436.

[3] The *prima facie* contradiction between the idea of divinization as the consequence and as the condition of 'knowledge' of God is more apparent than real.

the 'essential Man' immanent in us all. This οὐσιώδης ἄνθρωπος is the offspring of God, who in the beginning ἀπεκύησεν ἄνθρωπον ἑαυτῷ ἴσον. As we have seen, this heavenly Man has affinities with the Son of Man of the Fourth Gospel (see pp. 33–6, 43–4, 243–4).

Yet there was another strain in Greek piety, which acknowledged the distance between the human and the divine, and counselled humility.[1] Philo was not entirely without Greek precedent in his firm protests (e.g. *Leg. All.* 1. 49 φίλαυτος δὲ καὶ ἄθεος ὁ νοῦς οἰόμενος ἴσος εἶναι θεῷ).[2] But his main background here is of course the stern monotheism of the prophets. That any being should be 'like' God, or 'equal' to God is for them inconceivable: see for example Is. xl. 25 וְאֶל־מִי תְדַמְּיוּנִי וְאֶשְׁוֶה יֹאמַר קָדוֹשׁ (where Symmachus and Theodotion have ἰσωθήσομαι, Aquila ἐξισωθήσομαι); Ps. lxxxviii (lxxxix). 7 τίς ἐν νεφέλαις ἰσωθήσεται (יַעֲרֹךְ) τῷ κυρίῳ; καὶ τίς ὁμοιωθήσεται (יִדְמֶה, ἐξισάσει Symm.) τῷ κυρίῳ ἐν υἱοῖς θεοῦ; Exod. xv. 11 מִי כָמֹכָה בָּאֵלִים יהוה מִי כָּמֹכָה (LXX τίς ὅμοιός σοι ἐν θεοῖς, κύριε; τίς ὅμοιός σοι; Symm. has ἐξισωθῆναι and ὁμοιωθῆναι).

In the dramatic situation the charge, ἴσον σεαυτὸν ποιῶν τῷ θεῷ, is brought by Jews, and may be supposed to have relation to Jewish ideas.[3] Jesus is accused of the outrageous claim to be 'equal to God', in that his words, ὁ πατήρ μου ἕως ἄρτι ἐργάζεται κἀγὼ ἐργάζομαι, seem to imply collateral action with God in a field where God's competence is exclusive. In a Hellenistic context, this may be taken as tantamount to a claim to divinity in the sense in which a θεῖος ἄνθρωπος, such as Apollonius of Tyana, claimed to be ἰσόθεος or θεός, or in the sense in which the Hermetic initiate, 'making himself equal with God' (ἐξισάζειν), becomes identified with the divine Man whom God procreated ἑαυτῷ ἴσον, and so is θεὸς θεοῦ παῖς. Such would be the ideas which Hellenistic readers of the Gospel would have in mind. While however for a Hellenistic thinker such

---

[1] E.g. *Iliad* v. 440–2, where Apollo warns Diomedes, μηδὲ θεοῖσιν | ἶσ' ἔθελε φρονέειν, ἐπεὶ οὔ ποτε φῦλον ὅμοιον | ἀθανάτων τε θεῶν χαμαὶ ἐρχομένων τ' ἀνθρώπων, and the speech of Agamemnon in Aeschylus's tragedy, in which he protests against the extravagant honours paid to him, ending, λέγω κατ' ἄνδρα μὴ θεὸν σέβειν ἐμέ (*Agam.* 914–25). The strain is also present in those *Hermetica* which emphasize the transcendence of God; see p. 21 above.

[2] The very phrase of the *Iliad* is echoed in II Macc. ix. 12, according to the text of Codex Venetus: μὴ θνητὸν ὄντα ἰσόθεα φρονεῖν, but other MSS. have ὑπερήφανα.

[3] Odeberg *ad loc.* p. 203 says that 'a son who rejects the paternal authority is characterized as also משוה עצמו לאביו, "making himself equal with his father"'. This would fit the present passage admirably, but I have not been able to confirm the quotation.

expressions might imply deification or divinization only in the sense of partaking of the divine nature, or entering into an order of beings, the immortals, already numerous, for a strict Jewish monotheist they would imply that the person making such claims is setting himself up as a rival to the one God; since he is asserting his competence, in and by himself, to perform divine actions. His prototype is the 'Lucifer' who cries, ἀναβήσομαι ἐπάνω τῶν νεφῶν, ἔσομαι ὅμοιος τῷ ὑψίστῳ (Is. xiv. 14). The heresy of the 'two principles' arises; there is a δεύτερος θεός. This interpenetration of two realms of thought complicates the meaning of the passage.

We may perhaps best approach an understanding if we consider what kind of charge is answered in the *apologia* of v. 19–30. It seems clear that it is intended to rule out any suspicion that Christ claims to be a δεύτερος θεός, or a 'second principle' over against the one God. Its conclusion, οὐ δύναμαι ἐγὼ ποιεῖν ἀπ' ἐμαυτοῦ οὐδέν...ὅτι οὐ ζητῶ τὸ θέλημα τὸ ἐμόν, ἀλλὰ τοῦ πέμψαντός με, is a complete answer to the charge of 'making himself equal to God' in that sense.[1] This is the point that is emphasized also in v. 19 οὐ δύναται ὁ υἱὸς ποιεῖν ἀφ' ἑαυτοῦ οὐδέν, and in 26–7 ὥσπερ ὁ πατὴρ ἔχει ζωὴν ἐν ἑαυτῷ οὕτως καὶ τῷ υἱῷ ἔδωκεν ζωὴν ἔχειν ἐν ἑαυτῷ, καὶ ἐξουσίαν ἔδωκεν αὐτῷ κρίσιν ποιεῖν. The sole condition on which the Son exercises divine functions is that He acts in complete unity with the Father, a unity which has the form of unqualified obedience to the Father's will. Given such unity, every act which the Son performs is an act of the Father. The acts of ζωοποίησις and κρίσις of which He gives 'signs' are in the fullest sense acts of God, since in them God's will is fully effective. As this identity of operation is conditioned, on the Son's part, by unqualified obedience, so, on the Father's part, it is based upon His perfect love for the Son. We recall that in iii. 16 the total work of the Son in bringing life and light (and therefore judgment) is rooted in the love of God for the world. (Φιλεῖν here, ἀγαπᾶν in iii. 16, do not differ essentially in meaning, at least as used in this setting.)

Is the *apologia*, then, intended to justify, or to repudiate, the claim to equality with God?[2] It seems we are bound to answer that in the sense

---

[1] So in Philo, *loc. cit.* the Logos is the ἡνίοχος of the world-chariot, but God is the ἔποχος and gives orders. There is a formal similarity; but reflection will suggest the immense difference, all the more striking for the similarity, between Philo's cosmological speculations and the personal realism of the gospel.

[2] There is a somewhat similar formal ambiguity in Phil. ii. 6 οὐχ ἁρπαγμὸν ἡγήσατο τὸ εἶναι ἴσα θεῷ. The process of thought is different, but there as here the concept of equality with God is confronted with Christ's obedience, which wins Him the divine name κύριος.

in which ἴσος τῷ θεῷ or ἰσόθεος might be used by contemporaries, either Jewish or pagan, it is not true that Jesus was 'making Himself equal with God'; for the evangelist certainly does not intend to present Him as an ordinary θεῖος ἄνθρωπος; and equally certainly the Jew would be mistaken in supposing that He is presented as a 'second God', or 'second principle'. On the other hand, it is difficult to deny τὸ ἰσόθεον, in some sense, to one who exercises the supreme divine δυνάμεις. It seems that if the evangelist had been asked whether or not he intended to affirm that Christ was ἴσος τῷ θεῷ, he would have been obliged to reply that ἴσος, whether affirmed or denied, is not a proper term to use in this context.[1] He does not here offer any alternative term, but sets forth with great precision the actual facts, and leaves the reader to reflect upon them.[2] The immense importance of this careful definition of the relations of Father and Son for the whole structure of Johannine thought will emerge as we proceed to subsequent episodes.

(b) The latter part of the discourse (v. 31–47) is taken up with a fresh but related theme, that of μαρτυρία. Jesus has made remarkable claims. Upon what evidence do they rest? The theme has already had a large place in the gospel. Ch. i. 19–49 is in great part a series of μαρτυρίαι, from John the Baptist, Andrew, Philip and Nathanael. The theme was resumed in iii. 25–36,[3] where we started, once again, with the μαρτυρία of the Baptist, but in iii. 31–4 passed to the testimony borne by Christ Himself, who, descending from heaven, sent by God, and speaking the words of God, testifies to what He has seen and heard. To accept this testimony is to affirm the veracity of God Himself (to refuse it, it is

---

[1] Note that ἴσος and ὅμοιος are interchangeable.

[2] He finds a more fitting expression in the formulae (a) ἐγὼ ἐν τῷ πατρὶ καὶ ὁ πατὴρ ἐν ἐμοί, and (b) ἐγὼ καὶ ὁ πατὴρ ἕν ἐσμέν, and the unity of mutual indwelling is expressed in an act whereby the Son dedicates Himself wholly to the Father, xvii. 19–21.

[3] In iii. 11 ἀμὴν ἀμὴν λέγω σοι ὅτι ὃ οἴδαμεν λαλοῦμεν καὶ ὃ ἑωράκαμεν μαρτυροῦμεν καὶ τὴν μαρτυρίαν ἡμῶν οὐ λαμβάνετε, the plural verbs come in strangely. The sentence is almost identical (except for the number of the verbs) with iii. 32 ὃ ἑώρακεν καὶ ἤκουσεν τοῦτο μαρτυρεῖ καὶ τὴν μαρτυρίαν αὐτοῦ οὐδεὶς λαμβάνει. It is at first sight tempting to remove iii. 11 as an editorial comment, framed after iii. 32, the 'we' being the Church or its teachers (cf. xxi. 24 with xix. 35). But this temptation is to be resisted. Ἀμὴν ἀμὴν λέγω ὑμῖν (σοι) is often used by this writer to make the transition from dialogue to monologue, and iii. 11 is best taken as a kind of heading to the series of reflections which follow, which, as we have seen, expand the theme of the dialogue, iii. 1–10. The 'testimony' of iii. 11 is that of Christ, but, as occasionally elsewhere, the evangelist betrays the fact that it is mediated corporately by the Church.

implied, is to deny God's truth). This brief treatment is expanded in the present discourse.

Since the immediate matter at issue is the claim Jesus makes for Himself, He will not here offer His own testimony (though, as we shall learn elsewhere, self-testimony is, in fact, valid in the peculiar circumstances (viii. 14)). The testimony of John the Baptist He will adduce only as an *argumentum ad hominem* to those who set store by the Baptist's work and teaching (33–5). The finally valid testimony is that of God Himself. It is this testimony (it seems) which is referred to in 32, the following verses, with their reference to the Baptist, being parenthetic. The μαρτυρία of God is accessible to men in two ways. First, the works of ζωοποίησις and κρίσις which Christ performs are manifestly divine activities. If they are acknowledged to be real at all, they are acknowledged as 'works of God'; and since they are in fact performed by Jesus, they make His claim self-evident. Secondly, the testimony of God is given through the Scriptures, which, rightly understood, bear witness to Christ (v. 39).[1]

---

[1] The text, and the meaning, of v. 39 are somewhat uncertain. All extant Greek MSS. agree (minor aberrations apart) in reading ἐραυνᾶτε τὰς γραφάς, ὅτι ὑμεῖς δοκεῖτε ἐν αὐταῖς ζωὴν αἰώνιον ἔχειν· καὶ ἐκεῖναί εἰσιν αἱ μαρτυροῦσαι περὶ ἐμοῦ. The Curetonian Syriac reads ܐܘܚܝܐ ... , which would represent ἐραυνᾶτε τὰς γραφὰς ἐν αἷς δοκεῖτε ὑμεῖς ὅτι ζήσεσθε εἰς τὸν αἰῶνα, καὶ αὗται αἱ γραφαὶ περὶ ἐμοῦ μαρτυροῦσι, or the like. Similarly, the O.L. MSS. *a, b* have *in quibus putatis vos vitam habere hae sunt quae de me testificantur*, which might represent ἐν αἷς δοκεῖτε ζωὴν ἔχειν ἐκεῖναί εἰσιν αἱ μαρτυροῦσαι περὶ ἐμοῦ. This slightly attested reading can now claim the support of Pap. Egerton 2. 7–10: see Bell and Skeat, *Fragments of an Unknown Gospel*. There seems no doubt that the MS. should be restored: ἐραυνᾶτε τὰς γραφάς· ἐν αἷς ὑμεῖς δοκεῖτε ζωὴν ἔχειν ἐκεῖναί εἰσιν αἱ μαρτυροῦσαι περὶ ἐμοῦ (the transcription shows a stop between γραφάς and ἐν, but none between ἔχειν and ἐκεῖναι). If (as seems probable) the author of the papyrus was dependent on the Fourth Gospel, then it becomes our earliest witness for the text of this passage, and it agrees in the essential points with a text which may have left its traces in *a* and *b*. Whichever type of text is adopted, the crux remains, whether ἐραυνᾶτε is indicative or imperative. The passage in Pap. Eg. 2 is most naturally understood in the sense 'Search the scriptures; those (scriptures) in which you suppose you have life are the ones which testify about me.' The verb was clearly taken as imperative by the translator of the Old Syriac, and it was so understood by patristic writers who (if their MSS. are to be trusted) read the normal Greek text. (One wonders whether some of them may have been influenced by a text resembling Pap. Eg. 2.) But with this longer text it would seem more natural to understand ἐραυνᾶτε as indicative; for the antithesis intended is ἐραυνᾶτε...καὶ οὐ θέλετε (with καί adversative, as elsewhere in this gospel). Moreover, there are two serious objections to taking ἐραυνᾶτε as imperative: (i) the motive supplied in the ὅτι-clause is not cogent: it is a poor argument to say

This divine testimony, however, in both its forms, often fails of acceptance (cf. iii. 11, 32). Why is this? It is because in order to accept any outward testimony, whether of the works of Christ or of Scripture, there must be a certain prior inward acceptance of God's λόγος. The λόγος given outward expression in the Scriptures, or in the life-giving word of Christ (cf. iv. 50, v. 24), is itself more than any outward expression: for λόγος is never merely a 'word'. It is in the widest sense God's self-disclosure, in word or deed, or in silent operations within the mind of man. The unresponsive Jews have not the λόγος of God dwelling in them, and therefore cannot recognize the 'word'.[1] That they have not the λόγος in them is true in two regards: they do not love God, and they do not seek His glory but their own (v. 41, 44). The test is ethical. Consequently they cannot recognize or accept either the testimony of Scripture or the testimony of the works which God performs in the actions of His Son. Thus we come back to the theme of judgment. Jesus has spoken the life-giving word. The Jews, not having God's λόγος dwelling in them, have failed to recognize it. That is the count against them. Jesus is not their accuser. They are Israelites; they are the heirs of God's ancient revelation; they have His 'word' in the Scriptures. That is sufficient accusation (v. 45–7). It is a special case of the principle that men judge themselves by their attitude to the light they have.

In this discussion of 'Christian evidences' we can hardly be wrong in finding a reflection of the practice of missionary apologetics in the early Church. The importance of John the Baptist in early forms of the *kerygma*, and the place assigned to him in all the gospels, prepare us for the appeal to his testimony as a part of the evidence for the Christian claim. This testimony is certainly more explicit in the Fourth Gospel than in any of the others, but all of them point to its employment in the preaching of the Gospel. Yet the value of this appeal must early have

'Search the scriptures, because you suppose (wrongly) that in them you have eternal life'; and (ii) it would seem unnecessary to urge 'the Jews' (who in this gospel are generally the representatives of Jewish religion in its strictest form) to study the Old Testament. It is to be observed that while the Old Syriac ܘ܂ܣ is unequivocally imperative, it would not be impossible with the reading of Pap. Eg. 2, *a*, *b* to take ἐραυνᾶτε as indicative, if one were permitted to alter the punctuation so as to read, 'You search the scriptures, in which you suppose you have life: it is they that testify about me', though the asyndeton at that point is somewhat harsh. It may seem hazardous to go against so strong an ancient exegetical tradition, yet I cannot but think that the verb is more likely to be indicative, a view which has the support of Cyril of Alexandria, for what it is worth.

[1] Cf. I John v. 10.

declined, as the memory of the work of John receded in time and space.[1] The evangelist, though he recognizes in it a useful *argumentum ad hominem* in certain cases, is not prepared to stake much on it. The real evidence is μείзων τοῦ ᾿Ιωάνου.[2] Again, the appeal to Old Testament prophecy was an important part of Christian missionary apologetic from the earliest time: ἐκεῖναί εἰσιν αἱ μαρτυροῦσαι περὶ ἐμοῦ is a maxim to which every early Christian teacher would have subscribed. Yet once again, the evangelist is aware that its effect is limited. The presuppositions for understanding the Old Testament in a Christian sense are not always present. Though men may read the 'Word of God', they may not have His 'Word' dwelling in them; and without that, the Scriptures will not carry conviction. So he passes somewhat lightly over the biblical *testimonia* (though in their place he values them highly), in order to fix his readers' attention on the primary evidence—the self-evidencing power of the 'Word of God' working in the words and actions of Jesus. The theme of μαρτυρία awaits further elucidation in ch. viii; but it is clear that it has a rightful place in the present argument.

If we now look back over the second episode as a whole, it is not difficult to discern its unity of theme. It follows upon an intricate treatment (in the First Episode) of the idea that Christ initiates men into the life which is real life—ζωή in the pregnant sense which was not unfamiliar to contemporary Hellenistic thought, or ζωὴ αἰώνιος, as our writer prefers to call it. The reader is then confronted with two significant or symbolic narratives which represent Christ as conferring life by His word. It is then explained that these 'signs' are intended with full seriousness to bear the meaning that Christ exercises the functions of Deity, as represented by the δύναμις ποιητική as well as by the δύναμις βασιλική. Nevertheless, He is not to be regarded as a δεύτερος θεός. His exercise of divine functions is conditioned by a deliberately willed subordination of the Son to the will of the Father; a subordination correlative with the eternal love of the Father for

---

[1] The evidence for the continued existence of a 'Baptist' community at Ephesus is of the slenderest, and although 'Baptist' sects of various kinds are attested in and near Palestine, the assumptions (*a*) that they perpetuated the work of John, and (*b*) that they counted seriously as competitors with missionary Christianity— at any rate outside a narrow region—have little direct evidence in their support, in spite of the large amount that has been written about them. See p. 120.

[2] The awkward expression, ἐγὼ δὲ ἔχω τὴν μαρτυρίαν μείзω τοῦ ᾿Ιωάνου, has probably no very recondite meaning. 'The evidence of which we are speaking, and which I possess, goes beyond that of John', is probably pretty close to the sense intended.

His Son; a subordination so complete that it amounts to unity, or even identity, of will and of act. It is in this sense that the familiar expression υἱὸς θεοῦ is to be understood. The intelligent Hellenistic reader would recognize that he was being offered a new and admittedly difficult conception of the manner in which 'life' is mediated to men; new and difficult, and yet having its starting point in intelligible and widely accepted religious ideas. He might well ask, however, for evidence that Christ was to be recognized as mediating eternal life, with these fresh implications. The mere assertion is not enough. Hence the discussion of μαρτυρία. In effect, the evangelist suggests that, given a certain inward aptitude for recognizing the truth, the 'works' of Christ provide direct and luminous evidence of the divine power operative in them, and consequently of His own status as mediator of eternal life. We may, however, ask what, in reality, are the 'works' to which the enquirer is referred. He might well say that since he had not himself witnessed the healing of the boy at Cana or of the cripple at Bethesda, he still lacked actual evidence. But in fact, a serious enquirer in the Hellenistic world, though he might be impressed by such miraculous cures, would not be ready to find in them evidence for such claims as are here advanced. After all, such cures were frequently reported. He might have met thaumaturges of whom he did not think over highly. He could even learn for himself a spell for raising the dead.[1] But in the light of the discourse (especially v. 24) he would readily understand that the 'works' in question concerned, not some casual cure of invalids in Palestine, but the initiation into divine life which was the goal of the contemporary religious quest. He is thus being asked, in effect, to consider the evidence that a new kind of life really was to be found in the Church; and in the end, the evangelist holds that such evidence is forthcoming only if men will 'come to' Christ. But about this much remains yet to be said.

---

[1] It runs: Ὁρκίζω σε, πνεῦμα ἐν ἀέρι φοιτώμενον, εἴσελθε, ἐνπνευμάτωσον, δυνάμωσον, διέγειρον τῇ δυνάμει τοῦ αἰωνίου θεοῦ τόδε σῶμα (ap. Reitzenstein, *Die hellenistischen Religionen* (1920), p. 160). A 'splendid spell for casting out demons' is reprinted from the great Paris Magical Papyrus in Milligan, *Select Greek Papyri*, no. 47.

THIRD EPISODE. BREAD OF LIFE (vi)

The Third Episode occupies the whole of ch. vi. It consists essentially of a single significant narrative and a discourse which draws out the symbolic significance of the narrative. The dominant theme is that of Bread of Life, of which bread distributed by Jesus to the multitude is the symbol.

The whole passage, however, is provided with a continuous narrative framework, carefully composed with attention to dramatic verisimilitude. The introductory sentences, vi. 1–3, bring together motives which belong to the common substance of the Gospel tradition: a journey across the Sea of Galilee, the pressure of the crowd, the repute of Jesus as a healer, His withdrawal to Τὸ Ὄρος with His disciples. It is unnecessary either to attempt to identify the Mountain on a map of Palestine, or to seek for any recondite symbolic meaning. The Mountain is the place where Jesus goes either to teach His disciples (as here) or to secure solitude (as in vi. 15).[1] John does not appear to attach any further significance to it, as Matthew does.[2] Verses 1–3, then, do no more than provide a setting for the narrative, out of familiar traditional material. With verse 4, we arrive at a distinctively Johannine trait: the reference to the festival of Passover.[3] Here we are justified in seeking for something more than the surface meaning. Dramatically, the season is appropriate enough, and there is no reason why as a matter of historical fact the incident to which this passage refers may not have happened about Passover time. But the Christian reader could hardly fail to remember that the Christian Passover was the Eucharist, and it is probable that the evangelist intended at the outset to give a hint of the eucharistic significance of the narrative which follows.

With verse 5 the narrative of the Feeding of the Multitude properly begins. It is told with little substantial variation from the Synoptic versions,[4] either in the dialogue or in the action, though with no great

---

[1] So Mark iii. 13 (the commissioning of the Twelve), vi. 46 (solitude); the nearest to our present passage is Matt. xv. 29.

[2] For Matthew, Τὸ Ὄρος is the place where Jesus gives the New Law (v. 1 sqq.), and where He is enthroned as Sovereign of heaven and earth (xxviii. 16).

[3] The words τὸ πάσχα are present in all Greek MSS. and versions, and the fact that Irenaeus and others ignore them is not sufficient reason for excising them from the text.

[4] It may, however, be more than accidental that whereas in Mark vi. 42–3, viii. 8 the filling of the baskets with surplus fragments is a mere appendage to the main action, emphasizing the abundance of the supply by which the multitude were

degree of verbal similarity. As in the Synoptics, the Feeding of the Multitude is followed by the incident of Jesus walking ἐπὶ τῆς θαλάσσης; but in the Johannine version this incident does not follow immediately. The direct result of the Feeding is the recognition of Jesus by the crowd (as by the Samaritan woman in iv. 19, by some of the visitors to the Feast of Tabernacles in vii. 40, and by the blind man healed in ix. 17) as the coming Prophet. As such, they attempt to make Him king. This provides a motive for the separation of Jesus and His retirement to the Mountain while the disciples row away. The story is more perspicuous, better motivated, and dramatically more effective than the Synoptic version, whether or not it is more historically credible. But while John cares for dramatic propriety, he cares even more for the deeper meaning which he discerns within the ostensible facts, and we may reasonably ask what significance he intended to attach to this sequence of incidents: the Feeding of the Multitude, the attempt at revolution, and the walking on the water. I shall come back to this question.[1]

Meanwhile, we follow the continuity of the narrative. Verses 22–4 provide a procedure by which Jesus is reunited with the multitude, and a stage for the great discourse which is to follow, delivered (as the evangelist notes) in the synagogue at Capernaum (vi. 59). The effects of the discourse are drawn out in the remaining verses of the chapter. Many of the disciples are 'scandalized' and desert: only the Twelve remain, and through Peter as their spokesman confess their faith in Christ, who thereupon forecasts His betrayal by one of them. Here the episode closes. Dramatically, its unity is complete.

We have now to examine its contents more closely. We shall do well to begin with the examination of the discourse, in which the evangelist has provided a clue to the meaning of the whole episode. It takes the form of a sustained dialogue between Jesus and the crowd who, having partaken of the feast of loaves and fishes, have followed Him from the spot where the Feeding took place. The words in which He first addresses them, in verse 26, imply that although they had been witnesses of the 'sign'[2] which Jesus had worked in distributing bread to the multitude,

---

satisfied (ἔφαγον καὶ ἐχορτάσθησαν), in John vi. 12 the satisfaction of hunger is mentioned only in a subordinate clause (ὡς δὲ ἐνεπλήσθησαν), and the gathering of the fragments is a fresh stage, solemnly introduced by a command of the Lord, συναγάγετε τὰ περισσεύοντα κλάσματα, ἵνα μή τι ἀπόληται. John perhaps means to suggest the βρῶσις μένουσα in contrast to the βρῶσις ἀπολλυμένη (vi. 27). I owe this observation to Dr David Daube, in a communication to my Seminar.

[1] See pp. 344–5.   [2] So vi. 14.

yet they saw no further than mere food for the body, which perishes in the using, βρῶσις ἀπολλυμένη. Consequently, although they had not only seen and handled that which Jesus gave, but actually fed upon it, they had not, in the deeper, and true, sense 'seen signs': they had not received βρῶσις μένουσα εἰς ζωὴν αἰώνιον. The language recalls that of the discourse upon living water, where the water which men and cattle drink, only to become thirsty again, is contrasted with water which springs up εἰς ζωὴν αἰώνιον.

The discourse, or dialogue, thus initiated falls into three parts, in which the idea of Bread of Life is developed in three stages.

(i) In the first part, verses 26–34, the idea of the food of eternal life is developed with reference to the manna spoken of in the Old Testament (Ps. lxxvii (lxxviii). 24) as 'bread from heaven'. The dialogue is here based upon well-attested Jewish beliefs, or speculations, about manna. According to the Apocalypse of Baruch (nearly contemporary with the Fourth Gospel), 'it shall come to pass at that self-same time that the treasury of manna shall again descend from on high, and they will eat of it in those years (sc. the period of the temporary messianic kingdom on earth), because these are they who have come to the consummation of time' (II Baruch xxix. 8 Charles). Similarly in the fragment of a Sibylline Oracle cited in Theophilus ad Autolycum, which may be pre-Christian:

> Οἱ δὲ θεὸν τιμῶντες ἀληθινὸν ἀέναόν τε
> ζωὴν κληρονομοῦσι, τὸν αἰῶνος χρόνον αὐτοὶ
> οἰκοῦντες παραδείσου ὅμως ἐριθηλέα κῆπον
> δαινύμενοι γλυκὺν ἄρτον ἀπ' οὐρανοῦ ἀστεροέντος.
>
> (*Oracula Sibyllina*, ed. Geffcken, frag. 3. 46–9.)[1]

In later rabbinic tradition the renewal of the gift of manna becomes a fixed feature of Jewish eschatological expectation.[2] We may therefore take it that the Jews are here represented as demanding that Jesus shall establish His messianic pretensions by the well-recognized token of restoring the gift of manna, the 'bread from heaven', assuming that this is what He meant by βρῶσις μένουσα εἰς ζωὴν αἰώνιον. Jesus in reply

[1] The coincidences between the language of this oracle and that of the Fourth Gospel are striking: ἀληθινός, ζωὴ ἀέναος (for αἰώνιος), ἄρτος ἀπ' οὐρανοῦ.

[2] See the abundant evidence cited in S.-B. *ad loc.*, most of which is much later than the Fourth Gospel; but Baruch and the Sibylline Oracle are sufficient evidence of the belief about the time when this gospel was written. Schlatter, *Der Evangelist Johannes, ad loc.* cites a number of rabbinic passages, and shows how closely the language of our present passage corresponds with the rabbinic Hebrew.

denies that the manna was 'heavenly' bread in any important sense.[1] It came, no doubt, from the sky; but it was not ἄρτος ἀληθινός. Here we are passing from properly Jewish to Hellenistic ways of thought. The bread of which Jesus is speaking is 'real' bread, belonging to that order of existence which has been described (iv. 23) as πνεῦμα καὶ ἀλήθεια. The manna, however miraculous, does not belong to that order of existence, since it perished in the using, or became corrupt if it was not used (Exod. xvi. 15–21): it is, in spite of its miraculous origin, βρῶσις ἀπολλυμένη.

We are therefore to understand the discourse at its present stage as repudiating the crude and quasi-materialistic type of eschatology which was common in some primitive Christian circles no less than in some types of Judaism. The new age which Jesus inaugurates (of which it is said, ἔρχεται ὥρα καὶ νῦν ἐστιν) is not to be defined in terms of crude miracle on the phenomenal level, the plane of σάρξ (for, as we shall be told presently, ἡ σὰρξ οὐκ ὠφελεῖ οὐδέν, vi. 63), but in terms of that order of being which is real and eternal.

There is however another possible line of association of which we should take account. In rabbinic tradition bread is a standing symbol of the Torah.[2] This tradition can be traced back to the time of Eliezer ben Hyrcanus and Joshua ben Chananiah, not far from the date of this gospel. In later authorities the bread which Wisdom offers in Prov. ix. 5 is identified as 'bread of Torah'. I do not find evidence that this identification was in rabbinic exposition extended to the manna, but the equation of manna with σοφία in Philo almost necessarily implies that in some circles it was taken to be a symbol of Torah. The passage in Philo is worth quoting, for a certain resemblance to the language of our present passage. Commenting on the story in Exod. xvi, and in particular on verses 16–18, which speak of the *equal* distribution of the manna, he observes, 'The divine Logos distributes equally to all who will use it the heavenly nourishment of the soul (τὴν οὐράνιον τροφὴν τῆς ψυχῆς), that is, wisdom' (*Quis Rer.* 191).[3] If then we may suppose that our

[1] According to *Joma* 75[b] Bar. (*ap.* S.-B.) R. Aqiba declared, on the basis of Ps. lxxvii (lxxviii). 25, that manna was actually the bread which angels eat. His contemporary, R. Ishmael, repudiated this opinion, on the ground that it is not to be supposed that angelic beings eat bread. This seems to point to debates in rabbinic circles, at a date not far removed from that of the Fourth Gospel, upon the sense in which manna is 'heavenly bread'.

[2] See S.-B. *ad loc.* The discussion between Eliezer and Joshua is from *Genesis Rabba.* S.-B. date it about A.D. 90.

[3] Elsewhere in Philo the manna symbolizes the Logos itself.

evangelist was acquainted with a school of thought for which the manna was a symbol of the Torah, as the expression of divine wisdom, then we should recognize in this passage another exemplification of the maxim, ὁ νόμος διὰ Μωϋσέως, ἡ χάρις καὶ ἡ ἀλήθεια διὰ 'Ιησοῦ Χριστοῦ. The argument would then run: Moses did indeed give the Torah, of which manna is the symbol; but the 'bread of Torah' is no more the knowledge of God which is life eternal than the manna is ἄρτος ἀληθινός; so Moses did not, in the true sense, give ἄρτος ἀπ' οὐρανοῦ, which, as the Scripture itself says, is God's own gift, and which is given through Christ.

The people are not supposed to understand what is meant. Their request, Κύριε πάντοτε δὸς ἡμῖν τὸν ἄρτον τοῦτον, goes no further than the Samaritan woman's Κύριε δός μοι τοῦτο τὸ ὕδωρ. Indeed, thus far the discourse on Bread of Life is closely parallel to the discourse on Living Water.

(ii) With verse 35 the discourse takes a fresh turn, and advances beyond anything that has previously been said. To look back for a moment, the words of verse 33 have the kind of oracular ambiguity which this evangelist loves. It is possible to read the words ὁ καταβαίνων adjectivally, with the substantive ἄρτος supplied from the context.[1] The sense would then be, 'The bread of God is ἄρτος ἀπ' οὐρανοῦ in the sense that it descends from heaven and gives (eternal) life to the world.' But for the attentive reader the phrase ὁ καταβαίνων recalls at once ὁ ἐκ τοῦ οὐρανοῦ καταβάς of iii. 13, and it would be equally possible to construe it after the same manner, substantivally, in the sense 'The bread of God is He who descends from heaven and gives life to the world'—and this, as we know from iii. 13, is the Son of Man, the only one who has in his own right passage both ways across the frontiers of τὰ ἄνω and τὰ κάτω. In verse 35 the ambiguity is cleared up. Jesus expressly claims to be ὁ καταβαίνων ἐκ τοῦ οὐρανοῦ, and, therefore, Himself the Bread of Life. His function as life-giver is then explained in a passage which reads like a brief recapitulation of the great discourse on ζωοποίησις in ch. v. It is grounded in the will of God and in Christ's own obedience to it. By the will of God, he who 'sees' Christ[2] possesses eternal life here and now

---

[1] This is no doubt the construction primarily intended, cf. vi. 41 ἐγώ εἰμι ὁ ἄρτος ὁ καταβάς. Yet it remains true that ὁ καταβαίνων (καταβάς) is a concept complete in itself.

[2] In the sense otherwise expressed by θεάσασθαι τὴν δόξαν αὐτοῦ, i. 14, as distinct from the ineffectual 'seeing' of vi. 36.

(cf. v. 24), and will be raised at the Last Day (cf. v. 28–9). This is sufficient to recall to the reader's mind the whole elaborate exposition of ch. v, and the argument moves to another point.

Jesus has been described as ὁ καταβαίνων ἐκ τοῦ οὐρανοῦ, and the description is now repeated: ἐγώ εἰμι ὁ ἄρτος ὁ ἐκ τοῦ οὐρανοῦ καταβάς. But this raises a difficulty. Jesus is a man of known origin and parentage: how can it be said that He descended from heaven? There is no direct answer: the question is treated in much the same way as the problem of μαρτυρία in the latter part of the discourse in ch. v. As we were told there that the evidence for the claims of Jesus is convincing only to those who have the divine Word dwelling in them (v. 38), so here we are told that it is only those who are (in the words of scripture) διδακτοὶ θεοῦ, those whom God 'draws' to Christ and 'gives' to Him, who apprehend what it means that He descended from heaven. Here as in v. 40 to 'come to' Christ is the necessary condition for understanding what He is. One implication however of the 'descent from heaven' may be hinted at: He who comes from God possesses uniquely the vision of God (vi. 46), which, it is agreed, confers eternal life; and that is why it can be said that he who 'sees' Christ has eternal life (vi. 40). Descent from heaven means, among other things, the mediation of the vision of God to a world in darkness.

This matter briefly dismissed, the discourse comes back to the main theme: Christ as the Bread of Life. The contrast is now made explicit. Manna is no food of eternal life: those who ate it died. Those who eat the Bread which is Christ never die. He is not only the Giver of βρῶσις μένουσα εἰς ζωὴν αἰώνιον: He is Himself the Bread. To this point we are brought at verse 50.

(iii) The third part of the discourse begins at verse 51 with a reiteration of the statement, ἐγώ εἰμι ὁ ἄρτος ὁ ζῶν ὁ ἐκ τοῦ οὐρανοῦ καταβάς, and proceeds to draw out its logical consequences. If Christ is both Bread and the Giver of bread, then what He gives is Himself—His flesh and blood. The question, 'How can this man give us his flesh to eat?' receives no direct answer, any more than did Nicodemus's question, 'How can a man be born again?' The instructed Christian reader cannot miss the reference to the sacrament of the Eucharist. Indeed, the Johannine expressions, ἐγώ εἰμι ὁ ἄρτος τῆς ζωῆς...ὁ ἄρτος ὃν ἐγώ δώσω ἡ σάρξ μού ἐστιν ὑπὲρ τῆς τοῦ κόσμου ζωῆς, amount to an expanded transcription of the 'words of institution', τοῦτό μού ἐστιν τὸ σῶμα τὸ ὑπὲρ ὑμῶν, as we have them in I Cor. xi. 24 (written at Ephesus), and John's ultimate answer to the question 'How?' would undoubtedly have been given in sacramental terms. But the non-Christian religiously minded public to whom this work is in large part addressed could not be expected to have this clue.[1] Like other challenging statements in this gospel, the oracular saying about 'eating the flesh' is intended to be held in suspense in the mind, in expectation of further enlightenment. But while the 'how' is left in question, the essential meaning of 'eating the flesh and drinking the blood' of the Son of Man is stated in terms less foreign to the public in view: it means union with Christ by mutual indwelling (vi. 56).[2] This idea is not again referred to in the Book of Signs, but it becomes of outstanding importance in the Farewell Discourses.[3]

Yet the expression δοῦναι τὴν σάρκα,[4] however figuratively it is taken, can hardly fail to suggest the idea of death. And the expression πίνειν τὸ αἷμα, again, can hardly fail to suggest shed blood, and therefore violent death.[5] In such veiled terms the evangelist suggests that it is through death that Christ becomes bread of life to the world, just as in ii. 20 he hinted that it is through the destruction and resuscitation of the σῶμα of Christ that the new kind of life is inaugurated. Such hints await further explication.

In the second and third parts, then, of this discourse we have an important advance on what has gone before. In vi. 27–34 Christ is the Giver of bread, as in iv. 10–15 He is the Giver of water. Such a description could, at a pinch, be kept within the limits of Jewish eschatological beliefs which conceived the Messiah as a second Moses or, shall we say, as

[1] The importance which has often been given in this connection to the practice of theophagy in certain cults is probably exaggerated. The extent to which the practice, and the ideas associated with it, were really alive in the Hellenistic world of the first and second centuries A.D. is not altogether clear. In any case, the Hellenistic background of Johannine thought seems to lie, not in crude popular paganism, but in circles represented by Philo, the *Hermetica*, and the common elements of the great 'Gnostic' systems, which do, no doubt, borrow and 'spiritualize' some conceptions associated with 'mystery' cults; but the conception of theophagy is not among them. At most, it seems, we may say that theophagy belongs to a deep stratum of primitive thought and practice which, lying submerged in our minds, generates a natural and more or less universal symbolism; and such symbolism is capable of being re-vivified upon a higher level.

[2] See p. 195.　　　　　　[3] See pp. 411–12, 419–20.

[4] Δοῦναι τὴν ψυχήν is commoner for the idea of voluntary death, but παραδοῦναι τὸ σῶμα occurs in I Cor. xiii. 3. Expressions like 'to eat up his flesh' (Ps. xxvi. 2), 'to give his flesh to the birds and beasts' (I Sam. xvii. 44, Ezek. xxxii. 4–6, Ps. lxxviii. 2) indicate the range of association of ideas.

[5] Cf. Wetstein *ad* John vi. 53 Ubi sanguinis a carne separati fit mentio, violenta morte mortuus intelligitur.

a Moses-like figure sublimated or 'etherialized'; for Moses gave the people both water from the rock and 'bread from heaven'. But if Christ is Himself the food and drink of eternal life, we are well beyond merely messianic categories. It is God alone of whom it can properly be said that through union with Him (mutual indwelling) man enjoys eternal life (vi. 53, 56). Here therefore, as unequivocally as in v. 17 sqq., specifically divine functions and prerogatives are ascribed to Christ. We see therefore how important it is for our author's argument that the discourse in ch. v should precede the present discourse. For in v. 17–30 it is established once for all that in ascribing to Christ divine functions and prerogatives the writer never intends to present Him as a δεύτερος θεός, an independent source of supernatural life, or to infringe monotheism by introducing a 'second principle' (as the Rabbis said). It is by virtue of an unbroken identity of will and purpose, resting upon unqualified dependence of the Son on the Father, that Christ 'works the works of God'. This, as we have seen, was set forth clearly and at length in ch. v. The argument is presupposed here, and it is briefly and allusively re-capitulated in vi. 37–40. Finally, after the bold statement that union with Christ by mutual indwelling is eternal life, the author adds the words, 'As the living Father sent me, and *I live because of the Father*, so he who feeds on me will live because of me.' With that precise and emphatic statement of the role of Christ as Life-giver the discourse closes.

It follows that the proposal to re-arrange the work at this point, and to make ch. vi precede ch. v, a proposal which has been widely accepted by recent writers, is less convincing on consideration than it is attractive at first sight. It is of course true that ch. v leaves Jesus in Jerusalem, and it is not easy to start from Jerusalem across the Sea of Galilee; whereas it would be at least somewhat easier to start such a journey from Cana in central Galilee, where Jesus was left at the end of ch. iv.[1] But such topographical considerations are of less moment than the fact that the existing arrangement of chapters corresponds to the movement of thought: ch. vi presupposes the position established in ch. v, and makes a definite advance upon it.

With verse 59 the discourse reaches its formal conclusion. The remainder of the chapter, vi. 60–71, is of the nature of an appendix or epilogue, comparable with iii. 22–36, iv. 31–42. Like those passages, it consists

[1] But only as it would be somewhat easier to start a journey across the Channel from Oxford than from Birmingham.

340

partly of narrative and partly of dialogue (with editorial comments of the evangelist in verses 64, 71), and contains further reflections elucidating the main theme.

The characteristic feature of the appendix is the reappearance of the idea of πνεῦμα in verse 63. In ch. iii we learned that the realm of τὰ ἄνω is the sphere of πνεῦμα, and that rebirth into the eternal life of the higher realm is birth ἐκ πνεύματος. In ch. iv we learned that God Himself is πνεῦμα, and that the new approach to God opened up by Christ is worship ἐν πνεύματι καὶ ἀληθείᾳ, the two terms, πνεῦμα and ἀλήθεια, forming a virtual hendiadys: the sphere of πνεῦμα (τὰ ἄνω) is the sphere of ἀλήθεια, absolute reality, as distinct from the phenomenal order of σάρξ. In the discourse on the communication of eternal life in vi. 36–59 πνεῦμα is not mentioned; but the use of the term ἀληθινός sufficiently indicates that the food of eternal life belongs to the order of ἀλήθεια and therefore of πνεῦμα. In fact, the main tendency of the whole dialogue, with its sustained contrast between the ἄρτος ἀληθινός on the one hand, and any sort of material food on the other, whether it be the 'loaves and fishes' with which the multitude were fed, or even the manna 'from heaven', is appropriately summed up in the maxim, 'It is πνεῦμα that vivifies:[1] σάρξ is useless.' This is the clue that the reader must hold fast in attempting to understand the discourse. Whatever is to be said about the mode of communication, that of Himself which Christ communicates is πνεῦμα, for real life is essentially ἐκ πνεύματος. As Son of Man (the ἄνθρωπος ἀληθινός), He is ἐκ τῶν ἄνω. Yet in Him the eternal Logos (which comprehends the whole κόσμος νοητός) was made σάρξ, and in and through the σάρξ He established communication with men. The bare idea of attaining eternal life by 'feeding upon the σάρξ' was, as the author well knew, a 'scandalous' idea to his Hellenistic public.[2] It is to be rightly under-

---

[1] The association of πνεῦμα and ζωή is not specifically Johannine. Paul has the phrase πνεῦμα ζωοποιοῦν (I Cor. xv. 45); and Philo says that πνεῦμα figures in the story of creation διότι ζωτικώτατον τὸ πνεῦμα, ζωῆς δὲ θεὸς αἴτιος (De Opif. 30). See also pp. 216, 218–19.

[2] Σκάνδαλον, σκανδαλίζειν, are almost technical terms of the earliest Christian theological vocabulary denoting the process by which the Jewish people came to be rejected as the people of God; Rom. ix. 33, I Pet. ii. 8, I Cor. i. 23, Gal. v. 11, Mark vi. 3, Matt. xi. 6, xiii. 57, xv. 12, etc.; and dramatically the present passage has the same reference, since it describes a widespread desertion of Jesus by (presumably Jewish) μαθηταί: but I conceive the evangelist to have specifically in mind the great stumbling-block to the acceptance of the Christian faith by spiritually minded persons in the Hellenistic world, affected as they were by the depreciation of the material order which was almost universal among them.

stood, he says, only by those who 'see' Christ,[1] not only as the one who descended from heaven, but also as 'ascending where He was before'. He had already said much the same thing in iii. 13–15, where we read that the Son of Man ascends to heaven, and that it is necessary that He should be thus 'elevated' if men are to have eternal life through Him. In both passages the 'ascent' or 'elevation' of the Son of Man remains cryptic. It is only in the later course of the argument that the reader will learn that it is through suffering and death that Christ is 'elevated', and 'ascends to the Father'.[2] It is by the same action that He 'gives His flesh for the life of the world'. Meanwhile, however, the words which Christ spoke[3] are charged with the πνεῦμα καὶ ζωή (once again a virtual hendiadys,

[1] Θεωρεῖν is again used, as in vi. 40, for the discerning vision which recognizes the eternal reality behind or within the phenomenal facts of the life and death of Jesus Christ.

[2] See pp. 373–9 below.

[3] The view has found some acceptance, that ῥῆμα in verse 63 is a case of Semitism, and means, like the Hebrew דבר, 'thing', 'matter' (res). 'The matters of which I have spoken—viz. the sacramental feeding upon the flesh and blood of Christ— are spirit and life.' That is possible; but it is less easy to take ῥῆμα in verse 68 (which is clearly a response to verse 63) in that sense; and it becomes still less probable when we consider the treatment of the 'words' of Christ (ῥήματα, λόγοι) all through the gospel. It seems therefore that we must be content to understand the ῥήματα of verse 63 (as in v. 47, viii. 20, xii. 47–8, xiv. 10, xv. 7, xvii. 8, etc.) as 'words' spoken by Christ, and, in the context, as the preceding discourse in its totality. We are then faced by the difficulty that in the discourse Christ is said to convey eternal life through His flesh and blood, here, through His words. The difficulty is real. To postulate two authors of divergent views, the one a 'sacramentalist', the other a 'mystic', is easy, but it is unprofitable, since our task is to understand the work as it lies before us. It is clear that our author had an overpowering sense of the potency of the spoken word as the expression of rational and articulate thought; above all, when the word is spoken by one who, in the fullest sense, 'knows ἀλήθεια' and indeed is ἀλήθεια. It is then instinct with the energies of God's creative thought. That is one reason why λόγος is for him an entirely appropriate term for the divine as revealed in creation and in the history and experience of the human race. At the same time, he does not share the tendency to abstraction which is the bane of much Hellenistic thought. The word, or the truth which the word embodies, is not fully effective till it is expressed in action, concretely, as the Word of God expressed itself in creation. Christ speaks words of life, but they are, all through, correlative with the actions in which their meaning finds effective expression—the σημεῖα, which are in some sort verba visibilia. Above all, the final word of life can be spoken only in the decisive action of Christ's death and resurrection. It is, in the last resort, only there that the Word can be seen fully to be made flesh—there, where He gives His σὰρξ καὶ αἷμα for the world. Thus there is for our author no contradiction between the statement that life comes by feeding upon the flesh and blood of Christ, and the statement that His words are life. The total revelation of eternal life is expressed in the union of word and deed—the deed, that is, of Christ, who in dying gave His flesh and shed His blood for mankind. It is also communicated and appropriated by

meaning the life which is generated ἐκ πνεύματος) which He embodies, and work their effect on those who have faith, while remaining ineffectual for those who have not (64). The evangelist has in view the mission-field of the Church in the Hellenistic world, and accepts the fact that many who hear through Christian preachers the words which are 'spirit and life' reject them in unbelief. No ultimate human cause for this can be assigned. It lies within the providential rule of God. Faith is the gift of God (cf. Ephes. ii. 8–9); no one can come to Christ, ἐὰν μὴ ᾖ δεδομένον αὐτῷ ἐκ τοῦ πατρός. The teaching is essentially the same as that of the saying in Matt. xi. 25 sq., Luke x. 21 sq., where the observed fact that the appeal of Jesus to His people has met with rejection among the religiously instructed classes, while it has been effective with the simple, is traced to the εὐδοκία of the Father.[1] In its Johannine intention, the situation is one in which the utterance of the words of Jesus has effected an act of divine κρίσις, in the sense of iii. 16–21, separating those to whom faith is given from the unbelieving mass.

The dramatic situation therefore (to which we now return) has full symbolic value. The multitude is 'scandalized'. The twelve alone remain faithful. This is exemplified by an incident which is the Johannine equivalent of Peter's confession at Caesarea in the Synoptics (vi. 68–70). Here the confession, while using the title ὁ ἅγιος τοῦ θεοῦ, which is

men through a union of word and deed: both in the hearing, understanding and believing of 'the word of the cross', and also in the sacramental act which is the continuing σημεῖον, the *signum efficax*, the *verbum visibile*, through which the Church shares the life of Christ. Such I take to be the line of thought presupposed behind our present passage. Our author however is subject to a self-imposed limitation. In writing for a non-Christian public he will not directly divulge the Christian 'mysteries'. There is no description either of the rite of Christian baptism (or its prototype, the baptism of Jesus), or of the Christian Eucharist (or its prototype, the sacramental incidents of the Last Supper). Consequently, he can give no direct answer either to the question 'How can a man be born again?', or to the question, 'How can this man give us his flesh to eat?' In each case he can only assure his readers that he is speaking of the life of πνεῦμα. It is mediated through material channels, water and bread—bread, which those who 'see Him ascending' (or 'lifted up'), and they alone, recognize as His 'flesh'. The life, however, which these convey is first and last eternal life, or in other words, πνεῦμα καὶ ζωή.

[1] In the Synoptics, no one (apart from the Son) can know the Father, except ᾧ ἐὰν βούληται ὁ υἱὸς ἀποκαλύψαι: in John, no one can come to the Son, ἐὰν μὴ ᾖ δεδομένον αὐτῷ ἐκ τοῦ πατρός. But this might be held to be in some sort implied also in Matthew and Luke; for just as the maxim οὐδεὶς ἐπιγινώσκει τὸν πατέρα εἰ μὴ ὁ υἱός is limited by καὶ ᾧ ἐὰν βούληται ὁ υἱὸς ἀποκαλύψαι, so οὐδεὶς ἐπιγινώσκει τὸν υἱὸν εἰ μὴ ὁ πατήρ might be limited by a similar καὶ ᾧ ἐὰν βούληται ὁ πατὴρ ἀποκαλύψαι. In any case the ultimate determination lies in the Father's εὐδοκία.

current also in the Synoptics, contains the additional statement, ῥήματα ζωῆς αἰωνίου ἔχεις, which is not only properly Johannine language, but links the incident, in meaning, directly with the foregoing dialogue. As the Synoptics add to the confession a prediction of the Passion, so John adds to it a forecast of the betrayal (vi. 70–1). This is a back-reference to vi. 64, and bears the meaning that the process of κρίσις must go on even within the remnant of Christ's own disciples. They too are to be purged by His word; and the purgation is not complete until Judas departs into the night after the Last Supper (xiii. 11, 30).

We may now turn back to the question left unanswered on p. 334 above: What significance did the evangelist attach to the sequence of incidents: the feeding of the multitude, the attempt at revolution, and the walking on the sea? In the main, the discourse has reference to the single incident of the Feeding. It may be that the evangelist has simply taken the other two incidents from tradition, in which they were in-separably associated with the Feeding,[1] as indeed the walking on the sea is associated in Mark vi, and a voyage across the sea (though without the incident of walking on the water) in Mark viii. But even so, it would be unlike our author to take anything over from tradition without seeking its deeper meaning. His temporal sequences seem nearly always to be more than merely temporal. With respect to the present sequence, I put forward the following suggestion tentatively.

The discourse taken as a whole (and including the appendix or epilogue) indicates a progression from false or inadequate conceptions of the messianic status and function of Christ to more adequate conceptions. The multitude are prepared to find in Him a second Moses, who will restore the gift of manna. This is set aside. Christ gives something better than manna; He gives bread of life: more than that, He *is* Bread of life. He is the Ζωοποιῶν. Union with Him is eternal life. This progression brings about an act of κρίσις. It separates those who are unable to take the required step from the few who, in some measure at least, are willing to take it. The multitude are 'scandalized'; the twelve confess that Jesus is not only God's Holy One (or Messiah), but also the One whose words mediate ζωὴ αἰώνιος.

It appears that we have a similar progression in the sequence of incidents. After the Feeding, the multitude recognize Jesus as 'the

[1] There is, I believe, probable ground for accepting the sequence of incidents as a part of the historical tradition.

coming Prophet' (a quasi-messianic designation); and consequently seek by force to make Him king—a perfectly reasonable thing to do with a messiah. Jesus repudiates the attempt, and with it the inadequate conception of His status and functions underlying it. He then proceeds to separate His own men from the multitude. The latter He dismisses from His entourage. The disciples too are temporarily separated and in the dark (as in vi. 67 the possibility of their desertion is contemplated). But almost immediately they receive enlightenment. Christ appears to them 'upon the waters',[1] and He pronounces the sacred formula: Ἐγώ εἰμι. It is true that in the story, taken at its face value, these words might mean, as they do in the Synoptic parallels, no more than 'It is I'; but in view of the importance which the formula bears in other Johannine passages it seems more than probable that it is to be understood here as elsewhere as the equivalent of the divine name אני הוא, I AM.[2]

It appears, therefore, that the sequence of incidents gives a progression parallel to that which we find in the discourse. If so, then the narrative of the Feeding of the Multitude is not only significant or symbolical in itself, but it constitutes, in conjunction with the two incidents following, a complex σημεῖον which is elucidated, after the Johannine manner, in the appended discourse.

Fourth Episode. Light and Life: Manifestation and Rejection (vii–viii)

The central block of the Book of Signs, chs. vii and viii, bears the appearance of a collection of miscellaneous material. It consists of a series of controversial dialogues, often without clearly apparent connection, apart from a general reference to the conflict between Jesus and the ecclesiastical leaders of Judaism. There is no long continuous discourse, comparable with those in chs. v, vi and x. It will be well to have before us at once the general structure of the whole series, which is here arranged under rough catch-headings:

vii. 1–10 Introductory (see below, pp. 351–2).

  11–13 Scene at the Feast of Tabernacles in the absence of Jesus.

---

[1] Cf. Ps. xxviii (xxix). 3 Κύριος ἐπὶ ὑδάτων πολλῶν, lxxvi (lxxvii). 20 ἐν τῇ θαλάσσῃ ἡ ὁδός σου, καὶ αἱ τρίβοι σου ἐν ὕδασι πολλοῖς, καὶ τὰ ἴχνη σου οὐ γνωσθήσονται. Although there is no verbal echo, the picture of Christ walking upon the stormy waters of the sea may have been felt to suggest the symbolism of divine power and majesty employed in these and other passages of the Old Testament.

[2] See pp. 93–6.

vii. 14–24 Jesus at the Feast. First dialogue: theme, Moses and Christ.

25–36 Second dialogue: the messianic claims of Jesus. The interlocutors are mainly 'Jerusalemites', the 'crowd', 'Pharisees' or 'Jews'. Jesus has only two brief speeches.

37–44 Third dialogue, introduced by an oracular saying of Jesus, and carried on by the 'crowd'. Theme, the messianic claims of Jesus.

45–52 Fourth dialogue. The same theme continued. Interlocutors, the 'chief priests and Pharisees', their ὑπηρέται, and the senator Nicodemus. Jesus is absent from the scene.[1]

viii. 12–20 Fifth dialogue, introduced by an oracular saying of Jesus. Theme, the nature and value of the evidence for the claims of Jesus.

21–30 Sixth dialogue, consisting mainly of a discourse of Jesus interrupted by brief comments and questions of the 'Jews'. Theme, the challenge of Jesus to the Jewish leaders.

31–59 Seventh and closing dialogue. Theme, Abraham, his 'seed' and Christ. Interlocutors, Jesus and the 'Jews'.

The tone of the whole is markedly polemical. The debate in its earlier phases proceeds largely upon the plane of Jewish messianic ideas, though it moves into other regions before the end. The evangelist has brought together here most of what he has to say in reply to Jewish objections against the messianic claims made for Jesus. There are of course other controversial passages in this gospel, but scarcely another where the controversial note is so sharp and so sustained; and this in itself gives a certain unity to the whole episode.

This unity is emphasized by the peculiar literary structure of the two chapters. The interchange of debate is unusually rapid, especially in the earlier part. Jesus is not allowed a speech of any length without being interrupted by questions or objections. At some points the opponents are more vocal than Jesus Himself. Sometimes they hold the stage and He is silent. Towards the end their interventions become rather fewer and briefer, but even at viii. 52–3 they are permitted to develop their objection at some length. All this is unusual, even in the Fourth Gospel, and scarcely paralleled in the Synoptics. It helps to create a vivid impression of the constant presence, and urgency, of the opposition, and this is clearly part of the author's aim.

[1] The *Pericope Adulterae*, vii. 53–viii. 11 in the Textus Receptus, is omitted as being no part of the original text of this Gospel.

346

The point is further emphasized by his repeated statements that Jesus was in danger of His life, and that attempts were made to put Him under arrest, or to lynch Him on the spot. It will be well to review these statements.

vii. 1   Jesus was avoiding Judaea, ὅτι ἐζήτουν αὐτὸν οἱ 'Ιουδαῖοι ἀποκτεῖναι.

vii. 13   People in Judaea were afraid even to mention His name διὰ τὸν φόβον τῶν 'Ιουδαίων.

vii. 19   Jesus asks, Τί με ζητεῖτε ἀποκτεῖναι;

vii. 25   The Jerusalemites are surprised at the boldness of one ὃν ζητοῦσιν ἀποκτεῖναι.

vii. 30   Ἐζήτουν αὐτὸν πιάσαι, καὶ οὐδεὶς ἐπέβαλεν ἐπ' αὐτὸν τὴν χεῖρα.

vii. 32   The police are sent to arrest Him.

vii. 44   Τινὲς ἐξ αὐτῶν ἤθελον πιάσαι αὐτόν, ἀλλ' οὐδεὶς ἐπέβαλεν ἐπ' αὐτὸν τὰς χεῖρας.

viii. 37   Ζητεῖτέ με ἀποκτεῖναι.

viii. 40   Ζητεῖτέ με ἀποκτεῖναι.

viii. 59   Ἦραν οὖν λίθους ἵνα βάλωσιν ἐπ' αὐτόν.

The dialogues are in fact punctuated all through by these references to hostile action against Jesus. They help to build up a background against which the dialogues are to be read. As compared with other episodes in the Book of Signs, this fourth episode is dominated by the motive of conflict.

The action is staged at the Feast of Tabernacles. The introduction relates how Jesus came up from Galilee for the festival. The first dialogue takes place μεσούσης τῆς ἑορτῆς, and the second dialogue is clearly intended as its immediate sequel. The third dialogue is placed ἐν τῇ ἐσχάτῃ ἡμέρᾳ τῇ μεγάλῃ τῆς ἑορτῆς. There is no further explicit reference to the Feast. It is not quite clear that the address which Jesus gave 'in the Treasury while He was teaching in the Temple' (viii. 20) is (dramatically) continuous with the third and fourth dialogues, but such would appear to be the author's intention. We are to conceive the action taking place, as it were, upon a double stage. In the foreground Jesus is confronting the crowd attending the Feast. In the background, the authorities are deliberating and plotting. The first crisis comes in the middle of the Feast, when certain of the crowd are so impressed by what Jesus says that they are prepared to believe He may be the Messiah (vii. 31). The news reaches the authorities (in the background), and they despatch agents to arrest Jesus. Meanwhile the public debate continues, on the front stage, with no note of lapse of time, until on the final day of the Feast Jesus makes a momentous proclamation (which we must consider presently— vii. 37–8). The effect is to divide the crowd acutely. We are then returned to the back stage, where the authorities receive the report of their agents (vii. 45). Meanwhile (viii. 12), on the front stage, Jesus is continuing the public debate 'in the Treasury',[1] the attempt to arrest Him having failed (viii. 20, cf. vii. 45–6). The artificiality of this construction is patent, but down to this point at least it seems clear that the evangelist intended to place the whole action at the Feast of Tabernacles.

Beyond this point the connection is more vague; but there is no indication of a change of scene before ix. 1, and there are hints that viii. 21–59 is conceived as a continuation of the same episode.[2] The final attempt to stone Jesus (viii. 59) appears as the culmination of the various threats against Him, and it leads to an effective *exit*. The terms in which His retirement is described are significant: Ἰησοῦς δὲ ἐκρύβη καὶ ἐξῆλθεν ἐκ τοῦ ἱεροῦ. The whole episode began with Jesus ἐν κρυπτῷ (vii. 4). His attendance at the Feast is at first οὐ φανερῶς ἀλλ’ ὡς ἐν κρυπτῷ (vii. 10). Then at mid-feast He suddenly appears in public, to be met with opposition and threats. It is fitting that the episode of conflict, having ended in the rejection of Jesus's challenge, should be rounded off by His retirement into concealment once more. Thus the words ἐν κρυπτῷ—ἐκρύβη may be taken as clamping this entire series of dialogues into a dramatic unity, with the Feast of Tabernacles to provide a significant background to the whole.

It is probable that the dialogues themselves contain deliberate allusions to the ritual of the festival and the ideas associated with it. One of the most distinctive ceremonies of the Feast of Tabernacles was that of libations of water. The water was drawn in solemn form from the Siloam reservoir, conveyed to the temple, and poured over the altar of burnt offering. This took place on each of the seven days of the Feast (and, according to inferior authorities, on the extra eighth day also). It was associated with prayers for rain, and may have been the survival of

---

[1] Observe that Jesus is silent all through the scenes recorded in vii. 40–52, so that viii. 12 ἐγώ εἰμι τὸ φῶς τοῦ κόσμου is His first utterance after vii. 37–8 ἐάν τις διψᾷ κ.τ.λ. The two utterances in which Christ offers Himself as giver of living water and as the light of the world belong closely together.

[2] vii. 16 is taken up in viii. 28, vii. 20 in viii. 48, 52, vii. 28 in viii. 42, vii. 29 in viii. 55, vii. 33–4 in viii. 21.

a primitive rain-making ceremony, since the festival was celebrated about the time when the first rains of autumn might be expected. However that may be, the idea of the satisfaction of the need for water in order to live recurs in rabbinic discussions of the festival and its meaning, and water is made to symbolize various spiritual blessings.[1] The oracular saying which Jesus is said to have uttered 'on the last, the great day of the Feast' (vii. 37–8) certainly gains point if all this symbolism is in view.

> If anyone is thirsty, let him come to me;
> And let him drink who has faith in me.[2]

As the Scripture said, 'Out of His body shall flow rivers of living water.'

Another distinctive ceremony of the Feast of Tabernacles was the illumination of the Women's Court in the Temple, which, we are told, was so brilliant that every courtyard in Jerusalem was lit up by it.[3] It has often been suggested that there may be an allusion to the illumination in the oracular saying with which the fifth dialogue is introduced: 'I am the light of the world. He who follows me will never walk in darkness, but have the light of life.' If it be granted that the festival is conceived as background for the whole series of dialogues, the allusion would be natural enough, though no stress is laid upon it.

Another allusion to ideas or practices associated with the Feast of Tabernacles has been suspected in the sixth dialogue. There is some evidence for associating specifically with the ritual of this festival the use of a peculiar form of the divine name, אֲנִי וְהוּא, Ani-w'hu, which

---

[1] See S.-B. vol. II, pp. 799–805; Moore, *Judaism*, vol. II, pp. 43–8. Joshua ben Levi (early third century), like our evangelist, associated it with the gift of the Holy Spirit; see Moore *loc. cit.*

[2] This seems the better punctuation. It gives parallelism, though in a chiastic form not common in this writer (cf. however vii. 24, viii. 23, xvi. 28, xvii. 18, 23, and a few other traces of chiasmus). For ἔρχεσθαι and πιστεύειν in parallelism, in a similar context, cf. vi. 35. It also allows the αὐτοῦ of the quotation to refer to Christ as the source of living water. The difficulty of identifying the γραφή remains, but it is at any rate no greater than that of finding a *testimonium* for the statement that the individual believer is a source of living water, an idea of which there is elsewhere no trace in this gospel, or anywhere in the New Testament. It may be recalled that among the scriptures most frequently quoted in rabbinic authorities with reference to the libations at Sukkoth are Is. xii. 3, Ezek. xlvii. 1 sqq., Zech. xiv. 8. The first passage speaks of πηγὴ σωτηρίου (cf. John iv. 14); in the second, water issues from the temple; in the third, ὕδωρ ζῶν issues from Jerusalem. We know that for this evangelist the body of Christ is the true temple (ii. 21), and by implication it is the πηγή of living water (xix. 34). It may be therefore that the evangelist has interpreted the three γραφαί as tantamount to the assertion that streams of living water flow from the body of Christ. The idea receives symbolic expression in xix. 34.

[3] See S.-B. vol. II, pp. 805–7; Moore, *Judaism*, vol. II, pp. 44–7.

was regarded as the שֵׁם הַמְּפוֹרָשׁ, the hidden Name of God.[1] Its origin is uncertain, but it appears to be a mutation of the Old Testament formula אֲנִי הוּא, *Ani-hu*, which the LXX renders ἐγώ εἰμι. The form with the conjunction ו was interpreted to imply the intimate union of God with Israel. The inmost nature of God, it is implied, can be expressed only in a name which declares that 'I and he', God and Israel, are in union. Some such idea appears to be expressed in the dialogue, viii. 21–30. The words, 'Unless you believe ὅτι ἐγώ εἰμι, you will die in your sins' (verse 24), echo the ἐγώ εἰμι, אֲנִי הוּא, of the Old Testament. They are repeated in verse 28, with the addition (29), ὁ πέμψας με μετ' ἐμοῦ ἐστιν. Similarly in viii. 16 we have ἐγώ καὶ ὁ πέμψας με, which recalls even verbally the formula אֲנִי וְהוּא, *Ani-w'hu*, and the meaning attributed to it in rabbinic tradition, Christ taking the place of Israel (as often). This however is somewhat speculative.

It appears then that the Feast of Tabernacles affords an appropriate setting for this sequence of dialogues. One of the traditional lections for the festival is Zech. xiv, which describes the approaching Day of the Lord:

It shall come to pass in that day that living waters shall go out from Jerusalem.... And the Lord shall be king over all the earth. In that day shall the Lord be one and his name one.... And it shall come to pass that every one that is left of the nations that came against Jerusalem shall go up from year to year to worship the King, the Lord of Hosts, and to keep the Feast of Tabernacles.

The reference to 'living waters' here is in rabbinic exposition frequently applied to the libation ceremony of Tabernacles, together with Zech. xiii. 1, Ezek. xlvii. 1 sqq., and Is. xii. 3; and this line of association seems to be traceable to Eliezer ben Jacob (c. A.D. 90). The anticipation of the coming of the Kingdom of God, or the Messianic Age, which is so intimately connected with Tabernacles in Zechariah, is less prominent than might perhaps have been expected in rabbinic interpretations of the symbolism of the festival, but it recurs here and there, though not, it would appear, in contexts which can be definitely traced to an early date.[2] There is

[1] See above, pp. 93–6.
[2] See S.-B. vol. II, pp. 774–812: *Excurs: Das Laubhüttenfest*. The *Lulab* and *Ethrog* carried by the worshippers signify thanks to God for the promise of a 'new creation', Ps. ci (cii). 19 (*Lev. Rab.* 30. 3 *ap.* S.-B. p. 790); the celebration holds within it the promise of the Messiah (after R. Abba bar Kahana, c. A.D. 310, *ap.* S.-B. p. 793); the *Sukkoth* themselves signify the shelter which God will provide for His own in the Day that burns like a furnace (Mal. iii. 19), cf. Is. iv. 6, Ps. xxvi (xxvii). 5 (*Pesiqta* 186–7, *ap.* S.-B. p. 779). See also G. Klein, *Der älteste christliche Katechismus*, pp. 49–55, whose conclusions however are over-positive.

a somewhat vague tradition that the Messiah might be expected to appear in the month Tisri, to which Tabernacles belongs. It is by no means impossible that the evangelist was acquainted with these eschatological associations.

For him, at any rate, Tabernacles is the occasion when Jesus manifests Himself as Messiah in Jerusalem. His claims are canvassed in terms which show familiarity with various aspects of Jewish messianic expectation.[1] But messianic categories are transcended when Jesus offers Himself as the source of living water, and as the light of the world, and finally pronounces the ἐγώ εἰμι which affirms the mystery of His own eternal being, in unity with the Father. This threefold manifestation corresponds with the affirmations of the Prologue, which presents the Logos as the bearer of life and light, and as being both θεός and πρὸς τὸν θεόν, or εἰς τὸν κόλπον τοῦ πατρός.

With this in view, the narrative setting of the dialogues takes a special significance. In vii. 3–4 Jesus is urged to go up to the Feast of Tabernacles in the words φανέρωσον σεαυτὸν τῷ κόσμῳ. Choosing His own time, He goes up μεσούσης τῆς ἑορτῆς. What does this mean but a fulfilment of the prophecy, 'The Lord whom ye seek shall suddenly come to His temple' (Mal. iii. 1)? It is the Day of the Lord, which, according to Zech. xiv, the Feast of Tabernacles foreshadows.

We have here a striking instance of the characteristic Johannine irony. On the surface, we are reading about a rustic prophet who leaves the obscurity of the provinces to appeal to the great public of the metropolis. But the words φανέρωσον σεαυτὸν τῷ κόσμῳ have a weight disproportionate to the ostensible situation. In their deeper meaning they are an appeal to the Messiah to manifest Himself to Israel. But if we go deeper still, they speak of the manifestation of the eternal Logos, as life and light, to the world of human kind.

It follows that the narrative setting of the series of dialogues is itself a σημεῖον in the sense which that word bears in the Fourth Gospel. It might have been given as a simple narrative of an occurrence during the ministry of Jesus. After a period of retirement in Galilee, He went up to Jerusalem for the Feast of Tabernacles, and there made a public appeal in the temple. The result was that the crowd threatened to stone Him, and the authorities ordered His arrest. He therefore left the temple, and went into retirement again. But every stage of this narrative has symbolic meaning. The Logos was in the world unknown. He came to

[1] See above, pp. 88–93.

His own place (Jerusalem is the πατρίς of Jesus in the Fourth Gospel, iv. 44), and those who were His own received Him not. As a result, the manifestation of the Word is withdrawn from Israel: ἐκρύβη καὶ ἐξῆλθεν ἐκ τοῦ ἱεροῦ. The whole episode, from this point of view, might be taken as a large-scale illustration of the way in which this evangelist understands the primitive Christian doctrine of the blinding or πώρωσις of Israel, to which he has given a prominent position in the epilogue to the Book of Signs, xii. 37–41.

It appears, then, that this central episode, in spite of first appearances, corresponds in essential structure to the general pattern. It contains both narrative and discourse indicating the symbolic meaning attached to the narrative, though the discourse is expanded at great length in a series of dialogues, and the narrative forms a background.

Having established the point that the dominant theme which gives unity to this whole episode, narrative and discourse alike, is that of the manifestation and rejection of the Logos as light and life, we may now take note of certain elements in it which indicate the place it is designed to hold in the development of the great argument.

First, we have here several allusions, running through the two chapters, to the theme of judgment (vii. 24, viii. 15–16, 26, 50), resumed from ch. v. In iii. 17–21 the fundamental principle was enunciated that Christ came to give life and light and not to judge, but that when the light appears, men inevitably judge themselves by their attitude towards it. In this sense Christ is, after all, the agent of judgment, as He is said to be in v. 27. In viii. 15 we have the same paradox: Christ does not judge, but nevertheless, in virtue of His unity with the Father (as in v. 30), He is the agent of ἀληθινὴ κρίσις. His adversaries judge κατὰ τὴν σάρκα, or κατ' ὄψιν (vii. 24), and while they suppose themselves to be sitting in judgment upon His claims, they are in reality being judged by Him. Although the theme is not further elaborated here, the attentive reader will observe that the whole episode is an example of the working of the principle of iii. 15–17; and he is thus prepared for the more explicit treatment of the theme in the next episode (see pp. 354–62).

Secondly, κρίσις is in part a process of separation or discrimination (as indeed the etymology of the Greek word implies), and it is hardly accidental that the evangelist has emphasized in this episode the effect of Christ's presence and words in dividing His hearers. Already before He appeared at the festival 'some were saying, "He is a good man";

others were saying, "No, he misleads the people"' (vii. 12). When He appeared, some said, 'Have the rulers really concluded that this is the Messiah?'; but at once objections were raised (vii. 25–7). In the process of the debate, 'many believed on Him' but the Pharisees were hostile (vii. 31–2). After the proclamation of living water, 'some of the crowd who heard these words said, "This is indeed the Prophet"; others said, "This is the Messiah"', but again objections were raised, and a σχίσμα ensued (vii. 40–3). At the close of the sixth dialogue again 'many believed on him' (viii. 30), but this only led to more acute debate. We seem to have an echo of the theme, which appears in the Synoptic Gospels, that the coming of Christ brings not peace but division.[1] In this gospel it is fundamental that the impact of the incarnate Logos upon the world sifts men, and selects, through their actual response, those who are given ἐξουσίαν τέκνα θεοῦ γενέσθαι. From one point of view, indeed, the whole story of the ministry in chs. ii–xii is a story of sifting and selection, which results in the appearance in chs. xiii–xvii of a small body of men 'cleansed' by Christ's word and united to Him. As we have seen, the third episode culminates in a sifting of the early followers of Jesus; and the present, central episode carries the story forward, by showing how at every stage and at every level of Christ's auditors the process of 'polarization' goes on. In the next episode the theme will be further developed.

Thirdly, the continuous menace to the life of Jesus which forms the background of the dialogues points forward to the Passion. This theme has hitherto been approached with great reserve, and for the most part allusively. In ii. 19–21 it was hinted that the temple which is the body of Christ must be destroyed and raised again; and for those who are in the secret the 'elevation' of the Son of Man in iii. 14–15 suggests the thought of the cross; but the suggestion is left undeveloped. At v. 16–18 we have the first hint of opposition which will lead to a murderous attack, but for the moment nothing comes of it. In vi. 51 Jesus declares in cryptic terms that He gives His flesh for the life of the world, but there is no answer to the question, 'How can this man give us his flesh to eat?' Yet enough has been said to lead the attentive reader to look out for further clarification.

In the present episode we have further cryptic allusions to the coming Passion. The motive of a vicarious death, suggested by vi. 51, is not further pursued at present; but the idea of the 'elevation' of the Son of Man recurs in viii. 28, and in vii. 33–4 Jesus speaks of His departure for a mysterious destination, in words which are echoed in viii. 14, 21–2.

[1] Luke xii. 51–3, xvii. 34–5 (cf. *Parables of the Kingdom*, pp. 86–7).

All these allusions leave His auditors perplexed. At vii. 35 they surmise that He is planning a mission to foreign parts; at viii. 22 that He is contemplating suicide. Yet the intelligent reader, who knows that at every point in this stormy scene Jesus is in actual danger from the attacks of His enemies, can hardly fail to see that a violent death is a highly probable issue of His present conflict, and that it is to this that He is referring. Only, whereas those who are ἐκ τῶν κάτω die in their sins, for Him who is ἐκ τῶν ἄνω death is a return to the Father who sent Him (vii. 33, viii. 14, 21–4), and in death as in life His union with the Father is unbroken (viii. 14–16, 25–9). The meaning of ὑψωθῆναι is still left unexplained; but it is now placed in a context which speaks of the impending violent death of Jesus as a return to τὰ ἄνω whence He came. A clue to its meaning lies not far below the surface.[1]

The episode, therefore, taken as a whole, may be regarded as corresponding in some sort both to those passages in the Synoptic Gospels which depict the conflicts of Jesus with the authorities, leading to His arrest and condemnation (e.g. Mark ii. 13–iii. 6, xi. 27–xii. 12), and to those which contain explicit predictions of the Passion. The Johannine method of presentation is superior in dramatic force and in theological depth, but it has the same effect, of making the reader aware that, from this point on, all that is said and done takes place in view of an irreconcilable conflict destined to end in the death of Jesus.

FIFTH EPISODE. JUDGMENT BY THE LIGHT
(ix. 1–x. 21, WITH APPENDIX, x. 22–39)

Ch. ix contains a narrative—that of the healing of the blind at Siloam—and a dialogue in the form of a trial scene. The two are intimately connected, and together would constitute a simple Johannine unit of narrative and discourse. It is not however clear that the episode is to be regarded as closed at the end of ch. ix. It is not until the beginning of ch. xi that a fresh narrative begins. The relations of ch. x with its context demand examination, and it will be well to clear up this point first.

Ch. x falls into two clearly marked portions, the division being made after verse 21. Verses 1–21 contain a discourse on the theme of the shepherd and the flock. More precisely, they contain two short discourses developing the same general theme, each discourse being followed by a statement of its effect on the auditors. After the first discourse, 1–5,

[1] For a fuller discussion of this passage, see p. 376 below.

we are told that its hearers did not understand it. After the second discourse, 7–18, we are told that it caused a σχίσμα among its hearers. There is an obvious resemblance to certain parts of chs. vii–viii. A 'schism' among the hearers of Jesus is mentioned also in vii. 43, and although the word does not recur, the phenomenon itself is present all through the fourth episode. Again, in x. 20 the hostile party among the Jews accuses Jesus of demon-possession, as in vii. 20, viii. 48, 52.

The resemblance is even closer in the second part of ch. x, 22–39. Here we have, once again, a scene at Jerusalem during a festival. There is a controversial dialogue between Jesus and 'the Jews' upon the theme of His messianic claims; and as before there is a threat to stone Him (x. 31) and an unsuccessful attempt to put Him under arrest (x. 39). In general character and purport this controversial dialogue is closely similar to those of chs. vii–viii, though different particular points come up for discussion.

In view of these facts, it is not surprising that proposals for the re-arrangement of the material in this part of the gospel have found much favour. Certainly, if we were enquiring into the history of the composition of the work, it might plausibly be argued that ch. ix, which has a distinct character of its own, once existed as a separate unit, and that the discourse about the shepherd and the flock, x. 1–18, similarly may have had a separate existence, while the material in x. 19–21, 22–39 may well have been drawn from a store which included also the controversial discourses and dialogues which now form part of chs. vii–viii. But whatever may have been the history of composition, it does not appear that we could at present improve upon the existing order without disintegrating the work which has come down to us, and relying upon mere speculation. The following points are worth consideration.

First, the controversial dialogue in x. 22–39 is expressly placed at the Encaenia in winter. Either this statement occurred in the source (of whatever kind) from which the material was drawn, and in that case this dialogue was from the first separated from the kindred material in chs. vii–viii, which belongs to the Feast of Tabernacles; or else it was inserted by the evangelist, and in that case he intended the dialogue to stand apart from chs. vii–viii. In either case we should not be justified in combining this dialogue with other dialogues, however similar, from which the evangelist, or his source, expressly separated it.

Secondly, there are cross-references, quite in the Johannine manner, which strongly suggest that the existing order was designed by the writer.

Thus in x. 26–8 we have a reference to the shepherd and the sheep which is intelligible only to readers who have already been made acquainted with the discourse of x. 1–18. Nor can this reference be plausibly removed from its position in the controversial dialogue. The dialogue is clamped together throughout by the recurrence of the word ἔργον (verses 25, 32, 33, 37, 38), and the reference to the shepherd and the sheep is organically related to the first occurrence of that word. Again, the account of the 'schism' and the charge of demon-possession in x. 19–21, similar as it is to parts of vii–viii, seems to be anchored in its present place by the reference to the healing of the blind, which would be senseless unless ix. 1–7 had preceded it.

It would indeed be quite agreeable to the Johannine method to regard this back-reference as designed to clamp the whole of ix. 1–x. 21 into a unity, much as the echo of ἐν κρυπτῷ (vii. 1) in ἐκρύβη (viii. 59) marks the unity of vii–viii. We should then have in ix. 1–x. 21 a sequence of narrative, dialogue and monologue, dialogue passing into monologue at x. 1 with the emphatic words ἀμὴν ἀμὴν λέγω ὑμῖν. Similarly in ch. iii the brief narrative of the visit of Nicodemus introduced a dialogue which at iii. 11 passed into monologue with the same emphatic words, ἀμὴν ἀμὴν λέγω σοι. The same formula again marks the passage from dialogue to monologue in v. 19, though here it is provided with a transitional phrase, ἀπεκρίνατο οὖν ὁ Ἰησοῦς καὶ ἔλεγεν αὐτοῖς. With the same emphatic words, ἀμὴν ἀμὴν λέγω ὑμῖν, and this time with no transitional formula, a discourse follows upon an introductory dialogue in xii. 24.

It seems therefore that the fifth episode is comprised mainly in ix. 1–x. 21, and the controversial discourse, x. 22–39, with its change of time and place, forms a kind of appendix or epilogue, like iii. 22–36 appended to the discourse on Rebirth, and vi. 60–71 appended to the discourse on Bread of Life; and probably (as we shall see) xi. 45–53 appended to the sixth episode. On analogy we should expect this appendix to take up some point in what has gone before, and to prepare for what is coming; as iii. 22–36 takes up the theme of baptism from iii. 5 and in verse 35 points forward to the discourse of v. 18 sqq.; as vi. 60–71 takes up the theme of ζωοποίησις and points forward cryptically to the Passion in the prediction of the betrayal, vi. 70; and as xi. 45–53 connects the theme of Jesus's resolve to risk death in Judaea for the sake of raising Lazarus with the theme of the approaching Passion as a voluntary and vicarious act (see below).

Assuming, then, that chs. ix–x form a single episode with an appendix or epilogue loosely connected with it, we must now enquire what is the main theme of this episode, and how it takes its place in the development of the argument.

We recall that chs. vii–viii present Christ 'manifested to the world' as life and light, but rejected. This presentation, with its clear reference to the terms of the Prologue, fitly occupies the central position in the Book of Signs. In the three preceding episodes, the aspect of life was predominant (rebirth, living water, ζωοποίησις, bread of life). We are now to have an episode in which the aspect of light predominates. The key-word which indicates the connection with the foregoing episode is φῶς εἰμι τοῦ κόσμου (ix. 5, repeating viii. 12). Clearly the healing of the blind is conceived as a 'sign' of the triumph of light over darkness, in the sense of the Prologue: the φῶς ἀληθινόν shines in darkness, and the darkness, so far from 'overwhelming' it, is overcome and dispelled. This theme is subtly linked, in the author's manner, with the discourses on life by the recurrence of the symbol of water. As men enter the true life by birth from water, so they receive the true light by washing with water. But just as the water 'of the Jews' purifying' is turned into wine, and the water of Jacob's well is superseded by the living water which Christ gives, so the water of the pool is enlightening only if it is the true 'Siloam', the ᾿Απεσταλμένος, the Son whom the Father sent. We observe that in this episode the significance of the σημεῖον is divulged, not in an accompanying discourse, but by brief insertions into the narrative itself.

But there is a further point. In iii. 19–21 we were told that light brings judgment, in the sense that it discriminates between those who prefer darkness to light because their deeds are evil, and those who come to the light that their deeds may be made manifest, that they are wrought in God. This theme, as we have seen, is dealt with allusively in chs. vii–viii. It is now to receive more explicit treatment. With the sign of the giving of light is associated a dialogue which takes the form of a trial scene: judgment in action. As sheer drama, this trial scene is one of the most brilliant passages in the gospel, rich in the tragic irony of which the evangelist is master. The one-time blind beggar stands before his betters, to be badgered into denying the one thing of which he is certain.[1] But the defendant proper is Jesus Himself, judged *in absentia*. In some sort,

---

[1] The beggar on trial suggests to the Christian reader his own situation in the world—enlightened in baptism and called upon to confess Christ before men.

the man whom Christ enlightened pleads the cause of the Light. When he is 'cast out', it is Christ whom the judges have rejected. Then comes the dramatic περιπέτεια. Jesus swiftly turns the tables on His judges, and pronounces sentence:[1] 'For judgment I have come into the world, that the blind may see and the seeing be blinded....If you were blind, no guilt would attach to you; but now you say "We are the men who see": and you stand guilty.'

It appears then that the dominant theme of this episode is not the coming of light as such, but its effect in judgment. The fact that the coming of Christ brings light into the world is stated symbolically with the utmost brevity, and the weight is laid upon the elaborate dialogue which dramatically exhibits judgment in action.

At the end of ch. ix the judicial sentence pronounced by Jesus leads without interruption to the discourse of the shepherd and the flock, which in a purely formal sense is the direct continuation of the pronouncement in ix. 41, though, as we have seen, the emphatic words ἀμὴν ἀμὴν λέγω ὑμῖν serve, as elsewhere, to mark the transition from dialogue to monologue. How far, then, does this formal connection express a real continuity of theme? It is clear that the opening sentence of the discourse is in fact a judicial verdict upon a class of persons described as κλέπτης καὶ λῃστής. The theme of judgment is in any case not wholly dropped.

The discourse, however, is not to be fully understood without reference to a passage in the Old Testament which must have been in the author's mind. The comparison of the people of God to a flock is a piece of symbolism as well-established as it is natural. In the thirty-fourth chapter of Ezekiel it is made the basis of a lengthy and elaborate apologue. The prophet begins by denouncing the corrupt rulers of Israel as false shepherds of God's flock. Instead of feeding the sheep, they prey upon them; instead of protecting them, they allow them to wander unheeded, with the result that the flock is scattered and devoured by wild beasts. The shepherds therefore are to be deposed from their office, and God Himself will seek out His sheep as a shepherd seeks his flock in the dark and cloudy day. He will lead them out (ἐξάγειν) from their place of exile, collect (συνάγειν) the scattered flock, and lead them into (εἰσάγειν) the land where they will find good pasture (νομή). God will feed His sheep and give them rest and they shall know Him (γνώσονται ὅτι ἐγὼ Κύριος).

---

[1] Jesus acts as Advocate (παράκλητος) for His persecuted followers: but it is He who is persecuted (Acts ix. 4–5).

He will then judge between sheep and sheep, between the rams and the he-goats. He will save His sheep (σώσω τὰ πρόβατά μου), and will set over them one shepherd (ἀναστήσω ἐπ᾽ αὐτοὺς ποιμένα ἕνα), namely David (i.e. the Messiah of David's line). God will then eliminate the evil beasts and give peace to the flock. The prophecy ends with the emphatic proclamation, πρόβατά μου καὶ πρόβατα ποιμνίου μού ἐστε, καὶ ἐγὼ κύριος ὁ θεὸς ὑμῶν.

The resemblance to John x. 1–18 is far-reaching. Jesus speaks of sheep which are preyed upon by robbers, neglected by hireling shepherds, scattered¹ and torn by wolves. But the good shepherd leads them out (ἐξάγει); they are saved (σωθήσεται); they go in and out and find pasture (νομή); he rescues them from the wolf; he knows his sheep and they know him (γινώσκουσί με τὰ ἐμά); he will bring other sheep from a different fold, and there will be μία ποίμνη, εἷς ποιμήν.

The prophecy of Ezekiel is in the first place a sentence of judgment upon unworthy rulers of Israel, who are denounced both for robbing and killing the sheep (xxxiv. 3) and for abandoning them to beasts of prey (xxxiv. 8). Similarly the discourse in John x arraigns both those who rob, kill and destroy the flock (x. 1, 10) and the hirelings who abandon the sheep to the wolf (x. 12–13). It seems that the same class of criminal is in view. It is the false rulers of God's people upon whom judgment is passed²—the same upon whom judgment is passed at the conclusion of the trial scene in ix. 41. The 'Pharisees' have expelled from God's flock the man whom Christ Himself enlightened. They are scattering the sheep whom Christ came to gather. It would in fact be quite possible to read ix. 41–x. 5 as what it formally is, a single speech of Jesus, directly moti-vated by the situation depicted in ch. ix. He has said to those who have unjustly expelled the man He healed, 'You say, "We are the men who see"; and you stand guilty.' He goes on, 'Anyone who arrogates to himself (as you have done) an authority over God's people for which he has no proper qualification is no better than a robber.'

¹ John uses σκορπίζειν for Ezekiel's διασπείρειν, here as in the kindred passage xi. 52 ἵνα καὶ τὰ τέκνα τοῦ θεοῦ τὰ διεσκορπισμένα συναγάγῃ εἰς ἕν. Διασκορπίζειν occurs in some MSS. of the LXX of the kindred passage in Zech. xiii. 7, translating the same verb פוץ, and reappears in the citation of the latter passage in Mark xiv. 27.

² Observe that nowhere in this gospel, except in ch. ix, are we concerned with the relations between the Jewish authorities and the flock of Israel which is under their care, as distinct from their relations with Jesus Himself. There is therefore no other place where the discourse about true and false shepherds could be so fitly introduced.

In Ezek. xxxiv the severe judgment upon the false shepherds leads to a promise of deliverance for the flock. Similarly in John x the robbers and hireling shepherds serve as foil to the good shepherd, who doubles the roles of David, the 'one shepherd', and of God Himself; for in John it is Christ, as in Ezekiel it is Jehovah, who leads the sheep, provides them with pasture, brings them back when they were scattered, rescues them from the wolf, and effects their salvation. But in John the picture of the good shepherd is enriched with traits which go beyond Ezekiel's circle of ideas. In particular, the shepherd brings the sheep life, or, as x. 28 has it (where the theme is resumed), ζωὴ αἰώνιος. Thus the argument is switched back from light to the twin-concept of life. That however is not all. In the imagery of the discourse the heroic shepherd goes out to meet the wolf, and lays down his life in defence of his flock. This provides the evangelist with the clearest and most explicit statement he has yet permitted himself upon the Passion of Christ as a voluntary and vicarious self-sacrifice. The fourth episode, as we have seen, made it clear that Christ will die as a result of His conflict with the rulers of Israel, but the hint given in vi. 51 that His death is voluntary and vicarious was not carried further. In the discourse of x. 1–18 it is taken up and developed, on the basis of the illuminating image of the heroic shepherd. Life eternal, as the reader has known since ch. iii, is the gift of Christ, and since ch. vi he has been led to surmise that Christ gives life, in some sense, by giving Himself. Now the idea begins to assume concrete shape. Christ is actually going to be killed in His conflict with false rulers, and through His death He will bring life to others, as really as a shepherd might save the lives of his sheep by fighting the wolf at the cost of his own life. If that does not tell the whole story, at least it gives part of the answer to the unanswered question of vi. 52, 'How can this man give us his flesh to eat?'

It will shortly appear how effective a transition is thus provided to the theme of the next episode. But for the present we must note the significance of the collocation of the themes of judgment and of the life-giving death of Christ in this episode. His gift of life and light is met with rejection. Those who reject it are shown in the very act of bringing down upon themselves the inevitable judgment of God on those who prefer darkness to light. But in that same act they are preparing the death of Christ, through which He gives life to the world. By a slight shift of thought, His death is itself a judgment upon those who compassed it through their rejection of the light, as the heroic death of the noble shepherd arraigns both the greed of the robber and the craven desertion of the hireling. We are thus being prepared for the profound statement of xii. 31, that the death of Christ is κρίσις τοῦ κόσμου τούτου, while at the same time it is the necessary condition under which new life will spring from the buried seed (xii. 24).

We have now to examine the appendix or epilogue to the fifth episode, ch. x. 22–39. In x. 19–21 we were left with a 'schism' among Christ's hearers which is itself an aspect of the process of κρίσις (see pp. 352–3 above). The divine Shepherd is 'discriminating between sheep and sheep, between rams and he-goats', as Ezekiel said He would (xxxiv. 17). Verses 26–7 indicate that the scene at the Encaenia is designed to expose the attitude of those who have by their own choice excluded themselves from Christ's flock, and who, by a renewed attempt to seize and stone Him, align themselves with those who cause His death.

The theme of the dialogue is essentially that which occupies so much of chs. vii–viii: the messianic claims of Jesus; and here as there we observe a movement from Jewish messianic categories to categories more akin to Hellenistic religious thought—divine sonship, union with God, mutual indwelling. All through this gospel the evangelist, while aiming at convincing his readers that 'Jesus is the Messiah, the Son of God' (xx. 31), develops his doctrine of the person of Christ in categories which are substantially independent of the Jewish messianic idea; but from time to time he brings these categories into touch with that idea, so that messiah-ship is gradually reinterpreted for a wider, non-Jewish public. In the present dialogue the question raised is whether Jesus is Messiah (x. 24): the answer is given in the forms 'I and the Father are one' (x. 30), and 'The Father is in me and I in the Father' (x. 38), as well as in the form 'I am the Son of God' (x. 36), which belongs both to the traditional Jewish and to the Hellenistic world of thought. The question itself arises naturally out of the preceding discourse. Jesus has spoken of Himself as the shepherd of the flock. In Ezekiel the shepherd is 'David', that is, the Messiah. With complete dramatic appropriateness the Jews ask 'Are you the Messiah?' Jesus's avowal is all but explicit, but in the course of the dialogue we learn what the Messiah really is: He is the Son who being one with the Father is the Giver of eternal life.

The significance of this discussion at just this point in the gospel may perhaps be best appreciated if we compare it with a passage in the Gospel according to Mark which contains parallel material. The scene in John x. 22–39 begins with the demand (unprecedented hitherto in the gospel):

'If you are the Messiah, tell us plainly' (x. 24). The only place in the Synoptic Gospels where a similar demand is made is Mark xiv. 61 (and parallels), where the High Priest asks 'Are you the Messiah, the Son of the Blessed?' To this Jesus replies categorically, 'I am'. Similarly here He says plainly, Υἱὸς θεοῦ εἰμι (x. 36). In Mark he goes on to speak of the Son of Man at the right hand of God. It is in accordance with the developed theology of the Fourth Gospel that the corresponding proposition here takes the form, Ἐγὼ καὶ ὁ πατὴρ ἕν ἐσμεν (x. 30). In both cases the rejoinder of the interlocutors is a charge of blasphemy (Mark xiv. 64, John x. 33), which in Mark leads directly to sentence of death, and in John (agreeably to the difference of situation) to a temporarily unsuccessful attempt to arrest Him.

Whether John is borrowing from Mark and adapting his borrowings to his own purpose, or developing independently material drawn from a common tradition, is a question I reserve. In either case it is clear that the evangelist is using at this point material which represents the crucial moment when the claim of Jesus is brought decisively into the open, and provokes an immediate reaction which leads to His death. It is often observed that John does not accept the Marcan doctrine of the 'messianic secret', but represents Jesus as making messianic claims all through His ministry. And yet it is here for the first time that His claim is both public and explicit. Moreover, though much has been said all through the Book of Signs about the relations of Father and Son, the concise and conclusive expression of these relations in the maxims, ἐγὼ καὶ ὁ πατὴρ ἕν ἐσμεν, and ἐν ἐμοὶ ὁ πατὴρ κἀγὼ ἐν τῷ πατρί, is new, and forms a real climax. Nothing further remains to be said on the subject; and in fact nothing more is said about it in the Book of Signs.

Thus the appendix to the fifth episode, though in part it harks back to chs. vii–viii, is by no means mere repetition; nor could it without loss be transferred to another place in the gospel. It is organically related to the preceding discourse and amounts to a comment on the whole situation presented in this episode; while there is embedded in it a declaration of Christ—δίδωμι αὐτοῖς ζωὴν αἰώνιον—which will become the text, as it were, of the next ensuing episode.

SIXTH EPISODE. THE VICTORY OF LIFE
OVER DEATH (xi. 1–53)

In ch. xi. 1–44 we have a compact *pericope* which has the aspect of a single
continuous narrative—the longest in this gospel outside the Passion-
narrative. It begins, ἦν δέ τις ἀσθενῶν, and ends with the restoration of
the sick man, who meantime has died and been buried. The story is told
with an unusual elaboration of detail. No separate discourse is annexed;
after xi. 44 we pass, through a short connecting link, to a different scene.
On examination, however, the *pericope* xi. 1–44 is found to contain a large
proportion of discourse, in the form of dialogue, in which the interlocutors, apart from Jesus, are Mary, Martha and Thomas, as well as the
messengers from Bethany, the disciples in a body, and the 'Jews' who
serve as chorus and comment on the action. The lively interchange of
dialogue, which is characteristic of this author's style, runs through the
whole *pericope*. Most significant, apart from the saying of Jesus in verse 4,
which governs the whole, are the two relatively self-contained dialogues
contained in xi. 7–16 and xi. 21–7 respectively, both of which deal with
important theological themes. It seems clear therefore that we are to
recognize in this *pericope* a special variation upon the regular Johannine
pattern of sign + discourse. We have already observed that in ix. 1–7 the
fundamental motive of the whole episode is indicated by a brief dialogue
inserted into the narrative, and that in chs. vii–viii the narrative is
subordinated to the dialogue and partly interwoven with it, acquiring
from the contents of the dialogue a high symbolic value. In the present
episode the interweaving of narrative and dialogue is complete. Any
attempt to isolate a piece of pure narrative which may have served as
nucleus soon becomes arbitrary in its treatment of the text. There is no
story of the Raising of Lazarus —or none that we can now recover —
separable from the pregnant dialogues of Jesus with His disciples and
with Martha. On the other hand, these dialogues could not stand
by themselves. They need the situation in order to be intelligible,
and they not only discuss high themes of Johannine theology, but
also promote and explain the action of the narrative. Formally the
pericope is narrative containing discourse; in substance it might equally
well be described as didactic dialogue containing symbolic narrative by
way of illustration. Word and action form an indivisible whole, to a
degree unique in the Book of Signs, though, as we have seen, not without
partial parallels.

Of the twin themes, those of life and light, which dominate the Book of Signs, the latter, as we have seen, with its implicate of judgment, prevailed in the fifth episode, in so far as it had its centre in the Healing of the Blind and the Trial Scene; but the discourse of the Good Shepherd made a transition to the theme of life. The present episode is wholly concerned with the theme of life. In the programmatic discourse of v. 19–47, where the activity of the Father in the Son is characterized as consisting of ζωοποίησις and κρίσις, the work of ζωοποίησις is presented in two stages, or upon two levels. First, to hear and believe the word of Christ is to possess eternal life; it is to have passed from death to life. In that sense the time is coming *and now is* (ἔρχεται ὥρα καὶ νῦν ἐστιν) when the dead will hear the voice of the Son of God and come to life (v. 24–5). Secondly, the time is coming (ἔρχεται ὥρα) when all who are in the tombs will hear His voice and come out (v. 28–9). With this we may compare vi. 54, which also moves in two stages or on two levels: 'He who eats my flesh and drinks my blood possesses eternal life, and I will raise him on the last day.' The discourse of ch. xi clearly reverts to this line of thought, and once again we recognize the two stages, or levels, upon which it moves. 'He who believes on me, even if he dies, will come to life, and everyone who is alive and believes on me will never die' (xi. 25–6). *Prima facie*, all these passages affirm, first, that eternal life may be enjoyed here and now by those who respond to the word of Christ, and, secondly, that the same power which assures eternal life to believers during their earthly existence will, after the death of the body, raise the dead to renewed existence in a world beyond. (In v. 24–9 this final resurrection is associated not only with eternal life but also with judgment (v. 27), but in the present passage the theme of judgment is not in view.) The regulative idea is that Christ is the ζωοποιῶν on both levels. In xi. 23–6 this idea is set in contrast with the current belief in resurrection 'on the last day': set in contrast, for it seems that Martha is here playing the usual part assigned to interlocutors in Johannine dialogues; she is misunderstanding a saying of Jesus to open the way to further explication. 'I know he will rise again on the last day', says Martha. 'I am the resurrection and the life', is the reply. In other words, whether the gift of eternal life is conceived as a present and continuing possession ('he who is alive and has faith in me will never die'), or as a recovery of life after death of the body and the end of this world ('even if he dies he will come to life'), the thing that matters is that life is the gift of Christ—and Christ's gift to men, we know, is Himself (vi. 51).

Thus He is alike the life by which men live now and always, and the resurrection which is the final triumph over death. The terms ἀνάστασις and ζωή are correlative with the statements in verses 25 b and 26 a respectively, as follows:

I am the resurrection: he who has faith in me, even if he dies, will live again.
I am the life: he who is alive and has faith in me will never die.

We now observe that the two stages, or levels, on which Christ acts as ζωοποιῶν are here given in an order which is the reverse of that which obtains in v. 24–9, vi. 54. There it is (in effect) 'life and resurrection', here, 'resurrection and life'. The emphasis is upon ἀνάστασις, and, accordingly, the discourse we are now considering is integrally associated with a dramatic scene of resurrection. The story of the raising of Lazarus is so conceived as to present a picture of resurrection as it is described in v. 28.

Those who are in the tombs	He found Lazarus in the tomb (xi. 17).
will hear his voice	He cried with a loud voice 'Lazarus, come out!' (xi. 43).
and come out.	The dead man came out (xi. 44).

Are we then to conclude that the Raising of Lazarus is offered as a sample fulfilment of the prediction in v. 28? In a sense it is so. Any moment in which Christ presents in action a σημεῖον of His divine functions of ζωοποίησις and κρίσις is, in some sense, the destined ὥρα of His manifestation. At Cana, when His mother intervened, His ὥρα had not yet come (ii. 4); but when 'He manifested His glory' in giving wine for water (ii. 11), it had, in some sense, come. Similarly, when Jesus was in hiding in Galilee, His καιρός was not yet present (vii. 6), but when at the Feast of Tabernacles He declared Himself the source of light and of living water it was, in some sense, present. A certain similarity of structure in the Lazarus story would suggest that when Jesus delayed in Transjordan, His ὥρα was not yet, but the moment when the dead heard His voice and came out was the destined ὥρα in which His glory was manifested, and so, in some sense, a fulfilment of the prediction, ἔρχεται ὥρα ἐν ᾗ πάντες οἱ ἐν τοῖς μνημείοις ἀκούσουσιν τῆς φωνῆς αὐτοῦ, or at least a first instalment of the fulfilment. But it now becomes important to ask, In what sense? The resurrection of which v. 28–9 speaks is final. Of those who thus come out of the tombs at the voice of the Son of God to 'the resurrection of life' it must clearly be understood that they die no more. But Lazarus (upon the level of events in time on which the story moves) will die again when his time comes. If therefore his resurrection is, in some sense, a fulfilment of the prediction in v. 28–9, it must be in a symbolical sense. Not the raising of Lazarus, as σημεῖον, is the fulfilment, but that which the sign signifies. Now the resurrection to which v. 28–9 refers is the general resurrection 'on the last day' (cf. vi. 54); but the raising of Lazarus is set in contrast with the resurrection on the last day, to which Martha had pinned her faith. It seems we might put it in this way: the evangelist has taken an event associated with the 'last day', and transplanted it into the historic ministry of Jesus, thus making of it a 'sign' of the ζωοποίησις which that ministry (when consummated) brought into effect. The implication is that the absoluteness and finality which pertain to the resurrection on the last day belong also to the ζωοποίησις which Christ has effected. We might go so far as to say that if it were possible for us to contemplate the resurrection on the last day as a *fait accompli*, it would still be, as is the Raising of Lazarus, no more than a σημεῖον of the truth that Christ is Himself both resurrection and life—the giver of life and the conqueror of death; and this truth was as certain, as potent, and, for those who could 'behold His glory', as manifest in His historical activity and its consequences as it ever will be.

If something like this is the intention of the evangelist, we may say that the σημεῖον of the Raising of Lazarus adds to the presentation of Christ as giver of life, which has already taken such varied forms of expression, this especial new element: that the gift of life is here presented expressly as victory over death. Resurrection is the reversal of the order of mortality, in which life always hastens towards death. The Hellenistic society to which this gospel was addressed was haunted by the spectacle of φθορά, the process by which all things pass into nothingness, and which engulfs all human existence. It was a large part of the appeal of Christianity that it gave the assurance of a divine principle of ζωοποίησις implanted within the historical process, and countering the reign of φθορά. This assurance was grounded upon an instance in which resurrection actually took place; Christ overcame death in dying. If therefore the episode of the Raising of Lazarus is to be a true σημεῖον of resurrection, it must in some way find place for the dying of Christ by virtue of which He is revealed as the resurrection and the life.

It is at this point that we discern the significance of the preliminary dialogue between Jesus and His disciples in xi. 7–16. It refers back to the attempts to stone Him which were reported in viii. 59 and again in

x. 31–3. These attempts were followed by retreats from the place where Christ manifests His glory: the place of manifestation has become the place of that hostility which will cause His death. Hence to go to Judaea, while it still means to 'manifest Himself to the world', as in vii. 4, now means also to go to death. Thus the summons to go to Judaea, in order that the glory may be manifested in an act of ζωοποίησις (xi. 4, 40), is also a summons to face death; and so the disciples understand it. When it becomes clear that Jesus has fully made up His mind to go, Thomas calls to his fellow-disciples, 'Let us go to die with Him'—an utterance which we may regard as in some sort an equivalent for the Synoptic saying 'If anyone wishes to come after me, he must take up his cross and follow me' (Mark viii. 34, and numerous parallels). Thus the narrative before us is not only the story of dead Lazarus raised to life; it is also the story of Jesus going to face death in order to conquer death. In the previous episode we were told that the Good Shepherd comes to give life to His flock, and that in doing so He lays down His life for the sheep (x. 10–11). The episode we are now considering conforms exactly to that pattern.

It is in the light of this that we may consider the place occupied in the evangelist's scheme by the short narrative of a meeting of the Sanhedrin, and of the resolution to put Jesus to death, which follows upon the story of Lazarus, xi. 47–53. It corresponds to the brief notice in Mark xiv. 1–2, which however does not constitute an independent *pericope*, but is akin to the summaries which belong to the Marcan 'framework'. As we have it in John, it is a complete *pericope*, and might quite well have reached him in tradition as a separate unit, for which he had to find an appropriate setting. In any case, he has provided a connecting passage, xi. 45–6, which is clearly designed to bring the report of the Council-meeting into the closest relation with the story of Lazarus; while the summary narrative which follows it (xi. 54–7) effectively separates it from the material contained in ch. xii. We may therefore take it that the evangelist designed the Council-meeting as a pendant to the episode of Lazarus. Its essential purport is that Jesus is formally devoted to death by a vote of the competent authority. This is, in fact, the act by which, in its historical or 'objective' aspect, the death of Christ is determined.

We have observed before that the cryptic announcements of the coming death of Christ as a theological event (as His 'elevation', as the giving of His 'flesh' for the life of the world) were followed by the report of overt actions on the part of His enemies threatening His life; whereby it became clear that while on the one side His death is a free act of self-sacrifice, on the other side it is the assault of the powers of darkness upon the Light. Similarly here, Christ will go to Judaea to offer His life that Lazarus may rise from the dead; and the immediate effect of His action is to provoke a sentence of death upon Him. The sentence is delivered in terms which for the evangelist are acutely significant. The High Priest says, 'It is expedient for you that one man should die for the people'; and in saying this, adds the evangelist, he was unconsciously exercising the prophetic gift belonging to his sacred office (however unworthily discharged), for he was cryptically declaring the truth that Christ was to die 'to gather into one the scattered children of God'. It is clear that this carries on the allusion to the discourse of the Good Shepherd which we have already recognized.[1] The Good Shepherd not only lays down His life for the sheep, but also brings in the 'other sheep', that there may be one flock as there is one Shepherd (x. 11, 16).

It seems clear therefore that ch. xi constitutes a single and complete episode. Its theme is resurrection. This theme is elaborated in the dialogue between Jesus and the sisters of the dead Lazarus, as well as in the significant narrative of the raising of the dead; and its essential setting is provided by the dialogue between Jesus and His disciples which declares His intention of going to death, and by the appended report of the Council-meeting, in which He is devoted to death. Thus the theme is not only resurrection, but resurrection by virtue of Christ's self-sacrifice. More exactly, the theme is Christ Himself manifested as Resurrection and Life by virtue of His self-sacrifice.

Seventh Episode. Life through Death. The Meaning of the Cross (xii. 1–36)

The seventh episode of the Book of Signs is composed of two significant narratives and a discourse partly in dialogue form. The two narratives are those of the Anointing at Bethany (xii. 1–8), and the Triumphal Entry into Jerusalem (xii. 12–15). The discourse begins with the appearance of Greeks at the Feast of Passover, asking for Jesus (xii. 20–2). It is relatively

---

[1] The verb συνάγειν, xi. 52, is the verb used of the gathering of God's flock in the passage which underlies the Johannine discourse of the Good Shepherd, Ezek. xxxiv. 12–13.

short (for a Johannine discourse), and deals with the single theme of the approaching Passion and its significance. It seems probable, on a comparison with the introductions to the narratives of the healing at Bethesda (v. 1) and of the feeding of the multitude (vi. 4), that xi. 55–7 should be regarded as the introduction to this episode. The words 'Jesus departed thence to the country near the wilderness, to a city called Ephraim, and stayed there with His disciples' (xi. 54) wind up the preceding episode, and the words 'The Jewish Passover was approaching' make a fresh start, and govern the whole seventh episode, which closes with the pregnant words, 'Jesus departed from them and hid Himself', xii. 36 (cf. viii. 59). What remains of ch. xii is by way of epilogue to the entire Book of Signs.

As with other episodes, we must suppose that the clue to the meaning is to be found in the discourse. The theme of the discourse here is clear and simple. It treats throughout of death and resurrection: the seed that decays to give birth to a crop (xii. 24); the principle of dying to live (xii. 25); Christ's self-devotion; His death as judgment on the world, and as ὕψωσις (xii. 31–3). We shall therefore expect to find symbolic allusions to the same theme in the narratives.

Apart from details of the narratives themselves, we observe that the evangelist has provided them with a framework which at every point reminds the reader of the main theme.[1] Before Jesus arrived in the neighbourhood of Jerusalem, the authorities had provided for His arrest whenever He should appear (xi. 57). When He arrives at Bethany, we are emphatically reminded that this is the place where Jesus gave life to dead Lazarus at the risk of His own life[2] (xii. 1) and that Lazarus himself was there, a living witness (xii. 2). At the close of the narrative of the Anointing we are reminded once again of the presence of Lazarus, once dead, now alive, but included as a victim in the plot against the life of Jesus (xii. 9–11). After the narrative of the Entry we are reminded yet again, with an iteration that is clearly deliberate, that Lazarus stands as witness to the truth of life out of death (xii. 17–18). In the light of all this we turn to the narratives themselves.

The Anointing at Bethany (xii. 2–8) is related in a manner mainly similar to Mark, and with more than the usual degree of verbal similarity,

[1] If we divide the connecting passage, xi. 54–7, after verse 54, regarded as the conclusion of the preceding *pericope*, verse 55 becomes introductory to the new episode, and particularly to the *pericope* of the Anointing, and closely resembles other such introductions; cf. ii. 13, v. 1, vi. 1–4.

[2] For this identification of the significant place, cf. iv. 46, and see p. 319.

but with certain traits which rather recall the Lucan narrative of the Sinful Woman in Simon's House (Luke vii. 36–9). It seems clear that for John's purpose the significant point of the story comes in xii. 7, with its reference to the burial of Jesus. The exegesis of the verse presents difficulties, and the text itself is not altogether beyond question;[1] but it seems that the intention is, in any case, to associate the incident with the thought of burial, in preparation for the saying about the buried seed in xii. 24. If this be granted, then we may find in the narrative a σημεῖον (in the Johannine sense) of the burial of Jesus. Seated beside Lazarus, whom He 'called out of the tomb' (xii. 17), He is anointed as one would anoint a corpse. If in xi. 53 He is designated for death, here He is designated for burial.

The second narrative is that of the Triumphal Entry of Jesus into Jerusalem (xii. 12–15). It is related in terms not substantially different from the Synoptic forms, though shorter. Unlike Mark, John makes the crowd acclaim Jesus directly as βασιλεύς, as does Luke; and unlike Mark again, but like Matthew, he quotes the *testimonium* from Zech. ix. 9 which seems to be implied, though it is not quoted, in Mark and Luke. For John (as for Matthew in a different way) the idea of Christ's kingship has real importance.[2] The special significance, however, which John wishes to attach to the incident is best gathered from the 'editorial' additions in verses 16–19.

(i) The disciples, we are told, did not understand the purport of the Triumphal Entry until Jesus was 'glorified' (xii. 16). In Johannine terms, Jesus was glorified in dying to rise again. We recall that after the narrative of the cleansing of the temple, we were similarly told that 'when he rose from the dead, His disciples remembered that He had said this, and believed both the scripture and the saying of Jesus' (ii. 22). The cleansing of the temple is thus understood as a symbol of the destruction and resurrection of Christ's 'Body'. So here, it is Christ dead and risen who is symbolically set forth in the Rider on the ass whom the crowds acclaim king.

[1] In Mark the anointing is definitely a πρόληψις, or anticipation, of the anointing of the Body for burial. John does not so represent it, at least explicitly. According to the T.R., it would be possible to understand that John regards the 'day' on which Jesus was anointed at Bethany as the 'day of His burial' (in a symbolic sense). The better attested text, however, appears, though very obscurely, to contemplate the day of burial as still lying in the future.

[2] See pp. 229–30.

(ii) The person thus acclaimed, we are reminded, is He who 'called Lazarus out of the tomb and raised him from the dead' (xii. 17–18). The King who comes is the Conqueror of death (by dying).

(iii) Finally, by a characteristic piece of Johannine irony, the Pharisees make the most pregnant comment of all.[1] 'You are doing no good,' they say peevishly, 'the world has gone off after him!' (xii. 19). All that they mean, ostensibly, is that there has been a general landslide (as we sometimes say) among the populace in favour of Jesus: ὁ κόσμος is 'tout le monde'. But for John the word κόσμος bears a larger meaning: it is the 'world' of human kind, which God loved (iii. 16) and which Christ came to save (iii. 17, iv. 42).[2] The crowd acclaiming the coming King is a πρόληψις of all mankind united under the sovereignty of Christ.

To sum up, the Triumphal Entry is a σημεῖον of the universal sovereignty of Christ as Conqueror of death and Lord of life, and as such the sequel to His (symbolic) burial.

The transition from the narrative to the ensuing discourse is carried out with subtle art. The Pharisees have been made involuntary witnesses to the world-wide concourse of men to Christ. Immediately upon that, we read that a group of Ἕλληνες[3] approached Jesus through His disciples Philip and Andrew (the two among the Twelve who bore Greek names). In the dramatic situation we may suppose them to be proselytes, but in the intention of the evangelist they stand for the great world at large; primarily the Hellenistic world which is his own mission field. These Greeks are the vanguard of mankind coming to Christ. Their desire is to 'see' Jesus; a word chosen hardly without at least a side glance at the 'seeing' which is vision of God and eternal life (cf. vi. 40, though the verb is different).

The approach of the Greeks provides a setting for a discourse in which the note of the universality of Christ's work is prominent. It begins with the metaphor of the single disintegrated seed which produces a multiple crop (xii. 24), and culminates in the declaration that Christ is to 'draw all men to Him' (xii. 32). It is all spoken as if in the very presence of the approaching consummation of His work, which (as we shall learn) is His Passion. For ἔρχεται ὥρα we have ἐλήλυθεν ἡ ὥρα: the crisis is already here. Its significance is brought out in various ways.

[1] As Caiaphas (xi. 50–2) and Pilate (xviii. 39, xix. 15, 19–22) are cited as witnesses.
[2] It is the same play upon the word as we have in vii. 4 φανέρωσον σεαυτὸν τῷ κόσμῳ.
[3] Ἕλληνες here must signify persons of non-Jewish race and of Greek speech and culture, but not of pagan religion, since they attend the Jewish festival.

First, the necessity of the death of Christ to the universal effect of His work, which has already been hinted at (cf. x. 15–18, xi. 51–2), is enforced by the metaphor of the seed which, as an individual grain, disintegrates as a condition of reproduction.[1] Without the 'death' of the seed, no crop: without the death of Christ, no world-wide gathering of mankind. This strikes the key-note of the whole discourse.

In iv. 35–6, the harvest was said to be already come, and the reaper gathering the crop. Are we to understand the present passage as an afterthought correcting an over-optimistic earlier estimate of the situation? It is a common reading of the Synoptic narrative (though, I think, an over-simplified one) that Jesus at first expected rapid and overwhelming success through the simple proclamation of the Kingdom of God, and later was taught by circumstances that success could come only through His own suffering and death. Such a reading might seem to find support from a comparison of these two Johannine passages. But it is not likely to be John's view. All through the Book of Signs Jesus is represented as conferring on men the light and life absolute which belong to the supernal world, or the Age to Come: in that sense the time which is to come has come—ἔρχεται ὥρα καὶ νῦν ἐστίν. But it is after all only the 'signs' of life and light that are conferred: sight for the blind, healing for the sick, food for the hungry, bodily life for the dead and buried. Sign and reality are indeed intimately related, but the reality lies beyond the sign: and the *real* gift of life and light depends (as we have been led step by step to surmise) on the actual death and resurrection of Christ. In principle He is already devoted to death (xi. 53, 57, xii. 7), and to that extent the reality of that which the signs signify is secured. But in order that we may pass beyond signs to the reality, the death and resurrection must be actual, must be carried through into history. Whatever signs of harvest and ingathering the incidents of the ministry may afford have reality only on the condition that the seed shall be buried for the crop to grow. So now, at the last moment of the ministry, Jesus proclaims, ἐλήλυθεν ἡ ὥρα. The Passion looms in immediate imminence; the event is on the verge of happening, which will manifest in action the reality behind all the signs.

[1] The metaphor of the seed and the crop is well established in the Synoptic tradition of the sayings of Jesus, and it has Old Testament antecedents. But the intelligent Hellenistic reader would be aware of the widespread doctrine of a divine seed (σπέρμα) in man, derived from τὰ ἄνω and destined to return to its source. This doctrine was also set forth in the myth of the descent of the divine Ἄνθρωπος. This divine seed, or heavenly humanity, was conceived as preserved intact within

Secondly, after further comments on the implications of the situation, which recall well-known sayings in the Synoptic Gospels (xii. 25–6), the discourse develops the theme of the glory of God in the self-sacrifice of Christ, in a passage which appears to be a Johannine rendering of the tradition represented by the story of Gethsemane in the Synoptics, and by Hebrews v. 7–9. Jesus, aware of a human shrinking from the ordeal before Him, deliberately sets aside a petition for deliverance, and utters instead a prayer which is an acceptance of the Father's appointment: Πάτερ, δόξασόν σου τὸ ὄνομα. His act is ratified by a *Bath-qol*: καὶ ἐδόξασα καὶ πάλιν δοξάσω. God's glory has already been manifested in the ministry of Jesus; it is now to be conclusively manifested in His death and resurrection (xii. 27–32). In this interchange of prayer and response, the interior act of self-devotion is effected, which answers to the external action in which Jesus was devoted to death by resolution of the Sanhedrin (xi. 53).[1]

The reader is here offered a clarification of an idea which has been introduced, characteristically, step by step in various passages. It began in v. 44 with a simple contrast between the glory which men receive from one another, and the glory which comes from the only God. What the former is, we know well enough; it is worldly honour and fame. What the true glory is, cannot so easily be told. In vii. 18 we learn that the teacher who speaks ἀφ' ἑαυτοῦ is seeking his own glory (the glory that comes from men), while he who seeks only the glory of the one who commissioned him is a true teacher. It is not said, but implied, that Jesus is such a teacher. In viii. 50–5 we are brought a step further. Jesus, we are told, does not seek His own glory, but He is glorified by

its imprisoning receptacle of matter, and as liberated by enlightenment, or γνῶσις, to ascend again to God. John has made the profound observation that the disintegration of the seed, as a separate entity, is essential to its fructification. Accordingly, the Heavenly Man, who is the Seed, must *die* in order that the σπέρματα τοῦ θεοῦ may be collected (συλλεγῇ) and find a passage (δίοδος) into the Pleroma (Valentinus, cited p. 108 above): in Johannine language, the Son of Man must die in order that the scattered children of God may be gathered together, and all men drawn into the unity of the divine life.

[1] See pp. 353–4, 360, 367–8, where I called attention to the way in which passages which set forth the inner, theological, necessity for the death of Christ are balanced by passages which indicate the movement of external, historical, forces which ultimately brought about His crucifixion. This balance of inward and outward action is exhibited on the grand scale in the Book of the Passion, where the prayer of self-surrender in ch. xvii (which in some sort corresponds to xii. 27–30 in the analogous structure of the two parts of the gospel) is balanced by the narrative of the arrest, trial and crucifixion of Jesus which follows. See pp. 418–20, 432–3 below.

God. It is He, therefore, who receives 'the glory that comes from the only God'; but what this glory is, or how it is attained, we do not yet know. In xi. 4 it is intimated that the glory of Christ is not only received from God, but is bound up with the glory of God: Lazarus's illness is designed ὑπὲρ τῆς δόξης τοῦ θεοῦ, ἵνα δοξασθῇ ὁ υἱὸς τοῦ θεοῦ δι' αὐτῆς. In the sequel, Christ (after a prayer of thanksgiving to God (xi. 41)) restores dead Lazarus to life. Those who are the witnesses of it 'see the glory of God' (xi. 40). We have already noted that the whole Lazarus incident signifies that Christ is the ζωοποιῶν by virtue of the surrender of His own life. We are therefore prepared to surmise that it is in conquering death by laying down His life that Christ both glorifies God and receives the true glory which comes from God, though this is as yet far from explicit. Like all the σημεῖα, however, the raising of Lazarus has still only provisional reality. The rubric, Ἰησοῦς οὐδέπω ἐδοξάσθη (vii. 39), is still in force.

With all this in mind, the reader is ready to feel the importance of the proclamation: ἐλήλυθεν ἡ ὥρα ἵνα δοξασθῇ ὁ υἱὸς τοῦ ἀνθρώπου (xii. 23). He already knows something about the glory of Christ: he knows, negatively, that it has no taint of self-glory, and, positively, that it is bound up with the manifestation of the glory of God. He may have found reason to surmise that it is not only devoid of self-seeking, but actually involves self-renunciation. This element of self-renunciation is now made explicit in the metaphor of the seed, which suggests by contiguity that self-renunciation is included in the concept of the δόξα of the Son of Man. Then follows the prayer, Πάτερ, δόξασόν σου τὸ ὄνομα, which is at once an act of self-devotion and an ascription of glory to God. Such is the logic behind the so-called 'paradox' of the Fourth Gospel, the 'paradox' involved in using the term δοξασθῆναι to connote the death of Christ (more properly, the complex event which is His death-and-resurrection, and gives life to the world).

Thirdly, the act of self-devotion accomplished, its immediate effect is declared: it is the judgment of the world (which, we already know, is inseparable from the offer of eternal life). The proclamation, νῦν κρίσις ἐστὶν τοῦ κόσμου τούτου (xii. 31), is to be understood in the same way as xii. 23 ἐλήλυθεν ἡ ὥρα. The discourse is delivered as in the very presence of the catastrophe which looms imminent. On the assumption that the passion of Christ is already in process, the judgment of the world is also already in process; and its issue, the expulsion of the adversary, is fixed, though not fully accomplished until Christ's passion is also brought to its end in His resurrection: νῦν ὁ ἄρχων τοῦ κόσμου τούτου ἐκβληθήσεται ἔξω. (The combination of present and future tenses is significant of the peculiar situation.)

Popular Christianity expected the judgment of the world at Christ's second advent, when God would put all enemies under His feet. Paul divined that in His death He had already triumphed over principalities and powers. In the Johannine presentation of the Gospel there is judgment wherever the light is manifested; and 'signs' of this judgment have been noted from point to point in the Book of Signs. Yet again all such signs stand under the rubric: Ἰησοῦς οὐδέπω ἐδοξάσθη. The full reality of the signs awaits the act of death-and-resurrection, which is Christ's δοξασμός. The real Last Judgment therefore sets in with the beginning of the Passion.

We know, however, that judgment is not the last word. The final effect of Christ's δοξασμός is to draw all mankind to Him, and so into the sphere of eternal life. The expression πάντας ἑλκύσω πρὸς ἐμαυτόν (xii. 32) carries on the thought of x. 16 (the 'other sheep') and xi. 52 (the scattered children of God). Both these passages, be it observed, associate this universal effect of the work of Christ with His passion and death. In the present passage the protasis of the sentence is, ἐὰν ὑψωθῶ ἐκ τῆς γῆς. Here then, at last, we are to expect the clarification of an expression which has been left enigmatic though suggestive at earlier points in the Book of Signs.

We may first observe that the association of ὑψωθῆναι with δοξασθῆναι appears to go back to Is. lii. 13, where the LXX has ἰδοὺ συνήσει ὁ παῖς μου, καὶ ὑψωθήσεται καὶ δοξασθήσεται σφόδρα.[1] The Servant of the Lord is to be exalted and glorified in consequence of His passion and death. In primitive Christian usage, as we have seen, the term ὑψωθῆναι was used for Christ's exaltation[2] 'at the right hand of God'; and we must

---

[1] Cf. also Ps. xxxvi (xxxvii). 20 ἅμα τῷ δοξασθῆναι αὐτοὺς καὶ ὑψωθῆναι, cxi (cxii). 9 ὑψωθήσεται ἐν δόξῃ.

[2] It is to be noted that ὕψωσις, ὕψωμα, exaltatio, were used in astronomy and astrology, denoting either the maximum apparent elevation of a heavenly body, or the date at which it exerts its maximum influence: see Moulton and Milligan, s.vv. ὑψόω, ὕψωμα. In the calendar of Asia, it appears, the festival of Ὕψωμα Ἡλίου was celebrated on April 12. It is a curious reflection that our evangelist and his fellow-Christians at Ephesus would be celebrating the death and resurrection of Christ just about the time when their pagan neighbours were celebrating the Exaltatio Solis. Since Christ is the Light of the World, it is not beyond possibility that this astronomical or astrological usage has helped towards the use of ὑψωθῆναι in a highly mysterious and significant way in this gospel. See G. Weinstock, 'A New Greek Calendar and Festivals of the Sun', in J.R.S. vol. XXXVIII (1948), pp. 38–9.

suppose the Fourth Evangelist to have this usage well in mind. In iii. 14 ὑψωθῆναι would naturally be taken as an equivalent of ἀναβαίνειν, which appears in the context. But the comparison with the serpent in the wilderness requires some modification, or extension, of the meaning. In discussing that passage[1] I suggested that it might be understood by reference to the Hermetic doctrine of an εἰκών of God which draws the minds of men upwards (ἀνέλκει) towards the vision of God and eternal life.

The next passage to be considered is viii. 28 ὅταν ὑψώσητε τὸν υἱὸν τοῦ ἀνθρώπου, τότε γνώσεσθε ὅτι ἐγώ εἰμι. If it read ὅταν ὑψωθῇ... it might readily be understood from iii. 12–15, with reference to the doctrine of the εἰκών just mentioned. The context speaks of the contrast between τὰ ἄνω and τὰ κάτω, and of Christ's departure for an unknown destination (viii. 21–3). By implication, His journey is an ἀνάβασις from τὰ κάτω to τὰ ἄνω, and therefore a ὕψωσις (cf. iii. 12–13). This ὕψωσις is the condition of attaining true γνῶσις. That would be intelligible enough. It is the use of the active ὑψώσητε that causes the difficulty.[2] In the Old Testament ὑψοῦν with a human subject and with God as object is used in the sense of 'to pay reverence, homage or praise'.[3] The sentence in viii. 28 might possibly mean, 'when you pay divine honours to the Son of Man, you will know who He is'. But I find it difficult to integrate this with the thought of this gospel as a whole. In no other place does it use ὑψοῦν in any such sense. Nor is Christ the object of the verb ὑψοῦν in that sense in any other passage of the New Testament.

If we follow the argument of the whole passage, viii. 21–8, it appears to run somewhat after this fashion. Jesus announces that He is going away to a destination whither His hearers cannot follow Him, inasmuch as they will die in their sins. His hearers surmise that He is contemplating suicide. That is to say, they divine that the departure of which He is speaking is in fact death, though they imagine that death as self-inflicted. Jesus in reply affirms that He belongs to τὰ ἄνω, whereas His hearers belong to τὰ κάτω. It is no wonder they cannot follow Him in the journey He is about to take since (it is implied) His journey is to τὰ ἄνω: it is not denied that it may be by way of death. Now throughout the

[1] See p. 307 above.

[2] Where ὑψωθῆναι is used of Christ's exaltation to heaven, as in Acts ii. 33, either it is virtually intransitive, or it implies God as the agent, as Acts v. 31. A human agent for ὑψοῦν in this sense is difficult.

[3] Ps. xxxiii (xxxiv). 4, with μεγαλύνειν; xcviii (xcix). 5, 9, with προσκυνεῖν; cvi (cvii). 32, with αἰνεῖν; cxvii (cxviii). 28, with ἐξομολογεῖσθαι; cxliv (cxlv). 1, with εὐλογεῖν.

episode to which this passage belongs it has been made clear that the life of Jesus is in danger. At viii. 20 it is intimated that He escaped His enemies' attacks only because οὔπω ἐλήλυθεν ἡ ὥρα αὐτοῦ, and although at viii. 30 He is said to have received some response of faith, at viii. 37 He is still aware that His hearers are ready to kill Him. In view of all this, is not the phrase ὅταν ὑψώσητε τὸν υἱὸν τοῦ ἀνθρώπου a grim suggestion that they will help Him in His upward way—by killing Him? But the manner of His death will be such that then at last, and not till then, His true status will be known, for then will be manifested the true significance of the mysterious Name ἐγώ εἰμι (which is perhaps to be understood as the 'Shem Hammephorash' אני(ו)הוא = ὁ πέμψας με μετ' ἐμοῦ).[1] That all this should be supposed immediately intelligible to the interlocutors in the dramatic dialogue is unlikely; but it is perhaps not too extreme an example of the Johannine irony.

It is however possible that the harsh transition from the idea of exaltation to that of death might be eased by recalling what was apparently a popular play upon words. In Gen. xl there is a story about the dream-prognostications of certain palace functionaries of Pharaoh king of Egypt. The dreams are interpreted by Joseph. The interpretation in each case contains the phrase, 'within three days shall Pharaoh lift up thy head' (Gen. xl. 13, 19); but in the case of the 'butler' it turns out to mean restoration to his former high office, while in the case of the 'baker' it means decapitation and hanging.[2] It appears then that the expression נשא ראש[3] could suggest either promotion or execution. There is a similar play upon words in passages cited from the work of Artemidorus on the Interpretation of Dreams (second century A.D.), and even in a rabbinic parable in Pesiqta Rabbati.[4] Apparently the macabre play upon words

[1] See pp. 93–6.

[2] My attention was called to this passage by Dr David Daube in a communication to my Seminar at Cambridge.

[3] נשא is rendered by ὑψοῦν in some dozen places of the LXX, though not in Gen. xl. In Is. lii. 12 וְנִשָּׂא וְרָם is rendered by the single word ὑψωθήσεται.

[4] Artemidorus, Onirocritica, I. 76, εἰ δέ τις ὑψηλὸς ἐπί τινος ὀρχοῖτο, εἰς φόβον καὶ δέος πεσεῖται· κακοῦργος δὲ ὢν σταυρωθήσεται διὰ τὸ ὕψος καὶ τὴν τῶν χειρῶν ἔκτασιν, IV. 49 ἔδοξέ τις ἐσταυρῶσθαι, σημαίνοντος τοῦ δοκεῖν ἐσταυρῶσθαι δόξαν καὶ εὐπορίαν· δόξαν μὲν διὰ τὸ ὑψηλότερον εἶναι τὸν ἐσταυρωμένον, εὐπορίαν δὲ διὰ τὸ πολλοὺς τρέφειν οἰωνούς: similarly II. 53; Pesiqta Rabbati 10, cited by Walter Bauer ad loc. Pesiqta Rabbati however is a very late compilation, and it is not certain how much of its material is ancient. But Artemidorus is near enough in date (second century A.D.) to the Fourth Gospel to be useful evidence. Although he does not actually use the verb ὑψοῦν, ὑψηλός and ὕψος are used equivocally in much the same way.

was widespread, and might be familiar in various circles, Jewish and Hellenistic. It is therefore not impossible that such an expression as ὅταν ὑψώσητε τὸν υἱὸν τοῦ ἀνθρώπου might be sufficiently reminiscent of certain popular ways of speech to suggest to Jewish or to Hellenistic readers an equivocal meaning: either 'when you promote the Son of Man to honour',[1] or 'when you kill the Son of Man by hanging'. The passage however remains enigmatic, and probably intentionally so.

We now return to the passage in ch. xii which we have before us: ἐὰν ὑψωθῶ ἐκ τῆς γῆς πάντας ἑλκύσω πρὸς ἐμαυτόν. In view of various combinations of ideas which we have already noted, this might readily convey to a reader the sense that Christ, ascending, or being exalted, into the heavenly sphere, which is the sphere of eternal life, will attract all mankind into it after Him. A note, however, in xii. 33 states that it 'signifies' (σημαίνει) the death of Christ, and not only so, but the manner of His death, crucifixion. This note is very commonly attributed to a 'redactor'. Even if this be granted, it appears that the redactor has rightly understood the intention of the author. According to verse 34 the Jewish auditors take the expression ὑψωθῆναι to refer to death, since they are puzzled by its apparent contradiction of the scriptures which declare the eternity of the Messiah. The only conclusion they can draw is that the Son of Man is not Messiah. But if not, who is he? No answer is given, at least directly, but the implication appears to be that they are right in supposing Jesus to be referring to the death of the Son of Man, but wrong in propounding the consequent dilemma: either the Son of Man is not Messiah, or Jesus has contradicted the scriptures. The dilemma can be rebutted if the death of the Son of Man, so far from being inconsistent with the eternity predicated of the Messiah, is the means to His 'exaltation', as it is also to His glory. But if this is so, then the death of the Son of Man must be of such a kind that the term ὑψοῦν can be used of it, even literally, without straining the meaning of the word; and in fact the expression ὑψοῦν ἐκ τῆς γῆς might with perfect propriety be applied to death by hanging or crucifixion, especially in view of the apparently widely known *double entente* that we have noticed. It appears, then, that the note in verse 33 is the correct explanation of verse 32. There is no need to attribute to a redactor an explanation which clinches the argument implicit in the whole train of thought. The

---

[1] Upon the superficial level on which the auditors are supposed to argue, this might appropriately characterize such action as that attempted by the multitude in vi. 15, or that carried into effect in xii. 13.

evangelist has at last supplied the key to his use of the term ὑψοῦν, which he has employed from time to time in ways calculated to keep the reader in suspense. For him, of course, it is a good deal more than a play upon words. The death of Christ by crucifixion, the only method of execution which (along with other modes of hanging) can appropriately be described in the terms ὑψωθῆναι ἐκ τῆς γῆς, is a σημεῖον of the reality which is the exaltation and the glory of Christ.

The discourse ends with a brief peroration reverting to the idea of Christ as the Light. The crowd has cavilled at the statement that the Son of Man must be 'lifted up'. In reply Jesus brushes aside their attempt to debate points of scriptural exegesis with a grave warning that for a brief space they are in the presence of the Light and have the opportunity of entering into the knowledge of God through faith—the implication being that their efforts to put the matter on the plane of academic debate are an evasion: the truth is before them if they will acknowledge it. Shortly, since the Son of Man is to be 'lifted up', the moment of opportunity will have passed. It is the moment of decision. The scene closes with the pregnant statement, ἀπελθὼν ἐκρύβη ἀπ' αὐτῶν. It is the end of Christ's public ministry. The Light is withdrawn; the faithless are left in darkness.

EPILOGUE TO THE BOOK OF SIGNS (xii. 37–50)

Ch. xii. 37–50 is conceived as epilogue not only to the discourse of xii. 23–36, but to the whole Book of Signs. It falls into two parts. In the first part, verses 37–43, the evangelist, speaking in his own person, comments upon the story he has told. In the second part, verses 44–50, he gives a *résumé* of the salient points of the preaching of Jesus, as it has been reported in detail in the preceding chapters.

(i) The evangelist's comment indicates that the story of the ministry of Jesus, which he has set forth as a series of σημεῖα, or significant actions, is a story of man's refusal of divine life and light. Those who saw and heard did not respond with faith, or, if in their hearts they were convinced, they would not confess it for fear of the consequences, and so were self-condemned.

Like other writers of the New Testament he sees in this fact the token of divine judgment in the rejection of the unbelieving people, and cites two prophecies of Isaiah, liii. 1 and vi. 9–10. The latter is cited also in all three Synoptic Gospels, and in Acts xxviii. 26–7 (in the mouth of

Paul), where it forms, as here, part of an epilogue.[1] The former is cited by Paul in Romans x. 16, and it belongs to a *pericope* (lii. 13–liii. 12) of which almost every verse is cited somewhere in the New Testament. It cannot be doubted that these scriptures belonged to the primitive stock of *testimonia*, and represent the earliest reflections of the Church upon the failure of Jesus, and of His apostles, to win the Jewish people. For John they have the particular significance, that they point to the fact of divine judgment which has been one of his main themes. The Jews' refusal of the light, with its consequent withdrawal (xii. 36), is the 'blinding' and πώρωσις of Israel of which the prophet spoke. The whole of the Book of Signs is from this point of view an expansion of the statement in the Prologue: εἰς τὰ ἴδια ἦλθε καὶ οἱ ἴδιοι αὐτὸν οὐ παρέλαβον. That statement however has for background the broader statement, ἐν τῷ κόσμῳ ἦν καὶ ὁ κόσμος αὐτὸν οὐκ ἔγνω. The evangelist has in mind not only the rejection of Israel and the consequent extension of the Gospel to the Gentiles (though he has alluded to this in xii. 19–20, 24, and especially 32, as well as in x. 16, xi. 52), but also the principle of judgment by the light in its widest application. The prophecies of Isaiah will be equally applicable to all, of whatever place or people, of whom it can be said that they love the glory of men more than the glory of God [2]—or in other words, love darkness rather than light.

(ii) The remaining verses of ch. xii form a *résumé* of the leading themes of the discourses in chs. ii–xii. No new theme is introduced; yet the passage is no mere *cento* of phrases from the earlier chapters. It rings the changes afresh upon the themes of life, light and judgment, restating the central purport of what has already been said on these themes, in a series of concise, epigrammatic propositions. The principal passages of discourse which are here recalled are iii. 16–21 from Episode I, with allusions to the appendix, iii. 31–6; v. 19–47 from Episode II; and viii. 12–26 from Episode IV. It may be useful to review these passages, indicating the points which are echoed in this epilogue.

Ch. iii. 16–21 asserts that the Son has been sent into the world in order that ὁ πιστεύων εἰς αὐτόν (cf. xii. 44) may have ζωὴ αἰώνιος (cf. xii. 50).

---

[1] For the author of Acts, in harmony with the teaching of Paul, the emphasis falls upon the complementary citation from Ps. lxvi (lxvii). 3, which announces the extension of salvation to the Gentiles. The sequel to the story of rejection is treated by our evangelist along different lines. See pp. 402–3 below.

[2] The contrast of the true glory and the false echoes v. 44, with all the additional depth given to it by the treatment of the true glory in xii. 23–33. The mark of the true glory is precisely renunciation of personal security.

EPILOGUE

He was not sent into the world to judge but to save (οὐ γὰρ ἀπέστειλεν ὁ θεὸς τὸν υἱὸν εἰς τὸν κόσμον ἵνα κρίνῃ τὸν κόσμον, ἀλλ᾿ ἵνα σωθῇ ὁ κόσμος δι᾿ αὐτοῦ: cf. xii. 47). The unbeliever however is under judgment, in the sense that φῶς ἐλήλυθεν εἰς τὸν κόσμον (cf. xii. 46 φῶς εἰς τὸν κόσμον ἐλήλυθα) and men loved darkness more than light. On the other hand, since He whom God sent speaks God's words (cf. xii. 50), ὁ πιστεύων εἰς τὸν υἱὸν ἔχει ζωὴν αἰώνιον (cf. xii. 44 with 50). Similarly, iii. 36 ὁ πιστεύων εἰς τὸν υἱὸν (cf. xii. 44) ἔχει ζωὴν αἰώνιον (cf. xii. 49).

Ch. v. 19–30 deals with the subordination of Son to Father, as the condition under which the Son performs the divine acts of κρίσις and ζωοποίησις. The argument is resumed here with extreme brevity. The word which Jesus speaks, because it is dictated by God Himself, brings judgment (xii. 48b–49). The same word (as God's ἐντολή) is eternal life (xii. 50). A later part of the same discourse, v. 41–7, reverts to the theme of judgment, to which those are obnoxious who do not 'receive' Christ (οὐ λαμβάνετέ με) or believe His words (πῶς τοῖς ἐμοῖς ῥήμασιν πιστεύετε;) (cf. xii. 48).

Ch. viii. 12–26 begins with the proclamation, ἐγώ εἰμι τὸ φῶς τοῦ κόσμου· ὁ ἀκολουθῶν μοι οὐ μὴ περιπατήσῃ ἐν τῇ σκοτίᾳ, which is nearly repeated in xii. 46 ἐγὼ φῶς εἰς τὸν κόσμον ἐλήλυθα ἵνα πᾶς ὁ πιστεύων εἰς ἐμὲ ἐν τῇ σκοτίᾳ μὴ μείνῃ. It goes on to speak of judgment. Christ does not judge (ἐγὼ οὐ κρίνω οὐδένα, cf. xii. 47 οὐ γὰρ ἦλθον ἵνα κρίνω τὸν κόσμον). In another sense however He does judge, and His judgment is absolute, because it is also the judgment of God (ἡ κρίσις ἡ ἐμὴ ἀληθινή ἐστιν, ὅτι μόνος οὐκ εἰμί, ἀλλ᾿ ἐγὼ καὶ ὁ πέμψας με, viii. 16). In this sense, Christ has a word to speak and a judgment to pass. That which He heard from God who sent Him He speaks to the world (viii. 26). Similarly here, xii. 48b–50, where the echo is very clear.

The substance of the epilogue, then, is all resumed from earlier discourses, and the language, though never identical, echoes the language of those discourses in a subtly varied pattern. The only really new formulation is in xii. 44–45, which, though thoroughly Johannine in vocabulary (πιστεύειν εἰς, ὁ πέμψας με, ὁ θεωρῶν ἐμέ, cf. ὁ θεωρῶν τὸν υἱόν, vi. 40), shows the same mould as some sayings in the Synoptic Gospels (cf. Matt. x. 40, Luke x. 16). Its content however is implicit in the preceding discourses (cf. v. 23, 24, viii. 19, 47, x. 30, 38).[1]

From this analysis and comparison it appears that the passage under consideration, xii. 44–50, is appropriately placed as a postscript to the Book of Signs. It is no doubt somewhat awkward to introduce further

[1] It is to be further elaborated in the discourses of the Book of the Passion.

words of Jesus after the evangelist's comments, and after the solemn close of the ministry in xii. 35–6. It is not surprising that proposals have been made to lift the passage from its present context and place it elsewhere in the gospel. It cannot be said that it would have been altogether out of place as a postscript to one of the episodes of the Book of Signs (like, for example, iii. 31–6). Yet something seems to be needed at this point to pull the whole series of discourses together, and this *résumé* of salient points from the discourses, in language which echoes their language without repetition, does this effectively. The reader is not meant to understand that Jesus appeared in public once more for a final appeal after His withdrawal as noted in verse 36. If the writer had intended this, he would have inserted some such 'stage direction' as he is accustomed to use. The series of propositions is not presented (dramatically) as spoken upon one particular occasion. It sums up in brief what was spoken over a whole period. We may compare Mark's proleptic summary of the κήρυγμα of Jesus in Galilee (i. 14–15), or the summary of apostolic exhortations in Acts ii. 40, where the sentence, Σώθητε ἀπὸ τῆς γενεᾶς τῆς σκολιᾶς ταύτης, in spite of the *oratio recta*, is clearly not intended as a verbal report of what Peter said on this occasion. The preference of ancient authors for *oratio recta*, where we should use the oblique form, should be borne in mind. Thus the words Ἰησοῦς δὲ ἔκραξεν do not mean that on a particular occasion Jesus spoke the words following. They mean rather, 'This is the content of the κήρυγμα[1] of Jesus', the aorist ἔκραξεν being of the kind to which Moulton gave the not altogether felicitous name of 'constative'.[2]

[1] In the LXX κηρύσσειν and κράζειν are used as alternative translations of קרא (both being chosen, probably, because of the consonantal combination KR, according to the principle illustrated by Thackeray, *Grammar of the O.T. in Greek*, pp. 36–8, a principle more far-reaching, I believe, than his note would suggest). In the Synoptic Gospels, as indeed in most parts of the New Testament, κηρύσσειν is used for the public proclamation of religious truth, κράζειν being reserved for urgent emotional utterance, e.g. the outcries of the demon-possessed (Mark iii. 11, v. 5, 7, etc.), or of afflicted persons desiring succour (Mark x. 47, ix. 24), or the clamour of a crowd, whether expressing enthusiasm (Mark xi. 9), or fury (Mark xv. 13–14). With Jesus as subject it is used only of the inarticulate cry with which He expired (Matt. xxvii. 50). Κηρύσσειν does not occur in the Johannine writings with the exception of Apoc. v. 2, where it has its normal sense. Κράζειν is used in the Fourth Gospel (apart from the present passage) of John the Baptist's testimony to Christ (i. 15), and of 'proclamations' by Jesus in the temple (vii. 28, 37), but never for emotional or irrational cries. We must conclude that, for whatever reason, John used κράζειν where most other Christian writers used κηρύσσειν, and in the same sense.

[2] See Moulton, *Grammar of New Testament Greek*, I, *Prolegomena*, pp. 109, 115–18.

The passage however does not only serve to summarize the purport of the preceding discourses. It forms an apt transition to the second main part of the gospel, which I have proposed to call the Book of the Passion. The evangelist, in accordance with his general outlook on the evangelical facts, has made the account of the ministry end upon the note of judgment and rejection. Yet it remains true that Christ came ἵνα ζωὴν ἔχωσιν καὶ περισσὸν ἔχωσιν (x. 10), and this will be the dominant note of what follows. The closing words of ch. xii, ἡ ἐντολὴ αὐτοῦ ζωὴ αἰώνιός ἐστιν· ἃ οὖν λαλῶ, καθὼς εἴρηκέν μοι ὁ πατήρ, οὕτως λαλῶ, might stand as motto to a good deal of chs. xiii–xvii, and they are echoed in what was originally (we cannot doubt) the conclusion of the whole gospel: ταῦτα γέγραπται...ἵνα πιστεύοντες ζωὴν ἔχητε ἐν τῷ ὀνόματι αὐτοῦ (xx. 31).

CONCLUSION: CHARACTER AND STRUCTURE OF THE BOOK OF SIGNS

The foregoing review of chs. ii–xii has shown that they form an organic whole. A continuous argument runs through them. It does not move along the direct line of a logical process. Its movement is more like that of a musical fugue. A theme is introduced and developed up to a point; then a second theme is introduced and the two are interwoven; then a third, and so on. A theme may be dropped, and later resumed and differently combined, in all manner of harmonious variations. The themes are those of life, light and judgment, the passion and the glory of Christ, and the like. Each is enunciated and exemplified in various ways, and by the end of ch. xii they have all been brought into a unified presentation of the whole truth about Christ and His work; the whole truth, for although the story of His death and resurrection remains to be told, and there is much to be said about its far-reaching significance, yet in principle the Christ of the Book of Signs is the Christ who dies and rises again; and this truth about Him is the essential presupposition of the whole picture of His ministry. The works of Christ are all 'signs' of His finished work. The 'signs' are all true, provided that He who works them is the Son of Man who was exalted and glorified through the cross. In that sense, each several act of Christ contains within it the whole truth of the Gospel, and should disclose this truth if it is sufficiently pondered and probed. This conception of the purport of the story of the ministry has determined the structure of the Book of Signs.

The unit of structure is the single episode composed of narrative and discourse, both related to a single dominant theme. The incidents narrated receive an interpretation of their evangelical significance in the discourses; or, to put it otherwise, the truths enunciated in the discourses are given dramatic expression in the actions described. Act and word are one; and this unity of act and word is fundamental to the Johannine philosophy, and distinguishes it from the abstract intellectualism or mysticism of much of the thought of the time.

The episodes are constructed upon a common pattern, subject to endless variations. Each of them tends to move from narrative, through dialogue, to monologue, or at least to a form of dialogue in which comparatively long speeches are allotted to the chief Speaker. Most of them have an epilogue or appendix, which in part recapitulates leading ideas of the episode, and in part alludes to ideas contained in other episodes, earlier or later, in such a way as to form a series of links. I shall illustrate this presently.

Each several episode, I have said, contains in itself, implicitly, the whole of the Gospel. The apostolic *kerygma* was centred upon the saving facts of Christ's coming, His death, resurrection, and exaltation. In those forms of it which develop the historical, or narrative, element, such as are represented by Acts x. 36–43, xiii. 17–39, special prominence is given to the journey ἀπὸ τῆς Γαλιλαίας εἰς Ἱερουσαλήμ (Acts xiii. 31), as prelude to the Passion. From the Synoptic Gospels we may gather that this journey had early acquired in Christian thought the character of a solemn procession to the place of sacrifice (Mark x. 32–4, Luke ix. 51, xiii. 31–5). The way from Galilee to Jerusalem is a *via dolorosa*, in all gospels, and apparently in the *kerygma* which lies behind them. This symbolic value of the journey to Jerusalem is deeply embedded in the scheme of the Fourth Gospel. The central core of the *kerygma* is here represented by various combinations of the motives: Galilee to Jerusalem (Judaea), death, resurrection, ascent, exaltation—not, as in the Synoptics (and the Acts), by way of successive chronological stages, but as aspects of each single saving act of Christ. A glance backwards over the seven episodes will make this clear.

In the first episode, after the ἀρχὴ σημείων in Galilee (with which compare the ἀρξάμενος ἀπὸ τῆς Γαλιλαίας[1] of Acts x. 37), Jesus goes up

---

[1] It seems there is an Old Testament background to this. The great 'messianic' prophecy of Is. ix (cited at length in Matt. iv. 14–16) begins by proclaiming light to the benighted people of Γαλιλαία τῶν ἐθνῶν (cf. John viii. 12). In the LXX the opening words of the prophecy (addressed to Galilee) are τοῦτο πρῶτον πίε

to Jerusalem for Passover (which is the season of the Passion), and there enacts, in the cleansing of the temple, a σημεῖον of the destruction and resuscitation of His Body. This accomplished, we are told that the ὕψωσις of the Son of Man is the condition upon which men are able to receive eternal life; and although at a first reading the uninstructed reader cannot be expected to fathom the meaning of that cryptic phrase, we now know that it refers to His death and resurrection.

In the second episode, after a healing in Galilee, Jesus goes up to Jerusalem once again. There He takes action which leads to an attempt on His life. To this He responds by proclaiming Himself the ζωοποιῶν.

The third episode takes place entirely in Galilee, but has the Passion well in view. It is again Passover-tide. Jesus speaks of giving His flesh and blood for the life of the world; there is an anticipatory allusion to His ἀνάβασις;[1] and the episode ends with a forecast of the betrayal.

In the fourth episode the journey of Jesus from Galilee to Jerusalem, with the repeated attempts to kill Him there, is the main theme. The intricate controversial dialogues which accompany the action are a commentary upon it, indicating that the Christ who came from Galilee to Jerusalem and there exposed His life to His enemies is the source of life, the light of the world, the 'exalted' Son of Man.

The fifth episode lies wholly in Jerusalem, as the third lay wholly in Galilee, and the journey motive is lacking. It presents Christ as judged and rejected (in the person of the man He had enlightened) by the Jews, and as the shepherd who gives His life for the sheep, but takes it again and gives eternal life to men.

In the sixth episode we have a journey, not indeed from Galilee to Jerusalem but from Transjordan to Judaea, and this is emphatically represented as a journey which invites the risk of death. It is undertaken expressly in order that Christ's power over death may be manifested: in the very place of death He is the resurrection and the life. With characteristic Johannine irony, the High Priest is made to countersign the truth that Christ is to die for the people, to gather God's scattered children into one.

(ix. 1, in M.T. viii. 23: *sic legendum cum* B). It is tempting to find here a *testimonium* for the ἀρχὴ σημείων in Galilee, which provides wine for the people to drink. I owe this suggestion to Mr Hugh Montefiore in a communication to my Seminar.

[1] The question may be raised, whether even the banal ἀναβαίνειν εἰς Ἱεροσόλυμα (ii. 13, v. 1, vii. 10, 14), though it is an expression that every pilgrim to the temple had occasion to use, may not have had for this writer a suggestion of the ἀνάβασις of the Son of Man (iii. 13, vi. 62, xx. 17).

Finally, the seventh episode presents Jesus coming up from a place 'near the wilderness' and riding into Jerusalem to His death, and interprets that death in a sense which makes it also His glory and exaltation.

These brief pointers may suffice to indicate what I mean when I say that the Book of Signs is so constructed that each several episode contains in itself the *whole* theme of the Gospel: Christ manifested, crucified, risen, exalted, communicating eternal life to men. Over each of them might be written: ἔρχεται ὥρα καὶ νῦν ἐστιν. In each, Christ communicates life and light, and yet in a sense which points forward to that which is not yet (οὔπω, οὐδέπω, occur at least seven times in a pregnant sense in these chapters), but shall be when the crucifixion and resurrection shall have become concrete events of history.

While the several episodes thus constitute relatively complete and independent units, they are connected by a subtle system of cross-references and correspondences, in which recurrent symbols and catchwords play a part. In particular the passages which I have described as appendices or epilogues often serve as links. I will give some examples.

Ch. iii. 25–36 is an appendix to the discourse on rebirth. It takes up various expressions characteristic of that discourse (as I showed above, pp. 308–11). In particular, it takes up πνεῦμα from iii. 5, and associates it with Christ as the bearer or giver of πνεῦμα (or as both, see p. 311); and so points forward to vii. 39, where the association of πνεῦμα with living water, and both with Christ as their giver, elucidates what had been left vague in iii. 1–21. It also takes up the theme of μαρτυρία from iii. 11, and associates it with two ideas here mentioned for the first time, both destined to play an important part in the argument: the ῥήματα of God which Christ speaks, and the divine commission of Christ, resting on the Father's love for the Son. This threefold association of ideas is worked out elaborately in the discourse of ch. v, and underlies the controversial dialogue of viii. 14–19. Further, the appendix culminates in the statement that faith in the Son (whom the Father sent, and who speaks the ῥήματα of God) is the condition of attaining eternal life. This idea, after running through the discourse of ch. v, emerges in vi. 63, 68, where it is once more knit up with the idea of πνεῦμα. The little appendix, therefore, close-packed as it is, forms an important link.[1]

---

[1] The close-packed fullness of the short passage iii. 31–6, and its importance in the development of the argument, might appear to lend support to proposals which have been made to transfer it to an earlier point in the gospel, where it might serve

Again, iv. 27–42 forms an appendix to the dialogue with the Samaritan woman. In 32–4 it introduces the idea of the βρῶμα or βρῶσις of Christ, which consists in doing the will of God. The theme of Christ's obedience to the divine θέλημα is elaborated in v. 19–30, which ends with the emphatic statement, οὐ ζητῶ τὸ θέλημα τὸ ἐμὸν ἀλλὰ τὸ θέλημα τοῦ πέμψαντός με. In vi. 27 the idea of βρῶσις recurs: not, this time, Christ's own βρῶσις, but that which He gives, which, we learn, is His flesh and blood (vi. 55), given for the life of the world. He is able thus to give life, because He came from heaven οὐχ ἵνα ποιῶ τὸ θέλημα τὸ ἐμόν, ἀλλὰ τὸ θέλημα τοῦ πέμψαντός με. For it is the Father's will (and here we glance back at iii. 36) ἵνα πᾶς ὁ θεωρῶν τὸν υἱὸν καὶ πιστεύων εἰς αὐτὸν ἔχῃ ζωὴν αἰώνιον. It appears, then, that the reason why Christ is able to give Himself as βρῶσις μένουσα εἰς ζωὴν αἰώνιον is because His own βρῶσις is to do His Father's will; and this corresponds exactly with what is said in vi. 57 καθὼς ἀπέστειλέν με ὁ ζῶν πατὴρ κἀγὼ ζῶ διὰ τὸν πατέρα, καὶ ὁ τρώγων με κἀκεῖνος ζήσει δι' ἐμέ.

Once again, v. 41–7 is an appendix to the discourse on ζωοποίησις and κρίσις, and on the rejected μαρτυρία (v. 19–31, 32–40). Reflecting upon the situation—Christ, who speaks God's words and does God's works, is disbelieved and so dishonoured—the writer introduces the idea of true and false δόξα, which, as I have shown, runs through so many important passages. The present passage looks back to ii. 11, which states that in the 'signs' Jesus ἐφανέρωσεν τὴν δόξαν αὐτοῦ. The story in v. 1–18 is of a 'sign' which on this principle was a manifestation of the glory of Christ, and yet He receives no glory, but is disbelieved and even threatened. Clearly, therefore, there is a problem about Christ's δόξα which calls for deeper consideration, and such consideration it receives in subsequent passages to which I drew attention above (pp. 373–4). Here again, therefore, we find that the function of a passage appended to an episode is to tie it up to ideas which will be further explored, and after such exploration will throw back light upon the episode itself.

The appendix to the third episode, vi. 60–71, we have already noticed as looking back to iii. 13 (ἀνάβασις of the Son of Man) and iii. 34 (πνεῦμα, ῥήματα τοῦ θεοῦ—the latter already taken up in ch. v—both of them in connection with ζωὴ αἰώνιος, which has been a main theme of the discourse in vi. 26–59); and on the other hand as preparing both for the

as a programme. But I have given reasons above (loc. cit.) for concluding that the whole passage, iii. 26–36, is designed, in its present sequence, for the place where it occurs in our text.

development of the theme of κρίσις in chs. vii–viii and ix, and for the final catastrophe.

The fourth episode has no such appendix. In the fifth episode I have proposed to regard x. 22–39 as having the character of an epilogue, though it is longer and more elaborate than most of the appendices, and appears to have more substantial significance in and for itself than is usual. Yet it does perform the function of linking episodes. It clearly takes up the ideas of chs. vii–viii—so clearly that a large number of recent critics have wished to transfer it into direct connection with those chapters—and it equally clearly points forward, in its concluding sentence, ἐν ἐμοὶ ὁ πατὴρ κἀγὼ ἐν τῷ πατρί, not indeed to any coming passage in the Book of Signs, but to the Farewell Discourses where this idea is elaborately and significantly developed.

The appendix to the sixth episode is of a different character, and hardly conforms closely to the pattern we have been tracing. Yet in xi. 52 it implicitly refers back to the idea of x. 16, and taken as a whole it is the indispensable preliminary to the Passion-narrative (cf. Mark xiv. 1–2), and therefore to the proleptic treatment of the Passion in ch. xii.

The seventh and last episode has no appendix of its own, since it is followed directly by the passage which I have taken to be the epilogue to the Book of Signs as a whole.

The links therefore between episode and episode are intricate and subtle, and serve to knit the episodes firmly into the general structure of the Book of Signs. We have now further to note that, although in some sort each episode stands on its own feet as a presentation of the whole truth of the Gospel, yet in the order in which they stand they represent a progression of thought. On a broad view, it can hardly be accidental that a series of discourses dealing in the main with the general theme of (eternal) life should begin with birth (in the first episode, iii. 3–8), and end with the victory of life over death (in the sixth episode) and the transmutation of death itself into glory (in the seventh episode).

Further, we can trace a development in the presentation of the several themes which enter into the total presentation. I have illustrated, in the course of studying the several episodes in their sequence, how the theme of the Passion develops, and along with it (though not, at first, in explicit connection) the themes of ὕψωσις and δόξα. Similarly, a review of the episodes in their sequence will show a development of the theme of judgment from the first enunciation of the principle of κρίσις in iii. 19–21 to the final proclamation, νῦν κρίσις ἐστὶν τοῦ κόσμου τούτου, in xii. 31.

I will add one more example: the treatment of the theme of the relations of Father and Son. It is first introduced in iii. 35 ὁ πατὴρ ἀγαπᾷ τὸν υἱὸν καὶ πάντα δέδωκεν ἐν τῇ χειρὶ αὐτοῦ. This is fundamental, and pre-supposed in all that follows. In v. 19–30 it is repeated, and the πάντα δέδωκεν is particularized: the Father has committed to the Son whom He loves both power to give life and authority to judge. In vi. 51 (which must be read in conjunction with vi. 38, referring back to iv. 34) the Son's power to give life is expressly related to His personal dependence on the Father (dependence not only for power of κρίσις and ζωοποίησις, as in ch. v, but for life itself). In the fourth episode, at scattered points, the relation of Son to Father is stated in three ways, all of which are here made explicit for the first time, but clearly are either implied in considerations adduced in earlier passages, or represent a step in advance from the posi-tions there established:

   (i) the Son's 'knowledge' of the Father (viii. 55);

   (ii) the Son's origin from the Father (viii. 42);

   (iii) the continual 'togetherness' of Father and Son (viii. 29).

Finally, in the appendix to Episode V, the relation of Father and Son is stated in terms of mutual indwelling and absolute unity (x. 30, 38). This is the climax of the development in the Book of Signs, and in the Book of the Passion these ideas of unity and mutual indwelling come to be of regulative importance.

The Book of Signs, we conclude, exhibits a design and structure which respond sensitively to the development of the highly original ideas of the author. It constitutes a great argument, in which any substantial alteration of the existing order and sequence would disturb the strong and subtle unity which it presents, and which I take to be characteristic of the creative mind to which we owe the composition of the Fourth Gospel.

C. THE BOOK OF THE PASSION

I. The Farewell Discourses (xiii–xvii)

1. *Main themes*

The material of which these discourses are composed falls broadly into two classes: first, material corresponding to the 'esoteric' teaching comprised in the Synoptic Gospels, but enlarged and developed in a Johannine sense; and secondly, material corresponding to certain parts of the Book of Signs, but developed upon a new plane of significance. Under both heads there is much fresh teaching, but it may be regarded as expansion of topics already present under one or other of these heads.

(i) The discourses contained in these chapters are all represented as addressed to the disciples in private. In the Book of Signs there is no such 'esoteric' teaching, apart from the calling of disciples in ch. i. 37–51, the brief conversation with disciples at Jacob's Well in ch. iv. 31–8, and the scene of Peter's confession in ch. vi. 66–71.

In the Synoptic Gospels on the contrary private instruction of an inner circle occurs from time to time all through the ministry, alternating with public teaching. The themes of such teaching (if we neglect those places where it is simply a device of the evangelists to introduce interpretations of parables[1]) may be classified as follows:

A. Precepts, warnings and promises for the disciples.
  1. The mission of the disciples to the world (Matt. ix. 35–x. 16, Mark vi. 7–11, Luke ix. 1–6, x. 1–16).
  2. Precepts for conduct within the Christian community (Mark ix. 33–50, x. 35–45 and parallels).
     (The Great Sermon, Matt. v–vii, Luke vi. 20–49, is represented by Luke as delivered to the disciples in the presence of the multitude, by Matthew as delivered to the disciples with the multitude at a distance. We might perhaps call it semi-private teaching.)
  3. Predictions of the treachery of Judas, Peter's denial, and the desertion of the disciples (Mark xiv. 18–21, 26–31 and parallels).

---

[1] It is very generally held that the interpretations of parables in Mark iv and Matthew xiii are contributed by the evangelists (see my *Parables of the Kingdom*, pp. 13–15, 180–9). Other cases where the 'esoteric' motive seems to be an editorial device are Mark vii. 17–23, ix. 28–9, xiii. 3 sqq.

4. Warnings of persecution (Matt. x. 17–40, Luke xii. 2–12, Mark xiii. 9–13).

5. Promises of divine protection and of the help of the Holy Spirit (Matt. x. 18–20, 28–33 and parallels, Mark xiii. 11).

B. Predictions of the death and resurrection of Jesus Christ (Mark viii. 31–3, ix. 12, 30–2, x. 32–4, etc., and parallels).

C. Eschatological predictions.

1. Predictions of the signs of the end (Mark xiii. 5–23 and parallel and analogous passages).

2. Predictions of the second advent (Mark xiii. 26–7 and parallel and analogous passages).

It is to be observed that while such private teaching is to be found scattered all through the Synoptic narrative of the ministry, the Synoptic Evangelists show a certain tendency to concentrate it in the discourses or dialogues which either immediately precede the Passion-narrative, or are included in it. Thus, Mark gives the long 'apocalyptic discourse' of ch. xiii, composed out of disparate materials, some of which find a place in our other sources at earlier stages in the narrative; and Luke has introduced a dialogue at the table of the Last Supper containing material partly to be found at earlier points in Mark and Matthew. John, it may be, only carried to completion a tendency which had already been at work, in placing all the 'esoteric' teaching[1] at the Supper table. In any case the themes treated are those which I have enumerated as the themes of private teaching in the Synoptic Gospels. The topic, indeed, which I have numbered 'C1. Predictions of the signs of the end', is missing. It lies outside the evangelist's interests. And again there is comparatively little which corresponds to the semi-private teaching of the Sermon, since detailed ethical instruction formed no part of the evangelist's purpose. All the rest is here, as a brief survey will show.

If we examine, to begin with, ch. xvi, we shall find that it covers pretty exactly the themes A3, 4, 5, with the Johannine equivalents for B and C2, and that there is little in it which may not be regarded as expansions of these themes.

xvi. 1–4 contains predictions of persecution (A4). The expression ἀποσυναγώγους ποιήσουσιν ὑμᾶς may be compared with the forecast of the punishment of Christians by synagogues in Mark xiii. 9, Matt. x. 17, as well as with the beatitude pronounced upon the disciples when men

---

[1] Except iv. 34–8, corresponding to Matt. ix. 37–8 (A1), vi. 67–71, corresponding to Mark viii. 27–31 (B).

'cast out their name as evil' (Luke vi. 22). The warning of the danger of death for the faith (ὁ ἀποκτείνας ὑμᾶς) recalls the saying of Matt. x. 28, Luke xii. 4 'Fear not them that kill the body'. There is no suggestion of literary dependence on such passages, but it is the same tradition.[1]

xvi. 5 refers to the death of Christ, in a peculiarly Johannine fashion, as Christ's return to Him that sent Him (cf. B).

xvi. 7–15 contains the promise of the Holy Spirit (A5), which in Mark xiii and Matt. x follows, as here, upon the warnings of persecution. The promise takes a specifically Johannine form, which we shall have to consider further when we have other passages before us.

xvi. 16–22 deals with the theme of the death and return of Christ, and is the Johannine equivalent for the themes B, C2. Further consideration of this must again be postponed.

xvi. 23–4 contains the Johannine version (αἰτεῖτε καὶ λήμψεσθε) of the saying represented by Matt. vii. 7–8, Luke xi. 9–10 (αἰτεῖτε καὶ δοθήσεται ὑμῖν...ὁ αἰτῶν λαμβάνει), which must therefore, it would appear, have reached this evangelist as part of the private teaching of Jesus. It is however given, in xvi. 25–8, a peculiarly Johannine setting to which we must return later.

xvi. 30–1 contains a brief confession by the disciples, 'We believe that thou camest forth from God', which may be regarded as a kind of doublet of Peter's confession (vi. 68–9; cf. Mark viii. 29).

xvi. 32 is a plain prediction of the desertion of the disciples (A3). 'The hour is coming, and has come, when you will be scattered each to his home, and will leave me alone'; cf. Mark xiv. 27.

xvi. 33 closes the chapter with a renewed warning of persecution, and an assurance of victory (A4, 5)—which may be compared with the Marcan ὁ ὑπομείνας εἰς τέλος οὗτος σωθήσεται (xiii. 13).

Here then we have a compact section of the Farewell Discourses forming a real parallel to parts of the eschatological discourse in Mark, with references to other passages of esoteric teaching in the Synoptic tradition. With this in mind we may look at the preceding sections of these discourses (xiii–xv), and we shall find the same themes recurring,

[1] If we were enquiring into the probable sources of the Johannine discourse, we might pay attention to the fact that persecution here takes the form of excommunication and death at the hands of Jewish authorities, and that nothing is said about trials before 'kings and governors', or about 'Gentiles', as in Mark xiii. This would suggest, as some other phenomena in the Johannine Book of the Passion suggest, a Jewish Christian setting, little affected by the experience of the Church of the Gentiles.

with other themes belonging to the Synoptic tradition of the private intercourse of Jesus with His disciples.

The passage xiii. 1–30 corresponds to the Synoptic account of the Last Supper.[1] The incident of the washing of the disciples' feet in xiii. 1–17 dramatizes the saying placed by Luke (xxii. 27) in the context of the Supper: 'Who is greater, he who sits at table, or he who serves? Surely he who serves; and I am among you as he who serves.' The action is applied as an example to the disciples in words which recall the saying in Matt. x. 24, Luke vi. 40: 'The slave is not greater than his master, nor the apostle greater than he who sends him.' This clearly belongs to the general body of precepts for the disciples as a Christian community ($A2$), and echoes what may fairly be called the central purport of the Synoptic tradition on this theme (cf. Mark ix. 33–7, x. 42–5, Matt. xi. 29, as well as the passages already cited). For the rest, all that the Fourth Gospel has to say upon this theme is summed up in the 'new commandment' of mutual love in xiii. 34–5, repeated in xv. 12, 17; and in the general injunction to obey the commands of Christ, xiv. 15, 21–4, xv. 7–10, and to 'bear fruit', xv. 8, 16. All this falls under $A2$.

In xiii. 18–19 we have the Johannine version of the prediction of the treachery of Judas, which in all the Synoptics, as here, takes place at the Last Supper ($A3$).

In xiii. 20, the words, 'he who receives whomsoever I send receives me, and he who receives me receives Him that sent me', recall Matt. x. 40, Luke x. 16, Mark ix. 37 and parallels. This may be taken as a brief reference to the theme of the mission of the disciples to the world ($A1$), which recurs in the Prayer, xvii. 18, as well as in the post-resurrection section, xx. 21.

In xiii. 36–8 we have the prediction of Peter's denial ($A3$), which is placed at the Last Supper by Luke, while Matthew and Mark give it on the way to the Mount of Olives.

In xiv. 2–3 the key-words are: 'I will come again', that is to say, we have a Johannine equivalent for the prediction of the second advent ($C2$).

xiv. 13 is another variation on the theme, 'Ask and ye shall receive.'

In xiv. 16–19 we have an important collocation of the promise of the Holy Spirit ($A5$), and the prediction of the death and return of Jesus (ἔρχομαι πρὸς ὑμᾶς) (B, $C2$), in its peculiarly Johannine form, and the same combination of themes recurs in xiv. 25–31.

---

[1] The account of the sacramental acts and words of Jesus is omitted, probably because the evangelist will not divulge the Christian 'mystery'.

xv. 13 alludes to the death of Jesus as vicarious self-sacrifice (*B*); ψυχὴν θεῖναι = ψυχὴν δοῦναι in Mark x. 45.

In xv. 18–21 there are warnings of persecution (*A*4) and here again as in xiii. 16 we have the quasi-Synoptic saying 'The slave is not greater than his master' in a different application; while the Marcan prediction, ἔσεσθε μισούμενοι ὑπὸ πάντων διὰ τὸ ὄνομά μου (Mark xiii. 13), is echoed in the words, μισεῖ ὑμᾶς ὁ κόσμος...ταῦτα πάντα ποιήσουσιν εἰς ὑμᾶς διὰ τὸ ὄνομά μου.

xv. 26–7 repeats the promise of the Holy Spirit (*A*5), to witness concerning Christ, with the added injunction, ὑμεῖς δὲ μαρτυρεῖτε. We may compare Mark xiii. 9–11, where the prediction that the disciples will be brought before courts εἰς μαρτύριον αὐτοῖς is followed by the statement, 'It is not you who speak, but the Holy Spirit.'

It seems clear, therefore, that these discourses are an equivalent for the discourses which the Synoptic evangelists have placed in immediate contiguity to the Passion-narrative, and that their purpose is to give the Johannine version of Christ's teaching upon those topics which were traditionally the subject of private instruction given to the Twelve. I say the Johannine version of such teaching; and it is indeed clear that while the selection of topics is similar to that in the other gospels, the presentation of those topics is widely different.

In particular, I have included under the head of 'predictions of the death and resurrection of Christ' a number of passages which do indeed clearly refer to that topic, but which contain none of the words usually associated with it: no words meaning 'die', or 'kill', or 'crucify'; neither ἐγερθῆναι nor ἀναστῆναι. The nearest to an explicit word for 'dying' is ψυχὴν θεῖναι. For the rest, we have such expressions as ἀπελθεῖν, μεταβῆναι ἐκ τοῦ κόσμου, ὑπάγειν, πορεύεσθαι πρὸς τὸν πατέρα, and δοξασθῆναι. All such expressions, we may observe, would serve equally well to denote the ascension; and we may recall that in the Book of Signs the term ὑψωθῆναι, which in the primitive language of the Church was used of the ascension, denotes the crucifixion.

Similarly, while the resurrection is not spoken of in explicit terms, we have such expressions as ὁ κόσμος με οὐκέτι θεωρεῖ, ὑμεῖς δὲ θεωρεῖτέ με, or, μικρὸν καὶ ὄψεσθέ με, or, πάλιν ὄψομαι ὑμᾶς καὶ χαρήσεται ὑμῶν ἡ καρδία (with which we may compare the words used in recording the first appearance of Christ to the disciples after the resurrection in xx. 20, ἐχάρησαν οἱ μαθηταὶ ἰδόντες τὸν κύριον). There is no doubt that such expressions do refer to the resurrection; yet they would be equally applicable to the second advent, and indeed they are employed interchangeably with such expressions as πάλιν ἔρχομαι. In fact, it would appear that the distinction drawn in my classification between '*B*, predictions of the death and resurrection of Christ', and '*C*2, predictions of the second advent', though it is quite clear in the Synoptics, is a vanishing distinction in John. He has chosen to treat the death and resurrection as eschatological events. Christ's death on the cross *is* His ascent to the right hand of the Father; and His return to His disciples after death, which is closely associated, if not identified, with the coming of the Holy Spirit, *is* His second advent.

This reinterpretation, or transmutation, of popular eschatology is carried through at length in xiv. 1–24, which we must now examine more closely. The passage begins by speaking of Christ's 'journeying' away from His disciples (πορεύεσθαι), with the assurance, echoing the faith of the primitive Church, πάλιν ἔρχομαι (xiv. 3). This raises difficulties, which are discussed in a dialogue in which Thomas, Philip and Jude are interlocutors. It turns out that Christ's 'coming again' must be understood in the sense that (*a*) Christ will continue His mighty works in His disciples (xiv. 12); (*b*) the Paraclete will dwell in them (xiv. 15–17); (*c*) they will live by virtue of the living Christ (xiv. 19); and (*d*) they will continue in a perpetual interchange of ἀγάπη with Him (xiv. 21). In this sense He will come to them (ἔρχομαι πρὸς ὑμᾶς, xiv. 18); they will see Him (θεωρεῖν), though the world will not (xiv. 19); He will manifest Himself to them (ἐμφανίζειν, xiv. 21). That this language was intended to suggest thoughts of Christ's final 'epiphany', or *parusia*, is shown by what follows. A difficulty is raised which must have occurred to anyone who was aware of popular beliefs. 'Behold He cometh with the clouds, and *every* eye will see Him.' That, we know, was taught in the churches of Asia, where this gospel was written, about the time when it was written (Rev. i. 7). No wonder John's Asian reader, through the mouth of Jude, exclaims, 'Lord, whatever has happened, that thou wilt manifest thyself to us and not to the world?' (xiv. 22). The answer shows that the true *parusia* is to be found in the interchange of divine ἀγάπη, made possible through Christ's death and resurrection (xiv. 23).

There is another instructive passage in xvi. 16–22, where once again a difficulty is raised which must have troubled Christians of the period when this gospel was composed. Christ has said, μικρὸν καὶ οὐκέτι θεωρεῖτέ με, καὶ πάλιν μικρὸν καὶ ὄψεσθέ με (xvi. 16). This oracular utterance puzzles the disciples. They are particularly troubled by the use of the term μικρόν. Τοῦτο τί ἐστιν ὃ λέγει, τὸ μικρόν; they ask, as well they might (xvi. 18). There is sufficient evidence that, in some quarters at least, the interval between Christ's crucifixion and resurrection on the one hand and His second advent on the other was expected to be very short; and it was believed that He had said it would be. But by the time this gospel was written the short interval—τὸ μικρόν—was expanding unexpectedly. What had Christ really meant? The reply is given in striking terms. It speaks of a θλῖψις, which may best be compared to the pains of a woman in childbirth, and, like them, will be succeeded by joy at the birth of a man. This θλῖψις, these ὠδῖνες (Mark xiii. 8), are familiar enough in the eschatological thought of the time. They are the birth-pangs of the Messiah חֶבְלֵיה דִמְשִׁיחַ, חֶבְלוֹ שֶׁל־מָשִׁיחַ,[1] which will issue in the coming of the Son of Man. Yet the sorrow (λύπη) spoken of is *also* that of the stricken disciples on Good Friday, and the joy is that of Easter Day, as it is described in ch. xx.

It appears then that the evangelist had the intention to interpret the event which he is about to record in chs. xviii–xx—the death and resurrection of Christ—as the eschatological Event in the fullest sense, and in doing so, to offer a revision of the eschatological teaching current in the Church and embodied in the other gospels.

(ii) But beside themes which are drawn from the general evangelical tradition, there appear in these discourses other themes taken up out of earlier parts of the Fourth Gospel itself. Sometimes the language of the Book of Signs is echoed, but with significant modifications; sometimes it is actually repeated, but in a setting which gives it a fresh turn. The fresh turn often consists either in the substitution of present or past tenses for future tenses; or in the substitution of the second person plural for the third person; or in both. I give some examples.

One of the recurrent themes of the gospel is that of the divine δόξα revealed in Christ. It is announced already in the Prologue. In vii. 39 we are reminded that Jesus was not yet glorified. In xi. 4 we are told that the sickness of Lazarus was designed ἵνα δοξασθῇ ὁ υἱὸς τοῦ θεοῦ δι' αὐτῆς. In xii. 23 the moment has come ἵνα δοξασθῇ ὁ υἱὸς τοῦ ἀνθρώπου. After all this heightening of expectation the words of xiii. 31 come with dramatic force: νῦν ἐδοξάσθη ὁ υἱὸς τοῦ ἀνθρώπου.

[1] According to Moore, *Judaism*, II. 361, S.-B. 1. 950, these are the true forms, the current חֶבְלֵי הַמָּשִׁיחַ being incorrect. The expression can be traced back to R. Eliezer ben Hyrcanus, *c.* A.D. 90.

Another of the recurrent themes is that of the knowledge of God, which is also vision of God. From the Prologue and the Book of Signs we learn that there is no vision of God except through the revelation of the μονογενής (i. 18). He alone has seen the Father and declares what He has seen (vi. 46, viii. 38). He alone knows the Father, and through His works and death men may, or will, come to know (viii. 28, 32, x. 38: the verbs future or subjunctive). In xiv. 7–9 this prospect of knowledge and vision of God is declared to be realized in the experience of the disciples— ἀπ' ἄρτι γινώσκετε αὐτὸν καὶ ἑωράκατε (the present and perfect tenses are emphatic; ἀπ' ἄρτι, clearly, because Christ is already glorified).[1]

Again, the incarnate Word brings life. In vi. 57 we read, 'As I live because of the Father, so he who feeds upon me will live because of me.' In xiv. 19 this is restated in the form, ὅτι ἐγὼ ζῶ καὶ ὑμεῖς ζήσετε... γνώσεσθε ὅτι ἐγὼ ἐν τῷ πατρί μου καὶ ὑμεῖς ἐν ἐμοὶ κἀγὼ ἐν ὑμῖν. The second person of the verb replaces the third person. In other words, the benefits of the incarnation and work of Christ, set forth in terms of general application in the Book of Signs, are here concentrated and focussed upon the disciples.

The general effect of all this may be summed up if we say that the archetypal relation between Father and Son which is everywhere affirmed in the Book of Signs, and is there held forth as the final relation between God and men, to be realized through the incarnate Word—a relation which is knowledge, vision, mutual indwelling, the sharing of life—is now declared to be realized in the disciples. It is realized by virtue of Christ's departure and return, now seen, in yet another aspect, to be the eschatological Event. For it is the fulfilment of all the prophetic promises: it is the glory of God revealed; it is the knowledge of God made available for all, from least to greatest; and it is the dwelling of God with men.[2]

Thus the whole series of discourses, including dialogues, monologues and the prayer in which it all culminates, is conceived as taking place within the moment of fulfilment. It is true that the dramatic setting is that of 'the night in which He was betrayed', with the crucifixion in prospect. Yet in a real sense it is the risen and glorified Christ who speaks. This is emphasized again and again: Jesus knows that the Father has

---

[1] The effect is not really weakened by recollection of the anticipatory confession, ἐγνώκαμεν, of vi. 69. The present tenses in x. 14 may be regarded as 'gnomic', forming part of the definition of the καλὸς ποιμήν.

[2] Is. xl. 5, Jer. xxxviii (xxxi). 34, Ezek. xxxvii. 27 are typical specimens of a large body of prophecy whose terms are more or less clearly echoed here.

committed everything into His hands (xiii. 3) and given Him authority over all flesh (xvii. 2) (which is clearly the prerogative of the risen Christ at God's right hand, cf. Matt. xxviii. 18), and that He is on His way to God (πρὸς τὸν θεὸν ὑπάγει, xiii. 3; cf. xvii. 13 νῦν πρός σε ἔρχομαι); the Son of Man *has been* glorified (xiii. 31); He has already overcome the world (xvi. 33); He has finished His work (xvii. 4). All that is said about the realization of the benefits of the incarnation of the Word is said in view of this 'finished work'.

It appears, then, that it was part of the evangelist's intention in these chapters to show how the life eternal, which has been set forth in sign and promise in the Book of Signs, is realized in the experience of the disciples (i.e. of all Christian believers), and to exhibit its true nature and character. It is described in various terms, but chiefly in terms of the mutual indwelling of Christ and His disciples, reproducing the archetypal mutual indwelling of Father and Son (xiv. 10–11, 20, xv. 4–5, xvii. 20–3). This in turn is construed in terms of divine ἀγάπη, which exists eternally in perfect mutuality between Father and Son, is manifested dynamically towards men in Christ's self-offering, and is returned by them in trust and obedience towards Him and in charity towards one another (e.g. xiv. 31, xv. 9–10, 12–13, xvii. 23–6, xiii. 34–5, xiv. 21–3; note especially how mutual indwelling passes into ἀγάπη in xv. 1–17 and xvii. 20–6).

The importance of the conception of ἀγάπη in this part of the gospel may be gathered from a study of the vocabulary. In chs. i–xii[1] the key-words are ζωή and φῶς. In chs. xiii–xvii these words are notably rarer. The new key-word is ἀγάπη. The figures are as follows:

	chs. i–xii		chs. xiii–xvii	
ζωή	32		4	
ζῆν	15	50	2	6
ζωοποιεῖν	3		–	
φῶς	23		–	
φωτίζειν	1	32	–	
σκότος, σκοτία	8		–	
(in 'spiritual' sense)				
ἀγάπη	1	6	6	31
ἀγαπᾶν	5		25	
(of false love, 2)				

[1] Ch. i is here included because in this respect the Prologue goes with the Book of Signs.

The synonym φιλεῖν is used four times in each section, and φίλος twice in i–xii, three times in xiii–xvii; but except in v. 20, xvi. 27 φιλεῖν has not the weight which attaches to ἀγαπᾶν.

This change of vocabulary is hardly accidental. It means that terms of a metaphysical cast, current throughout the religious world of Hellenism, recede, and their place is largely taken by terms of a strongly personal and ethical cast, characteristic of the Hebrew-Christian tradition. This does not mean that the teaching of these chapters is different from that of the earlier chapters, or designed to supersede it. Although ζωή and ζῆν are comparatively rare, they occur at crucial points (e.g. xiv. 18, xvii. 3), and although φῶς is not found, the thought of φῶς γνώσεως is never far from the mind of any Hellenistic thinker when he speaks of knowledge of God (and γινώσκειν is frequent enough in these chapters). The evangelist does not intend for a moment to abandon the belief that Christ brings life and light, or even to subordinate that belief. His intention is to emphasize the truth that the final reality of life and light is given in ἀγάπη. It is in the exercise of ἀγάπη that man knows God and shares His life, that God and man are made one, and that the creature returns to the Creator through the eternal Word through which all things were made.

2. *Design and argument*

The evangelist, then, appears to have had a twofold intention in composing these discourses: first, to interpret the death and resurrection of Jesus as the eschatological event in the fullest sense, and in doing so to reinterpret the eschatological beliefs of the early Church; and, secondly, to set forth the nature of the new life into which the disciples (and all Christians) are brought through Christ's death and resurrection. We have now to enquire how far this twofold intention has determined the structure of these chapters.

The logical development and coherence of the discourses are not always immediately obvious. There are many repetitions. The argument often seems to return upon itself. The thought appears to move on different levels, sometimes concrete and historical, sometimes abstract and 'mystical'. Here as elsewhere in this gospel these phenomena have often been explained by hypotheses of the use of various sources, imperfectly combined by a writer who might be regarded as redactor rather than author, or of accidental displacement of pages. Here, however, as elsewhere, I conceive it to be the duty of the interpreter to attempt in the

399

first place to understand and account for the actual text which lies before him, and if possible to discover the plan on which it is arranged, whether or not any other possible plan might be discovered behind it.

I propose, then, to examine the formal structure of chs. xiii–xvii as they lie before us, and to attempt to relate the structure to the argument. They begin with a dramatic scene which combines action with dialogue, like so many other passages in the gospel. This is followed by passages of pure dialogue, in which the part assigned to Jesus is progressively increased, and the part assigned to other interlocutors diminishes, until monologue prevails. Then there is a short concluding dialogue (xvi. 29–33). To all this is appended a monologue of a unique kind, the long prayer of ch. xvii. To this we shall find no full parallel in other parts of the gospel.[1] But if for the present we confine ourselves to chs. xiii–xvi, we observe that the same general pattern holds in various episodes of the Book of Signs. For comparison we may recall the following:

ch. v. 1–9   action (healing at Bethesda)

      10–18   dialogue (Sabbath healing)

      19–40   monologue (the work of Father and Son in κρίσις and ζωοποίησις, and the question of μαρτυρία)

      41–7   appendix

ch. vi. 1–23   action accompanied by dramatic dialogue (Feeding of the Multitude, etc.)

      24–59   dialogue tending to monologue (Bread of Life)

      60–5, 66–71, two brief concluding dialogues

ch. ix. 1–7   action (healing at Siloam)

      8–41   dialogues (trial scene and two brief colloquies)

ch. x. 1–18   monologue (the shepherd and the sheep)

      19–21   brief concluding dialogue between parties of the Jews

      22–39   appendix

These parallels will suffice to show that the thought of the Farewell Discourses has taken shape in a form which reproduces broadly a standard Johannine pattern, though here it is elaborated on an unparalleled scale. We must now inspect the pattern in greater detail.

[1] Yet the brief self-communion issuing in prayer, and answered by a *Bath-qol*, in xii. 27–8 is a real parallel on a small scale, and its theme is the same: it represents Christ's self-dedication to His appointed destiny. But *formally* there is little resemblance.

(a) Opening dramatic scene, xiii. 1–30

The opening dramatic scene runs from xiii. 1 to xiii. 30. It is based upon the incident of the washing of the feet of the disciples by Jesus. This is treated as a significant action (σημεῖον) in the Johannine manner Its symbolism is complex. Clues to it are not wanting. We are to bear in mind, first, that the action takes place δείπνου γινομένου [1] (xiii. 2). That is to say, it has its setting within the κυριακὸν δεῖπνον,[2] the focus of the rite which carries the ἀνάμνησις of Christ crucified and risen. This would be enough to put the instructed Christian reader at once on the right track. The idea of washing with water would further suggest to him by associa-tion the sacrament of baptism (λουτρὸν παλιγγενεσίας, Titus iii. 5).[3] The uninitiated reader would not be aware of all this; but if he had read the Book of Signs attentively he would not lack clues, especially if his background was that kind of 'Hellenistic mysticism' represented by the Hermetic and kindred writings.

The moment at which the incident takes place is clearly significant. Jesus, fully aware of His divine mission, origin, and destiny, is about to leave the world and return to the Father (xiii. 1, 3). This gives peculiar emphasis to His act of humility:[4] it is a κατάβασις. Christ, the eternal Son of Man, who descended from heaven to ascend to heaven again, to whom all authority is given (cf. iii. 13, 35, vi. 62), descends to the lowest place of service. We are reminded not only of Paul's words about Him who ἐν μορφῇ θεοῦ ὑπάρχων assumed the μορφὴ δούλου (Phil. ii. 5–8), but also of the place in the *Poimandres* which speaks about the heavenly Ἄνθρωπος: 'Being immortal, and having authority over all things, he suffers mortality in subjection to fate. Being above the frame of the universe, he has become a slave within the frame' (*C.H.* I. 15). The *Poimandres* indeed speaks of a 'fall', John of an act of condescension, but there is a real analogy of ideas, which a Hellenistic reader might be expected to discern. The washing of the feet, therefore, is a 'sign' of

[1] The alternative reading γενομένου has inferior attestation.

[2] So I Cor. xi. 20, written, like this gospel, at Ephesus. The meal is not explicitly called δεῖπνον elsewhere in the New Testament.

[3] In xiii. 10 λούεσθαι, to take a bath, is contrasted with νίπτειν, to wash a part of the body. Baptism is a bath (λουτρόν, Eph. v. 26, Tit. iii. 5). The Christian reader is assured that having undergone the λουτρόν he is καθαρός, yet may need some kind of recurrent washing. The thought may perhaps be understood by reference to I John i. 8–ii. 2, with iii. 4–6 and 19–20. See my commentary on that epistle.

[4] For the washing of the feet as a servile duty, and as a mark of exceptional deference or consideration, among the Jews, see passages cited by S.-B. *ad loc.*

the incarnation of the Son of God, consummated by His self-oblation in death. Further, the attentive reader of the Book of Signs will be aware that 'water' is the instrument of regeneration (iii. 5), the vehicle of eternal life (iv. 13–14), even the Spirit which is given when Christ is 'glorified' (vii. 39), and that it sheds φῶς ἀληθινόν on blinded eyes (ix. 5–7). Again, the present passage itself indicates that the washing of the feet is a means whereby the disciples 'have part with' their Master (μέρος ἔχεις μετ' ἐμοῦ, xiii. 8), and the sign of final and effectual καθαρισμός (unlike the ineffective καθαρισμός τῶν 'Ιουδαίων (ii. 6), and the καθαρισμός about which the disciples of John the Baptist disputed with a Jew (iii. 25)). The washing completed, Jesus pronounces, ὑμεῖς καθαροί ἐστε (xiii. 10; cf. xv. 3 ἤδη ὑμεῖς καθαροί ἐστε διὰ τὸν λόγον ὃν λελάληκα ὑμῖν).[1] Similarly in the Hermetic tractate *De Regeneratione*, Hermes says to the regenerated Tat, καλῶς σπεύδεις λῦσαι τὸ σκῆνος· κεκαθαρμένος γάρ (*C.H.* XIII. 15). Thus the whole complex of ideas to be expounded is implicit in the symbolism of the opening scene.

The narrative of the Last Supper is now completed by the prediction of treachery among the disciples, the designation of Judas as the traitor, and his departure into the night. The sentence ἦν δὲ νύξ (xiii. 30) is not only intensely dramatic; it also recalls the whole symbolism of light and darkness in the Book of Signs (cf. ix. 4 ἔρχεται νύξ). The agent of death who goes out into the night is one who loves darkness rather than light, because his deeds are evil (iii. 19).

We are reminded therefore of the theme of κρίσις which ran through the Book of Signs; of κρίσις in the sense which it has borne all through: a sifting of men by their varying responses to the words and actions of Christ. The sifting is now complete. With the departure of Judas the faithful remnant is finally selected out of the unbelieving world. Here we have a clue to the relation between the Book of Signs and the Farewell Discourses in the scheme of the gospel. The evangelist himself has characterized the Book of Signs as a story of rejection: the rejection of Christ by 'the Jews', and their rejection by God, as declared by Isaiah (xii. 37–42). Thus the statement of the Prologue is made good: εἰς τὰ ἴδια ἦλθεν, καὶ οἱ ἴδιοι αὐτὸν οὐ παρέλαβον. But the Prologue goes on, ὅσοι δὲ ἔλαβον αὐτόν, ἔδωκεν αὐτοῖς ἐξουσίαν τέκνα θεοῦ γενέσθαι (i. 11–12).

[1] The disciples are καθαροί through washing with water: they are καθαροί, also, διὰ τὸν λόγον. Similarly, eternal life comes by eating the flesh and blood of the Son of Man (vi. 54) and also, τὰ ῥήματα ἃ λελάληκα ὑμῖν are ζωή. The treatment of the two sacraments seems analogous (see p. 342 n. 3).

Thus the chapters which exhibit the rejection of Christ must be supplemented by chapters which exhibit the blessedness of those who receive Him, and through Him become children of God. These are represented by the loyal group who are left with Jesus when the traitor has gone out, and to them our attention is now directed.

(b) Dialogue on Christ's departure and return, xiii. 31–xiv. 31

After the opening dramatic scene, comprising action and dialogue, we come to the first cycle of discourse, which is in dialogue form, extending from xiii. 31 to xiv. 31. Ch. xiv is clamped together by the repeated use of the expression μὴ ταρασσέσθω ὑμῶν ἡ καρδία in verses 1 and 27. Ch. xiv is linked with what precedes by the recurrence of the theme of Christ's departure (xiii. 33, xiv. 2, 4, etc.). The whole dialogue, indeed, is dominated by the ideas of going and coming. Verbs expressing these ideas (ὑπάγειν, πορεύεσθαι, ἔρχεσθαι) occur at least fourteen times, with Christ as subject; and the longest passage without direct reference to going and coming is no more than five verses. This dialogue in fact is occupied with the interpretation of the death and resurrection of Christ.

The dialogue opens with the proclamation, νῦν ἐδοξάσθη ὁ υἱὸς τοῦ ἀνθρώπου καὶ ὁ θεὸς ἐδοξάσθη ἐν αὐτῷ. The past tense of the verses is chosen because Jesus is in effect already accomplishing His passion. He has been devoted to death by vote of the Sanhedrin (xi. 47–53), and has accepted death by a voluntary act of self-oblation to the glory of God (xii. 28); and Judas is already on his way to perform his fatal act of treachery. In all that follows it is Christ crucified who speaks, the living Christ who has already passed through death, although dramatically He speaks on the eve of death (see pp. 397–8).

After this introductory proclamation, Jesus recalls the words He spoke to the Jews (vii. 33–4, viii. 21): 'Yet a little while I am with you; you will seek me and not find me; where I am going you cannot come.' These words, He now says, apply equally to the disciples. Where He is going they cannot at present follow Him. 'Why?' asks Peter. The reply is given in the traditional form of the prediction of Peter's denial: ἀμὴν ἀμὴν λέγω σοι, οὐ μὴ ἀλέκτωρ φωνήσῃ ἕως οὗ ἀρνήσῃ με τρίς. The wording of the prediction is close to Luke's λέγω σοι, Πέτρε, οὐ φωνήσει σήμερον ἀλέκτωρ ἕως τρὶς ἀπαρνήσῃ μὴ εἰδέναι με. In its Lucan setting it is a rejoinder to Peter's profession, μετά σου ἕτοιμός εἰμι...εἰς θάνατον πορεύεσθαι (Luke xxii. 33–4), much as, here, Peter expresses his willingness ψυχὴν θεῖναι. In John also, we are to understand, the journey which

Christ is about to take is, in the first intention of the words, the journey of death, and for this journey Peter is not yet prepared. But that is not all that is to be said about it. He is going to prepare a place for His disciples within the Father's house, and will return to bring them home with Him. Here we have the closest approach to the traditional language of the Church's eschatology. In I Thess. iv. 13–18 Paul assures his correspondents, ἐν λόγῳ κυρίου,[1] that Christ, who 'died and rose again' (and, although he does not add the words, ascended to heaven), will descend from heaven, and living Christians will be caught up to meet Him—καὶ οὕτως πάντοτε σὺν κυρίῳ ἐσόμεθα. This, we may fairly assume, was the current belief about the departure and return of Christ and His disciples' reunion with Him. It is echoed in xiv. 3 πάλιν ἔρχομαι καὶ παραλήμψομαι ὑμᾶς πρὸς ἐμαυτόν, ἵνα ὅπου εἰμὶ ἐγὼ καὶ ὑμεῖς ἦτε. From this position the Johannine reinterpretation starts.

In the dialogue which ensues, the disciples Thomas, Philip and Jude, like Peter, play very much the part which is assigned to interlocutors in the dialogues of the Book of Signs, misunderstanding the words of Jesus to give an opportunity for further elucidation. Through question and answer it is explained (to put it shortly) that the journey Christ is undertaking (in dying) is the journey to the Father, and Christ Himself (Christ crucified) is the way on which the disciples must travel to the same goal. Christ is the way to the Father; that is to say, He mediates the knowledge of God, or the vision of God; to see Him is to see the Father, since He is one with the Father by mutual indwelling, and His words and deeds are those of the Father. This divine activity on earth will not cease when He goes to the Father (when He dies). It will continue in those who believe in Him, and continue on an even greater scale, since He will act in answer to their prayer, and through Him the Spirit will be with them and in them. In this sense, He adds, οὐκ ἀφήσω ὑμᾶς ὀρφανούς· ἔρχομαι πρὸς ὑμᾶς—which is the promise of His 'return'

[1] The expression, λέγομεν ἐν λόγῳ κυρίου, it seems, indicates that Paul is here having recourse to the accepted tradition of the sayings of Jesus, as in I Cor. vii. 10, ix. 14. That he is citing a saying verbally does not necessarily follow: even in I Cor. vii. 8–12, 25, 40, where he lays some stress upon the distinction between a 'commandment of the Lord' and his own γνώμη, it does not appear that he gives a verbatim quotation without note or comment. How much of I Thess. iv. 15–17 he regarded as representing what Jesus actually said, remains doubtful, but he does seem to be appealing to some traditional saying, as distinct from instructions for which he made himself personally responsible. Without enquiring here into the value of the passage as evidence for the teaching of Jesus, we may safely conclude that it represents a pre-Pauline tradition of the primitive Church.

in a slightly altered form (xiv. 5–18). But the words which follow put it in a fresh light. The time will shortly come when, although He is invisible to the world, His disciples will see Him; seeing Him (and therefore possessing the vision of God) they will have life; they will have that knowledge of God which is actual sharing of the mutual indwelling of Father and Son (xiv. 19–20). These statements are to be understood in accordance with all that has previously been set forth, in sign and discourse, about Christ imparting life and light to men by giving Himself to them (that is, by dying for them), but they will be brought into greater prominence in a later discourse (see pp. 410–13).

By now it is surely clear that the 'return' of Christ is to be understood in a sense different from that of popular Christian eschatology. It means that after the death of Jesus, and because of it, His followers will enter into union with Him as their living Lord, and through Him with the Father, and so enter into eternal life. That is what He meant when He said, 'I will come again and receive you to myself, that where I am you too may be' (cf. also xvii. 24). This is the true 'epiphany',[1] and it is essentially an epiphany of the love of God, as the evangelist has set forth clearly and emphatically in xiv. 21–4.[2]

From this point we can recognize the importance of the 'new commandment' of mutual love (xiii. 34), which I passed over in its immediate context, but to which we must now return. After the cryptic announcement of His death, Jesus adds, 'I give you a new commandment, to love one another. As I loved you, you must love one another.' We are intended to bear in mind that the entire process of man's salvation is set in motion by the love of God for the world (iii. 16). The love of God is expressed in action by the Son whom He sent. The Father loves the Son, and the Son responds in obedience (iii. 35, v. 19–20). That is why the words and deeds of Jesus are the words and deeds of the Father (cf. xiv. 11, 24). Hence it is with the eternal love of God that Christ loves His own and loves them to the end (xiii. 1). So much we have already been told. We now learn that (as a sequel to the death of Christ) His followers are to reproduce, in their mutual love, the love which the Father showed in sending the Son, the love which the Son showed in laying down His life. Such love, among Christians, is a revelation to the world: ἐν τούτῳ γνώσονται πάντες ὅτι ἐμοὶ μαθηταί ἐστε, ἐὰν ἀγάπην ἔχητε ἐν ἀλλήλοις

---

[1] 'Emphany', John would say. His verb is ἐμφανίζειν (xiv. 21–2). Ἐμφάνεια is a synonym for ἐπιφάνεια, e.g. Josephus, Ant. xv. 11. 7, § 425 ἐμφάνειαι τοῦ θεοῦ.

[2] See what has already been said on p. 395.

(xiii. 35). That is all that is said here. It looks forward to further developments. But we may anticipate. In xvii. 21, 23 Christ prays that His followers may be in unity, ἵνα ὁ κόσμος πιστεύῃ...ἵνα γινώσκῃ ὁ κόσμος ὅτι σύ με ἀπέστειλας καὶ ἠγάπησας αὐτοὺς καθὼς ἐμὲ ἠγάπησας. Although there is to be no outward manifestation, after the manner of popular eschatological expectation, by which the world might be compelled to believe, yet there *is* to be an epiphany to the world—the revelation of the divine love in Christ, as it is active in the loving unity of His people. Only by such a revelation, and by no crude miracle of coming on the clouds, can the world be led to faith and knowledge, and so to the eternal life which God designed for it when in love for the world He gave His Son.

It would seem that the evangelist was conscious of putting forward a bold reinterpretation of what was believed to be the teaching of Jesus. This would appear to be the motive of his recurrence to the subject of the Spirit in xiv. 25–6. Jesus, he means, had indeed spoken on these themes to His disciples before His death, but His words were imperfectly understood and remembered. After His death the Church received the Spirit, and the evangelist is convinced that by inspiration of the Spirit he has himself been taught what Jesus truly meant, in accordance with His promise. These verses are a kind of explanatory—or even justificatory—postscript to the dialogue, which is now substantially complete. It turns out to be a coherent treatment of the one theme—the meaning of the death and resurrection of Christ, as departure and return. In the course of the argument certain ideas are briefly introduced (after the Johannine manner) which are to become later the subjects of more extended treatment; in particular, (*a*) the mutual indwelling of Christ and His disciples (xiv. 20); and (*b*) the role of the Paraclete (xiv. 15–17).

In xiv. 27–31 we have a kind of appendix, which (after the Johannine manner) resumes some of the contents of the main dialogue, but also reverts to the historical, or dramatic, situation. Jesus speaks words of farewell and of comfort. Then suddenly He exclaims, ἔρχεται ὁ τοῦ κόσμου ἄρχων...ἐγείρεσθε ἄγωμεν ἐντεῦθεν.

We here encounter one of the most difficult problems in the structure of these discourses. The words ἐγείρεσθε ἄγωμεν appear to imply an immediate movement to meet the approaching enemy.[1] Yet in ch. xv

---

[1] Ἄγειν intransitive means properly to 'march'. It is a military term, apparently derived from ἄγειν='lead', by the suppression of the object (στρατιάν, ναῦς, etc.). Thus in Thucydides VII. 81 τὸ δὲ Νικίου στράτευμα ἀπεῖχεν ἐν τῷ πρόσθεν καὶ

Jesus goes on speaking as if there had been no interruption, and it is not until xviii. 1 that a move is made. It is no wonder that many critics have felt obliged, here at least, to posit some disarrangement of the text, and to attempt a rearrangement. The trouble is that no simple rearrangement will remove the difficulty. Even if chs. xv and xvi be in some way got rid of,[1] ch. xvii remains. To place anything at all after xvii. 26 would be to create an intolerable anticlimax, and the long pause for prayer after ἐγείρεσθε ἄγωμεν would be as difficult as the continuation of the discourses. Something more than mere rearrangement of the material seems to be called for. It is suggested, not without plausibility, that chs. xv–xvii may have been introduced as an afterthought, either by the original author of the work or by another writer supplementing it—a writer who was careless enough to overlook the difficulty thereby caused. Or again, it is suggested that the author may have written xiii. 31–xiv. 31 and xv–xvi (and perhaps xvii) as alternative versions of the Farewell Discourses, intending to incorporate one or other in his finished work; and this too is plausible, since so many of the topics of xiii–xiv recur in xv–xvi. We might then suppose that the author left his sheets without final arrangement, and a redactor did the best he could. Either of these hypotheses is possible. Yet we are still faced with the problem of explaining the existing text. Unless the 'redactor' was strangely irresponsible, he must have given some thought to the arrangement of the material, and unless he was more obtuse than we can easily believe, he must have seen the difficulty about ἐγείρεσθε ἄγωμεν as clearly as we do. Presumably he thought the words had some intelligible meaning as they stand. And after all it is still not proven that the evangelist himself was not his own redactor. So we may enquire afresh how these two verses may be understood, in their present position.

πεντήκοντα σταδίους· θᾶσσόν τε γὰρ ὁ Νικίας ἦγε, κ.τ.λ., it is easy to supply στράτευμα as object; but in Xenophon, *Hellenica* IV. ii. 19 ἦγον δὲ καὶ οἱ Λακεδαιμό-νιοι ἐπὶ τὰ δεξιὰ καὶ οὕτω πολὺ ὑπερέτεινον τὸ κέρας ὥστε κ.τ.λ., the verb has become intransitive: 'the Lacedaemonians *advanced* to the right', etc. (see L. and S. *s.v.*). So here ἄγωμεν ἐντεῦθεν suggests, 'let us *advance* from here': καὶ γὰρ προῄδει ἥξοντα· καὶ οὐ μόνον οὐκ ἔφυγεν, ἀλλὰ καὶ ὁμόσε ἐχώρει (*Catena Patrum* ed. Cramer *ad* Mk. xiv. 42).

[1] The proposal to place xv–xvi before xiv has sometimes been supported by the argument that xiv. 30, οὐκέτι πολλὰ λαλήσω μεθ' ὑμῶν, implies that the discourse is nearing its end. This is an example of precisely the kind of wooden criticism which ought never to be applied to the work of a mind like our evangelist's. However long these discourses may be, they are burdened from beginning to end with the sense of parting, and the time is short.

It will be well to recall the context in which the words ἐγείρεσθε ἄγωμεν occur in Mark. Jesus has returned a third time from the place of His agony in the Garden of Gethsemane, to find His disciples again asleep. In strong agitation He cries, 'Still sleeping? Still taking rest? Enough of this! The moment has come.' Then, as the posse begins to appear among the trees of the garden, 'Look, the Son of Man is being betrayed into the hands of sinners. Up, let us go! Look, my betrayer is at hand' (Mark xiv. 41–2). And with that Judas comes on the scene and the betrayal follows. Now compare John xiv. 30–1: 'The ruler of this world is coming....Up, let us be going!' It seems to be essentially the same situation as that of Mark xiv. 41–2. The enemy is approaching; only it is not Judas but the Archon of this world (in Hellenistic terms). Even this is not very different from Luke's rendering of Jesus's address to His assailants: 'This is your moment; it is the dominion of darkness' (Luke xxii. 53). In Luke and John alike the real enemy is the devil (who had inspired Judas to his act of treachery, xiii. 2, and has now taken possession of him, xiii. 27); and to this Mark would scarcely have demurred. Yet Mark and Luke are relating an incident which John has described differently in xviii. 1–11, while John xiv. 31–2 refers to a moment some time before this incident. May we not say, John has transferred the inner or spiritual aspect of the situation immediately before the betrayal, as described by Mark, to the context of the discourses at the supper-table? It was not only in the Garden that Jesus faced His enemy. There He met the Adversary in the person of Judas and went to meet him, but the power and wickedness of the Archon were not confined to his human agent. Christ was already engaged with him; He was already advancing to the conflict, spiritually, while He yet spoke with His disciples in the upper room. That at least is a possible way of understanding the passage, and one well in accord with the evangelist's manner.[1]

Assuming that something like this is the line of thought, and that ἐγείρεσθε ἄγωμεν ἐντεῦθεν means, 'let us go to meet the advancing enemy',

---

[1] We may compare the way in which the prayer in Gethsemane appears in altered guise in John xii. 27–8, and the essentials of the dialogue in the High Priest's court of Mark xiv. 62–4 in John x. 24, 36. It is not necessary to suppose that John was here using Mark as a source, and moving his material about. Such material as this must certainly have been continually used in oral tradition, and might well be incorporated by different writers at different stages in their accounts. Similarly, we need not suppose that John has lifted ἐγείρεσθε ἄγωμεν out of Mark and displaced it, if we may assume (what is by no means improbable) that this stirring battle-cry sounded through the oral tradition.

we may examine the connection of clauses in verses 30–1. There seems to be grave linguistic difficulty about putting a stop at ποιῶ and taking ἐγείρεσθε ἄγωμεν as an independent sentence. The ἵνα-clause is left in the air, and attempts to supply an apodosis appear clumsy. On the other hand it seems natural enough to take ἵνα γνῷ. . .as the protasis of a final sentence, and ἐγείρεσθε ἄγωμεν ἐντεῦθεν as the apodosis, with ὅτι ἀγαπῶ . . .καὶ. . .ποιῶ as a double substantive-clause in dependence on γνῷ, and καθὼς ἐνετείλατο. . .as a sub-dependent clause qualifying οὕτως. This gives an intelligible meaning. In order that the world may learn (a) that Jesus loves the Father, since (b) He is obedient to His command (cf. iv. 34, v. 19–20, vi. 38–9, xii. 27–8), He goes to meet His assailant. His real assailant, meeting Him at this very moment, though His encounter with Judas and the posse is still in the future, is the Archon of this world. But the Archon has no *claim* on Him. There is therefore no *necessity* for Jesus to fall into his hands. He voluntarily takes His decision, as the only remaining way of demonstrating to the world what the love of God and obedience to God really mean. I propose therefore some such translation as this: 'The Ruler of this world is coming. He has no claim upon me; but to show the world that I love the Father, and do exactly as He commands,—up, let us march to meet him!'

So understood, verses 31–2 represent in one more form Jesus's acceptance of His destiny (like xii. 27–8), and therefore fittingly conclude the first dialogue, which has been concerned all through with aspects of His departure and return (death and resurrection). With the words of verse 31 the journey has begun. There is no physical movement from the place. The movement is a movement of the spirit, an interior act of will, but it is a real departure nevertheless. As we shall see, the next stage of the discourse takes definitely a standpoint beyond the cross.

(c) *Discourse on Christ and His Church, xv–xvi*

I have described the whole passage, xiii. 31–xiv. 31, as dialogue, although after xiv. 8 the rapid interchange of speech which has continued from xiii. 31 gives place to relatively long speeches of Jesus. It is, as we have seen, Johannine practice to move from dialogue to monologue, and it would be possible to mark such a transition at xiv. 12, with the customary formula ἀμὴν ἀμὴν λέγω ὑμῖν. The dialogue form, however, is resumed at xiv. 22–4. Perhaps we might speak of this part of the discourse as monologue within a dialogue framework, ending with an epilogue spoken by Jesus (xiv. 25–31). Yet all through the passage I believe we can feel the mood of dialogue rather than of continuous monologue.

With chs. xv–xvi it is different. From xv. 1 to xvi. 15 we have pure monologue—the longest in the whole gospel. In the rest of ch. xvi we have what might be described again as monologue within a dialogue framework, but the framework is slender. After the theme is announced in xvi. 16 there is a question of the disciples which sets the course of the succeeding exposition; and in xvi. 29–30 they respond to what Jesus has said with a confession of faith. This leads once more to a brief epilogue spoken by Jesus. Since in the whole two chapters there are only two brief interpellations by the disciples, we shall not be far wrong in finding, in the arrangement by which the (mainly) dialogue passage xiii. 31–xiv. 31 leads to the (mainly) monologue section xv–xvi, one more example of the pattern which we have recognized elsewhere: dialogue giving place to monologue.[1]

The long monologue, xv. 1–xvi. 15, forms a connected and continuous whole. The dialogue of xiii. 31–xiv. 31, we saw, dealt throughout with the problems presented by the death and resurrection of Christ in relation to the eschatological beliefs of the early Church. In the course of the discussion certain themes were introduced and briefly dismissed, after the author's manner, for future discussion; in particular, the mutual indwelling of Christ and His disciples, and the work of the Paraclete. These now become major themes of discourse. Whereas in xiii. 31–xiv. 31 attention was directed almost continuously to the actual crisis of Christ's departure and return, the long monologue looks beyond that crisis, and contemplates the situation of those who have already passed through it, first within the fellowship of the Church and in relation to their risen and exalted Lord (xv. 1–17), and then in relation to a hostile world (xv. 18–xvi. 11), reverting briefly to the internal life of the Church in the concluding verses, xvi. 12–15. In xv. 1–17 the theme of mutual indwelling prevails, in xv. 18–xvi. 11 the theme of the Paraclete. We must now trace the course of the argument.

The discourse begins abruptly, with the proclamation, ἐγώ εἰμι ἡ ἄμπελος ἡ ἀληθινή. The similar proclamations in vi. 35, viii. 12 are preceded by introductory words, εἶπεν αὐτοῖς ὁ Ἰησοῦς, and, πάλιν αὐτοῖς ἐλάλησεν

---

[1] In xiii. 31–xiv. 31 there are 5 interpellations in 39 verses, in xv–xvi two interpellations in 60 verses. It is clear that the movement is from dialogue towards monologue. This is a strong argument, on purely formal grounds, against any attempt to place xv–xvi before xiv.

ὁ Ἰησοῦς λέγων, but in both these cases Jesus is resuming after others have spoken. Here there is no change of speaker, and no such introductory phrase is needed. Yet the words ἐγείρεσθε ἄγωμεν ἐντεῦθεν have so emphatically brought the preceding discourse to an end that the fresh departure is evident. The closest parallel is the transition from ix. 41 to x. 1.

The figure of the vine dominates the discourse down to verse 8. The thought is at first that of God's care for His vine. As I showed in an earlier chapter (pp. 136–7), the idea of God as the γεωργός, who plants and cultivates the world, mankind, and the individual soul, would be familiar enough to Hellenistic readers. But soon we reach the second stage of the allegory, in which it is no longer the relation of cultivator and vine, but the relation of the vine and its own branches that is in view. Here we must start from the frequent use of the vine-figure in the Old Testament for the people of Israel, especially, perhaps, in Ps. lxxix (lxxx), where the poet tells how God brought a vine from Egypt, and planted it, so that it grew and put forth great branches (κλήματα, as here), but the vineyard fence was broken down, and the vine robbed and ravaged by men and beasts. The poet then appeals to God to look upon His vine—

κατάρτισαι αὐτὴν ἣν ἐφύτευσεν ἡ δεξιά σου,
καὶ ἐπὶ υἱὸν ἀνθρώπου ὃν ἐκραταίωσας σεαυτῷ (l.c. 16).

In the LXX rendering[1] it is even clearer than in the Hebrew that the Vine and the Son of Man are equivalent concepts (cf. verse 18), both standing for the people of God, exposed to death and destruction but saved by the hand of God, who raises them to life again (ζωώσεις ἡμᾶς, l.c. 19).

To these Old Testament associations of the vine-figure we must add, for Christian readers, its eucharistic associations. In the Synoptic accounts of the Last Supper the contents of the cup are expressly described as γένημα τῆς ἀμπέλου, which is hardly a mere synonym for 'wine'. In the eucharistic prayers of the Didache the thanksgiving over the cup runs, Εὐχαριστοῦμέν σοι, πάτερ ἡμῶν, ὑπὲρ τῆς ἁγίας ἀμπέλου Δαυὶδ τοῦ παιδός σου, ἧς ἐγνώρισας ἡμῖν διὰ Ἰησοῦ τοῦ παιδός σου.[2] The thought is probably that of the Church as the true people of God, His vine, now revealed through Jesus.[3] John advances upon this: Jesus is the Vine, including in Himself all members of the true people of God, as the

[1] Which certainly represents a false reading, but is not the less important for that.
[2] See above, pp. 138–9.
[3] We may compare Paul's use of the figure of the olive-tree (Rom. xi. 17–24), the olive being another Old Testament figure for the people of God, Jer. xi. 16.

branches of the vine. This might be no more than the natural corollary of Ps. lxxix. Even in the Psalm the Vine, which is also the Son of Man, represents the people of God passing through destruction into newness of life. And both the eucharistic associations, and the position which the present passage occupies in the development of the discourses, put it beyond doubt that it is Christ crucified and risen who is the ἄμπελος ἀληθινή.

This once granted, the organic union of the branches with the vine and so with one another provides a striking image for that idea of the mutual indwelling of Christ and His people which the author wishes to develop. Soon it appears that the principle of such indwelling is ἀγάπη: Christ's love for His 'friends', reproducing the love of the Father, and issuing in loving obedience on the part of the disciples, which is the 'fruit' the branches bear. And the practical upshot is 'love one another'; an injunction which, already promulgated at xiii. 34, is now seen to have even deeper implications.

The thought of the love between Christ and the Church now suggests by way of contrast the hatred which the Church endures from a hostile world. This introduces the traditional warnings of persecution (xv. 18 sqq., xvi. 2);[1] but they are given a peculiarly Johannine turn. 'Because you are

---

[1] In the context of the warnings of persecution, Jesus adds (xvi. 4) that He had not warned His disciples earlier because it was unnecessary while He was with them. He warns them now in order that they may not be 'scandalized' through being unprepared for trouble after His departure (xvi. 1). John therefore agrees with Mark, who places such warnings just before the Passion (xiii. 9–13—though there is a hint in iv. 17), against Matthew, who places them at earlier points in the ministry (v. 11–12, x. 17–25, etc.). In xvi. 5 there is a sentence which has caused much speculation. Jesus says, νῦν ὑπάγω πρὸς τὸν πέμψαντά με, καὶ οὐδεὶς ἐξ ὑμῶν ἐρωτᾷ με, Ποῦ ὑπάγεις; In xiii. 36 Peter asked, ποῦ ὑπάγεις; and in xiv. 5 Thomas's protest, if not a question, comes near it. The desire to remove the near-contradiction has been a strong motive for attempts at rearrangement. I believe, however, that any attempt to place this passage, with or without much or all of the rest of xv–xvi, before xiv, would raise more difficulties than it would solve. Other critics have suspected the work of different hands, not fully brought into harmony by the redactor. But the apparent contradiction does not perhaps go so deep as is sometimes supposed. In xiii. 33–xiv. 3 the destination of Christ's approaching journey is elaborately kept secret. In xiv. 4 the reading ὅπου ἐγὼ ὑπάγω οἴδατε καὶ τὴν ὁδὸν οἴδατε, supported by ΑΔΘ and by ancient versions, is to be rejected, in favour of the reading of ℵBW, etc. What Jesus is saying is, 'You know the way: you do not need to know where it leads.' Thomas objects, 'If we do not know the destination, how can we know the way?' which is the voice of common sense. But Jesus replies, 'I am the way.' This is the whole purport of the mystification of xiii. 33–6. No revelation of the ultimate goal is necessary before Christians can do what it is their business to do—follow Christ at whatever cost and obey His commandment of charity

not ἐκ τοῦ κόσμου, therefore the κόσμος hates you' (xv. 19). For a full understanding of the sense, we must again anticipate what is said in the prayer of ch. xvii. Here Jesus says, 'The world hated them, because they are not of the world, as I am not of the world' (xvii. 14). This harks back to the discourses of vii–viii. In viii. 21 sqq. Jesus says to the unbelieving Jews, 'Where I am going, you cannot come.... You are ἐκ τῶν κάτω, I am ἐκ τῶν ἄνω. You are ἐκ τούτου τοῦ κόσμου, I am not ἐκ τοῦ κόσμου τούτου.' He now declares that the disciples, in contrast to the unbelieving Jews, are not ἐκ τοῦ κόσμου: that is to say, they belong to the sphere of τὰ ἄνω—in virtue, obviously, of their union with Christ as branches of the true Vine. In other words, they have passed from death to life (v. 24) or have been born again out of the sphere of flesh into that of spirit (iii. 5–6). This, evidently, is true only proleptically in the supposed historical situation, but here, as all through the Farewell Discourses, Jesus speaks as one who has already passed victoriously through death, and to the disciples as to those who after His death experience His coming in power.

Persecution, then, is a sign that the disciples no longer belong to 'the world'. It is also itself a form of communion with Christ, since He too is hated by the world (xv. 20–21, 23). But again, this very fact, that the world hates Christ, manifests God's judgment on the world (xv. 22). The theme of judgment thus returns, and is in the foreground down to xvi. 11. The sentence pronounced in xv. 24 recalls that of ix. 39–41. With this clue, we perceive that there is a certain parallel between this passage and the story of the trial of the man born blind. As we saw, he represented in some sort the disciple of Christ, enlightened by Him through washing with water, persecuted by false rulers, and excommunicated (the phrase is, ἀποσυνάγωγος γενέσθαι). But in passing this judgment, which is implicitly passed on Christ Himself, the false rulers incur His judgment. So here, the disciples who, having been cleansed by Christ (xiii. 5–10, xv. 3), are in union with Him (xv. 7–10), are hated by the world, and brought

(cf. xxi. 22). When they know the way, then the goal will reveal itself, for the way Christ goes must be the way to the Father. It is in this order that the revelation is given: first the way, then the goal; not vice versa. At xvi. 5, on the other hand, the disciples are in full possession of Christ's disclosure of His (and their) goal (xiv. 12 πρὸς τὸν πατέρα πορεύομαι, idem xiv. 28). Consequently, they are no longer puzzling themselves about the destination, and that is as it should be; but that being so, it is quite unreasonable to be sad about it. Jesus is reproaching them, not because they are not enquiring about His destination, but because in spite of knowing that He is going to the Father they are dismayed about the future.

to judgment, to be excommunicated (the phrase is ἀποσυναγώγους ποιεῖν) and put to death. But thereby the would-be judges show that they do not know God (xvi. 3) and that they hate Him, since they hate His Messiah, according to the prophecy (xv. 22–5). That is the sign that they are found guilty in God's judgment.

It is in this context that the doctrine of the Paraclete is expounded. Παράκλητος is properly a forensic term. A paraclete is an advocate, who supports a defendant at his trial. In ix. 35–41 Jesus appears as advocate for His persecuted confessor, and (being judge as well as advocate) secures a reversal of sentence. The disciples in the situation here contemplated, after the departure of Christ, will be on their trial, and they will need an advocate ('another advocate', as we have it in xiv. 16). They must give their testimony; but it is their Advocate who testifies (xv. 26). Then the tables are turned. The Advocate becomes a prosecuting counsel, and 'convicts' the world (xvi. 8–11). It is the same procedure as in ix. 35–41, only with the Spirit in place of Christ. Thus the coming of Christ after His death, which for the disciples means the attainment of eternal life, means for the world the Last Judgment. As this coming is mediated for them by the Spirit, so the Last Judgment also is mediated by the Spirit. All this is intelligible in view of the teaching in the Book of Signs about judgment through the light. In one sense, the light was already in the world during the ministry of Jesus, as eternal life was already there in Him. But as it needed His death to seal and to universalize His saving work, so it needed His death to seal and to universalize the judgment which men passed on themselves by their attitude to Him. The crucial event has now happened (has happened, that is, in spiritual intention)—the death and resurrection of Christ, which is the judgment of this world, issuing in the expulsion of the Archon of this world (xii. 31). This judgment is made effective through the work of the Spirit in the Church: ὁ ἄρχων τοῦ κόσμου τούτου κέκριται (xvi. 11).

In this context the idea of the Paraclete, in the ordinary meaning of the term, is perfectly appropriate and intelligible. Where it appears earlier, at xiv. 16–17, and xiv. 26, the title παράκλητος does not seem so well in place. It would in some ways be simpler if we could read xv. 26–7, xvi. 7–11, before xiv. 16–17. But there is one quite fatal objection to any such rearrangement. In xiv. 16 the Spirit is called ἄλλος παράκλητος— 'other' than Jesus, one readily understands. But if xv. 26–7, or xvi. 7–11 had preceded, then ἄλλος παράκλητος could only mean another paraclete beside the one already mentioned; that is to say, it would inevitably suggest to the reader that there were at least two Holy Spirits. We must suppose that for John παράκλητος has become a fixed title for the Holy Spirit in the Church, so that he uses it even where the specific functions of the advocate are not in view. That a reference to the Spirit as such is needed at xiv. 16–17 is clear, since the Johannine doctrine of the departure and return of Christ cannot be set forth intelligibly without it; and it is needed at xiv. 26, I suggested, because the author wishes to justify his bold reinterpretation of the 'return' of Christ by appealing to the guidance of the Spirit in the Church.

The remainder of the long monologue (xvi. 12–15) is based upon the work of the 'Spirit of truth' as teacher of the Church, and mediator of the knowledge of Christ and of the Father. It takes up and elaborates the theme of xiv. 26, though this time, quite properly, without using the term παράκλητος, when the functions in view are not those of an advocate. These verses form a short *coda* to the monologue, bringing the reader back from the thought of the Church in conflict with the world to that of the Church in living dependence on its Lord.

Thus far, the passage we are considering constitutes a closely knit process of thought, dealing with various aspects of the life of the Church after the death of Christ. With xvi. 16 we seem to be brought back to the theme of the dialogue in xiii. 31–xiv. 31. The passage begins with the oracular utterance, μικρὸν καὶ οὐκέτι θεωρεῖτέ με, καὶ πάλιν μικρὸν καὶ ὄψεσθέ με, and this provokes a question from the disciples which gives an opening for a restatement of the eschatological interpretation of Christ's death and resurrection which we have already examined (pp. 395–6 above). In some sort it is a doublet, or alternative, to xiv. 19–24, which similarly begins with ἔτι μικρὸν....[1] Yet it seems we must resist the temptation to rearrange the discourses so as to find a place for this section in contiguity with xiv. 19–24. In the first place, the difficulty which the disciples raise is founded upon a combination of words to be found in xvi. 10 and 16, and nowhere else. It is true that similar expressions are found elsewhere (xiv. 12 πρὸς τὸν πατέρα πορεύομαι with xiv. 19 ἔτι μικρὸν καὶ ὁ κόσμος με οὐκέτι θεωρεῖ, ὑμεῖς δὲ θεωρεῖτέ με), but the verbal

[1] It is however to be observed that xiv. 19 and xvi. 16 are by no means identical. In the former place, after a short interval, Christ will be invisible to the world, but visible to His own; in the latter place, after a short interval He will be invisible to His own, but after a second short interval He will again be visible to them. The standpoint is different, even though in some respects the ground covered is similar.

form quoted in xvi. 17 is that of xvi. 10 with xvi. 16, only. This seems to confirm the present sequence of sections. Again, the present passage ends by saying that Jesus has been speaking in παροιμίαι—which would be a very proper description of the imagery of xvi. 19–22—but in future He will speak παρρησίᾳ (xvi. 25). He then makes the statement, 'I came from the Father and entered the world; again I am leaving the world and going to the Father' (xvi. 28). Upon this the disciples comment, ἴδε νῦν ἐν παρρησίᾳ λαλεῖς καὶ παροιμίαν οὐδεμίαν λέγεις. That is, xvi. 28 is the explicit statement to which the metaphors of xvi. 19–22, drawn from current eschatological thought, correspond. This 'plain statement' is clearly meant to be the close of the exposition, which passes from παροιμία to παρρησία. We must conclude that in xvi. 16 sqq. the evangelist has deliberately brought the discourses back to their starting point, the meaning of Christ's death and resurrection, without which there is no assurance of divine ἀγάπη, no abiding in Christ, and no power in the Church to judge the world.

The comment of the disciples, which we have already noted (xvi. 29), leads to a confession of faith which is to be taken as their response to the whole series of discourses: 'We know you know all things: we believe you came from God' (xvi. 30). Jesus replies by communicating the humiliating fact that they are all to desert Him in the coming crisis;[1] while nevertheless He gives them reassurance. There is peace for them in Him, and they may be of good courage, because victory does not depend on them: ἐγὼ νενίκηκα τὸν κόσμον. His action, not theirs, is decisive.

As the first cycle of discourse ended with the summons to advance against the enemy (xiv. 31), so the second cycle ends with the announcement of victory. The attack and the victory are both upon the inward, spiritual plane. They will be consummated upon the plane of overt action in the sequel.

[1] The damping down of an enthusiastic confession of faith might seem surprising, if we did not remember that it corresponds to a constant pattern, not only in the Fourth Gospel but elsewhere: cf. John vi. 68–70, xiii. 38; Mark viii. 29–33 (and parallels), x. 28–31, 38–40, xiv. 29–31. It is part of the character and genius of the Church that its foundation members were discredited men; it owed its existence not to their faith, courage, or virtue, but to what Christ had done with them; and this they could never forget.

(d) The Prayer of Christ (xvii)

The resounding conclusion of the discourse, 'Courage! I have conquered the world', forms also an effective transition to the prayer which follows, if we bear in mind that the fight is fought and the victory won upon the field of the spirit and by the power of God. The prayer gathers up much of what has been said, both in the Book of Signs and in the Farewell Discourses, and presupposes everywhere the total picture of Christ and His work with which the reader should by this time be amply acquainted. Almost every verse contains echoes.

After words which place the prayer within the supreme moment of fulfilment (in terms similar to those of xii. 23 and xiii. 1, 31): ἐλήλυθεν ἡ ὥρα,[1] δόξασόν σου τὸν υἱόν, the exordium (xvii. 1–5) recites Christ's commission (ἐξουσία πάσης σαρκὸς ἵνα. . . δώσῃ αὐτοῖς ζωὴν αἰώνιον) and reports His full discharge of it (τὸ ἔργον τελειώσας), to the mutual glory of Father and Son. The following verses (xvii. 6–8) review briefly the ministry of Jesus and its results: He has revealed God's name[2] (and nature) to His disciples, and transmitted to them the ῥήματα of God; they have received the divine message and attained faith and knowledge.[3]

The central portion of the prayer (xvii. 9–19) contemplates the disciples in their situation in the world after Christ's departure (οὐκέτι εἰμι ἐν τῷ κόσμῳ καὶ αὐτοὶ ἐν τῷ κόσμῳ εἰσίν); commissioned to carry on His work (xvii. 18) and exposed to the hatred which brought Him to the cross (xvii. 14). He prays that they may be kept in God's 'name' (11), preserved from evil[4] (15) and sanctified in the truth (19); that they may be one (11) and have fulness of joy (13).

Finally the scope of the prayer broadens to include all future believers (xvii. 20–6). Christ prays that they may all be brought into the perfect

---

[1] By way of distinction, we might say that in xii. 28 the ὥρα is the crucial moment in the relation of Christ to the world of mankind (cf. xii. 20–1, 31–2), in xiii. 31 in the relation of Christ to His disciples, and in xvii. 1 in the relation of Christ to the Father. But in all it is the same ὥρα.

[2] The revelation of the 'name' of God is associated with Christ's enunciation of the ἐγώ εἰμι (=אֲנִי הוּא) which is bound up with ἐγὼ καὶ ὁ πατὴρ ἕν ἐσμεν. See pp. 93–6, 257, 349–50, 361 above.

[3] The content of πίστις and γνῶσις here is Christ's plenary commission from the Father, and similarly in xvii. 25; but in view of what has been said in other places (e.g. v. 19–30, vi. 57, viii. 14–16, 28–9) this is tantamount to the knowledge of God which is eternal life (cf. pp. 168–9, 182–3 above).

[4] Note here the echo of the Paternoster, ῥῦσαι ἡμᾶς ἀπὸ τοῦ πονηροῦ (Matt. vi. 13): cf. also πάτερ ἅγιε.

unity of the divine life as shared by Father and Son. Christ will thus be manifested to the world, and His own will be with Him, will have the vision of the glory of God, and will experience the divine ἀγάπη in its fulness.

We have now to enquire in what precise way this prayer is related to the discourses which preceded it. If we look back on these discourses, we see that they turn upon one central theme—what it means to be united with Christ (with Christ crucified and risen). This theme is treated in a kaleidoscopic variety of aspects. Let us briefly recapitulate a few of them. Jesus washes His disciples' feet that they may 'have part with Him' (μέρος ἔχεις μετ' ἐμοῦ, xiii. 8). They are to be bound together with the ἀγάπη which is a reflection, or reproduction, of His ἀγάπη (xiii. 34). Such ἀγάπη is capable of transcending the separation made by death between Christ and His own: His 'return' to them is a realization of ἀγάπη (xiv. 19–24). After He has passed through death they will be united with Him as branches of the true Vine (xv. 1–9), and the fruit which the branches yield is once again ἀγάπη, proceeding from the ἀγάπη of God revealed in Christ (xv. 8–10). Even in suffering persecution they are in union with Him,[1] who is also hated by the world (xv. 18–21). In conflict with the world they have the support of the Paraclete, whose indwelling perpetually mediates the knowledge of Christ (which is the knowledge of God) to His disciples (xiv. 17, xvi. 7–15).

These are only a few pointers to the way in which this theme dominates the discourses. As we read, it becomes clear that Christ is not merely telling His disciples about life in union with Him and how to attain it; He is actually imparting it to them. Here the passage, xv. 13–17, is especially illuminating, because here Christ emphatically addresses His disciples as φίλοι (not δοῦλοι Χριστοῦ, as the phrase went), and φίλοι are those bound by ἀγάπη. They are His 'friends' by virtue of His choice, sealed by His supreme act of ἀγάπη in laying down His life for His friends; He has given them knowledge of God, and appointed them to 'bear fruit' (which, as we already know from 7–12 above, means loving one another in obedience to His command), and consequently to have access to all the resources of God's grace. All this is the sequel

---

[1] Cf. Acts ix. 4–5, where Christ addresses the persecutor of His people: τί με διώκεις;... ἐγώ εἰμι Ἰησοῦς ὃν σὺ διώκεις. As Albert Schweitzer pointed out, this has deep roots in the Synoptic sayings of Jesus (*Mystik des Apostels Paulus*, pp. 106–10).

to the figure of the Vine, which puts in the strongest possible terms the idea of union with Christ through mutual indwelling.

The implication is that the interchange of intimate conversation among 'friends', which makes up these Farewell Discourses, is itself the process of uniting men with Christ. They are actually (even if proleptically) being invested with the benefits which are theirs through Christ's supreme act of ἀγάπη. They are being incorporated with Christ in the ἀγάπη which is mutual indwelling, and in which knowledge of God, vision of God, eternal life, are given to men.

But this relation between Christ and His followers is always, in this gospel, grounded in the archetypal relation in which He stands to the Father. If therefore the washing of the feet, with the intimate converse of Christ with His friends which flows out of it, in some sort represents dramatically the union of men with the eternal Son, we still need something which will represent the archetypal union of the Son with the Father; and this is supplied in the only way in which such union can be truthfully represented in human terms. The prayer in some sort *is* the ascent of the Son to the Father. Let us recall its key-phrases:

πάτερ, δόξασόν σου τὸν υἱόν . . .
δόξασόν με σύ, πάτερ, παρὰ σεαυτῷ . . .
πρὸς σὲ ἔρχομαι (*bis*) . . .
ἁγιάζω ἐμαυτόν . . .
σύ, πάτερ, ἐν ἐμοὶ κἀγὼ ἐν σοί . . .

and finally the emphatic and pregnant

ἐγώ σε ἔγνων.

In such words we apprehend the spiritual and ethical reality of that ἀνάβασις or ὕψωσις of the Son of Man which is hereafter to be enacted in historical actuality on the cross. This is what is ultimately meant by the words, 'I am going to the Father . . . that where I am you may be also.' Christ's 'journeying' to the Father is neither a physical movement in space, such as a bodily ascension to heaven, nor is it the physical act of dying. It is that spiritual ascent to God which is the inward reality of all true prayer. And this ascent in prayer carries with it all those who are included in the intercession which is, again, inseparable from all true prayer. In thus praying, Christ both accomplishes the self-oblation of which His death is the historical expression, and 'draws' all men after Him into the sphere of eternal life which is union with God: first, the

419

faithful group of His personal disciples, and then all who are to believe in Him to the end of time. Consider again these key-phrases:

περὶ αὐτῶν ἐρωτῶ. . .

ὑπὲρ αὐτῶν ἁγιάζω ἐμαυτόν. . .

ἵνα καὶ αὐτοὶ ἐν ἡμῖν ὦσιν. . .

ἵνα ὦσιν τετελειωμένοι εἰς ἕν. . .

ἵνα ἡ ἀγάπη ἣν ἠγάπησάς με ἐν αὐτοῖς ᾖ κἀγὼ ἐν αὐτοῖς.

This is the climax towards which everything has been moving from the moment when Christ, in full consciousness of His unique relation to the Father, washed His disciples' feet that they might have part in Him. It is also the climax of the thought of the whole gospel.

The significance of the intercessory prayer in relation to the preceding discourses will become still clearer if we approach the whole of this great episode—the Farewell Discourses with the prayer following—from a fresh point of view, a point of view which may well have been that of many of the first readers of this gospel, nurtured in the mystical piety represented by such literature as the *Hermetica*.

In the Hermetic writings, it is noteworthy that several times a dialogue is concluded with a prayer or hymn.[1] In particular, the *Poimandres* and the *De Regeneratione* (Περὶ Παλιγγενεσίας), which we have noted as having definite affinity with the thought of the Fourth Gospel in certain respects, are concluded in this way.

The theme of the *Poimandres* (*C.H.* i) is the way to eternal life through the knowledge of the nature of God and His relations to man and the world. The closing hymn (i. 31–2) begins with a triple *trisagion*, praising God for His creation and for His self-revelation to man. It then passes into an act of spiritual sacrifice—δέξαι λογικὰς θυσίας—and a prayer for knowledge, and for power to declare the truth to the human race. Finally the worshipper confesses: εἰς ζωὴν καὶ φῶς χωρῶ· εὐλογητὸς εἶ, πάτερ· ὁ σὸς ἄνθρωπος συναγιάζειν σοι βούλεται, καθὼς παρέδωκας αὐτῷ τὴν πᾶσαν ἐξουσίαν. The hymn therefore is more than a mere embellishment of the dialogue; it is the crown of the process of initiation. In reciting it, that is to say, in praising God, presenting spiritual sacrifices, and dedicating himself to the mission of revealing the knowledge of God, the initiate is also 'entering into life and light'. In speaking of himself as ὁ σὸς ἄνθρωπος, to whom all authority is given, the initiate seems to identify himself with the οὐσιώδης ἄνθρωπος, or Man from heaven. He has

[1] So *C.H.* i. 31–2, v. 10b–11, XIII. 17–20, Latin *Asclepius* (= Λόγος Τέλειος), 41.

420

described (§§ 24–6) how the Man, liberated from the bonds of matter and mortality, ascends to the Father and joins the 'powers' who praise God in the highest heaven. The hymn then may be taken as an echo of the praises of the powers, and in reciting it the initiate ascends to the Father—enters into life and light.

The *De Regeneratione* (*C.H.* XIII) refers back to the *Poimandres*, on the assumption that the unnamed prophet of *Poimandres* is no other than Hermes. The work is a dialogue between Hermes and his son Tat, in which we are given a dramatic representation of the process of initiation or rebirth, by which a man becomes θεὸς θεοῦ παῖς. Tat is born again as the divine 'powers' invade his soul, expelling the passions of mortality, until the entire divine Logos is constituted in him (εἰς συνάρθρωσιν τοῦ λόγου). 'Do you not know', says his father, 'that you are born a god and a child of the One, as I am?' Tat responds, 'It is my wish, O father, to hear the benediction of the powers in their hymn, which you said I should hear when I came to the eighth sphere.' Hermes assents, and bids his son keep silence while the hymn is recited. Like the hymn in *Poimandres*, it begins with the praise of God for His creation and His self-revelation. 'All powers within me, praise the One and the All.... Holy Knowledge, enlightened by thee, by thee hymning the noumenal Light, I rejoice with the joy of Mind.... O Life and Light, from you [1] unto you the benediction proceeds.... Thy Logos hymns Thee through me; through me receive the All by the Logos, a λογικὴ θυσία.... Save, O Life; enlighten, O Light.... Thou art God! Thy Man cries this through fire, through air, through earth, through water; through all Thy creatures.' Tat now confesses, 'From thy hymn and thy benediction my mind has been enlightened', and adds a benediction of his own: 'I, Tat, send up to God λογικαὶ θυσίαι. O God—Thou O Father, Thou O Lord, Thou O Mind—receive the λογικαὶ θυσίαι which Thou desirest from me; for by Thy will all things are completed.'

Here it is even more clear than in the *Poimandres* that the hearing and reciting of the hymn form the final stage of initiation. Tat's exclamation, σοῦ γὰρ βουλομένου πάντα τελεῖται, may be compared with the τετέλεσται which is the last word of the dying Jesus in the Fourth Gospel.[2]

---

[1] MSS. ἡμῶν, but the emendation, proposed by Reitzenstein and accepted by Nock-Festugière, gives a finer sense.

[2] If, as is possible, the *De Regeneratione* has been affected by Christian influence, it still shows us how a person with the religious background of 'Hellenistic mysticism' would read the part of the Fourth Gospel with which we are now concerned.

While therefore in one aspect the Farewell Discourses may be regarded as growing out of the tradition represented by the esoteric teaching, and particularly by the eschatological predictions, of the Synoptic Gospels, in another aspect they are analogous to Hellenistic documents of the class of the *Poimandres* and the *De Regeneratione*. That is to say, they are a dialogue on initiation into eternal life through the knowledge of God, ending with a prayer or hymn which is itself the final stage of initiation. Removed from their historical setting, the discourses might be taken as a timeless colloquy between the Son of God, or Heavenly Man, and those who by His mediation are initiated into eternal life. Christ speaks these words, 'knowing that the Father had given all things into His hand, and that He came from God and was going to God'. Proclaiming His own eternal unity with the Father, He explains to the candidates for initiation how they may become one with Him, and so enter into that eternal unity. In union with Him they are not of this world, they belong to the sphere of τὰ ἄνω, to which He belongs. He is ascending to the Father, and will take them with Him that where He is they may be also. Having thus prepared them, He offers the prayer in which He brings them with Him into the Father's presence, and accomplishes their union with God.

It is in this sense that these discourses would be read by members of the Hellenistic public which the Fourth Gospel has in view. The language and ideas would so far be familiar and acceptable. But having recognized this, we are in a position to define what distinguishes this gospel from all such Hellenistic teaching.

First, while in both Hermetic tractates (as in this kind of literature generally) the dialogue is a secret colloquy[1] between the individual and his initiator, in the Fourth Gospel the whole process of initiation takes place within a body of 'friends' of Jesus. The corporate character of the transaction is essential. It is only within the body that the individual finds eternal life; he is one branch of the true vine, and without the other branches he cannot live and bear fruit.

Secondly, that knowledge of God, or union with God, which is eternal life is here interpreted in personal and ethical terms as ἀγάπη. God's

[1] This is especially emphasized in the *De Regeneratione*. 'Now that you have learned this from me,' says Hermes, 'promise silence about the marvel, and do not disclose to anyone the mode of transmitting rebirth, that we may not be counted betrayers of the doctrine. Each of us has been sufficiently occupied, I in telling, and you in hearing. You have learned to know, by the power of mind (νοερῶς ἔγνως), yourself and our Father' (*C.H.* XIII. 22).

knowledge of man, in Christ, is His love for man. Man's knowledge of God is his response to the love of God in Christ, by love, trust and obedience to Him and charity towards his fellows.

Finally, the knowledge of God which is life eternal is mediated by an historical transaction. Only through the 'departure' and 'return' of Christ, that is, through His actual death on the cross and His actual resurrection, is the life He brings liberated for the life of the world. If the goal is the unity of mankind with God, it is only by dying that Christ can 'gather the scattered children of God'; it is only by being 'lifted up' on the cross that He can 'draw all men to Him'. The prayer, 'that they may all be one, I in them and thou in me', finds fulfilment only because He who offers it has laid down His life for His friends. The reader is thus placed at the right point to begin the reading of the Passion-narrative.

II. The Passion-narrative

We have seen that the Book of the Passion corresponds in structure with the several episodes of the Book of Signs, in that it consists of a narrative accompanied by an interpretative discourse. In this case the discourse precedes, in the form of the dialogues of Jesus with His disciples on the eve of His Passion. The narrative is that of the arrest, trial and crucifixion of Jesus, His burial, the discovery of the empty tomb, and His appearances to the disciples.

We have further observed that in the Book of Signs the narrative is sometimes given in a relatively pure form, unaffected by the theological significance which is attributed to it in the accompanying discourse—as for example the healing at Bethesda—while sometimes discourse and narrative are so fused that the narrative itself conveys that significance— as for example the Raising of Lazarus; and there are intermediate types, in which unobtrusive pointers to the theological significance are incorporated in the narrative, as in the healing at Siloam. It will be of interest to enquire to which type the narrative of the Passion and Resurrection belongs.

The question immediately before us is this: to what extent, and in what points, does the Passion-narrative in the Fourth Gospel appear to have been affected by motives arising out of the Johannine theology? All forms of Passion-narrative contain an interpretative element as well as a factual record. We shall naturally expect to find a similar element in the Fourth Gospel. By this time we should have formed a fairly precise idea of the specific character of Johannine theology, as it is disclosed in the Book of Signs and the Farewell Discourses. It is this that provides the test we shall apply in examining the Johannine Passion-narrative, and not any generalized *Gemeindetheologie*. Our standard of comparison is of necessity the Passion-narrative as it is found in the Synoptic Gospels. That it is, in a broad sense, the same story that is told, is clear; yet there are characteristic differences.

In the first place, the Johannine chronology of the Passion differs from that which we find in the Synoptic Gospels. In recording the Last Supper, Mark makes it clear that he regards it as a paschal meal, and in this the other Synoptics seem to follow him, though it is not clear that either he or they are entirely consistent. John on the other hand gives an account which is throughout consistent with the view that Jesus was crucified on Nisan 14, the day on which the Paschal Lamb was killed, and consequently that He was dead before the paschal meal was eaten. This change of date is often taken to be due to theological motives, the death of Christ being synchronized with that of the paschal victims.

That Christ was the Paschal Lamb of the Christian Passover is an idea at least as early as I Cor. v. 7. It is possible that John alludes to it in the phrase ὁ ἀμνὸς τοῦ θεοῦ (i. 29, 36), though I do not think it probable (see pp. 233–5). Again, it is possible that the quotation in xix. 36 is from passages in the Pentateuch referring to the Paschal Lamb, but it seems more likely that it comes from Ps. xxxiii (xxxiv). 21 (*ibid.*). But even if these references were accepted, they are far from showing that the idea of Christ as Paschal Lamb was a distinctive or regulative idea of Johannine theology. Nowhere in the discourses is it adduced in explication, or even illustration, of the meaning of Christ's death—not even where we read about 'eating His flesh' in a scene which is placed at Passover time (ch. vi). It is not therefore very likely that the evangelist has himself remoulded the chronology to suit this idea, especially as he gives no hint that he regarded the synchronism as significant. On the other hand we have reason to believe that there was an ancient tradition which dated the death of Jesus on Nisan 14, since (*a*) this date seems to be implied in quartodeciman usage, which was immemorial at Ephesus, and (*b*) there is a statement from the Jewish side that Jesus suffered on the eve of Passover (Baraita in *Sanh.* 43 a). I do not here discuss the question whether or not this tradition is historically to be preferred to the one followed by Mark. In any case it seems highly probable that the evangelist is following a pre-Johannine tradition in the date he assigns to the crucifixion, and not shaping the narrative to suit his theological preconceptions.

We may further note certain traits of the Synoptic narratives which do not appear in the Passion-narrative of the Fourth Gospel (chs. xviii–xx (xxi)).

(i) In general, the Johannine narrative is free from prodigies of the kind included in the Synoptic narratives—in Mark, the darkening of the sun[1] and the rending of the veil of the temple; in Matthew, the earthquakes accompanying the crucifixion and the resurrection, and the apparitions of departed saints; in Luke, the healing of the servant's ear. The Johannine narrative is equally free from tendentious accretions such as Matthew's stories of Pilate's wife and the bribery of the guard. The issue of water and blood, John xix. 34, is certainly a σημεῖον, but perhaps not a τέρας (see p. 429).

(ii) John does not give a eucharistic character to the Last Supper. But the eucharistic idea has already been embodied in the narrative of the Feeding of the Multitude with its accompanying discourse.

(iii) There is no Gethsemane story in John. But its purport is represented, in effect, by xii. 27–8. Its omission, therefore, has no theological motive, though the recasting of the prayer in xii. 27–8 may betray such a motive, at least in its wording.

(iv) Nothing is said of the charge of blasphemy preferred against Jesus in the High Priest's court, or of His confession of Messiahship on the same occasion. But, as we have seen, both these themes have had a place in the Book of Signs (x. 30–9). This omission therefore is not due to theological motives.

(v) John not only omits Mark's report that the cross was carried by Simon of Cyrene, but appears deliberately to contradict it (βαστάζων ἑαυτῷ τὸν σταυρόν (xix. 17)). That this has an anti-gnostic tendency is possible but questionable.[2]

[1] That the darkness has symbolical significance cannot be doubted; yet it appears that the darkness on the day of the crucifixion, as a fact, has independent attestation, if it be true that it was mentioned by Thallus the Samaritan, who flourished round about A.D. 50 (see Goguel, *Life of Jesus*, Eng. tr., pp. 91 sqq.). Before deciding that an incident of this kind which lends itself to symbolical interpretation is necessarily legendary, it would be well to read various accounts of the promulgation of the Vatican Decrees of 1870, in a violent thunderstorm. See, e.g., Wilfrid Ward, *Life of Newman*, II, pp. 304–6 (letter of J. R. Mozley). The rending of the veil I take to be purely symbolical, in the sense of Heb. x. 20.

[2] The idea that Simon of Cyrene was actually crucified in place of Jesus is attributed to Basilides by Irenaeus, *Adv. Haer.* (ed. Harvey) I. 19. 5, and after him by Epiphanius. But this does not prove that the idea was abroad at the time this gospel was written.

(vi) John has no reference to the mocking and reviling of Jesus on the cross, recorded in all Synoptics, or to the tokens of sympathy from the women of Jerusalem and from one of the crucified robbers, recorded in Luke alone, and he has omitted the cry of dereliction, as Luke also has done.

On the other hand, John includes details not given by the Synoptics. It is unnecessary to attempt a complete list of the innumerable variations, but the following characteristic points may be considered.

(i) He has emphasized the voluntary character of the sufferings of Jesus at various points. In the Garden, when His assailants hesitated to arrest Him,[1] He gave Himself up; and did so on condition that His disciples should be let go (xviii. 6–8). At this point (xviii. 9) there is a note referring back to a passage in the section of Farewell Discourses (xvii. 12). Here therefore a theological motive is explicitly indicated. In deprecating Peter's attempt at a rescue He said, 'Shall I not drink the cup which my Father has given me?' (xviii. 11). Here the phraseology (ποτήριον) belongs also to the Synoptic tradition. The same emphasis upon the voluntary choice of Christ is to be seen in the account of His death (xix. 28–30). Not until He knew that all was accomplished did He yield up His spirit. All this certainly goes beyond the Synoptics, but it develops a tendency already present in them, and not peculiar to John.

(ii) He has laid much greater stress upon the political charge brought against Jesus in the Roman court (while reducing the significance of the examination in the Jewish court). In the other gospels we learn that Jesus was condemned by Pilate as King of the Jews, but here everything turns upon the claim of Jesus to kingship, over against the exclusive claim of Caesar (xix. 12, 15). This is not related to the distinctively Johannine theology, but seems to belong to a non-Synoptic version of the tradition. In xix. 7 the υἱὸς θεοῦ of Mark xiv. 61, xv. 39 reappears, but as compared with the Synoptics its importance is reduced rather than enhanced.

(iii) When the Jews decline jurisdiction in the cause of Jesus, the comment is interpolated that this took place 'in order that the word of

---

[1] In xviii. 6, the ἐγώ εἰμι might well suggest (and be intended to suggest) the divine Name, yet this is in no way essential to the narrative; nor need the recoil of the assailants (ἀπῆλθαν. . .καὶ ἔπεσαν χαμαί) of necessity imply an *Allmachtswunder*. It is tempting to adopt the poorly attested reading, ἀπῆλθεν. . .ἔπεσεν, and understand it of Judas.

Jesus might be fulfilled, which He spoke signifying the kind of death He was to die' (xviii. 32). This is a clear reference back to xii. 32–3. We are intended to observe that by the transfer of jurisdiction from the Jewish to the Roman court, it was assured that instead of being stoned, Jesus should be crucified, and so 'lifted up', as a symbol of the 'lifting up' or exaltation of the Son of Man. It is common to all Passion-narratives that Jesus was condemned to crucifixion by a Roman court. The Johannine narrative may or may not be historically exact in implying that but for the expressed desire of the Sanhedrin Pilate might not have claimed jurisdiction. In any case, the Synoptics also imply that Pilate was unwilling to take responsibility for the death of Jesus. But the note in xviii. 32 is a clear pointer to a theological interpretation of the fact of crucifixion.

(iv) While in the Synoptic account of the trial Jesus breaks silence only to make His messianic confession before the High Priest (Mk. xiv. 62), and to reply to Pilate's Σὺ εἶ ὁ βασιλεὺς τῶν Ἰουδαίων; with the ambiguous σὺ λέγεις, in John He defends Himself vigorously in both courts. Yet in xix. 9 the traditional motive of the silence of Jesus reappears. His protest to Annas in xviii. 20–3 is not unlike in tone to His protest in the Garden in Mark xiv. 48–9. His reply to Pilate's threat in xix. 10–11 may reflect early Christian discussions about the incidence of responsibility for the death of Jesus. In His reply to Pilate's interrogation about the claim to kingship (xviii. 33–8) there is nothing specifically Johannine down to the end of verse 36, unless it be the mere phrase ἐκ τοῦ κόσμου τούτου, but definitely Johannine conceptions emerge in the further elaboration of the theme: ἐγὼ εἰς τοῦτο γεγέννημαι καὶ εἰς τοῦτο ἐλήλυθα εἰς τὸν κόσμον, ἵνα μαρτυρήσω τῇ ἀληθείᾳ· πᾶς ὁ ὢν ἐκ τῆς ἀληθείας ἀκούει μου τῆς φωνῆς. This is Johannine language, and the ideas are characteristic of John: the kingship of Jesus consists in His witness to the truth, and the allegiance He claims is that of obedience to the truth. Here then we note a theological intrusion into the narrative.

(v) John has emphasized the innocence of Jesus (xviii. 38, xix. 4, 6) somewhat more than Mark, but hardly more than Luke.

(vi) In the record of the crucifixion John has in part a different set of fulfilled prophecies. While he cites explicitly a passage to which the Synoptics only allude, 'They divided my garments...' (xix. 24), he cites also the following: 'I thirst' (xix. 28), 'No bone of Him shall be broken' (xix. 36) and 'They shall look upon Him whom they pierced' (xix. 37), which do not occur in the Synoptics. But these are drawn from parts of Scripture which traditionally supplied such *testimonia*,[1] and there is no apparent allusion in them to ideas specifically Johannine.

(vii) The episode of the Mother and the Beloved Disciple (xix. 26–7) is peculiar to the Fourth Gospel. Whatever its motive, it does not seem to be dictated by the Johannine theology.[2] It may belong to a special form of the tradition.

(viii) In recording the death of Jesus, the evangelist has substituted for the inarticulate cry reported by Mark (for which Luke gives a prayer such as might be uttered by any devout person in the hour of death) the highly significant Τετέλεσται. We are almost certainly intended to understand this with reference to xvii. 4 (τὸ ἔργον τελειώσας). It is therefore closely related to the Johannine theology. Whether the unusual phrase παρέδωκε τὸ πνεῦμα (for Matthew's more natural ἀφῆκε τὸ πνεῦμα) is to be understood in the sense that Jesus in dying bequeathed the Holy Spirit to the world He was leaving, or whether it simply means that He surrendered the spirit (or vital principle) to God who gave it (cf. Eccl. xii. 7),[3] I do not feel able to decide.

(ix) Immediately after the death of Jesus, the evangelist records that a spear-thrust brought water and blood from His side. To this he draws especial attention (xix. 34–5). A reference must surely be intended to the symbolism of water and blood in the Book of Signs. From the crucified body of Christ flows the life-giving stream: the water which is the Spirit given to believers in Him (vii. 38–9), the water which if a man drink he will never thirst again (iv. 14), and the blood which is ἀληθὴς πόσις (vi. 55). That we are to understand the incident theologically, as a σημεῖον, in the Johannine sense, seems clear. It is not so clear that the record is itself the product of theological motives. The incident of the piercing

---

[1] Διψῶ is probably from Ps. lxviii (lxix). 22 (cf. ὄξος in 29), a psalm which has afforded several other *testimonia*; xix. 36 is more likely from Ps. xxxiii (xxxiv). 21, which is about the sufferings of the righteous, than from Exod. xii. 46 or Num. ix. 12, but even if it refers to the Paschal Lamb, that is no peculiarly Johannine concept; xix. 37 is from Zech. xii. 10, a chapter which is echoed in several eschatological passages of the New Testament, this verse, notably, in Rev. i. 7, in a context very remote from the theology of the Fourth Gospel.

[2] Attempts to give a symbolic meaning are in general singularly unconvincing. If a 'tendency' is present it seems more likely to have something to do with claims made in the Church at Ephesus for the enigmatic 'Beloved Disciple' than with theology.

[3] Ἀποδοῦναι is the proper verb for restoring a gift to the giver, or delivering property to its rightful owner. Παραδοῦναι is more often used of 'handing on' a piece of property (or a piece of information, or the like) to a successor; yet it is quite properly used of 'surrendering' (a city, ship, or person, for example) to a superior; and that is not far from a sense which would be quite appropriate here.

of the side is introduced as a fulfilment of prophecy—of prophecies drawn from a common 'testimony' source. It is therefore likely to be pre-Johannine. At most, the issue of water and blood might be thought to be a symbolic construction of the evangelist.[1] Yet the terms in which he draws attention to it are remarkable. He guarantees the truth of his statement by a solemn appeal to eyewitness. It is the only such direct appeal in the whole gospel, and I cannot think it should be summarily dismissed. Even if verse 35 is attributed to a redactor, he must surely have had some particular ground for saying, ἀληθινὴ αὐτοῦ ἐστιν ἡ μαρτυρία, καὶ ἐκεῖνος οἶδεν ὅτι ἀληθῆ λέγει.[2]

(x) John asserts, what the Synoptics implicitly deny, that the body of Jesus was anointed for burial (xix. 38–40). Accordingly, the purpose attributed to visiting the Tomb on Easter morning is absent from John xx. The motive here may be the desire to avoid the ignominy of a burial without anointing: it is scarcely theological.

(xi) In the narrative of the resurrection, John is concerned to emphasize the testimony to the empty Tomb. Not only the women, but Peter and the Beloved Disciple can attest the fact, and not only so, but they can attest the position in which the grave-clothes were found (xx. 2–10). This may have apologetic value, but it does not proceed from the specifically Johannine theology.

(xii) In the account of the appearance of the risen Christ to Mary Magdalene, the repeated use of the verb ἀναβαίνειν (xx. 17) points back to passages in the Book of Signs (iii. 13, vi. 62) where it has a specific theological significance.

(xiii) After the resurrection, Christ is said to have breathed on His disciples, saying, λάβετε πνεῦμα ἅγιον (xx. 22). It may be that the

---

[1] It is worth noting that at least two medical writers (W. Stroud, *The Physical Cause of the Death of Christ*, 1853, and W. B. Primrose, 'A Surgeon looks at the Crucifixion', in the *Hibbert Journal*, vol. xlvii (1949), pp. 385–8) have accepted the phenomenon of the discharge of blood accompanied by a watery fluid in the circumstances indicated, though they interpret the symptom in completely different ways. For a recent full discussion see R. Schmittlein, *Circonstances et Cause de la Mort du Christ* (1950).

[2] The discussion of the questions, who is meant by ἐκεῖνος, and who by ὁ ἑωρακώς, seems to be inconclusive. For the present purpose it is enough that verse 35 amounts to a solemn attestation of the veracity of the statement in verse 34. I find myself reluctant to think that either author or redactor would have committed himself to such an attestation unless he had good reason to believe that *someone* whose word could be accepted had seen what he describes, if he had not seen it himself.

evangelist has introduced the giving of the Holy Spirit into the Gospel narrative[1] because in i. 33 (and so perhaps iii. 34) Jesus is directly pointed out as He who baptizes with Holy Spirit (though this is in no way peculiar to the Fourth Gospel; cf. Mark i. 8 and parallels, Acts i. 5), while in vii. 39 we are told that the Spirit was not given until Jesus was 'glorified'. Since He has now been 'glorified', in the Johannine sense, in His death, the time has come for the Spirit to be given. The conception of the Spirit here implied is strikingly different from that of the Farewell Discourses—so different as to suggest that the story of the 'insufflation' may have come to the evangelist out of a different tradition, rather than that it was created by his own theology. This may perhaps be supported by the observation that xx. 23 is clearly drawn from a tradition parallel, though not identical, with Matt. xviii. 18. Yet even so, the placing of the incident is so directly congruous with Johannine ideas that it may fairly be treated as part of the evangelist's theological interpretation.

(xiv) The scene in which Thomas figures prominently (xx. 24–9) is different from most post-resurrection appearances in the gospels, in that a specific individual is cited as witness to the facts (recalling the list of *testimonia* in ch. i), and his evidence is enhanced in value by his initial scepticism. There are three main motives: (*a*) the reality of the resurrection body of Christ; (*b*) the relation of faith and sight; and (*c*) Thomas's confession of faith: ὁ κύριός μου καὶ ὁ θεός μου (xx. 24–9).[2] Of these the first is not specifically Johannine.[3] The second brings up again a theme which has been in view in one way or another all through the gospel, and says the evangelist's last word upon it. The third invites comparison with the series of confessions of faith with which the whole narrative is punctuated. Such comparison shows that it goes beyond all the others, and links up with the opening of the Prologue: θεὸς ἦν ὁ λόγος. Thus the identity of Jesus with the incarnate Logos is finally affirmed on the testimony of the disciple who having seen Him after His resurrection

[1] It is in some sort the Johannine equivalent for the story of Pentecost in Acts ii. See Bishop Cassian (Serge Besobrasoff), *La Pentecôte Johannique* (Valence-sur-Rhône, 1939).

[2] Ὁ κύριός μου identifies the one who appears as 'the Jesus of History' (cf. xiii. 13–14); ὁ θεός μου adds a theological valuation of His person. I remember hearing F. C. Burkitt paraphrase Thomas's confession thus: 'Yes: it is Jesus!—and He is divine!'

[3] In affirming the quasi-physical character of the appearances John goes beyond Matthew, but not so far as Luke, who says that Jesus ate with His disciples after the resurrection (xxiv. 42, Acts x. 41). John does not say this, even in xxi. 13.

'became not faithless but believing'. Here we have unmistakably a piece of Johannine theology embodied in narrative.

(xv) For the sake of completeness we may here take note of the appendix (ch. xxi). It has the effect of compensating for the exclusive attention to Jerusalem in ch. xx (where the Fourth Gospel resembles the Third) by introducing an appearance of Christ in Galilee (thus assimilating the Fourth Gospel to the First, which has appearances both in Jerusalem (Matt. xxviii. 9–10) and in Galilee (xxviii. 16)). The interest in Jerusalem and the south is in general characteristic of the Fourth Gospel, and the motives of the appendix are more akin to those of the Synoptics. At most we may recognize Johannine traits in the scene between Jesus and Peter in xxi. 15–17. The emphasis on ἀγάπη as the link between Christ and His disciples, and the idea of the flock, recall earlier passages. But it can hardly be said that theological motives have been at work; and the naïve conception of Christ's second Advent in xxi. 22 is unlike anything else in the Fourth Gospel. For the rest, it may be that those critics are right who surmise in the background some adjustment of the claims of Rome (for Peter) and Ephesus (for the Beloved Disciple).[1]

It appears then that the Passion-narrative is given in the main as a straightforward story, with only a minimum of intruded interpretative elements. If we were estimating its strictly historical value, we should have to take account of various apologetic motives which may have helped to mould it; but these motives are such as are in greater or less degree common to all Passion-narratives, and do not depend on the Johannine theological interpretation. Returning then to the question, to which type of narrative among those represented in the Book of Signs the Passion-narrative belongs, we must report that it is not like the narrative of the Raising of Lazarus, where story and interpretation are inseparably fused, but like those where the story is given in traditional form, and its meaning is to be understood from accompanying discourses. At most, there are small and unobtrusive hints at the inner meaning, similar in principle to those which appear, for example, in the Feeding of the Multitude and the Healing at Siloam. It is as though the evangelist, having sufficiently set forth the meaning of the death and resurrection of Christ, turned to the reader and said, 'And now I will tell you what

---

[1] It may be added that the meal of bread and fish which Jesus gives to the seven disciples (an obvious parallel to the feeding of the multitude upon the like fare) is treated in early Christian art as an alternative expression of the eucharistic idea; but the text of the gospel gives no hint of this.

actually happened, and you will see that the facts themselves bear out my interpretation.'

For we are, of course, intended to understand the Passion-narrative in the light of all that has been said in earlier parts of the gospel, directly and indirectly, about the meaning of Christ's death and resurrection. If now we put together those occasional sentences in chs. xviii–xx (xxi), in which we have noted that Johannine theological ideas come to the surface, we shall find them instructive pointers to the meaning beneath the surface, of which the evangelist expects his discerning readers to be aware all through. I shall consider first those five passages in the account of the arrest, trial and crucifixion of Jesus which we have noted as conveying a theological interpretation.

(i) In the story of the arrest, after recording how Jesus gave Himself up to the police on the understanding that His followers were to be allowed to go free, the evangelist adds: ἵνα πληρωθῇ ὁ λόγος ὃν εἶπεν, Οὓς δέδωκάς μοι, οὐκ ἀπώλεσα ἐξ αὐτῶν οὐδένα (xviii. 9). The reference is to a sentence in the prayer, xvii. 12. Critics have often attributed this note (which is readily detachable from its context) to a somewhat unintelligent redactor, on the ground that xvii. 12 obviously refers, not to the protection of the disciples from the police, but to their protection from spiritual perils that menace their eternal salvation. This objection, I conceive, rests on a failure to appreciate the way the evangelist's mind works. For him, each several act and word of Jesus, upon any particular occasion, holds within it a meaning going beyond the particular occasion. It is, of course, true that the meaning of xvii. 12 cannot be confined within the limits of xviii. 9; yet the action of Jesus in the Garden was a σημεῖον of His action upon a larger scale and a higher plane; and this action upon a larger scale and a higher plane is the true meaning of His action in the Garden. To elucidate this meaning the evangelist refers us to xvii. 12. But we have further to note that xvii. 12 in turn refers back to earlier passages. In vi. 37–40, Jesus, having offered Himself as Bread of Life to men, regretfully recognizes that the offer is in large measure rejected in unbelief. Yet there is a limit to the extent to which the contumacy of men can hinder the work of salvation. He goes on, 'All that the Father gives me will come to me, and I will never reject anyone who comes to me, because I came down from heaven, not to do my own will, but the will of Him who sent me. This is His will: that I should lose nothing that He has given me, but raise it to life on the Last Day. This is my Father's will: that everyone who beholds the Son and believes on him, should have eternal life and that I should raise him on the Last Day.' The same idea occurs in the context of the image of the shepherd and the sheep, in x. 27–8: 'My sheep hear my voice; I know them and they follow me; and I give them eternal life. They shall never be lost and no one shall snatch them out of my hand.'[1] The reader of these sentences will not have forgotten the words which occur a few verses before: 'I lay down my life for the sheep' (x. 15). Here we have the full, rich content that lies in the words of xvii. 12, and consequently lies behind the citation of those words in xviii. 9. In a hostile world, the will of God for men's salvation challenges the powers of evil in the incarnation and work of Christ, through which eternal life is opened to men. Once a man has responded (by God's grace alone) to Christ in faith, Christ (in whom the whole Godhead is at work) takes responsibility for his salvation. He can do this only because He is entirely devoted to the will of the heavenly Father, to the point of laying down His life, and that will is set towards men's salvation. With all this in mind John would have us read the story of what happened at the moment when Jesus encountered His enemies. Having already devoted Himself to the Father's will (xii. 27–8, xvii. 19), He went to meet them, attended by the meagre remnant of faithful men whom God had given Him: 'If it is I you are seeking, let these men go.' The Shepherd went to meet the wolf to save His flock. To say that this 'fulfilled' what Christ has said is not to impose an arbitrary or fanciful interpretation; for the ethical and spiritual quality of the action whereby Christ gives eternal life to men is precisely the quality exhibited within a restricted situation in His self-surrender in the Garden. And that, the evangelist would have us observe, is, fundamentally, how Jesus came to fall into the hands of His enemies, as a matter of history.

(ii) When Jesus is transferred from the jurisdiction of the Sanhedrin to that of Pilate, the comment is inserted: ἵνα ὁ λόγος τοῦ Ἰησοῦ πληρωθῇ ὃν εἶπεν σημαίνων ποίῳ θανάτῳ ἤμελλεν ἀποθνήσκειν (xviii. 32). This is

---

[1] The words which follow, x. 29, offer a notorious crux to the textual critic. The reading ὁ πατήρ μου ὃ δέδωκέν μοι πάντων μεῖζόν ἐστιν is found in B* alone in its pure form, but has influenced the text of other MSS. and is followed by the Old Latin. It would mean either (a) that Christ's flock is greater than all forces that oppose it (ὃ δέδωκέν μοι as in vi. 39)—which I think John would never have said—or (b) that the authority God gave Christ is supreme (cf. xiii. 3), which is Johannine, but not obviously appropriate here. The alternative reading, more widely if less weightily supported, is probably to be adopted, ὁ πατὴρ ὃς δέδωκέν μοι πάντων μείζων ἐστιν, which is like vi. 37–40 in sense though not in grammatical form.

clearly a back-reference to xii. 32–3, where a similar note is appended to the expression ἐὰν ὑψωθῶ ἐκ τῆς γῆς πάντας ἑλκύσω πρὸς ἐμαυτόν. Here, as there, many critics have thought the note to be due to a redactor, on the ground that the play upon the word ὑψωθῆναι, signifying on the one hand crucifixion, and on the other hand exaltation, is too crude for our author. Yet it is characteristic of his mind that he seeks symbols of spiritual truth in the most banal features of nature and human experience: in the noise of the wind that you cannot see, in running water, in wine for a wedding party, in washing one's feet after a journey. In particular, since in Jesus Christ the eternal Word was made flesh, everything He did or said or suffered must be scrutinized for inner meanings. There must therefore (the evangelist holds) be significance in the fact, not only that He died, but that He died not by stoning (like Stephen), or by the sword (like James), or by burning (like Nero's victims), but by crucifixion; and the evangelist has found the clue to this significance in a grim play upon words which, it appears, had some currency in Jewish and in Gentile circles. In any case, in xii. 32 ὑψωθῆναι must refer to the death of Jesus, as the context shows, whether the note in 33 be accepted or not.

Here once again, as at xviii. 9, the primary back-reference brings with it a chain of other references, to passages which I have reviewed above (pp. 375–9) in discussing xii. 33. We may here briefly recall some of them. In iii. 13–16 we have a passage bearing upon the answer to Nicodemus's question, 'How can a man be born again?' To be born again is to enter into the life of πνεῦμα, which belongs to τὰ ἄνω. There is no way of entering that realm through initiations or raptures, as the mystics do vainly talk, for 'no one has ascended to heaven but He who descended from heaven—the Son of Man'. And He must be 'elevated' (δεῖ τὸν υἱὸν τοῦ ἀνθρώπου ὑψωθῆναι) in order that men may have eternal life. Thus the process of man's salvation is a process of κατάβασις and ἀνάβασις, carried through by the Son of Man on behalf of all men (πάντας ἑλκύσω, xii. 32). The Son of Man, or eternal Man from heaven, descended from τὰ ἄνω into the temporal order, to ascend again, and so to make a way—or rather to be the way (xiv. 6)—for men to ascend to the Father. To say that the heavenly Man descended is to say in other terms, ὁ λόγος σὰρξ ἐγένετο. The κατάβασις is set forth in the very fact that He who was in the beginning with God (i. 2), and shared His glory before the foundation of the world (xvii. 24), lived in the flesh, was weary and thirsty (iv. 6–7), wept at a friend's grave (xi. 35), and suffered indignities at the hands of men. We have just read how He was betrayed

PASSION-NARRATIVE

by a false follower, put in chains, and insulted with blows. Now the final indignity awaits Him: crucifixion. It is the lowest step in the κατάβασις of the Son of Man. But for this final step the evangelist's word is ὑψωθῆναι. There lies the paradox: the bottom of the descent is— 'exaltation'. But even if it is a paradox it is far from being a mere 'conceit'. The descent is ethically conditioned. It is not simple loss of status. It is a voluntary condescension. This has been made clear in xiii. 1-15, where Jesus, in full consciousness 'that He came from God and was going to God', went down on His knees, stripped like a slave, to wash His disciples' feet. This is set forth as an expression of divine ἀγάπη (xiii. 1, 34). Similarly, He *chose* to die: 'The good shepherd lays down his life for the sheep'; 'no one has greater love than this: to lay down life for his friends'; 'for their sake I consecrate myself'. It follows that if Christ chooses to die, He is indeed choosing the final stage of His 'descent' into mortality; but in the act of choice He is glorified with the glory of God. For the glory which the Son possessed with the Father before the foundation of the world is the glory of the divine ἀγάπη, and this ἀγάπη (to return to our starting point in iii. 13-16) is the ultimate reality behind the whole story: 'God loved the world so much that He gave His only son.' The act of self-devotion for the sake of His followers, 'that the love with which thou lovedst me may be in them' (xvii. 26), is, as we have seen, in a spiritual sense, Christ's return to the Father, or in other words, His 'elevation', or 'exaltation'. But when that pure act of will is translated into a concrete event, it takes the form of crucifixion. Thus, paradoxically in a sense and yet not illogically, the death of Christ is at once His descent and His ascent, His humiliation and His exaltation, His shame and His glory; and this truth is symbolized, for the evangelist, in the manner of His death—crucifixion, the most shameful death, which is, nevertheless, in a figure (by way of σημεῖον), His exaltation from the earth.

(iii) In the account of the trial before Pilate, where Christ's kingship is in question, the process of examination of the Prisoner leads up to a statement in which we have recognized characteristically Johannine ideas and language: ἐγὼ εἰς τοῦτο γεγέννημαι καὶ εἰς τοῦτο ἐλήλυθα εἰς τὸν κόσμον, ἵνα μαρτυρήσω τῇ ἀληθείᾳ· πᾶς ὁ ὢν ἐκ τῆς ἀληθείας ἀκούει μου τῆς φωνῆς. Here we have the evangelist's definition of true kingship: it is essentially the sovereignty of ἀλήθεια.[1] We are reminded of many

[1] I retain here the Greek word, because ἀλήθεια moves between the meanings, 'truth' and 'reality', or, as we might say, between the Real as it is in itself, and the Real as revealed and apprehended in word and action (see pp. 170-2).

DFG

passages in the gospel. In His controversy with 'the Jews', Christ 'speaks ἀλήθεια' (viii. 45–7): to 'dwell in His word' is to 'know ἀλήθεια' and to be liberated by it (viii. 31–2). Thus His kingship is one that does not oppress or enslave men, but sets them free. This liberating word of ἀλήθεια is the word of God Himself: indeed His word *is* ἀλήθεια[1] (xvii. 17). The reader is further to bear in mind (though it is not necessary that it should be disclosed to Pilate) that Christ is Himself ἀλήθεια (xiv. 6), as He is the Word.

So much may serve briefly to recall the associations of the term ἀλήθεια in this gospel. It is however significant that the pronouncement we are considering (xviii. 37) is placed in the context of a trial scene. Where ἀλήθεια is, there men are judged, as we may learn from iii. 18–21: ἀλήθεια and φῶς are closely akin: and it is only ὁ ποιῶν τὴν ἀλήθειαν—the man whose deeds express the divine reality (which, having read the gospel through, we know is ἀγάπη)—who can stand the scrutiny of the light. So once again we have, as in ix. 13–41, the theme of judgment treated with Johannine irony. As there the 'Pharisees' sat in judgment upon the claims of Jesus, and in the end found the tables turned and sentence pronounced against them, so here Pilate believes himself to be sitting in judgment on Jesus, while he is actually being judged by the Truth. His scornful question, 'What is truth?' marks him as one of those who will not 'come to the light' (iii. 20). In this Pilate stands for the unbelieving world. Thus the trial of Jesus, with its issue, illustrates what is meant by xii. 31 νῦν κρίσις ἐστιν τοῦ κόσμου τούτου.

We now recognize what lies behind the whole question of kingship, which has bulked so largely in the Johannine Passion-narrative. It is the question of authority to judge, which Pilate claims in xix. 10, but which in v. 27 is the divinely assigned prerogative of Christ. In the end Pilate himself confesses that Christ is king, by the inscription which he places on the cross. Asked to withdraw it, he confirms what he has written (xix. 22). He is thus, as it were, subpœnaed as an unwilling witness to Christ's authority, as Son of Man, to judge the world (as Caiaphas was subpœnaed to testify that He died to gather the scattered children of God (xi. 50–2)). In view of this, we may recognize the ironical appropriateness (to the evangelist's mind) of the fact that it is by Pilate's judgment that Christ is crucified, that is, that the Son of Man is 'lifted up', to draw all men to Himself. 'When you lift up the Son of Man,' Jesus

---

[1] Hence, the liberating kingship which Christ exercises is the Kingdom of God (though the evangelist does not use the term in this sense).

had said to His enemies, 'you will know that I AM' (viii. 28). Then may not the famous *ecce homo*, ἰδοὺ ὁ ἄνθρωπος (xix. 5), contain a disguised confession of Christ? Ostensibly, the words are contemptuous: 'Look! the fellow!' But the evangelist was hardly unaware that 'Son of Man' means 'Man', and it would be entirely consistent with the Johannine irony that ἰδοὺ ὁ ἄνθρωπος should have the veiled meaning: Behold the heavenly Man, now about to be exalted to reign over mankind! The early Christian perversion of Ps. xcv (xcvi). 10, ὁ κύριος ἐβασίλευσεν [ἀπὸ ξύλου] (the bracketed words being added in R*), is true to Johannine thought.

(iv) In recording the death of Jesus, the evangelist gives as His last word the pregnant τετέλεσται. The verb τελεῖν sometimes has the meaning 'bring to an end'; but its dominant meaning in all periods of Greek is 'fulfil', 'accomplish', 'perform', 'bring to completion'. It thus approximates in meaning to τελειοῦν,[1] and I have suggested that it is intended to echo xvii. 4, which uses the latter verb of the 'completion' of Christ's earthly task. But τελεῖν has a special sense which may have dictated its use here. It is used of the due performance of religious rites, such as sacrifices or initiations. Thus in the Hermetic *De Regeneratione*, the newly initiated Tat gives thanks for his regeneration in the words: δέξαι λογικὰς (θυσίας) ἃς θέλεις ἀπ' ἐμοῦ· σοῦ γὰρ βουλομένου πάντα τελεῖται (*C.H.* XIII. 21). As therefore the liturgical term ἁγιάζειν is used of Christ's self-oblation in xvii. 19, so here His death is declared to be the completion of the sacrifice, regarded as the means of man's regeneration, or initiation into eternal life. In xvii. 4, τελειοῦν is used of the completion of Christ's task, which is defined as the disclosure of the 'name' of God (6) and the deliverance of His ῥήματα (7) to men (which, as we know, are the vehicle of πνεῦμα and the media of eternal life (iii. 34, vi. 63, 68)). We may recall some earlier passages which use the same verb of Christ. In iv. 34 we learn that His βρῶμα (that by which He lives on earth) is ἵνα ποιῶ τὸ θέλημα τοῦ πέμψαντός με καὶ τελειώσω τὸ ἔργον αὐτοῦ. Again in v. 36, among the primary evidences of Christ's plenary commission are τὰ ἔργα ἃ δέδωκέν μοι ὁ πατὴρ ἵνα τελειώσω αὐτά, αὐτὰ τὰ ἔργα ἃ ποιῶ. Thus it appears that the very existence of the incarnate Word on earth is bound up with the accomplishment (τελείωσις) of the work of man's salvation according to the will of God. In the prayer of ch. xvii the work is

---

[1] How close the two verbs are in meaning and usage in Hellenistic Greek may be illustrated by a comparison of Acts xx. 24 (*Paulus loquitur*)...ὡς τελειώσω τὸν δρόμον μου with II Tim. iv. 7 τὸν δρόμον τετέλεκα.

declared to be completed (τελειοῦν)—on the plane of pure spiritual activity, that is, since Christ then and there offers Himself in sacrifice; but it is completed (τελεῖν) as a concrete act on the plane of history only when the sacrifice is consummated in His death.

(v) In xix. 34–5 the evangelist draws special attention to the fact that after the death of Christ on the cross water and blood issued from His side. The reference to vi. 55 and vii. 38 is inevitable. In ch. vi it was left undefined how Christ could give men His flesh and blood, though, as I suggested (p. 353), the attentive reader might divine it, especially from vi. 51. In vii. 38–9 the water which issues from His body is equated with the Spirit, which cannot be given until Christ is 'glorified'; but again we are left in doubt what is meant by δοξασθῆναι. Now we know what it means, and it becomes finally clear that the sustenance of the eternal life in man depends on Christ's death as self-oblation in fulfilment of the will of God (cf. vi. 38–9).

Guided, then, by the pointers which the evangelist has provided, we find in the story of the arrest, trial and crucifixion of Jesus Christ a σημεῖον on the grand scale, to whose significance each detail contributes: Christ's self-surrender in the Garden, the transference of His case to the Roman court, His *apologia* upon the charge of claiming kingship, the way He died, and the efflux of blood and water from His body after death. Each of these details calls up by association a chain of ideas already expounded in the course of the earlier parts of the gospel and concentrates them upon this crucial event. Our attention thus directed, we can hardly fail to see that the motives of a whole series of σημεῖα are gathered up in this supreme σημεῖον: the sign of the wine of Cana, which we now perceive to be the blood of the true Vine; the sign of the temple (which is the Body of Christ) destroyed to be raised again; the signs of the life-giving word (at Cana and Bethesda), since the Word Himself is life and dies that men may be saved from death; the sign of the Bread, which is the flesh of Christ given for the life of the world; the sign of Siloam—the light of truth which both saves and judges; the sign of Lazarus—life victorious over death through the laying down of life; the sign of the anointing for burial; and the sign of the 'King of Israel' acclaimed on His entry to Jerusalem to die. Along with these, other symbols, which although they have not been embodied in dramatic incidents have been woven into the discourses, have their significance clarified and enhanced in this supreme σημεῖον: Moses's serpent (the σύμβολον σωτηρίας), living water, the good shepherd, the grain of wheat, the woman in travail. As everywhere, so most emphatically in the story of Christ's arrest, trial and crucifixion, what happens and is observed in the temporal and sensible sphere signifies eternal reality: the life eternal given to man through the eternal Word. In this sense the Passion of the Lord is the final and all-inclusive σημεῖον.

Yet it differs from all other signs. The difference might be expressed in this way. The healing of the blind, the feeding of the multitude, the raising of Lazarus, doubtless happened (or so the evangelist was persuaded), but the happening had no lasting 'objective' effect in history. The multitude might 'eat of the loaves and be filled', but there the matter ended, unless they 'saw signs'. They were soon hungry again. Not the event, but the eternal reality it signifies, brings real satisfaction of man's hunger for life. Lazarus is raised to life, but in the course of nature his body will die again; the only lasting effect is that which his bodily resurrection *means*: 'He who lives and believes in me will never die.' With the event of the cross it is not so. Here is something that happened in time, with eternal consequence. Though individual men may miss its significance, nevertheless the thing has happened and history is different: the whole setting of human life in this world is different. It is an 'epoch-making' event; in history, things can never be the same again. But more: in it the two orders of reality, the temporal and the eternal, are united; the Word is made flesh. It is an event in both worlds; or rather, in that one world, of spirit and of flesh, which is the true environment of man, though he may fail to be aware of its twofold nature. Thus the cross is a sign, but a sign which is also the thing signified. The preliminary signs set forth so amply in the gospel are not only temporal signs of an eternal reality; they are also signs of this Event, in its twofold character as word and as flesh. They are true—spiritually, eternally true—only upon the condition that this Event is true, both temporally (or historically) and spiritually or eternally.

When however we contemplate the story of the event in this way, it is clear that it cannot end with the death of Jesus. His crucifixion may *signify* in the fullest possible way His glory and His exaltation, but in historical actuality it remains a miserable and humiliating end to a gallant struggle. That which happened, on the historical plane, and by happening changed the setting of human life in this world is not simply the death of Christ, but His death-and-resurrection, as one complete event. So the central tradition of the Church affirmed, and our evangelist, faithfully following the tradition, records how Christ rose and appeared to His disciples. In its character as σημεῖον the resurrection can, consistently with the Johannine theology, do no more than carry on the significance already recognized in the crucifixion. While in some other parts of the New Testament it would not be untrue (though perhaps it would almost everywhere fall short of the whole truth) to say that the death of Christ is temporary failure and humiliation, subsequently retrieved and more than retrieved by the glory of the resurrection, for John the crucifixion itself is so truly Christ's exaltation and glory (in its meaning, that is to say), that the resurrection can hardly have for him precisely the same significance that it has for some other writers.

It will perhaps help to clarify this point if we compare the treatment of the post-resurrection appearances in John and in other gospels. In Matthew, after a brief, passing allusion to an appearance of Christ to the women who visited the Tomb (xxviii. 9), we are given a scene on a mountain in Galilee where Jesus appears to His disciples invested with universal sovereignty, and sends them out with plenary commission to claim the allegiance of all nations for Him, their rightful King (xxviii. 16–20). We may interpret the meaning of the scene out of Matthew's own record. 'When the Son of Man comes in his glory...all nations will be assembled before him.... And the King will say...' (xxv. 31 sqq.). 'Thus shall it be at the consummation of the age: the Son of Man will send his messengers (angels) and they will collect all scandals out of his kingdom...' (xiii. 41–3). In other words, the scene in xxviii. 16–20 is in all essential respects a proleptic *parusia*-scene: Christ comes in glory to reign over all mankind. This is for Matthew the significance of the resurrection. In Luke there is no comparable scene. For him, the appearances of the risen Christ have evidential value. By them the apostles know that the Lord is indeed alive, and will come again. Even the scene of the ascension in Acts i, in spite of clouds and angels, falls far short of the character of a *parusia*-scene. It speaks of a parting and of glory deferred.[1]

---

[1] I am here indebted to the exposition of R. H. Lightfoot in *Locality and Doctrine in the Gospels* (1938). His argument that Mark, from whom we have no account of a post-resurrection appearance, took substantially the view of the resurrection which we find in Matthew, I find convincing, though I cannot follow him in believing that Mark xvi. 8 is the ending which the evangelist intended. It would be consistent with his own general view of Mark to suppose that he intended to end his book with a scene analogous to that of Matt. xxviii. 16–20, or alternatively that such a scene was actually written, but disappeared when the autograph of Mark was damaged. Where no certainty, no strong probability, even, is attainable, my guess would be that the 'lost ending' of Mark is more likely to be represented by the end of Matthew than by anything else that has survived. In view of Mark xiii. 10, xiv. 9 it should have contained something like the 'great commission' of Matt. xxviii. 19a.

If now we compare the Fourth Gospel with the others, we observe, first, that there is nothing in John remotely resembling the scene of Matt. xxviii. 16–20. There is indeed a commission to the apostles (xx. 23, cf. xxi. 16–17), but it is much nearer to Matt. xviii. 18, and it says nothing about preaching to the nations. On the other hand, in place of the curt reference to an appearance to the women in Matt. xxviii. 9 we have the story of the appearance to Mary Magdalene (John xx. 11–18), which is the most humanly moving of all the stories of the risen Christ. The same humanly moving quality is to be found in a marked degree in the appendix (John xxi); and it is almost equally present in Luke's story of the two at Emmaus (xxiv. 13–32). Not only so; in John as in Luke there is an obvious interest in the evidential value of the post-resurrection appearances (John xx. 16, 27, 29, and so in the appendix, xxi. 12–13; cf. Luke xxiv. 30–1, 34–5, 39, 43).

Here then are two questions demanding an answer: (a) Why does John, with his prevailing interest in the heavenly glory of Christ, keep out of the resurrection narratives all such obvious suggestions of divine majesty as we find in Matthew, and emphasize the element of human feeling? (b) Why does the author of the 'spiritual gospel', who is often said to give to his picture of the 'Jesus of History' a hieratic tone scarcely consistent with real humanity, insist so strongly on the quasi-physical character of His resurrection? (I say quasi-physical, since in spite of xx. 20, 27, the resurrection body of Christ passes through closed doors, and He is not immediately recognizable even by His most intimate friends, xx. 19, 14–15; and so in the appendix, xxi. 4.)

I suggest that an answer to both these questions may be given if we allow full weight to the Johannine doctrine that Christ is glorified and exalted in His death. This is meant to be understood in the most absolute sense. No higher exaltation, and no brighter glory, is to be conceived than that which Christ attained in His self-oblation, since it is the absolute expression of the divine ἀγάπη. This is the glory which He had with the Father before the foundation of the world (xvii. 5, 24). It is veiled from the eyes of men by the shame of the cross; but not veiled from those who know what the ὕψωσις on the cross really means, and in that ὕψωσις 'see the Son of Man ascending where He was before' (vi. 62). Thus, in narrating the crucifixion the evangelist is concerned to keep before his readers the truth that what is *prima facie* an event on the plane of the temporal and the sensible—the death of a good man unjustly condemned— is really an event on the spiritual plane. To this the resurrection can add nothing; for the spiritual reality of resurrection is already given in the act of self-oblation. In dying, Christ is 'going to the Father' (xiv. 28, xvi. 10, 16), and this is to *live*, in the fullest sense possible (xiv. 19). In other words, resurrection is *prima facie* a reality on the spiritual plane, and the evangelist is concerned to show that it is also an event on the temporal, historical plane. In order that the death-and-resurrection of Christ may constitute an 'epoch-making' event for mankind, it is necessary that it should actually happen—that the entire event, death-and-resurrection together, should happen—*in this world*. That is what the quasi-physical features of the post-resurrection appearances are intended to affirm. From this point of view, it is not the resurrection as Christ's resumption of heavenly glory that needs to be emphasized, but the resurrection as the renewal of personal relations with the disciples. It is this side of the resurrection which is emphasized in the Farewell Discourses (xiv. 18–19, 23, 28, xvi. 16–22), and it is this which is so movingly represented in xx. 11–23, as well as in the appendix.

From this point of view we can understand how it is that although it is declared that at the moment of the death of Jesus on the cross all is accomplished, and that the life-giving stream, which is the Spirit (vii. 38), is now released (xix. 34) for the salvation of man,[1] it is yet necessary that the Spirit should be given by the risen Lord to His disciples (xx. 22). *Sub specie aeternitatis*, all is fulfilled in Christ's one complete self-oblation. Yet there was a moment in history when men received the Spirit as they had not received it before, and this moment is represented by the incident of the 'insufflation', which is securely anchored to the empirical history of the Church by the commission to forgive sins—a commission strictly relative to the existence of the Church in time.

From this point of view, also, we may perhaps understand the enigmatic reply to Mary Magdalene, xx. 17 οὔπω ἀναβέβηκα πρὸς τὸν πατέρα... ἀναβαίνω πρὸς τὸν πατέρα μου καὶ πατέρα ὑμῶν καὶ θεόν μου καὶ θεὸν ὑμῶν. The reappearance of οὔπω, which is so natural and so significant at its frequent occurrences in the Book of Signs, is surprising here, after the hour has been declared come, and all things accomplished. While Christ's ascent, or exaltation, is fully accomplished on the cross, *sub specie aeternitatis*, it cannot be fully accomplished in relation to men and to human history until the resurrection, as return to His disciples, in this world, and at a particular time, is an established fact. Thus the process by which

[1] Possibly also, that in dying He 'delivered' or bequeathed the Spirit to those He left behind, xix. 30; see p. 428.

Jesus is establishing renewed contact with His disciples after His resurrection is accompanied by a process of ascent, which can be (temporally speaking) complete only when this renewed contact is consolidated; that is, in the sense of xiv. 15–18, xvi. 13–16, when they possess the Spirit. When therefore the disciples have received the Spirit through His 'insufflation' (xx. 22), we may know that Christ has finally ascended. And this seems to be implied when Thomas is invited to touch His hands and side,[1] in contrast to Mary Magdalene, who was not permitted to touch Him,[2] because He was not yet ascended.

In the story of Thomas, in fact (xx. 26–9), we are already on the confines of the empirical and the spiritual worlds. At the beginning, we are still at the point where Christ reveals Himself at a particular moment of time, at a particular place, and to certain historical individuals, who are to attest to succeeding generations the fact that He rose from the dead, in this world. But when Thomas confesses Him as God, He is already in the eternal world; and for the disciples the stage when He was known through the sight of mortal eyes has yielded to the stage at which faith is the medium of the saving vision of Him (see pp. 185–6). From this moment the company no longer consists solely of the eleven disciples gathered at that particular time and place; every reader of the gospel who has faith, to the end of time, is included in Christ's final beatitude: μακάριοι οἱ μὴ ἰδόντες καὶ πιστεύσαντες. This is the true climax of the gospel; the rest, however true and however moving, is mere postscript.

---

[1] It is not said that Thomas did actually touch the Lord's body, nor may we infer from I John i. 1 αἱ χεῖρες ἡμῶν ἐψηλάφησαν that it was believed that he, or others, had done so, since ψηλαφᾶν here almost certainly refers to contact with Jesus before the crucifixion; but it certainly is implied that Thomas might have touched Him, though he no longer felt the need to do so, and may have refrained out of reverence.

[2] The sense of μή μου ἅπτου (xx. 17) is not entirely unambiguous. According to a well-known grammatical maxim, μή with the present imperative means 'stop doing...'; thus μή μου ἅπτου might mean, 'stop touching me', with the implication that Mary was already doing so. But the present ἅπτεσθαι differs from the aorist ἅψασθαι in more than mere *Aktionsart*. Ἅψασθαι means 'touch' (so invariably in Matthew and Mark), ἅπτεσθαι means 'hold', 'grasp', even 'cling'. Μή μου ἅπτου, therefore, might mean 'Do not cling to me', without any necessary implication that Mary was doing so (since μή with the present imperative may simply negative the specific meaning of that tense). Yet it would be pedantic to press it to mean that Mary might touch but must not cling. It seems difficult to avoid the position that some change in reference to what is called ἀνάβασις is implied between xx. 17 and xx. 27. It is at all events clear that for John the ἀνάβασις is not a movement in space, but a change in the conditions under which Christ is apprehended as the glorified and exalted Lord.

APPENDIX

Some Considerations upon the Historical Aspect of the Fourth Gospel

It will have become clear that I regard the Fourth Gospel as being in its essential character a theological work, rather than a history. Nevertheless, the writer has chosen to set forth his theology under the literary form of a 'Gospel', a form created by Christianity for its own proper purposes. A gospel in this sense consists of a recital of the historical narrative of the sufferings, death and resurrection of Jesus Christ, prefaced by some account of His ministry in word and deed. To this type the Fourth Gospel entirely conforms, and in this it differs from all other contemporary literature which has the same aim—to set forth the knowledge of God which is eternal life. In one sense it might be said that in the Fourth Gospel the narrative is a dramatic presentation of theological ideas, for the incidents narrated, including, in one aspect, those of the Passion, are treated as 'signs' or symbols of unseen realities; and this symbolical character, as we have seen, goes very deeply into the whole scheme of the work. But this is not an entirely satisfactory description. In tracing the various lines of thought, and comparing them with analogous ideas in contemporary theology, we have time and time again been led to recognize the *differentia* of Johannine teaching in the fact that it finds the eternal reality conclusively revealed and embodied in an historical Person, who actually lived, worked, taught, suffered and died, with actual and direct historical consequences. The concise formula for this fact is ὁ λόγος σὰρξ ἐγένετο. We must therefore conclude that the narrative is for the author much more than a dramatic vehicle for ideas. His aim, as I have said, is to set forth the knowledge of God contained in the Christian revelation. But this revelation is distinctively, and nowhere more clearly than in the Fourth Gospel, an historical revelation. It follows that it is important for the evangelist that what he narrates happened.

In the process, however, of bringing out the symbolical value of the facts he has used some freedom. Like many ancient writers, he has put into the mouth of his characters speeches which, since they bear not only the stamp of his own style, but also the stamp of an environment different from that in which the recorded events took place, cannot be regarded as

444

historical.[1] This use of freely composed speeches to elucidate the significance of events does not in itself impugn the historical character of the narrative in the Fourth Gospel, any more than in Thucydides or Tacitus. There is however good reason to suspect that in some cases and in some respects the narratives which provide the setting for such speeches may have been moulded by the ideas which they are made to illustrate. We may perhaps express the evangelist's attitude to history in this way. He accepts without qualification the general tradition of the ministry, death and resurrection of Jesus, as it was expressed in the apostolic preaching, and entered into the earliest confessions of faith; and he is concerned to affirm with all emphasis the historical actuality of the facts which it transmitted. He has meditated deeply upon the meaning of the Gospel story, taken as a whole. He then turns back upon the details of the story, and seeks in each particular incident the meaning of the whole, expressing that meaning partly by the way in which he reports the facts, partly by the order in which they are placed, and partly through carefully composed discourses and dialogues.

In seeking to interpret the facts he records, the Fourth Evangelist is not necessarily exceeding the limits proper to history. For it is the function of the historian, as distinct from the chronicler, to expose the course of events as an intelligible process, in which the human spirit interacts with its environment; and that means, both to envisage events as arising (on the one side) out of human thoughts and motives, and to make perceptible and intelligible the influence they in turn exert on the thoughts and motives of men, through which fresh events are prepared.[2] From this point of

---

[1] The form of discourse selected is mainly that of dialogue. The use of dialogue for the transmission of philosophical teaching goes back to Plato. There is no reason to suppose it had ever entirely lapsed, even though the Stoics preferred the form known as διατριβή. At any rate in the second century it became widely popular. The Hermetic dialogues on the one hand, and those of Lucian on the other, are two obvious examples which attest the renewed popularity of the dialogue form in very different circles. The Fourth Gospel is earlier than these, but it may well have been affected by the same general tendency. In dramatic power, characterization, and general liveliness, the Johannine dialogues are far superior to the Hermetic, while they have a depth and seriousness of purpose which cannot be looked for in the brilliant journalist Lucian. John no doubt was under the influence of the 'dialogues', if such they may be called, which were used to set forth the teaching of Jesus in the tradition represented by the Synoptic Gospels, and were in turn akin to forms used for the preservation of rabbinic teaching. But in John the Hellenistic influence is stronger. The Johannine dialogue, however, is an original literary creation, for which there is no really close parallel.

[2] See what I have said in *History and the Gospel*, pp. 25–9. Cf. Hugh Last in *Journal of Roman Studies*, xxxix (1949), p. 4: 'All the parties so far involved in the

view, the question of the historical value of the Fourth Gospel means asking, To what extent does this work, retelling in a fresh medium of thought the episode out of which Christianity arose, offer a true and valuable account of its significance in history?

In asking that question, we shall still have to pay much attention, as critics have long done, to a comparison of the Fourth Gospel with the Synoptics. But we shall recognize, as some older critics did not, that the Synoptic Gospels also have an inseparable element of interpretation in their record.[1] It is indeed inevitable that an episode which stirred men so deeply (on any showing), and which (in Christian belief) possessed unique spiritual significance, should impose on its reporters the necessity of relating it to their most profound thoughts and feelings, and indeed to their ultimate beliefs about God, man and the universe. For the Synoptic evangelists, that meant relating it to eschatological conceptions derived from Jewish religious tradition. For John, it meant relating it to more rational, and more universal, ideas such as those which we have studied. The question is, whether the fundamental significance of this episode in the history of mankind (in history regarded as an adventure of the spirit in the domain of nature) is expressed more adequately, or less, through the one set of conceptions or through the other; or whether the two modes of expression are complementary to one another, and both essential to a view of the facts which shall be historical in the widest sense. I believe that the course which was taken by *Leben-Jesu-Forschung* ('The Quest of the Historical Jesus', according to the English title of the most important record of that 'Quest') during the nineteenth century proves that a severe concentration on the Synoptic record, to the exclusion of the Johannine contribution,[2] leads to an impoverished, a one-sided, and finally an incredible view of the facts—I mean, of the *facts*, as part of history.[3] I have elsewhere argued that the early recrudescence in the

present debate would, I think, agree in the view that the primary concern of history is with the various elements—ideas, sentiments, emotions and passions—which together make up the conscious life of men; that events produced by human agency are of very little interest except as clues to the motives and purposes of the agents; that such motives and purposes are the essence of the experiences which the historian has to recreate.'   [1] See R. H. Lightfoot, *History and Interpretation in the Gospels* (1935).

[2] This proved to carry with it (as might have been expected) the rejection of elements in the Synoptics themselves which seemed to critics reminiscent of the Fourth Gospel: a notable *circulus in probando*.

[3] A great historian of ideas, the late A. J. Carlyle, many years ago admonished me not to neglect the 'implicit history' contained in the Pauline Epistles and the Fourth Gospel; and I have found the observation fruitful.

Church of an over-emphasis on eschatological expectations for the future has in many places tended to overshadow the element of 'realized eschatology' in the ministry, teaching, passion and resurrection of Jesus Christ.[1] John, it appears, drew upon a tradition in which this over-emphasis had at any rate not gone far. His formula ἔρχεται ὥρα καὶ νῦν ἐστιν, with the emphasis on the νῦν ἐστιν, without excluding the element of futurity, is, I believe, not merely an acute theological definition, but is essentially historical, and probably represents the authentic teaching of Jesus as veraciously as any formula could. If that is so, it follows that a picture of the ministry of Jesus largely controlled by that maxim cannot be without historical value.

It still remains, however, a part of the task of the student of history to seek to discover (in Ranke's oft-quoted phrase) 'wie es eigentlich geschehen ist'—how it actually happened. To what extent and under what conditions may the Fourth Gospel be used as a document for the historian in that sense?

The answer to that question depends upon the sources of information which were at the disposal of the evangelist, if we assume (as I think we may, in view of what has been said) that he intended to record that which happened, however free he may have felt to modify the factual record in order to bring out the meaning.

In the first place, he can be shown to have followed the broad general outline of the ministry, death and resurrection of Jesus Christ which is presupposed in the Synoptic Gospels, reproduced in the apostolic preaching in Acts, and attested up to a point in the Pauline epistles.[2] This outline we have good reason to believe primitive, and by his fidelity to it the evangelist gives proof of his intention to expound the meaning of *facts*, and not to invent a dramatic plot.

In the filling in of this outline in the other gospels, we observe a difference in the treatment of the Passion-narrative as compared with that of the ministry. The Passion-narrative is continuous and detailed, with the succession of incidents well marked, and varying but little in the different accounts. The narrative of the ministry, on the other hand,

[1] See *Parables of the Kingdom*, pp. 34–110. The not altogether felicitous term 'realized eschatology' may serve as a label. Emendations of it which have been suggested for the avoidance of misunderstandings are Professor Georges Florovsky's 'inaugurated eschatology' and Professor Joachim Jeremias's 'sich realisierende Eschatologie', which I like, but cannot translate into English.

[2] See my book, *The Apostolic Preaching and its Developments*, 1936, especially pp. 164–75 (in later editions, pp. 65–73).

is largely discontinuous and episodic, and the order is freely varied. These phenomena are consistent with the view that the essential core of a 'Gospel' as such is an account of the Passion, with an introduction which might be expanded at will with a varied selection of material, and which followed no fixed order. The same is true of the Fourth Gospel. The Passion-narrative follows the well-marked pattern. The earlier narrative shows an even greater measure of freedom than the other gospels show.

The actual order of events as they appear even in Mark can no longer be regarded as strictly chronological. It is always in some measure topical, and subject to the more or less arbitrary scheme of arrangement favoured by the particular evangelist.[1] The Fourth Evangelist sits more loosely than the others to any kind of chronological arrangement. As we have seen, the construction of the Book of Signs is dictated by the order of thought. We should therefore be wasting time in trying to harmonize the order of Mark with the order of John directly, by such puerile expedients, for example, as the assumption that the temple was cleansed twice over, or in attempting to fit the movements between Galilee and Jerusalem into a precise chronological scheme. So far as the Fourth Gospel may be laid under contribution for determining the order of events, it must be through considering single episodes, and connecting paragraphs, severally, on their merits, and attempting to determine from internal indications their probable relations in time.

It is nevertheless true that in one part of the gospel, vi. 1–vii. 1, we seem to have a kind of shadow of the Marcan order, in the sequence of incidents which may be tabulated as follows:

Feeding of the multitude (vi. 1–13; cf. Mark viii. 1–9).[2]

Demand for a sign (vi. 30; cf. Mark viii. 11).

Cryptic saying about bread (vi. 32 sqq.; cf. Mark viii. 14–21).

Peter's confession and prediction of betrayal (vi. 68–71; cf. Mark viii. 27–31).

Retirement in Galilee (vii. 1; cf. Mark ix. 30).

---

[1] Yet I believe the tendency to treat the Marcan order as wholly arbitrary has sometimes gone too far. See my article, 'The Framework of the Gospel Narrative', in *The Expository Times*, vol. xliii (1931/2), pp. 396–400.

[2] But the Johannine story of the Feeding corresponds (in some respects, including the numbers) with Mark vi. 34–44, and, like it, is followed by the Walking on the Sea (John vi. 16–21, Mark vi. 47–51); which demands consideration at leisure.

In both Mark and John, as it happens, this sequence of incidents is followed by the final abandonment of Galilee.[1] The degree and kind of significance to be attached to this coincidence is bound up with the question whether or not John used the Synoptics as a source. A majority of critics, for many years past, held the opinion, almost as a dogma, that he did so use them—or Mark at least—altering them in accordance with special motives of his own. Since the 'alterations' are so drastic at times, the dogma tended to throw a cloud of discredit upon the Johannine narrative. That opinion however rested upon an assumption, which was not usually avowed, and of which the critic perhaps was hardly aware, that the writings of early Christianity must have formed a documentary series, in literary dependence on one another. It is now widely recognized that the main factor in perpetuating and propagating the Christian faith and the Gospel story was oral tradition in its various forms. There is therefore no strong *a priori* presumption that resemblances in early Christian documents are due to literary dependence. The presumption is rather the other way. It is because of specific evidence of various kinds (which need not here be particularized) that we are led to recognize documentary sources behind the Synoptic Gospels (though they may not be so extensive as was formerly believed). Definite evidence pointing to documentary relations between John and the Synoptics is seen to be singularly sparse, when once the presumption in favour of such relations is abandoned. The *prima facie* impression is that John is, in large measure at any rate, working independently of other written gospels.[2]

I am not in this book discussing the question of the authorship of the Fourth Gospel. I should not care to say that the hypothesis is impossible, that the Johannine narrative rests upon personal reminiscences, transformed through the changing experiences of a long life, after the manner imagined by Browning in *A Death in the Desert*. We do not know what effect many years of active intercourse with Hellenistic circles may have had upon a Palestinian Jew—even upon a Galilaean fisherman—with an agile and adventurous intelligence. But some of the evidence which has been adduced in favour of authorship by an eyewitness is subject to

[1] See my article, 'The End of the Galilean Ministry', in *The Expositor*, 8th series, vol. xxii (1921), pp. 273–91.

[2] See P. Gardner-Smith, *St John and the Synoptics* (1938), a book which at least shows how fragile are the arguments by which the dependence of John on the other gospels has been 'proved', and makes a strong case for its independence.

a heavy discount. For example, the convincing characterization and dramatic actuality of parts of the gospel are urged in its favour. But two of the passages which most powerfully display these features are represented by the evangelist himself as occasions when no eyewitness was present—the conversation with the Samaritan woman,[1] and the examination before Pilate.[2] There are, besides, indications which seem to point to the use of previously existing material. It was, I think, Eduard Meyer who first pointed out that the extremely artificial way in which the healing at Bethesda is made to lead up to the discourse in v. 19 sqq. is much more readily explicable if the evangelist was using a narrative that had come down to him (by whatever channel) than if he was composing freely—or, we may add, recollecting what he had himself witnessed—and the same observation may be made elsewhere. Without pronouncing dogmatically upon questions which it would be preposterous to purport to settle in this offhand way, we may say that it is a reasonable hypothesis that the evangelist is giving us a rendering of oral tradition as it had come down to him, sometimes containing material which reached Mark or the others by different channels, sometimes material of similar character which may be supposed to have belonged to the same general store, and sometimes material of a character so different that it is difficult to institute a comparison.

If, taking this hypothesis, we start (as is right) with the Passion-narrative, we find a long and highly wrought passage where the main run of the story is, as we have noted, undoubtedly conformed to the standard traditional pattern. Yet the variation in detail is considerable, and the amount of verbal resemblance to the Synoptics is almost the minimum possible if the same story is to be told at all. Certainly there is not nearly so much as is ordinarily required to prove literary dependence. I have already pointed out that the passages in which definitely Johannine motives are to be recognized are brief and comparatively few, and appear rather

---

[1] Only two persons were aware of this conversation. I find it impossible to imagine a situation in which either of them would have repeated it in this form. If it be replied that either of them may easily have told the evangelist in general terms what the conversation was about, I should be obliged to point out that the dramatic colour—all that was at first invoked to prove eyewitness—would in that case still remain the evangelist's own creation.

[2] I suppose Pilate's secretary was present; but to suggest that he later became a Christian and recited the conversation would be a very long shot; and I do not suppose anyone would wish to argue that the sentry at the door, recruited who knows where, but hardly from the intelligentsia, produced this highly intelligent and most vivid account from memory.

to have been inserted into a narrative already shaped than to have determined the course of the narrative. The character of the whole seems to be consistent with an independent rendering of oral tradition, parallel with Mark's, and with the non-Marcan tradition which, as I believe, forms the main basis of the Lucan Passion-narrative. Upon this hypothesis the Johannine Passion-narrative should be examined and estimated; not as a tendentious manipulation of the blameless record of Mark, but as representing a separate line of tradition, to be compared with Mark, with the possibility that it may be inferior to Mark in some respects and superior in others.[1]

The examination of other narratives should similarly be conducted in each case on its merits. Some of them evidently refer to incidents also recorded in the Synoptics; for example, the Feeding of the Multitude, the Walking on the Sea, the Cleansing of the Temple, the Anointing at Bethany, and the Triumphal Entry. Others possibly or probably do; for example, the Healing of the Nobleman's Son. Others again reproduce patterns of narrative familiar from the Synoptics, so closely that we may justly regard them as drawn from the same general reservoir; for example, the Healing at Bethesda. Then there are those which, in form and pattern as well as in contents, seem to be peculiar to the Johannine tradition; for example, the Raising of Lazarus and the Meeting of the Sanhedrin. In examining each, it is desirable to have regard, not only to verbal and linguistic similarities and divergences, but also to form or pattern, which may have much to tell about the shaping of the particular narrative in the oral stage.

Similarly, embedded in the discourses and dialogues which are certainly an original creation of the evangelist, we find sayings which appear sometimes to be variant forms of sayings known from the Synoptics, and at other times to have been moulded upon patterns of which the Synoptics also have examples. These are all the more significant when we find a run of such sayings, having some similarity to the sequences of sayings in the

---

[1] Is John's dating of the Crucifixion more, or less, probable than Mark's? The question is freely arguable, with no necessary presumption in favour of Mark. Again, for John the political charge against Jesus is the one which clearly decided His fate. Elsewhere he has made Caiaphas explicitly lay stress upon the political danger which His ministry evoked ('the Romans will come and take away our place and nation'), as well as recording an abortive attempt to make Him king. On general principles, is it more likely that Mark, writing almost under the walls of the imperial palace at Rome, should have soft-pedalled the suggestion that it was a case of 'another βασιλεύς, one Jesus', or that John should gratuitously have emphasized this highly dangerous political note in a narrative in which it was not previously prominent?

Synoptics which some would regard as representing a very early stage in the transmission of the sayings of Jesus (prior to comparatively voluminous collections of sayings such as the hypothetical 'Q'). Such sequences, for example, seem to occur in John iv. 32–8, xii. 24–6, xiii. 13–20.

In examining such passages, whether narrative or didactic, we have always to ask, how far it appears that the specifically Johannine concepts (often indicated by the use of a quasi-technical vocabulary) have worked to produce the form of story or saying. That is why a detailed examination of Johannine thought such as we have here essayed is an indispensable preliminary to any estimate of the historical element in the gospel. Even when we have a fairly clear and comprehensive picture of what the distinctively Johannine types of thought and expression really are, the task of estimating the forms of the various units is a delicate one; but I believe it is not altogether without prospects. Where we have units which have the appearance of having been framed independently of the specially Johannine motives, we may provisionally set them down to the credit of a special branch or channel of oral tradition.

Another question which needs to be asked is how far a given passage, though it does not evidently reflect the theological concepts or vocabulary of the author, may nevertheless have been moulded by special interests in the place where the gospel was written—that is, as I think we are justified in saying, at Ephesus. There is, I believe, at least one element in the narrative which cannot have been due to any such moulding influence; I mean the topographical data. All attempts that have been made to extract a profound symbolical meaning[1] out of the names of Sychar, the city of Ephraim, Bethany beyond Jordan, Aenon by Salim, of Cana and Tiberias, or again, of Kedron, Bethesda (or Bethzatha),[2] and Gabbatha, are hopelessly fanciful; and there is no reason to suppose that a fictitious topography[3] would in any way assist the appeal of the gospel

[1] Siloam, it is true, is given a symbolical meaning; but that marks it out as an exception. It would be possible to concede that in this case the evangelist introduced a name for symbolical reasons; but I think it more likely that his discovery of the etymology of the name Siloam was a lucky bit of erudition, like some of Philo's etymologies.

[2] A strong case for the originality of the form Βηθεσδά, as well as for the identification of the place, has been made out by Joachim Jeremias, *Die Wiederentdeckung von Bethesda*, 1949.

[3] I do not think it can fairly be compared with the fictitious περίοδοι which had some vogue. The suggestion that these names represent a kind of pilgrims' manual is, so far as our evidence goes, anachronistic; and in any case, what would be the point of directing pilgrims to Aenon near to Salim, unless there was a previously established tradition that John baptized there?

to an Ephesian public. The names, whether we are able to identify them on the map or not, cannot reasonably be supposed to have got into the gospel except out of a tradition which associated certain episodes in the life of Jesus (or of John the Baptist) with those sites.

It may then be of some significance that most of the place-names which occur in John but not in the Synoptics belong to southern Palestine. The only two new names in Galilee are Tiberias and Cana, while Chorazin, Nain, Decapolis, Gadara (or Gerasa, or Gergesa), Caesarea Philippi, as well as Tyre and Sidon, are absent from the Fourth Gospel. I can see no theological motive for the difference, nor can I think that the Ephesian reader either knew or cared anything about the geographical situation of these places. The natural inference is that the tradition from which the Fourth Evangelist was drawing had some original association with southern Palestine. If so, that might also account for a certain southern, or even metropolitan, outlook which has often been noted.

Along such lines as these I believe that some probable conclusions might be drawn about the pre-canonical tradition lying behind the *prima facie* historical statements of the Fourth Gospel. If it should prove possible to identify such a tradition, then we should have material in hand which we might compare with our other data, drawn from the Synoptic Gospels or from sources outside the gospels altogether. Through such comparative study of different strains of tradition we may hope to advance our knowledge of the facts to which they all refer.

INDEX LOCORVM

I. IN SCRIPTVRIS VETERIS TESTAMENTI

[References are primarily to the LXX, ed. Swete (C.U.P.). Where necessary
references to the Hebrew enumeration are added in brackets]

II. IN APOCRYPHIS

III. IN SCRIPTVRIS NOVI TESTAMENTI

INDEX LOCORVM

INDEX LOCORVM

IV. IN LIBRIS VETERVM CHRISTIANORVM

INDEX LOCORVM

V. IN LIBRIS IVDAICIS

A. PHILO OF ALEXANDRIA (ed. Cohn & Wendland, 1896–1906)

B. Miscellaneous works included in *Apocrypha and Pseudepigrapha of the Old Testament* (ed. R. H. Charles, 1913, vol. II)

C. RABBINIC WRITINGS

VI. IN LIBRIS ETHNICIS

INDEX NOMINVM

Merx, A., 264
Milligan, G. (*see also* Moulton, J. H.), 332
Monoimos, 109
Montefiore, H., 385
Moore, G. F., 68, 75, 92, 146, 243, 267, 324, 325, 349, 396
Moulton, J. H., 147
Moulton, J. H. and Howard, W. F., 35, 382
Moulton, J. H. and Milligan, G., 375
Mozley, J. R., 425

Nathan (Rabbi), 261
Nock, A. D., 11, 12, 37
Nock, A. D. and Festugière, A. J., 13, 17, 18, 28, 29, 34, 37, 39, 45, 218, 421
Norden, E., 189
Nygren, A., 199

Odeberg, H., 245, 246, 306, 312, 326
Otto, R., 242

Pallis, S. A., 115, 117, 124, 129
Papa (Rabbi), 80
Pinchas (Rabbi), 321
Pinchas ben Jair (Rabbi), 93
Posidonius, 10
Primrose, W. B., 429
Ptolemy (Gnostic), 102

Ramsey, A. M., 206
Reitzenstein, R., 31, 32, 33, 34, 37, 40, 43, 46, 47, 52, 111, 120, 121, 128–9, 219, 222, 243, 421
Robinson, H. W., 141, 214, 254

Schlatter, A., 74–96 *passim*, 322, 335
Schmidt, C., 240
Schmittlein, R., 429
Schweitzer, A., 193, 418
Scott, W., 11, 13, 18, 24, 27, 28, 29, 30, 33, 34, 37, 39, 40, 46, 47, 52, 182, 216, 221
Simon of Gitta, 99, 101
Skeat, T. C., *see* Bell, H. I.
Spitta, F., 237
Strack, H. L. and Billerbeck, P., 68, 74–96 *passim*, 167, 205, 261, 320, 322, 336, 349, 350, 401
Stroud, W., 429

Tarn, W. W., 250
Thackeray, H. St J., 382
Thallus the Samaritan, 425
Theodore bar Khonai, 115, 126
Theophilus of Antioch, 335
Torrey, C. C., 74

Valentinus and Valentinians, 100–10 *passim*, 314, 373

Ward, W., 425
Weinstock, G., 375
Wetstein, J. J., 325, 339
White, Bouck, 4

Yannai (Rabbi), 245

Zosimus, 12, 30